Marshal South
and the
Ghost Mountain Chronicles

Marshal South and the Ghost Mountain Chronicles

An Experiment in Primitive Living

Edited and with a Foreword by

Diana Lindsay

Introduction by

Rider and Lucile South

"Adventures in the Natural History and Cultural Heritage of the Californias"

Sunbelt Publications
San Diego, California

Marshal South and the Ghost Mountain Chronicles
Sunbelt Publications, Inc.
Copyright © 2005 by Sunbelt Publications
All rights reserved. First edition 2005

Edited by Diana Lindsay
Cover design by Handmade Graphics & Computer Concepts
Book design by W. G. Hample & Associates
Project management by Jennifer Redmond
Printed in the United States of America

ISBN: 0-932653-66-9

Sunbelt Publications, Inc.
P.O. Box 191126
San Diego, CA 92159-1126
(619) 258-4911, fax: (619) 258-4916
www.sunbeltbooks.com

08 07 06 05 04   5 4 3 2 1

"Adventures in the Natural History and Cultural Heritage of the Californias"
A Series Edited by Lowell Lindsay

Library of Congress Cataloging-in-Publication Data

South, Marshal.
  Marshal South and the Ghost Mountain chronicles : an experiment in primitive living / Marshal South ; foreword by Diana Lindsay ; introduction by Rider South ; [edited by Diana Lindsay].— 1st ed.
      p. cm. — (Adventures in cultural and natural history)
  Includes bibliographical references and index.
  ISBN 0-932653-66-9
  1. South, Marshal—Homes and haunts—California—Anza-Borrego Desert. 2. Authors, American—Homes and haunts—California—Anza-Borrego Desert. 3. Authors, American—20th century—Family relationships. 4. Wilderness survival—California—Anza-Borrego Desert. 5. Anza-Borrego Desert (Calif.)—Social life and customs. 6. Anza-Borrego Desert (Calif.)—Description and travel. 7. Outdoor life—California—Anza-Borrego Desert. 8. Authors, American—20th century—Diaries. 9. Anza-Borrego Desert (Calif.)—Biography. 10. South, Marshal—Diaries. 11. South, Marshal—Family. I. Lindsay, Diana, 1944- II. Title. III. Series.

PS3569.O75Z473 2005
818'.5209—dc22

                                    2004027437

CREDITS:
Cover Photograph: Tanya South
Cover Illustration: "Barrel Cacti & Yucca," linoleum block and watercolor by Marshal South, Yaquitepec Press
Back Cover Photographs: Marshal South
Inside Front Cover Map: Lowell Lindsay, digitized by Ben Pease
Inside Back Cover Portrait: Thomas Crocker, used by permission of Rider South
Articles by Marshal South originally appeared in *Desert Magazine*, used by permission of Rider South
Plat of Yaquitepec: Adapted from a sketch by Rider South
All photos courtesy of Rider South and Marsha Rasmussen unless otherwise credited
All animal and plant sketches by Jon Lindsay except for those on pages 71, 138, 161, 183, 186, 243, 245, 247, and 273
    taken from *Our Historic Desert* published by Copley Books and used by permission. Drawings and sketches by
    Marshal, Rider, and Rudyard South are credited as they appear.

Barrel Cacti & Yucca   Marshal South

The Desert! Either you will love it or you will hate it. If you hate it you will fly from it and never wish to see its face again. If you love it, it will hold you and draw you as will no other land on earth.

—Marshal South

CONTENTS

FOREWORD

by Diana Lindsay

For over 50 years an adobe house on windswept waterless Ghost Mountain, on the western edge of California's Colorado Desert, has been slowly disintegrating. A one-mile-long, steep trail from the southern edge of Blair Valley, in Anza-Borrego Desert State Park, leads up to the site—on a flat just below the top of the mountain. The skeletal remains of the house, known as Yaquitepec, still stand—a rusted bed frame, the base of a large adobe oven, the frame for an arched doorway, and the many cement and barrel cisterns that once caught the seasonal rainfall—the only water available other than what was hauled up the trail. Here is where poet, author, and artist Marshal South and his family lived from 1930 to 1947, pursuing a primitive and natural lifestyle that became well-known through South's monthly columns written for *Desert Magazine*.

Ruins of Yaquitepec on Ghost Mountain. Photos courtesy of David Baumann.

In the years since the park acquired the property in 1958, curious desert explorers have hiked that trail, off San Diego County Highway S-2, to view the ruins. Invariably, hikers will ask themselves why someone would have chosen to live in such a dry, desolate area with small children for all of those years? Questions about the Souths are frequently directed to volunteers at the Anza-Borrego Desert State Park Visitor Center, but the responses have been based on limited information. When more information is wanted, it invariably leads to searches on the computer web pages or to libraries where past editions of *Desert Magazine* can be read.

Marshal South authored a total of 102 articles and poems for *Desert Magazine* from 1939 to 1948—80 articles about life on Ghost Mountain, 15 articles about the Anza-Borrego region, and 7 poems. All of these have been reproduced in this book. South introduced hundreds, perhaps thousands, of people to the desert through his monthly columns. He had a very loyal following, deservedly so. South wrote with a lyric quality, painting word pictures as only a poet or artist could. He wrote with passion about the desert—its silence, beauty, and natural history; its healthful qualities; its early inhabitants and their lifestyle. He deserves the recognition accorded to other desert writers such as J. Smeaton Chase, Charles Lummis, George Wharton James, John C. Van Dyke, and Mary Austin.

South was an inspiration to *Desert Magazine* publisher Randall Henderson and contributed to the early success of the magazine. Henderson said that his columns were "the most popular feature in the magazine."

Although South explained in his articles what drew him and his wife Tanya to the desert and Ghost Mountain, how they built their home, and why they chose an unconventional lifestyle, questions still remain. There has always been an aura of mystery and secrecy surrounding the Souths' past—especially their life before Ghost Mountain. The Souths' abrupt and acrimonious divorce, rumors of fictionalizing accounts of life at Yaquitepec, Marshal's early death, and Tanya's years of silence did not help matters. Attempts to learn more about Marshal South have led to dead ends, and the extent of his writing career beyond his novels, one or two short stories, and his articles in *Desert Magazine* was unknown.

The unanswered questions and general interest in the Souths have led to over 40 published articles and website postings since 1969 that speculate about the Souths. Some of those articles were well-researched, using the limited facts and materials that were available. There are academics who are currently studying Marshal South's contribution to western literature, and even an opera is being considered as a vehicle to tell the story. But the real story, based on previously unknown facts, has never been told—until now. It is a story long overdue.

Roy Bennett Richards—The Early Years

Marshal South, like a character out of one of his western novels, was part fiction. His real name was Roy Bennett Richards. A man much more complex and talented than previously supposed, he was a widely-published writer of poems (over 50), short stories and essays (over 40), novels (8), and *Desert Magazine* articles and poems (102). His writings were published in South Australia, Great Britain, and the United

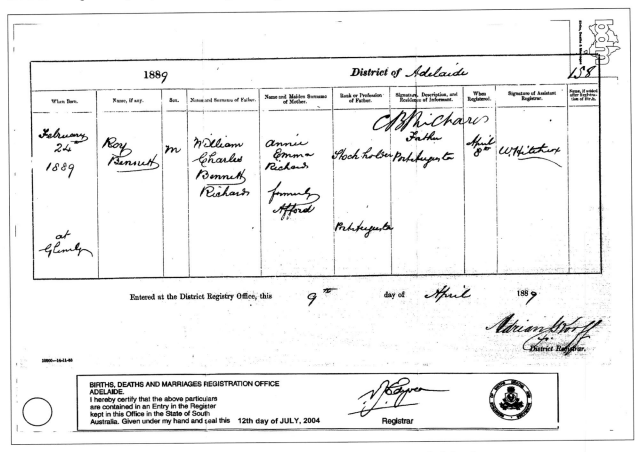

Birth certificate for Roy Bennett Richards—Marshal South.

States—in local and syndicated newspapers and magazines in New York, Pennsylvania, California, Arizona, and Texas. An artist who painted watercolors and oils, made pottery, carved wood and designed iron sculptures, he also worked in silver and leather, made weavings, and ran his own printing press—creating booklets, greeting cards, and newsletters decorated with colored blocks hand-carved from linoleum.

Roy Bennett Richards was born on February 24, 1889, in the seaside suburb of Glenelg, possibly at his grandmother's house, about six miles southwest from the center of Adelaide, South Australia. He was raised on his father's sheep ranch (station) at Pandurra, about 24 miles west of Port Augusta, a town approximately 200 miles north of Adelaide.

His mother, Annie Emma Afford Richards, was born on March 1, 1859, in Adelaide. She married William Charles Bennett Richards on August 6, 1877, when she was 18 years old and "Charlie" was 29. Charlie was born in the United States, in Wisconsin. When Charlie was nine years old, his father Thomas Richards moved the family to Australia in the hopes of building a better life there. Charlie's marriage to Annie was not his first. When he was 20 he married Annie Longmire and had two sons by that marriage, which ended in divorce in 1875—something very rare in those days.

Charlie was a sheep rancher who owned and leased many large estates, called stations. The *Adelaide Observer* (December 1, 1894) stated that he was "one of the pioneer pastoralists in the province." He was described as "a most energetic and fearless man among the live stock," and in *Pioneers of the North-West of Australia, 1856-1914*, there is a description of an incident in which he lost a horse while crossing some sand hills and "promptly roped a wild steer, and harnessed it up in the horse's place in the shafts of his wagon and proceeded on has [sic] way." His intense drive and persistence was illustrated in the *Adelaide Observer* (September 26, 1902) when they reported that "C.B. Richards.... With one team of ponies...drove over 320 miles of a heavy bush road in five days, accomplishing on the last day in twelve hours driving, 120 miles.... We question if such a feat has been performed by anyone else in the colony."

The same paper also reported (April 23, 1898) a visit by the Pastoral Commission in early April to inspect drought conditions and their effect on sheep country northwest of Adelaide. They visited Charlie's ranch and met Roy, at the time nine years old:

> *We now arrived at the Pandurra Woolshed, but where the only living things were one horse and one small boy, distinctly of the Australian species, in age about ten, in stature appearing to be barely six, but in precocity of intellect something approaching closely to twenty years. This elderly youngster, with hands in his pockets, evidently enjoyed a confab with strangers, and gave us clear and useful information on various subjects. As the Pandurra Station was some distance further on, and the time and appetite for the midday meal had arrived, one of the Commissioners anxiously enquired if the lad thought Mr. C.B. Richards (the lessee of Pandurra) expected us at the station. Then this Australian child, eying one of the party who presented a robust and well-fed appearance, said, with a broad grin and a decided wink—"Well, I spect [sic] he does, for he's killed a calf an' a sheep."... Our precocious little friend had other information...."*

The commissioners made their way to the station house for lunch and then went on to inspect another piece of property leased by Charlie, called Caroona. They later reported that Charlie was "pleasant company."

Charlie, who owned and managed large ranches and was a man to be reckoned with, could easily afford to send Roy to St. Peter's College in Adelaide, South Australia's most prestigious boy's school, affiliated with the Church of England. While he was a student, Roy began his writing career.

On December 23, 1904, the *Port Augusta Dispatch* published a short story entitled "A Terrible Christmas Eve." It is probably Roy's first published piece—he was 15 years of age. It is the story of a tomb discovered in Cairo and of the Indiana Jones-like escape of the two explorers.

Between 1904 and 1907 Roy had several works published by the *Port Augusta Dispatch*—prose, poetry, fiction, humor, satire, and commentary on political and social issues. He also had articles published in *The*

Gadfly—a humorous Adelaide weekly. The *Dispatch* was very proud of him, and the editor stated so in their May 5, 1905, issue when Roy was 16 years old:

> *We, this issue, publish another short story from the pen of our boy-author—a coming and promising second to the late Mr. Guy Boothby* [a popular and prolific South Australian writer in his day]. *Several very interesting short stories have already been published in our columns from the pen of our youthful contributor (a Port Augusta boy)—and have been published by us with a considerable amount of pride—several under a nome* [sic] *de plume. The Dispatch was the paper in which was published his "maiden effort," as well as his succeeding stories, which, to say the least, were all very readable....should he continue to show this literary talent, some day we may hope to see his abilities displayed in a greater effort, or in the production of a volume—comprehensive, and worthy of our youthful author.*

"Roy—Our Boy Author"
Illustration courtesy of State Library of South Australia.

During this period he may have been a cadet journalist for the *Dispatch*. The newspaper published a caricature of him captioned "Roy—Our Boy Author." The caricature is the last of a series of 12 entitled "Our Portrait Album" that was printed between March 9 and May 25, 1906. There is a possibility that Roy drew these for the *Dispatch*. The identity of the artist is unknown, and the initials that appear on the caricature are "JK."

Even at this early age Roy enjoyed using pseudonyms. Several of his articles in the *Dispatch* were published under the name "Cryptic." A series of humorous letters to the editor regarding the "pace of funerals" also could have been written by him under the names "A.B.C.," "J. Woodforde," and "Non Itchia Mala."

Not lacking in a sense of humor, Roy announced his departure from Port Augusta through another series of letters to the editor of the *Dispatch* built upon a complaint about holes in the street. Very likely he wrote all of the letters using various pseudonyms in addition to his own name. One poem is dedicated to himself, signed "'Walking Man' nee 'Pedestrian,'" which appeared in the June 28, 1907, edition of the *Dispatch*, asking all to "Bow to our Royal Richard now." His last published piece appeared the following month on July 12, 1907. In it he confesses his various pranks.

Sometime soon thereafter, Roy left the Port Augusta area with his mother and brother, Norman Afford Richards (born January 4, 1897). According to the family, Annie and the boys abandoned Charlie, taking all the money they could find in the house with them. Apparently, Charlie wanted Roy to work on the sheep ranch while Roy wanted to pursue a writing career. That may have been the reason why Roy did not attend St. Peter's College after 1906. Also, Annie's marriage to Charlie may have been difficult, much in the same way as Charlie's first marriage, which had led to a divorce.

Annie and the boys left Australia. As there are no shipping records of her having left from Adelaide, in all likelihood they took a train east from Adelaide to either Sydney or Melbourne where they boarded a ship to the United States. Because Charlie had been born in the United States, the boys were American citizens, which made it easier to obtain passage. They arrived on the West coast sometime in 1908.

Oddly enough, it took Charlie awhile to figure out where Annie and the boys had gone. On November 19, 1909, the *Port Augusta Dispatch* reported that he took the Sisters of St. Joseph and 33 of their pupils on a holiday excursion to Curlew Island and back in his motor-launch. It was reported that "all enjoyed themselves immensely." And just a few weeks later on December 3, 1909, he posted this notice offering a reward for the name of the person who escorted his wife to Saltia "on the morning of the 18th September, 1907, from the Greenbush Gaol [police station], where she had been harboured for a time against my consent." It appears that no one had offered him information prior to that time, and perhaps during that recent excursion he had received some clues, which led to the advertisement.

It was always Annie's concern that Charlie would follow them to the United States. The family believes that they moved around for a couple of years before settling in Oceanside, California, because of their fear of being located. Annie claimed on a later census survey that she had lived in California since 1908 and had been a resident of Oceanside since October 1911.

Roy traveled on his own in Mexico and the Southwest during this period as his early writings in Oceanside reflect intimate knowledge of these areas. In *Desert Magazine's* April 1948 "Desert Trails," he stated that he was in Guadalajara when Porfirio Diaz was president of Mexico and Miguel Ahumada was governor of Jalisco. Diaz served as president from 1884 to 1911 (and also an earlier period from 1876 to 1880) and Ahumada was governor from 1903 to 1911. Roy was there in 1911 or even earlier. There are also family stories about him "riding the rails," but that could have been later in 1920 when he moved back to Oceanside from Douglas, Arizona.

Whether Charlie actually followed them to the United States in later years is unknown. He was reported in the October 2, 1914, *Port Augusta Dispatch* as living in Adelaide, but a death notice has not been located in South Australia.

Lines dedicated to
"Walking Man"
nee "Pedestrian,"
on his departure from Port Augusta.

Farewell, farewell, thou'st passed away,
We miss thee sadly day by day,
No more with coat and headgear neat
We view thy figure in the street,
Nor will we, tho' we fume and fret
Again behold thy cigarette.

The matches that thou used to strike
In numbers that we did not like,
Ne'er more shall we again behold,
Thy pipe is out, thy hearth grows cold,
The railings of the churchyard fence
All lack their paint since thou went hence.

The ten inch nails and dog-spikes too
That thou drove in so straight and true,
Still languish in the shattered walls,
And each to heaven loudly calls
For vengeance, on the head of him
Who hammered them with such a vim.

The swinging lamps that used to fall
Upon the helpless heads of all,
Their leaden weights no longer melt,
And darkness can no more be felt.
On vanished seats thy flock stick not—
The paint brush rotteth in the pot.

No longer does the Public swear,
Nor Editors tear out their hair
Through reading literary rot
That thou thought fine—which it was not.
No longer do we sit and pine
From seven o'clock till half past nine.

Farewell, farewell, our swords have crossed,
And fights we've fought—which thou has lost.
Alas, alas, that thou hast gone,
Our luckless town is all forlorn,
No longer are our minds perplexed
With asking what thou wilt do next.

Farewell, farewell, then "A.B.C."
"Non Itchia" too, farewell to thee,
Farewell, farewell, to "Walking Man"
Who called himself "Pedestrian."
Farewell, farewell, farewell, to thee,
May thou die happy—so may we.

— ROY B. RICHARDS

Enter Marshal South—Oceanside's Poet Laureate

When the family settled in Oceanside, they used the Richards family name. It may have been a concern for them if Roy were again to publish using his name—it could lead Charlie to them. Roy had already shown a penchant for using pseudonyms, so in all likelihood, it was an easy decision for him to select a nom de plume.

Roy was also a word wizard and may have liked the double meaning found in the name "Marshal." Used as a noun, it could be someone with a high military rank or a deputy, as in a frontier marshal. Roy had an early fascination with the American West and set one of his first stories in Texas when he was writing in Adelaide. The only thing missing from his author photo on the back cover of *Child of Fire*, published in 1935, was a badge. He was pictured with a western hat, leather jacket, and an ammunition belt across his chest. Used as a verb, "marshal" means to usher or lead in ceremoniously. Perhaps he saw himself as taking the lead as an author of western fiction—one who would be recognized for his writing skills.

"South" also may have been a reference to his fascination with the Southwest, or it could have been a reference to *Terra Australis*—southern land—an early name for Australia. He was also from the province of South Australia.

The selection of a pseudonym for Roy was just one of the many ways that the members of the family chose to hide themselves. The earliest documents they filled out listed England as their land of birth, not Australia, and all

"Marshal" South, author of Western novels (left); in Arizona in 1918 (right).

documents through the death of each one usually listed England. Marshal even listed London, England, as his birthplace on one of his documents. Perhaps this was done to make it harder for Charlie to find them, or it could have been done to avoid questions about their background in Australia. Australia was known to have been a penal colony, and it would have been easier to say they were from England rather than having to explain Charlie's background. There is yet a third possibility. It could have been a practice for those living within the British Empire to simply say they were from England, as they were ultimately British citizens.

Sometimes birth dates and years, as well as given names, were changed on documents or surveys, which made it even more difficult to trace the family back to Australia. Roy changed his middle name from Bennett to Benjamin or B. Richards and dropped Roy. Norman changed his middle name Afford—his mother's maiden name—to Allen and listed New York as his mother's birthplace on his wedding certificate. Annie listed herself as a widow of "W.C." Richards rather than "C.B." Richards, the initials used by Charlie.

Using his new pen name, Roy's first known published work in the United States appeared in the *Los Angeles Tribune* on May 7, 1912. It was a poem entitled "Intervention." The *Oceanside Blade* of December 27, 1913, reported that "A poem by B. Richards who writes under the pseudonym of Marshal South, and entitled 'Lights of Vera Cruz,' appeared in the magazine section in last Sunday's *Los Angeles Times*." This is the earliest known reference of B. Richards writing as Marshal South.

By 1914 B. Richards was again in writing stride and had once again become the darling of a local newspaper. The *Blade* began making regular comments about his poems and stories and even made note of the volume of works produced that year, which were at least 10 poems and two short stories.

On May 2, 1914, the *Blade* stated: "Oceanside's favorite poet, B. Richards, who writes under the name of Marshal South...is surely some poet, and as he is still young, the *Blade* looks for him to make a name for himself." On October 3, 1914, this was printed: "B. Richards, Oceanside's poet laureate, has an uncommonly well-written poem in the *L.A. Times*." The following week on October 17, the editor of the *Blade* commented about the poem "Finis," stating that

Marshal South, Oceanside's Poet laureate, has written a poem called "Finis" recently printed in the Blade that puts B. Richards...on the map. Now when a poet gets on the map lesser mortals have to be careful and look into their poetical antecedents.... Now we have read over "Finis" a number of times and while finding it pretty high class poetry we see between the lines certain poet laureate tendencies.

On November 7, 1914, the editor of the *Blade* told readers that "the irrepressible person, Marshal B. Richards South, has again broken into verse and good verse, which we print this week. If the Poet Marshal—not city marshal—goes on like this our equally irrepressible poetical editor threatens to let himself loose with an 'Ode to a Blind Pig.' The *Blade* dreads this effusion and trusts Brother Richards South will try and curtail his poetical crop."

But Richards did not "curtail his poetical crop," and the "Ode to Blind Pig" ran in the November 14 issue—signed by "General Shelly North," the editor of the *Blade* who was having fun with a play on words while standing in awe of Oceanside's poet laureate.

The *Blade* was reporting on more than Richards' writing ability in 1914. Richards had decided to take an active role, outside of his writing, to stir up interest in patriotism and the need for defense. His first activity was to call for a display of military arms. On September 9, 1914, the *Blade* reported that "our distinguished local poet...sounded the alarm, and all Anglo Saxons, and others rushed to the Hansen store with arms." The Hansen store, where Richards worked as a clerk, was converted to "Fort Hansen" and an assortment of arms was placed on view in the show windows.

It was reported in the paper that an army in force had descended from "Fort Richards" and "Fort Hansen" and "all arms and ammunition, ancient and modern, that could be found within 50 miles of Oceanside and Denmark was saved." On display in the store windows were a variety of arms. Richards contributed the following: a sword used in the Maori war in New Zealand, spurs from a "Mexican bandit who died with his boots on," and a "luger pistol of great velocity used by European armies." The *Blade* stated that "such a display was never before seen in Oceanside, and the *Blade* trusts will never be needed again."

B. Richards then called for the formation of the Oceanside Debate Club, and over 100 people attended its first meeting, according to the December 26, 1914, *Blade*. "Marshal South" spoke on "National Defense and the fallacy of disarmament," and before the meeting adjourned, a local rifle club was organized.

By the end of 1914, the local paper was referring to B. Richards more often as Marshal South. South was also becoming much more militaristic in his poetry and outlook. On December 5, 1914, the *Blade* reported that he had received a letter from the German Ambassador in Washington D.C. praising his poem "The Emden," which he had read in the *Los Angeles Times*, and when the *Blade* reported that South's story "The

Sword of the Flame" would appear in the January issue of *Black Cat*, it stated that "Marshal is very military even in his titles." The *Blade* also called him "a warrior poet" on January 30, 1915, and said he was "gifted," citing his poem "Beware" as an example of his ability." In a stanza from "Beware" Marshal wrote:

Awake! O Land of Liberty, awake. No longer may thy wealth and people lie,
Wrapped in false dreams of safety and content—those drowsy dreams in which great nations die.
No "politics" nor "theories" here have place; this is a matter for the nation's care;
By heroes was thy banner planted wide—by men and guns must ye maintain it there!

As impassioned that he was in his poetry so did he become in his efforts to create a Defense League. He placed a notice in the *Blade* that ran on January 2, 1915, asking for all marksmen to attend a meeting to complete the organization of the Oceanside Rifle Club. At the meeting he read the by-laws of the National Rifle Association and said that he would be forwarding the names of all who joined to the national office in Washington, D.C. He said that all who wished to take part in military drill would be enrolled as members of Company A, Oceanside.

His interest in national defense did not come out of nowhere. He had actually called for the need for national defense as early as 1906, when he was 17 years old in South Australia, when he wrote an essay entitled "Peace and Australian Defense" for the *Port Augusta Dispatch* on June 15, 1906. He also wrote a poem entitled "The Coming of the Yellow Man" on February 1, 1907, where he warned about the threat of Japan and China as sleeping giants who would soon awake. He saw the situation in Europe in the same light and knew that the best defense would be preparation for the coming onslaught.

On January 16, 1915, the *Oceanside Blade* headline read: "SAFE AT LAST!" The article stated, "The American Defense League, an organization for the encouragement of public interest in matters of national defense was formed on Tuesday. Marshal South, President…." Another article in the same paper said, "A sigh of relief was sighed all over Oceanside for no longer need our fair city fear invasion from either Hun, Japanese, or idle tramps."

By the following month the newly formed Defense League was 20 strong, and with new uniforms they attended a commemoration service at Grace Episcopal Church to celebrate the 100th anniversary of peace between the United States and Great Britain.

South continued to hammer his point about readiness. "The Protest of the Dead" was published in two parts on January 25 and February 6, 1915. The *Oceanside Blade* said that it "should be carefully read by all. No doubt, at heart, many of us are pacifists but after seeing the horrible spectacle of untold millions trying to destroy each other in Europe, pacifism seems impossible without general disarmament. In this poem Mr. Richards is at his best."

Marshal South, president, the American Defense League.

THE PROTEST OF THE DEAD

Was it therefore for this that we perished?
  To this end that we struggled and wrought?
Just for this that we warred and adventured?
  For this that we suffered and fought?
Was it only for this we pushed westward
  through the long weary trail of the plains?
Toiling on in the dust of the ox trains,
  or the foundering mire of the rains?

Was it only for this we fought Savage,
  fought Wilderness, Famine and Death?
That we toiled in the heat to the southward,
  or died in the north blizzard's breath?
Was it all to this end we faced empires,
  and wide planted the flag of the free?
Just for this that we builded a nation,
  who's wide bounds are but stayed by the sea?

JUST FOR THIS?
For this! That ye, ye who come after,
  stand so careless to guard and to hold;
That ye value the nation we gave you far
  less than the worth of your gold.
That ye prate of "expense" and "taxation"
  and the era when all war shall cease,
And the day (God! How far) when the he-wolf
  with the lamb of the fold shall make peace.

That ye sit, chanting nostrums and plaudits
  in the face of the guns of the world;
That ye follow the creed by which Egypt
  and Rome to destruction were hurled.
That ye suffer your arms to lie dormant,
  while ye labor your wealth to increase,
While ye stifle the voices of warning with
  your empty dream-chatter of "Peace."

"Peace!" Aye, peace! With our swords
  we obtained it. With your swords ye must
    hold it, or pass—
Soothe your souls not to comfort with "visions"
  as frail as the wind in the grass.
Are ye blind? Look ye back through the ages;
  look ye back at the powers that held sway;
They passed careless to wreck and destruction
  by the path ye are treading today.

Give heed; that is not the Millennium!
  While this earth and man's passions endure,
Ye may not match palm boughs against cannon;
  neither peace with soft plaudits secure.
Guns and arms are not forged in a moment;
  and ye may not train men in a day—
Give ye heed. Lest the freedom we gave you,
  like your "peace-dreams," shall vanish away!

After the publication of this poem, the *Blade* never mentions B. Richards again. The complete transformation had taken place, and only Marshal South now existed. The same issue also announced the dates for the next two meetings of the Oceanside Debate Club in which Marshal later debated such topics as "Resolved that Trusts are necessary and to be encouraged by the American people" and "Resolved that the Sympathy of the United States for England against Germany in the European War is Misplaced."

In the next several months South was busy recruiting more members for the Defense League. His title was now "captain." The *Blade* announced on March 27, 1915, that South "will be the founder and editor of *Defense*"—a monthly magazine "devoted to the encouragement of public interest in matters of National Defense." It would be the official organ of the American Defense League, locally represented by Company A.

The *Blade* continued to lavish praise for his efforts stating on April 10, 1915:

Marshal South, ex-officer in the British Army and poet of no mean ability…. To this man…Oceanside may some day owe the placing of her name upon the map of the nation in capital letters—for it is in Oceanside that South has succeeded in organizing the "American League of Defense," destined, perhaps to become an institution with branches in every part of the Union.... As founder and president of the league the poet-soldier declares that an organization for the encouragement of public interest in matters of national defense is not only a thing of patriotic beauty, but an absolute necessity for the welfare of the nation.... South is still a young man. He has just passed 27. But he has had vast experience for one of his age.

Just as in earlier years when Roy created characters to write letters to the editor for the *Port Augusta Dispatch*, he was now beginning to build on the character of Marshal South by claiming that South was an "ex-officer in the British Army"! Other claims would be made in the future that built on the partially fictional character of South in order to appeal to audiences.

In his role as captain of the Defense League he received a letter of support from Prof. George A. Dickson of New Castle, Pennsylvania, who wrote that "it is considered quite remarkable that in so few weeks, with limited practice, Company A, has been whipped into military shape. Marshal South really deserves great credit and more should join the company." The *Blade* also reported on May 29, 1915, that the rifle club received "a consignment of sixteen Krag rifles, and 1500 rounds of ammunition from the United States Government."

South now began a surprising and gradual disengagement, slowly scaling back his own involvement as the momentum of activity and praise continued to mount through the end of the year. Was South suddenly feeling that he had gotten in over his head—perhaps going in a direction that he did not want to pursue? Or, had he reached a level of competency that satisfied him and thus began seeking a new challenge? We can only guess at his motivation.

The July 10, 1915, edition of the *Blade* reported that South was stepping down as president of the Oceanside Rifle Club and as captain of Company A so that he could devote more time to his duties as president of the American Defense League. The same issue reported that *Out West Magazine* of Los Angeles had announced that they were inaugurating the publication of a special department to report the activities of the league and that South would be its editor. And a final article in that edition, with the headline "Oceanside Citizen Receiving Much Publicity," recognized South as "a very energetic and earnest resident."

South's work for the American Defense League even attracted the attention of Theodore Roosevelt who met with South to discuss the policies and objectives of the league. The July 31, 1915, *Blade* reported that "The Colonel displayed deep interest in the movement and expressed his hearty support of the league.... Before leaving Marshal South on behalf of the Defense League presented Mr. Roosevelt with a memento of his visit to San Diego in the shape of a special souvenir copy of the poem of 'Welcome' written by Mr. South which was first published in the *San Diego Sun* on the day of his arrival [July 26]." The *Blade* later reported on August 28 that Roosevelt heartily endorsed the motto of the American Defense League, which South created—"Adequate Defense is the Safeguard of Liberty."

On December 20, South, as president and founder of the Oceanside league, sent a resolution from the board of directors to the American Defense League of San Diego calling for the amalgamation of the Oceanside league with that of San Diego. The resolution was accepted and the amalgamation was announced in the December 25, 1915, issue of the *Army & Navy Call*—the official organ for the American Defense League. South's poem "Prepare" also appeared in the same issue. South accepted a position on the advisory board of the newly reorganized league and became its national representative and organizer. He called for an aggressive campaign to educate the public about the "pressing need" for "adequate national defense without the perils of militarism, and to do all and every possible thing to prevent war by assuring peace through adequate preparation."

Marshal's activity through the Fall had reached a crescendo, just as his poetry had. The greatest praise to date came with the publication of "Progress" in the November 1915 issue of the *American Magazine*. In the foreword to the poem, Albert Miller of the *Los Angeles Express* had this endorsement: "I have read nothing

PROGRESS

I

"Behold our progress!" the Assyrian cried,—viewing
    beneath the brilliant blazing sky
The lofty towers, the walls of sun-baked brick,
    the brazen gates, the ponderous ramparts high,
The roll of chariots in the narrow ways, the glittering
    crowd close thronging mart and street,
The gleaming flash of spears beneath the sun,
    the shaking tread of conquering legions' feet—
"Behold our progress and enlightenment! *We* are the
    people! We shall surely stand."
        —AND SPEAKING THUS THEY PASSED.

The moon shines cold above the desert sands,
    The thin winds whimper lone across the waste;
The shifting dunes long since have rolled and closed
    Above dead cities ages-long effaced.
The monuments and towers are overthrown,
    The tablets molder in the sword blade's rust,
And all the glory that the past has known
    Has crumbled, like the builders,—into dust.

II

"Behold our progress!"—Hear proud Egypt's boast:
    temples and pyramids and painted stone;
Column on column reared beside the Nile; throughout
    the world for wealth and science known;
Rich galleys clustering on the river's flood; learning and
    wisdom sheltered in the halls;
Vast monuments of power on every hand; ranked gods
of stone and massive sculptured walls—
"Behold our progress and enlightenment! *We* are the
    people! We shall surely stand."
        —AND SPEAKING THUS THEY PASSED.

The jackal whines among the fallen stones,
    The painted tombs no longer guard their dead;
The desert winds disport with mummy-dust;
    The gods are fallen and their glory fled.
The bats at even flitter forth from holes
    Wherein aged shreds of human clay are thrust;
The silken sails and gilded galley poles
    Have crumbled, like the builders,—into dust.

III

"Behold our progress!"—Hear the tramp of Rome:
    legion on legion on the stone-paved ways,
Clatter of chariots; tread of marching feet; standards
    ablaze beneath the morning rays;
Mistress of all the world, from pine to palm; art and
    adornment filched from every land;
Monarchs in chains behind her chariot wheels; States
    that pay tribute to a conqueror's hand—
"Behold our progress and enlightenment! *We* are the
    people! We shall surely stand."
        —AND SPEAKING THUS THEY PASSED.

The broken pillars in the Forum lie,
    And shattered fragments strew the Circus floor.
The loathsome beggars cluster in the shade
    Of walls whose echoes legions wake no more.
The brazen bucklers turn no foeman's steel,
    The short, keen sword no longer makes its thrust,
And all the Empire that hailed Caesar lord
    Has crumbled, like its builders,—into dust.

IV

"Behold our progress!"—Emperor, King and Czar:
    navies far flung and battle flags unfurled;
Europe a checkerboard of blood and flame; their legions
    mustering throughout the world.
Hear once again, while red the ruin roars, the puny voices
    shouting each to each.
Each on the other shouldering the blame; hear once again
    the weary, age-old speech—
"Behold our progress and enlightenment! *We* are the
    people! We shall surely stand."
        —AND AS THEY SPEAK THEY PASS.

The dreadnaughts fade beneath the Channel tide,
    The cities flame; the fields are black with dead.
The highways shake beneath the tread of hosts
    Pouring to meet the flame-shot storm of lead.
Women, sad-eyed, the hushing hamlets fill;
    The needy seek in vain starvation's crust;
And all the gain of hard-wrought centuries
    Is crumbling, with its builders,—into dust.

bearing on the war by any American or English poet that takes rank with the verses I send you herewith in his behalf." The *Oceanside Blade* of November 6, 1915, had this to say: "Every lover of good poetry and everyone who is able to appreciate a remarkable piece of literature is advised to get a copy of the *American Magazine* and read 'Progress.'" The *Los Angeles Tribune* paid tribute to South and reported in a headline that his poem was "Being Complimented And Copied Widely." They wrote this about South and his latest poem:

> *The futility of human endeavor that is not rooted in righteousness is the lesson taught by one of the notable poems of the year from the pen of Marshall [sic.] South, who fairly may be claimed as a Californian by adoption. The poem appears in the American Magazine for the current month and is reprinted on this page. If its philosophy offers rude challenge to the vanity of our civilization the music of the verse and stately progress of the measures through the melody of their rhythm cannot but delight. Once in a long, long weary while, the intervals of waiting being stuffed with mediocrities, is heard the note of some real singer rising high and clear, and, grateful for its coming, men listen while it lasts and themselves are silent for a space in reverie when it ends. We indulge the hope that in Marshall [sic.] South America has found such a singer, that rarest of rare comers—a true poet.*

There is a sudden silence of activity for the next several months, and the only notifications that appear are in regard to South's poems. On March 25, 1916, the *Blade* reported that "Progress" had won a gold medal at the annual "elocution contest" at Erasmus Hall in Brooklyn, New York. A second gold medal had been awarded for the recitation of Alfred Noyes' poem "The River of Stars." The paper also reported that South's "America" had been chosen by the Knights of Pythias in Monrovia, California, to be read at their annual meeting on March 30. On May 24, 1916, the paper stated that South had received a personal note from Theodore Roosevelt thanking him for the recently published poem "The Nation's Call—To Theodore Roosevelt."

A New Life in Arizona—The Army and Margaret

Margaret loved cats. Marshal called her "Pusstat."

Sometime before July or August, Marshal South was tapped by the draft. He was 27 years old, but from this point on, all documents—including his death certificate—show that his birth year is actually three years earlier, making him 30 years old in 1916. Rider South recalls his mother telling him that Marshal's mother Annie went into the draft board and told them Marshal's birth year was 1886 and not 1889. Why was this done? Did it have any relationship to the fact that he was sent to Camp Henry J. Jones in Douglas, Arizona, rather than to Europe? Did his mother insist on the change? Norman was also serving, and she may have feared losing both sons and having no family to comfort her. Or, it may have been Marshal's decision to change the date.

Marshal served with the Transportation Division of the Army Quartermaster Company—the QMC.

Portrait of Margaret taken about 1920.

Unfortunately, his military records were burned in a massive fire in 1973 at the National Personnel Records Center in St. Louis, so the details of his service are sketchy. It is known that he was sent to Arizona before September because the poem "The Last March" was printed in the *Los Angeles Daily Times* on September 8, 1916, with a note at the bottom of the poem by Marshal's name stating it was written in Douglas, Arizona. It is also known that he served as a clerk in the office of the QMC where he met Margaret Frieda Schweichler who also worked in the same office as a civilian secretary. While he served in Douglas, his poetry was regularly published by the *Los Angeles Times*, the *New York Forum*, and the *Douglas Dispatch*.

A relationship began between Marshal and Margaret, who was 21 years old when they met. She was born on July 6, 1895, in Juliette, Idaho. Her father was a German Jew, but Margaret was a Lutheran. She was an artist who painted oils on canvas. The only thing that is known about their courtship year is that they would go out to the desert and paint and sketch side by side. They took out a marriage license on December 21, 1917. Margaret must have had second thoughts about a marriage because in a poem dated January 9, 1918, Marshal begs her to give him a second chance:

TO MARGARET: THE DEAREST GIRL IN ALL THE WORLD

You have shattered the spell of my ancient gods; you have shadowed their altars glow
  And never again shall their voices call, with the call that I used to know.
You have fettered my life with a rose-leaf chain,—but ere ever its links shall part
  They will tear the heart-strings, one by one, from the depths of a broken heart.

For never again shall the South wind harp, with the lure of the Spanish Main
  For the charm is gone from the southern seas—and I cannot return again
And never the Southern Cross shall flare by night from the star-splashed blue
  And the call of its orbs shall pale and die when Fate parts me from you.

For I cannot follow the same old trails, nor steer by the same old lights
  And my memory weaves me a thousand ghosts in the still of the lonesome nights
And I feel again the touch of your hand and the fragrant breath of your hair
  Then the visions vanish and naught remains,—but silence, and despair.

I am not all that I ought to be—as none knows better than I
  You know my faults and I need not strive to shield them or to deny
But I love you, love you with all my heart, and my life—tho you may not care—
  Is laid for ever beneath your feet,—and none shall remove it there.

I cannot speak the words that I ought, nor pen the things that I feel
  (For my rhymes sing better of war and hate, and fire and the gleam of steel)
So I cannot paint you my love in words—true words that might explain,
  So I must suffer and stand aside; dumb, foolish, and full of pain.

But my life is laid in your hands to keep; to mould it as you desire
  To build with it all of the dreams you dreamed;—or cast it into the fire
With you it can reach to the heights of fame;—without; it will touch despair.
  In your keeping its making or marring lies,—for Fate has placed it there.

What doubts Margaret had were washed away with this poem. They were married by the Justice of the Peace on January 17, 1918, in Bisbee, Arizona. She resigned her job with the QMC on March 1, 1918, and on December 5, 1919, Marshal Jr. was born in Douglas.

The 1920 *Douglas City Directory* listed Marshal and Margaret as living at 531 7th Street and indicated that Marshal worked for the Army QMC. Marshal was discharged from the Army sometime in early 1920.

An editor's note from a poem Marshal wrote in 1937, dedicated to his friend E.W. King, fills in some missing details from the years he served in the Army. The poem was written for *Presidio News* upon King's 85th birthday and reprinted with the editorial note in *The Big Bend Sentinel* on October 22, 1937. The editor of the *Presidio News* stated that King reenlisted for the service when he was 65 years old by presenting his service record to Major Elliott, quartermaster at Ft. Bliss in El Paso, Texas. King was sent to Camp Henry J. Jones to serve in the QMC where he was soon joined by Marshal South. They "served together until the Eighteenth Regiment, United States Infantry, was entrained for 'somewhere in France.' Following the entrainment of the Eighteenth, Mr. King and Mr. South were transferred to El Paso, where they served until the A.E.F. [American Expeditionary Forces] returned from 'over there.'"

Photo of Marshal in Arizona taken about 1918, probably on base at Camp Henry J. Jones.

The poem also gives hints of how Marshal spent his time while serving in the Army. They would "wander down to Mike's café" and dunk their doughnuts while swapping stories "with the boys of the Q.M.C." about the latest "lies of some Border scare." They would sit at their desks and "hammer the Waybills out" and on Sunday hikes they would "cross the line" and "sniff Sonora air, while the music plays and the dark-eyed girls parade in the plaza there." They would head for the dusty plain where they would "search on the field, where Villa fought, for the war-scraps that remain."

More information is also found in the *Oceanside Blade* of September 16, 1916. The newspaper reported that it had received a letter from "Capt. South" stating that he was now living in Douglas, Arizona—"a city of some thirteen years growth from the sage brush, some 13,000 population; one mile from the Mexican line and the present base of some 12,000 U.S. Troops." He said that there was considerable military activity in town, a share "of which has fallen to the part of Oceanside" in that the Transportation Division of the QMC was solely staffed "by two representatives from your city—Mr. E. [Edmund] W. King, a former resident of Oceanside for many years [from 1909 to 1914], and myself." Marshal also said there was a lot of activity in town due to the fighting centered in the Mexican town of Agua Prieta, a mile south of Douglas.

South served while General John J. Pershing was in pursuit of Pancho Villa from 1916 to 1917. He became fully informed about the activities of the Carranzistas and the Villistas, which provided the

Margaret and Marshal about 1918.

Marshal called his son "Ratzin."

background for several of his western novels. In his later writings for *Desert Magazine* he also recalled days of exploring Sonora and staying at rickety hotels that bore bullet holes from the revolutionary days.

In June 1920, a few months after Marshal was discharged from the Army, Margaret asked him to leave. Marshal was distraught and spent nights sleeping out in the open desert "sinking into hopeless degradation; sleeping on boxes and out in the desert in an overcoat; chased off by the police." He hoped Margaret would take him back and he repeatedly tried to return only to be rebuffed.

Marshal moved back to Oceanside and wrote letters to Margaret. She responded that she wanted nothing to do with him, writing "I can never be happy with you." She said she preferred to live alone.

The marriage failed because they had different expectations. Marshal was never interested in money. He grew up in wealth and never valued it. He lashed out against the drive for money in his earliest essays written for the *Port Augusta Dispatch* in 1906. He valued creativity and freedom. Margaret was practical and ambitious. She wanted a spouse that could provide a comfortable home and living—one that would find a good job and stay with it.

In a letter to Margaret written on December 18, 1922, from Oceanside, Marshal wrote:

...we follow different stars. For you the material success counts. The earthly prosperity and comfort. For me these things mean nothing or next to nothing; it is toward the world of ideals and thought and philosophy that my steps lead. I crave companionship of soul, someone who can understand and accompany me in my wanderings—be they earthly or spiritual, someone who will not oppose me or crush me down with a heavier and more inflexibly immovable spirit. I want someone who can laugh with my foolishness and sympathize with my deeper moods. And who will not try to suppress me or to re-make me into a successful provider which I am not or never can be.

In the same letter he reflects about the bitter lessons they have learned and "inflicted upon each other. Upon you I have brought trouble and financial disaster, disillusionment, and shattered dreams. For me you have brought the unspeakable torture and agony of useless and rejected love and the tearing separation from the love of my boy. God forgive and comfort both of us."

Marshal continued to write letters from Oceanside, sending money and gifts when he could. Margaret always wrote back, sometimes including drawings that "Ratzin" (Marshal Jr.) made—choo-choo trains and two

Margaret and Marshal Jr.

headed elephants. His days of writing were essentially over except for a poem that was published in the *San Diego Tribune* on December 2, 1922, entitled "Futility." In a foreword to the poem, the editor called Marshal "a poet of disillusion" and said that "Futility" expressed the "Philosophy of a Pessimist." The editor wrote, "what a futile thing is human existence after all its struggle to shape a destiny contrary to that which was foreordained from the beginning! ...For, within the narrow cycle of Man's feeble, trivial, futile endeavor he invariably returns upon his own track and pursues again and again the same delusions, the same false lights, the same vain aspirations, dreams and chimeras."

Thus Marshal sunk into depression and stayed there until he met Tanya.

One rumor that has surrounded Marshal South can be put to rest. He has been accused of abandoning Margaret and leaving her to fend for herself in Arizona. That rumor is partially based on comments made by Marshal Jr. as an adult. He remembered that his father had left them when he was about six years old and that he and his mother were left to survive by selling her paintings and raiding trash cans for food. These are true memories, but they are not memories of Marshal but of Margaret's second husband. Margaret married Augusto Carlestedt in the early 1920s. He was Peruvian and was deported by the INS in 1925. In 1926 Margaret moved to Los Angeles, changing the spelling of her last name to Carlstedt. She became a small store owner and later a realtor in Inglewood.

Tanya—A Kindred Spirit?

Tanya at the Rosicrucian Fellowship about 1921.

Tanya South was born on November 4 (Gregorian calendar), 1897, in Zhmerinka, Podolsk, near Brahilov in the Russian Ukraine near the Romanian border. She was the sixth child of Nahoom (Nathan) and Seepa (Celia) Oocheetal (Lehrer)—orthodox Jews. Her father was a school teacher who was drafted into the Russian Army and served 20 years in the medical corps performing surgeries—mainly amputations. After he was discharged he opened a small shop that was subject to periodic raids (pogroms) by the Czarists. The family regularly witnessed atrocities during these raids. Fortunately for them, they were able to immigrate to the United States, arriving in New York in October 1906 when Tanya was eight years old.

Tanya grew up and attended schools in New York and was called Tessie. She may have attended some classes at Columbia University. In later years Marshal claimed she graduated from Columbia (in articles he wrote using her name), but there is no record of her having attended any classes. Tanya became a secretary on Wall Street. She was a small woman—five feet, three inches tall—with blue eyes and light brown hair (Marshal was five feet, eleven inches tall, weighed less than 140 pounds, and had brown eyes and brown hair).

In September 1920 after her father died, Tanya moved to Oceanside and began working immediately for the Rosicrucian Fellowship. She gave up a well-paying position in New York, according to Marshal, to work for a fraction of the earnings at the Fellowship. She was interested in astrology, the occult and spiritual pursuits. Tanya worked as the healing department secretary for Augusta Foss Heindel. Augusta's husband Max Heindel was the founder of the Rosicrucian Fellowship in Oceanside. When he passed on in 1919, Augusta became the head of the organization. The Heindels believed that astrology was the key to unlock the mysteries of man's inner nature. Augusta Heindel taught Tanya how to read palms.

Tanya had been involved with the organization while she lived in New York. Her poem "Smile" appeared in the Rosicrucian Fellowship Magazine *Rays from the Rose Cross* in May 1920. Using the name of Tessie Lehrer, she also wrote an article in the July 1920 issue posing a question and then providing an answer to "Why Is It Necessary for Man to Evolve Through Matter?" Other poems were published in the August ("Only God") and December ("I am Thought") 1920 issues. She continued writing articles and poems on a regular basis for the Fellowship magazine at least until 1923 when Marshal and Tanya wed.

When Marshal moved back to Oceanside, he began working as a carpenter for the Rosicrucian Fellowship. On July 23, 1920, the Fellowship had laid the cornerstone for their temple, and for the next several years they employed many builders.

Marshal was depressed and contemplating suicide when he met Tanya. She began counseling him through

Wedding photo of Marshal and Tanya South taken March 8, 1923.

astrology, doing horoscopes for Marshal and Margaret. In the December 2, 1922, letter to Margaret, Marshal told her about Tanya and confessed that the stars were not fortunate for him in many ways: "They give genius…but they do not give earthly success (and I do not crave that anyhow) also they give loneliness and suffering. And if I followed their impellings I would die either by grief or by my own hand." He credited Tanya's influence in overcoming that desire.

Marshal explained to Margaret that Tanya had brought great peace into his soul and had "awakened me to the uselessness of seeking love in earthly things when it is only the cause of broken hearts." Crediting Tanya with binding up his "broken heart" and bringing "the rest of peace to a tortured soul," he told Margaret that where she had opened the door of life to him that Tanya had opened the door which leads beyond life.

In that same letter of December 11, 1922, Marshal asked Margaret to grant him a divorce, stating that "it is not fair of you to keep me tied to you and at the same time refuse to be a companion to me....for two years you have pushed me from you and urged me to seek someone else. And I could not do it. I clung to the hope of

Honeymoon accommodations on an Oceanside beach.

you. And finally Fate has intervened." He told Margaret that he did not know if Tanya could love him, but he did know this: "whatever happens, that little girl—and she is more than a girl, almost more than human, in her spiritual faith and understanding—has done more for me than any other human being or religion ever did. She has not changed my philosophy but she has thrown sunshine upon it. And she has brought peace and understanding."

In describing Tanya to Margaret he referred to her purity of thought, her kindness, her priceless words of good counsel, and her lonesomeness and starvation for affection, which Marshal equally felt. He said that Tanya "is the only genuine soul I ever met whom I believed had fixed their ideals on something above this earth." He worried about her because while "She is wise in the ways of God and the great unknown, in the ways of…the world she is helpless." He prayed that "God guard her and send her someone whom she can love, to be her protector, in some measure, against the horrors of life."

He advised Margaret to hold fast to her talent of painting—to paint every opportunity she could "for the sake of the beautiful that it will develop in you—never mind the fact that they will sell or not. Have trust in the care of a Higher Power which will watch over all of us for our own good." He also told her that he didn't know what the future would bring, but he was "determined on one thing and that is that my salvation and purpose in life lies in holding fast to my talent for writing and developing it, no matter what the result may be financially."

In the next few months, Tanya and Marshal decided to wed. As divorce proceedings between Marshal and Margaret had not yet taken place, Marshal claimed on his wedding certificate that it was a first marriage for him. They were married on March 8, 1923, in Santa Ana, California. They moved to Los Angeles where Tanya took a job with an oil company and Marshal began work for an "office building concern."

He wrote Margaret after Easter (the letter is undated but mentions that Easter has just passed) to tell her the news and to send her some money:

I have something to tell you which I sincerely hope will not hurt you, because, in spite of the unhappy course of our married life, we have been, and always will be, the dearest of friends, and I do not want to hurt your feelings. You know I told you about the little Jewish girl that I met in Oceanside who was so wonderful and who cast all of our horoscopes (also she recommended all those astrology books which I sent on for you. She helped me pick them out for you). Well, Margaret dear, we are married; and we are both very happy; the only shadow that at all dims our happiness is the feeling that you may feel wounded and deserted. Truly that is worrying us both. We don't want you to feel that way. We want you to feel that you have not lost one friend but that you have rather gained another…. Tessie talks so much about you and loves you so much. She knows you pretty well from your horoscope and the things I have told her about you and she wants so much that you and Ratzin should feel that we are all one in friendship and love….we are trying to make ends meet, that is why we both have to work. However Tessie is cheerful and brave about it all and I am doing my best. If you could only be friends with us both our happiness would be complete.

To read this letter it would appear that just as Marshal has described, he and Tanya were very happy and very much in love. But was that really the case? Perhaps Marshal was just a hopeless and impassioned romantic bent on having someone to love who he hoped would love him, understand him and acquiesce to his desires. His original description of Tanya to Margaret may have been framed more in his hopes and desires rather than what she was really like. He had told Margaret that if Tanya loved him she "would go with me to the end of the earth…. And she has risen far above money. For she does not want it nor value it. She lives simply and dresses simply. She is not afraid of poverty and it is the higher things of life that she desires—not the material."

Tanya later expressed to her children that she married Marshal because he hounded her and she finally gave in. The children are not sure whether Tanya ever really loved him. She told them that they fought on their wedding night. She was also not as disinterested in material comforts as Marshal wanted to believe. She later wrote, "I can't say when the so-called depression hit us because with Marshal we were always suffering in a depression."

Sometime after Marshal's marriage to Tanya, Margaret married Augusto Carlestedt. Whether either Margaret or Marshal obtained a divorce is unknown. No record has been found in Arizona or California. It is possible that Margaret obtained a divorce in Mexico with Augusto's help.

Marshal moved back to Oceanside in either late 1923 or early 1924 while Tanya kept the apartment in Los Angeles. Marshal's mother was ill and Norman, who had married in 1921 and was working for the railroad in Colton, was not available to help. Annie Richards died on August 1, 1924. The house that she had lived in since 1914 (the old Capt. Pishon house on Pacific Street between Second and Third) and her estate were left to Norman. It can only be assumed that Marshal had encouraged her to leave everything to Norman. After Annie's funeral service, Marshal returned to Los Angeles.

Portraits of Tanya and Marshal taken in 1930.

In the following years Tanya continued to work while they both pursued their interest in writing. Marshal worked on short stories and novels while Tanya wrote poems. Marshal chose not to concentrate on poetry himself while he was married to Tanya—perhaps not to compete with her. Marshal had some success with his own writings when two of his short stories were published in 1926 and 1927, but he was unable to find a publisher for his novels until a later date.

In 1925 or 1926 Marshal and Tanya began taking camping trips to the desert, exploring sites along San Diego County's unpaved Highway S-2. They stayed often at the Vallecito stage station (before it was restored), until Tanya was frightened by an apparition of a white horse she claimed to have seen. In 1928 they moved back to Oceanside and continued to struggle to make ends meet.

A Primitive Lifestyle—A Source of Income

What really encouraged Marshal to drop out and to seek such an isolated place miles away from anything? His article in the *Saturday Evening Post* of March 11, 1939, explained the surface reasons—they "were tired" and "out of step….temperamental misfits and innate barbarians…not equal to the job of coping with modern high-power civilization." They did not want to be slaves to making money, and they wanted to pursue more creative and spiritual endeavors. They wanted peace and solitude, and they wanted to experience a total sense of freedom—mentally and physically.

It is understandable that with the Depression their options for supporting themselves became very limited. There was no longer the cash needed to pay for both housing and food, and there may have been

The original house was 8 x 7 feet, which expanded as the family grew.

difficulties finding outlets to publish Marshal's stories. Moving someplace where they could homestead or live on free land made financial sense to two writers with little income. But why choose an isolated area and a natural and primitive lifestyle?

There are a few possibilities that may have led to this choice. Marshal was well read and may have been influenced by popular writers of the day. He undoubtedly read books by Ralph Waldo Emerson, Henry David Thoreau, and Hermann Hesse (*Notes of a Nature Man* and *Siddhartha*). He may also have read Adolph Just's *Return to Nature!: The True Natural Method of Healing and Living and The True Salvation of the Soul*—considered a health classic. Also, during the late 19th and early 20th centuries German natural-living movements—the Lebensreform (life reform), Naturmenschen (natural men), and Wandervogel (migrant birds/free spirits)—were taking place and spreading to the United States. Contemporary with his own

lifestyle on Ghost Mountain was a growing movement in Palm Springs centering in Tahquitz Canyon from which evolved the first of the Hippies—Gypsy Boots (who later became a health food advocate in the Los Angeles area) and eden ahbez (who wrote the song *Nature Boy* about Gypsy in 1948, which was later made famous when it was sung by Nat King Cole). Gordon Kennedy in his book *Children of the Sun* explains why so many left the cities, their jobs, and their clothes to live in tune with nature. His explanations sound like Marshal's pages from *Desert Magazine*, as do eden ahbez's lyrics for the album he later recorded.

Also, Marshal had come to accept Tanya's Rosicrucian beliefs about the ability to move closer into the spirit world as one surrounds himself with silence, peace, harmony, the rhythm of a disciplined life, natural foods, and nature. Hard work and discipline were seen as a way of strengthening the resolve for spiritual connection. They had already connected with the desert through years of camping, and this particular desert was reminiscent of Marshal's boyhood home in South Australia. Not only was the landscape similar, but the very isolation must have reminded him of Pandurra. In the desert Marshal could be free to spend time on his writing and artistic interests while Tanya could practice her religious teachings and develop her poetry skills. They were both strong-willed and energetic, and probably the challenge of building their own home had its own appeal.

Living without clothes had a practical side. There was no water on Ghost Mountain. Every drop had to be hauled up. There was no extra water for washing clothes and clothing holds body odor. Although Marshal felt very comfortable with no clothes, Tanya was not. She told her daughter that Marshal had insisted over her objections. When company came to Ghost Mountain, Tanya always wore a dress.

Whatever the final motivation was, the Souths packed their Model T with all of their possessions and headed to the desert on January 15, 1930, despite the objections of friends and Marshal's brother Norman (the engineer referred to in the *Saturday Evening Post* article of March 11, 1939). They drove their car to Blair Valley, which was land owned by the Bureau of Land Management years before it became part of Anza-Borrego Desert State Park. They camped in the valley and explored the "thin, ghostly trails" that led to their eventual abode on the obscure ridge they named Ghost Mountain.

*Yaquitepec as envisioned and sketched by Marshal South
in the early 1930s.*

In later years they cited different dates for the beginning of their "great experiment," depending on the article and the audience. Sometimes it was stated as February 1, 1931, but in *Desert Magazine* they used the date of February 1932. In all likelihood, they probably spent quite a bit of time in town purchasing building supplies and planning the basic construction of their adobe, and they may have had to work some to pay for the supplies. Perhaps this is why different dates may have been cited for the beginning of their sojourn.

Tanya cited the January 15, 1930, date in her short biography and on Victoria's birth certificate. The year is also cited on the 1930 census records as well as in a letter written by Marshal to the "Chief of the Division of Parks" in Sacramento, California, in 1936. The year 1930 is also when they had a series of professional portrait shots taken of them. Marshal would use these later as author photos for the covers of his books.

They spent years building their house. Marshal's years of building expertise was put to the test as he hand-built Yaquitepec, engineering an extensive system of cisterns and catch basins to store rainwater.

They called their house Yaquitepec—from Yaqui, the fierce freedom-loving Indians of Sonora, Mexico, and "tepec" referring to the hill (the pronunciation, according to Rider, sounds most like YAKeete-PECK), and referred to it as the "House of the Sun." Five years after they began their adventure, they could point to a comfortable small adobe home that would provide the basis for continual expansion as their family grew.

Although there was always something under construction and work to be done, Marshal could now take the time to concentrate on publishing his works.

Manuscripts that he had previously written were finally accepted by a London publisher, and by 1936, he had four published books: *Flame of Terrible Valley*, *Child of Fire*, *Juanita of the Border Country*, and *Gunsight*. His publisher, John Long, Ltd., had this to say about his first two novels: "*Flame of Terrible Valley* and *Child of Fire*…are strong stuff, but in the best senses, that of excitement, colour and originality. There is, in our opinion, no doubt that Marshal South is to be classed as one of the finest Western storytellers of today."

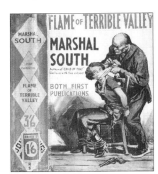

Flame of Terrible Valley is particularly interesting because of the setting, which is Vallecito, Mason, and Earthquake (Shelter) Valleys (all located within the immediate vicinity of Ghost Mountain). The Vallecito stage station is described as "a sinister, crumbling ruin, which is said to be haunted." The story, according to the publisher's promotion "deals with the dogged vengeance of a Chinese Tong and the quest for stolen gold." Certainly the inspiration for this story came from Tanya's experience of camping at the old ruins and from stories that Marshal had heard from his neighbor Stuart Hathaway who had purchased the old Las Arena Ranch, originally owed by Edward R. Burts. It was rumored that Burts was involved in smuggling Chinese into the United States from Mexico.

There was high praise for his first two novels found on the cover jacket of *Juanita of the Border Country*. The *East Anglican Times* reported that "Marshal South is an American who is capable of producing vivid fiction, and these examples of his creative ability will win appreciation. They are distinguished by resourceful inventiveness and power of expression…." The *Bristol Evening Post* stated: "Marshal South should speedily rise to the fore as one of the most original and interesting writers of Western stories," and the *Dundee Courier* said, "Mr. South is a newcomer to Western fiction, but he is likely to create a permanent place for himself in the affection of the public."

Other books would follow, with all of them following a basic formula, differing only in the setting and the characters. There was always a treasure, a damsel in distress, a hero with sterling qualities that prevailed over the villains and won the heart of the damsel, and all the books were cliffhangers. To his London audience he promoted himself as an American western novelist with "a drop of Red Indian blood in his veins."

Whether he actually had "Indian blood in his veins" is unknown. His grandfather Thomas Richards was from Wisconsin, and it is possible that he could have had an Indian ancestor. On the other hand, it could just have been marketing hype to help the book sell. Marshal did have a history of embellishing his credentials for his audience, having claimed to have served in the British Army and that Tanya was a graduate of Columbia University (an impression intended to allay his readers' concerns about her ability to effectively home-school their children.).

By 1936 Marshal began noticing more traffic along Highway S-2 and in Blair Valley below Ghost Mountain. Some of the motorists were hunters and others were picnickers who were driving carelessly and destroying native plants. Marshal became "much distressed" by "indiscriminate shooters" who he observed driving along trails with gunners perched on car fenders "shooting everything that moved—and letting it lie." He wrote to James A. Snook, Chief of the Division of Parks in Sacramento on September 13, 1936, expressing his concern about protecting native wildlife. Marshal knew that the state was in the process of acquiring lands for the state park, and he wanted to know what he could do until such time that the land could be acquired. Marshal told the state that on his own he had been posting "no hunting" and "game refuge" signs in the hopes of protecting the area. He received a letter back from Newton B. Drury on September 21, 1936, stating that the state did not have the authority to forbid hunting or to protect

Carrying water up the mountain. For the first year, all water was carried up to Yaquitepec in this manner, 12 gallons at a time.

wildlife until they obtained title. Marshal was instructed to work with Guy L. Fleming, district superintendent of Southern State Parks, who could address his concerns.

In later years Marshal would explain to his readership the steps he took to conserve the surrounding desert. He also felt a strong affinity to wildlife, which was in keeping with Rosicrucian beliefs.

Marshal was aware that all BLM land in the area was scheduled to be transferred to the state. To protect his holdings, he filed for a 160-acre homestead that included Ghost Mountain. Whether his next move was precipitated by this application or some other factor is unknown. On September 19, 1938, Tanya and Marshal were remarried in San Diego. This time on the application he indicated it was a second marriage and that he was divorced. Ten months later his land record for a homestead was recorded for Township 013S, Range 006E, Sections 32 and 33.

Interestingly, Margaret finally filed for divorce from Augusto Carlestedt on December 22, 1938. She received a final decree on April 7, 1944, and then 11 days later she married Earl Rector.

The following year, on March 11, 1939, South's article on Ghost Mountain entitled "Desert Refuge" appeared in the *Saturday Evening Post*. It was a milestone. It led to a contract with *Desert Magazine* to publish a one-year series entitled "Desert Year" that would feature life at Yaquitepec month by month. The children were the highlight of the series.

Three children were born while the Souths lived at Ghost Mountain. All three were born in Oceanside, where Tanya spent her last month of pregnancy with each child. Rider Del Sol South was born January 22, 1934; Rudyard Del Sol South was born December 20, 1937; and Victoria Del Sol South was born September 15, 1940.

The reaction and response to the initial series was best summed up by Wallace M. Byam, designer of the Airstream travel trailer, whose letter to the editor of *Desert Magazine* was printed in the March 1941 edition:

> *More people than I believe you realize will be missing Marshal South's article. It seems that we all ought to get together and do something to get him back.*
>
> *You see, Marshal South is the "escape" of a lot of people running on tread mill, racing in squirrel cages, slaves to businesses, jobs, possessions and conventions. Lots of us know full well that our striving is futile and the more we get the heavier the load, but convention and modern life has so cast its spell upon us that we can't pull away from it.*
>
> *So we escape through Marshal South. He does the things we would like to do...he lives our dream life for us...and boy we are going to miss him terribly. Do try to get him back.*
>
> *Of course, I sometimes wonder if Marshal South really is a person, and if he actually does live up there on his unpronounceable mountain.... But whether fictional or real, for heaven's sake keep him going. We are going to be plumb lost without him.*

Editor Randall Henderson assured Byam that there would be more of South—that manuscripts were being prepared that would appear in future editions of *Desert Magazine*.

Beginning in May 1941 a new monthly series began entitled "Desert Home." In introducing the series, Henderson wrote that the Souths "have found happiness in primitive living and close association with Nature." He said that the series would give "some interesting glimpses of their daily life on Ghost mountain [sic]." The series name changed to "Desert Refuge" after three months and continued until December 1946. The series now included a poem written by Tanya that would appear at the end of almost every article.

Tanya's poems most always reflected her religious thoughts as a selection of titles will indicate: "Faith," "Fate," "Aspiration," "Growth," "Hope," "Persistence," "Contentment," "Kindness," "Inner Power," and "The Golden Way." Knowing that life on Ghost Mountain was not always the utopia that Marshal's writings reflected, the poems actually hint at how Tanya was able to accept and endure years of a very hard life—by turning inward for strength:

FAITH (May 1941)

Lose not your Faith. Whatever may befall,
Your Faith alone can carry you through all,
And give you inspiration to renew
Your life, and guide you clearly what to do.
Count every other loss a paltry thing
Compared with Faith, to which your soul must cling.
Faith is our special candle in the night
Which, burning, guides our wandering steps aright.

There are three poems, however, that do not fit Tanya's style—either in subject matter or poetic cadence. They are "Prospector" (January 1942), "Path of Empire" (February 1943), and "Handicraft" (February 1944). They are typical of Marshal's style and were probably written by him:

THE PROSPECTOR

His hard old face is sour and bleak,
*   The face of one who's had to seek,*
'Mid frowning rock with prying steel,
*   His substance and his daily weal.*
He shrugs at rain or stormy weather,
*   His days—his years—merge all together*
Into one common goal alone,
*   As he holds up—a bit of stone.*

His burro waits not far away,
*   Nibbling a bit of grass or hay,*
His old pack shifts; he paces on,
*   Intent with eyes far-sighted grown,*
In eager search—for bits of stone.

PATH OF EMPIRES

There lies the Past,
*   For every eye to see.*
The ancients could not last—
*   Neither shall we.*

A climb to height,
*   And we relax, benign,*
As if our special might
*   Must stay divine.*

And in that hour,
*   While we forget to pray,*
Our cherished super-power
*   Starts to decay.*

HANDICRAFT

Give me the feel of a handmade thing.
*   Though crude and rough it be,*
A soul and purpose seem to cling,
*   Unto its form for me.*

The high perfectional results
*   Machines can bring to bear*
My instinct cherishing insults
*   By mass production fare.*

A fevered "factory output" goal
*   Machine work may demand,*
But there is greater charm and soul
*   To things all made by hand.*

A few of her other poems also reflect heavy editing from Marshal and are distinctly different from poems she clearly wrote herself before her marriage and after the divorce. Rider South has indicated that Marshal even wrote the two magazine articles credited to Tanya that appeared in *Holland's* (November 1940) and *Tomorrow* (January 1944), respectively.

Readers were thrilled to see South's articles again. Elsa A. Livingston wrote in August 1941 that she was "happy…to see that Marshal South has again contributed his art of writing for the Magazine…for I don't think anyone brings one closer to the desert and its wonders than he does."

Marshal had struck a chord that vibrated within his readership. They not only loved his descriptions of the desert but they also bought into his philosophy. William C. Chandler wrote in October 1941 that he:

> …*appreciate*[d] *his messages, which he translates from the Great Spirit, in words that are understandable, to hungry souls who are unable to comprehend the blessings of Nature. In our mad scramble for material gain we are missing the wealth of beauty so aptly pictured by Mr. South. It is people like him, with their spark of love, received from living in close harmony with the Great Spirit, who enable us to see, through their eyes, in their word pictures, what we long to be able to see.*

The praise heaped on South did not go unnoticed. He had become the desert prophet. And he fell into character, giving his audience what they demanded. He spared them the difficulties of living on Ghost Mountain and focused on the positive aspects while emphasizing his own brand of philosophy.

Some readers didn't like it. In May 1942 a reader complained telling Henderson that he wanted to hear more about the family and less about philosophy. That was a call to arms, and a loyalist responded in defense in June 1942:

> *Bum philosophy, the man writes. From a letter like that you can see that he is interested in the material things of life. He is not interested in getting the peace of mind that the desert gives one, and which Marshal South puts forth so well in his articles…. I for one rely upon such good philosophy about the desert….it's articles like South's that help the desert lovers through these times.*

Most of the comments by readers were very positive and supportive through the years as the Souths had a very large following. Every so often a negative comment would appear, but it was always countered in successive issues. Comments about Marshal were never passive.

Tanya relaxing on a rock at Yaquitepec

In November 1943, someone complained about South's "diatribes against the artificialities of conventional civilization." In August 1944 someone complained about the "'I-am-better and wiser-than-you-are-because-I-live-on-the-desert' spirit manifested," while a newspaperman "chained to a desk" wanted South "and his remarkable family" to know how they were envied. A woman in October 1944 wrote in protest about South's "superciliousness" and said he had "gone off on a tangent" and had "no sense of values." She found more truth in Tanya's poetry. Someone in November 1944 complained about all the squabbles regarding Marshal that were in the previous issue and wanted them to cease. Henderson commented in February 1946 that "some readers turn first every month to Marshal South's story on the adventure in primitive living" while others "think Marshal should have his head examined by a sanity board." He concluded that it "would be a very dull place…if we all had the same ideas about the art of living."

Trapped by an Image

Henderson periodically provided background on the Souths for new *Desert Magazine* readers. This biography always began with their move to the desert during "the Great Depression." He helped to create the image of who they were, making them larger than life. It was good marketing hype, and it helped to build his readership. He wrote that the Souths were "free and independent—and happy." They built their home working "from sunup until dark, long hours of hard labor, but it brought them added health and a serene philosophy of life." Of the children, Henderson said, "Tanya is teaching them from books. Marshal is teaching them from Nature…. For them, their experiment in primitive living has been a glorious success and they have no desire ever to return to the world where humans fight each other for food and shelter and power and gold." He said the monthly articles "give a vivid cross-section of their daily lives, and a fine insight into the philosophy of their way of living." Henderson had created the perfect family.

And he helped to paint Marshal into a corner. As the desert prophet, Marshal wasn't mortal, and he had the perfect family. When the Souths left Yaquitepec for Utah in October 1942 in search of a new home that would provide a reliable source of water, their quest was doomed from the start. They did not have the funds to buy property. If Marshal had to get a job to support them, he could no longer be

Marshal had become the desert prophet.

who he was. He required the isolation to keep up the image of the character that had been created. So they returned to Yaquitepec in November 1943 with the determination to expand their system of cisterns. If they could increase their water supply, they could maintain the charade and their source of monthly income.

Henderson was joyful about their return to Ghost Mountain. In December 1943 he wrote,

I am sure that…readers will share my pleasure at this news. They will never find another home that means as much to them as the little cabin they built with their own hands…. The Souths personify that element in the human family which puts independence above security…. We like and admire the Souths because we know instinctively that theirs is the kind of faith and courage that will keep freedom alive in this world.

Readers were also relieved when they returned. Like Henderson they desperately wanted to maintain the image that had been created. Ethel York wrote in September 1944 that she "felt uprooted because everything I had ever read about them centered around Yaquitepec. Now all is well."

But things were not well. Tanya and Marshal fought "like cats and dogs," according to Rider. Although there were times when they were happy and got along (more so before the children came), overall, they did not have a happy marriage. They argued over money. Tanya was mainly unhappy because Marshal was not interested in providing a steady income and security for the family. He wanted to do his own thing. Though he worked hard at what interested him, once he achieved a certain level of success, he lost interest and turned to other things. This was a major source of tension between the two of them. Tanya would see the demand for Marshal's pottery, his newsletters, his greeting cards, and his short stories. Pursuing any of those would have generated extra income and added to their only other source of regular income, which was the monthly check from *Desert Magazine*. But Marshal did not like the idea of "work," at least when it involved deadlines or money. And he did not want to be supervised.

Once when he was contacted by the editor of *Ranch Romances* to do a series for the magazine, he responded that he was above writing for such publications now that he was a published book author. Tanya was furious because they needed the money.

Marshal became restless and unhappy with Tanya who was getting grouchier day by day. She did not encourage him. She made sarcastic and biting comments and called Marshal "lazy," and she may not have been happy about the return to Yaquitepec.

They had talked about separation at different times. One time before Victoria was born they packed the car to take Tanya to Santa Ysabel, but on the way there, they changed their minds and returned to Yaquitepec. Tanya did not want a divorce—her religion may have had something to do with it. A failed marriage might have been viewed as spiritual failure. But she felt more and more trapped on Ghost Mountain, especially after Victoria was born. She was worried about the children and felt they needed to adapt to city life while they still could. Tanya and Marshal were also getting older, and the hikes up and down the mountain were getting harder.

To add to the tension, the Souths were forced to move by the U.S. Navy in July or August 1945 because their property had become part of the "Naval Air-to-Air Gunnery Range." Neighbors Everett and Lena Campbell provided temporary housing for them on a remote piece of property they owned at the foot of the Laguna Mountains until the Navy notified the Souths in April or May of 1946 that they could return to Ghost Mountain. Although the Navy transported their things back to Blair Valley in June 1946, Marshal would not allow them to haul things up the mountain because the caterpillar tractor they wanted to use would have left

THE HOUSE OF THE SUN

By Divine command proclaiming anew the ancient, fundamental religion of the Fatherhood of the GREAT SPIRIT and the Brotherhood of all of His Creation.

an unsightly scar on the mountainside. Everything was left at the foot of mountain for them to carry up by hand. In addition, they had not been at Yaquitepec during the rainy season and had missed the opportunity to fill their cisterns with water.

But to *Desert Magazine* readers, all was well, and maybe in Marshal's mind it was also. His truth was in his character—a prophet of the desert. He believed in his philosophy even though it was at odds with reality.

While they lived in the little house on the Campbell's property, Marshal had produced a booklet on their own Yaquitepec Press that was entitled *The House of the Sun*. He wrote the contents, Tanya wrote a poem entitled "Contentment," and the children ran the press. The booklet outlined their philosophy of religion: "By Divine command proclaiming anew the ancient, fundamental religion of the Fatherhood of the GREAT SPIRIT and the Brotherhood of all of His Creation." The booklet introduced the sacred symbol of the House of the Sun—"that of a sun, an eagle and a cactus—carrying thus, in symbology, the truth of the upward passage of men's souls from the thorny bitterness of earth to the higher realms of light." He wrote:

The Souths had many guests visiting Yaquitepec. Here an unknown guest stands with the Souths down in their parking area at the foot of Ghost Mountain. From left: Marshal, guest, Rudyard, Rider, Victoria, and Tanya.

Let my House be a house of Love and of Understanding.
Let the pillars thereof be the mountains and the trees and its pavement be the wide earth.
Let its roof be the arch of the sky, and its music the songs of the birds and of the wind and of the harps of the rain.

> *Let its lights be the lights of the sun and the moon, and of the glow of the everlasting stars.*
> *Let Fellowship and Peace and Brotherhood dwell therein. Of man and of very creature.*
> *And I, the Spirit, shall dwell in that House, and walk beneath its arches, and bless it, from*
> *Everlasting unto Everlasting.*

Marshal had intended this to be one of several publications from Yaquitepec Press. There is a note at the end of the booklet suggesting that further offerings were in the works, however Rider does not recall that any other booklets were ever actually produced.

Through the years the Souths maintained their privacy and never disclosed their own personal feelings regarding each other. Just as in the *Desert Magazine* articles, they represented themselves as happy with their choices and lives. Their large correspondence to others reflects this as well, and they were considered gracious hosts to their many guests.

Their guest book is filled with signatures: 40 visitors in 1940, 33 in 1941, 20 in 1942, 18 in 1943, 23 in 1944, and 17 in 1945. Many of the guests were neighbors (Everett and Lena Campbell—Vallecito Valley, Louis Bushore—Earthquake Valley, and Louis and Delores Strahlmann—Mason Valley), and friends from Julian (Myrtle and Louis Botts, George Foote, Arthur Kalstrom, and others), or surrounding areas. Others were from northern and southern California, as well as throughout the United States and Peru. Some of the more interesting guests included representatives from the Peruvian Consulate, the Missouri Botanical Garden, J.L. Kraft (from the cheese company), and of course, Randall Henderson. There were probably a lot more who did not sign in.

Guests who visited them in 1946 (who did not sign the guest book) included two families who shot footage of the Souths in 16mm (Manner family on July 1) and 8mm cameras (Pettinger family in late summer or early fall). Tanya looks particularly shy and reluctant to smile in these films, but there was a reason. Due to dental problems, she had all of her teeth extracted that summer (she was later fitted for dentures).

Most noteworthy among the guests of Yaquitepec were Marshal South Jr. and his family. As an adult Marshal Jr. learned about his father from an article in *Desert Magazine*. He wrote to his father through the magazine and received a letter in reply dated June 27, 1946, in which his father invited him to visit Ghost Mountain. In the intervening years Marshal Jr. had attended schools in the Los Angeles area, including Pepperdine University and UCLA, and had become an aeronautical engineer. He worked at North American Aviation, Inc., and with J.A. Keith had invented and developed the supersonic wind tunnel in the early 1940s. He also helped to design the T-28 Air Force trainer and other aircraft in addition to the Apollo spacecraft in later years. He married Mae Berthelsen on August 28, 1943, and they had had two children, Carol, age four, and Marsha, age two, when he received his father's letter. The letter expressed Marshal's joy in hearing from his son:

> *Dear, dear boy:*
> *If your daddy has a few foolish tears in his eyes as he writes this,—and he has—forgive him. It has been so long. Always and always I have felt that you would comeback to me—and in just this way....*
> *...through all those years I have seen you, as I still see you today, a dear little boy in his mother's arms waving one little hand at me as I disappeared around the corner.... But the memory and the picture have never dimmed and in the silence of many a long night it has brought tears and agony. You were wearing a little blue jacket that day. You have always remained to me my "little boy blue" ever since.*

Marshal and Margaret had long since lost track of each other. Marshal told his son that many years before he had been given an address from a mutual friend who had seen Margaret while she was visiting

*Marshal and Marshal Jr.
in July 1946 (left).*

*Marshal Jr. and his mother, Margaret,
during the same approximate
time period (above).*

Oceanside. But some time had passed before he had received the address, and though he wrote several times, there was never a reply. Nevertheless, he had been overjoyed by his friend's description of Marshal Jr. as a "wonderful" young man.

He congratulated his son on his marriage and family and asked that they pay a visit to Yaquitepec because their "old car—partly tied together with baling wire and binder twine—might prove unequal to the strain" for a drive to Los Angeles. Besides, "it is about 18 years since we were in the 'wicked city' and we'd probably be arrested as wandering natives from Borneo."

He warned Marshal Jr. that he would "doubtless be greatly disappointed" because his "daddy has spent the years meandering down all sorts of by-ways where the wheels of 'Progress' passeth not and the illusions of 'prosperity' is just another of 'those durn things,'" but he felt they would "understand each other pretty well," based on comments made in Marshal Jr.'s letter to him. Like his father, Marshal Jr. believed in the benefits of natural and healthy foods and of long exposure to the sun.

Marshal gave detailed directions to find Yaquitepec and invited them to stay overnight if they camped, alerting them that they had no accommodations and that things were "primitive." He also warned them that they were "no-clothes-ists" but said "if such unconvention is shocking to either your wife or yourself, we will wear something in your honor." Marshal also told his son that the house was not in the best of condition due to the period of neglect while the Navy was using it as part of their gunnery range. They had only recently returned to their home and had not yet lugged all of their possessions back up the hill.

Marshal asked his son to give "every good wish and blessing" to his mother and said he would be very happy if Margaret wanted to come along. He closed by stating that Tanya and the youngsters would all give them a hearty welcome.

They visited sometime in July and stayed overnight. Mae's recollection is that Tanya served a nice meal and watermelon. Tanya wore a dress and Marshal wore a loincloth. During the visit Tanya passed a note to Marshal Jr., addressed to Margaret. What was in the note is a matter of conjecture.

Upon returning to Los Angeles, Marshal Jr. gave the note to his mother who gave it to her husband Earl Rector to read. Somehow the letter frightened them when it "stuck" to Earl's hand and they had to burn it to remove it from his skin. Some members of the family thought that Tanya had somehow conjured up some evil spirits. The story of the burned letter has become a family legend.

The Mold Breaks—End of the Experiment

Tanya filed for divorce on October 18, 1946, about three month after Marshal Jr.'s visit. Neither guests to Ghost Mountain nor the *Desert Magazine* readership suspected that things had reached such a point, but there were subtle indications that things were not right.

Tension in the South household had been running high since the return from Utah. Tanya's concerns for financial security and the children's future were not being met. She constantly worried about the children's safety and wondered what would happen if an accident occurred and Marshal was gone. She would be literally trapped on the mountain with no access to emergency medical services. Marshal turned a deaf ear to her concerns and was unhappy with Tanya's complaints. The closing lines in his July 1946 "Desert Refuge" article could have been directed toward Tanya: "There are some who will try to tell you that life is grim and earnest and a most serious matter. Do not believe them. Life…is a glad song of Eternity….all that matters is how you accept it. For, like a mirror, it will return to you in full measure just what you give it—either in scowls or in smiles."

The last time that Marshal mentions Tanya's name in a *Desert Magazine* article is August 1946 when he describes their joy at being able to move back home when they receive permission from the Navy. Subsequent articles discuss the children's activities, desert features, or expound Marshal's desert philosophy, but Tanya's name is conspicuously absent.

A few of Tanya's poems in 1946 may also indicate her increased inner turmoil. In June *Desert Magazine* printed "Awakening," in which she wrote, "There is awakening through strife./There is a deepening through grief./Thus do we earn a higher life,/…Fear not that evil days have come,/But rouse your courage for the fray." In "No Choice," appearing the following month, she wrote, "There is no choice but to do right./And for the Truth to staunchly fight." In her August poem, entitled "Courage," she seemed to be calling up the courage she needed to move toward her goal:

> ### COURAGE
>
> *It guides my weary feet o'er crags*
> *And jagged rocks and endless moor.*
> *And yet my spirit never sags,*
> *And still I rest in Truth secure.*
> *With Faith that God is at the helm*
> *And knows in fullness and the whole,*
> *No earthly storms shall overwhelm,*
> *Nor keep me from my hoped for goal.*

And, finally in September appeared "On Fate." She wrote, "How then can Fate betray us?/'Tis we who make our Fate./No, no one can delay us,/Nor cause our sorrow great,/But we ourselves…."

Even with all of the hardships of living on Ghost Mountain and the personal tensions, Victoria feels that her mother might have continued to endure and adapt had Marshal met her part way and if the "incident" had not occurred.

The actual incident that set Tanya off in a direction that led to divorce occurred during a family trip to Julian. On arrival, Marshal left to go shopping—he was the one who handled the money. Tanya and the children went window shopping, and when they got to the library, they went in to talk to Myrtle Botts, the town librarian. Myrtle was a good friend and had been supplying them with books to read for years. While they were visiting with her, Marshal came into the library with one ice cream cone— for Myrtle. This was after he had told the family there was not any money for ice cream cones on this trip. Tanya read much more into this than was probably warranted.

Tanya was very possessive, according to Rider, and couldn't handle the idea that Marshal might give attention to another woman. Buying that ice cream immediately changed Tanya's outlook on Myrtle. The trip back home that day was "awful," according to Rider, and "from there on it went downhill."

Tanya was convinced that something was going on—and sustained that belief for the rest of her life. There also could have been some jealously on her part. Marshal may have been praising Myrtle's qualities while he was having disagreements with Tanya, much the same way that he had previously praised Tanya in letters to Margaret. The bottom line, however, was that Myrtle was the last straw, and things quickly unraveled.

Marshal began spending more time away from Yaquitepec (probably in an attempt to get away from Tanya's harping), which only fed her fears and concerns. When an opportunity was offered to paint a frieze

Marshal in Julian in 1947 or 1948 standing in front of the museum building—the Foster house—before it was restored. Photo courtesy of Jeri Botts Wright.

on the walls of the Julian Library, he took the job. The frieze is still there. The library is now a realty office next door to the chamber of commerce. The mural depicts the progression of life beginning with spiritual symbology to the early Indians, the arrival of the Spanish, early homesteaders and the Butterfield overland stage. Marshal lived at the library while he painted the frieze. This left Tanya and the children alone on the mountain with no transportation, no way to summon help in an emergency, and no groceries apart from what Marshal was willing to deliver to them. Tanya felt compelled, at this point, to take action on her own for the sake of the children. Victoria believes that her mother's decision took great courage.

Sometime in October Tanya gathered up the children and walked them three miles down to Highway S-2. There she flagged down a vehicle to carry a letter to San Diego asking for help. The Red Cross responded some days later and provided her transportation to San Diego to file for divorce. Her attorney advised her that in order to get the divorce, there needed to be cause as incompatibility was not sufficient to grant a divorce in those days.

In the affidavit filed on October 28, 1946, she made several statements, some of which were probably exaggerated under the advisement of her attorney. She claimed that Marshal threatened to kill her or to put her into an institution and take her children away from her. She said that she feared for her life and that Marshal was hot-tempered and on two occasions struck and beat her severely. She asserted that Marshal wanted to move to South America or organize a polygamy colony and that he became very angry when she would not agree to go. She also claimed Marshal wanted his freedom so that he could remarry. In her petition for divorce she stated that they had been separated since September 1945 and that Marshal had been a resident of Julian since that time. In actuality, during that time period the family had just moved from Ghost Mountain to the home that their neighbors had made available to them and they were planning the publication of *The House of the Sun.*

Judge Arthur L. Mundo issued an order to show cause and placed a restraining order against Marshal, ordering him to appear in court on November 12. At that time the court assigned custody and care of the children to Tanya and ordered Marshal to provide financial support and to bring food and supplies to the house once each week. Marshal was also ordered to refrain from striking, beating, or molesting Tanya or attempting to take the children away from her.

Desert Magazine editor Randall Henderson discovered what happened when he opened a San Diego newspaper and saw the headline "Divorce Plea Breaks Up Hermit Family." He related to his readers in the January 1947 issue that the "news was no less disillusioning to me than it will be to thousands of *Desert* readers." He told his readers that he drove to Ghost Mountain with the hope that he could contribute something to "Operation Salvage." He had considered both of them friends and had "always found them kindly and sincere people." He summed up their "domestic difficulties" with this sentence: "Two temperamental poets lived so close together in such a small world they finally got on each other's nerves." He also announced that a serial based on a home life of a family that was no longer united could not continue, but he would continue to run Tanya's poems, which he did until February 1959. Henderson reported that Marshal would be living in Julian where he had a position. Although Henderson said the position was with the chamber of commerce, it was actually with the Julian Library to paint the frieze. He said Tanya and the children would remain on Ghost Mountain in their "comfortable home." In actuality, that would have been impossible for any length of time.

Marshal did not contest the divorce. He sent a letter to Judge Mundo on January 21, 1947. He told the judge that the "divorce is only the culmination of an intolerable domestic friction which has existed over a number of years…it had to come—for the good of all concerned." He explained that Tanya was "a city girl" and "has no love for the country….my wife has never accepted whole-heartedly my ideas. She has always complied unwillingly." He said he had hoped the divorce "could have been obtained quietly, by mutual consent." But since "the break has come," what he "most earnestly" wanted was "to PROTECT [his emphasis] her and the children." His main concern was their welfare and his ability to provide for them if they left Ghost Mountain. On the mountain they could live very well on his limited income:

> *I can take care of them on the ranch—where for the past fifteen years we have lived very well— amazing as it may seem—on an income that has never exceeded $40.00 per month. This was an "experiment" in close to nature living, it is true. But it has been a very successful experiment. My children are of much more than ordinary intelligence. The little girl played chess when she was four years of age—and with such skill that I never could beat her in a game. The middle boy, Rudyard, drew pictures and wrote poems and little stories from the time he could use a pencil. At seven he was writing his own little fiction stories and setting them in type and printing them. Rider the eldest boy has always been precocious. He has a mind beyond his years and behaves more like an adult than a child. None of the children have ever been sick or ever needed a doctor. I think this is a fairly good record. All of them, due to home schooling, are in advance of the regular school-educated child.*

He explained to the judge that if they lived in the city, he would not have the means to provide for them. He said that Tanya had the opportunity to remain at the ranch and to write a regular monthly feature, "BUT SHE REFUSES TO WRITE IT [his emphasis]."

Marshal asked Judge Mundo to award the 160-acre homestead to Tanya with the proviso that it not be sold until the youngest child was of legal age. He was afraid that Tanya would unwittingly sell it "for a few hundred dollars." He pleaded, "I beg of you to protect her from herself—for the sake of the children, whom I dearly love." He wanted to make sure that it was "secured so that she and the children will be able to return to it at any time and find there a rent-free home awaiting them" if things did not go well in the city.

He told Judge Mundo that it was fine with him if everything was awarded to Tanya—the property and the 1929 Ford. He wanted to make it clear that he was not trying to evade his responsibilities, explaining that his "earning capacity at present is such that I cannot meet unreasonable demands. But I am more than willing to do all that I can…not from legal pressure but because I love my children."

Marshal also said that he could "probably fight this" and prove Tanya "incompetent" and be awarded custody of the children, but he felt that it would be a hardship on them and that they were probably better off with their mother "IF [his emphasis] she does not go entirely off the 'deep end'…. She has some fanatical religious ideas. But they love her."

The Souths appeared in court on January 27, 1947. At that time Rider was called to the witness stand and testified that "his father struck and abused" his mother. He was instructed by Tanya's attorney to say that in order to show cause. In fact, Rider recalls that his father never beat his mother as she had originally stated, although he may have pushed or even struck her in the heat of an argument.

Tanya and the children did not return to Ghost Mountain. They were placed in temporary housing in Carlsbad, and on the 27th of January, the boys received their first haircuts. Newspapers exclaimed that the children had taken their first steps into civilization. Randall Henderson took exception to the reporting, commenting later to his readers about the meaning of "civilization." It has to do with the "state of social culture characterized by relative progress in the arts, science and statecraft," not on the condition of the length of hair, he explained. He said that by the reporter's logic, the children—who had lived on a remote mountaintop and had been taught to respect life—were "uncivilized," but now that they had their hair trimmed and no longer lived on the mountaintop but in a "community where hundreds of people meet death every year," they were at last becoming civilized.

On February 11, 1947, Judge Mundo granted an interlocutory judgment awarding Tanya exclusive custody of the children and of the Ghost Mountain property with no restrictions. Marshal was awarded his 1929 Model A Ford and his printing press and was ordered to pay court fees and $25.00 per month to Tanya for financial support. The affidavit for final judgment of divorce was granted on February 13, 1948.

It was an acrimonious divorce. Tanya had nothing good to say about Marshal, and she was quick to accuse him of not sending the $25.00 each month as ordered by the court. In the September 1947 issue of *Desert Magazine* she had written a poem entitled "The Law." Marshal read it and wrote out his own version of the poem:

THE LAW
by Tanya South

Thus is the Law. And there are none
Who follow it but will succeed.
Whate'er in life we may have done
To win, the Law we had to heed!

Guard you the Law, and well obey
Its mandates and its covenants.
For what we think and do and say
Make all our Fate and its events.

THE LAW
by Marshal South

Obey the Law—for if you don't
Your "wife" will get you, by-and-by—
"My five and twenty bucks don't come—
I'll have you jailed"—I hear her cry.

Unto the San Diego Court
In frenzied tones I hear her call
And when you "call" her bluff she says:
"Oh yes, I got it, after all."

So Heed the Law—or you'll be damned—
Or even worse, my dear young friend—
So here's a tip: Be very sure
You "REGISTER" the cash you send.

After Ghost Mountain

Tanya and the children lived in Carlsbad for six months until a four-room unit became available at the Frontier Housing Project in Point Loma. While they lived in Carlsbad, Tanya found a job cleaning movie theaters to help support herself and the children. After they moved to Point Loma, she found a position as a secretary with the Welfare Department. As she adapted to her new situation she expressed the terror she felt in striking out on her own, along with her pain and anger, in a poem that was published in *Desert Magazine* in August 1947, entitled "You Are Still You." She wrote, "Whate'er the evil luck you drew,/Whate'er the terror, pain or hate,/You still are you, vital and warm." The poem ended on a note of hope for the future.

But for Marshal, the separation and divorce was arguably more difficult. It had shattered his world and had taken its toll on him physically. He was ill. The newspapers had cast him in a dim light as "the cruel poet" with allegations of "privation." Few reached out to befriend him, with the exception of Louis and Myrtle Botts of Julian and Bill and Ad Mushet of the Banner Queen Ranch.

The Bottses felt compassion toward him. Along with their daughter Jeri and Myrtle's mother, they basically became his new family. After Marshal finished painting his frieze at the Julian Library, he painted a scene on the walls of the chamber of commerce (today found downstairs in the Julian Town Hall hidden behind furniture), and did a few odd building jobs that the Bottses found for him in Julian and San Diego.

Marshal contacted Henderson at *Desert Magazine* and began writing again—first an article about the Banner Queen Ranch and Bill and Ad Mushet, which appeared in April 1947, and then an article about Agua Caliente Hot Springs in the July issue. Henderson was happy to have Marshal writing again, and he told his readers that Marshal was making frequent trips to the desert and hoped to open up a shop where he could sell his leather and silver crafts. Beginning with the August issue, a new South series began, entitled "Desert Trails," which included explorations of the surrounding desert.

Marshal at the restored Vallecito stage station in 1948. Photo courtesy of Jeri Botts Wright.

In April 1948 a doctor told Marshal that he needed to avoid high elevations, like those found in Julian, because of a heart condition. He was admitted to a hospital in mid September and a few days later he was released. When he suffered a relapse, Bill Mushet brought him down to his ranch at Banner Queen for a few days and then took him out to "Burro Spring," a half-mile from Agua Caliente.

Marshal wrote Henderson and told him that he was "very weak, but if a cure is possible the desert will do it." He told Henderson that he was working on two new articles. He also wrote a letter to Myrtle that included depressing thoughts about his end being near. The letter worried the Bottses, and they drove down to the desert to retrieve him. They brought him back to Julian and set him up in a trailer in their back yard. A month later, on October 22, he died with Myrtle by his side. He was 59 years old.

Tanya always felt that there had been an intimate relationship between Marshal and Myrtle. Jeri Botts Wright believes there could not have been. Her parents were very close, and if there had been anything going on, Louis Botts would have known. Jeri said the whole family loved Marshal, although they thought him eccentric and peculiar. Myrtle and Jeri did attend one of the court proceedings, at Marshal's request, to provide support for him. They also thought that Tanya had exaggerated her claims in court.

Just as Tanya had come into his life when Margaret had rejected him, Myrtle provided Marshal with a sense of hope and love that he desperately needed. It's true that he wrote love poems to Myrtle, but he also wrote them to Myrtle's mother and to Jeri. The family read and shared all of the letters, and they treasured the poems. The Bottses had provided comfort to him in the end and hopefully provided the love and understanding that he so desperately craved. Jeri Wright believes that rumors grew about a possible relationship because they were fanned by a few local women who were jealous of Myrtle. She was well read and respected as the town librarian and often received praise from local townsmen who were happy when she found references or ordered books they needed for mining or farming.

Marshal's last photograph, taken in front of the Banner store by Myrtle or Louis Botts, either en route to Agua Caliente Hot Springs or after he was picked up and taken back to Julian. He died a month later. Photo courtesy of Jeri Botts Wright.

Marshal's body was taken to Paris Mortuary in El Cajon. The Bottses contacted Marshal Jr. and his mother Margaret. Together they all paid for a plot in the Julian Cemetery and planned the funeral arrangements. Tanya was notified. As she did not drive and there was no public transportation to Julian, she chose to take the children to the funeral home in El Cajon to pay their last respects. They took the bus from Point Loma. Victoria recalls being afraid to get close to the body that was laid on a slab. She remembers her mother standing silently by her father for a long time, and she thinks she may have cried on the way home.

For years Tanya has been unjustly accused of not caring that Marshal had died. Outside of the family, no one knew that they had gone to the funeral home. Myrtle had written scathingly to Marshal Jr. on January 12, 1965, that Tanya did "not see fit to even attend his funeral…."

Final rites were conducted by the Reverend Robert Scott Wallace at 11 a.m. on Saturday, October 30, 1948, at the Julian Baptist Church. South was buried next to John Hutson in an unmarked grave because no funds were left to pay for a gravestone. In later years a fire occurred in a house in Julian that contained all of the cemetery records, and until recently, the actual location of his grave was unknown. Rider South arranged to have a marker placed on his father's grave in January 2005. It reads: "Father, Poet, Author, Artist," and it includes the logo for *The House of the Sun* (the logo is found after each *Desert Magazine* entry in this book).

Desert Magazine announced Marshal's death in the December 1948 issue, which included his last published story. Henderson's final comments are particularly apt in understanding South:

He was a dreamer—an impractical visionary according to the standards of our time, but what a drab world it would be without the dreamers. Marshal's tragedy was that he tried too hard to fulfill his dream. He would not compromise. And that is fatal in a civilization where life is a never-ending

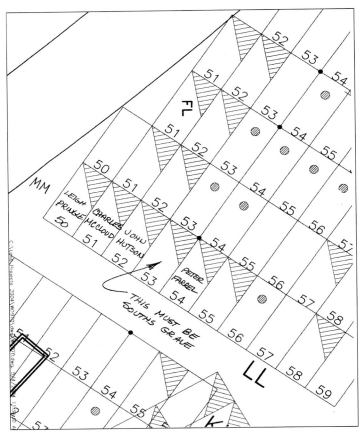

David Lewis of Julian determined the site of Marshal's grave using information contained in a letter written by Myrtle Botts.

The location of Marshal's unmarked grave was lost for years after cemetery records were destroyed in a Julian fire. Photo courtesy of David Baumann.

compromise between the things we would like to do and the obligations imposed by the social and economic organization of which we are a part.

Marshal wanted to live a natural life, and so he moved out to Ghost Mountain to be as close to Nature as possible. If he had been a hermit that would have worked very well. But Marshal was not a hermit by nature. He wanted to raise a family—and impose upon his family his own unconventional way of life.

Therein lay the weakness of his philosophy. He despised the rules and taboos of the society he had left behind, and immediately set up a new and even more restrictive code for his own household. And therein lies the explanation of the break in the South family life....

....Marshal's magazine stories were popular because of the beautiful prose with which he expressed the dreams which are more or less in the hearts of all imaginative people. Those of us who knew him well, felt for him the respect that is always due a man with the courage of his convictions.

We'll miss his stories of the desert trails. We will remember him for the artistry with which he expressed ideals we all share.

Marshal South was a brilliant, complex, and creative man who never wavered from his early beliefs about money, progress, and civilization. As he became older, he became more inflexible and rigid and would not change or compromise them for anyone. He has been misunderstood and misjudged, and rumors often hid the truth.

Marshal was a creative genius who could work in any medium. He was motivated by his own sense of creativity—not by money. He built and created for the sake of perfecting his creation. When he achieved a level of perfection that satisfied him, he would look for a new challenge. He was also a religious person in the sense that he felt a deep connection to a higher power that he called "the Great Spirit," and he felt a genuine spiritual kinship with Native Americans and all living things. In his later years he had combined and professed a mix of scientific thought with Rosicrucian beliefs, superstitions and myths. He was a hopeless romantic and an idealist, and he deeply loved his children, Margaret, and in all likelihood, Tanya.

As a naturalist, he paid keen attention to his surroundings and had a strong environmental awareness. He was an ardent conservationist, and he passionately loved the desert and the freedom it represented. He was an outspoken advocate of naturism and promoted the benefits of nudism. He was not afraid of a life filled with hard physical work or discomforts. In fact, he relished the idea of overcoming those discomforts by sheer will. He was a heteroclite in every sense of the word—totally unorthodox and eccentric.

He was a good communicator and marketer. He knew his audience and wrote for them, embellishing when necessary. Like his novels, he relied on set formulas for the success of his *Desert Magazine* articles. The children had set "characters" based on who they really were. He would put words in their mouths and kept baby talk for Rudyard and Victoria well after they had grown out of it in real life—but the readership liked it. He used real incidents and created stories around them, describing accurately the natural features of the area. He never wrote about the difficult times or the disagreements with Tanya. It was much like *The Waltons* or *Bonanza*, as Rider South explained, "They never showed it like it really was. They never worked and the families were always happy….he just made life there sound interesting." Marshal focused on, or maybe really only saw, the good things, as opposed to Tanya who would only focus on the hardships, which were real. He continued writing to the end, developing a new much more "guidebook" approach. But it was really too late to start anew. With a weakened heart, his will to live disintegrated. All that he and Tanya had striven to create had been destroyed. It killed him; but for Tanya the result was years of bitterness over the shattered dreams of what could have been.

Marshal's brother Norman did not attend his funeral. He was at the Naval Hospital awaiting his own heart surgery. He sent a letter to Margaret and Marshal Jr. on December 19, 1948, thanking them for making the arrangements for Marshal's funeral. He told Margaret that he knew she thought "a great deal of him." Norman died in his home a year later on January 14, 1950. Margaret died August 11, 1975, and Marshal Jr. died December 25, 2002.

Tanya raised the children who all grew up to lead very successful lives. She continued writing her poetry for *Desert Magazine* until Henderson stepped down as editor in 1959. Her name is found on 202 poems in the magazine. A few of those had been edited by Marshal and at least three of them were actually written by him. The total number of poems she authored in her lifetime is unknown, as only a few survive. She destroyed almost all of them just before she died. She was very proud of her poems. Victoria has fond memories of waking up in the middle of the night and seeing her mother write poetry by the light of a kerosene lamp while everyone slept. Tanya also wrote "A Sequel to Ghost Mountain" for the April 1949 issue of *Desert Magazine* telling readers how well the children were doing since they left the mountain.

Tanya sold Ghost Mountain to the state park in 1958 for $950. Victoria believes that her mother felt compelled by the state to sell because they had sought her out and asked about the property, which was an inholding within the park boundaries. She thinks her mother really did not want to sell but felt she was being forced to sell. In the end, she did meet Marshal's request. The property was not sold until the year that Victoria turned 18.

In 1983 the state contacted Tanya about creating a cultural preserve at Yaquitepec. Tanya objected. She wrote on May 1, 1983: "The idea of establishing a cultural preserve to 'honor' the stark, miserable existence that Yaquitepec represented is quite absurd to me. Marshal has glorified our existence on the mountaintop in his articles in the *Desert Magazine*. He was a superb fiction writer." She asked the state not to bother her again.

Tanya's bitterness intensified in the years after she left Ghost Mountain. She felt that people blamed her for the divorce—for destroying the great experiment. People could not understand how she could leave "such a great man." Indeed, the curious would seek her out to ask her questions, and they would be met with anger. She always felt that no one understood her position, which was that she simply wanted to protect her children.

To that end, Tanya wrote her own story about life on Ghost Mountain, which she later sent to her daughter to read. Victoria told her that it expressed too much bitterness and that people would not want to read it as it was. She suggested that her mother rewrite it so that it would be a little more upbeat. Tanya did not take the criticism well, and she destroyed the manuscript.

The only thing that does exist today is a short biography in which Tanya gave her own family background and a little information about Marshal's. This is what she wrote about the years at Yaquitepec, which indicate that despite the hardships there was love: "I have to confess that I've minimized and eliminated a great deal of the information flooding me about those terrible years. I couldn't force myself to write about them—they were so horrible. The only beauty in them was our love and loyalty for each other. No I haven't exaggerated either."

The biography does have one very curious item in it—a reference to Margaret. She wrote: "Marshal married Margaret, a woman already pregnant, who insisted on a divorce as soon as her child was born." This was actually the second or perhaps third reference to this. The first time is possibly in the mysterious letter given to Marshal Jr. for Margaret that was burned; and the second time is in a letter she mailed to Marshal Jr. after the divorce and just before Marshal died—both Marshal Jr. and Margaret read that letter. It is curious that she did this because she certainly knew the truth about Margaret as she had played counselor for awhile in that relationship. Marshal Jr. was Marshal's son. He was born a year after the marriage. It is also obvious from the letters Marshal wrote to Margaret that Marshal Jr. was his son. We will never know her motivation in making these statements.

Tanya maintained her privacy after the children were grown and gone, and she never granted an interview. She did return to Yaquitepec years later with Rider in 1963 or 1964. They drove up through Julian and visited with Myrtle Botts. Victoria believes that her mother was not "that unhappy in later life," but "as her health began to deteriorate…she pushed people more and more away from her." Tanya gradually cut off her relationships with each of her friends (and some family members) and she would have nothing to do with neighbors. She never lost her anger toward Marshal, and she always cherished her Rosicrucian books. Victoria said, "Her focus was very much inward and her faith sustained her, even if she didn't show it to others." She died of old age on May 31, 1997, just months short of her 100th birthday.

Tanya at age 85.

Remembering Marshal

Marshal had wondered how he would be remembered, and he projected those thoughts in an article about Paul Sentenac in the August 1948 "Desert Trails." He wrote,

> *…how shall we form opinions of a man about whom the vague threads of gossip and misunderstanding have been woven for many years since his death…. The thing which is enduring is something which cannot be seen, touched or measured by material standards. It is the spirit of a man. His ideas—the inner light or urge by which he moves…. In the ruins of his desert castle…[he] has left his monument and his epitaph. He was one who dreamed dreams. He had something of the divine fire of the poet. The tumbled stones of his hilltop Gibraltar prove it.*

INTRODUCTION

by Rider and Lucile South

The Great Experiment

While Mother had a very different childhood in New York City, she accepted living in the desert as an adventure when she was a young person. Father had been raised on a sheep ranch in Australia, and he was comfortable living outdoors, but he did not want to run a sheep ranch. His love was writing. In the United States he was able to carry on with his dreams. In the desert they both found peace and quiet and an escape from a hectic and harsh world. Then I came along. Mother was 36 years old and Father was 44 years old when I was born. By then they had been living in the desert for several years. The house was partly finished and became bigger as I grew older. The routine had been established. My parents each had ideas about raising children that eventually polarized their differences.

While at first glance one might think the desert would be a dangerous place for a child, in our case, it wasn't. I only remember seeing three or four rattlesnakes in my years there. If we ran out to the front yard, there were no cars to run us down, no strangers to stay away from, and no dogs to bite us. For a child it was a reasonable place to grow up.

Father sometimes called it an experiment in desert living. Now the question comes up—when does a good thing turn bad? One candy bar is a great treat, but 20 makes you sick. As we three kids got older, our parents, each in his or her own way, realized that the great experiment had to end. But how?

Mother, coming from city life, wanted us to adapt to city living while we were still pliable in thought. She was more practical and cared for us in that way. Father wanted us to be comfortable with people as he was and not become part of the masses. He was an artist and a writer, and in his own way he cared for us. While each loved us, they had different plans for our upbringing. Eventually, Mother's plan of making us comfortable in the city won out.

Baby Rider with his mother, Tanya South.

Watercolor of Rider, painted by his father, Marshal South.

41

In the years to come, we three children benefited from the quiet peace on the mountain in which we had grown up. I was born in 1934 in the middle of the Great Depression when a lot of people were cold and hungry. I do not ever remember being cold or hungry or unloved by either parent.

—Rider South, Silver City, New Mexico

[Editor's note: Rider is the oldest of the three children who grew up on Ghost Mountain. He was almost 13 years old when he moved to San Diego. His recollections of the years on Ghost Mountain are in sync with details described through the monthly articles written by his father. Years later as an adult, Rider returned to Ghost Mountain with his wife Lucile. What follows is a description of a personal tour of Yaquitepec as recalled by Lucile, followed by small vignettes Rider later shared with Lucile about his early childhood. Lucile then recounts the first time she met Rider and the long relationship she has had with him and Tanya.]

A Visit to Yaquitepec

Ouch! A cactus needle pierced my finger. Drawing it out and tossing it aside, I could see cactus plants all around me. Behind me, my husband Rider South was carefully making his way up the steep incline. I had supposed he would lead the way, but now I realized he was behind me to protect me from falling to the bottom of the mountain we were climbing.

We were climbing Ghost Mountain in the Anza-Borrego Desert in southern California. Marshal and Tanya South, Rider's parents, had chosen this place to homestead. I had expressed the desire to see where Rider had spent his early years. This trail was more difficult than I had imagined, but we finally reached the top. Then Rider took my hand and led me to what remained of the house where he had lived until he was almost 13 years old.

"This is Yaquitepec!" he exclaimed.

"You lived here?" I could not hide my surprise.

"Of course it's in ruins now, but it really was a nice house. The park people took off the galvanized roof because they thought it a hazard. Without a roof the weather has practically destroyed it."

I followed him, and he showed me the place where a big bed had been. He said that it had to be big because in the winter the entire family shared it. Further on in the room, I could see the remains of a large fireplace. He pointed out the far side of the fireplace where his mother had done the cooking.

I asked Rider what his mother had cooked on the big stove. He answered, "Pink beans, lima beans, potatoes and onions. She also baked bread in the oven."

"Where did she get the flour for the bread?"

"We would grind wheat to make flour. It was sort of a family affair," he responded. "Mother, Father, and I took turns in turning the handle on the little grinder. I still have it at home, and I will show it to you sometime."

"Our table was opposite the fireplace. Father had made it from two 12 x 10 inch boards that he had carefully smoothed and stained. Standing nearby were the two large coolers. They were both about 3 feet wide and 6 feet high and probably two 2 feet deep with fine-screened doors to protect the food from flies and other insects. The four legs were in small cans of kerosene that kept bugs from crawling into the coolers. When something had to be kept even colder, Father would take it outside to the cellar. Next to the coolers there was a cabinet where Mother kept all the dishes. This cabinet and the coolers had occupied half of the northern wall of this large room."

He led me across the room and described where there had been an archway that had led into the front room. A screen wall divided this area into two rooms, and the one on the west was mouse proof. It was made

The iron doors for the adobe cooking range were cut and hammered from tops cut from iron drums.
The broom to the right is made from mescal/agave stalks and blades.

to hold perishable items. Its west wall continued the walls of the house. The screen wall was set into a foundation. This was probably the first room they had built—when it was just the two of them.

"The same length running north and south was our east room," he continued. "This was the front of the house, and it faced the east to get the morning sun. From here we could see the rest of the small valley and the distant Carrizo Badlands.

"The east wall of the house had three large pillars approximately 2 feet square. Between the pillars, for about 2 1/2 feet, rose a solid wall of adobe mud capped with cement. This made a wonderful place to sit to watch the big black ravens soaring in the beautiful clear blue sky.

"My Father had bought eight window frames, each one containing six panes of glass. Half were set on top of each other and securely fastened with a vertical board on either side. The side next to the pillar had hinges and opened wide. All of the windows were done this way. There was a large catch in the lower part of the window, which hooked into an eye on the inside of the house. In this way the windows could be left open for fresh air.

"At the extreme northern end of this eastern room my Father made a large door at least 4 feet wide and 6 feet tall. It was secured with a latch on the inside. Both ends of this room had archways. The one going into the kitchen was on the south while the northern one went into a small storage area. It eventually was intended to lead into another room. This comprised the basic house in its best condition. We lived there in comfort for several years," he concluded.

We went outside and Rider showed me where the cellar had been that his father made. The state park had since filled it in. Rider said that the bottom of the cellar was always cool even in the summertime. It was about 12 feet deep and 8 feet in diameter with a roof of adobe about 12 inches thick. A trap door made of wood covered with sheet iron was hinged to the roof. Rider added, "After opening it we could go down the ladder to the bottom. I don't remember when they made it because I was very young."

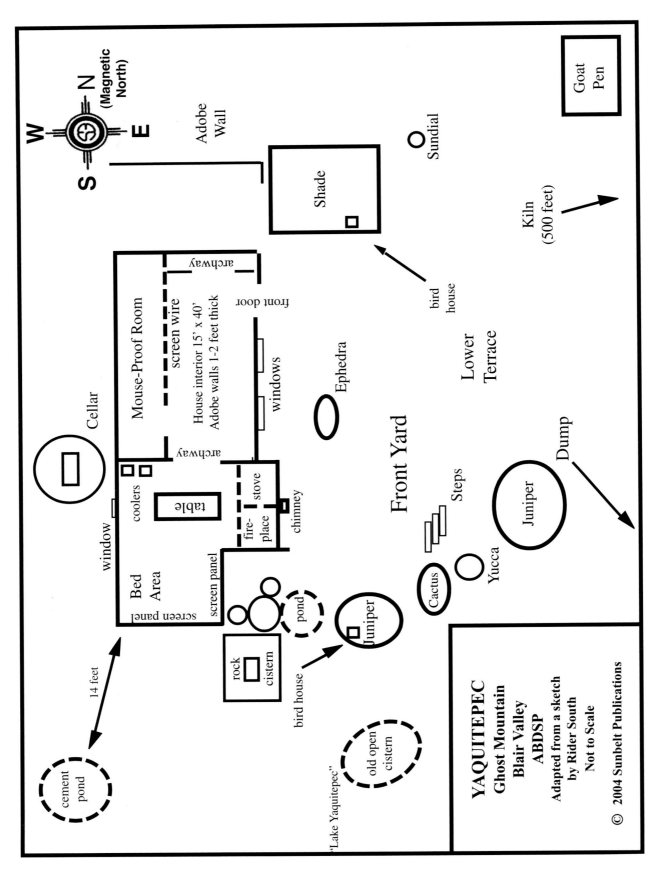

YAQUITEPEC
Ghost Mountain
Blair Valley
ABDSP
Adapted from a sketch
by Rider South
Not to Scale

© 2004 Sunbelt Publications

Side view from the cisterns of Yaquitepec.
(See page 60 for side view of the house from the shade.)

Front view of Yaquitepec. The home faces magnetic east.

The roof of the house was corrugated iron, which slanted to the east with a gutter on the front side of the house. When it rained the water would run into the gutter and go into one of the cisterns.

The first few gallons of water were discarded because it had cleansed the roof of dust and sand. Then the following rainwater could be used for drinking. The first water storage containers were actually large steel drums painted on the inside with heavy cement tops. Next to the steel drums was a low cistern about 3 feet deep and 8 feet in diameter made of cement with a canvas top. Rider said that they were pretty much in place "before my memory started."

On the other side of the steel drum was the largest of the cisterns. "It was the size of a small car on the inside," Rider recalled. "Father built it with cement and rock. It also had a canvas top. There were several cisterns that were planned and never finished because of a lack of time, money and energy."

"What happened when it didn't rain?" I asked.

"Daddy was very strong. He carried up most of the water that we brought from Julian or Banner by car. He would carry it in 5-gallon metal Army surplus cans. They were much larger than the 2 1/2-gallon canteen that Mother would carry or the 1-gallon canteen that I would carry. Father and I were the main water bearers because Mother needed to care for Rudyard and Victoria and attend to her usual household duties.

"One year we had a heavy rain that was followed by a year of drought. Then all the water had to be brought in. Otherwise there were infrequent trips for water."

Rider described the house while we walked around it. He added, "About 200 feet from the house was the edge of the cliff where we could look down on our parked car [It is 100 feet to the edge from the house but further to get a view down to where the car was parked.]. Almost always a breeze or a strong wind blew up from the valley below. Because the cliff was so steep and then became level, the wind would just sail over the top of a large rock found along the edge. That was where Father used to sit and think, basking in the warm sun. Although the wind blew almost constantly over the face of the cliff, Father never wanted to put in a windmill to generate electricity. He wanted us to grow up in a free and natural environment and not be constrained by anything modern.

"When Father realized we would need an area sheltered from the intense sun, he constructed an open building rather like the carports people use. It was big enough to have sheltered two cars and had a cor-rugated roof higher than the house. The shaded ramada provided a nice cool area where we would play. Because it was positioned right next to the house, it was convenient for our parents to use when they made clay pots.

"In the summer time we would sleep under the shade. In the morning the house was cool, but in the late afternoon and early evening the sun warmed the house up. It was much more enjoyable to sleep outside under the shade with the cool night breezes blowing.

"A large olla held our drinking water and was quite picturesque in its macramé basket. It hung from a rope in the shade ramada. The pottery would sweat because it was porous. The wind would keep it cool.

"To the east and north of the shade was a little terrace that had a large rock in the middle. On top of the rock Father had put a flat rock approximately 18 inches square with a rod that pointed to the North Star. Many people that came to see us said that our sundial was only 20 minutes off. After we had left the place, some know-nothing straightened the rod and ruined the sundial.

"In front of the house between the shade and below the cisterns we had our front yard. The front of the house and the eastern part of our yard were approximately 40 feet wide. It stretched in a sort of semi-circle with nice clean gravel in front. In the middle of the yard stood a small Indian tea bush [*ephedra*]. To the east of our lowest cistern grew a large juniper tree where Father had put a birdhouse. The north part of the front yard was bordered by our house's shade. The eastern end of our front yard had steps leading down to a lower terrace, a large area that had been planned for a garden. I don't remember anything actually growing there except maybe two or three stalks of corn. Steps going down from this terrace led us to a large juniper tree. The trail went around the trees and across a flat area about 400 square feet in size. On the northern end of the flat, Father had made a pen for our two goats out of century plant [mescal or agave] stalks. We had a dedicated area near the dump that was used as an outhouse.

"The trail up the hill went to the back of our house, which was the practical way to enter it [and the way used by park visitors today]. However, about 300 feet from the house, Father had made a trail, which carefully went around the hill where we viewed the valley and the badlands. Further on, it went past our dump, then through an area where there was an Indian mescal [agave] roasting place. We would travel around the big juniper and up the steps to our front yard. With the exception of passing the dump, this route was much more scenic and better looking than having people come to the back of our house," he explained.

Rider noticed I had slowed down. We decided to eat the lunch we had brought with us and to take a rest. He started to tell me about the various areas near the house where they had spent their days.

"From the front big juniper our trail went directly east through the flat area and up a little incline over a rocky area for about 500 feet. The path went past another Indian mescal roasting area. It was here that we built a kiln from the surrounding rocks to fire our pottery. Further on, about 100 to 150 feet, there was a place where water had come down from the hillside until several large boulders blocked its path. This resulted in a natural clay pit. One of Father's friends in the U.S. Border Patrol—Arthur Kalstrom—had some experience at water witching. He said he thought there was water down about 60 feet in the flat area where we dug clay for pots, but we never did dig down through the rocks to find water.

I asked Rider what he first remembered about living at Ghost Mountain. He halfway closed his eyes and became thoughtful, and then a little smile appeared on his lips.

"One thing I can recall was the day my father came to me while I was playing outside the kitchen door and informed me I was about to have a baby sister or brother. We drove to Oceanside and moved into an apartment on the oceanfront. I also recall that when we were leaving to go home to the desert, Dad went to the garage where the old car was and started to crank the 1929 Model A Ford. There was a loud backfire, and the engine caught fire! Fortunately, there were a number of men in the garage. They pushed the car into the open and put out the fire. There was no damage to the motor, and we took off for Ghost Mountain without further mishap."

There was another incident Rider remembered. He told me about the time that the family was climbing the trail by moonlight. "I was clutching a small box of crayons I had been given," he recalled. "Suddenly my foot slipped on the gravel, and I fell headlong into a century plant [agave or mescal]. My scream stopped my parents, and they quickly examined me to see if I had suffered any injury in my fall. They gently removed my hand from where I was holding my head. A spine of the plant had entered the top of my skull. We climbed the rest of the way to the top where they could see what they could do for me. Several days later, unable to remove the tip of the agave, they decided I needed a doctor. After a 60-mile drive to San Diego, we went to a doctor's office and he removed it."

I wanted to know if there was a scar. Rider said, "Look for one." A few minutes later we both began to laugh because in my search for the old scar, I looked as though I was seeking fleas like a monkey grooming her mate.

"What happened to the crayons," I asked.

"I had them for years," he laughed.

I was also curious about Christmas. "Did you have a tree?"

Watercolor, by Marshal South, of pots made from clay found on Ghost Mountain.

"Father usually went to where the car was parked at the bottom of the hill to find a nice rounded juniper for our Christmas tree. The junipers at the bottom of the hill always seemed bigger than the ones on the top of the hill, perhaps because they received a little more rain. The junipers were too large to be carried up the hill and into the house. Instead, he would cut the upper part of a large tree, and we would have a Christmas tree just the right size for us.

"He would carry the cut tree, which was usually about 8 feet tall, to the house and set it up. Mother would go through cartons containing all the decorations accumulated throughout the years. The decorations were not so hard to attach to the tree as the tinsel was. This was more exciting than a month later when each piece of tinsel and ornament had to be wrapped and carefully put away for next year.

"Since Father had been raised in Australia, he liked to have a plum pudding. Cans were carefully sterilized in a big pot of boiling water. Mother made the pudding of flour, sugar, suet, and all the other ingredients before the raisins and dried fruit were added. We watched the goings on with anxious eyes hoping some little tasty tidbit would come our way. When the pudding had been spooned into the sterilized cans, they were placed inside a pot of boiling water and cooked for about four hours. Mother placed the contents of each can inside a piece of cheesecloth and stored them in the screened cupboard."

I wanted to hear more and asked, "What did you do at Christmas?"

"On Christmas morning we could hardly wait until breakfast was over and we could open the toys Father had carefully chosen for each of us. Besides, each year *Desert Magazine* readers would send us many boxes of toys, candies and cookies. When Victoria was 15 months old, it was really like her first Christmas. While Rudyard and I would carefully untie the ribbons and bows enclosing the packages we had been given, Victoria would gleefully rip hers apart until she was surrounded by torn tissue and colorful ribbons.

"Rudyard looked forward to the balloons we received and became an expert in popping them. Tiny pieces of rubber were all over the place when he had finished his noisy occupation of bursting the balloons. He seemed to like to destroy things. One year he received a paint set and also a hammer. With that hammer he spent all afternoon reducing that paint set into 1-inch fragments on the dirt floor. Mother had to sweep them up with her broom made of dried mescal [agave] leaves."

I decided to ask Rider about other special occasions, and he shared these memories: "New Year's was just another night for us, and I do not remember any time we did anything special. We never celebrated other holidays like St. Patrick's Day, Valentine's Day or even Easter. However, birthdays were big events. Mother always made a cake with the traditional candles for us to blow out. Father had learned to make boiled icing, so it was always decorated with his artistic touch."

It was time for us to go down the mountain and head home for San Diego. I made Rider promise to tell me more about Yaquitepec, and in the days that followed he shared more stories and memories.

Recollections of Life on Ghost Mountain

Daily Routine

Every day on Ghost Mountain was somewhat the same. The sun would rise and cover the little house with warm sunshine. I would go to the woodpile to get the wood for the fire to cook our breakfast, and afterwards Mother proceeded to cook mush for Rudyard, Victoria and me. When it was ready she poured it into each of our pottery bowls. When we had finished our breakfast, Father came back from looking down at our car in the parking lot. He could see from the edge of our lookout that it had not been disturbed.

I remember one day Mother said, "We should do some housework today." This meant there was firewood to collect and wheat to grind. Father decided to start grinding the wheat. First he took out the little hand mill and secured it to the table. Then he went to the large container of wheat and filled a bucket of it to grind into flour. Later that day one of us hand-sifted the results. The finer flour would go into its container and be used to make bread or tortillas while the coarser grain went into a second container for our daily mush or hot cereal.

Rudyard and Victoria stayed with Father in the house while Mother and I went in search of wood to replenish our woodpile. For me, going out with either one of my parents to collect firewood was special. Then I had Father or Mother all to myself. We would walk a long way from the house so as not to spoil the landscape by taking nearby foliage.

On this day we went west until we found an old dead juniper tree below the house. We tugged at some of the big branches until they broke off. When we thought we had enough for one load, we took it back to the house. After several trips to the same place we decided to rest on a big rock for awhile.

Mother told me about her life in New York when she was a young girl. She never had any trouble getting work in an office because she could type fast and also was proficient at taking shorthand. I wanted to hear more but she said it was time to get back to work.

Marshal carrying firewood up the hill followed by Rider (center) and Rudyard.

We were about halfway home when Rudyard met us with the news that there was a strange car in the parking lot. We hurried to stack the branches in the woodpile and then hastened to see the car. Instead of a car, all we could see was the dust it made as it was driving away down the road. Evidently they had decided the trail was too hard to climb. This would happen every so often.

We returned to where Father was cooking, and we could smell the potatoes that he had been roasting for us. He was cooking tortillas on a sheet of metal he had cut from a large honey pail because he did not have a frying pan. The tortillas were made from the freshly ground flour.

After lunch Mother and I were tired, so we lay down for a little nap. We must have looked comfortable because before long the others joined us.

Trips with Father

Walks with my father were a highlight of living at Yaquitepec. The trips were so vivid because we had a lot of time together to talk about each trip.

Father began taking me for walks when I was quite young, and though my legs were far shorter than his, my youthful energy enabled me to keep up with him. One morning Mother said, "If you two will bring back a rabbit, I will make a rabbit pie for you." Since we had never seen a rabbit on top of Ghost Mountain, we took the long trail down to the flat area where our car was kept [the Souths had a rifle that they used to shoot rabbits]. We had to be careful to avoid the cactus needles and other things that would try to attach themselves to us. It was much easier to walk on top of the mountain where we had learned to jump from one rock to another.

We headed north, passing interesting creosote bushes with their tiny yellow flowers. We walked for an hour until we came to a cave containing Indian pictographs [the Morteros area of the park]. Father explained the stories the pictures told while we sat on a rock in the cave's shade and rested our tired feet.

Before long we heard the sound of a car approaching, and when it reached us it stopped. The occupants were city people who thought we were Indians. They came over to us and asked what we were so interested in. Father pointed to the pictographs and offered to explain the drawings that had been made by Indians many years before. Very soon they realized this interesting man was not an Indian after all.

They asked if Indians still lived in the Borrego Desert. Father told them they had left long ago. After they had asked Father more questions about the region, Father warned them if they were traveling further into the desert they would need water. Then we left for home after wishing them a safe journey.

We had started early so the sun was still low in the sky. A few lizards had left their holes and were basking in the warm sun, but we had not seen a rabbit all morning, and when we arrived home we were tired and empty-handed.

Father would take me on walks more often as I grew older. One time our destination was a dry lake. It was a long walk to the middle of the lake and we encountered fewer and fewer creosote and cactus bushes along the way. The sand gave way to dry clay where even grass could not survive. Father showed me a big crack across the lake that had been caused by an earthquake long before I was born. He explained that the earth was continuing to move and these movements had shut off old springs and had opened new ones. It was a desolate land and even our sparse vegetation at home seemed lush in comparison. We were glad to go home to more comfortable surroundings.

Father told me that before I was born, while he and Mother were still living in Oceanside, they would often go on camping trips in the desert. One time they stopped at the old Butterfield stage station at Vallecito. This was before the WPA [Works Progress Administration—a federal agency] restored it. They were sound asleep one night when they were awakened by the ghost of a big white horse [Tanya saw it but not Marshal]. Needless to say, they fled and never wanted to sleep there again. In the 1930s the place was rebuilt and no one ever saw the horse again.

Marshal and Rider in a cave.

From our mountain home we could see the old Butterfield station. Father would stand looking toward the station, frequently saying, "I wonder if it is close enough to walk to?" Finally Mother said, "You will never find out by standing here looking at it. Why don't you try walking to it?"

The next day after a good breakfast and after Father had filled a small canteen with water, he and I started off for the station. The south side of Ghost Mountain had a lot of "jumping" cholla cactus. They were even nastier than the cholla cactus on the other side of the mountain. Perhaps they did not actually jump at you, but it seemed as if they did.

About halfway down we reached a small valley that was still higher than the station. After a rest we continued down a canyon wash that eventually led us to the flat land. We plodded on forever, it seemed, before we arrived at the old station. We wanted to see the improvements, but first we rested beside the small spring in a box flush with the ground. Soon we were cooling our arms and faces with the cool water, and when Father put his feet in the spring my feet happily joined his.

The sun was high above us and we knew we had to get home before it set. We retraced our way along the flat land, but when we started to climb up to the valley we slowed down because it was more difficult. When we finally got home we were really tired. Mother said, "I hope you are satisfied now, and you won't have to wonder how far it is anymore." He said, "Yes, it is a long, long way." After a long night's sleep, I still felt tired. I was glad we probably would never make that hike again.

We always had a clear sky, and visibility was usually good, but one day was special. All of us could see where two hills came together in the distance. Between them there was a big flat rock. Rudyard claimed he could see a cave below that rock. Father said, "From there one could see the whole valley. We will call it the 'Cave of the Watcher.' Tomorrow we will get up early and go there." Rudyard said, "I saw it first and I want to go there too."

So the next morning, the three of us prepared to go. Mother always had us drink lots of water before we went on our expeditions. We didn't want to carry water with us. After we had our fill we started our descent of the mountain. The weather seemed cooler on the way down because of a gentle breeze, and Father told us we were lucky to have the cool breeze for our journey.

After a short rest we started off on the long journey across the flatland. The "Cave of the Watcher" was southwest of us. Although Rudyard had to struggle to keep up with us, he didn't complain, even though it must have been difficult with his little legs. When traveling on flatland you never seem to get anywhere. You just keep going on and on.

Suddenly in front of us there was a huge pile of rocks, probably 60 feet in length. They had blended in so well with the background, we had not known they were there. Rudyard and I scrambled up to the tallest rock and looked all around. We called Father to come up and see what we were seeing. He studied the scene for a minute and then said, "It looks as though we have found a fortress."

At the lower level we could see where someone had camped in the shelter behind the largest rocks. By the smaller rocks we could see ashes from ancient fires. We could not decide if we were viewing the remnants of an Indian or soldiers' fort. Only when you were atop this structure could you realize its purpose.

When we were rested we found a wash that came from the two hills. It led us between a corridor of large smooth rocks. The canyon became steeper and steeper as we struggled to reach the top of one of the hills. Halfway up we had to rest. It had been much harder to climb the smooth rocks than we had expected. At last we found the cave. We realized the entrance was only about as tall as Rudyard, but it was very deep. Carefully entering the cave we discovered ashes showing it had been used as a shelter at some time. From where we were standing, we had a grand view of the entire valley. We knew why Father had named it the "Cave of the Watcher."

When we descended we chose to go down another side of the hill that looked much easier for us. Reaching the bottom, we looked straight to our own mountain. It seemed nearer, and we reached it faster than if we had returned the way we had come. Our own trail down had not come over this far, and the climb was steeper until we reached our own trail. The three of us were grateful for the cool water Mother had for us when we arrived home, and we immediately went to sit under our shade.

Making Pottery

For awhile Father and Mother were interested in making pottery. They brought clay from a place about 650 feet from the house. Father would dig out some of this clay, and then it had to be cleansed of twigs and separated from the sand. So, they added water to the clay in a 5-gallon bucket. The twigs came to the top where they could be removed and the sand accumulated at the bottom. This was done several times until there was enough fairly pure clay, and then it was carried back to the house where it was fashioned into various objects.

Someone had given us a treadle pottery wheel. Besides the pottery made on the wheel, my folks also used the Indian method. Rudyard and I would patiently stand and watch how they fashioned clay into a beautiful vase or a new breakfast bowl.

When we began using the water for making pottery we would have uninvited guests. We had beehives down below in the parking area and the bees would come up to share our water. We were wary of our winged visitors but they were polite and didn't sting us.

We would go out often to where the pottery was left to dry. To our disappointment sometimes the pottery would crack and break. The pieces were put into water where they would melt and be used again. We were always happy and relieved when they dried without cracking.

The pottery needed to be smoothed before it could be painted and fired. A small flat polishing rock was dipped in water and lightly rubbed over the piece. Then came the part I liked the best—watching Father paint the pots.

He usually painted them with red oxide. He told me he used it because it would withstand the firing. His best pictures were those showing the old west. There were Indians with their tepees, horses and wagons, but sometimes it was just scenery. Mother would paint her pots differently. They were more symbolic, using designs she had seen on Indian blankets.

When the painting was finished the pottery was set out to dry again. Because the smallest bit of moisture could cause them to crack when fired, even in the dry air they usually took two or three weeks to dry.

Father and Mother had built the kiln out on the flat before I was born. It was a barren area perhaps because of the ashes left there from the Indians' fires. Using fire-blackened rocks from the mescal roasting area, my parents made a semi-circle for the kiln.

The fuel was old juniper wood to make a hot clean fire without any smoke. For a different effect, green juniper was used when they wanted the pots

Marshal making pottery under the shade.

to look smoky. The pots were placed on the coals and additional wood was put on top of them. The firing lasted for several hours.

The next day we anxiously checked the cooled pots to see if they had cracked. If they were cracked we crushed them, putting them in with fresh clay for the next time. The finished pots were taken to the Julian grocery store where they were displayed in the window. They were a favorite with the tourists who came for the annual "Apple Days" celebration.

If Father liked the more unusual shaped pots, he would make a plaster of Paris mold for them. Then he would duplicate them.

Whenever Father made a batch of plaster of Paris, he always had me stand up-

Rider making pottery.

wind from the mixing bowl. He never wanted me to breathe the dust. He said, "If it gets into your lungs, it will kill you." Father also painted landscapes, but they did not sell as well as his pottery.

From Schooling to Printing

One morning when there was not a cloud in the sky, I was sure it would be a fun day. I was wrong. When breakfast was over, our parents brought us pencils and paper and said, "This is going to be a school day." We were to have school even though the day was beautiful.

When it was not so nice outside our lessons were inside on the big table. My parents had decided we needed more schooling and fewer lessons in pottery and basket weaving or walking somewhere because it was a nice day. I did not like the idea of so much schooling at first, but as we advanced, I liked it better than when it was haphazard.

Rudyard and I reluctantly went to the big table. Mother started to work with Rudyard while Father wrote out a small sentence for me to copy. He watched me copy it about a dozen times. Then he gave me another sentence to work on. After I did both sentences in block letters, he told me to write them in script.

We continued this for what seemed like hours and I thought lunch would never come. I remember I ate my lunch as slowly as I could, but they caught on to my little plan. When they said I would not be copying more sentences I was relieved, but only for a moment, because I was told arithmetic was my next subject.

I'll never forget the trouble I had learning the multiplication table. It was weeks and weeks until I learned twelve times twelve. My brother only had to go up to six times six because he was three years my junior. Victoria was the lucky one. She sat in the corner and played with her dolls while we did arithmetic.

I guess it was because Father was an author and Mother was a poet that reading was of primary concern to them. Even little Victoria was given books to read, perhaps because Victoria was getting to the age where she would have gone to kindergarten had we lived in a town.

There were few days that we did not sit at the big table wrestling with the three R's. But it was geography that captured our imagination. On the days Father told us about Australia, the country "down under," we looked at him with awe. How wonderful it must have been to sail in a big ship and visit other countries.

Both Mother and Father had been to the different states they showed us on the map. One thing that seemed so strange to us, living as we did on top of our desert mountain, was Father's description of mighty rivers. We just could not imagine seeing so much water.

Lesson time—plenty of air and sunshine in this desert classroom.

My parents encouraged my schoolwork and told me that there was a big project coming up. I would have to be able to read well. I did not know what the big project was, but I knew I wanted to be a part of it.

When you live a long ways from a town everything is saved. It might come in handy in the future. Among our collection of odd things was an old piano stool. Father would often look at it with a faraway look in his eyes. Then he would ask me, "How is your reading coming along?" I would proudly show him the books I had read. We all read many books that came from the library in Julian. Father was always looking for instruction books.

Finally the day we had been waiting for arrived. Father said he was ready to make a printing press. He began to cut up pieces of a 2 x 4 inch board and then bolted some of the pieces together. Taking the piano stool apart, he tossed the seat aside. The screw that had made the seat go up and down he fastened upside down to a board. The nut, that was now at the top, was where he fastened a wrench. We watched fascinated when he used it to raise and lower the board he had fastened to the bottom of the screw.

Next he brought out a box that had been holding something mysterious. We saw it contained small letters of the alphabet which he called type. Our first job was to place the type into a large flat box with many compartments. It took us quite an amount of time to place all the capitals, lower case letters, spacers and punctuation marks into the large tray of compartments. Most of the type was easy to identify except for B, D, P, and Q.

In order to print the message he wanted, Father set the type in a small hand held tray. When completed, he carefully put it into a steel frame with small blocks of wood around it. The lines all had to be the same length. If not, spaces were added. Between the wood and the metal frame were two pieces of slanted metal. They were called a "coin" and could be expanded with a key. When it was all set up the coins were tightened with the key and everything was solid.

After the printing was done, it was my job to take each letter and return it to its own compartment. To find individual letters was difficult. Then I found by reading the words, I could find the letters easier and place them where they belonged.

Over the years Father and Mother had each acquired a large following from their articles and poetry in *Desert Magazine*. So they decided to print a newsletter. When the press that Father had made wore out, he purchased a small metal press. It was so heavy that it had to be disassembled and hauled up the trail in pieces. When it was assembled and placed in front of the window in the east room, we all marveled at how many moving parts there were.

Pictures were inserted amid the text by cutting designs out of heavy linoleum pieces and setting them in the type tray. All the hard work proved to be a success. Yaquitepec Press printed newsletters, booklets, and note cards.

Father as a Writer

Father wrote his articles for publication in his little writing house. It was about 6 feet wide and 10 feet long. A small desk held his typewriter and tons of paper and magazines were everywhere. The little hut was made of lath and tarpaper but somehow it held up even when we had adverse weather. It was sheltered between two big rocks and did not receive any direct wind [and was located about 200 feet southeast of the house].

One morning each month he would go to his room after telling us he did not want to be disturbed. We knew he was going to write the article for the magazine. Then he would reemerge and tell us that he did not have anything to write about, and for the rest of the afternoon he would complain to us, "I am losing my grip." The next morning he would retreat to his little house and by noon he would have the article ready for Mother to proofread.

When he was living in Oceanside before I was born, he wrote several western books that were later published in England. He typed his novels with two fingers. Mother had to retype them before they could be mailed to the publisher. When first submitted they were rejected. They were not accepted until there was interest in Americans with the beginning of World War II. He worked with the Charles Lavelle Literary Agency to place his books. His first books were published in 1935, a year after I was born, and several years later he began writing for *Desert Magazine*. His books sold well because he had a wonderful way of describing the Southwest. His characters were alive and vibrant. His stories of adventure were fascinating and held the reader's attention until the last page. Before he had married Mother he had traveled in Arizona, New Mexico, and Mexico, which gave him the background material for his stories.

While in Oceanside he had worked on local fishing boats, but he never wrote anything about the sea. With the exception of the *Curse of the Sightless Fish*, his stories were always about ranch life and gunfights, a lost treasure, and a beautiful damsel in distress. As the years passed, he became more thoughtful. The readers of *Desert Magazine* found his stories interesting in three ways: philosophy, environment, and family life. Father and Mother always cared for nature, and while living at Yaquitepec they became even more environmentally conscious. When they had children and experienced family life, they appreciated the living plants around them even more.

The passing years changed their views and consequently their stories became more philosophical. Mother mentioned God more often in her poetry. While Father still had the talent for writing the Wild West stories, he didn't care to write them anymore.

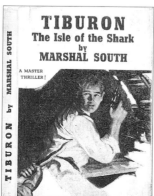

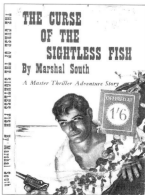

All of Marshal South's novels are cliffhangers.

Happiest Memories

Like most children, I have good and bad memories of places where I have lived. Even though we did not have the usual games, playing catch, roller skates, marbles, and all the things "city kids" had, we had parents that read to us and even taught us how to play chess.

Looking back on my childhood, some of my happiest moments were when all of us were sitting around a kerosene lamp listening to Mother read stories from many books. Besides children's stories, we heard the classics, and then there were adventure books like *King Solomon's Mines* by H. Rider Haggard. My parents liked his work so much that I was named after him. Other favorites were *Around the World in Eighty Days* by Jules Verne and the writings of Rudyard Kipling, for whom Rudyard was named. Some of the books were more for Mother and Father but we listened raptly. Then they told us about the authors. Because we realized Father was an author, the writers became real to us.

Rider—a Ghost Mountain Indian.

Father always had informative books, and we kids liked them too. We loved to hear everything that Mother read. Most of the books were borrowed from the Julian Library, but we also were given many books, and these we liked especially well. We enjoyed hearing them over and over again. We were better educated in literature then most of our peers because of our circumstances. Since we did not have electricity to run a radio, Mother's stories were a wonderful treat at the end of a long day.

As a rule Father did not want us corrupted by a lot of things that were from the outside world, but once we did have a battery-powered radio. It was a gift from James Kraft, founder of the Kraft Cheese Company who once came to Yaquitepec to visit Father and to discuss his interest in growing cacti in Wisconsin. While it lasted, it was fun listening to the radio, but new batteries were expensive and Father preferred not to have the radio. Kraft, incidentally, sent us cheese each year as a gift.

Even water, which had to be collected or hauled up to the top of our dry mountain, provided some fun activities and memories.

Occasionally, after a heavy rain when all our cisterns for drinking water had reached capacity, Father would let the water run to an open cistern. We were allowed to play there. We would use either a piece of wood for a raft or Father's cement-mixing pan for a boat. Sometimes, Father would crack a walnut very carefully, and remove the meat from the shell. He put a drop of pitch in the bottom of the shell and stuck a toothpick in it before it hardened. He made the sail from a very small piece of paper. Sometimes it would be just one boat, and other times we would have a fleet of sailboats.

We had a drink we liked when the summer heat became unbearable. Mother would add some vinegar, sugar and soda to a glass of cold water. Victoria called it "fiz-wake" because it fizzed up just like a can of soda pop. It became our favorite drink until wintertime.

When it snowed we would scoop up some snow, sprinkle it with honey from our beehives and have our own snow cones. It did not snow very often, but the snow cones made up for the shivery cold, which we were unaccustomed to. When there was enough snow we would make a snowman, and then we would have a snowball fight. We didn't have fog very often either, but when we did, it became quite chilly. Rudyard and I would go to the car overlook where we could see what looked like an ocean ending at the base of Ghost Mountain. We would look west where this imaginary ocean held islands. In reality they were the tops of nearby hills and mountains rising up through the dense fog.

Our fireplace was best when it was cold. When Father started a fire for us we enjoyed watching the pictures the flames made. One evening Victoria was too close, and when a coal exploded, in its flight it hit her leg and burned it. She kept a good distance from the fireplace after that.

A Gift for Victoria

When Victoria was almost four she began to lose her baby fat and baby-like ways. We thought she looked like a Christmas Angel because of her blue eyes and long blond hair. She was strong and could run fast. It was hard to catch her when Mother wanted her for something. Victoria, who had been named after Queen Victoria, was all girl. Rudyard and I played with little trucks and our wagon while she loved to play with the numerous dolls people had sent to her. Her favorite doll cried when she laid it down. We thought Father favored Victoria because she was so cute.

Before her fourth birthday we secretly built a crib for her dolls. The males of the family went to find dried century plant stalks for the project. When Father had three and Rudyard and I each had one, we carefully took them to the house. After laying them on the workbench in the shade, we removed the small leaves from the stalks. It was like cleaning the leaves from asparagus. When they suited Father, Rudyard and I were instructed to hold them firmly together while he cut them evenly across.

Victoria hovered around us asking, "Watcha doing?"

Mother tried to keep her occupied, but it was like holding quicksilver. In desperation, Mother took Victoria down the mountain to the parking space. We then had several undisturbed hours in the afternoon to complete our task, but it was not easy.

First my brother and I held the stalks while Father drilled the holes for the binder twine that would tie everything together. To make the bottom we laced the twine back and forth through some of the stalks about an inch apart. When it was finished the little bed measured about 18 inches wide and 2 feet long.

When we agreed we had made a fine crib, Father carried it down to the cellar out of view of Victoria's inquisitive eyes. It was just in time because Mother returned with Victoria right after we had finished taking away the tattered remains of the stalks. Mother also had been busy in the past weeks making a blanket for the crib during the wee hours, while the rest of the family slept.

On the big day Mother made a cake. Father decorated it with his specialty, boiled icing. After lighting the four candles we all sang "Happy Birthday." The crib was a big surprise for Victoria, and she was delighted to have a bed for her favorite doll. We were relieved to have the chore finished. It had not been easy to keep it a secret.

Good Things to Eat

One bright Spring morning Mother got up early and cooked a big pot of beans for us and took a loaf of bread out of the cooler. Father had decided we were going to roast mescal [agave] hearts, so Mother was preparing a picnic lunch for us.

After walking 15 minutes from the house, we found an old mescal roasting place. Mother asked Rudyard and me to find some large rocks. When she was satisfied with three of the rocks, she arranged them to suit her. Between them she made a small fire to keep the pot of beans warm for our lunch.

Father had been digging out the old roasting pit. The ground was soft because of the ashes left there by the Indians long ago. He continued to dig until he had a pit 5 feet deep and 5 feet across. The rocks he took out were as big as cannon balls. When he needed more, he gave Rudyard the job of finding them. Father kept me with him. When my brother had made a huge pile of the rocks, we lined the bottom and the side walls of the pit with them.

Mother could see we were tired from our labors and set out our lunch. We gratefully ate her delicious bread and beans. Too soon lunch was over, and Father put us back to work. Victoria was told to guard the rest of the lunch. The rest of us went scouring the hillside for dry mescal and juniper wood for Father to build a big bonfire in the pit. The dry mescal burned very fast and we were kept busy replenishing it.

After an hour Father instructed us to keep the fire going while he went to find some mescals that had just started to sprout their long tall thin stalks. We watched while he carefully extracted a plant from its neighbors. Then he warned us to be careful of the pointed ends of the leaves when we peeled them from the heart of the plant. We were glad when he said half a dozen would be enough.

The fire died down until just the coals were left on top of the rocks deep down in the pit. He put the mescal hearts on the top of the coals, pushing the rocks on the wall down on them. He finished by covering the rocks with dirt. We were five thirsty and hungry people—tired but happy and really glad the job was done. We trudged back home.

When we finished our supper it was dark and time for bed. Because it was springtime, our beds were outside, and gratefully we stretched out on them. Usually we watched the stars, but this time, sooner than usual, we all fell asleep.

Three days later Father said we should go after the roasted mescal. We found it was not hard to remove the mescal because the dirt was soft and the rocks had cooled. Father inserted a shovel under the big rocks and threw them out of the

Tanya grinding corn—she began using a hand mill after she discovered the Indian way left too much gravel in the meal.

pit. He had brought his pack for carrying things on his back, and soon he had the cooked mescal strapped on his pack. I took the shovel and we left the pit just as the Indians had done so long ago.

The mescal was our lunch that day, and it tasted better than the usual tortillas because it was sweeter. We feasted on half of it and saved the rest of it for another time.

Dry roasted mescal was a special treat—a dessert. Our mouths would start to water when Father would go to the cheesecloth bag where he kept the dry roasted pieces of century plants. They were kept there so they would dry out rather than mildew.

Like mescal, the elusive chia plant was also a special treat. When we found this pretty plant with blue flowers in bloom, we would try to remember where it was so we could find the seeds later. It made a fine dessert when we sprinkled the seeds on bread and cake.

The wheat, rye, and corn that Mother used to make bread from came in 100-pound bags purchased from the feed store in Julian. They also purchased other supplies in quantity, such as potatoes, onions, and beans. When fruit was in season we would get lug boxes of pears and apples, which always tasted good. Once in a great while, we would go to Escondido to the orange packing plant and buy big boxes of oranges.

Trips to Town

Every month Father would go to Julian to send his article to *Desert Magazine*. Usually he would go alone and come back with the new mail and articles of food. A couple times each year we would all go to Julian together where our post office box was. We could go for four or five months without seeing other people. At first the trips were made to Santa Ysabel. Then Father changed post offices from Santa Ysabel to Julian. I don't know why. Reasons for such decisions were not shared with little kids.

I always knew when we were going to town or when visitors were expected. It was always preceded by each of us having a bath down in the parking lot. All we had was a small basin that held a little water poured from 5-gallon cans that were stored in the parking area.

My hair was really bright red. It was braided on each side of my head and went down past my shoulders. My father and I both dreaded bath days, because my hair would be a mass of snarls containing twigs and other miscellaneous objects that had to be removed, and it took him almost a whole day to accomplish the task. When it was clean and dry, Mother would rebraid my hair in the two strands.

Rudyard was lucky. He had fuzzy, curly-looking black hair that would now be considered an Afro. It stuck out in all directions but was easy to take care of. Victoria had beautiful yellow hair that I envied because for some reason her hair did not tangle like mine. Usually it took only a short time to have her hair done for a trip to town, even though she really disliked having her hair washed. I would hold the basin of water on one side, and Father would hold it from the other while Mother washed her hair. Even when she was two or three years old, she would upset the basin.

When we ventured into the outside world, Victoria, Rudyard and I wore clothes that Father had made. They were designed to look like Roman togas and were held in place with elaborate clasps that Father had fashioned. Mother always wore a dress, and Father usually wore regular clothes. Sometimes the clothes he wore in town and when we had visitors were more spectacular. Of course when we were atop our mountain by ourselves, we did not wear anything.

It was quite a project to go to town. If Father thought the day had worked out right, he would buy us ice cream cones.

The only place I have ever seen cones with places for two scoops of ice cream was at the Julian Drug Store. I am sure there are side-by-side two-scoop cones in other places. Most stores just put the extra scoops on top of the first one. Our treat was from the drug store that had double scoop cones.

When we returned home, everything had to be taken up the mountain. We found going to town was not a total joy. Of course for awhile we had our special treats to look forward to.

My little sister and brother were able to carry some of the smaller items up the long winding trail. They could not carry much since they were so much smaller. It was almost more trouble than it was worth to watch over them as they tried to help with this chore. I was bigger so I usually helped Father carry things up to the house while Mother stayed with Victoria and Rudyard. None of us was ever left alone.

Pets

One day when we were taking a little ride in the car, we saw three tortoises crossing the road. Father put them in the car with us, and we were able to keep them because in 1940 it was before the Endangered Species Act was passed. We placed them in a little cage outside in summer. They were kept in the house in the mouse-proof room in the winter so they would be warmer in their winter hibernation. Because there were three of us children and three tortoises we would each guard our own tortoise when they were eating outside of their cage.

Sometimes we would line them up for a race. We were always frustrated because they would never stay in a straight line for a race but would go their own way. Somehow they never caught on to the race idea. They were a lot of fun, but they were deep thinkers and didn't have much personality. When we moved to San Diego we gave them to the San Diego Zoo.

The two goats we had were a different story. One was brown and the other was sort of russet, and they were very lively. When we bought them they were giving milk. Father made a pen for them out of mescal stalks. The pen was about 10 by 10 feet and had a roof. It was divided in half because otherwise they would fight.

Each had a bell and a collar around its neck. They were turned loose after they had been milked in the morning. They were sure footed, and they would climb on top of rocks. Out of reach they would prance around in places where I would not dream of going, and I was pretty nimble on my feet.

Side view of the house from the shade with the goats and the children.

There were times when they would be gone all night. In the morning when they returned they would have sheepish looks on their goat faces. If we hadn't had the only water for miles and miles, they probably would have never come back. It took at least an hour-and-a-half to remove the thorns from their hides.

They had a sort of love-hate relationship. Even though they loved to fight they would otherwise remain close together. I don't know what they thought of us kids, but we were fond of them.

While the large animals were of more interest to the younger members of the family, Father was more interested in a little mouse. When the big fireplace was lit and it was warm at night, that was the only light in the room. Once in awhile a tiny mouse would come out and look for any left-over crumbs it might find. Father would throw a kernel of wheat on the floor and watch to see how long before the mouse came out and got it. Another kernel would be thrown closer to see if the mouse would venture to claim it. We never did find a mouse nest in the house, or even outside. It came from somewhere and intrigued Father.

There was some other kind of animal that scurried around the floor at night. Father had painted the bed legs with creosote for about a foot from the floor. That kept us from having any strange creatures in our bed, but it didn't keep us from hearing it. We never found out what it was.

Because we had mice, you would think there would also be snakes. The few rattlesnakes never came close to the house. Once we saw a brown racer and a king snake. We all marveled at the king snake's long black and white checkered skin.

Those were all the living things we had at Yaquitepec except for flies in the summer. Because we never had any association with dogs and cats, except for a very brief period while in Utah, I am still inclined to give them a lot of space.

Ghost Mountain Guests

One of the many friends that Mother and Father had was a dancer named Jade Rhodora who worked in Tijuana. She was between shows and marriages and had come to visit us for a few days. She told Mother she wanted to be where it was quiet and peaceful. They were great friends because Jade understood Mother's problems living at Yaquitepec.

Jade was probably in her middle thirties. Her reddish brown hair hung below her shoulders. When she arose in the morning she would stretch and raise her arms to the sky. She was beautiful. Father liked to talk and laugh with this slim attractive woman.

One morning Father left to mail his article to *Desert Magazine* and to get some supplies in town. He was glad Jade was with us. Besides being so pretty, she was a very practical person.

The weather changed after Father had been gone for a few hours. Large black thunderclouds covered the sky, and a clap of thunder startled us. Jade was the first one who realized we were going to have a rainstorm. Rudyard and I rushed to the car overlook to look to the northwest from where the storm was coming. We were alarmed when there was another flash of lightning, and we saw it had hit a juniper tree down by the parking lot. We called Mother to see the fire.

Fearing it would go straight up the mountainside, Jade, Rudyard, and I grabbed shovels and ran down our trail. Even though she had longer legs than Rudyard and me, we were able to stay ahead of her because we knew the trail so much better. In no time we were at the burning tree in a small wash. Although we were breathing heavily because of our rush downhill, we were able to shovel sand over the juniper. Jade said we should stay awhile to be certain the fire had been put out. We were in need of rest anyhow before we went back up the trail. While we rested, she told us about her travels and about the places where she had danced.

The shovels were much heavier when we carried them back home. We were glad we were dry, as it had never started to rain. Jade's long legs carried her easily up the steep winding trail. We could not keep up with her because we had lost our enthusiasm.

Jade visited us often and remained Mother's friend after we moved to San Diego.

Other visitors to Ghost Mountain included some of the surrounding neighbors.

The Mushet family, who ran a guest ranch at Banner Queen, would sometimes bring guests to Ghost Mountain for "entertainment," occasionally without warning.

I remember one time it was dusk and we were outside under the shade in bed. We were still awake, just talking about the stars that seemed closer than ever that night.

Out of the silence we heard two young men's voices calling, "Hello out there." It was Buzzie and Mike Mushet, and they told us their parents were down at the parking space. They wanted us to join them at a barbecue. Father told them we would join them in a few minutes. After hastily scrambling into our clothing, we started down the trail that we knew by heart. Because it was an especially bright night, we didn't take long.

They had built a large bonfire. Steaks were on the griddle, and the folks were already imbibing in hard and soft drinks. Bill Mushet introduced us to the group of people they were treating to a barbecue. They were long-time guests of the Mushets.

They divided the guests into two groups. Father told one group Wild West stories, interspersed with some philosophical comments. As usual, when he had an audience he really shined. Mother and we three children were with the second group, enjoying the soft drinks and the unusual treat of steaks.

Gradually the conversation focused on Mother's ability to read fortunes. While she was at the Rosicrucian Fellowship, she had learned the art of palmistry. As different subjects appeared on their palms, she began relating details about people's lives, which really amazed them. She could read palms very accurately. Her group was just as thrilled with her fortune telling as Father's group was with his tales.

The party broke up probably about midnight. I am glad we were afoot and not driving in one of those party cars. The Mushets left several cases of Coca-Cola with us and asked us to just save the bottles for them.

Leaving Home

In 1942 Mother and Father decided that the family needed to live in a place that had more water and was less isolated. Father had many friends that had written to him about Utah and southern Arizona. He also had traveled through both states as a teenager. When my parents had accepted the idea of finding a new home, they made plans for the move.

There was no big moving van to take our belongings. Slowly we sorted possessions according to what was to be taken and what was to be left behind. This process took months, and then there was the slow laborious task of moving everything down to the car in the parking lot. Even though it was easier to take boxes down a mountain than it is to take them up, it was still a difficult project.

When the boxes were at the foot of the mountain, we put them in a pile and then covered them with canvas. Special care was taken to protect books, pictures, and delicate objects from the rain. The pilot printing press was disassembled and carried down piece by piece. Finally everything was ready to be packed into the Model A Ford. We hitched a two-wheeled trailer that we had used often in the past to the car, and it too was soon packed solidly.

We were concerned about our goats, Juanita and Conchita. They were a bit different from the usual goats because each had just one horn. They were the last things that went into the trailer. They accepted the move more placidly than we had expected, a relief to Father. Once the goats were taken care of, we were off to our new adventure.

Hot and dusty, we traveled for days across barren land. When we reached Boulder Dam in Nevada and saw all the water in the lake, it was like arriving on a different planet. I remember going across Boulder Dam in a convoy with a Jeep leading the group. A Jeep at the end of the line of cars carried soldiers with real guns, and we kids became very quiet. They looked awesome, really fierce. After crossing this massive structure we saw the sign that said we were now in Arizona.

About 10 miles from Kingman we found an old deserted gas station, made ourselves a camp, and stayed there a few days. Here we found a giant fig tree with delicious fruit that we enjoyed very much.

We went into Kingman to mail Father's article and to purchase needed supplies. It was really hot in Kingman, and Father took a quart-size water bottle with us. There was a water fountain by an ice plant. Father went to it and filled the bottle. On a second trip to the fountain, he found that the water had been turned down so low that he could not get any water for the bottle. We could not understand how anyone could be so mean as to deprive us of water.

We also found the countryside inhospitable. We had to avoid an ugly thorn that we had never seen before, a solid seed with three spikes sticking out of it. One was sure to be sticking out at all times. I think they were called goat heads.

Then there were rattlesnakes. When we walked away from the highway and came across a rattlesnake, it would follow us. We were used to snakes on our mountain that would try to get away from us as fast as possible. To have them following us was a new experience, and we learned to be careful when we went on our hikes.

One day after we had started to travel again, we parked off the road in a grassy area. Our two goats in the back of the trailer started to make a commotion. We soon found out the darker one of the two had given birth to a baby goat that was blue-black with white patches and had two small tassels under its neck. Father was the only one who didn't want to call it Betty. He wanted a Spanish name similar to the other goats' names. Somehow we prevailed, and it was named Betty. It was the cutest little thing I had ever seen.

We eventually arrived in St. George, Utah, and saw an old vacant motel. Father contacted the owner, and she let us stay in one of the cottages. We tethered the goats in a big field in back of the motel.

All was going well, until Betty, the baby goat, started to tangle the chain around two posts. I would go out and unwind her. She was frisky and looked cute because of the two horns about a 1/2-inch long. One day, when I was trying to remove her from the tangled chains, she butted me in the head with her two horns. It bled a little, and Father and Mother saw I was bleeding when I returned to the motel. They decided I was lucky I had not been blinded. Victoria, Rudyard, and I protested, but my parents decided to sell all three goats.

Shortly after that episode we moved to a vacant farm with a reservoir about 200 feet long. We kids had a lot of fun on a raft that we built. It was lucky none of us drowned because we could not swim. We also had to be careful because of the broken glass on the bottom of the reservoir.

Realizing that this was not suitable for us, Father drove off to look for a better place for us to stay. When he returned he told us he had not found anything and that we would return to Yaquitepec. We repacked the car and trailer and went back to the mountain.

Some things went back up the mountain, but before we had finished, Father heard from the Navy. They had approved the area for an airplane target range because it was remote and barren. We had to leave. Before we could pack again and leave, we saw planes shooting at prominent rocks.

A section of the frieze at the Julian Library painted by Marshal South.

Our friends and neighbors Lena and Everett Campbell heard of our plight and offered us refuge on some of their leased land. They also offered us an unoccupied house on acreage where they were raising cattle. The nice stone house had a large cement porch, which became the place for us to play.

A 3-inch pipe brought water to the backyard. The pipe stopped there, and the water was free to run across the yard. My brother and I set out to build a dam. We were like two busy beavers hauling rocks and dirt to build a really big dam. That was a fun time. Mr. Campbell was happy with our project because it provided a place for his cattle to drink.

In time the Navy said we could return to our home. Moving our possessions from the Campbell house to our parking lot was no problem for a few big trucks. Returning everything back up the mountain was another challenge. The Navy wanted to use a large tractor to carry things up the mountain, but Father did not want them using the tractor and tearing up the hillside. Eventually, Father convinced the Navy chief that leaving our possessions in the parking lot was all right.

But overall, things were not right. The trip to Utah and living at the Campbell house had disrupted our way of life. Nothing would ever seem the same again.

Shortly after the Navy had moved us back, Father started to paint a mural or frieze inside the Julian Library. The western scenes were reminiscent of the old days in the West. The mural ran along the top of the four walls. He stayed at the library while he was doing the artwork. The mural is still there but the room has become a realty office next door to the Julian Chamber of Commerce.

It was about this time that Mother began thinking that we kids should be going to regular school. For awhile there were harsh words spoken between my Father and Mother, which ultimately led to a divorce.

Life Goes On

One of Mother's friends helped us move to San Diego. We lived in Carlsbad for several months. While we were there, Mother wanted me to join the Boy Scouts, and eventually I did. When the troop went to summer camp in the Laguna Mountains, I went with them. On our return home, we drove through Julian, where I was happy to see my father walking on the street. We stopped and talked to him, and he bought all of us ice cream cones. We talked happily until the troop had to leave. It was the last time I saw him alive. I was glad I had had the unexpected opportunity to see him once more.

Rider's ring.

I cherish the silver ring he sent to me shortly after I saw him in Julian. The ring has a turquoise stone setting, and it is a fine example of his expertise in making jewelry. I keep it in its small box that my father made from a century plant stalk.

We moved to San Diego when housing became available in Point Loma, and we attended schools there. It did not take us long to adjust to all the modern conveniences in the city. Rudyard and I took advantage of the mirror in the bathroom to check out our new short hair, which made us look just like the other kids. Mother appreciated the luxury of a real kitchen. It became her domain.

Getting to know other kids took a longer time. We had only known adults and no children our own age except for the Mushet boys. We had to catch up to their mannerisms, which was hard on them too, as they thought that we were a little strange. Our lifestyle had been so different that it made us different.

Victoria became Vicky and probably felt at ease with her new friends in first grade. It was easier for her because she was so much younger. Rudyard and I had a harder time of it. When the fellows talked about baseball, basketball, and football, they might have been speaking a foreign language; it was so new to us. We had not even played catch on the mountain! When teams were made up I usually wound up on the bench. I spent my gym classes wandering around the field or examining the strange equipment in the gymnasium.

Rudyard melted in with his peers faster than I did. He did not have to cope with red hair, being taller than most other boys, and feet that had to overcome years of no shoes. He was also a good talker—something that would come to me in time.

After I graduated from Point Loma High School in 1952, I began my four-year training to become an aircraft mechanic while

Rider South, U.S. Army Signal Corps.

working for the Navy at North Island Naval Air Station. I served in the Army Signal Corps from 1956 to 1958, and retired from North Island in 1989.

As an adult I have been back to Yaquitepec to see the old place slowly fade away. One time I happened to be there when a state park ranger was giving a talk. He had read my father's articles, which had made life on the mountain sound like a cross between a fairy story and Camelot. Father always put the best possible face on our life there. He was an exceptional writer and made everything seem real.

To a city person that had never driven off a paved road, it all seemed wonderful, which in a lot of ways it actually was. However, to a person who has experienced desert life and has been up to the house, it should be evident that Father had written about the good days—not about the daily battle of living life on a rocky mountain with no water or living things except century plants and juniper trees.

It was called "The Great Experiment," and it lasted for about the right length of time. We have the memories that Father wanted for us, and Mother's desire for us to have an education was realized. We all graduated from Point Loma High School in San Diego, California.

Father died less than two years after we had left the mountain. Mother lived another 50 years. Each of them had his or her own vision for the family, drawn from their own experiences. They both desperately wanted to do the right thing for their children, but they both wanted to have their own dreams fulfilled too.

*   *   *

[Editor's note: Lucile Iverson South has spent her whole life involved with dancing—first as a child prodigy and vaudeville star, then as a nightclub performer and producer of USO shows, and finally as a ballroom and ballet instructor at San Diego State University for 18 years. Now in her 90s, Lucile continues to lend her dance expertise to young women who compete in the Miss New Mexico pageant each year. Her choreographed routines have helped these women to go on to higher levels of competition. Lucile is the author of *Dancing Thru Life on Toes of Gold*. In addition to describing her long and active dance career, the book gives details about her early relationship to Rider. Those details have been highly abbreviated below. Lucile also writes about her friendship with Tanya South, her mother-in-law.]

Lucile's Story

It had been a long time since I had read an article about the South family in our local paper. So when a young man named Rudyard South came to my studio in 1954 to take dance lessons, I did not connect the name with the story I had read.

One night after his lesson he asked if I could take another pupil. He told me he had an older brother who was quite shy. Rudyard thought he would gain more confidence if he learned how to dance. I told him I would be happy to have his brother for a pupil.

Rudyard and his mother came to the studio with Rider for his first lesson. I talked briefly with their mother but my only recollection of her was how small she was compared with her tall sons. It was the first time I met Tanya.

Rider was six-foot-two to my five-foot-four, and since I gave my ballroom lessons in ballet slippers, he had to look down at me. I became a bit self-conscious from his intense attention. It was the beginning of a long relationship that eventually led to marriage.

The second time I met Tanya is when Rider returned from Germany after his stint in the Army. He asked me to visit his mother. It was a very chilly June afternoon. His mother barely acknowledged me. We talked awhile, but I did not stay very long. I had a cup of tea and left. I thought it was disapproval of the age difference between Rider and me, but I was to wonder many years later if that was the trouble.

Wedding photo, Rider and Lucile South.

Over 20 years passed before we actually wed. We had the wedding in my backyard in front of a blooming gardenia plant on October 26, 1980. Our guests were mostly composed of his family. My brother gave me away, and my sister-in-law was my bridesmaid. My nephew took the pictures. Rider's mother was there along with his sister Vicky and her husband and four children. Rudyard was there with his wife and two children. Rider and I limited ourselves, and each had two friends to complete the wedding reception.

Through the years, Rider began to share stories about his family and their life in the desert, but his own family never talked about it, especially my new mother-in-law.

I tried to create a bond with my new mother-in-law, but could not. I would invite everyone over to our home for dinner on Tanya's birthday and also on Mother's Day. That lasted for two years. Then Tanya said it was too much work for me and would not come anymore.

I did have lunch with Tanya a couple of times. The only thing I would hear about the life on Ghost Mountain was that it was a difficult time, and she did not want to talk about it. She was proud of her poems and showed me some of them. She also showed me some of her paintings. I was interested in paintings, and we did talk about that.

Tanya's condominium was immaculate. She never made friends with the other residents. She just read and watched television. Our visits stopped when she said I was too busy and she did not want to take any more of my time.

The entire family would visit her at Christmas time. A few times Vicky, Tanya, Rider and I would have lunch together, but I do not recall ever being included in the conversation. Occasionally, Rider and I would visit her until she made it obvious that it did not matter whether we came or not. Rider was not too happy about that.

When Rider retired we moved to Silver City, New Mexico, and our visits were really rare. Rider would see her alone. I was not invited. There was not any reason; she was just cutting herself off from any friendships.

My memory of her is sad. She was a brilliant woman and had a delightful laugh when she did laugh. She was very correct in all she did. I think she brooded too much and had come to the decision that life had not been too kind to her, and she did all she could to withdraw from it.

—Lucile Iverson South, Silver City, New Mexico

Tanya South at age 70.

DESERT MAGAZINE ARTICLES

PART ONE — DESERT DIARY

[Editor's note: All articles that appeared in *Desert Magazine* are in chronological order with the exception of Marshal South's five non-series articles, which are grouped together at the end in Part Five—Miscellaneous Articles. Tanya South's "Sequel to Ghost Mountain" is also found there. Tanya's poems, which appeared with Marshal's articles beginning in May 1941, have not been included due to space restrictions. Subject breaks * * * have been added to the text where Marshal changes subjects abruptly. Marshal's comments appear within (parentheses) while the editor's notes are found within brackets as in this notation. Marshal's use of the British spelling of words, such as mould for mold or the use of double "ll" as in quarrelling, has not been changed. Obvious typographic errors found in the text of the articles in *Desert Magazine* have been corrected. Punctuation has been added or changed where necessary, and names have been made consistent, such as Juana Maria Better Than Nothing, which is used each time rather than the occasional Juana-Maria-Better-Than-Nothing. No change has been made to mescal, which sometimes appears as agave.]

DESERT DIARY 1
(February 1940)
January at Yaquitepec

THERE is always something tremendously exciting about beginning a New Year. Especially in the desert. Here at Yaquitepec we don't make "resolutions"—out in the brooding silences of the wastelands one doesn't need to bolster confidence with such trivial props. But every time January first rolls around we greet it with joy. It is the beginning of a new page; a page of some fascinating, illumined parchment. An ancient page, but to us still unread. What will it hold? The desert is full of mystery and surprise. No two years are ever the same.

And New Year's Day is always an event. Perhaps it is because it draws added lustre from the recent memories of Christmas trees and the mysterious visit of Santa Claus. Yes, Santa comes to Yaquitepec. Silently, in the dead of night, his gold-belled reindeer speed between the swaying wands of the ocotillos and the tall, dry stalks of the mescals and whisk his gift-laden sleigh to the summit of Ghost Mountain. And always when the old saint comes to stuff the stockings of the two little tousled-heads who dream on expectantly he finds a decked Christmas tree awaiting him. The Christmas trees of Yaquitepec are carefully cut branches of berry-laden mountain juniper. They are never large—for we are jealously careful of our desert junipers. But what they lack in size they make up in beauty.

The white clusters of berries glisten against the dark bunched green of the tiny branches. And the silver star that does duty every year at the tree tip sparkles in rivalry with the shimmering, hung streamers of tinsel.

The little desert mice, which scamper trustfully and unmolested in the darkness of our enclosed porch, explore timidly the rustling crepe paper and greenery piled about the base of this strange, glittering spectacle. And I am sure that the old Saint, as he busies himself at his task of filling the two big stockings hung before the old adobe stove, must pause often to glance at the gay tree and to smile and chuckle. Yes, Christmas is a glad time at Yaquitepec.

And New Year is somehow a joyous finale of the glad season. A wind-up and a beginning. And it doesn't matter much whether the wind is yelling down from the glittering, white-capped summits of the Laguna range and chasing snowflakes like clouds of ghostly moths across the bleak granite rocks of our mountain crest or whether the desert sun spreads a summer-like sparkle over all the stretching leagues of wilderness. New Year's day is a happy day just the same. The youngsters, eager in the joy of a lot of new tools and possessions, are full of plans. Rider, desert-minded and ever concerned with the water question, is usually full of ideas concerning the digging of cisterns. Or perhaps with the manufacture of a whole lot of new adobe bricks. Rudyard, with all the imitative enthusiasm of two whole years, follows eagerly in big brother's lead. He is fond of tools, too.

One of his cherished possessions is an old wooden mallet…"wooda hammah," which he wields lustily upon anything conveniently at hand. And prying into Rider's toolbox and helping himself to punches and hammers and, saws and nails, is his favorite indoor sport.

"Don't you get lonely, away up here on the mountain?" visitors ask sympathetically at times. And they stare when we laugh at them. Lonely! How is it possible to be lonely in the desert? There are no two days the same. Always, on the mighty canvas of the sky and the stretching leagues of the wasteland, the Great Spirit is painting new pictures. And constantly, through the tiny thoroughfares and trails of our world of mescals and rocks our wild creatures hurry. The flowers have gone now and the chill of winter is in the air. But life goes on just the same.

Coyotes range their beats with nightly regularity. We have been officially placed upon the coyote highway system and almost every night they come to sniff about our cisterns and to nose over the ash dump in search of possible eats. And sometimes grey foxes wander in on friendly calls. The snakes have holed up and the lizards are mostly all hid out. But owls come and sit on the corner of our ramada at night and regale us with woeful discourse. And the white-footed mice are always with us. There is something amiable and companionable about a white-footed mouse. Long experience with us has given them confidence. They slip in and out in the evenings like cheery little grey gnomes; squatting on the edge of the great adobe stove and nibbling tidbits, held daintily in their forepaws, while their big, beady, black eyes watch us attentively.

We have our birds too, though not the population of spring and summer. But quail whistle at times from the distance of the rocks and shrikes chatter advice from the summits of dead mescal stalks. The world moves on slowly but surely towards spring. The new grass is green in sheltered nooks and, already, some of the early fishhook cacti are putting out their flowers. The fishhooks are temperamental. If they feel like it they will flower, in defiance of seasons or regulations.

The house is bigger this year than it was last. Yaquitepec grows slowly. Almost everything in the desert grows slowly; and, like all the rest, our house-growth is controlled chiefly by water. When there is water in plenty there is adobe mud for walls. And when the cisterns are low, building necessarily has to stop. But the heavy walls are slowly replacing all the temporary ones. And we have a new window on the desert this year through which the winter stars can shine by night and through which, each dawn, we can watch the winter sun come up, red and swollen like the gilded dome of some great mosque, across a dim horizon that is studded by the phantom shapes of the Arizona mountains.

We like to sit in our window seats at dawn and sunset. It is then that the desert is most beautiful. The old sea bed, where once rolled the headwaters of the Vermilion Sea, is still a ghostly memory of its former state. And a memory not too dim, either. At dawn all the hollows of the badlands swim with misty haze that startlingly suggests water. And when sunset flings the long blue shadow of Coyote Peak [Carrizo Mountain] far out across the dry reaches the effect is breath-taking. There they are again, all those ancient bays and winding gulfs and lagoons. And beyond them the purple grey of the great sea. It is not an illusion that is part of our own make-up.

Recently we had a visitor, a young scientist from the east whose pet study is desert insects. He sat with us one evening and gazed out over the lowland desert, and marvelled. "It's a real sea," he said in puzzled bewilderment. "Why, I can see the play of the wind on the water, and the streaks of tide-rips!" Truly mystery broods in the desert. It is not hard, gazing out across the phantom bottoms, to give credence to the story of the ancient Spanish galleon that legend has it lies rotting parched timbers somewhere amidst the sand dunes.

Desert mystery—and a new year in the dawning. "It will be a good year," Tanya says confidently, as she proudly takes a huge tray of golden-brown whole wheat biscuits out of the great oven. "Rudyard is two years old now, and Rider is six. The garden is ready for spring and the cisterns are full. It will be a good, happy year for work and for writing." And she sets aside her pan of biscuits to cool while she snatches up a pencil to scribble the first verse of a new poem. Fleeting inspirations must be promptly captured—and she is a conscientious poet as well as a desert housewife. But she is a good prophet also. Yes, it will be a good year.

DESERT DIARY 2

(March 1940)

February at Yaquitepec

THE clear, metallic calling of quail in the grey dawn. There is something particularly fascinating and "deserty" in the call note of the quail. On Ghost Mountain our quail have confidence. They seem to know well that no gun will ever be raised against them. And they repay our protection with friendliness.

Sometimes in the nesting season they bring their energetic, scurrying broods on exploring expeditions right around the house; the lively youngsters, looking for all the world like diminutive ostriches, padding and pecking everywhere, while the old birds patrol proudly on watchful guard, or dust themselves luxuriously in the dry earth at the base of our garden terrace. There are few birds more handsome and decorative than the quail.

They nest regularly on Ghost Mountain, but not often do we discover where. They are adept at concealment. Once the glint of the sun upon broken eggshells betrayed an old nest that had been made scarcely 18 inches from our foot-trail. Screened by a bush and under the shelter of a granite boulder it had been hidden perfectly. Scores of times we must have tramped past, almost scattering gravel upon the sitting bird. But we had never glimpsed her.

Dawns decked with grey cloud and sometimes rain-streaked are a feature of our season now. There is nothing "regular" about the desert. Uncertainty is its keynote and its eternal fascination. Last night the drumming beat of rain made music on the iron roof of Yaquitepec and this morning we woke to a shower-splashed dawn. The sky to eastward was piled high with scudding mountains of white and grey mist, their summits tinged pink in the rays of the rising sun.

Away out above the lowland desert, sun and cloud-wrack fought a battle for supremacy. About nine a.m. the sun won through to complete victory. Against a backdrop of silver showers that screened the footslopes of the Laguna range the desert flashed up in dazzling brilliance. And over all, like a jeweled scimitar, its hilt in the desert and its point upon the summit of Granite Mountain, a mighty rainbow arched the sky. It will be a warm and brilliant day today. Tomorrow there may be snow. *Quién sabe!* This is the desert.

February touches always a warm spot in our hearts. For it was in a February that we first came to Ghost Mountain and set up the beginning of our desert home. That, too, was a year ordered in the desert's consistently irregular fashion. For spring was exceptionally early. Warm breezes blew through the junipers and the days were hot.

We like often to go back in memory to that day. Tanya carried an axe and a can of pineapple. I carried a rolled seven-by-nine palmetto tent. Already, on exploring ascents, we had made seven previous climbs on as many different days seeking an easy trail to the summit. And we had convinced ourselves that there was no easy trail. On this day of "homefounding" we cast caution to the winds and made a frontal attack, toiling upward through the cholla and the mescal bayonets and the frowning boulders and the slides of loose, broken rock.

It was a savage climb. But at last we reached the east-facing slope of the little sub-ridge that we had named Yaquitepec. We dumped our burdens in the shade of a juniper and dropped breathless beside them. A tiny, jewel-eyed, turquoise-hued lizard, sunning itself on a weathered hunk of granite, cocked its head at us speculatively.

Tanya and Marshal carrying corrugated roofing up to Yaquitepec.

Past our feet, through the pattern of shade flung by the branches above us, a huge pinacate beetle, solemn and dignified as an old rabbi in a long frock coat, ambled, wrapped in meditation. Overhead against the dazzling glint of the blue sky a lone buzzard wheeled. All about was the drowsy hush of peace. "It's heaven," Tanya said softly. "Oh, why didn't we come here years and years ago?"

There was work, that first day, as well as climbing. Among the rocks and sagebrush and mescals that crowded around us there was no space even for a tiny tent, there was scarce room to pick wary footsteps. Space had to be made.

Mescals are stubborn things at times. Especially when attacked with such an unsuitable weapon as an axe. And the chollas were frankly hostile and had no intention of being evicted without wreaking vengeance. I chopped and hacked and Tanya carried, lugging the ousted vegetation and heaving it off to one side in a bristling heap. It is astonishing how heavy a swollen-leaved, lusty mescal plant can be. And what a devilish thing it is to carry. Sweat ran down our faces and our bodies. Before beginning we had piled our clothes in the cleft of a great rock. Nevertheless, we were desperately hot. We were glad enough, after a while, to call a halt. We sat down in the thin shade of our friendly juniper and stove in the head of the pineapple can with the axe. We munched the juicy yellow slices and drank the syrup. Ever since that day we have had a particular affection for pineapple.

A space to accommodate a seven-by-nine tent doesn't sound excessive. But by the time we had removed all the rocks and shrubbery we felt as though we had cleared at least an acre. Then we set up the tent. That was triumph. We stored the axe and the empty pineapple can inside it, carefully tied the entrance flap shut, and weary but happy, turned to go back to our base camp at the foot of the mountain.

It was late. The sun had already reached the jagged mountain crests to westward, and across the lowland desert to the east fantastic shadows were gathering about the buttes and washes. We knew we would have to hurry, for we had to run the gantlet of a myriad bristling lances before we reached the mountain foot. It wouldn't be a pleasant thing to attempt in the dark.

Despite wearied muscles, we forced ourselves to speed. At the edge of the cliff, just before we swung over to tackle the long downward trail, we paused to look back. There it stood, the brave little brown tent, amidst a tangled desolation of rock and thorn. The long leagues of desert shadows were chill and purple behind it. It looked very tiny and lonely, standing there where never tent had stood before.

It brought a queer lump to our throats. "It's going to be *home*," Tanya said huskily. "It *is* home, already. I wonder why we didn't come here before?"

Then we scrambled away down the mountain to a campfire and welcome supper and bed. And that night, as we stretched weary limbs in our blankets and watched the march of the desert stars, coyotes sat on the ridges and yammered at us. And the wind came up across the long stretch of yucca-staked wilderness and skirled through the tall, dead mescal poles and through the junipers with eerie whisperings. But our hearts were warm. They were with that brave little tent, keeping guard amidst the mescals and the shadows and the wistful brown ghosts upon the summit, far above us.

That was in a February. Yes, we like February. It is a grand month.

DESERT DIARY 3
(April 1940)
March at Yaquitepec

OUR personal Herald of spring has already made his call at Yaquitepec. No, not the traditional lion who is supposed to usher in the month of gales. Our March announcer is a Western Robin. He comes every year. We like to think that it is the same bird—and probably it is, for we have never seen more than the one each year. Oddly he seems out of place here in the desert among the frowning rocks and the cholla. But he has all the friendliness of the robin family.

Annually he gives our domain a thorough inspection, hopping about our tiny garden patches and peering, with knowingly cocked head, at everything through amiable yellow-rimmed eyes. He usually stays around for two or three days and then vanishes. But he leaves our Desert Spring firmly underway behind him.

There will still be roaring gales, yes, and the surfy churning of the yelling wind through the junipers upon the summit of the cliff. Even we may have flurries of snow.

But the iron grip of Winter is over. The earliest of the Spring flowers are out. And away below us in the green carpet of grass that tints the dry lakes and desert hollows there are already broad brush strokes of delicate yellow gold.

The roadrunner, who is one of the cheery company of feathered and furred friends who share Ghost Mountain with us, sat out on a big boulder the other day and for a long time voiced his opinions of things in general. A cheerful rascal, for whom I hold sensitive memories. The first time—now a long while ago—that I heard his weird, querulous call-note, startlingly like the whining complaint of a sleepy puppy, I set out to trace it to its source.

Roadrunner

The thing was a mystery. It did not sound like a bird. And the whining complaint "Uuuummm…uuuum…uummm!" seemed to flit ghost-like amid the junipers and rocks. It defied location. And in the exasperated pursuit of it, I forgot caution—and trod squarely upon a mescal spine. That ended the search. For six months afterward the ache of the point, deep-driven into my heel, served to keep fresh in my mind the mysterious cry. We know now that it was a roadrunner. But I still have a remarkably tender feeling for the sardonic rogue.

Yes, Winter is moving out. But we bear him no ill will. Rather his going is tempered with a little regret. For Desert Winter, on Ghost Mountain, has a charm all its own. A fierce charm perhaps. But there is fascination in the abrupt and roaring changes that come charging over the wastelands. The days—the very hours—are unpredictable. To a sunny, summer-like warmth, when clothes are superfluous, a short half hour may bring the shivering chill of the arctic and a hasty snatching for blankets and a kindling of fires. It is then, when the wind yells savagely above the roof and grey, rolling mountains of cloud close in upon the sun, that we are grateful to the spiny myriads of mescals which crowd our jagged wilderness. For our chief fuel is the dry butts of the dead plants. Savage, spiny fuel. It must be handled with respectful caution. But in the maw of our great adobe stove its roaring flames and fiercely intense heat more than atone for the painful wounds that it sometimes inflicts on uncautious hands.

There are classes and degrees to this swift burning firefood. The butts of last season smoke and roar fiercely with a gassy fury that glows our iron stove-top to a cherry red. The older butts, those that have weathered down to grey, solid-cored, bundles of fibres, burn more slowly and must be stirred with the fire-irons and pounded occasionally lest they smother themselves in their own ash. The ancient, venerable remnants—relics of who knows how many score forgotten years—take long in lighting, but

when once alight glow with the bright, even heat of coal. They are hard, these blackened, weathered cores of long-perished agaves. Utterly denuded of leaves and fibres they are more like oddly shaped pieces of hardwood than anything else. And when once lighted they burn like mesquite and provide almost as satisfactory a bed of coals.

In the dark winter evenings when the gales, yelling along on the 3,500 foot level—often from a lowland desert that is utterly calm—slam and shudder from the summit of Ghost Mountain and thunder over our low roof. We have a lot of warm feeling in our hearts for the mescal. In the dancing glow of the flames the youngsters sit before the great open firedoor and draw patterns on the gravel floor and discover fairy castles and palaces amidst the glowing embers. Yes, Winter is going. But it leaves regrets.

* * *

We have been making *Carne seca*—jerky, if you prefer, though to us the Spanish name always seems more appropriate. Like most everything else there are ways and ways to the process. We have tried two methods—and each has its advantages. One way is to dip the long, thinly cut strips of meat into a deep kettle of boiling, well peppered strong brine. We lower them in slowly and extract them in the same measured fashion—a slow dip that leaves the meat white from the boiling liquid. Then it is hung out on the line to dry. The advantage of this method seems to be that it sears the juice in the meat and at the same time gives a uniform coating of salt and pepper that discourages the flies. The disadvantage is that it tends to make a rather tougher finished product.

The other method is to cut up our meat in as thin sheets or strips as possible and, salting and peppering it lightly, set it away on a platter for a few hours. The salt will draw the blood out, and the drained meat is then hung out on the lines in the evening. By morning, in the average desert weather, it is dry enough to discourage, to a great extent, the attention of flies. A little less tough product is the result of this plan. But we have used both systems with very satisfactory results.

For those who crave the genuine Mexican method I append the recipe of my old friend Don Juan Fulano de Tal: "Señor, you jus cutting up thee carne en thee beeg, then sheet an' rubbing heem weeth some *sal* an' a leetle chili an' one pint of *vinagre* to every *viente kilos*. Then you

Curing jerky at Yaquitepec (Rudyard, at left, and Rider).

hanging heem out on corral fence to dry." There are advantages to this method too. But no matter how you do it there are few things more tasty than desert dried meat.

* * *

The hummingbirds are moving in. This morning one raced into the porch, through the big, open window, and hung like a vibrant, suspended jewel, above our heads. He was utterly fearless and in the level rays of the morning sun, striking in across the mountaintop, he switched here and there, a flashing, buzzing ball of iridescent flame. A brightly flowered scarf of Tanya's lay across the foot of the bed and he sampled it curiously—thrusting at the painted flowers with slender investigative beak. Then, with a whir, he was gone—a flash of fire away over the cliff edge.

The morning sun was a glint of gold over our hilltop. In the cleft of the great boulder near the house the hardy little creosote bush gleamed cheerfully in its new dress of shiny green leaves. There was the faint but unmistakable hum of bees among the junipers.

Somewhere, away off in a world that calls itself "civilized" cannon foundries are roaring and men who preach "brotherhood" are dropping bombs upon the homes of little children.

Here, in the "savage wilderness" of the "merciless desert" there is peace.

DESERT DIARY 4

(May 1940)

April at Yaquitepec

ALL about the desert wastelands where the mescals grow there are ancient roasting hearths. Unvisited and forgotten, almost obliterated, many of them, by rains and storms and the slow march of uncounted years they nevertheless hold in their blackened stones an uncanny power to turn back the flight of Time.

Standing beside these lonely circles it does not require much imagination to see again the old days when the fires roared and the wind skirled fountains of sparks across the gullies and dusky forms moved in the glow, bearing loads of fuel or new, fresh mescal hearts to the roasting.

Many brown feet trod these deserted trails in those old days. In the sunlit silences or beneath the low hung stars the desert was then, as now, a great land of mystery. But it was not deserted. The mountain sheep were here. And great flocks of quail. And on the secluded ridges and in quiet canyons the tiny, timid, Chihuahua deer [southern mule deer]. Chia bloomed along the trails and beans of the catsclaw [acacia] and the mesquite swayed and ripened in the wind above grey rocks deep with mortar holes worn by the labors of many generations of dusky squaws.

The Indian, then, was part of the picture. He was as much a part of it as the desert wild life and the spiny plants whose food secrets he knew. A kindlier, brighter desert in those days; a bountiful mother to her simple, dusky children. Many things they did not have, many things they did not know. But it is all a question of values. Is the white man happier? Does he really *know* with any more certainty, from whence he came—or to where he will depart?

"The Spaniards, the white people, were too mean to the Indians," a philosophic snowy-haired old Mexican señora told us once. "The good *Dios* became angry. Many of the springs he dried up so the white men should not have them. In the old days when the *indios* dwelt in the land there were many, many more *ojos de agua.* Now they are gone. Where? It is the work of *Dios.* No one can sin without punishment!"

Yes, the dusky feet have departed from the old trails. But the old camp spots remain—and the mescal pits. No one wants roast mescal any more, in these enlightened days, except barbarians who have deliberately turned their back upon "progress." Even the reservation Indian is, to a great extent, too modern and civilized to accept such coarse food. Some there are who still roast the ancient delicacy. But the company of them is few and fast dwindling.

Silence is over the old hearths. When our fires flame at Yaquitepec and we, treading in the footsteps of the shadowy company who have passed on, bear fuel and the sprouting mescal hearts of April to the old stone circles, we feel somehow ghostly and unreal and part of a phantom picture that is all but forgotten.

But there is more to April than mescal roasting. All the desert is awake and rejoicing in Spring. Fountains of wax-like white flowers tower above the green, bristling bayonets of the yuccas and the emerald wands of the newly-leafed ocotillos are tipped with points of flame. Color! Sharp, vivid color! That is the keynote of the wasteland's awakening. And the knowledge that the vanished Children of the Desert found in many of these gorgeous blossoms a source of nourishing food takes nothing from their charm. Both the flowers of the yucca and the ocotillo are good to eat. But, lest the knowledge should tempt the transient wastelands visitor to sacrifice beauty to experiment, it should be stated that they are not food for the

Rider is sitting on a rug that was made at Yaquitepec. A homemade earthen pot is next to him.

unaccustomed. Like most desert bounty the taste is bitter, according to civilized standards.

Then there is the chia. The chia is a companionable little plant which seems especially to like the vicinity of the old mescal roasting hearths, spreading its circle of dark green, earth-hugging leaves, in the very shadow of the ancient fire blackened stones. Its flower spike bears round, compact, multiple-flowered blooms, set in stages, one above the other, on the slender stem. And the little gray-brown seeds that follow the tiny, short-lived blue flowers are one of the most important "Indian grains" of the desert. It is microscopic and tedious to collect. But there is high nutrition in these sand-like seeds. They were ground into meal which was eaten as mush or baked in cakes or combined with the tiny, pounded seeds of many other desert herbs and grasses. It was real labor to collect food in the old days. But it was healthy labor and healthy food. And not all of the desert harvest was so difficult.

The gathering of the golden mesquite beans, and the job of reducing them to a brown, sugar-rich meal, must have had its joys. Then, as now, there were birds and butterflies among the swaying branches and soft, drowsy breezes stirring in from the silver-glinted mirages of the lowland desert. Some of the old Indian camps, with the steady thumping of the stone pestles in the granite mortar holes and the low chatter of the busy squaws blending with the happy laughter of brown youngsters chasing each other through the aisles of patterned mesquite shade, must have been rather pleasant places.

There is a new adobe wall going up at Yaquitepec. There is always a new wall in progress. They grow slowly for there are many more things to do than building walls. But when ever we have built a new bit we always feel proud. It takes us back in retrospect to the days when there were no walls. The days when the wind gods, whenever they came yelling over the mountain crest, would heave the tent, and our cooking pots and household effects stored within would jump and rattle and sometimes upset with deafening crashes. We would have to rush frantically and pile rocks on the beds to keep them from blowing away.

We could build only a tiny section of wall at a time when we first came, because the only water we had was what we could catch in old tomato cans and such receptacles. But now we have a cistern, and the adobe walls grow more rapidly.

"King 'nake! king 'nake!" Rudyard notified us this afternoon. He stood on the top of a big boulder, pointing excitedly and shouting with all the lusty power of two-year-old lungs. Tanya and Rider ran out to investigate. Yes it was the king snake—our old friend of several seasons. He came now, sliding his handsome ringed cream-and-black length down one of our garden terraces, his alert little brown eyes beady and twinkling, his sensitive eager nose and flickering tongue moving investigatively here and there.

But he was disappointed as he slithered confidently towards the porch. The wall gap of yesteryear, through which he was accustomed to wander inside, was gone. The wall had been built up. There was almost hurt accusation in the glance he gave us as he turned slowly away and slid along the foundation, looking for mouse holes. Rudyard came over and screwed a belligerent face after the departing streak. "King 'nake!" he said definitely.

"Gun, Shoo', bang!" "King snake won't hurt you," Tanya comforted. "It's not like a rattlesnake, precious."

We all went down and sat on the great flat rock at Lake Yaquitepec—which is a little stone hollow which every rain fills with water. Here Rider sails his fleet of tiny boats. The snakes were out, we said, bad ones as well as good, and we would have to be cautious—as though caution was ever relaxed in an existence where caution becomes a vital part of life. It was warm and sunny and pleasant, sitting there on the broad rock top. A glinting, crystal silence was over all the desert.

Away to the west, Granite Mountain, its reef-lined slopes tawny and savage as the claw-scarred flanks of some sullen monster, hunched against the sky and in the lowering sun the dry lakes and all the wasteland hollows, far away below us, flashed their myriad tiny flowers in sheets of mingled wine and gold. An Arizona hooded oriole swept past our heads with a dazzling flash of yellow and jetty black. The green and brown plumes of the bunch grass swayed in the slow-moving air and the massed ranks of jumbled granite boulders shimmered in a warm, drowsy glow...Desert April!

DESERT DIARY 5

(June 1940)
May at Yaquitepec

AWAY down on the lowland desert the herbage on the dry lake beds is a wine-rusty brown, and through the brilliant sunshine that floods the crest of Ghost Mountain comes the drowsy cooing of mourning doves. These May days are pleasant ones at Yaquitepec; days when it is good to be alive for the sheer joy of living; when the skin tingles to the soft touch of the warm desert wind and the heart seems to lift eagerly to all the magic of spring.

Man is a strange animal. He is usually so busy making a living that he has no time to live. The birds and four-footed creatures are wiser. They have not saddled themselves with a host of taboos and fetishes and bogie men—of their own creating—to rob their lives of joy and make bleak their every moment with worry.

The little red-roofed bird house in the summit of the juniper tree by our water cisterns is occupied again. Just as we were preparing breakfast this morning 7-year-old Rider rushed in with the news that the two fly-catchers

Rudyard (left) and Rider building an adobe wall.

juniper just behind the wood pile. The day Rider and I installed the hollowed mescal butt for her home she sat on the tip of a neighboring tree and watched us. And ten minutes after it was in place she was busily lugging twigs and leaves into it and making herself very comfortable. She may be temperamental—but not in the matter of houses. She wanted a new one with all the gloss still on it.

All kinds of birds come to Ghost Mountain. They like the peace and quiet here—and the utter security. And a great many of them have

were back. They have a lease on the little house and come every season to nest in it. This year they were a few days late, and we had wondered.

But here they were at last, and as happy to arrive, it seemed as we were to see them. Cheerful, trustful little birds—and full of remarks. *"Chee-kwerk!"* and *"T-quip!"* Such a popping in and out of the round entrance hole of their box! Such a raising of crests and side-cocking of heads as they fly here and there about it, perching on the juniper twigs and examining it from every side. "My dear, do you think that horrid wren has been snooping around here while we have been away?" "No, no, darling! I'm sure she hasn't! Everything is exactly as we left it."

Rider said that he thought the "Mrs. Bird" looked a bit older this year. And she cocked her head at him severely and said *"Ti-churrr!"*

We have quite a few nest boxes hidden away in the thick summits of our junipers. Most of them are made from the hollowed butts of long-dead mescals. The birds appreciate them. But the boxes have to weather a bit and become part of the scenery before they will move into them. All except the wren—who actually *does* spend her time occasionally exploring the fly-catchers' cottage when the occupants are away. But she has better sense than to attempt to nest there. She has a house of her own in the

discovered the little bowl of water, hidden in the shade of a low-branched juniper, which we keep filled for the benefit of all our resident birds, including our tame chukar partridges. Many a thirsty wanderer has slipped gratefully down through the interlaced branches to drink at that hidden bowl—and flown away happily after flinging us an appreciative trill of song.

But high monarch above all our orioles and sparrows and wrens and shrikes and roadrunners and ravens and hosts of other birds is our condor. Ghost Mountain has its California condor. He does not live here. But his home is somewhere within easy cruising range. And he pays us fairly frequent visits of inspection, passing by high up in the turquoise sky, the distinctive white patches under his great wings clearly visible as he sails over our heads. A mighty bird, a survivor of a species that is almost extinct. There is a thrill in watching this royal voyager of the air whose tribe was once numerous—and whose great feather quills made such handy receptacles for the storing of gold dust.

This year there was water to spare for the making of adobe mud, and we have taken advantage of it. Mud is one of the simple and fundamental things. Being humbler and less obtrusive than water, civilization has treated it with greater scorn. But in spite of uptilted noses, mud manages quietly to persist. And if you stop to think, you will realize that today's empires—like those of the past—are still built *on* mud and *of* mud. It is true we camouflage it by fancy names, such as "plaster" and "cement" and a score of other genteel sounding titles. But these masqueraders are nothing more than glorified compounds of the same mixture of earth constituents and water as was used by the first savage to daub the chinks of his pole and reed dwelling. Good honest mud is as fundamental as life itself. And what a joy to work with! He who has not felt the thrilling, clinging touch of mud upon his hands; felt the oozy squelch of it between his bare toes and seen the honest brown wall or the coat of moist, satisfying plaster grow under his labor, has missed something of existence.

Our mud on Ghost Mountain is composed of the ruin of weathered granite rocks, of the age-accumulated rot of dead mescals and of the wind blown dust of the far leagues of desert. Yet it stands up to the weather startlingly well. Two years ago I made a temporary wall of mescal poles, chinking and plastering them with a hastily mixed mud that had but little fibre in it and far too great a content of quartz gravel. Nowhere was that sketchy pole-and-plaster wall more than three inches thick. It was put up for an emergency. I did not expect it to stand up more than three or four months—certainly not through the rains of winter.

Yet it is still standing. Gales have hammered it, fierce rainstorms have charged over the summit of Ghost Mountain and deluged it again and again with torrents of hissing water. It has sagged a little. Some of the poles are now bare to the weather, and in one or two places there are small gaps in it. But it is still standing defiantly. I have given up wondering when it will fall. I am hoping now that it will continue to stand up until the 18-inch wall of solid adobe—which is now creeping slowly up outside of it—has reached the top. Mud!…mud and water—and the labor of bare hands and feet! Thus was mighty Babylon built.

There is a tremendous amount of material in an 8-foot high adobe wall that is 18 inches thick. It consumes a lot of earth and a lot of water. Sometimes we reflect, as we splash on buckets of water and, barefoot, puddle the sticky mixture, just how hard and how slow it was to build our first structures of mud. Our first bake-oven in particular. It is still standing—a low, dome-shaped Indian oven of mud. For that we carried water up the mountain on our backs after first hauling it 14 miles across the desert. That oven wasn't very big, naturally. But it baked to perfection. Sometimes we still bake in it. Slowly the mescals among which it was first built have been rooted out and the rocks that crowded about it have been smashed up and rolled aside. Soon the growing roof of the house will cover the old oven and walls will surround it. It will be a part of the new kitchen. It has long since been supplanted by a much more elaborate adobe cookstove. But we intend to keep the old oven—and to bake in it sometimes. It brings back precious memories.

Hummingbirds shuttle and whiz between the bursting yellow buds of the tall swaying mescal shoots, and across the warm gravel come whiptail lizards, ready to flash into lightning bursts of speed should anything disturb their endless, bloodhound-like tracking.

It is hard to click the typewriter these days. It takes real will power. Even Tanya, the energetic, stops often to sit in the sun and watch the desert distances with dreamy eyes. Rider and Rudyard roll happily on a rug beside the stocky little squaw-tea bush [ephedra] that breaks the white stretch of windblown gravel in front of the house. Sometimes they squabble noisily and at others they just lie and speculate about the wheeling buzzards that describe effortless circles far overhead. I catch a chance remark:

"There will," Rider tells his young understudy, with mysterious importance "be honey-an'-whole-wheat cookies for supper."

DESERT DIARY 6

(July 1940)

June at Yaquitepec

THE Ghost Mountain strawberry crop is ripe, and this morning Rider begged so hard that we laid aside other work and went out on a gathering expedition.

Our desert "strawberries" have little in common with their civilized namesakes. As fiercely characteristic of the desert as is the Apache Indian they are the fruit of the long spined cactus which grows in bunches or clusters and is variously known as the "hedgehog cactus," the "torch cactus" and the "strawberry cactus" (*Echinocereus engelmannii*).

Their fruits are scarlet, with a network of small white—and particularly villainous—spines. In size they range from that of a large grape to a small plum. Though the job of brushing off the spines and skinning the fruit is a bit tedious the resultant delectable morsel is more than repayment—a little ball of cool snow-white pulp shot through with a multitude of tiny black seeds, like glistening grains of gunpowder. The taste is somewhat reminiscent of the strawberry, but with a flavor individuality which induces a demand for more and more.

Our collecting expedition was a grand success—as to amount collected. But strangely, the baskets we had taken along to bring back the fruit were as empty on our return as at the start. However a pair of contented little "tummies" were visibly expanded. About the best way to pick the fruit is with a loop of yucca leaf, as one picks the fruit of the tuna cactus.

Our desert is aflame with the glory of the mescals. Far down over the slopes and lowlands and staking the summit of Ghost Mountain everywhere their swaying banners of yellow-gold glint dazzlingly beneath the hard turquoise arch of the hot sky. It is only when their endless ranks of yellow plumed lances stretch away and away through the shimmering heat haze, that one can begin to get some faint idea as to the incalculable number of individual mescal plants that crowd upon the wasteland spaces. Each fountain of bloom represents a cycle run a long individual history flaming to extinction in one supreme burst of glory. Every yellow banner is the gesture of a departing life. By just the number of plumed lances that dazzles the eye this June will the ranks of the desert mescals be depleted. Yet how stubbornly Nature preserves the balance by slow, new growth. Each flowering—and dying—mescal represents anywhere from seven to 20 years of dogged growth and struggle. Myriads of the slow growing plants pass to extinction each year. Yet the numbers of them that cover the wastelands in the regions where soil and elevation are suitable remain balanced, or seem slowly to increase. For thousands of years the cycle has been running smoothly. There is food for thought here. Either singly or collectively there are some excellent parables to be gathered from the desert mescals.

These are the days when the tortillas dry upon the roof. That is one of the advantages of the desert springs and summer—there are many things that will "sun-cook." Not only is this the easiest method of cooking but it is also the most healthful. Our roof at Yaquitepec is of iron and almost flat. When the temperature begins to climb it provides an ideal surface upon which to lay out a batch of whole wheat tortillas. A few hours—and one turning— and they are dry and sunbaked enough to lay away in the storage sacks in the big earthenware cookie jar that is a product of our own hands.

The *tortilla* is another one of those simple things that has an honorable record dating from the dim ages when the earth was young. The simplest baked product of grain it still holds its own on an unshakable foundation of health and honest nourishment which no modern glorified creation of inflated yeast sponge can approach. It was not for nothing that certain periods for the eating of

unleavened bread were made mandatory upon the ancients. The old lawgivers knew their people; the craze for things "refined" and the idea of going the Jones and the Smiths one better was as strong in the days of Moses as it is now. Simple things are rarely appreciated—and the tortilla is fundamentally simple. A little meal, a little water—salt and grease if you wish to be luxurious—and for baking equipment a thin, flat stone or a sheet of iron over an open fire.

The other day, in one of the books of Lumholtz— whose exact and delightfully human records of desert and Mexican exploration are unrivalled—I came upon an enthusiastic eulogy of the tortilla. And the baking apparatus which he declared to be the most satisfactory was the same as that which we use ourselves in winter and on other occasions when we employ fire—the flattened side of a square, five gallon coal oil can. Lumholtz, earnest scientist as he was, knew his desert—and his tortillas.

Perhaps one of the chief virtues of the tortilla is the fact that it is, under all conditions, largely uncooked food. It must be whisked from the fire before it is scorched to a chip. Therein lies its tastiness and healthfulness. And never, *never* attempt to use a rolling pin in making tortillas! Theoretically, pressing the dough out to a flat, wafer-like thinness on a board by such means may be all right. But actually it is disastrous. The resultant product, when baked, is a dreadful thing, as tasty as a piece of old leather. A tortilla *must* be patted out by hand, patted lovingly and with the discernment and care of an artist. Then, when the limp disk of dough is of the correct wafer-like thinness, it must be dropped quickly upon the sizzling hot iron sheet, let stand for just the right number of seconds, flicked expertly over, toasted for a like space on the other side, then whisked off. So made, it is a delectable morsel—a little cake over which the gods might fight.

Tortillas should be served and eaten while still fresh and warm if possible. There is significance to the words of the Mexican song—of Villa days:

> *...I come to thy window*
> *Porfirio Diaz.*
> *Give him, for charity,*
> *Some cold tortillas....*

Nevertheless the tortilla, even when cold, is pretty good too. Those that we sun dry never fail to have the attention of enthusiastic and appreciative appetites. Particularly if Tanya mixes a little honey in the dough, as she often does.

* * *

The big rock is gone. It was the last of four—a hunched granite quartet of graduated sizes that, ever since the days of our first tent pitching, crowded upon the north flank of the home site. In those first days they looked too formidable to battle with. We had no tools. And their size made mock of our puny strength. But steadily, as the house has grown, we have cast thoughtful eyes upon them, and plotted. Now they are vanquished. One—the smallest—we left where it was. It now forms part of a foundation wall of what will be a big fireplace. The second largest succumbed to persistent, gnawing attacks with a heavy hammer. The third was doomed from the day we proudly brought home our first set of miner's drills and iron wedges.

The fourth was different. Huge and squat and flat-topped like an Aztec altar it defied even the drilling for a long time. Drilling holes by hand with steel drill and singlejack is a long process. And the granite was tough; many times it defied the wedges to split it. But, bit by bit, the big rock has been going. Now the last great, unmanageable fragment has been broken into blocks that can be boosted out of the way with the iron bar.

Rider harvesting cactus fruit.

We feel a little sorry for the old monarch, weatherer of so many thousands of years of desert wind and sun and storm. But our regret is overbalanced by satisfaction at the greater space his going gives us. Rider and Rudyard however are genuinely depressed. When granite rocks are drilled a fascinating white powder of pulverized stone is spooned from the drill hole. This, with much chatter and consultation, is collected and carefully saved in bottles and cans—later to be used in all sorts of weird experiments, concoctions and mixtures—and so no more powder. Rudyard is accusingly glum. And Rider, eyeing his hoarded store of bottled rock dust with much the eye of a thwarted miser, has already begun to offer suggestions as to other rocks that "ought to be broken up."

But the ear of the driller is deaf to hints. Over the gravel lie the jumbled remains of the huge monolith. They have to be laboriously rolled away before the new walls can go up and the roof beams of the north room can span the space. Somehow the site looks like a quarry just now and the air is still fragrant with the scent of aromatic shrubs and sage that the rolling fragments have crushed.

But already Tanya is planning where the beds shall stand in the new bedroom, when it is built.

DESERT DIARY 7

(August 1940)

July at Yaquitepec

*H*EAT! And the distant phantoms of mirage. Desert summer is with us now and Yaquitepec shimmers in the heat of a midday glare that is thirstily metallic. Birds cower, droop-winged and panting, in the shelter of the junipers; and upon the dry, scorching earth the snaky wands of the ocotillos throw sharp-edged shadows that are black as jet.

It is hot these days. But not too hot. The human system is adaptive; it adjusts speedily to its environment. The desert dweller becomes used to his summer with its tingling strike of dry sunshine. The heat that really sets him gasping and complaining is the humid choke of supposedly more favored sections.

There is a good deal of myth about the terrors of desert summer. It is born, most of it, from inexperience and from a curious American trait of deliberately refusing to conform to climatic conditions. The "old people" and the early Spaniards were wiser. It was not indolence but sound sense that created the mid-day siesta habit. With a common-sense adaptation to conditions. The desert in summer is as much a region of enchantment as at any other season, and has charms peculiar to itself.

Nowhere but in the desert, and in summer, can you see such magnificent cloud effects as those which tower into the hard, turquoise sky above the heat-dancing wastelands. These mighty mountains of dazzling white and ominous grey cease to be clouds. Rather they are the Titan sculptures of invisible gods. Sinister they are often. And awe inspiring. Small wonder that you will find no glib atheists among the dwellers of the unspoiled wasteland. Such things belong to the shadows of smoky walls; to the dulling thunder of machinery and the milling of tired crowds.

Out where the little thirsty winds run panting across the shoulders of sun-furnaced buttes there is no room for disbelief. The message is in the sky and in the wide sweep of the glowing earth. To Indian and to white man alike the mighty thunderheads that march across the blue vault, their crests lifting white into staggering immensity, their footsteps tracking league-long blots of indigo upon the panting earth and their voices calling each to each in hollow rumble, speak of the Great Spirit. The arrows of His wrath are in their hands and the rain of His infinite mercy is in their hearts. Atheists do not flourish in desert solitudes.

But the marching cloud giants that come stalking up out of the mystery of the Gulf of Cortez [California] are but one of the attractions of Yaquitepec in summer. There is the heat. Heat is not just "heat." It is something that grows upon one. It is fundamental with life. Desert heat is electric. Scientists, whose mission in life it is to make simple things as confusing as possible, will tell you that it is ultraviolet rays. Possibly! But shorter terms for it are life and health. The Indian knew nothing about ultraviolet rays. But he did know about health; before he was spoiled.

And some still remain unspoiled. The Tarahumare Indians of Mexico belong—or did belong, if they have not been changed within the last few years—to the unspoiled clan. One of the Tarahumare joys was to bask naked in the sun in temperatures that would almost frizzle a white man. And the Tarahumares were noted for their endurance. One of their sports, indulged in by both men and women, was long distance running.

Perhaps it is another indication of how far and how shamelessly we of Yaquitepec have slipped from the skirts of civilization in that we also like to bask on the rocks in summer. Sometimes the rocks are pretty hot, and they have a damp appearance afterwards as though something had been frying on them. But as you lie there you do not think of these things. All you can feel is the tingle of life and of electricity striking healing rays through every bone of your body. Try it sometime; but little by little and gradually at first.

* * *

Yesterday a whirlwind came and charged down upon the house in an attempt to scatter our shade ramada. These summer whirlwinds are mysterious things. You hear them coming up the mountain, roaring and grumbling. And, because of the absence of light soil among the rocks that would make dust, you can see nothing. It is like listening to the approach of a disembodied spirit; often not until it leaps upon you can you tell just where it is. Yesterday's was a big one. Rider and Rudyard were up on the garden terrace, watching the uncouth antics of Satan, the big black scaly lizard who makes his living up there catching flies. And all at once, from the shoulder of the mountain rim, there was a coughing roar. Rudyard took one peek at emptiness and twinkled brown heels in headlong flight for the house. Rider, with something of the spirit of a scientist, stood his ground, peering and squinting. He at least knew what the roaring invisible thing was. But he could not locate it.

Not until suddenly, a dead bush and a couple of dry mescal poles leaped into the air from just behind him and went sailing a hundred feet into the sky. And the next instant, as he crouched, grabbing at a big boulder for support, the thing yelled past him and fell upon the house. Doors banged and roof iron strained. There was the shrieking hiss of wind through the porch screens and the tied bundles of mescal poles of the ramada roof surged and rattled as Tanya came darting out, snatching at wildly slamming window shutters, Rudyard yelling lustily at her heels. Then the thing was gone, hurtling away in a wild leap back over the mountain rim. We saw dry bushes, bits of paper, an empty sack and the two mescal poles hung grotesquely in the sky—far up and still spinning. Then the hot stillness flowed in again; the wildly threshing ocotillos quieted. Satan came out of his rock cleft and waddled his fat metallic sheened bulk back onto the terrace, headed for a new fly victim. Rider came down the trail blinking the sand grains out of his eyes. "Phooey!" he said. "That was the biggest one ever. You ought to put some more screws in the roof iron, Daddy."

But it is not often that our desert twisters are so large or hit us so squarely. Usually they are just phantoms, rushing out of nowhere and tearing off into silence along the ridges. We feel rather kindly towards them. Their mood of mystery suits the atmosphere of Ghost Mountain.

Summertime is "bug time" it is true. But really there are worse bugs in other sections than the picturesque crew that inhabit the desert. The scorpions perhaps are the most fearsome. Especially the big ones, four to six inches in length and with a corresponding spread of claw. But these big fellows are in about the same proportion in the scorpion world as are city gangsters in our own social setup. The sting of these magnates we have so far managed to avoid. But the venom of the rank and file—little fellows ranging in size from an inch upward—is no more painful than that of a honey bee.

For a long time, remembering the prowess of the scorpions of Durango, the hot country of Jalisco and of other parts of Mexico, we trod in fear of them. Then one day Tanya, groping for a new typewriter ribbon in the depths of a box filled with old letters, was stung. Her prompt recovery from the pain, with no ill effects, exploded the scorpion myth. Both of us have been stung on several occasions since and we pay little attention to it. This is no attempt to whitewash the scorpion tribe. Some of the Mexican "hot-country" ones, especially where children are concerned, are deadly. The small Ghost Mountain variety is practically harmless.

The centipedes however are not so pleasant; especially when the spirit moves the six and eight inch ones to take tight rope exercises along the roof beams over the beds. The big ones are "bad hombres," to be wary of. But here again the little fellows are in the majority. Their chief sin, as far as we are concerned, is that being flat and slender they can squirm through negligible crevices; and therefore the covers of water cisterns and all other regions barred to bugs must be exceptionally tight fitting.

And this also goes for the ants. Our Ghost Mountain ants are well behaved and seldom drink to excess. Except in the hot reaches of summer. Then they go crazy for moisture. They will go anywhere, and to any lengths, to obtain it. It's not enough to screen a water cistern. It has to be absolutely ant tight or it is likely, at the end of summer, to contain less water than dead ants. In a way they seem a bit confused in their knowledge of water. They will walk down into it and under it until they drown, as humans might walk to destruction under some heavy, invisible gas. Their habits in this respect are annoying. But with food supplies they give us little trouble. We have found a certain defense against them. When we first came to Ghost Mountain we religiously kept the legs of all food cupboards in tin pans filled with either water or kerosene. This was effective if properly attended to. But the pans were always running dry, or grass stems and wind blown twigs would make bridges for the marauders, so one day we shifted to the trick of just painting the legs with ordinary creosote. It worked marvels. It doesn't look particularly handsome, but it is 100 percent effective. And the painting is renewed only at long intervals. Not only ants but all sorts of other bugs give creosoted cupboard legs a wide berth.

The yellow glory of the Ghost Mountain mescal flowers has departed. But the seed pods which have succeeded the flowers are full and plump. They look like elongated green pecan nuts, arranged in bunches somewhat like small upstanding clusters of bananas. The mountain squirrels like them, and many of the mescal heads are already denuded of seed pods by their raidings.

We are watching anxiously for rain. Each day now, when the mighty thunderheads form upon the horizon and march in upon the shimmering glare of the wastelands, we watch them with hopeful eyes. But so far Ghost Mountain is not on their schedule. Their shadows fall black and mysterious over the distant buttes; their cannonading rolls across the wasteland and the black skirts of their local torrential downpours beat dust from a thirsty desert on our very borders. But the crest of Ghost Mountain they ignore. They will come, however, in time. Patience is a virtue that is a desert necessity. Mayhap they will come in August.

DESERT DIARY 8

(September 1940)

August at Yaquitepec

*W*E HAD a grand thundershower. At a long last the rain gods suddenly remembered Ghost Mountain and trailed a veritable downpour across our thirsty roof. These desert thunderstorms are always thrilling. Especially when they come at night, as this one did. Here on the bald mountaintop the electric display is terrific. We have our iron roof well grounded with wire cable, but one cannot help but feel very small and helpless in the presence of the forked streams of electric fire that split the sky from horizon to zenith. It is no wonder that all primitive peoples had a deep awe of lightning.

But the rain was a life saver. Our cisterns were down, well beyond the danger mark. Adobe construction had long since been halted. The garden, save for a few stalks of experimental corn from which we hoped to develop a desert strain of drought resistant seed, was clinging to life only by virtue of a meagre daily ration of wash-water. Water is a precious thing and even on the scanty amount which wasteland dwellers soon learn to get along with, it is astonishing what inroads just bare necessity can make in a dwindling cistern. We had begun to be seriously worried. Now, however, that is past. The storm, though short, was torrential. From our main roof we caught one cistern brim-full and several barrels from a smaller catchment area.

But there is usually a flaw somewhere in the scheme of things. This storm was no exception. It presented us with a new problem. Taking advantage of the fact that one of the cisterns had been completely emptied in the dry spell we had seized the opportunity to give its interior a protective coat of paint, which it badly needed. And, unwisely, we had used a recommended preparation which we knew nothing about.

The result was that the water from the newly filled cistern had a chemical taste and odor which had not been noticeable in the paint coating after it had dried. Here was disaster. The children flatly refused to drink any of the new catch. "Bad!" Rudyard said definitely, spitting it out. "Too much i-o-dine in that thunderstorm, Daddy."

And then, out of the bleak prospect of having to lose a whole cisternful of water, I recalled something about the properties of charcoal. And we did have charcoal. There was quite a heap of it, left-over and wind-cleaned remnants from baking fires that had been swept out of our old beehive mud oven. We hunted out a big stoneware crock that we had used once for salting down meat. When it was cleaned out and filled with the odorous and undrinkable water, I heaped in a generous amount of the clean juniper charcoal, covering the whole crock with a floating layer almost six inches deep. After letting it stand for a day we experimented, siphoning off the clear water from below the charcoal layer.

Success! Taste and odor had almost entirely disappeared. So the cistern itself was treated with a liberal filling from the same charcoal heap. We have saved our drinking water. But it will be a long time before we take a chance again with unknown waterproofing preparations.

As a matter of fact concrete, if carefully made, needs no waterproofing. Our trouble at Yaquitepec has been that we have rarely been able to get the materials for making the walls thick enough. When the cement has to be carried up a long, steep trail on one's own shoulders there is perhaps excuse for making the cistern walls thinner than the six or eight inches that they really should be. The alternative was to coat the interior of the tanks with waterproof preparations. Out of a long list of experiments the only thing that has so far given satisfaction is a heavy asphalt emulsion. This can be applied cold, like paint, and dries out to a black, impervious, non-tasting, coating.

Tanya harvesting ephedra.

Also the bugs don't like it and will generally give the asphalt tanks a wide berth.

* * *

The nuts of the Jojoba sometimes called also the goat-nut or the quinine bush are ripe. This is the stocky little shrub with woody stems and rather large, leathery, oval-shaped, green leaves. The nuts, shelled out from their covering, somewhat resemble unroasted coffee beans. A couple of days ago we went out on a gathering expedition on the south slope of our mountain crest and brought home a quantity. The crop is variable. Some years there will be an abundance and at others practically none. Properly cured and roasted they make a good substitute for pea-nuts in candy. But a little caution is to be observed with the curing. There seems, just as with walnuts, to be a slight-ly poisonous quality to the uncured beans. At least that has been our experience with the Ghost Mountain crop, which we are now careful to cure well before using. They have one other quality too. They do not keep well in can-dy—not here. They are so inviting that our husky little Indians flatly refuse to let them alone. Whether made up into a clear sugar brittle or a candy of the peanut brittle type they just melt and disappear. One day the candy jar is full—the next it is empty. Rider, grinning, blames it on the hot weather. Rudyard, more plain spoken, says frank-ly "We just eated it all up."

Like most desert products these nuts have more than one use. The oil pressed from them was in favor with some of the aborigines as a hair tonic. On this, however, we cannot speak from experience, never having tried it. It is true that at Yaquitepec we have cast convention aside in the matter of hair styles—wearing it, as Nature intend-ed, uncut. But we have not so far needed any tonic for it. We wear no hats and the desert sun and winds give it all the stimulation it needs.

Heat shimmers over the wastelands and thunderheads pile upon the far off crests of the Mexican sierra. Each day, almost, there is the threat of thundershowers. But often the ominous cloud masses draw in towards Ghost Moun-tain only to be caught up and swirled into nothingness in the vortex of hot air which churns invisibly above us. It is strange sometimes to lie at noonday beneath the shade of the ramada and staring upward at the turquoise sky, see these great threatening clouds drift in and melt. We seem to be the very center of a giant, inverted funnel of hot air which draws in from the panting wastelands, swirls up the slopes of Ghost Mountain and pours in unseen volca-nic eruption into the high levels of the sky. It is a hot air whirlpool in which the thunderheads, drifting in, are caught and dispersed. Slowly and ominously they churn together right above us, holding momentarily a promise of downpour. Then, discouragingly, they dwindle and fade. Soon they are gone. We find it hard sometimes, when even a light sprinkle would be a benediction upon a parched earth, to watch day after day the inexorable workings of this mighty hot air engine that functions overhead.

Rain from a Cloudless Sky

But at times we have reward in experiences that are odd. The other night, from an absolutely cloudless sky blazing with desert stars, rain fell. Not a heavy shower, a generous sprinkle of big drops only. But they banged upon our iron roof in a fashion that was startling because so unexpected. This rain freak is said to be an occasional peculiarity of Baja California. But we have had it several times on Ghost Mountain. These out of the ordinary inci-dents contribute to the fascination of the desert.

The basket that Tanya made from braided yucca leaves for gathering *tuna* is empty now. But it served its purpose and bears a generous pattern of crimson juice stains to attest its honorable service. The chances are that in a very short time it will be the only visible memento of this month's fruit harvest. Like most other desert delica-cies tuna syrup and preserves vanish mysteriously at Ya-quitepec. And each year, as our sun-browned desert sprites grow in size and capacity, they vanish faster. Which is, of course, as it should be. What is the bounty of the desert for if not to be promptly eaten?

The fruit of the tuna cactus deserves greater popular-ity than it has. In Mexico it is used extensively and a va-riety of delicacies such as syrups and candies and *queso de tuna* are made from it. The fresh fruit is delicious, and being high in sugar content, is nutritious and well fitted for human consumption. But it is another natural food for which a hasty civilization has no patience. The old pa-dres knew the value of this cactus. The extensive plant-ings of it around the Missions were not only for hedges of defense but also for food.

There is a little trouble, of course, on account of spines. But this is easily overcome. We pick the fruit with a looped yucca leaf, dropping each fruit, as picked, into a collecting basket. When a sufficient quantity have been gathered we roll them on the gravelly soil, sweeping them to and fro with a broom of twigs or yucca. This rids the fruit of most of the tiny spicules and they can then be peeled. If care is used in the peeling one will encounter only a minimum of stickers. Divested of their thick, prickly rind the crimson-juiced fruits are delicious morsels which amply make amends for the trouble of spitting out the mass of woody little seeds they contain. The Indians fre-quently eat them as is—seeds and all.

For syrup the fruit is pressed in a coarse cloth, or through a screen fine enough to remove the seeds, and the juice is boiled to the desired thickness. *Queso de tuna* (tuna cheese) is merely a matter of boiling of the syrup until it cooks down to a delicious paste.

Does it store well? Yes, I believe so—in other places. But not here. The decorative properties, however, of both syrup and preserve, are some compensation for their quick vanishment. Judging by the war-paint designs acquired by our young Yaquitepecs while the tuna products last I am of the opinion that the term "red Indian" is directly traceable to the tuna.

DESERT DIARY 9

(October 1940)

September at Yaquitepec

THERE is a cool wind drawing in over the summit of Ghost Mountain this morning, and far off to the southwest, the mighty crests of the sierras are asmoke with a topping of fog. But Yaquitepec is wrapped in the sparkle of cloudless sunshine. Almost anything can happen at this season, from driving cold snaps to choking summer heat. But today is perfect—one of those dazzling, flawless days of which there seem to be more in the desert than in any other section of the earth. Scouting bees drone contentedly to themselves as they rove among the *ramarillo* [*romerillo* is a common name for various plants in Mexico. South may be referring to a rabbitbrush, rubber rabbitbrush, or a goldenbush—*Ericameria* (*Chrysothamnus*) sp.] bushes and about the opening pods of the dry mescal stalks.

Out under the juniper tree where the bird fountain is, three fawn-colored little desert chipmunks are prowling sociably in the shade and thrusting appreciative noses first into the grain pan and then into the drinking water. All the desert is drowsing.

But there is sound across the silence, for Yaquitepec's daily session of school is in full swing. Out at the big, plank table under the shade ramada Tanya is guiding our two young hopefuls along the mysterious trail of "Education." A fascinating business, this. Eager voices come to me through the stir of the breeze. Rider is reading from the printed page about a boy named Tom and a girl named Jane, who seem to have cats and rabbits and birthdays—and a lot of other simple things that can be briefly tabulated in big type. And there come often Rudyard's strident

remarks. When he gets going he has a voice that is out of all proportion to his size. And he cannot see why he should be outclassed in this "education" business. He has to read too—and count. "Purple!" he states definitely, poking with his finger at a color chart on the book. "—An' blue…an' yellow…an' gween…an' orange…an' – "

There is the sound of hasty movement by the disciplinarian. "Rudyard! . . take your hands off that book. You mustn't disturb Rider when he's doing his reading lesson. Wait until you .... "

"—Owange! Owange!...OWANGE ! !...I wanna read my colors! I wanna wead too! Owange an' purple an' red an'….No, I don' wan' that ol' magazine. *I wan' my lesson book!*"

Storm and tribulation. Brief tempest that settles to the sound of a grumbling monologue and intermittent hammer blows, as Rudyard is finally shunted from "education" to a job of blacksmithing.

Thus it goes. Not too long these daily school sessions. Just enough of the simple things, reading, writing and figures, to whet the childish interest without taxing too heavily the growing brain. It takes time for steel to be tempered and hardened to a keen cutting edge; fully as many unfolding minds have been ruined by overload as by neglect.

But school at Yaquitepec does not really end with the short open air sessions each day beneath the ramada. In actual fact it never ends. From dawn to dark our "little Indians" are soaking up knowledge gleefully. It is all a game—as all life is a game. Everything that the grown-ups do, that must our understudies do also. If Tanya sews, then they must have needle and thread and a scrap of cloth and sew also. If we paint a picture then must paints and brushes be produced also for two clamorous budding artists—and much paper be covered with all manner of fantastic and original designs. The Yaquitepec pottery industry has two industrious apprentices. "My potterzee" Rudyard says proudly as, generously clay daubed, he stands contemplating with artistic pride a lump of mud that he has poked and pummeled into some weird shape. "See, mamma! Lookit my nice pottery."

And all hands accordingly have to admire. All, that is, on most occasions. For sometimes Rider, with all the impatience of a finished artist for the amateur, gets impatient.

"Huh! what do you call it? What do you call that thing?" He demanded once, leveling an accusing finger at a clay lump over which Rudyard was loudly jubilating. "What do you call that mess?"

"Call it! *Call it?*" Sputtering, stunned almost with outraged indignation, Rudyard recoiled a pace as though unable to believe his ears. His eyes blazed; his mud-stuck fingers clawed the air wildly. "Wat I call it? Wat I call it, you *naughty* boy! I call it this-my-*not*-a-mess! I call it my *beau*-ti-ful pottazee stat-you of Vee-nus!"

But—dubious "statues of Venus" notwithstanding, the "potting" activities at Yaquitepec during the last few days have filled a few long standing gaps in our domestic needs. Every once in a while it is necessary to do this. For primitive clay utensils are fragile things. Capable of long lives under fortunate conditions they are also the most transitory of possessions if subjected to ill fortune. We are not alone in this drawback. The ancient dwellers of the desert faced the same

---

YAQUITEPEC TRAIL SIGN

In The Name Of The GREAT SPIRIT, PEACE.

This is Yaquitepec—Our Home

And In Accordance With The Ideals Of Peace,

Sunshine, Health, Simplicity, Bodily Freedom

And The Simple Faith In The GREAT SPIRIT

For Which This Desert Mountain Retreat

Was Established

NO CLOTHING IS WORN HERE

Therefore

If You Cannot Accept And Conform To,

In Clean-minded Simplicity,

This Natural Condition Of Life,

We Ask In All Friendship,

That You Come No Further,

But Return By The Path You Came.

The Peace Of The GREAT SPIRIT

Be With You Always

Marshal & Tanya South

---

problem. All over Ghost Mountain and vicinity you can find shattered chips of earthenware—mute evidence of industry and of tragedy. A long, long time it must have taken to have sown the desert so thickly with these chips of shattered jars.

An ancient art, potting. And perhaps it is only when one tries to work under similar conditions to the old-timers—that is, without a potter's wheel or any other mechanical aid—that one can fully appreciate the really high degree of skill they attained. The Indians of our vicinity rarely decorated their pots. Sometimes they ornamented them with simple incised designs, but such efforts of artistry were quite rare. For the most part the ollas were plain.

But their workmanship was superb. There must have been pride along the makers. For very few of the old pots show crudity. Built by eye and by hand the most of them are almost as exact as though machine made. The side walls are uniform in thickness; the mouths well-shaped in graceful line. Art and pride of work is not a product of civilization. To the contrary, civilization tends to destroy true art. If you doubt this, a little study of modern

grotesque horrors, not only on battlefronts but in art galleries also, ought to convince you.

There is a lot of work in the making of an olla. And when one has worked at the job, from the digging of the clay on through to the moment when one takes the fired and finished pot from the ashes, one is likely to have a tremendous appreciation of the industry of "lazy Indians." It is then that it is hard to repress actual shudders at the glib tales of some of the unimaginative early white settler—tales of how, when they were boys, one of their sports was to hunt for Indian ollas and, having found them, to set them up as targets to be gaily smashed by flung stones.

Hand potting, by the Indian method is not easy. And even after long practice one cannot be too certain as to results. So much depends upon little details. Maybe the clay has just a fraction too little sand in it. Maybe the heat of the weather dries the pot too quickly. Maybe the fire is too hot—or too cold. One never knows until it is all over and done just what the luck will be. Nor did the ancients. One of the best and biggest storage ollas that we ever found has a tiny crack in it—a crack that must have developed in the firing. It has been mended with a black gummy substance that is now as hard as the earthenware itself. It's an encouraging crack, anyway. Whenever one of the pots of our own manufacture crack we can always console ourselves by remembering it. Our shadowy predecessors had the same troubles.

But after all, potting is a great art, albeit a futile and a fascinating one. For—to strike the lyre and sum up, after the manner of old Omar:—

The potter potteth all the lifelong day,
  Toiling with muddy fingers in the clay,
But soon it is perceived his hope is nought.
  And to destruction shall his art be brought.
For, lo, each pot, o'er which he slaved his wit,
  Behold some careless damsel busteth it,
And of the potter's toil no trace remains,
  Save shattered fragments, strewing hills and plains.
And all thy tears and all Le Page's glue
  Shall not suffice to make the pot anew.

…And that is *that*. But despite these painful facts our shelves, from our last pottery session, are richer by quite a few things that we needed, including water dippers, water bottles and a few cups.

DESERT DIARY 10

(November 1940)

October at Yaquitepec

AN important event at Yaquitepec is to be recorded this month. The Thunder Bird, who for the dwellers of Indian sun-land takes upon himself the duties of the civilized stork, has made his long looked forward to visit, bringing from the Hand of the Great Spirit a precious gift—a tiny, lively little maiden whom we have named Victoria.

There is rejoicing upon the mountaintop and two "big brothers" are visibly swelled with importance at the prospect of having a little sister to look after. Rudyard, who has been automatically moved up a notch—being now no longer the "littlest" clan member is very conscious of his new dignity. Every once in a while, chest out and strutting, he lugs some treasured possession to exhibit to the new arrival. "See kid, this my bow-arrow. See!" And quite satisfied that he has made a good impression he trots off to get some other "exhibit." Rider smiles at such show-off with lofty amusement. But he is not one fraction less excited than his brother. Both of them spend most of their time hanging around watching every movement of this fascinating new playmate—and speculating on the wonderful times they will all have together when she grows up a bit.

* * *

The tall mescal stalks are dead and dry now and the seed pods have mostly all cracked open. To knock against a stalk in passing is to have a shower of the thin, jet black seeds rustle down upon you. Very carefully and marvelously packed in their seed cases, these tiny, wafer-like discs. The wind, swooping over the desert, scatters them far and wide as they shake out and fall.

There is one uncanny fact about mescal seeds which I have never been quite able to explain; you find them often, fresh and shiny looking, under the very centers of heavy flat boulders. Boulders which, until this moment of moving, seem to have lain undisturbed for centuries. How do they get there? What is the explanation? Ants, possibly. But I have never been able to discover traces of ant workings or runways under the stones where I have found these mysteriously hidden seeds.

Our bird friends are more in evidence again. A number of them drift away during the hot months, presumably summering in localities where water is easier. But they are beginning to return. And a few "visitors" with them. Yesterday we saw a bluejay. Ghost Mountain holds an attraction at this season. The days are pleasant and the crest is a sheen of gold from the myriad flowers of the *ramarillo* [rabbitbrush] bushes that cover the rocky ridges. These small crowding flowers, like little spreading paint brushes dipped in yellow hold a lure for the bees and drifting butterflies. Other species of tiny plants are opening blossoms also. We can generally count on a few showers in October, a sort of forewarning of the approach of winter.

* * *

Night before last there was a great thump on the roof, and almost immediately a heavy scrambling along the water gutter. Rider sat up abruptly in bed. "Skunk!" he said, blinking the sleep from his eyes. "I'll bet that's another of those spotted ones!"

It was a good guess. For presently there was another thump on the awning over a little arched window that stood open. Then, against the moon, an inquisitive peering head and lifted plume of tail appeared as our visitor scrambled onto the sill and paused, gathering himself for the jump inside.

But it was *outside* that he jumped. For, just at that instant, I flung a pillow at him. It slammed against the narrow window opening with a smack that must have robbed our unwelcome caller of seven years' growth. With a thud of utter rout he hit the ground and fled for safety in a spatter of flying gravel. We don't like the little spotted desert skunks at Yaquitepec, for we share the well founded conviction of most desert dwellers that their bite is likely to cause hydrophobia. We have had several bouts with them, for they are exceedingly bold. October in particular, seems to be skunk month. They are said to range a good deal. So it may be that on this month Ghost Mountain is the fashionable social center for the skunk "four hundred."

We have had other furred visitors during the past few days, who have been more welcome. Particularly the squirrel and the old packrat. There is usually a tiny pile of food scraps set out on the edge of the terrace at the north end of the house. An old brown squirrel who has gradually become tamer and tamer has developed a habit of coming down there to squat and stuff. Several days ago a big packrat, evidently scandalized at such gluttony, summoned courage enough to sample the free provisions also.

But his antics were funny. Plainly he was torn between nervous apprehension and a burning desire to get hold of some plunder. He would come scooting out of the bushes with long nimble leaps, pause, glance around, then dash for the food, snatching a morsel from under the squirrel's nose and fleeing with it as madly as a thief with a jittery conscience. Sometimes, in his haste he would drop the scrap half-way and too scared to stop, would go tumbling into shelter without it. Then presently, his nose and bright eyes would thrust cautiously out again. With a nervous rush he would dart for the morsel and race to safety with it. Soon he would be back again for more. Back and forth, grabbing and scooting, streaking away with his loot between the mescals and rocks. For a long while, sputtering with suppressed giggles, Rider and Rudyard watched the show through a narrow little window. Meanwhile, undisturbed and with a sort of bored air, the squirrel sat stolidly munching. When he had reached for the last scrap and stuffed it into his mouth he turned with dignity and tailed off to his own diggings.

* * *

The kitchen clock has again been under fire. Every once in a while there is an agitation to dispossess it and evict it from its niche over the stove. It is a battle between the "ayes" and the "noes"—and so far the "noes" have always won by a narrow margin. It is the only clock Yaquitepec possesses. And, as Rider points out, it is a good clock for it never varies. There is truth in this argument, for it is one of the most constant of clocks. One can always rely on it. Without variation for five years its hands have pointed to 4:33. Tanya contends that it is dumb and static and that she is a little tired of glancing at the unchanging expression on its face. There are other things, she says, that she would like better to see in the clock niche. "It won't tick!" she says, shaking it.

"It may go in the winter," I suggest mildly, "It went once."

"You say that every year," she counters, "and in the winter you say that the works are probably frozen and that it will maybe go in the summer. What's the good of keeping a clock that won't tick?"

"The sundial doesn't tick either," Rider said mischievously. "So we ought to keep the clock, Mother. Maybe some day we'll need to check up one against the other." He giggled at his own joke.

Rudyard (left) and Rider at the sundial.

Victoria is the newest member of the family.

"An excellent argument," I said. "I think Rider is quite right. One never knows what may happen; one should be prepared for every sort of emergency. Besides the clock is decorative and its presence lends a sort of social standing. And if there should be an eclipse of the sun and the sundial... "

"Oh well, never mind the rest of it," Tanya said resignedly. She put the old veteran back in his niche.

So again, in peace, with neither tick nor tock time marches on at Yaquitepec and the unhurried, silent shadow moves round and round on the chisel-marked granite block that stands on the terrace. There is nothing elaborate about the Yaquitepec sundial. But it does its work with fair accuracy and we are satisfied with it. It wasn't originally intended to be a sundial. In the beginning it was part of a crude homemade grain mill. But another mill superseded it and in the course of time the upper millstone of the discarded apparatus was broken. Then one day the old clock folded its hands at 4:33 and we were without the time. Which didn't matter much, for "time" is an illusion anyway. But there is a sort of habit to the counting of it. So I resurrected the nether millstone with its central iron pin—which was a long iron bolt cemented into a hole in the stone—and set forth to make a sundial.

When you set out to make a sundial you are likely, unless you have given some study to what seems an artlessly simple matter, to discover several things. Things about angles and directions and so forth. It isn't a matter of just marking the passage of a shadow with a line

denoting each hour. Oh no! Several things—simple enough things, of course—must be taken into consideration. All of which, by the aid of a carpenter's square and level, an old gun barrel and a borrowed watch, we eventually solved. It was winter when I made the sundial and I still have chilly recollections of "shooting" the North star through the old gun barrel, lashed to a post—an operation which, in conjunction with the square and level, gave me a pattern for the gnomen angle. There are teeth-chattering memories too of levelling and wedging and sighting under the chill starlight as I arranged the granite block on a big boulder pedestal in the exact position necessary, so that in the morning it could be permanently secured with cement. The cutting of the hour lines, checking with the borrowed watch, was a sunny job that was easy.

They are crude but the final result was comforting. Our sundial works. Sometimes it proves, when checked against the haughty mechanism of expensive visiting watches, to be fifteen minutes or so out. But who would worry about a little thing like 15 minutes' error? Certainly not here on Ghost Mountain, where there are no "limiteds" to catch and where the golden sheen of the sun wraps the desert distances in a robe of glow and dim mystery that is timeless.

What is Time, anyway?

DESERT DIARY 11

(December 1940)

November at Yaquitepec

Y ESTERDAY morning dawned grey and with the drift of heavy rain clouds working in from the southeast. For a long time we have been expecting rain, but had about given it up. It looked so threatening this morning however that I decided to go down and bring up a sack of potatoes, the only item of a recent load of supplies that still remained uncarried. Before I had climbed the mountain with it, however, the first rain sprinkles were upon me and I made the last section of the trail in breath-less haste.

There was a lot to be done. I dumped my pack load under shelter at the house and hurried to get things ship-shape. There is always a scurrying in preparation for rain. Things to stow away. The roof guttering to be cleaned and down-spouts to be inspected. By the time I had everything in order the rain was upon us in earnest; a steady light fall that bore all the earmarks of a long, slow storm.

Rain! – how the desert seems to rejoice at these drenchings. We have always work that can be done in-doors; some odd jobs that have waited for just such an occasion. This time it was soap making, for which we had collected a big stock of fat scraps and trimmings from the kitchen. But as we busied ourselves we spent much time at the windows. It is hard to keep away from the windows on occasions of rain. With all the lowland desert wrapped in a curtain of grey, the rocks and junipers on our mountain seem to stand out in clear-cut freshness. The ocotillos stretch their wands across the white, damp glint of the rocks. All the yellow flowers of the *ramarillo* [rabbitbrush] bushes have changed to creamy masses of seed tufts that, in the steady fall of the showers, give the low bushes the appearance of being coated with a mantle of yellow-white snow.

Rudyard and Rider perch in one of the broad win-dow seats, their noses pressed close to the glass, watch-ing a pair of white-crowned sparrows hopping beneath the shelter of the damp bushes that crowd upon the house. The chukka partridges came in to be fed with the first drizzle and after their meal sat around mournfully in the damp, heads cocked to one side, bright eyes watchful for hawks.

The chukkas do not like the rain. But our garden does. It was in perilous straits. For two weeks the carrots and beets have been on famine rations of water. And the corn has been sternly denied anything for so long that the tas-selled heads had begun to wear a chronically dejected look. Now in the downpour it is standing up bravely and wav-ing bright green banners of triumph. "Co'n getting plenty watah!" Rudyard says, pointing. He claps his hands in sheer joy. Rider, for his part, is speculating on how much water he will catch in his individual reservoir. There has been great engineering on that reservoir. He dug it him-self, struggling determinedly with a grown-up size mat-tock. It is about two feet deep and three feet across. Rider is desert minded when it comes to water. He spends a good deal of his time, when it rains, running around and setting up empty cans to catch stray drips from roofs and rocks. A good habit, perhaps. It is building a foundation that, in later life, may be useful. For, after all, an understanding of conditions is the first step towards mastering them.

Plenty of water falls upon most parts of the desert, if only it could be intelligently conserved. The desert plants have mastered conditions. There is no reason why human beings cannot do the same. An all-wise Providence sends copious drenchings of water from time to time upon the wastelands; the fact that these rains are often irregularly spaced is only another challenge to ingenuity. Man how-ever lets these thousands of tons of precious fluid rush to waste—and then complains about "desert conditions."

Our soap came out well. With the drumming patter of the steady fall beating upon the iron roof overhead we achieved a fine batch, stirring in the lye solution and beat-ing up the creamy mixture and turning it finally into moulds. It will be enough soap to last for several months.

When night shut down we drew the curtains and lit the lamp and Tanya made whole wheat doughnuts, cook-ing them in deep fat in the iron kettle. And of course, as we sat around the light and munched doughnuts, books had to come out and stories had to be read until the eager faced audience nodded sleepily and had to be lifted up bodily and piled off to bed. And still the rain fell. Wind came up out of the night and swirled over the house, and the ship's lantern swinging from the iron chain above the long table, flickered and danced, sending shadows scam-pering up and down the whitewashed walls. Night hush; the peace of falling rain; the haunting mystery of vast space—where else, save in the desert, does the heart thrill so deeply to such fundamental things?

* * *

A good deal of our spare time these days goes to fuel gathering. November is a warning that Winter is hurrying towards us and we must be prepared. It is quite a job. For it is astonishing the mountain of fuel that a few days of "cold-snap" can eat up. So there are expeditions down the trails and up the trails in search of dead trees and any material that will burn. Dead mescal butts, if they are last season's, make roaring winter fires. But the more ancient butts absorb dampness from the atmosphere and are tem-peramental when most needed. Dry juniper is our chief reliance for the cold days. Our fuel heap is growing—and I am reminded thereby of the fact that Rider is growing also. He is much a part of the fuel gathering trips and I am astonished sometimes to realize how materially his contributions help to swell the stack. I fear Rudyard gets a bit jealous at times. He hates to be outdone. I catch him sometimes struggling and puffing to uproot a dead mes-cal butt about six sizes too big for him. And when the dry stuff crumbles under the desperate clutch of tiny fingers and he sits down suddenly with a breath-taking flop he scrambles hastily to his feet, still holding the wispy hand-ful, and rushes to the fuel pile. "I am a *good* boy!" he announces loudly, tossing his scrap onto the heap. "I bring in *almost* as much fuel as Rider!"

But fuel gathering is rough on sandals. Ordinarily, bare feet are the rule at Yaquitepec. Wood gathering however calls often for the navigation of savage sections of rock and thorn where barefoot caution would consume too much time. So we dig out our Yaqui sandals for the job. Probably the oldest and simplest human device for foot protection, the sandal is still the most comfortable and healthiest thing man has ever fashioned in the way of footwear. You have to get used to wearing a sandal it is true. Generations of abuse in "thoroughly scientific" shoes have spoiled civilized feet to such an extent that they have to be entirely re-educated. But once the sandal technique is learned the foot enters upon a new and better life of freedom.

There are all kinds of sandals. The "scientific" ones are infinitely more destructive on the human foot than even the "scientific" shoes. But the good old primitive ones are the nearest thing to barefoot comfort ever invented. The ones we use at Yaquitepec are the Yaqui style. There is very little to them—just a piece of leather and a thong. The Mayo sandal is more elaborate; a weaving of thongs over the foot in a good deal of fanciness. But it is comfortable too. If you are lucky and can talk enough Spanish and will sternly insist that you want the old fashioned, country style ones, you can sometimes buy a pair of Mayo sandals in Mexican stores across the border. But not often. In sandals, as in everything else, the modernists are getting in their deadly work. You are likely to be offered some arch breaking device all tricked out in "cute" little leather knots—and with a heel.

However, sandals wear out—even the barbaric Yaqui ones. The granite rocks on Ghost Mountain are about as kind to leather as is an emory wheel. So the fuel gathering season at Yaquitepec is also the season when the cobbler plies his trade—splicing broken thongs and cutting new soles. But there are compensations. The sandal maker, as he squats at his bench, slitting and shaving leather, always has an appreciative audience. They are on the lookout for discarded scraps of leather. Leather scraps are hoarded away in boxes and jars amongst a host of other weird, childish treasures. Yes, winter and the season of roaring fires is on the way.

* * *

The sun rises late these November mornings. And beneath our mountain summit the morning shadows lie deep and long across the lowland desert. And there is a peculiar crisp freshness and beauty to the dawns. The sun gets up from his southern haunt, away south on the reaches of the Rio Colorado, with a leisurely deliberation, as though reluctant to begin the day. Through the low mists and shadows that lie purple and smoky along the old sea bed the great golden ball of fire heaves into view, flattened and distorted and coppery gold, a fantastic creation of dazzling gleam. Not like the hot, hard sun of summer, this mighty, rising disc. Vast, bulged and quaintly flattened as it breaks the far line of the horizon, it seems less like a sun than the dome of some Titan temple reared in the desert wastes by the labor of giants. Rider, who has an eye for beauty, is particularly fond of these sunrises. This morning, more than usually enthused, he hauled Rudyard out of a dozy sleep and dragged him outside.

"Now, you look at all that," he commanded. "See the purple and the pink and the gold and how beautiful it is. See it! Look at it! Now, don't you think it's beautiful?"

Then, as his fervor failed to elicit more than a sleepy grunt from his scarcely awake understudy, he added encouragingly, "Don't you understand what it *means?* It looked like this just about this time last year. *It means Christmas is coming.*"

Little Victoria, our newest clan member, is growing by leaps and bounds. A sturdy, lively little girl. The tint of the desert sun is in her cheeks and limbs and the mystery of the desert is in her eyes. Thoughtfully she lies, watching by day the dance of the sun-patterns on the wall, and the weaving tapestry which the lantern-flame draws from the shadows at night. What does she dream about? We wonder. Rider is sure that she is figuring out the design of bigger and better water cisterns. Rudyard loudly disagrees and asserts she is thinking of going to town to eat ice cream cones. The question remains unsettled in spite of loud arguments. Victoria says nothing. She just wrinkles up her tiny features and smiles.

DESERT DIARY 12

(January 1941)

December at Yaquitepec

DECEMBER! And another desert year winging to its close. All too swift they flit, these desert years of solitude and silence and peace. One could wish that they were twice as long. The span of them is not great enough to accommodate all the joy and eagerness of life. Happy years—close packed with a simple happiness that is free to all for the taking. Yet a mad world sets its hands only to robbery and slaughter.

Far down in the dim lowlands the sun rose this morning from a spreading pool of molten gold. It was as though the thin line of a vast flood of melted metal lay upon the far horizon. On the blue line of the distant desert it spread to north and south, glinting and flashing, a torrent levelling from some overturned crucible. And in the very midst of the wide thin spreading flood the sun rose, an upwelling bubble of dazzling fire. The desert foreground lay dusky velvet before its blinding rays, and in the shadowy robes that wrap the dim mountain bulk which we call the Sleeping Squaw, darting sunbeams woke a strange illusion of movement as though the Sleeper stirred in her aeon-long slumber and opened her eyes to the miracle of dawn.

Today I took the sand screen down to a point beyond the tiny rock hollow which we call Lake Yaquitepec and began to sift sand for the final coating of a new cistern. Rider and Rudyard came too, and while I worked, shovelling the rough sandy earth from the little watercourse and throwing it upon the inclined screen, they fished in the tiny rock pool. It was still brimming from a recent shower and into its mirror surface they toss handfuls of the short-broken lengths of golden yellow bunch grass stems. These were the "fish" and they are "caught" upon the ends of slender sticks of juniper, to which they adhere. A serious and intent business. But punctuated with much merry laughter. Good music by which to work.

A desert solitude? What are wealth and possessions? What can they buy to compare with such priceless things of simple happiness?

Today's coat of cement plaster marks the finishing touch to this last cistern. Mostly trowel and brush work, for the uneven portions have to be trowel-smoothed—and much of the cement is laid on with a brush. It gives a better surface and it is easier to reach the hollows in our rough rock construction.

In our early days at Yaquitepec—when we had no trowel or money with which to purchase one—our cement work was done with a tool fashioned from an old automobile license plate. And we did a lot of good work with it too. Good tools make for good and easy work. But there are many times when one need not neglect work just for the lack of them.

* * *

Fires roar merrily in the big stove these nights for there is a crisp snap creeping into the air. And it is a crispness that is enjoyable. After all, Winter when it comes brings its own special gifts. And not the least of those gifts are fireglow and story-telling. There is a new iron top to the stove this year as well as a new and much appreciated damper that works with a lever. The old one was a tin slide, of sour disposition—at times, a sore trial to cheerful temper. But it served long and faithfully and we forgive it its faults in remembering its virtues. There is a new adobe arch too, that closes in the north end of the kitchen. It will be warmer and cosier here this year—even though Santa Claus will maybe have to pause a moment and figure out the changed arrangement before he comes stealing in with his pack. "You ought to put up a sign to make it easy for him," is Rider's practical suggestion. But Rudyard, guided less by logic than by anxiety, is chiefly concerned about the time-honored chimney route. "Daddy, I t'ink you ought to wemove that new damper! I t'ink Sanda Klaws catch his neck on it an' choke to deaff! Yes, I t'ink so!"

There is fuel to collect against the possibility of savage snowstorms, there are Christmas trees to select and cut and carry home—diminutive, cheerful little trees that are in reality big, berry-laden branches of mountain juniper. There are sandals to repair and wreaths to make—evergreen wreaths to trim the windows with. And there is an extra supply of flour to be ground and tall candles to make so that Christmas eve may be ushered in with no stint of cookies and candlelight.

And to top it all there is Victoria! Victoria grows and grows. Her eyes are blue. The little desert mice squeak and scurry in the night hush—and she listens to them wide-eyed and speculative. For this is her desert too, and her land to which she has come. The boys perch about her bed and watch her with worshipful eyes. "An' we'll hang a stocking up for little sister too, won't we, Daddy," Rider says proudly. "Yes, old-timer, we sure will," I tell him. And Tanya smiles. Two little sons and a daughter! The Great Spirit has indeed shed his blessings upon Yaquitepec.

It is night now and the house is hushed, save for the soft rustlings of the friendly mice. There are dying coals glowing in the fireplace, and beyond the shaded glow of the lamp the shadows are soft upon three little heads, sleep-wrapped, upon their pillows. On the other side of the table, where the yellow lamplight falls in a pool, Tanya sits sewing. As she pauses a moment to thread a needle she looks up. "Listen to the wind whispering up the mountain," she says. "Do you remember …."

Yes, we remember. And for a space, while the old, old wind whimpers about the outer walls and talks to itself through the junipers we go back into memories. Memories of dear, happy days that have fled. There is much to remember. And more to be humbly thankful for. Above the desert the stars gleam. The footsteps of the Great Spirit are in the rustlings of the wind and the promise of His infinite mercy is written in the glow of circling worlds and in the testimony of the granite rocks. Peace! Faith! Assurance! These are the messages of the silence and the solitude.

* * *

And so we come to the ending of the year and to the ending of the year's Diary of Yaquitepec. It has been a year of friends and of good wishes. And if, to the ending of the chronicle, we were to attach any special thought or message it would be the message of Faith. In a world that is grim and shadowed by the blackness of war and of greed and of brutality let the lamp of Faith be kept burning brightly. Faith in things that are good; Faith in those simple, fundamental things that have been so much neglected. There are not many things in life that really matter. And he who would seek peace and contentment of body and spirit must seek it among the simple, fundamental, "old-fashioned," things which the blind, roaring rush of a greed-crazed age has so largely thrust aside.

Wealth, possessions and mechanical gadgets do not make the man—nor the nation. These are just the gilded bubbles flying in the wind, the chasing of which leads too often into the morass of destruction. Neither is greatness to be measured by weapons of war and conquest nor by marvels of science. These things go down into the dust and are the sport of the winds in all the deserts of the earth. For there have been "others"—others in the past who have built upon these same perilous foundations. Assyria and Egypt and Rome …and, further in the shadows, Atlantis and the ghost-memory Mu. Nor were these the first. Nor will they be the last.

> *For heathen faith that puts its trust,*
> *In speaking tube and iron shard.*
> *All valiant dust that builds on dust*
> *And guarding calls not Thee to guard…*

These be the breed of the World Conquerors—and of them so grimly wrote Kipling. These are they who build on Steel—and Progress. Things that crumble into rust and perish in their own madness.

But there are other things that do not change; things that endure and spring in eternal rebirth to uphold every age and every race, be it "Savage" or "Civilized." Simple, these things—and fundamental. A simple faith in the all-guiding beneficence of The Great Spirit is the chiefest of them. And next to that a simple life lived in close contact with the earth. From these things alone spring nearly all of the worthwhile joys of life; peace, contentment, and the glad laughter of little children. For him who sets up for himself other ideals these words are not written.

And so, in farewell from the Diary of Yaquitepec, we would say to those who are weary of turmoil and of

Rudyard (left) and Rider working on crafts.

sham: Return to the earth. Return to planting and reaping and the raising by personal effort of those things for which life calls. Return to the peace of the soil, which is not to be found in cities. And return to Faith. It matters not what the label of the Faith, so long as it is sincere Faith. For Faith is the chiefest of the fundamental things. And it is the chief thing that our Age lacks. For a long time our "clever" people have enjoyed themselves poking fun at the "God myth"…And they have made their doctrines a sorry mess of our times.

So hold fast to Faith—to an implicit faith in the mighty shadowy Power that not only tints the wing of the butterfly but also steers the hurtling suns upon their pathways. For him who holds thus fast to Faith there are no doubts nor terrors.

And in this thought, from a mountain in the desert, we bid you farewell: May the peace of the Great Spirit be with you always:

MARSHAL, TANYA, RIDER, RUDYARD and VICTORIA

PART TWO—DESERT HOME

Desert Home 1
(May 1941)

*S*O IT is spring again at Yaquitepec. But the free desert knows little of set seasons and cares less. It has been spring on Ghost Mountain for a long time. Everything is early this year. Some of the mescals had begun to thrust up shoots by the very first days of February. And there were ocotillo flowers too. As we tramped up and down the trail, carrying loads of supplies for fuel, it was 7-year-old Rider's game to see how many new ocotillo blossoms he could pick out.

The ocotillo is a temperamental thing. It will flower when it feels like it and it cares nothing for precedent. Resolute little banners of scarlet flame wave from the tips of bare, grey wands that still seem held in the torpor of winter. We never cease to be amazed at the tenacity of life and the indomitable purpose that seems to dwell in all desert things. A lesson here that is well worth pondering over.

The life of all desert organisms is hard—not soft. For them there are no cushioned corners or easy short cuts. They have to fight—to steel themselves against adversity, to carry on in the face of seemingly hopeless odds. And it has done something to them; to their spirit; to their very fibre. Perhaps this is most strikingly illustrated in the mescal.

A mescal never knows when it is beaten. Chewed off by rodents and toppled over, hanging by the veriest thread, the bud shoot will still right itself with unbelievable tenacity and go on to flower. Even if entirely beheaded the shoot will often thrust out flower buds from the ragged stump. Purpose! Determination! Do you think it an accident that, all down through history, desert peoples have builded mighty civilizations?

The heavy rains of winter have left their mark on Yaquitepec. In front of the house the whitewashed adobe is scarred with patches of brown where sections of the

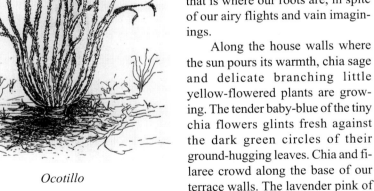

Ocotillo

lime plaster have crumbled and fallen away. And the mescal-and-mud facing of a rear wall is a forlorn skeleton of bare poles. Surprisingly little damage though, in actuality, and until new plastering and whitewashing cover the scars we shall rather enjoy the comfortable, warm look of the brown adobe patches on the walls. There is something sterling and heartening about the appearance of honest adobe. Some deep reminder of man's fundamental kinship with the earth. For, after all, that is where our roots are, in spite of our airy flights and vain imaginings.

Along the house walls where the sun pours its warmth, chia sage and delicate branching little yellow-flowered plants are growing. The tender baby-blue of the tiny chia flowers glints fresh against the dark green circles of their ground-hugging leaves. Chia and filaree crowd along the base of our terrace walls. The lavender pink of the filaree flowers glows against the grey and orange stones. Among them are white flowers too—the delicate little morning-glory-like blossoms that open only at night and in the early morning. A host of varied desert flora, gay with life and promise.

The squaw-tea [Mormon tea or ephedra] bush in front of the house is sprinkled thickly with clustering chrome-yellow blossoms; and down by the yuccas the white and yellow headings of my tiny desert daisy bushes nod beside the budding beavertail cactus. The barrel cacti too are crowned with flower circlets and the lone creosote bush by the great rock is already dressed in its bright new covering of varnished green leaves and is sprinkled with yellow blossoms. New pink and cream heads nod on the buckwheat. The whole world of desert growth throbs to spring.

There was corn to grind this morning, for we had a craving for corn hotcakes—and the meal can was empty. It is such a satisfaction to grind cornmeal from the glistening whole grain; one can almost see the strength and health spill from the crushed-yellow kernels. There is no "separating" and "grading" and "sifting"—and robbing— of the meal here. We get all of it without "improvements." It is too bad that man's chief commercial ambition seems to be to devise elaborate means to spoil and rob the simple, healthful foods that the Great Spirit provides in such abundance.

How well I remember, when a child, being solemnly told how, in less fortunate parts of the world, many children did not get fine white bread such as we ate. The poor little things had to eat coarse black bread. And naturally I was at the time, in my childish ignorance, duly sorry for them. Well, we know better now. But sometimes knowledge is long in coming. Bread, whether corn or wheat, is perhaps "the staff of life." But all too often it is a staff upon which the termites have been working. Bread at Yaquitepec is made of meal ground from the whole grain, and it is made without even yeast. No, it is not as "impossible" as you might think. Try making it that way sometime. I think you would like it.

The mornings these days are still chill enough for a little fire. Rider and Rudyard like to squat before it while breakfast is cooking, cheered on and encouraged in their tribal plottings by Victoria, who lies on her bed nearby and burbles an unceasing string of weird comment. We have gone back to using mescal butts for fuel. Winter has made tremendous inroads on our juniper pile; it is almost gone. And now, with the lesser need for great fires, the butts serve splendidly. Tanya and Rider go almost every day, searching over the rocky hillslopes, and bring home great loads which Tanya carries in a basket poised on her shoulder while Rider totes long mescal poles with the dry, dead butts still on them.

This season was so early that most of our mescal roasting is already over, a month ahead of usual. But that is the desert. It is delightfully unpredictable. You never know what sort of a year you are going to have or even what sort of a day it is going to be. No two days or two years are just alike. And changes from calm to storm come with staggering rapidity. Therein, I think, lies the fascination

of the desert—and its healthfulness. For one must constantly be on the alert; it is this that keeps one young.

Stagnation is a deadly thing. And so are routine and monotony. Some day we as a nation will learn this, and, learning, will embark on a new lease of life. A nation that has perfectly mastered the art of moving in perfectly ordered lock-step is "perfectly" lock-stepping itself down into oblivion. But this is drifting aside from the matter of the mescals. They are not all gone. There will be enough late comers for several April roasts.

Winds roar in plenty over Ghost Mountain these days. But sandwiched between is enough brilliant spring weather to make one rejoice in just the simple fact of being alive. Work is constant—there is always more of it piled up than we can ever hope to accomplish. But perhaps that is what makes the charm of it all. Out under the turquoise arch of desert skies, where the very silence seems to throb with the peace and purpose of the infinite, work ceases to be a drudgery. It slips into its rightful place as a joyful diversion.

When work is something which one does for oneself and from which tangible personal benefit to life and home can be discerned, it is no longer a slavery. This was the keen joy which the pioneers knew—and was the soaring force of spirit that enabled them to accomplish almost superhuman feats. Work! Work in freedom and in intimate contact with the earth.

Somehow everyone at Yaquitepec is singing these days. Tanya's pencil is busy as she snatches odd moments between tasks to capture verse from the chasing cloud shadows and the rustle of the windstirred junipers. Three-year-old Rudyard expresses the joy of life in long, rambling chants, half mumbled and half dramatically declaimed. Distinctively savage creations which cease instantly and self-consciously if anyone is so unwise as to let him know that he is being listened to. The chant won't end until someone interrupts. Rudyard is like that. When we have story telling competitions Rider always firmly rules Rudyard out from competing. Rudyard does not tell stories. He tells serials. They go on and on and on and never stop.

The bright warm days that we get now with increasing frequency are ideal for yucca shampoos. And now that we have plenty of good soft rainwater, we are revelling in them. You take the fibrous interior soapy-sapped wood of the yucca, preferably from the butt or lower portion of the trunk, and pound it. Then work the spongy mass up and down in water until you have a creamy lather. Then shampoo the hair with it. It is wonderfully cooling for the scalp and leaves the hair wavy and with a gleaming glint that no civilized soap can give. Yucca root is reported to be a hair tonic too. It is beneficial, beyond question. But I have no personal data to enable me to pass judgment on the story of an old prospector who solemnly assured me that an Indian squaw, of his acquaintance, being challenged to the feat, produced a luxuriant crop of new hair on the head of a white miner whose cranium was previously "as bare as a billiard ball." This she accomplished by repeated washings with yucca root.

A number of the squaw-tea bushes around Yaquitepec are already generously sprinkled with young seed cones. These green, immature little cones boil up very nicely as a vegetable, provided you get them young and tender enough. As they ripen they develop a quinine-like bitterness. But young and tender and put through the food grinder, which hastens the cooking process, they form a vegetable that is something of a cross between peas and spinach. A quite satisfactory dish. A little limey-bitter in taste, as are most desert plant foods. But it is this very ingredient that carries health with it. The desert animals know these things. You will find the packrats and other rodents chewing extensively on the bitter yucca leaves at certain life seasons. The wild creatures that are close to the earth as the Great Spirit intended life to be, do not need experts on diet to tell them things.

Rain! A sudden hammering drive that scuds in the wind and bangs upon the roof with the lash of flying buckshot. Startled I glance out of the window to see that the sun is gone and the sky is roofed with grey. All the valleys and canyons deep down below are blotted by a smoke of driving, rolling cloud. This is Spring.

Desert Home 2
(June 1941)

THE plaintive notes of the kildeer close around the house in the grey light before dawn. The sun rising out of the cloudbanked distance of the lowland desert to fade into the greyness of an overcast sky. Wind! Down on the cliff edge this morning as I scrambled among the boulders and junipers collecting fuel the wind roared up out of far down emptiness with a fury that threatened to hurl me from the rocks. Desert wind is a living thing. There is mystery in it and elemental, untamed freedom. A tiny sharpshin hawk, wings close furled against its sides, dropped like a whirling Plummet over the cliff edge and away into the churning gulf below, planing and drifting expertly into the gusts. Wind and threshing trees!

But here is the sun, bursting suddenly from overhead and blazing leagues on leagues of wasteland to a pattern of dazzling silver. Cloud shadows race like scattering coyotes across the writhing course of sandy washes and over the towers of cinnamon-colored buttes. A white-rumped shrike whirring down from the crest of a tall dead mescal stalk to snatch an unwary bug from a granite boulder. Yes, the chances are good that it will be a brilliant spring day after all.

There is always something electric and vibrant about desert in spring. You sense so plainly the stirring of the mysterious Force in all Nature; the mighty, unceasing throb of Earth-life that goes on and on, steadily and purposefully. Always it gives a fundamental sense of security. Wars may rage and nation battle against nation and turmoil and hate shatter the edifice of human frailties. But the steady, unruffled beat of the Great Heart goes on. You have only to pause in the silence of the desert peace to hear it.

Nighthawks are abroad these evenings, flitting and whirling through the dusk like dark, silent leaves. Masters of camouflage too, these ghostly wingers of the night. By day they sleep upon the ground, near bushes or among the open scattered stones of ridge slopes or in the lee of huge boulders. Low huddled to the earth, their heads sunk into the hollow between their folded wings, they look, with their sooty and faintly white pencilled plumage, so exactly like sun-bleached ancient mescal roots that it is hard to believe that they are birds. I have almost trodden upon them sometimes. And even then, standing over them and peering at them from a distance of three feet, it is often impossible to say with certainty that they are living things, until, abruptly, they take wing. Camouflage in Nature is a marvelous thing. There is a law behind it that is not well understood. Like everything else in Nature it has a definite reason, and one not quite so obvious as is popularly supposed. Like the airplane and other applications of natural forces man makes use of what he knows of camouflage—for destructive purposes.

The warm, bright run of the very best season of all the desert year is ahead of us. Golden sunshine, just right in temperature, and the caress of soft winds. Not that there will be no gales and storms and other brief interludes that make our Ghost Mountain climate interesting. But spring

Side view of Yaquitepec showing the cisterns. Open cistern becomes "Lake Yaquitepec" after rain.

is now no longer an infant. She is a bright maiden who is blooming towards the queenly womanhood of summer. Wrens sing in the juniper tops and carpenter bees bumble along the eaves' troughs of the house in the warm white mornings before sunrise. Pinacate beetles amble on their philosophic journeys and lizards flash across the rocks in pursuit of unwary flies. And Rider and Rudyard hold boat races on the new lake.

Oh yes, Yaquitepec has a new lake. It is tiny enough, it is true. But it is the biggest body of water that has ever collected and stayed in one place on Ghost Mountain for some centuries. Some day the "lake," when the side walls

are raised and the top put in, will be a cistern. Now it is a spoon-shaped excavation lined with chicken wire and cement. When the wind swoops over the mountain crest and strikes down among the junipers real riffles and waves heave in the lake.

Constructed hastily, working against time and with the lower level of it already full of water before the upper cement courses were laid, the lake has already justified itself a hundred fold. For we did not have to turn precious rain water to waste this year—the first year that we have ever been so fortunate. Always, previously, with our limited cistern capacity, there would come a time in the rainy season when, with everything brimming, we would have to switch the down-spouts and let the precious fluid run to waste. Always a bitterly heartbreaking thing to do, knowing full well that we would, later on in the year, be in need of that very water.

This year we switched the rainspouts from the brimming cisterns into the "lake." And the rain gods filled it full, almost to peril of overflowing. Now water beetles play and boats sail where but a few short weeks ago mescals spread their spiny daggers. Many and weird are the boats that sail the stormy waters. The latest is a round dish pan equipped with a stern wheel driven by a tiny steam engine that Santa Claus left this Christmas for Rider. Rider is proud of this boat—the result of his persistent begging of daddy to make a Mississippi river steamer. Rudyard has boats too. They are of strange shapes and material sometimes. The other day he tried to sail a hammer—and was scandalized to discover that it would work only as a submarine.

Our resident chukka partridges have hatched their broods. Three days ago as I went down to the lower terrace to replenish the grain in the feed pan, which we keep beneath a juniper tree for the chukkas and the wild birds, warning cluckings and scooting chukkas drew my attention to one little hen bird crouched beside the steps in the shelter of a tiny bush. She was sheltering under her wings a downy yellow and brown streaked brood of chicks. The cock bird strutted guardingly near by.

Hastily I withdrew. There had been such darting and scooting of little down covered atoms when I blundered into the group that I was afraid some were lost among the rocks. This must have been the case. For when I cautiously resumed some time later the little hen bird had gone, very evidently to round up stragglers. But she had left her main body of chicks still in the same place. Huddled close in a cleft of a rock and partly sheltered by the bush they were packed one upon another in a motionless, downy mass, glinting here and there with tiny, bright watchful eyes. They were almost invisible in their protective coloring which blended perfectly with their surroundings. They made no sign or stir of life. Only their eyes watched my every move as they waited obediently for their mother's return. Tender little atoms of life in a hard fierce world of rock and thorn! So many perils! As I tip-toed softly away I remembered a certain little quail and her mate. That had been stark tragedy of another season. The little desert quail and her mate had been quite tame, calling and talking to themselves all around the house and coming regularly for food. After nesting, the little hen bird came back attended by but a single tiny chick; her mate and all the rest of the brood had disappeared, victims of some wildlife tragedy. Lonely and disconsolate she hugged close about the house

for some days, keeping well beneath the juniper shadows and followed always on her stealthy comings and going by the tiny, uncertain little ball of fluffy life that ran like a shadow at her heels and over which she cooed and clucked in pitiful solicitude.

A skunk or some other marauder of the night got them both. For, one morning, going out across the flat for fuel, I came suddenly, not far from the house, upon a litter of freshly torn quail feathers beside a tiny cave under a big rock. Stooping down I peered into the little hideout. Feathers! Torn feathers and down—nothing more. The lonely, courageous little mother and her chick had gone together down the long, long trail. There was gloom over Yaquitepec when I came back with the news. Rider cried. And his were not the only eyes that were damp. For the little mother and her chick had somehow become part of the scheme of things. We missed them.

This afternoon one of the big, black scaly lizards got into the house—after flies probably. I swept him into a deep can from which he could not jump, carried him to the open window and dumped him gently on the ground outside. He lay there looking at me a long time— outraged. Then, when I went outside to plug up a little chink in the adobe wall that suggested danger as a snake entry, he suddenly took to his heels and scooted off in such a wrathful fury that I had to laugh. There are some people who tell you smugly that animals have no souls. These are the people who think the whole starry universe was made just as a picture frame for man. No souls? Rubbish! If you really want to understand humans study animals and birds and all living things. Their reactions throw much light on the antics of the human family. You will find the dour natured ones and the misers, the investigative ones, the hail-fellow-well-met type—and the plodders. They go by clans and classes too. The red racer snakes on Ghost Mountain belong to a guild of comedians.

There is a new adobe arch finished at the north end of the kitchen. But there is still a lot of wall to build to replace temporary structure. There is this about personal building—you are always adding something or enlarging. On the principle of the sea creatures that build their shells bigger and bigger as they grow. If it were possible I think that every family ought to build its own house. A house is a personal thing—or ought to be. Houses acquire souls. They absorb the spirit of the builders—and also the personality of those who live in them. It isn't necessary to be super-sensitive to realize the truth of this. Almost everyone can recall certain houses that carried with them an air of depression and gloom. And others that seem to be always smiling. The Indian knows this. You will find, if you will go to the trouble to dig beneath the surface of silly superstitions that they are usually founded upon concrete fact.

Mourning doves calling from the ridge somewhere. A pair of them comes here every year. We have never found their nesting place but it is somewhere among the rocks and junipers. Wild creatures have fixed habits. They take likes and dislikes to certain spots. And, outside of birds, desert creatures do not as a rule range very widely. Home is home, and they take root. The coyote is an exception. He is a wide ranger. But then he is a sardonic brigand, anyway. An example of polished roguery that can bring scant satisfaction to those who prate loudly of the "broadening influence" of travel.

Desert Home 3
(July 1941)

BENEATH the ramada, just outside the house, the carpenter bees are booming and bumbling amidst the thatch of dead mescal poles. Away to the east is the morning star, soaring upward like a shining angel above the whitening paleness of the far horizon.

Why is it, I wonder, that on these hushed, early desert mornings I think so much of my father? It is as though the mists roll away from an old, old trail that leads back to childhood. I see him again as he used to be; with his team and buckboard, driving on lonely roads, silent, keen-eyed for the trail in the faint light that wraps the world long before sunrise. Again I hear the slur of wheels through the sand, the strike of steel tires against a stone, the squeak of singletrees and the creak of leather. The swiftly moving hoofs of the team drum back the dead years in memories that bring, now, an odd, choked tightening of the throat as I see again the shadowy forms of the horses—and my father, his eyes upon the dim road, driving on and on into the star studded dawning.

But the droning of the busy carpenter bees breaks through the mists of childhood memories. Busy fellows, these big, shiny black bees. With all the swelled pomposity of some petty official, impressed with his own importance. They are always blusteringly officious. They take possession of the long channels cut in the pithy, dry stalks of the mescal shoots by the big butter-yellow amber-headed grubs which develop later into the slender, scarlet-winged, dashingly handsome, mescal beetles. The carpenter bees move into their dark, abandoned tunnels. And fall busily to their own carpentering.

From the thatch of the ramada these warm days there drifts a fine scatter of sawdust. And every once in a while, from a neat round porthole in a dead, overhead stalk, some shiny black artisan dumps an extra big accumulation of wood waste down on our heads. It is all right, so long as it does no damage. But at intervals we get an eyeful. Then we say violent things about the carpenter bees and wish heartily that we had not provided them with such an abundance of pithy labyrinths to work in.

This last week we have transferred our breakfast allegiance from wheat to corn—in the Yaquitepec version of the Pueblo Indian *piki*. We make a water-thin batter of home ground yellow corn meal, with nothing added but a little salt, and spill it out on a very hot griddle. The result is a paper-thin, much perforated, lace-like wafer which, as it crisps stiff enough, is whisked from the fire. Cooking *piki* is fun. And eating it is better. With a little butter and honey it is hard to beat. Crunchy and with the delicate flavor of the fresh grain. I don't know if you can make this sort of *piki* with "civilized" corn meal. Maybe so. But *quién sabe?* Civilized corn meal—like a lot of other things—seems to have acquired something of the hard, tinny brittleness of the modern age.

Yesterday the salt-cellar went the way that all things go—eventually. Being home made pottery and not hammered from a block of solid silver (as was the one fashioned in the early days of an Arizona mission for a visiting bishop) ours went quicker and more completely. So it had to be replaced. Investigation of the clay bin revealed that our supply of prepared clay was entirely exhausted. "Not even 'nough for not even one very *small* salt-cellar, Daddy," Rudyard reported solemnly as he leaned far into the bin and studied its vacancy intently for at least two long minutes. "But I think that in *this* corner there might...." Then his little brown heels went wildly into the air as he leaned too far. He disappeared into the box with a startled yell.

After he had been duly rescued and comforted we set out for our "clay mine." This is some distance from the house. There is plenty of clay on Ghost Mountain, as is natural in a district of much weathered granite. But it is patchy. Some deposits are too full of impurities, or too shallow, to be of any use. Every once in a while we run across a good spot. Then we mark the place and draw our supplies from there until we have worked it out.

The three of us—Rider, Rudyard and I—carried containers in which to pack home the clay. Graduated according to the size and strength of the bearer—after the time honored example set by the Three Bears. Rudyard cannily selected an empty baking powder can. Hefting it appraisingly, and with much wrinkling of his pudgy little nose, he declared he would "bring home plently heavy enough for Rudgy." Rider, however, had to be dissuaded from toting along a basket as large as my own. He is doggedly ambitious to be all grown up and it is hard sometimes to keep him from overtaxing his strength. We compromised finally on a smaller basket—and my allowing him to carry the light shovel as well.

The trail was thick-bordered, and in places almost obliterated by the herbage that was the result of this year's exceptional rains. But the grass now was all dry and tawny brown. It rustled beneath our bare feet and in the thin shade of it foraging ants hurried busily upon their duties. The wind that came down from among the rocks and junipers was warm and drowsy and the yellow flowers of the late mescals swayed against the blue desert sky like the last tattered banners of the retreating hosts of Spring.

Away up on the ridge somewhere a sleepy roadrunner intoned at intervals his puppy-like whining call. A buzzard wheeled overhead and two garrulous desert ravens flapped heavily. And down by the old mescal roasting hearth, where the trail skirts the blackened ring of stones where we usually fire our clay pots, we came upon a plump little horned toad [lizard] fast asleep upon an ant nest. But no ants were visible. Those that had not already been picked off by the artful little marauder were keeping discreetly underground. Sun warmed and drowsily content, with a full tummy, he had succumbed to pleasant dreams.

We reached our destination and dug our clay, first carefully clearing out the accumulation of dead sticks and gravel that the winter storms had piled in the shallow depression. Then homeward. The human head is a good, and natural, place to carry a burden. In Indian file, so laden we made our way back, Rudyard in the middle of the line, Rider bringing up the rear. Presently a stifled chuckle made me look back. Rider was sputtering with suppressed laughter, and pointing. But Rudyard, oblivious of the merriment, plodded stolidly on. He had hoisted his tiny baking can full of clay to the top of his head and, with plump little arms much too short for the job, was holding it there. His face was set in lines of grim determination, as of one who performs a serious duty. And there was satisfaction there, too. Was he not doing exactly as we were? He looked so funny that I turned away quickly. To have let him see me laugh would have been unforgivable.

And so we arrived home with our clay. And duly ground it and sifted it and made us a new salt-cellar—and several other things as well. Rider made a special little vase for himself. And so did Rudyard—or at any rate he got himself nicely mussed up with mud. Which is almost the entire joy of "potting" when one is three years old. So everyone was happy.

* * *

The garden grows. It is a tiny garden—the most of it protected by muslin covered frames. The beds are microscopic. But we have more water in our cisterns this year than last and the green stuff forms a welcome addition to the diet. Right now we have chives and pinto beans and bush beans and lettuce and scarlet-globe radishes growing. In the warm, sunny days one can almost see the plants grow.

We spend much of our time beneath the shade of the ramada these days. Here there is shade without walls and the little wandering breezes from out the wastelands can come and go as they please. It is a cool place to eat, too. Victoria is especially fond of it because there are generally fascinating little lizards to be seen wandering about on the top of the low, bordering adobe wall in search of flies. Some of these turquoise studded little rascals grow very tame. One, this noon, sat and glinted trustful jewelled eyes at me as I gently stroked it under the chin with my finger. They grow saucily insolent, too. There is one in particular that makes a point of scampering over Tanya as she lies on the rug in the shade, putting Victoria to sleep. Tanya does not particularly mind being scampered over. But the other day when the same inquisitive little sprite, breathlessly driving for a fly, tumbled into her paint pot as she sat decorating a desert gourd, she *almost* said something very loud. She got up so suddenly that she upset Rudyard, who fell against Rider, who was sewing a basket with mescal fibre. And in the wreckage his prize wooden needle got broken.

So, as there had to be another needle, we raided the nearest juniper tree for a likely twig, and whittled out a new one. Reflecting, as we sat there in the drowsy shade about the long, long road humanity has trodden from the time of the first primitive wooden needles to today's roaring machines. A long road. Humanity has lost something during that long trek. Something of incalculable value; something the loss of which is now driving it into insanity and red ruin. It has lost the knowledge of how to live. It has lost its faith. It has lost its sense of kinship with the Great Spirit. Dazzled by a greed for material things it has sold its birthright for a "mess of pottage." Pottage that is now, alas, red with torrents of blood.

Not a cheerful line of reflection. As we sat there in the peace of the silent desert, whittling upon our primitive needle, there came back to us a fragment of Kipling. Just a fragment. But a grim one. And aptly descriptive of humanity's gleanings on its march of "Progress."

"…The worst we took, with sweat and toil. The best we left behind."

PART THREE — DESERT REFUGE

Desert Refuge 1
(August 1941)

THE DAYS are hot now. Through the chinks of the ramada thatch the noonday sun searches the patch of black shade with thin, burning fingers. It is breathless in the house, even with every window flung wide. Our little thermometer, tacked against a temporary inside wall, hovers around 110 degrees, and often goes higher.

The big open unfinished cistern that we have grown used to calling "lake" is dry. Where, awhile back, toy boats sailed and water beetles played, hot, thirsty cement now glares to the scampering lizards and the hopeful bees.

It is hard on the bees. Both our own and the wild ones have gotten used to the lake as a water supply. Now, again, they must make long flights across the desert for their drinks. And, in consequence, they are mad. Habit is as strong in insects and all other living creatures as it is in humans. Like the needle of the phonograph, action impulses follow little grooves among the thought cells. Until there is a worn track which it is hard to turn from. "Thus did my father, and my grandfather!" "Behold, this is *right* and this is *wrong*!" Thus and so is "the custom."

It is a good thing that the Great Spirit, in His infinite wisdom, sees fit, every once in a while, to drastically upset the order of things. Else there would be no development of mind or soul or initiative. Just a ghastly lock-step—everything growing more and more crystallized and stereotyped and patterned until the whole universe mummified. After all it is disaster and upheaval that are the stuff from which *real* progress is built.

Our tame chukka partridges have learned to fit themselves to conditions. They come for their drinks at fairly regular times, morning and evening. And at such times we go out and serve them their portion in a tiny pan beneath the shade of the juniper tree. If they come in and find the pan dry they walk up and down prominently on the white gravel in front of the house, eyes cocked expectantly, until noticed. They are not the only ones who have learned, however. The squirrels, chipmunks and birds have learned too. Speedily, as the meal call sounds guests begin to assemble for the banquet. The chukkas do not like the big grey squirrel, who is a hoarder. They scold

angrily as he wolfs the grain. They don't like, either, the large red racer snake who comes periodically, trailing his long handsome length for a drink of water. But the racer is a good sport and fills his appointed place in the scheme of things. He is an adjuster in Nature's balance. Our mouse population, a problem a short time ago, is now back to normal.

Our tiny garden continues to do well, though it is rationed now on water from the drinking water cisterns. Every year the water situation improves a little, as we get more and more toehold. The thing is like a rolling snowball. The bigger it gets the quicker it grows. We get a lot of comfort sometimes in thinking back to beginnings. It's encouraging, and it is also an illustration of inter-dependence. It takes water to mix cement—and it takes cement to catch more water. Sometimes we think we haven't gone very far. Then we remember that we carried the first water to mix the first tiny batches of cement up the mountain on our backs. And remembering this—as we now dip a bucket into a sizable cistern for our supply—we feel better. And sizable cisterns mean the ability to make bigger cisterns. So it grows. So *everything* grows. A fundamental law. Germs and mescal plants and humans—and civilizations and universes. Until, like an over-inflated bubble, they grow too big to stand the strain of their own expansion. Then they blow up and return to beginnings, to start all over again. Hopeless? By no means. On the contrary, if you will reflect upon this mysterious, unswerving law, you will find there the most definite assurance of Hope and of Immortality. Life is a busy thing. And packed full of joy if it is lived sanely and sincerely.

And the richest joy of life is work. Work and accomplishment. Not treadmill work, but individually constructive work. I don't think there are many pleasures equal to

A level section of trail winding across summit of a Ghost Mountain Ridge.

The next garden was a trifle bigger. And only a trifle better and more successful. Plants are like people. They acquire certain habits and needs over long periods of reincarnation. A long line of ancestry had accustomed our garden vegetables to certain civilized conditions. They did not like the desert. The harsh soil upon which the mescals and the junipers and the *ramarillo* [rabbitbrush] bushes throve was too crude for them. So, as we had no time to wait upon evolution, we had to compromise—make soil that they *did* like.

Far and wide, on desert excursions, we collected fertilizer, carrying it home and up the mountain in sacks. When the grass and herbage flourished in the spring we collected that too. All of this enriching material we buried and dug in, into the stubborn earth. Then came the yelling winds, and the savage beat of the sun; the appreciative bugs; the mice and the squirrels and the joyful birds. Many times, before these individual or collective blitzkriegs, the garden went under. But, stubbornly, having an inability to know when it was licked, it always somehow got up on its hind legs and shook a defiant fist at the land hosts and the air hosts.

And it won out. Today it flourishes merrily, protected by frames—low enclosures completely covered with cheesecloth. Maybe you can't have a "garden estate" under such conditions. But you *can* have vegetables. In desert locations where water is scarce and high winds and pests are serious problems these garden frames are the answer. Five or six feet wide, and of any length convenient, they give complete protection. If you have had trouble with your desert vegetable garden and have not hit upon this device, try it out. Make the side walls from old lumber, or anything else that is handy, and build them from 12 to 18 inches high. If the materials are available it is an improvement to make the sides of fine mesh wire netting, as this lets in the air and light. There should be curtains of burlap or canvas, to let down when hot or heavy winds blow. The tops of the frames can be covered with cheap unbleached muslin, tacked down along one side and weighted with a long strip of wood on the other. It should be wide enough to lap well over. Lath covers, or covers of fine mesh wire, are perhaps better if they are tight enough to exclude pests. Or glass can be used. The garden frame is a practical thing for dry locations. It is economical as to water, too.

that of overcoming a seemingly hopeless problem. At any rate we get a thrill out of every cool green salad that comes up to the table these days, a thrill that is maybe childish and out of all proportion to the size of the salad, but a thrill nevertheless. Sometimes our rare visitors smile slyly as we enthuse. They are thinking of the lush fields where water in abundance flows docilely in ditches, and green things wax fat in pampered ease. But we are thinking of our first garden. It was 12 by 18 *inches* in size. And, for lack of anything better, we fenced it around with cholla cactus—a rampart against the mice and rats.

We planted mustard in that garden. And doled it scanty portions of drinking water that we carried up the mountain on our backs in a hot summer. And the little plants came up. It was a new world to them—new and harsh conditions. Ten thousand generations of mustard seed behind them had never faced conditions such as these. When they were three inches high, dwarfed and spindly and tough, they realized that the end was upon them. And, with the marvelous prompting of the Great Spirit (a circumstance from which one can derive more assurance than from all the books and preachers in the world), they began to seed—to put their last remaining flickers of life into a desperate effort to perpetuate their kind. We had one salad from that garden. It was a salad that might have served as an appetizer for a squirrel. But it was a salad.

Hot days and desert sunshine. How little any of us know about life, despite the learned delvings and soul-crushing science of our Age of Progress. What did the Chaldeans think, and discover? And the Atlanteans, and the Egyptians—and all the shadowy company before—who groped and swaggered and toiled through their respective cycles of growth and death. Dust in the wind! Mayhap I have the dust of dead world conquerors in the moist mud of the olla that grows in size and shape under the workings of my fingers. Perhaps in the dumpy little toy dog which Rider fashions from the moistened earth lurks the ashes of a forgotten saint.

> *Imperial Caesar, dead and turned to clay*
> *May stop a hole to keep the wind away.*

...And the world rolls on among the stars—a throbbing, living atom amidst a glorious universe of unnumbered myriads of other throbbing, living atoms. A universe of eternal, universal life, in which the fleeting shadow that we call Death is no more than a brief, recurring night between the glow of endless days.

* * *

The wind this afternoon whirls and roars. Perhaps that is the charm of our desert mountain. There is no sameness, all is constant change. The hot sunshine streams into the house through the open back window and the three ears of golden corn, with their stripped-back husks—corn of our own raising—sway and swing from the twisted fiber cord that suspends them from a ceiling beam. The back shutter of the kitchen window is open and sways and bangs at its confining hook. From the shade of the ramada, outside, come the mingled voices of Rider, Rudyard, Tanya and Victoria, who are out there in the warm wind trying to keep cool. Sketchily Tanya is wrestling with the job of reading an instructive story aloud. Comes a sudden stop to the narrative—an abrupt termination upon which the small, determined voice of Rudyard throws explanation:

"I am thoroughly se-gusted (disgusted) with that book," he says firmly, as he calmly removes it from Tanya's hand. "But I am not 'gusted with this other one,"—picking up another from the table and holding it out to her. "Read this. There's *fairy stories* in *this* book."

Beat of the wind. And heat in it. A hummingbird hurtling past and out over the little juniper studded flat with a sharp whirr—a flick of sound passing in the dry, driving air like the swish of a speeding arrow. Or was it really an arrow? A ghostly arrow from the ghostly bow of one of the long dead dusky warriors who roamed Ghost Mountain in the dim fled years? Who shall say? The "old people" were free. Their hearts were fierce and wild and brave

and beat with every shade of human love and a quenchless worship of Freedom. They died. But they were not enslaved. And their spirits live on. Their arrows still speed across the ridges; their ghostly chants still eddy in the whimpering wind.

Dawn to noon—and to Dark. But the trail of the bare, resolute brown feet and the thin twang of the desert bowstring lead out across the wastelands. A thin, resolute wilderness trail that has passed aforetime—and shall pass again—through the red rust of crumbled machines and the weathered mounds of forgotten cities.

Dawn to Dark!...And on to Dawn. The winds swirl out of emptiness. But the old, old trail goes on and on. On towards the Sunrise.

Desert Refuge 2
(September 1941)

THUNDERHEADS bank often upon the horizon these August days and the hard arch of the turquoise sky is a thirsty metallic backdrop for cruising cloud-mountains of dazzling white. There is something magnificent about these mighty, desert thunderclouds. It would be a warped soul indeed who could stand amidst the hush of the wasteland leagues and gaze at them unmoved. "Just clouds" would you say? "Simple aggregations of vapor. Drifting mist banks. Nothing more."

Well-perhaps. But as one stands in the hot, stretching silence of the endless desert and gazes upward these towering white sky mountains don't look like that. They don't look simple and commonplace or tagged with matter-of-fact scientific explanation. They look like something very different. They carry with them an ominous, disquieting sense of POWER. Of a living Power that is as far beyond science as the light of the sun is beyond the glimmer of a rushlight. A Power that moves in mighty silence; that is clothed in the swirling drive of stuff as unsubstantial as vapor. But a Power, nevertheless, before which the human soul shrinks in awe. Small wonder that the ancient dwellers of the desert sensed the might of the Great Spirit in these glittering pinnacles of cloud and conceived their dim, rumbling black caverns as being the haunt of the mysterious Thunderbird. Maybe we at Yaquitepec have gone back; mayhap the spirits of the old people have laid hold upon us. But science can keep its explanations—and its ideas.

* * *

One of our cisterns is dry, and several days ago I washed it out to be ready for the first heavy shower. I left the hatch off so the dry air and sunshine would freshen the interior. And I forgot about it for a couple of days. When I remembered and went to close the opening there were a couple of little desert mice in the bottom of the cistern. Victims of false steps—or perhaps of venturesome curiosity—they were huddled now in a little furry ball in the coolest corner. The smooth cistern sides had proved too much for them to scale. Without movement, in a beady-eyed hopelessness, they sat and watched me while I maneuvered a long pole down into the depths of the dry tank.

Then, suddenly, as the butt came to rest a couple of inches from them, they understood. Hope electrified the huddled grey ball to action. With nimble, clinging feet they scooted one after the other up the steep inclined plane, leaped over the edge of the man-hole and scuttled to safety amidst the bushes. I had to climb down into the cistern to mop it out again before I replaced the lid. But I didn't mind. A cheap enough price to pay for the privilege of another sidelight on animal behavior.

* * *

We have about decided that the Ghost Mountain "spring" is a myth. Oh, yes, there have been rumors of a hidden spring. Vague, elusive tales, something like the lost mine stories of which the wastelands are full. In winter, when chill winds sweep over Ghost Mountain and when everything that can hold water is full, we don't take much stock in the spring legend. But every summer, when the heat waves shimmer far out across the glinting badlands and our cisterns begin to drop their water level, we get out the spring story and dust it off—with all its vague, fascinating detail.

"...There was an old Indian. And he told a prospector....It was on the *south* side of the canyon....The mountain sheep had quite a trail there....No, It's hidden by now, maybe....The Indians filled up a lot of those springs, so the white men wouldn't find them....Anyway that place used to be called hidden well...."

And so forth, and so on. Regular desert stuff. Just enough mystery—and maybe truth—in it to make it alluring. In summertime!

It was Rider who resurrected the legend this year. Sitting by the side of the hatch of the big cistern where he acted as doorkeeper against the thirsty wild bees—shutting down and opening the cloth cover as I drew the buckets of water—he said suddenly: "Daddy, let's go look for the spring tomorrow. You know that old man said...."

So the next morning when the dawn was drawing a faint pencil of red behind the phantom blue outlines of buttes and mountain ranges away off in Arizona, we set out. Hot, blinding sunlight was glaring on the barren ridges by the time we reached the brink of Mystery canyon. Over the cliff edge a gnarled dead juniper, age-blackened in the sun, reached fantastic arms. The swimming gulf below was silent with the breathless, ear-ringing hush of the desert. Already heat was pulsing from it. The white sand of the little wash, far down on the canyon floor, was a writhing blur.

"It was on the south side of the canyon, about half-way up," Rider said hopefully, quoting from the legends. He took off his sandals to secure safer foothold among the tumbled, windscoured boulders, and we began to go down.

And we went down—and down. And sideways, west and east. All through that forenoon and far into the afternoon we worked back and forth along that almost perpendicular wall of sun-seared rock. Beetling cliffs where the wild apricot trees, roots deep driven into fissures, waved siren green branches that hinted falsely of water. Hushed caves where the shallow shadows were carpeted thickly with drifted, dry desert leaves. Scorching gullies where, in the choking heat of an oven, we threaded our way perilously between teetering, giant boulders—many of them big as an office building—picking our footing along the brink of menacing chasms that yawned blackly amidst the jumbled rocks. Buzzards wheeled high in the hot silence. Ghostly little brown birds, voiceless as shadows, slipped away into the gloom of stirless junipers. Once a big hawk, silent and grey like some malignant spirit, launched himself startlingly from a black cleft and swept away down the canyon.

"It was on the south side," Rider kept saying gamely, "about half-way up the canyon wall. Maybe if we keep on...."

But his voice was slowly getting dryer and hoarser and his eager scramblings less and less nimble. The canteen was about empty. The beat of the sun in the open gullies was killing. "It...was...on the south side...Daddy. And...and maybe...."

But we quit, finally, after a stubborn argument, for Rider hates to abandon his purpose. "We'll come again then, maybe in the fall or winter," he said at last, grudgingly. "And then we'll look on the *north* side, too. If this spring is just a fairy story we've got to know for certain."

Hot and weary we clambered down into the bed of the canyon and headed on our roundabout course homeward, skirting the base of the mountain. The sand was hot and the catsclaw bushes, gloating at our aching muscles, slashed at us vindictively. Rider's feet were dragging. But he made no complaint. And, even as we tramped, he stooped every once in a while to pick up pottery sherds [shards]. The desert about Ghost Mountain is littered with scraps of the shattered earthenware of the old people. How long? From whence—and to where? Silence and heat and scattered chips of old jars upon the sand. It isn't so much what you can see on the desert; it's what you can *feel*.

It was a weary tramp. But there was no help for it. We were a long way from the trail that threads up Ghost Mountain. But we knew well, from ample experience, that the longest way around was the easiest way home. We had made frontal attacks on the mountain before—to our undoing. A coyote got up presently out of a thin band of shade beneath a scorched butte and loped thirstily down the wash. He stopped, after a bit, and stared at us. Soon, as we paid no attention to him, we saw him trotting back.

It was a day for whiptail lizards. They were out in extraordinary numbers, scampering their handsome forms across the hot sand. There is something of the stage villain's slink about the gait of a whiptail. It is so exaggerated that it seems deliberately assumed. It is a play-acting pose that goes perfectly with the devil-may-care expression on their faces. Rider forgot his pottery collecting presently in the excitement of seeing one of them pick up and run on its hind legs. The whiptails, in common with some other desert lizards, will do that once in a while. Folding in their forelegs against their breasts and balancing by their long tails they will scoot like the wind in queerly human two-legged fashion. It is then that one can glimpse the family connection between the lizards and the prosaic domestic chicken.

It was a day for bell spiders too. Their webs were everywhere. Weary, as we were, we blundered often into their lowstrung nets and lines before we could turn aside. Bell spider is probably not the official name for these ingenious little desert dwellers. Without doubt they, unknowingly, shoulder some fearsome Latin appellation. But Rider calls them bell spiders because of the tiny fairy-like bell-shaped house they build for themselves. This sun-and-rain tent, open only at the bottom, hangs like a bell in the midst of an artful arrangement of supporting cables. Usually about an inch and an eighth long and three eighths of an inch in diameter at the bottom, it is ingeniously woven of white silk and camouflaged on the outside by scraps of dry buckwheat flowers, bits of dead grass or tiny dry leaves. Beside it, or around it, the little tent dweller weaves a marvelously elaborate catching net, almost invisible and of a texture resembling fine white crepe.

The spider itself is a ghostly whitish color, sometimes faintly marked, and with slender, brownish legs. It resembles, somewhat, the black widow; another point of similarity being its extremely tough web. Until one peers closely and discovers the neat and beautifully woven net which this spider makes amidst its sprawling and untidy arrangement of cross cables, its web has a striking resemblance to that of the widow. Whether its bite is harmless however, or charged with poison similar to its sinister relative, we do not know.

It was late when we plodded up the last stretch of the home trail. Even Rider had had more than enough. Tanya, Rudyard and Victoria were at the door to welcome us. "Did you find the spring?" Tanya asked hopefully.

Headed for the water *olla*, Rider shook his head:

"We've got a better idea," he said huskily. "We're gonna get a lot more cement and just build a spring for ourselves."

Which is the way it is likely to be. And, after all, there is a deal of comfort in the thought. Necessity is the goad which spurs to accomplishment. And a thing won by work has a value far in excess of anything that comes easily. Perhaps it is a good thing that there was no spring upon the summit of Ghost Mountain when we settled here. If there had been there might perhaps have been, today, no Yaquitepec—and a lot of other things.

With a spring, and abundant water, we might have found life in the desert "just too hard"—and moved away.

Desert Refuge 3
(October 1941))

THERE is rejoicing upon Ghost Mountain, for once more all our water cisterns are brimming over. Even the "lake," as we term the big cement lined excavation that will some day be an additional reservoir, is half full. For three days ago, after a long "torture of hope" during which heavy thundershowers marched in complete circle around us—drenching the lowlands and mountains within a mile and leaving us bone dry—the rain gods relented.

There was drama in their storm-sending too. And rebuke. For we had gone to bed dispirited and, let us confess it with shame, rather a little angry and full of complaint. All the day long we had sweltered in the hot heavy atmospheric breathlessness which precedes a desert deluge. And all day the sullen thunderheads had banked around us, glooming the sky everywhere except for one clear spot, seemingly not greater than the area of our mountain, that hung directly over our heads. And it had rained. In sheets and curtains of slashing grey the forked flails of the lightning had ripped waters from the heavens—to north, to east, to west, to south. But not here.

"All we get," said Rider bitterly, sniffing the damp fragrance of the breeze that came up in the evening from the distant lowlands, "—all we get is the *smell*."

So we had gone to bed disgruntled, trying hard to be philosophic in the knowledge that sooner or later our turn would come. But, after the manner of frail humans, not succeeding very well.

But the grey, still whiteness of the next dawn crept across the desert to the hollow rumble of heavy thunder.

to use our gently sloping house roof each night as a dance floor. Which would be all right, for they are lovable little animals, if they did not also use the water gutter as a check booth in which to park bits of cholla, the dry rinds of cactus fruits, mescal pods, dead juniper sticks and all the thousand and one other classes of trashy "valuables" which packrats—exactly on the order of humans—lug along with them and regard as "very important." And which they conveniently forget—in the water spout. It isn't any good to

Rider (left) and Marshal building an adobe wall.

Far off, but approaching. Hardened by so many previous disappointments, I noted it with a drowsy mental shrug. And went to sleep again.

"Daddy! Daddy! Wake up! It's *raining!*"

I woke with a jerk—in more senses than one—for Rider's hand was upon my arm and he was shaking me vigorously. "Real rain," he said breathlessly. And, as I sat up, fighting the sleep from my eyes, I heard Rudyard's shrill refrain piping from the next bed: "Yes, weal *wain! You* gotta get up an' fix the 'pouts! Hurree Daddy! *Hurree!*"

So I got up hastily—Rudyard is very definite in his commands and has all the authority of extreme youth—and rushed out to "fix the spouts." The spouts and water gutters always have to be "fixed"—that is, swept out and cleaned—immediately before a rain. It is a last minute chore that no previous planning can avoid. The reason is that the Ghost Mountain packrats, secure in the truce of brotherhood which reigns at Yaquitepec, long ago decided

clean the spouts the night before, except as to a reduction in labor. For the next morning will find a new collection.

"Hurree, Daddy! Hurree!" shrilled my imperious taskmaster, racing, a bare-skinned sprite, after me into the dawn, "Hurree! *Hurree!*"

And there was need of hurry. For ominous big drops were already plunking in wide-spaced intervals upon the iron roof. Far aloft we could hear that weird, sinister rushing sound—like the churning of a great wind—which is the advance message of released rain masses already plunging downward towards a thirsty earth. Rider was dashing here and there, closing shutters, dragging dry firewood into the kitchen and setting the innumerable pots, pans, pails and jars that are his own personal water-catching outfit, beneath the run-off and drip point of every inclined flat surface not connected with the main gutter system. We all worked fast. But I had barely tossed out the last bit of cactus joint and given the clean metal gutter a final wipe with the damp cloth when the deluge struck in a blinding white fury. Junipers, rocks, ocotillos and tall podded mescals blotted suddenly in a sheet of falling water. Rider and I reached shelter in a spume of stinging drops that seemed to tingle with the electricity of the forked fire that of a sudden split the sky overhead with a deafening crash. Rudyard bolted in at our heels like a little drenched duck, water pouring from his tangled brown curls. Then it *rained!*

The storm lasted half a day, with the first fury—when the water fell in solid curtains, succeeded by scattered and dwindling showers. The day previous Rider and I had collected a bundle of yucca leaves, with which to put a new seat in one of our chairs. A lucky circumstance, for now there was an indoor job all ready to hand. So, while Tanya sat in the window seat explaining the rain in complicated baby-talk to wide-eyed little Victoria, I and my two eager assistants hunted up awls and began to shred the long green bayonet-like leaves into quarter inch strips. The big leaves shred readily, following the lines of the fibers that run from butt to tip. When the leaves are fresh cut these strips are very pliant and braid or twist easily; but if they are dry they quickly can be gotten to the right condition by soaking in water. When we had accumulated what looked like a sufficiency of strips—in spite of Rudyard's "assistance," for he has rather elastic ideas at present on what constitutes a quarter-inch width—Rider brought the forlorn chair that needed fixing. It was in a bad way, never having recovered from the time when Rudyard invented a dramatic game called "Beeg fire on Bwoadway. Peoples jumping into net." He had used the canebottomed chair as the "net," jumping lustily into it from the height of a box set upon the table. The drama had been suppressed quite suddenly by unimaginative grown-up "police." But not in time to help the chair much.

Well, what is one chair seat, anyway, in the scheme of things. Kingdoms, we have been told, have crumbled for the want of a horseshoe nail. And heaven alone knows how many automobile classics have been lost to unprogressive speed drivers who neglected to use "whoozawizz" spark plugs. So why worry about a chair seat? I cut out the old torn bottom and began to braid in the new one. We have found that braiding, after the manner of the South Sea Islanders with their coconut fiber, is the best treatment for yucca.

It is a fairly long job to braid the seat into a regular sized chair, braiding as one goes and lacing the completed cord back and forth, basket fashion. So by the time the rain was over and the children were racing up and down through the puddles in the hot sunlight that had broken through the scattering clouds the chair was about finished. Not a brilliant example of weaving, perhaps, but

something that would serve well enough. I clipped the last strand end, set the chair by the table and went out to sniff the fragrance of the damp, rejoicing, sun-sparkled desert. Tanya and Victoria were already out, sitting on the damp rock step beside the "lake" watching Rider and Rudyard sailing their long-stored boats. Over the crests of the clean-washed juniper trees winged, like migrating fairies, a wide scattered drift of gauzy-winged flying ants. "Plush bugs," as Rider calls the bright many-legged, fluffily scarlet little round insects which appear mysteriously after warm weather rains, were already ambling about underfoot.

It is true enough, as Kipling said, that "Smells are stronger than sounds or sights to make your heartstrings crack…." But of all the scents that can stir up haunting memories and sheer delight for the human nostrils I know of none half so potent as the fragrance of the desert after rain. It is something too deep and subtle for description. If you know it you know what I mean. And if you have never lifted your head and drunk in the winey, aromatic fragrance that wells from the grateful earth and stretching leagues of wasteland after a heavy shower, you have missed something—missed one of the greatest and most mysterious thrills that the wilderness holds. To stand in the midst of a sunlit, rain-washed silence and drink deep of this prayer of thanks, welling up like incense from plant and shrub and rock and spiney thorn to the Great Giver of all Mercy, is a moment—a sacred moment. One stands awed, listening to one's own humble heartbeats. Thus stood our dusky brothers, the "savages" of the dim, fled yesterdays. With them the Great Spirit was something *real*—not an empty thing, blurred in a tinsel mockery of Sunday clothes and stereotyped ritual and hollow words.

But rain at Yaquitepec means not only water in the storage cisterns. It means mud. Mud is a valuable thing. So long we have been without it. Or, having it, have had it in little dabs—as much, maybe, as one can obtain from a pint of wash water, or from the frugally saved unused portions of a brew of tea. Such dabs take a tedious time in making a showing upon an adobe wall—though we can point to considerable areas of the mud walls of Yaquitepec that were built in just such piecemeal fashion.

But now is one of our widely spaced periods of abundance when we *revel* in mud. There is mud upon my hands as I write, and mud upon my feet. Dried mud that has been imperfectly scraped off. Rider, still working at outdoor jobs, is pleasingly decorated all over with wet, clayey signs of toil. Rudyard has mud in his hair. Purposely put there, we discovered later, as a result of his having remembered a story told some time ago by a visitor to the effect that the Apaches plastered their heads with mud as a hair tonic. Even Victoria has had her innings. For seizing an opportunity, she crawled off her rug and into a gooey batch of adobe which I had just trampled to the right consistency. In the ensuing cleansing operations, to the accompaniment of lusty yells, Tanya got well mudded too. So that makes it unanimous.

But a lot of new wall has gone up, built with a shovel and a trowel and the plain bare hands, and in breathless haste—racing against the swift soaking away of the surface water in the open pools, from which we take it. In some of the pools that have been previously well trampled by our bare feet—after the manner of the old buffalo wallows on the plains—there is still water standing. So for a day or so yet there will be mud—and wall building. Then again operations will stop. Thus, in such fits and starts, goes our building. Woefully primitive, of course. But we are shamelessly unashamed of the method. And it is likewise quite true that the house isn't finished as yet. Nor are we anxious to have it so. "Finished" is an ominous word, reminiscent, somehow, of the practice of sending elegant young ladies and young gentlemen to an elegant "finishing school." Too many things, now, in this era's progressive set-up, are regarded as "finished." And a lot of them frequently are.

Desert Refuge 4
(November 1941)

THE WALL of the new room on which we worked with such frantic haste after the last big rain—racing with mudmaking against the evaporation of our open waterholes—stands bravely. What there is of it. It must now wait for more rain and more mud. Which is perhaps just as well. For it will get a chance to thoroughly sunbake before the next course is laid.

It is a good wall and we are proud of it. Not a thing of classic beauty, but rugged and strong—as a wall should be. Eighteen to thirty inches thick—the variation in width depending on the necessities of the foundation—it stands now like the rampart of some ancient fort. A circumstance from which we draw no little satisfaction. For it is a comfort, when the imagination balks at peering forward into a future of machinemade hells of destruction, to turn backward in thought to the days when every home was a castle and warfare could claim at least the honesty that marks the struggles of the beasts.

Not that the past held any magic over the present—save in degree. But it held more hope. It was swayed by

the same laws, marching in the same changeless cycles. But men's hearts then held more simple faith and truth. They were groping towards an ideal—towards a light. Now they stand in the light and the light blinds them, they have become mad. "Onward, Progress! Onward!"—To where?

But the days march past on Ghost Mountain without benefit of "Progress." The little lizards scamper along the sunny summit of our new, three-foot high wall and the butterflies drift and float over the summits of the age-gnarled junipers.

Yesterday, upon the summit of a barren ridge, where the ocean had forsaken it, who knows how many centuries ago, Rider found the desert-bleached fragments of a big, ancient sea shell.

And this morning, as I set out a newly decorated pottery bowl and olla to dry upon a rock the bright-eyed chipmunks and lizards came out of the bushes and thorn thickets to investigate—and to speculate. Drift of cloud and stir of wind. Clock ticks on the endless ribbon of eternity. Time. Time. Somewhere there are tooting whistles and shrieking sirens. Time. Time. "Hurry! Hurry! Hurry, or you'll be too late!"—For what?

* * *

The hand of Winter begins to reach towards the world. Here at Yaquitepec the movement is only a gentle stirring, as yet. But there is warning in it. Warning that the winter wood must be gotten in; that the carefree methods of summer fuel-gathering will no longer suffice. There must be a generous woodpile against storms. It is a problem that we face each year, and one that must be attacked well in advance. For it seems that no matter how high a stack of dead juniper wood and ancient mescal butts we collect in the fall, winter demands always manage to get away with every scrap of it.

So Rider and I devote every opportunity these days to wood packing. Sometimes Rudyard comes along. But, though he is intensely eager, his little legs are short yet for hazardous rock scrambling and for long trips. We have a brand new specially designed pack-board this year which makes the home-bringing of the loads much easier. Some day Yaquitepec will go "modern" and add a faithful burro, or a pair of them, to the establishment.

And, so doing, we will, of course, begin within our own immediate sphere, another age-old cycle. All things move in cycles—and all according to immutable laws. Smooth infallible automatic laws of action and re-action, by which everything and every happening of the universe, either good or evil, carries with it, in its borning, the seed of its own destruction.

And where does this concern the burro, you ask? Well, in its own personal "cycle" it concerns the burro a great deal. But what we have reference to, particularly, is own concern. For the acquisition of a beast of burden is one of the first steps along the path of man's desire for greater ease. A simple step—and a long, long path. Very pleasant, some stretches of it. But the inevitable end of it is grim ruin, physical, individual and national. The beast of burden makes life a little easier. The machine makes it easier still. It is easier to ride in a cart than to walk. Easier still in an automobile; easier yet in an airplane. Pleasant the road— and deadly. But it is the law. And it is the law also that, beyond the inevitable ruin, starts again the hard, lonely little path of toil and sweat. "It can't happen here—or again," you may say. "Times have changed; we are more enlightened now. We have harnessed and conquered the forces of nature. We are just emerging upon man's most glorious epoch and destiny."

An ocotillo to be used for firewood or building material.

So? Well, who would dispute. And does it really matter? Meanwhile the winds come on whispering feet across the old desert, stirring the dead grass over shattered bits of forgotten pottery and playing with the dust of sea creatures that only "yesterday," in the depths of an ocean that "would last forever" called these very spots home.

Deserts and oceans are the record keepers of cycles. But only to a limited degree. It is in a desert that you can dig in the ruins of great Babylon, where now little lizards sun themselves in the dust of the one-time palaces of "mighty" kings. But when you have dug down and down through all the strata of man's building of cities, age after age, one upon another—with the dust-built drift of human forgetfulness and oblivion separating each from each like blank leaves in a printed book—you come finally to a layer where, deep down, the earth holds silence as to record and in blank sand and stone guards her secrets tight lipped. But if you turn away in your "science" and smug certainty, satisfied that you have come to both final endings and first beginnings, there will be grey ghosts among the dusty tombs and the heaps of shattered pots to laugh at you. For, before the "very first" tombs and broken pots, there were still other tombs and broken pots. Before the sand and the gravel and the deep granite there was the fire-mist. And before the fire-mist there was other sand and gravel and other granite. And before that…

But why grope the universe with the feeble flame of a sputtering match? How old is the desert wind? Or the desert stars. And what has all this to do with carrying firewood for winter and plans for a burro? Well, *quién sabe?* But maybe more than some might think.

And so, on these things, and on many another, Rider and I muse and speculate as we tramp over the rocks gathering sticks. We classify these expeditions as "work." And work they are from the point of industry and the expenditure of lots of physical energy. But it is natural "work" of the sort that the Great Spirit, in His wisdom, designed for all His creatures. Work such as the birds do, and the foxes and the squirrels and the packrats and the hard-working beavers. Work of this sort is a natural thing. It is something you can sing over as you do it—as do the birds. It is a very different thing from that black slavery which man has invented.

Man's work too often isn't work. It is "toil." A different thing; a grimmer thing. No bird or animal or other industrious wild thing "toils"—except such misguided creatures as the ants and the bees and others of their ilk who are fanatical followers of some crazed "ism" that submerges the individual to the "good of the mass." They are very busy, seemingly, on some "plan." Getting somewhere—or nowhere at all. For brilliant examples of utter dumbness and intellectual depravity I commend you to these "intelligent" mass slaves.

Lots of brown moths were whirling over the rocks as we came home yesterday with our last load of wood of the afternoon. The wind across the shoulder of the mountain was brisk and in the swirl of it the big brown flutterers, each of them brilliantly splashed with scarlet, went scattering and blowing across the ridges like an eddying drift of autumn leaves. Across the rim of the mountain they were trailing away out of sight into the dimness of the far grey desert. Shadows lay there, for the sun was setting, and the jagged peaks to westward stretched a ragged coverlet of indigo haze across all the lowlands. Lances of dying sunlight fell through the gaps on the rim of the world and bathed the summit of Ghost Mountain in a shimmer of golden pink, through which we moved with the unreality of ghosts, throwing long, unearthly shadows. On the trail, as he carried carefully the fragments of ancient sea shells that he had picked up away back on the ridge, Rider found another whitened shell—that of a long dead desert snail—and beside it a brown, lichen-crusted chip of pottery, with the faint imprint of the potter's fingertip still upon it....Whose fingertip? And how long ago?

Tanya, Victoria and Rudyard were in the doorway to welcome us, and behind them, in the house, the candles were already lit. The faint, aromatic odor of juniper smoke and the warmly sweet fragrance of newly baked corn bread. Sunset and dark. Another day.

Desert Refuge 5
(December 1941)

REAL winter draws closer to Ghost Mountain. But these present fall days are full of a charm that is all their own. On the ridges the yellow flowers of the *ramarillos* [rabbitbrush] are still in evidence and invite the attentions of methodical bees. The sun has lost its fierce fire. But the rocks glow warm at noonday and the wandering breezes that come to whisper around the walls of Yaquitepec still have tales to tell of drowsy solitudes and the clean fragrance of yucca-studded, sunglinted washes where the hours, marked only by the slow-moving shadows of greasewood and of ocotillo, drift by in silence that is marred by no tick of clock or pulse of progress.

Except when it storms. But that is another story. Storms are another mood, the charm of the desert lies in its ever changing moods. Fierce. Tempestuous. Vibrant with life and passion. Like a primitive woman, blending fierce love and savage fury. There lies the fascination of the desert. Do you seek for something calm and ordered, methodic, dependable—and listlessly "dead"? Then turn your search elsewhere; you will not find it here. Civilized man seeks stability for security—and its accompanying stagnation and ultimate decay and ruin. But nature is wiser. Not along flower scented paths does real development, either of soul or body, lie.

Turn back the pages of recorded history. There you will find that it was always the barbarian—he who knew heat and cold and bitter privation—who came forth, time and again, from his bleak wildernesses and overthrew the pampered dwellers in the cities of ease…himself, in turn, to succumb to luxury and in time be overthrown by his hard-muscled barbarian successor. Wave upon wave from the north and from the wastelands. Hard ice melting in the tropic sun. But that is nature's way. Flow and ebb. Storm and sun. Thus does she preserve the balance. Do not look for advancement in "mass." It is not done. It is done by the *atom*—by the *individual*.

* * *

These are the evenings of fires, and the primitive thrill and family bond that the leaping flames of the hearth can waken as can nothing else. We are building a new fireplace at Yaquitepec. Sometimes we think that if we are not careful we shall find ourselves dwelling in a fireplace instead of a house—that the fireplaces, by sheer weight of numbers, will swallow the rest of the building. There are four of them now—existent—incomplete—and just commenced. Of one the foundation only has been started. That will be the big one. Another has its side walls half up—that is to be a double one that will warm two rooms. The third is the old standby, whose fire-blackened maw, yawning beneath our big adobe stove, has flung cheer already over a range of desert winters.

The fourth is an addition that rises now, with mud and granite rocks, beside the "old faithful." Perhaps we should call it the Wild Geese Fireplace. For the wild geese started its building by their high, lone honking one night against the desert stars. Going south. And *early*. We took counsel together. This was another "sign" in a string of signs that spoke of the possibility of a hard, cold winter. "We cannot finish the new room and its big fireplace in time," we said. "And we may need, this year, more warmth than the old stove can give. The quickest way is to build a brand new fireplace."

So, in the course of time—things move slowly at Yaquitepec, not because of indolence but because there are many other things to do—the workmen assembled as for the building of the pyramids. And the seven-year-old lugged rocks. And the three-year-old fetched mud—in an old can. And the one-year-old sat in her high chair and yelped encouragement. And Pharaoh—himself—gat him his trowel and hefted him his hammer and began the fireplace. A good fireplace. And now it is all but finished. Adjoining the old stove, and with an arrangement of smoke flues that would be an architect's nightmare, its yawning mouth will swallow with ease the very largest mescal butt that grows upon Ghost Mountain. Or log of juniper. "Blow, blow, ye bitter winter winds!" The flames will roar and the sparks crackle. A successful fireplace! Victoria approves it. "Bee Hay!" she remarks solemnly every time she looks at it. Victoria has academic leanings. She confers B.A. degrees upon everything that strikes her fancy. She has 12 teeth now and is walking and starting to talk.

A week ago Rider and I voted ourselves a day's vacation and went on a long tramp. Rider looks forward eagerly to these excursions which constitute a rare holiday in the regular routine of school lessons. Already he is a veteran "prospector." But his prospecting is for strange plants and bits of pottery and bugs, for which he totes along a little sack and a small paper box or two. This time we abandoned our mountain and struck out across the lower desert, among the barren rocky buttes and the creosote-studded slopes and washes. The day was perfect; one of those glowing days of desert fall when the sun-warmth is just right for comfort and one can tramp for miles and miles without fatigue. Far off the distant mountains stabbed a sky that was a dazzling blue. The nearer ridges glowed above us in a mosaic of tumbled boulders and shadow-etched clefts. Through the crystalline air the gnarled junipers that clung along their escarpments seemed close enough to touch. A sleepy breeze drifted from the hills, carrying with it the winey, aromatic tang of greasewood and *ramarillo* [rabbitbrush] and yucca and the odor of clean space. Underfoot the gravelly earth, weatherings of ages from the gaunt, surrounding mountains, crunched beneath our hide sandals. The grit of it and the soft, occasional rustle of a creosote branch, springing back from the crowding of our bodies, were the only sounds that broke the hush of a vast bowl of desert silence.

And so, through a wilderness of blessed silence—for which years of familiarity have only whetted our appetite—we moved on. We had no plan save to tramp and explore. Chaparral cocks slipped away through the creosotes; an occasional jackrabbit flicked vanishing ears through the cactus.

Under an aged silver cholla near the rocky toe of a ridge we came upon a big mortar hole worn in a flat granite slab. The blunted stone fragment once used for a pestle still lay beside it. The ancients had been here before us. But earth now filled this forgotten grinding bowl. And the brown hands that had held the old pestle have long since returned to earth too. An inquisitive little antelope squirrel perched upon a nearby boulder and watched us with bright, beady eyes; then with a saucy flirt of his tail disappeared merrily—a symbolic atom of bubbling life.

And so, in the glow of midday, amidst a wild clutter of rocks on a lonely ridge, we came to a mine. We came upon it suddenly. And stopped, startled. A mine—or rather an abandoned shaft, such as this was—was about the last thing we would have imagined. We stood staring into it. The shallow shaft was partly filled. In the debris that

formed its bottom lusty bushes grew. On the weathered mound by the opening lay a miner's drill, rust-eaten. On a rock beside it an old knife from which the years had stripped the wooden handle. The gently swaying branches of a big creosote bush wove a moving tapestry of light and shadow over the ancient prospect. In the hushed stillness one listened instinctively for footsteps. And heard none.

"I guess," said Rider presently, "this is 'The Lost Pick' mine." He pointed into the deeper shadows at the base of the creosote bush. And there lay the pick. Old and rusty as the drill, and with its handle weathered into crumbling grey rottenness. I stepped softly across and picked it up.

The Lost Pick mine! Was this abandoned shaft really the one to which a desert wanderer had referred more than two years ago? Perhaps. We had almost forgotten. There had been several nebulous lost mines in the rambling reminiscences of the old man. The "Lost Pick." The "Lost Blanket Roll." The "Lost Canteen." Rambling, disconnected stories—yarns which the narrator himself hardly troubled to believe. Fabric of dreams and desert shadows; the dancing mirage of gold—which it is more blessed to pursue than to find. A fairy tale. Yet here was the old pick—and the old shaft. We stared curiously into the shallow digging and poked speculatively at the sides with the old pickhead. Rider even clambered into the hole—and promptly forgot gold in the excitement of finding a perfectly magnificent specimen of a dead and dried beetle.

No, there wasn't any gold there. At least not the foolish kind of yellow stuff that humanity sells its soul for. There was gold of the sun and the silence and the whisper of the wind. And—for us—treasure in the shape of the old pickhead which despite its years of weathering was in excellent order. For a long time we dwellers on Ghost Mountain, had needed a pick. And had been forced to do without one.

So we took our prize and went away as softly as we had come. We had found the "Lost Pick Mine"—and we lost it again, leaving it to its memories and its silence. There is no trail and we shall not tell. Someone—sometime—dug there in hopes. Let the peace of the desert hold safe its memories.

But the old pickhead, on a new handle, is now part of the Yaquitepec tool equipment. Despite the fact that we share the Indian belief that it is not lucky to meddle with old relics, the pick was something else again. It was "meant." And we took it in gratitude. There is a feel to such things which you will not find in the textbooks.

Maybe we are superstitious. Well, the desert Indians were superstitious too.

Desert Refuge 6
(January 1942)

THE earth—and the desert—wings on towards the turn of the year. Cold days of storm mixed with days when the sunshine sparkles over Ghost Mountain as warmly as in late spring.

There is this great charm to the desert: every season seems to be, of itself, perfect. In the summer when the heat drenches mountain and lowland and weaves fantasies of mirage across the swimming distance we assure ourselves solemnly that now the desert really is at its best. Then come fall and winter. And the storms beat and the house fires roar. And there is crisp joy in the tangy air. And the southern-drifted sun comes up each morning in sunrises that are the most beautiful to be found in all the world—heaving up from a vast couch of mysterious blue velvet and wading knee-deep through all the gold and pearls and rubies and flashing diamonds of ten thousand overturned treasure chests to light the fires of day. Beauty in prodigal measure. And, revelling in it all, we forget. And we declare with equal assurance that undoubtedly fall and winter are the desert's best seasons.

But it is the same old tale in spring. When all the facts are assembled, we have to admit we have been hasty. There are no "best" seasons on the desert; or rather, they are all "best." At least so they seem to us. Which is perhaps to be taken as a confession of a satisfied frame of mind. But then that is the sort of peace and contentment that the desert gives, if only one will live close to its heart.

* * *

Last night, misled by sky indications, Rider and Rudyard put out pans of water, in the gloating hope that it would freeze. Ice somehow holds a fascination for them. And the winter storms that sometimes mantle Ghost Mountain in snow are hailed as supreme holidays. But this time it was a false alarm and the patter of eager bare feet and the clack of the wide-flung door which roused the chill house in the early dawn, gave advance notice only to murmurs of disappointment.

"Huh! Just *water!* Why *didn't* it freeze?"

Then a sudden yell: "Daddy! Mother! Quick! Quick! Get up! Come and look at the sea!"

It took several yells—and much frantic urging. For only the enthusiasm of youth finds attraction in leaping from a warm bed to dash forth into a chilly desert dawn. However, protesting excuses and violent threats were alike ineffective. And sleep, with a couple of excited young savages clamoring at the bedside, was out of the question. We got up finally and with Victoria, blanket wrapped and voicing no uncertain protests, tramped out into the cold.

And stood suddenly still, ashamed of our unwillingness. The sight that greeted our sleepy eyes was almost terrifying in its weird magnificence. Grey fog filled the great desert valley below us. High above it we looked out over its tumbled upper surface as over the surface of a stormy sea. This was by no means the first time that we had beheld the mist phantom of the old ocean that long ago rolled in this now dry sea bed. But it was the first time we had seen it in such terrible reality. Ghosts! You talk of ghosts! Well, here in grim actuality was the ghost of a great sea. And in a sullen, angry mood. Above it, here and there in the cold morning light, the hard, barren summits of desert mountains projected as the lonely islands they had once been. And against them dashed the spume of grey waves. You could see the smoky spray drifting to leeward, tossing in the wind. Great grey rollers came plunging in and broke upon the rocks; leagues and leagues of heaving water that lunged in silent thunder against the very foot of Ghost Mountain.

Down below, at our very feet, was a rocky beach and a weird black blot of shadow that lifted and rolled in the foam in uncanny semblance of the wreck of an ancient ship. Strange shaped. An old thing. The wind was coming out of the east and it was cold. There was a sense of fear in it. One had an uneasy sensation of looking at something that was long dead; of something so far out of the forgotten past that it was frightening. For in spite of all our reasoning, it is sometimes frightening to be brought abruptly face to face with truth. With stark proof of the deathlessness of that substance out of which we and our whole universe are fashioned; proof of the thing which we call immortality. A fact of the universe; so fundamental, so plainly displayed. Yet men go mad, seeking frantically in musty books for the thing that is ever before their eyes.

The naked savage of the deserts and the mountains is closer to the truth than his civilized brother. The savage knows that nothing ever really dies or completely disappears. He knows these things without need of reasoning because he is still close to the source of his being; his feet have not travelled so far along the dubious road of "progress." The savage shows his implicit faith in immortality by such actions as putting out dishes of food for the spirits of the dead to eat…And for this demonstration of a supreme faith in something we prate about glibly—and mostly *do not* believe in—we dub the savage as depraved and superstitious. And we send missionaries to him—to make him like ourselves.

The sun rose presently and the ghostly sea began to break up. We went inside and started a fire for breakfast. We were all quite silent and thoughtful. Including the youngsters.

* * *

Tanya made the Christmas puddings today. They are made early and put away to mellow. Once, tied in the stout cloths in which they were boiled, we used to hang them from a ceiling beam in old fashioned style. Until one year, going blithely to unhook the New Year's day pudding, to make it hot for dinner, we found only a shell. The suspending string was there, and the pudding cloth, and the sturdy shape and semblance of a hearty pudding. But all of the inside was gone. There was a neat round hole in the top of the cloth, near where the string was tied. Some industrious little squirrel had also liked the pudding. Busily, with many trips, while we slept, he had hollowed out the pudding and carried all of it away.

Now we cook our puddings in tin cans, boiling them in a big iron kettle which swings by a chain over a fire of juniper chunks and ancient weather-hardened mescal roots. And we store them away on a shelf in a tightly screened cupboard. Not yet is the whole house rodent-tight. And bright-eyed friendly little marauders come along the beams at night, or perch on the high top of the fireplace, daintily nibbling at crumbs.

Pudding making is an event. Attended by much cheerful chatter, and frequent shrieks of delight. Everyone has to have a stir at the pudding for sentiment's sake. Even Victoria had her turn. Braced firmly on sturdy little legs she clutched the spoon with both hands and lunged determinedly at the batter in the mixing bowl which Tanya held down to her. She wrinkled up her mouth and laughed and got batter on the tip of her nose. "Such funny customs my family have," Victoria seemed to be reflecting. But she relinquished her batter spoon unwillingly—and only after a bribe of raisins in a cup. Tanya has to watch the raisins. Else there would be none of them in the pudding. The hovering sprites who circle the mixing bowl are nimble fingered and very fond of raisins and citron.

But this event of pudding making serves to bring home to us the fact that another year at Yaquitepec is almost over. Over—and it seems only yesterday that we were beginning it. So fast the years go! It has been a happy year for us on our desert mountain. So many new friends and so many cheery contacts with old ones. Almost all of these contacts, old and new, have been through the far stretching net of the postal system. But these good friends whom we have never seen are as real to us as though we had wrung their hands and looked into their eyes. The thin lines of the winging letters are very real and very strong bonds of friendship.

If there be a shadow to cloud the bright retrospect of the year it is that many of these good friends have had often to wait long for answers to their letters. But this is something which we cannot help. Our days are crowded with tasks. Sometimes there is scant time for writing. The spirit is more than willing, but the physical flesh is limited as to accomplishment. But perhaps our worry is needless. Friends—especially desert friends—need little explanation or apology. They understand.

Soon now Rider and I will go out across the flanks of Ghost Mountain on our annual Christmas tree hunt. Usually it is a long trip, for the Christmas tree is selected with care. It is a tiny one always—a mere branch of desert mountain juniper in truth. But it must be a symmetrical branch, one that looks like a real little tree. And its cutting must inflict no great injury upon the tree from which it is taken. These Ghost Mountain junipers are of slow growth and most of them are very old. A count of the rings on dead ones leaves one a little awed. Not wantonly, even for Christmas, must one of these sturdy living things—fellow sharers with ourselves of the all pervading life of the Great Spirit—be injured.

* * *

Rudyard has just called me out to inspect his "mine of pwecious stones." It proves to be a shallow hole which he has dug in the lee of an ancient granite boulder. He has filled the depression carefully with a miscellaneous collection of granite chips, bits of limestone, and lumps of dry clay. "See," he says, swelling with all the pride of the proprietor, "I c'lected them all myself. Pwecious stones! Jus' as good as silver an' diamonds. See, Daddy!"

So I complimented him on his industry and left him happily fingering his hoard while I came back to the typewriter.

"Precious stones!" Bits of clay and scraps of granite—"Just as good as silver and diamonds. See, Daddy."

And I have seen. And I am thoughtful. Not without cause wrote the ancient writer, in the ancient Book, so long ago: "Out of the mouths of babes and sucklings ye shall obtain wisdom."

Desert Refuge 7
(February 1942)

SO CHRISTMAS is over and another New Year is well launched upon its flight. We took down the tree today stripping it of its finery and carrying it up beyond the garden terrace amidst the boulders to the little open air storage space to which all Yaquitepec Christmas trees proceed after their reign is over.

A melancholy business this, consigning a friend of gladness to oblivion. At one time, when he was younger, Rider invariably wept at this "burial" of the tree. Now, though he no longer sheds tears, he is always silent, as are all of us. We always put off the doleful task as long as possible. And this time, due to Rudyard's entreaties, we did not dismantle it until well after the New Year was established. The tree is a symbol. And as we lay it away we always recall "The Fir Tree"—Hans Andersen's charming little fairy story on the subject.

But it was a grand and memorable Christmas—and we are still picking up from the most unlikely places scraps and tatters of colored rubber, remnants of gay balloons. Rudyard is crazy about balloons. Which would be all right if he were not also possessed of a gift—amounting to positive genius—for bursting them. Always unintentionally. Santa never fails to bring him balloons. And always Christmas day, with its detonations sounds as though Ghost Mountain were the center of an air raid.

Yes, the youngsters had a wonderful Christmas. Especially Victoria. Last year she met the season with the mild tolerance of infancy; this time, with all the vigor of a most precocious young lady of 15 months, she welcomed it with hilarity. Victoria has lots of strength and vivacity. She fought stoutly all proffered offers of assistance and sailed into the job of unlimbering her well stuffed stocking with zest. Soon she was entirely hidden in a violently agitated mound of crumpled tissue paper and tie ribbons. Every once in a while, like a seal she would come up for air; then, shrieking in excited joy, would disappear again beneath the litter. Shamelessly she stole all the show. Rider and Rudyard, grubbing in hastily opened boxes and wrestling with the knots of packages, didn't get a look in. Which bothered Rider not at all. But Rudyard, still with memories of the time when he was the youngest, must have felt a bit jealous. For he observed loftily, between philosophic helpings to a box of candy, "You have jus' *got* to excuse her, Mother. She is weally only a *very* little girl yet."

A grand holiday season. Not only did Santa leave a generous portion of his sleigh load to delight the hearts of our three little "desert Indians," but there were many other packages and cards. Gifts and cheery greeting cards from friends everywhere. A lot of these packages and cards, due to the hit or miss system of our widely spaced trips to the post office, did not arrive for Christmas day. But we got them before New Year. And the Yaquitepec observance of Christmas takes in the whole week any-

how, so it was just the same. It gives us a warm, crinkly feeling around the heart, these remembrances from folks whom we have never met. There will be many happy letters to write in answer. They will go out as fast as we can manage it. Till then, however, to all, these words are a partial, happy acknowledgment.

* * *

The weather today is beautiful; one could believe it was midspring. On the window sill of the little one room house, set off by itself among the rocks, where I usually do my writing, a tiny lizard basks and cocks a watchful eye for flies. He is a writinghouse pet. He has dwelt here a long time and has assumed a different coloring from the lizards that play on the outer rocks. My little friend lacks their flashing colors; his body is darker—almost black. A result of getting less sunlight I suppose, for he seldom goes outside. Also he is more stunted in build. A lively little lizard. Pert and active and very friendly. But these differences of size and coloring that mark him off from the general run of wild lizards are very noticeable. Here is another of Nature's sermons without words. Sunlight and freedom are life. Confinement and even a slight deprivation of light and air mean degeneration.

Not that my little "civilized" lizard isn't some lizard in his own eyes. He acts as though he were very proud of the education which he has doubtless absorbed from the many books over which he scrambles in mad pursuit of flies. Sometimes with a prodigious leap he lands on the moving carriage of my typewriter and has to be carefully chased off to save him from being jammed in the mechanism! An industrious hunter. The amount of insects that one of these little fly lizards can consume is tremendous. The daring ones get away with bees—though how they avoid stings is something which I have never solved. I have seen them gulp and look a little surprised after the capture and swallowing of a big black bee. But a few moments later they are invariably back on the job again. Possibly a lizard is immune to bee stings.

* * *

A lot of rain drenched Ghost Mountain this fall. Upon some of our new walls it was disastrous; they had not had time to acquire the toughness which comes with age and long drying. If one can protect the summits well it helps immeasurably. And even a good healthy coat of simple whitewash on the face of them is a weather resistant much more potent than it sounds. Summer is really the only time for adobe work. But, unfortunately, we generally have to be sparing in our use of water in the summer.

The scheme that works best for us is to run up a temporary wall of poles, plastered or covered with tar paper.

The interior of Yaquitepec the night after Christmas.
Moonlight and candles illumine the tree and gifts.
The statuettes in the niches were home-modelled and home-cast in metal.

Then, when the roof is on, at our leisure, we build the main mud wall against and behind the temporary one. This is easy, since most of our walls are built up by adding the adobe directly to the wall and not by using individual sun-dried bricks. At one time I had the haunting worry that a wall built in this fashion, indoors, so to speak, would be less strong than one raised in the open air. This doubt bothered me until just lately, when it became necessary to demolish a small section built in this wall, that had been standing for several years. After completing the downright toil required to remove this bit of rock-hard adobe I had no further fears on the subject.

To our notion walls built up of mud rather than by bricks have certain advantages. Not the least of these is that if one feels affluent enough to afford it (not a condition which many Yaquitepec walls have enjoyed) one can work a generous amount of barbed wire into the wall. This reinforcement laid back and forth along the wall every few courses, to be buried in the added mud, is a capital insurance against earthquake damage. And in any case it gives one a warranted sense of confidence in the wall's stability.

Bees are drifting lazily about among the *ramarillo* [rabbitbrush] bushes, seeking chance remaining blossoms. And across the top of the rocks and junipers, faint splashings and much laughter serve to remind me that the Yaquitepec boating season is already in full swing. Oh, yes, to its other attractions Ghost Mountain now adds canoeing. Thanks to the rains, the little cistern-to-be lake is brimming and our two ingenious young braves now spend much of their time voyaging on the romantic waters—using my cement mixing trough for a boat and wielding a toy shovel for a paddle. These canoe trips are a great success. But though much game, in the form of amazed chipmunks and startled squirrels can be observed on the shore, the voyagers report dolefully that there are, as yet, no fish in the lake. Well, that will come later. I recall now, with some misgivings, that long ago, I assured a too-curious acquaintance the reason we had selected Ghost Mountain as our homesite was because it was an ideal spot for the raising of goldfish. Which proves that it is *never* safe to depart from the noble example set by George Washington. Dangerous! Setting out maliciously to mislead I may have uttered the sober truth.

* * *

We have had cause enough already to congratulate ourselves on the new fireplace. Even to date it has more than repaid the labor of its building by the good times it has provided during storms. And the amount of mescal butts it has consumed so far is amazing. Queer fuel, these straw-yellow, bristling, dry agaves. One has to be super-cautious in handling them. But long practice develops a sort of subconscious dexterity. We seldom get "stuck" these days, unless by down right carelessness or by unusual accident. Strange fuel! There is savagery in its flaming. The butts do not last long. A furious heat, then they die down. But in death they are weirdly beautiful. Fire roses—flowers of glowing ember, perfect in every leaf. Then slowly crumbling to grey ash.

We had one thing to do in connection with the fireplace building that we had not counted on. We had to build the chimney higher to get an increase in draught. Casting about for a quick way to do this we had the inspiration to use three empty five gallon honey cans. Tops and bottoms cut out, the can, fastened into a long flue, formed just the core we needed. With the outside loosely wrapped in some old chicken wire this improvised tin pipe, set upon the summit of our slender chimney, solved the extension problem to perfection. Now we are plastering the outside of the square tin core with cement—a job made easy by the chicken wire wrapping. Not yet has all the cement casing been put on. But it will be when the cement bin has been replenished. Which is the usual way with Yaquitepec improvements. Rarely is a job completed in one run. Usually there are several sessions, with long waits between. And a half dozen jobs that are running simultaneously. It is this, somehow, that gives life its spice.

* * *

And so in confidence—the confidence that one draws from the good earth and the stars and the healing strength of the desert silence—we take our course out along the new trail across Nineteen Hundred and Forty-two. What will the year bring? *Quién sabe?* Why should one speculate. It will bring what it will bring. And I am not of the melancholy frame of mind of so many of my old Mexican friends down on the border who, years ago, when mulling over the havoc and upheavals of politics and revolution which had forced them to flee from their beloved "patria" would declare dolefully: "*No hay garantias,* señor. *No hay garantias!* "

No, it is true that there are no guarantees. Less perhaps now than ever. But it is well to reflect also that perhaps there never have really been any "*garantias.*" Life is a stormy passage at the best. And of necessity it must be passed dangerously. Not all the perils that threaten it lie in war or in unleashed evil. Stagnation and greed and false values will wreck the body and spirit as surely as will violence. And, as for money or possessions, over which so many tremble, fearing the loss, these are less than a puff of dust on a desert trail. The thing that makes or mars a man or a nation is the thing that cannot be seen—

the intangible *quality* of the Spirit that dwells within. That is the anything that really matters.

Desert Refuge 8
(March 1942)

THE lizards are coming out again on Ghost Mountain. For quite a period—all through the severe weather—they have been holed up in snug crevices and in deep runways beneath boulders. Now, tempted by increasing warm days, they are returning to their regular beats. A cheerful note. We have a happy, busy lizard population around Yaquitepec. Their jewelled scales as they scurry to and fro seem to give an added glitter to the sunlight. Each year their brief winter absence gives us a sense of real loss.

But the lizards have no taste for snow. And Ghost Mountain has had its share of the white, driving flakes this season. Even Rider and Rudyard—that pair of enthusiastic wishers for "ice"—got almost enough of chill blasts and frozen cistern surfaces. But they had a grand time snowballing each other; wild, hilarious romps outside, spaced by breathless dashes indoors to warm their bare feet.

Snow does not last long on Ghost Mountain. Usually a few brief hours and it is gone. But while it is here the grim rocks and the cactus tangled ridges are a breath-taking fairyland of glittering beauty.

Victoria, I think, got the greatest thrill from the storms. To her it was a first experience and a tremendously puzzling thing. She could not keep away from the window, running to peer out! Then trotting back to tug at us with insistent fingers until we too should come to look. Over and over again. "Snow" we told her. And she stared at us, a deep wonderment in her blue eyes. "No," she repeated softly, "No." She reached her little hand towards the flakes, whirling, like a cloud of fluttering white moths just outside the window pane. "No." This miracle held her in awed silence; even her big Christmas dolly was forgotten for a while. How fresh and wonderful is the world when one is young. Which reflection leads one to remember sorrowfully that it is not the world or the everlasting miracles of life which change their freshness. It is only that with the years we grow calloused. We burrow

Rudyard (left) and Rider in the snow.

deep under a self-made shell of trivialities and falsity and inhibitions.

But spells of cold weather are ideal for dipping candles. There is something about a candle, the soft friendly glow that makes night shadows assume their real character of cheerfulness. Shadows are temperamental things. They were never intended to be grim. The harsh glare of civilized electric light has made hatchet-faced villains of them; sinister, merciless, soulless things that haunt the dark corners of a mechanical age. But the shadows of firelight and candlelight are man's friends. The candlelight shadows that weave joyous tapestries and chase each other in and out of archways and across the whitewashed walls of Yaquitepec are a happy breed. They play pranks with the roving white-footed mice; luring them on with promise of concealment, then impishly whisking aside to reveal the startled, bright-eyed explorer in the very midst of his cautious investigation of cake box or flour bin. Inquisitive shadows. They perch in rows along the roof beams watching us like attentive little gnomes, very still and well behaved. Then, suddenly, as the desert wind chuckles through a crack, they are gone, tumbling over each other in a frantic rush for safety.

It is impossible to regard our candlelight desert shadows as anything else than friends. Victoria tries to catch them toddling determinedly through the darker reaches beyond the long table and snatching with eager fingers. She has had no luck so far. But she comes back each time with a whimsical screwed-up grin and a determined hunch of her little shoulders that says as plainly as words, "Never you mind. You just wait."

Candles, in their aristocracy, should be made of beeswax. There is nothing so clearly glowing and so vital as a beeswax candle. But not always is our supply of beeswax equal to the demand. Then we substitute paraffin, with a moderate mixture of tallow, which does well enough. Candles are a cold weather item anyway. With the approach of summer all the Yaquitepec candles are hustled into the cellar. Any that are forgotten are not long-lived as candles; they wilt into pools of grease.

Dipping candles is a job that takes patience. But it is lots of fun and well spiced with a flavor of old-time romance. Perched in the window seat the other day, plowing through his school reader, Rider was wildly excited by the picture and story of candle dipping in early Colonial days. Exactly the same method that we ourselves use. The orderly rows of cotton wicks hung on little wooden rods; the kettle of hot wax. Each rod of wicks dipped quickly down into the hot wax and withdrawn, to be set aside on a rack or across chair backs for the hanging dips to cool while the next rod of wicks is dipped. Then, when all rods have been dipped, back again to the first. And so

on, over and over, till the candles are thick enough. For gay effect, after all the dips are done and are hanging plump and firm and white we generally dip them once or twice more in another kettle of wax that has been colored red or blue or green. A colored candle doesn't burn any better, but it looks festive. Life is the better for cheery little touches of color.

A little while back we made ourselves a new chandelier—a word which today, with its modern version of a glittering cluster of electric bulbs, it is hard sometimes to remember, simply means "candle holder." Ours, however, hold no commission from modernity. We simply took a hefty limb of desert mesquite and hewed it with an axe until the top side was flat, and the log, everywhere, was cut away so as to show the warm, rich, brown and yellow tints of the inner wood. Then, in the flat side we bored five holes, candle diameter, and about an inch and a quarter deep, at equal distances along its length; cutting around each, with a chisel, a shallow trough to catch the wax gutterings. With a short length of old iron chain attached to each end of the log, by which to swing it from the ceiling beams, and with a hasty coat of oil to bring out the fine, rich grain of the mesquite wood, our chandelier was complete. Not a large one. But the ceilings of Yaquitepec are low, anyhow; and the room is not wide. When the curtains are drawn against the gathering desert evening shadows our mesquite log chandelier with its five wavering-flamed candles, standing steadfast like a line of George Washington's soldiers, gives light and cheer enough.

Candles! There is a romance to candles. And there is something else to their soft, mellow light that is worth remembering. Candle light, like old fashioned lamplight, is a *natural* light, the same as firelight. Some of these days when you have been listening to the enthusiastic remarks of some of our proponents of modern lighting you might do well to go out and stand on a street corner and count the passersby—old men to mere infants—who are wearing glasses. Then you may like to remember that the desert Indians—all primitive American Indians—had marvelous eyesight. And it may give you food for thought to reflect on the fact that the only artificial light these primitives knew was the light of torch and of campfire.

* * *

Many of our Ghost Mountain juniper trees these days are rusty brown and yellow with clustering myriads of flower cones; tiny things about the size of an extra plump grain of wheat. And when one brushes past the trees the bloom-dust whirls out in stifling clouds. These little cones, though, have other uses. For a long while Rider and I, tramping over the rocky slopes on fuel gathering expeditions, were puzzled by the neat little collections of green juniper bouquets we would come across in the most un-expected places. Sometimes these little tufts of twigs and leaves, surprisingly regular in size and all clipped in or-derly manner from the trees, were piled beneath squaw-tea bushes, sometimes in the shelter of chollas, sometimes in clefts between boulders.

We knew that it was the work of packrats, because the old patriarch, who for years has made his home in the box back of our discarded car, had covered the whole floor of his quarters with the green bunches. But the reason for it all was a mystery. Rider's joking explanation that all the packrats were putting up Christmas decorations soon failed to satisfy. For the accumulation of piles of green-ery persisted long after even the most ignorant rat must have known that Santa Claus had gone back to his home at the North Pole.

Then, by accident, we discovered the truth. The busy packrats were eating the juniper flower-cones. Nimbly they would climb the branches and nip off a cone-laden tuft, just as we would pick a bunch of grapes. Then they would race to a place of safety and leisurely proceed to nibble off every cone, abandoning the stripped bunch and returning for another. Thus the little heaps of plucked branch tufts grew. We had known, of course, of the fond-ness of desert animals for the mature juniper berries—relished by many besides the antelope squirrels and the coyotes—but this was our first introduction to flower cone harvesting.

The tiny cones are not bad eating, if one can forgive a distinct turpentine flavor. Their chief human disadvan-tage is that it takes a huge quantity of them to make a man-sized meal—in which bulk the turpentine might pro-duce unpleasant results. The little rodents that feast upon them, however, have the benefit of more equal propor-tion. For its animal children the desert is, in many re-spects, a land of plenty; even if it is also a region of eternal strife, where life depends for its existence, on unceasing vigilance.

Desert Refuge 9
(April 1942)

THIS morning, when I sat down to the typewriter, it would not work. The keys tangled and jammed, even the carriage had locked itself immovable. The ma-chine is of the "noiseless" variety and hard to peer into.

The family was called in consultation. We gathered round the mechanism as surgeons about the bedside of a patient desperately ill. Rider fetched his Christmas flashlight. By its beam we peered deep into mysterious mechanical cav-erns. Heavens! The whole interior of the machine was carefully crammed full of wheat!

Desert mice! The mystery was solved. But where, we asked ourselves when we had recovered from our as-tonishment, had they gotten the wheat. Then, suddenly, we remembered. A few days previous, Rudyard, running with a can of grain to feed the chukka partridge, had tripped and dropped his burden. Wheat had been scat-tered widely over the gravel floor. We had retrieved all that we could. But night was shutting down and in the gloom we necessarily made a very poor job of it. "Well, anyway, our little mice will enjoy it," we had said. The floor was clean in the morning, so we knew they had found the wheat.

They had stored it all. The typewriter, standing on a high shelf, had been unused for several days. What prompted the little desert workers to carry the grain into this extremely difficult-of-access hiding place is a mys-tery of mouse psychology. It must have been quite a job. Noiseless typewriters have intricate mechanisms. It took us an hour of shaking, and key jiggling, and poking with fine wires, to dislodge the wheat and get the machine working again.

However our Yaquitepec animal friends are remark-ably well behaved. White footed mice, pocket mice and packrats have all alike accepted us as part of their world and give us very little trouble. Once in a while, in moving some box or basket that has stood in a quiet corner for a long span, we disturb a terrified mother mouse who, with her half-naked brood of clinging babies, has to be care-fully transferred, nest and all, to some safe place on the outdoors. And more than once we have come upon weird collections of sticks and cholla joints and mescal pods wedged in the spaces behind our storage barrels; proof that an industrious packrat has found, somewhere, an en-trance hole to the porch—usually one that takes us a long time to locate and block. These occurrences however are no more than friendly contacts with our neighbors and serve to remind us that we are all one big family—all of us with busy lives and loves and family problems. Man is

Pocket mouse

so blundering and blind. One wonders sometimes on what grounds he demands mercy from his Creator when he himself gives so little to the wild creatures among whom he lives.

* * *

Last night was warm and at midnight I went out to open up another shutter of our screened sleeping porch. The gravelly earth was hard and chill to bare feet and in the ghostly moonlight the grey rocks and shadowy junipers and mescals had an eerie look, as though one wandered homeless through the dim landscape of some deserted planet. High overhead the moon, just past its first quarter, rode coldly gleaming through the thin grey murk of a cloud-filmed sky. The ghostly reflection of it was wan silver in the dark waters of our little pool. Silence! Not even the whisper of a wind. The silence and mystery of the desert.

Everyone in the house was asleep. Through the unshuttered screens its interior was a dim cavern of hushed shadow and half glimpsed form, through which the low-turned flame of the old ship's lantern gleamed as a soft star of peace. What a strange thing is sleep. And how symbolic. The comforting, protecting arm of the Great Spirit drawn tenderly about tired children at the close of the day.

I did not at once go back into the house. Instead I sat down on the upper of the two rock steps that lead past the cisterns to where the woodpile is. Upon my bare body the chill of the night air struck with a tingling, electric glow that was almost warmth. Far off, through a mist-rift above the shadowy ridges, the North Star gleamed. Almost I seemed to hear the deep, measured breathing of the earth.

I must have sat there a long time, hunched knees to chin, staring out into the silence and the stretching dimness of tumbled rocks. Just how long I do not know, for one does not keep record of such musings. The night air was like a garment of peace, and the overhead arch of the desert stars, appearing and disappearing through rifts in the canopy of haze, was as a glorious procession of the Heavenly Hosts, streaming forward triumphantly across the fields of Paradise.

Peace! Assurance! Joy! A triumphant upwelling of the heart which no temporary storms of disaster and mortality can shadow or destroy. One gets very close to the heart of things, sometimes, in the desert silence. Close to the mysteries which the old Chaldean astrologers traced in the night skies, close to the joy of the desert shepherds who saw the gleaming of the strange Star in the East. Not often, amidst the glare of man's garish lights or the turmoil of man's boasting, can such things be sensed. But always—even through the blatant din that is called "progress"—it brings soothing peace to know that, eternally, beyond the passing tumult, these things ARE.

* * *

Mescal roast time is approaching. Several plants close to the house are already sending up their plump shoots. The crop will not be as generous as last season. That is the way with most desert growths. Everything proceeds in cycles; a high crest is followed by lean years. If one could devote several lifetimes of careful study to this maze of intertwined cycles—varying with each plant and organism—many of the mysteries of Nature might be unlocked.

But this season, in the matter of mescal roasting, we approach the task with one more new scrap of knowledge. Our desert Indian predecessors did not always use their hands or a convenient flat stone, as we had supposed, when digging or uncovering their mescal pits. They sometimes used shovels—wooden shovels.

An interesting discovery. Not so much from the actual fact of the implement itself as for its demonstration of the ordered path of invention and evolution. We had known of the ancient "digging-sticks" for a long time, having unearthed several specimens of these time-weathered ironwood relics from hiding places near long forgotten roasting hearths. But we had never found a shovel. And, until recently, when one was brought to our attention by another desert dweller, we were unaware of their existence.

Comparatively rare, these shovels, apparently. But nevertheless some were in use in ancient times. About 28 inches long from the end of its stumpy handle to the tip of its flat, square blade, the specimen shown us had been discovered hidden away in a crevice under a huge granite boulder not far from Ghost Mountain. Carefully hewn from a single piece of wood—and that, seemingly, the rounded slab split from the outside of a large tree—this age-grey relic bore evidence of skillful workmanship, and of much use. How old? Who can say? Long antedating the white man, evidently. The dry air of the desert is kind to wood if it is at all sheltered. What ancient tales of fire-flame and mystery might this grey piece of man-hewn tree trunk reveal if it could speak. Somehow it raised odd, wistful sensations in our hearts as we examined and handled it.

Wood! There is something about wood—man-shaped wood—and also about ancient, man-chipped stone, which stirs the imagination.

The Age of Wood. The Age of Stone. The Age of Bronze. The Age of Iron. Today the Age of Steel. Stages of the trail—the trail of man's progress.

Dawn to Dark. The old, old trail. A long trail. It is good that upon it there are sections where one finds chipped flints and wooden tools. And it is good, sometimes, even in an age of "efficiency" to stand naked and free upon a high rock in the chill dawn and watch as did primitive man the sun flame up in glory across an untamed wilderness. Thus, and thus simply, may man discover the Great Spirit in his own soul. When sham and hypocrisy and artificiality are shed, assurance is born in a steady burning flame of faith and beauty that needs no progress or logic for its adorning. Did you ever pause to muse upon that mysterious Stone Age race, called sometimes the Cro-Magnons, whose trace is preserved in the dim grottos of Europe? There are things about them worth musing over. Some of their art work, still to be found in deep caverns, is remarkably skillful and fine.

* * *

Bees droning in the desert sunshine. And out along the terrace wall in front of the house a couple of speculative butterflies hovering over the new heads of the chia sage. In the kitchen, before the adobe stove, Tanya is expertly flipping whole wheat *tortillas* onto and off a sheet of tin, flattened from a five gallon honey can. The tin is smoking hot. Beneath it are flames of juniper sticks and mescal leaves. Primitive? Yes.

Flick! And the thin, round wafer of dough drops upon the hot surface. A momentary toasting. Then over, on the reverse side. Then as swiftly off onto the waiting plate. Or into an eager, outstretched hand. For she is ringed with an attentive, appreciative audience. There is nothing quite so primitively toothsome as a new-made *tortilla*, fresh from the fire. Even little Victoria dances and shouts, stretching eager baby fingers and munching with a satisfaction that leaves no doubt as to its wholesomeness. She has nothing to be ashamed of in her appetite, which matches that of her two brothers. When the three of them decide to sit in on a *tortilla* bake Tanya is lucky if she has anything besides an empty plate to show at the conclusion of her labors.

Desert Refuge 10
(May 1942)

RUDYARD and I were under the shade of the ramada. It was a warm, drowsy afternoon and the sleepy little breeze that came stirring through the junipers carries with it the faint incense of desert flowers. Everything was very quiet and still. All around us the rock-tumbled summit of Ghost Mountain lay glowing in the sun. Lizards basked on the warm boulders and the sharp, dark shadows of the junipers were like patterns cut from black paper.

In the house Tanya was hushing Victoria to her afternoon nap; and at the table Rider was wrestling with his daily arithmetic lesson. Occasionally, according to the manner in which the problems proceeded, he emitted soft, under-breath sighs or growls or chuckles. The faint, intermittent sounds seemed to accentuate the silence.

Last week we went upon a spring picnic. It was Rider's idea—a suggestion which, in the beginning, encountered a rather chilly welcome from "the Powers," for the work budget was over full. We might as well have spared ourselves the trouble of argument however. Once the magic word "picnic" had been uttered the day was utterly lost.

We surrendered gracefully. I filled a canteen with water and Tanya packed a lunch. And after we had gently, but firmly, dissuaded Rudyard from attempting to lug along about 15 pounds of old stones and other treasures, we set out.

I suppose we at Yaquitepec are abnormally primitive frank rebels, if you will, against the straight jacket and all-too-often hollow mockery of the thing called civilization which perches like a strangling "Old Man of the Sea" upon the shoulders of most of the world. Yet I think we can claim no different urge from that which stirs the heart of almost everyone, no matter how "custom tailored," over this matter of picnics. A good sign! A cheering sign—and with hope in it! See how the most jaded of tired eyes will light; how the most wearied of "finance" saturated bodies will tense and the most rabid addicts of "System" and "Progress" will forget for a moment their jangling tin gods of telephone and machine at the mention of a picnic. Deep down, the seed—the seed of freedom and simplicity which the Great Spirit implanted in every breathing thing—still sleeps. It is not dead. In good time, when man has battered himself weary and bleeding into the dust, it will waken again to save him and to set his feet anew upon the trail.

Thus, we reflected as we tramped happily away across the mountain crest, picking our way along the narrow path that wound among mescals and bisnagas. The morning was perfect; the sort of perfection which seems to exist nowhere else but in the desert at springtime. Rider carried the lunch and Tanya the canteen. I carried little Victoria in a blanket. Rudyard, thwarted in his original plan to tote along "pwecious rocks" and other ballast, carried a scratch pad and a pencil with which to "Dwaw sketches an' wite pomes." Down the trail ahead of us a friendly roadrunner scooted for a few moments, then turned aside and vanished over the rocks with a flirt of his long tail. Far off the dimness of early morning haze still lingered among the buttes and washes of the lowland desert.

At the edge of the ridge, where our steep foot-trail dips downward over the precipitous edge of Ghost Mountain, we stopped and took off our sandals. Bare feet are infinitely safer on these slopes; especially when one carries a precious burden. The loose litter of rocky fragments clicked and gritted underfoot as we made our way carefully downward, and the mica flakes in the stones sparkled in the sunlight as though the trail had been strewn with powdered gold. On the topmost twig of a wind-gnarled juniper a canyon wren watched us, pert-eyed, as we passed and poured forth a sweet trill of song. A grand morning—especially for a picnic.

We were headed for a tiny valley among the rocky buttes that clustered the foot of Ghost Mountain to the north. A microscopic thing, scarce larger than a giant's pocket handkerchief, but we had never been there. And it was not too far off. What better combination than a picnic mixed with exploration?

From the foot of Ghost Mountain we struck off across a space of lowland desert, threading our way between the creosotes and the yuccas and with a wary eye for bristling chollas that grew here and there, half concealed, among the clumped galleta grass. Bees hummed. And presently, in the blackened hollow trunk of an ancient, dead yucca that stood beside the white sands of a little wash, we came upon a big colony of them—a stream of busy workers passing back and forth through a round gnawed hole that probably, in the beginning, had been made by some rat or chipmunk. Peaceable enough, these desert bees—if left alone. Molested they are likely to reveal tempers as ferocious as that of an angered desert Indian. A mixed breed. Most of them are blacks.

We reached the foot of the butte presently and started to climb. The tiny valley that was our objective lay high up, rimmed in a skirt of rocks. The going was tough, but as we clambered upward we came all at once to the trace of an ancient Indian trail. The "old people" had been here before us. Clumps of later-grown cactus and mescals blotted the old path in places and its dim trace, in sections, was deeply trenched and rutted by long years of storm. But it was an infinitely easier route than straight climbing. Slipping and stumbling, following its dim, zig-zag windings, we passed at length over the top of the ridge and down into the little depression that was our goal.

It had been a stiff, breathless climb. But here was reward enough. The tiny valley was a creosote and yucca studded bowl, rimmed by stony ledges. And, used though we were to the beauty of the desert, it looked like a little bit of sunlit fairyland. It was a patterned carpet of gold. Myriads of little yellow flowers grew everywhere between the bushes, so thickly that the foot trod down dozens with every step. The clean white gravel between the plants sparkled in the sunshine like crushed marble. In the deep shade beneath the wide-branching creosotes crowded a luxuriance of sheltered grass, green and tall, its massed verdure lit by the glint of unnumbered blue blossoms which the children promptly christened "corn flowers." Above, the bayonet-fringed heads of the drowsing yuccas lifted great fountain plumes of white, wax-like flowers, round and about which hummingbirds whirred—darting and poising in flashing sparks of color. There was a breeze too. It seemed to belong to the valley, for we had not noticed it before. It stirred softly among the yucca plumes and swayed the long slender branches of the creosotes and fanned a bewildering breath of fairy perfume down the sunlit aisles between the bushes as it went about softly on noiseless feet. It seemed something more than a breeze. Perhaps, as Rider suggested thoughtfully, it was the Spirit of the Flowers.

We ate our lunch in the narrow shade of a clump of yuccas which reared brown-skirted, palm-like trunks above our heads. Out in the warm, still beat of the sun, torch cacti spread great blooms of scarlet, and tiny, gay mimulus blossoms did sentry duty amidst the crowding ranks of yellow daisies. From brush thickets to yucca clumps orioles winged. The heady incense of millions of flowers rose in the warm sunshine and the fan of the breeze stirred rippling waves in the thick masses of the tall grass clumps. The glint of gold from the flowers was dazzling to the eyes. Our spread of blanket was a tiny island in the midst of a gorgeous rug of yellow and white, green, blue and pink.

We finished our simple lunch and then lay and sunned ourselves in the warm drowsy peace, letting our bodies drink deep of the healing strength of the earth. Overhead a couple of desert ravens passed, flapping heavily across the sky and commenting on our presence with a long-spaced, philosophic "chowks." Rudyard wrote a "pome," scribbling industriously weird pencil marks of alleged writing upon his scratch pad. Victoria went to sleep, a tiny fragment of uneaten tortilla in one hand and a bunch of yellow flowers in the other. After a while Rider and Rudyard wandered out to a small clear patch of glinting white gravel and began to build fairy houses. Fashioning them with walls and roofs of carefully collected little flat colored stones, doors and windows and paths and gardens, all complete. It is a favorite play job.

If ever, when wandering through untrodden sections of the wasteland silence, you should come suddenly upon a tiny clearing, wherein cluster a group of little Pueblo Indian houses, shaded by tiny twig trees and with proportionately sized bordering corn patches, all carefully planted with bits of leaf and grass and cactus spines, you may know that you are somewhere in the vicinity of Ghost Mountain and that you have stumbled upon one of Rider's and Rudyard's fairy villages. They build them and go away and leave them, with wistfulness and love and good wishes, in the silence of the desert. They are for the fairies to come and live in. And mayhap the fairies do just that. Why not? Are we all so old and crusted and "scientific" that we do not believe in fairies any more? Of course not! Of course there are fairies! We of Yaquitepec believe in them anyway.

It was almost sunset when we got home. The great ball of day-fire was slipping to its western rest in a flaming glory of crimson and of gold. The long shadows of mountains were marching across the lowland desert. The children were tired as we came up over the last section of the trail and the little homehouse, low crouched among the mescals and giant boulders looked wonderfully welcoming and friendly. A quartet of desert quail whirred away from the lower of our tiny garden terraces as we came up the path. They too had been having a picnic—amongst our radishes. But they had not done much damage.

Marshal looking down into the valley from Yaquitepec.

Desert Refuge 11
(June 1942)

RIDER and I got up very early this morning, just as soon as the cool desert dawn brought light enough to see. There were fresh seeds to plant in the garden frame and we wanted to get the job done before breakfast. Our tiny garden at Yaquitepec would be less than a joke to any one accustomed to the broad sweep of lush, fertile acres. But it is surprising the amount of vegetables its microscopic expanse will yield. Here in North America we have not yet begun even to scratch the possibilities of our land. The average Chinese farm is about an acre and a quarter in area. And we have a long, long way to go yet before necessity brings our limit to anything near that.

A long while ago Bolton Hall wrote a book entitled *Three Acres and Liberty* and another *The Garden Yard*. Old books, now. But they still should be obtainable in most libraries. They are more than worthwhile reading. The truths they set out have a deeper meaning today than ever before. For in that direction—and in that direction only—lies salvation for an industrially maddened world. The Earth! Individual contact with the earth. It is a kind Mother. The Chinese are a nation of small, individual farmers. They have existed for 4,000 years or more; and are probably good for at least another 4,000—if they have the good-sense not to go entirely "modern." It is a fundamental truth that a nation whose roots are deep-struck into the good earth cannot be destroyed.

So Rider and I dug and weeded in the clear, white dawn. Burying all the tiny waste leaves and grass stems deep in the soil for fertilizer, and sowing our seeds—Black Seeded Thompson lettuce this time—in the little vacant spaces between the rows of other growing stuff. The main thing with a garden frame is that you have to keep it busy, as soon as one row is harvested new seed must be planted promptly in the vacant space. And never waste a dead leaf or the tiniest scrap of humus producing material. Dig it all back into the earth. Thus the little plot grows richer and richer—the best and only safe bank in the world. Only too well we remember when our soil was so poor that it would not grow anything. Now it is all hand made and does fairly well, though some of the fertilizer was gathered, and carried home in sacks, over a radius of five miles.

The sun came up as we worked. Somehow we have never yet gotten to the point where a desert sunrise is commonplace. We still invariably exclaim over it, as over some daily recurring miracle that is never twice the same.

This morning, as we ceased our labors a few moments, watching the first point of blinding fire among the rocks of the eastern ridge grow and grow as the mighty circle of the sun heaved up behind the shadow lace of juniper branches and tall mescal poles, it seemed to us—as it always does—to be the most beautiful desert sunrise we had ever beheld. The air was clear and quiet and summery.

Carpenter bees droned and bumbled, and in the long sunrays that came striking through the glistening patches of bunch grass among the granite rocks the whole summit of Ghost Mountain seemed to take fire in waves of dazzling metallic sheen. A humming bird whirred in and lit, delicate as a tuft of thistledown, upon the tip of a gently swaying wand of ocotillo; pausing a moment to peek, with cocked head, at its glinting reflection in the tiny rock pool which Rider keeps filled with water for his wild bird pets. Somewhere up the hill a quail called, and a couple of purple finches winged low across the house roof. From the chimney a pale skein of smoke lifted as Tanya lit the breakfast fire. And against the faint clatter of pots and dishes rose laughter and shrill squeals of delight as Rudyard and Victoria romped on the bed in their regular morning pillow fight. Yes, just another sunrise.

Another day. New life. New hope. New joy. Somewhere there are cannon booming. Steadily, hate maddened, their voices draw closer. With truth was it said, a long time ago: "My house is a house of prayer, and ye have made it a den of thieves!"

These have been busy days, lately. "Cement days"—for we are striving to enlarge the Yaquitepec water reserve. As we grow here in numbers—five now, where in the beginning there were but two—our consumption of water increases alarmingly. Also our gardening increases, and our livestock. The well has not yet been located. Therefore the only answer, so far, is cement. Cement and more cement!

For long we have had a standard joke that when there is sufficient water with which to mix cement there is no cement. And when we have cement, then there is no water to enable us to use it. This time, amazingly, however, we had both—several sacks of the precious stuff and ample water remaining in the outdoor pool to turn it into concrete. So we dug and plastered merrily—establishing, before all our supplies were gone—three new potential reservoirs. One on the slope south of the house; one in a deep excavation among the rocks north of the garden; and another in a depression beside the hollow-topped granite boulder which, when rain full, is known as "Lake Yaquitepec."

No, these new catch basins are not finished—only well started. But we take abundant hope and satisfaction from them, and from the sight of their still thirsty-looking concrete glaring white beneath the turquoise sky. Some-day, in those thirsty depths, there will be cool, gleaming water—water for more garden; for livestock; for every purpose. Life is good. "If you could only see the fine cabbages which I raise with my own hands," wrote that old ex-emperor of Rome proudly, when urged to return to the capital, and to power, "you would not wish me anything so unkind as that I should again assume the hollow pomp of office."

And lately there has been pottery to fire, too. Always a nerve wracking job. For apprehension, like a gloomy owl, perches always upon the shoulders of the potter until his wares come safely from the fire. It was ever thus. The old Greek potters made pilgrimages to the temples and sought, by gifts, to bribe the favor of the gods. For the clay is temperamental and the finest of pots, wrought with loving care and bearing every promise of sturdiness, will crack and shatter in the flame—like so many promising humans who wilt and crumble under the test of adversity. The old-time Indians—and the modern ones too—knew the same troubles. "If the dirt don' like you it

Rudyard (left) shows his clay pot to Rider.

crack right away" a dusky skinned potter advised me once, with glum philosophy. And it is true. The clay, seemingly, has likes and dislikes and whims and notions. Ah, how many gay pots and bottles and jugs and bowls go blithely to the fire—as to the testing furnace of war—and come forth only in the bitterness of ruin.

Mayhap the potter deluxe has better luck. Dimly it is our notion that, beyond our horizon, there exist vainglorious kilns, fat with magnificence, in whose polished interiors haughty pots are "fired" by gas-flame and by electricity. We have read of such things and, shudderingly, at times we have even peeked, for just a flash, at the king's-ransom prices at which such supercivilized kilns sell. But that is as far as our knowledge or our envy—goes. Yaquitepec pottery has need of no such frills. In the blaze of the open fire-hearth, as was the way of the ancient dwellers of the desert, it must take its trial. "Old ways are best" says the contented proverb. Well, at least they are often the healthiest and happiest.

Primitive man evolved all sorts of plans and notions for the outdoor firing of pottery. The two main essentials are, however, a dry spot of ground and an abundance of fuel. The first is comparatively easy to find; the second not always so simple—especially in the desert.

There are two types of fuel that are our chief reliance for pottery firing. One is the dry, dead mescal butts of last season's blooming. The other is ancient yucca trunks. The latter is the best, but there is more of the former. Mescals come, in greater or less quantity, every year. But the yucca is of slow growth. The supply of ancient, dead trunks is strictly limited.

For this last firing, however, we were in Fortune's path. By accident Rider and I had discovered, in a secluded little spot on the lower desert, a veritable treasure of yucca fuel—enough for a generous firing, and to spare. Since it was easier to take the pots to the fuel than the fuel to the pots, we packed our sun-dried clay ware in back baskets and, one bright morning, tramped away down the mountain. Rudyard came too. Our Rudyard is growing and his feet are easier now to keep shod with sandals. Baby feet are too small to handle sandals successfully; and for a long while this was the main reason for leaving him at home. Now, to his great delight, this difficulty is passing, and more and more he plods along on our excursions. Usually well armed with his bow and arrows for protection against "savitg cweatures"—for which he always scans the desert attentively.

A load of fragile, unfired pottery is not the least worrisome burden that one would choose to pack down a precipitous mountain trail. We picked our steps carefully. But about half-way down a wild yell and a cascade of loose stones brought me to a sudden face about to discover that Rider's feet had slid from under him on a treacherous ridge of shale and, clutching frantically at his burden, he sat down heavily.

"Ow! Ow! All the potteree is bwoken! All the potteree is bwoken!" yelled Rudyard, dancing with excitement and brandishing bows and arrows as he peered into the basket. "All bwoken! Every bit! Daddy, can I have *all* the pieces."

"It's not broken. Not any of it!" Rider scrambled to his feet. "I just managed to save the basket from hitting the ground." He was a bit breathless.

"But isn't anything hurted?" Rudyard demanded. There was distinct disappointment in his tone.

"Yes," Rider said briefly, as he resumed his way down the trail. "Those stones I sat on were hard."

"Oh, is *that* all," said the mighty hunter of "savitg" creatures. "I am sowwy." With which ambiguous remark he dismissed the matter. His arrow whizzed across the mescals and another ferocious "rhynosterous" fell dead.

We reached the bottom without further mishap. In spite of our early start the sun was well up and it was getting hot. By the time we had trekked through the creosotes and over the little intervening rise to our destination we were glad to ease down our burdens in the shade of a friendly juniper.

There is an asserted thrill to treading where no man has ever trodden before—though so ancient and well trodden is our old earth that I believe it is safe to say that no man has ever experienced it, no matter what seeming evidence to the contrary. A greater thrill, I think, comes from the continual proof that, no matter where we may happen to be, fellow human beings have, at some time, preceeded us. At any rate it was so here. For, on the brown, glowing earth, not 10 yards from our tree, a roughly circular scatter of big, flattish stones told of an old-time mescal hearth. And, stirring the deep mulch of fallen juniper leaves with the point of his arrow, Rudyard found beneath our shade tree the fragments of a small, broken olla. One large section had been part of the neck. In it there was a neat hole—evidently one of a pair of holes through which a string of fiber or raw hide had once been passed for carrying purposes.

We piled the ancient hearthstones together and made a little paved floor. On this, carefully arranging the pieces so that all should get as even a heat as possible, we set our clay ollas and bottles. Some of the nearer dead yucca trunks we brought and laid around our pile of earthenware somewhat after the fashion of a fence. But not too close—the heat must come gradually at the first. Then we dragged in all the dead tinder-like trunks we could find. It is astonishing—and heartbreaking—what a vast amount of fuel a single firing of pottery will consume. We worked until we had a small mountain of dead wood at hand

Then a carefully arranged priming of dry mescal leaves in a strategic corner of the pottery corral. Rudyard struck the match. Smoke lifted and the red forks of flames ran right and left. With long mescal poles Rider and I poked and shifted the yucca trunks, shoving some closer, others farther away. Too great a heat at the start will crack the pottery. It must be warmed gradually. Sometimes it is necessary to protect fragile pieces with leaned barricades of old, broken ware.

We had forgotten our temporary weariness now as we became engrossed in the job of tending the fire. While Rudyard ranged the immediate district, slaying "fewocious beasts" with well aimed arrows, Rider and I poked and watched the burning trunks, laying on new ones here and there; gradually working the flame-ring closer and closer to the pots as they became more heated. Finally we decided that they were safe enough for the main fire. Warily, for the heat was intense, we began to roof them completely over with dry fuel; piling dead trunks over and across until the pots were the center of a hollow, blazing mass. Dead yuccas can develop a tremendous heat. Through the crevices between the logs we could glimpse, here and there, our pots glowing a fierce, cherry red.

For half an hour we kept the fire going at full heat, filling in burned-out gaps with new fuel. Then we dropped our fire poles and sat in the shade of the juniper to rest.

We went home in the early afternoon, leaving our pottery standing, like the grim survivors of a battlefield, in the midst of a ring of smoking ashes. It was still fiercely hot—too hot to get near. It is best for fired pots to cool slowly and it would be a long while yet before the fire completely died. The coyotes and the brown ghosts would not harm our wares and the desert starlight harbored no vandals. We left them alone in the silence.

They were cold enough next day, standing cheerful and ash-flecked in the midst of a fire ruin that was as chill as they. Eagerly—for this is the supreme moment—we thrust hands among the soft, gray-white ash banks and drew the pots forth one by one, examining them critically, tapping them with appraising fingernails while we listened for the clear, metallic ring that indicates a perfect piece. The day was warm and glowing; the silence was like wine. Against the brown earth the fire-ash was a tumble of snow. Piece by piece, with mounting excitement, we tested our pots.

Yes, the "dirt" had "liked us." Nothing was cracked. By some miracle it had been a hundred percent perfect firing.

☀ ♏ 🌵

Desert Refuge 12
(July 1942)

VIVID yellow plumes of the tall, blossoming mescals against the morning sun. The silence is lazy with the faint drone of a myriad bees. And before the open windows of Yaquitepec little shoals of tiny insects hang suspended on vibrating wings. In their poised watchfulness and darting movements their likeness to microscopic fish in some clear tropical lagoon, is startling. And why not? We all dwell at the bottom of a mighty air ocean; exactly the same, except for density, as that in which the marine creatures live. How close together the Great Spirit has placed the different planes of Life! And how little we know about even the most obvious of them. The world of the ocean adjoins our own. And what do we really know of its secrets and life conditions? Yet we pretend, many times, an arrogant knowledge of realms much more mysterious.

Tanya and Rider are up the slope gathering mescal fuel. Their voices drift down to me through the still air. And with them the faint, musical clank of goat bells. For Conchita and Juanita, our two four-footed friends, have rambled off with them, following at their heels like pet dogs, cropping a bite here and a mouthful there. Skipping from rock to rock and butting each other playfully.

Have I chronicled Conchita and Juanita before? Perhaps not, for it is only recently that they became members of our Ghost Mountain population. Already, though, they are a firm part of the picture and their drowsily tinkling bells have brought to Yaquitepec an added flavor of Old Mexico and the colorful lands of sunshine.

Small, active little goats—a Nubian Toggenberg mixture—their brown coats and graceful antelope outlines fit perfectly into our desert landscape. They are popular with our young Yaquitepecos, for more reasons than one. Rider, Rudyard and Victoria now hold milk drinking contests.

I pause a moment to watch the primitive picture which my fuel gatherers and their four-footed attendants make

as they come down the rocky face of the northeast ridge. Rider glints lithe and sun-bronzed against the sky. On his shoulders he balances skillfully two dead mescal plants of last season's vintage. With their long poles and attached butts of yellow, bristling dry leaves they seem to completely overshadow their eight-year-old carrier as he steps carefully from foothold to foothold on a trail that is marked—Indian fashion—by occasional guide stones.

Tanya's filled basket is poised high upon her shoulder, steadied with one arm. Her unbound hair waves free in the sunlight as she picks her way through the pattern of purple-gray rocks and blooming buckwheat, pushing aside the emerald green wands of scarlet tipped ocotillos.

And before her, or behind, or on either side, as she moves, range the goats. A pair of little brown antelope, skipping from boulder to boulder. The musical *clink-tonk-tink* of their bells swells louder as they draw nearer the house. Primitive, fundamental life in a primitive, fundamental setting! Only the desert, it seems, holds such scenes now. Scenes of a simple life, in a changing tapestry of color, that are both a joy and a despair. One longs to paint them—to catch their color and appeal upon canvas. But the longing is vain. The desert defies you. Even as you reach for a pencil or snatch for your colors the pattern has changed; dissolved and re-arranged and re-blended as the patterns of the drifting clouds and the elusive shadows that fleck the wasteland distances. Well, perhaps it is better thus. This is the stuff of which dreams are woven. And one cannot freeze dreams upon canvas or imprison them in glass containers. For then, instantly, they cease to be dreams.

Fuel gathering these warm days is a minor chore. Something to be done in odd moments; not the imperative "has to be" that drove us during the winter. But nevertheless we often look back regretfully on our roaring winter fires. Not alone from the primitive bond that an evening fire has upon the human heart but also from the cooking angle.

Big fires mean abundant banks of glowing coals. And a plentitude of hot coals helps a lot in cookery. Almost every evening, during the cold months, Tanya would take a great iron pot with a close-fitting lid and, having filled it with some sort of varied stew ingredients—jerky meat and potatoes and onions, or beans and chili and corn, or what not, all generously seasoned with garlic or wild sage—she would rake out the glowing coals of the big fireplace, clear down to the hot, baked-clay paving, and setting the huge pot in the hollow, would cover it completely with coals and banked ashes. In the morning we would rake away the grey, still warm ash banks and lift the iron lid from a cauldron of delectably cooked food; all the component ingredients tender and spicily fragrant with a fragrance which only cookery by wood heat can give.

We have never found a substitute method for this primitive way of cooking—a substitute, that is, which gives anything like the same results. It is only a variation, of course, of the pit oven of the savage or the buried bean pots of our ancestors. But it has a "something" to it. Different ways, and different heat mediums—especially this latter—affect strikingly the flavor of food. And its healthfulness. As he has followed the siren song of his shiny modern gadgets of food preparation up the ladder of ease, man has lost something. Perhaps much more than he would believe possible.

* * *

Humming birds whirr in the sun. And all over Ghost Mountain the strawberry cacti are beginning to yield their harvest of cool, delicious fruit. Rider and Rudyard are busy, most of their spare time, in scouting for them. Their healthy young appetites, plus Victoria's, make heavy inroads on the supply. There never is quite enough to satisfy the demand—which is perhaps why the delicious morsels never lose their popularity.

Pink in color and protected by spines, the fruits, when freed from their savage overcoats, are tempting snow-white or pink-tinted balls of coolness, plentifully speckled with tiny, shiny black seeds. Other residents of Ghost Mountain like them too including the chipmunks and packrats. Sometimes we wish the packrats, in particular, were not so crazy about the delicacies. Not that we envy them their just portion of the fruit. But we do object to their thrifty habit of saving every thorn-cluster in the rind and placing it at strategic points either in the vicinity of their own homes—or ours. Very often ours. There are few things more exasperating to step on, with bare feet, than these very efficient little thorn bunches. At the moment one is apt to lose sight of the intelligence the packrat displays in using this perfectly natural defense against enemies.

Packrats are remarkable little desert dwellers. They provide a never ending source of diversion as well as an unfailing field for study. We have one old fellow who has chosen to live in a big rough outdoor cupboard in which we store miscellaneous odds and ends. His nest, a big affair, is composed mostly of the cotton padding which he industriously stole from an old automobile cushion. This is his home. But all the aisles and open spaces among the cupboard's contents constitute the "grounds" of his estate.

Periodically—according to the season of the year—he decorates this pleasure park either with tufts of green from juniper branches or with an artistic litter of cholla joints and chewed yucca leaf scraps. In one corner of the cupboard stands an old quart jar without a lid. This is his crystal treasure chest. He is always filling it and emptying it. The costly loot that it contains is composed of everything that strikes his fancy—bits of sundried orange peel, small clusters of cholla thorns, sections of chewed yucca leaves, dry juniper berries, bits of sun-whitened bone, bleached twigs, scraps of paper, dried ocotillo blossoms. There seems no end to the variety of hoarded trinkets. When the jar is full he starts, methodically, to unload it. And when it is empty fills it again. Over and over. A serious business; one to which he has evidently dedicated his life.

Undoubtedly he is an "eminent personage" of some sort. Perhaps a Rajah or a Baron. Or an Antiquarian of note. And if you are going to smile at his antics and his "stupidity" it might be well to remember what some humans do. Even to the hoarding of diamonds and rubies—and other bits of glorified glass.

Not all packrats however have a "purpose" in life, or take it so seriously. In direct contrast to our collector friend is the one who lives on our roof. He is a gay soul. One who believes, evidently, that life was meant to be tossed away in careless gaiety. A short life and a merry one. He is a cynic. Collect property? Not he! His home is a careless affair of unhandsome sticks tossed together in a sheltered nook where our main roof overhangs that of a small outhouse. He has no pride in it. It is merely a place in which to sleep when he comes reeling home from wild parties. And he is out on a wild party almost every night. He is quite regular and has developed a technique all his own.

When coming home he first climbs to the top of our rock built water cistern. From thence to a jutting beam: From this vantage point, as a springboard, he takes of; in a wild leap, landing with a resounding crash in the midst of our sheet iron roof. Sometimes, in tipsy jollity, he is lugging a juniper stick bigger than himself. This adds an artistic note to the "sound effect." Perhaps you think a desert packrat too small to make much noise. But if you could be jerked from sleep at two o'clock in the morning by the sound of our hilarious friend landing on the roof you would think you were listening to the explosion of a demolition bomb. Almost nightly we swear dire vengeance upon our gay roof tenant. And, as regularly, when the desert morning breaks in peace, we forgive him. After all he is "one of the family." It takes all kinds to make up a world—in the desert as elsewhere.

* * *

Warm days and sun. Far, far away the dim, phantom leagues of the lowland desert lie wrapped in a smoke-blue shimmering haze. Upon the horizon bulk the distant out-lines of sleeping mountains. The whiptail lizards scoot across the white gravel before the house, nosing, in search of prey, from bush clump to bush clump.

We appreciate the cool water in the drinking olla these days. Also the shade. The children have discovered a way to combine the two. They spread a blanket near some friendly juniper and bring forth from the house an earthen jar of cold water a little flavored with honey or—if it is to be had—a little lemon juice. Then they sit around, Indian fashion, and sip cool drinks from small home made pottery cups, stirring the brew every once in a while with a big wooden spoon. Victoria plays hostess. And very well—if she can be prevented from upsetting the water jar.

Quite ceremonious the youngsters make these tribal drinkfests. Sometimes, watching them, we wonder just what the friendly spirits who lurk in the tree shadows must think of all this—here on their ancient ranging grounds. Ghosts? Oh yes. There *are* ghosts on Ghost mountain. But that, as Kipling would have said, is another story.

Desert Refuge 13
(August 1942)

WHEN, some time ago, Tanya and I decided that the increasing family needs called for an improved transportation system up the trail of Ghost Mountain we turned naturally to the *Desert Magazine* to solve our problem. Somewhere, we felt sure, among the vast army of desert dwellers and friends, we could find the owner of a couple of good burros who would be willing to part with them.

And we were not disappointed. You can get most everything from the desert if you ask for it in the right quarter. To our modest advertisement came not one but many replies. But the one that intrigued us most was from our fellow wilderness dweller—whom we knew well but had never met—Paul Wilhelm of Thousand Palms oasis. Paul wrote that he had a couple of gentle burros he would be glad for us to have. The matter was settled.

And settled too, almost as speedily, was the problem of getting them to Yaquitepec. Randall Henderson of *Desert Magazine* offered to drive to Ghost Mountain and transport me to Thousand Palms oasis in his car. "You can then," wrote Randall, cheerfully, "return with the burros at your own sweet leisure."

Thus it was arranged. And thus it came about that on a late Sunday afternoon, when the wind was snoring through the lofty palm summits of Paul's little desert Eden, I headed through the low mesquites of the wash with two new—though somewhat reluctant "friends" in tow. Rhett and Scarlett. Dust swirls scudded underfoot. In a bright flash of feathers a scarlet tanager winged through the bushes. The grim, jagged mountains beyond the oasis stood sharp against the sky like the painted backdrop of a stage scene. We had over 120 miles of trail ahead of us. There was a spice of adventure in the air. It was good to be afoot—and footloose. I found myself adapting and humming half forgotten fragments of an old ballad of the Pony Express: "Shake along, little burros; shake along….A hundred and twenty miles to go….Remember that the mail must go through."

I had brought along a couple of blankets for the trip. And these with a gay orange-colored bag—once the container of a hundred pounds of dog biscuit and now pressed into service as a packsack were roped upon Rhett. He was a wise old campaigner of the trails and sniffed a bit contemptuously at the lightness of his load. Scarlett I had planned to ride on occasion. She was a good saddle burro, Paul said. Her ears were longer than Rhett's and her expression a trifle more sophisticated.

We left the fringe of mesquites behind, turning from the trail to make a short cut across the bleak wastelands along the flanks of the desolate hills. The wind tore down and scurried the dust; the far, grim summits of the Santa Rosas towered against the sky. Ahead, the town of Indio was a distant, dim blue cloud. I climbed aboard Scarlett presently, having decided that by now she should have gotten over the first pangs of home-parting. With Rhett in tow—for I dared not turn him loose so close to his old home—we jogged on.

We reached the highway in the lowering dusk. Trucks thundered past and cars came charging at us glaring eyed. A concrete highway is no place for peace loving burros. But we could not help it. Civilization has robbed life of many another bit of peace and freedom. We hugged the far shoulder of the road and made the best of it.

We spent the night at John Hilton's—after being first halted in the dim darkness of a lone stretch of road by a patrol car of Uncle Sam's immigration service. But, as we knew most of the local force, the inspectors waved us cheerily on our way. But there was drama in the encounter. Somehow it made us feel like a "*Contrabandista*" guiding his pack train of stealthy, heavy laden mules along mysterious trails. We regretted bitterly that we had no black *mastachios,* or a sinister dagger, or a sable, scarlet-lined cloak. We determined to have at least the cloak next time.

Paul Wilhelm (left) and Marshal South at Thousand Palms oasis.
Photo by Florence Silver taken just before Marshal started the 120-mile trek to
Ghost Mountain with Rhett and Scarlett.

Tanya and the children could judge the flavor.

From John Hilton's the burros and I trailed contentedly on. A grand day of desert sunshine with distant mountains wire-edged against the turquoise sky. Scarlett and Rhett were resigned now. They munched at bushes and weed patches with an air of stoic endurance. Most of the time I walked. We all enjoyed ourselves better that way. Foot-pace burro travel may be slow. But one gains by it something which cannot even be sensed when one goes charging across country in a soulless gas-burning machine.

Inspector Smith and his brother officer whirled their patrol car out of the darkness again that night and stopped to inquire after the good health of the pilgrimage. They rendered the cheerful information that they hadn't seen many sidewinders on the highway at night so far this year. Which was consoling—for we had been thinking about sidewinders, for whom we have a great respect. After the big car had purred away into the mystery of the night we went on beneath the starglow in a cheery frame of mind. Not alone because of the reported scarcity of sidewinders. It always gives one a warm feeling to rub shoulders with Efficiency, especially in wartime. And this was the second time on the trek that we had evidence that the border patrol is very much on the job.

We finally camped for the night at Coolidge Springs, in a ghostly dark with the wind sighing through the tall lines of shadowy athel trees.

I watered and packed the burros and we were off on the road again before anyone was astir. "DANGER. ARTILLERY FIRING," said the big red-lettered sign in the wash, marking the edge of a military reserve. But there was no evidence of artillery nor any sound of firing. Only, in the distance, the grim waterline of the old vanished sea, whose waves had beaten against these now dry scorched desert buttes far back in the mists of Time, stretched like a black, ruled line. Somehow there was in that old bleached sea-stain something that carried a note

Perhaps to say that we spent the night at John Hilton's is scarcely the truth. There was not much of it to spend. John had arranged in advance to leave a light burning. But by the time I had unpacked and hitched the burros to a telegraph pole and tiptoed into the bedroom the morning star and a worn moon were hanging high in the east against a glow of dawn. I suppose I slept all of 15 minutes before John summoned me to breakfast.

John Hilton needs no introduction to *Desert Magazine* readers, and it was hard to get away upon the trail again. By art and subtlety he and his wife Eunice convinced me—no hard task—that I must stay to lunch also. There is so much to see at John's—his cactus gardens, his gorgeous paintings, his fascinating collections of desert gems and minerals. I finally got away about two-thirty in the afternoon, bearing, among a varied assortment of other souvenirs sent to the family at Yaquitepec, a special treasure. A priceless bottle of genuine Mexican hot sauce which John had brought from Sonora. It was positively guaranteed to possess a potency capable of burning a hole through a copper pot in five seconds flat. And the bottle would, John assured confidently, last me "almost indefinitely"—one had to use such a minute quantity in order to transform one's "innards" into a raging conflagration.

It really *was* a good sauce. Compounded, I believe from sulphuric acid, *chillis pepinos,* T.N.T. and dynamite. I blush to say that I consumed most of the bottle that night for supper. But thoughtfully saved a small sample so that of ironic laughter regarding Man and his "works"—his wars and his achievements. Dust! Yesterday the ocean. Today the puny voices of the guns. Tomorrow the old sea-line and the very mountains upon which it is graved will be gone.

A glorious desert morning, with the stretch of the Salton Sea glinting like the blue steel blade of a giant's sword beyond the stretch of the sandy desert to our left. Early in the forenoon Rhett and Scarlett discovered a luscious pile of dusty hay beside the roadway. Evidently a hay truck had come to grief. We paused right there. And while I loafed in the warm sunlight they industriously made a clean sweep of the precious provender. A burro's life, I reflected, as I munched one of my own dry sandwiches, has certain advantages.

And so, through desert silence and sunshine and the shimmer of desert mirage, the burro Pony Express moved on, slowly but surely eating up the miles. A hundred and twenty miles is nothing to an automobile. But to the leisurely jog of burro travel it is a respectable distance. As we ambled along, however, across thirsty stretches where mesquite-grown dunes shimmered in the sunglare, or through the wind-whispered starglow of night, we remembered always that "…the mail must go through."

And through it went. Even a little ahead of calculated time. Three more night camps—the last one only a couple of miles from the rugged base of Ghost Mountain—then on a bright morning, as the sun lifted well above the ridges, a couple of weary burros plodded the last stretch up the precipitous Yaquitepec trail. We were met by three excited youngsters who, while dancing for joy over daddy's safe return, still managed to find time to shower their new four-footed friends with an amazing variety of edible tidbits.

It was a joyful homecoming—with the savory aroma of breakfast and the cheerful clatter of dishes, as Tanya mixed her greetings with the bustle of setting out a meal. The mail had gone through. Scarlett and Rhett had come to their new home. The trip was over.

Yes, over. But a wealth of memories would long endure. Highlights and shadows; mirth and tribulation. For not in a space 10 times as great as this could one compass all the incidents. But they are safe in memory's album for future scanning. Somehow, as I watered and fed Rhett and Scarlett, I could not help recalling one of them—the meeting with another artist friend. Mr. Crocker, whose home is near Julian, California. With his daughter he had come whirring out of the mirage-blinking distance as we had been plodding along with the Superstition Mountains on the horizon. We had not seen each other for a long time and, when sight of our cavalcade had jerked his car

to an amazed halt, he had dipped back into his own memory of past days.

"You may not know it," he said a bit wistfully, "but once I myself, ran a pack train. How well I remember …And how they would scatter…And run under trees…And try to rub their packs off…And…." He sighed. And we looked at him in a new fellowship. For, with the manners and bearing of Boston's most exclusive set, he is the last person in the world whom you would ever remotely suspect of having run a pack train. "Yes," he said regretfully "…those were the days…But cuss!...Ah, not even yet have I succeeded in breaking myself of the habit."

And when he and his daughter had whirred on, leaving the burro express the richer by a welcome gift of grapefruit and dates, which Rhett, Scarlett and I ate, share and share alike, I had chuckled a little.

I chuckled again now as I turned my two faithful trail companions loose to a long, well-earned rest. "…But cuss!..." Yes, he had in truth run a pack train—there can be no secrets among fellow members of the noble fraternity of packmasters.

But it is a good world, nevertheless. And how else, anyway would one run a pack train—or a couple of burros either?

Desert Refuge 14
(September 1942)

IT IS hot. As I sit in the shade and tap the keys of the typewriter, our whole desert world, clear to the distant rim of the horizon, is a shimmering glare of sunlight. Something of the same summer blaze that prevails in the Yaqui country of Mexico, and in the lands of the Seris Indians, who range the island of Tiburon and the adjacent mainland. Such light is hard on unaccustomed eyes. Just as the primitive foods of the desert are hard on unaccustomed stomachs.

But there is a priceless compensation for every hardship the desert has to offer. The compensation is freedom, and wide range, liberty of body and of mind. And these things are part of the desert dwellers' fiber and bone.

For over 400 years the Yaqui has fought fiercely against his "civilized" aggressors who have sought to rob him of his freedom. A wild land, a savage land, a land of mountains and rocks is the homeland of the Yaqui. A desert land. Such locations breed fierce love of freedom. It is the people of the mountains who fight on—and survive. The ease-pampered dwellers of the lush lowlands too often bow the neck to the yoke of the conqueror.

Desert heat is a strange thing. Not nearly so fearsome as the story-writers would have us believe. But one must use the practical common sense of the desert Indian in dealing with it. It does not take kindly to "high-pressure" exertion and "hustle." One must respect the very real power of the desert sun. Early morning and late evening are the periods for work. For the rest of the day, the shade—and it is surprising how tiny a patch of shade will suffice. "The shadow of a great rock in a weary land," wrote the prophet long, long ago. And there is a peculiar appreciation of the words by all dwellers of the wasteland. The writer of them dwelt in a desert land; he knew whereof he spoke.

And desert heat plays strange pranks sometimes. In the vicinity of Ghost Mountain we have come, several times, into areas of those uncanny heat pockets, which, for want of a better term (never having encountered any previous writing concerning them) I call "desert vacuums." These phenomena are not frequent. But when one runs into them they are terrifyingly real. Sometimes you walk into them and sometimes they seem to form, without warning, around you. There is nothing to see; no hint of a change. But of a sudden you are oppressed by a sense of heaviness and dizziness. Every muscle and fiber of the body seems suddenly changed to lead. Every motion, every movement becomes difficult. The head swims and the solid earth goes round in dizzy circles. You are gripped with a very real fear of fainting. About all you can do is to stagger to the nearest patch of shade—if any bush or rock offers it—and sit down. Usually, after a bit, the air condition passes. Or mayhap you recover enough strength to plod on and pass beyond the area of the "pocket." The whole thing is uncanny. But it is no myth. I have had the same story from several hardened desert dwellers. I have had testimony to the effect that animals—even semi-wild desert cattle—are susceptible to the numbing lethargy which these "pockets" induce.

Explanation? Well, I have not much to offer by way of explanation. My personal theory is that the hot dry air rising from the heated desert is, by the contour of certain sections of the terrain, sucked into funnels, something on the order of the centers of cyclonic storms. And these "vacuum" centers in some way rob the atmosphere of ingredients necessary to life…possibly oxygen. Hence the feeling of collapse when one walks into them. This theory may be all wrong. But the matter is worthy of study. The several cases on record where old prospectors have been found dead beside full canteens of water, suggests

that under certain extreme conditions these mysterious "vacuum" pockets may be deadly.

Air pockets are however so infrequent that thought of them need deter no one from summer trips. Other tricks of the sun are equally unexpected. I recall that once, while packing up a load of supplies along the steep foot trail that leads to the crest of Ghost Mountain, I was startled by a very distinct whiff of smoke. I stopped instantly and, after the manner of the savage or the four-footed creatures of the wilds, sniffed the air carefully. One's nose becomes very sensitive to odors in the wilderness and scents carry—tobacco smoke, for instance, can often be detected over long distances, sometimes as far as two miles.

In this instance I was baffled. The smell of smoke was there. But from whence did it come? All points of the compass seemed to give the same reaction. Possibly, I told myself, Tanya, on the summit of the mountain, had tossed an old woolen rag into the stove.

So I went on. But presently to my amazement I not only smelled smoke but actually saw smoke. It was all around me in thin spirals. My pack was afire.

Hastily I backed up to a convenient rock and disentangled myself from the pack straps. Yes, it was afire. A small woolen blanket, used as a back-pad, was smouldering merrily. But there had been no matches in the pack; nothing to start a fire. What could have caused it? Then, as I worked, smothering out the burning cloth, the explanation dawned on me. There was a glass jug full of water among the articles I was carrying up. The summer sun, striking through the curved, water filled glass, had acted as it would have done through a lens. It was only about nine o'clock in the morning. But the sun was hot. It had actually set the pack afire. Glass bottles around Yaquitepec, since that day, have been regarded with suspicion. And we have ceased to scoff at the old story of the prospector who packing a load of powder on his back, was blown up and killed—just because he had a magnifying glass stuck under one of the straps of his load.

There is abundant charm to desert summer, though. Much more than enough to outweigh any trifling tricks and discomforts that the heat may bring. Colors glow in the far reaches of the wastelands and the glint of mirage is weird on the white sands of every distant wash.

* * *

Tarantula hawks—those gay dashing wasps—sail through the warm still air above the junipers and around the crests of the dead mescal stalks. Sinister, romantic fellows. With their orange wings and shining black bodies they always remind us of conventional devils from the operas…black velvet tights and scarlet cloak complete. They are a tough breed of free-booters and seem to have few enemies.

Once I saw a lizard make a dash and snap an alighted tarantula hawk in his mouth. But before I could reach the spot the big lizard dropped his prey. I had just a glimpse of a shiny black insect and his jaunty cloak scuttling to safety under a low thicket of *ramarillo* [rabbitbrush] bushes, while the lizard moved away more slowly. Had he been stabbed by some jeweled dagger? Possibly. It must have been a keen dagger. These wasteland lizards are not soft in constitution. Even the small ones think nothing of dining upon savage black bees.

* * *

The garden has dried up. A few wisps of dead leaves, scorched now to a crisp brownness beneath the contempt of even our nibbling goats, are all that remain to remind us of the crisp salads which it so lately yielded. The main water cistern is dry. And so far the great white thunderheads which sail the blue vault above Yaquitepec have spilled no fresh rain upon us. Water is too valuable now for gardens. We have moved our two burros to distant pasturage, where they will remain till the rains have filled our cisterns again. Rudyard and Victoria shed a few tears as they took sorrowful leave of them. And even Rider, now right hand man of Yaquitepec, was downcast. But water is water. Until our supply is replenished we do not dare dole out, even the comparatively small amount that the burros require. Even Conchita and Juanita—our two active little goats—are not allowed to waste the precious fluid.

* * *

One advantage of our Ghost Mountain weather is that it is never constant. Even in summer. And stretches of glowing heat are sandwiched with spells when the sunglow is tempered with the drive of a cool, fragrant wind. Such days are the cream of summer. And on such days Rider, who is eagerly interested in bugs, butterflies, rock specimens and every natural thing, usually persuades me to go on a hike somewhere. "We might find a spring, you know" is his most artfully used argument.

Well, we have never found the spring. But we do find all manner of other things. Last week we found a grim

Scarlett the burro under the ramada with Rudyard and Rider.

Rhett and Scarlett packing supplies up Ghost Mountain.

rocky hill where our predecessors, the Indian dwellers of the wasteland, had probably staged more than one sanguinary encounter with their enemies. A humble little "Gibraltar" of the desert. A few piled walls of stones in strategic points. A few caves walled and loopholed, in which defenders could crouch. But in the silence of the desert, as I scrambled about the mute evidences of some Indian "greatest war of history" I reflected that a man could be killed just as dead by an obsidian pointed arrow as by the most expensive weapon of modern science. And that the heartaches and misery of war are neither lessened nor increased by the methods employed.

The ancients slew with an arrow or a club. We in our vaunted civilization hurl death from the skies. But death is death. And grief is grief. It makes no difference what the setting or the period. Or how "barbaric" or "civilized" the actors in the drama. Man is commonly reputed to have come a long way upward out of savagery. Sometimes it gives one pause to wonder if he has not forgotten, in his scramble for culture, the most important ingredient of life. We have electric iceboxes and radios; we have airplanes and marvelous cannon. We can shout the price of soap or the latest quotation of the stock exchange around the world. "But what shall it profit a man if he gain the whole world and lose his own soul?"

Desert Refuge 15
(October 1942)

A THIN wisp of desert road, leading on into the dim mystery of vast distance. What is at its end? We do not yet know, but soon we shall. For our feet are upon it; our eyes are towards far horizons. For this month's chronicle is a chronicle of search—of search for a new location in the great friendly silences of the desert. Already the little house upon the summit of Ghost Mountain is far behind us. Its door is shut and the stillness that has closed about it is unbroken save for the hushed footfalls of the wind, wandering lonely around the corners of the white walls and among the scatter of old, abandoned toys beneath the shade of the ramada.

But it is well not to write much of these things or to awaken memories; the ache of them is as yet too close. For it is not easy to wrench oneself from things beloved and from things which long years have tangled so closely with the fibers of one's very soul. Man, it is true, has graduated to a stage in the scale of evolution which enables him, unlike the plant, to move from place to place. But he is still a creature of the earth, and attached to it. The roots which he strikes deep into the earth are not physical roots, but they are none the less very real roots. And their up wrenching can often cause more than physical pain. A deeper pain. Heartstrings go deep into the soil of HOME. On this and on this alone is Patriotism founded. The love of home—of the bit of earth where one's roots are. It is hard to break such ties.

Nevertheless we have turned our faces to the open road and to the wide mystery of the further desert. Already we are deep in its distance-hazed reaches. New plains surround us, new buttes, new mesquite-grown arroyos and new silences beneath the night stars. The sun this morning rose from behind the ragged, purple peaks

of weird, unfamiliar mountains, climbing into a cloud flecked sky that was a glory of gold and pink and purple. "Here sun coming!" cried little Victoria, eagerly, clapping her hands. "We tum to new home today, muvver?"

"Maybe not today, baby," said Rider, gravely, taking it upon himself to answer. "Maybe not today—but very soon. Won't we Daddy?"

"Of course," I reassured him, "It's there, waiting for us; with everything we need. All we have to do is to keep right on and we'll find it."

"I wan' lots, an' lots an' LOTS of water!" declared Rudyard emphatically. "I wan' even as much as—as much as—" He struggled for some expression of volume truly colossal. "—I wan' even as much as TWELVE GAL-LONS."

"And you shall have it, precious," Tanya promised him. "You shall have 12 gallons, for your very own."

And we all laughed. For while the desert sun shines and the creosote bushes glitter and the hills on the horizon are clothed in their witchery of indigo and purple one cannot lose faith. The Great Spirit watches over the wilderness; all the dwellers therein are beneath the protecting shadow of His wing.

But our four-year-old's remark about water puts the whole reason for our move in a nutshell. Water! It has become vital. It is the lure which day by day beckons us deeper into the desert.

Perhaps in normal times our ears would have been more deaf to the call which finally wrenched us from Yaquitepec. We had built our dreams there; we tried hard to convince ourselves that someday we could, by adequate cistern capacity, overcome the water handicap. We did not want to move.

But these are not normal times. Today our beloved nation is engaged in a grim battle for the freedom of the world. It is a battle that will be won largely by the conservation of foodstuffs and natural resources. Every bushel of grain and pound of food that each one of us can produce for ourselves, releases just that much more of national supplies to aid in the winning of the struggle. And even on our mountaintop we felt very definitely that we ought to be producing more. It is true that not a great deal of outside supplies were needed for Yaquitepec. But we did need some—particularly as the demands of our growing family increased. We should, we felt, be able to produce more. Corn, food, larger gardens.

And this was the urge that finally tipped the scale of the long debated water problem. We could not afford to wait years for the development of the necessary water. We must set forth and find it in some new location.

With the decision once made we shut our eyes and ears to all else and fell to packing and preparing. Rider set about dismantling his glass cases of treasured specimens and bugs—packing them carefully for transit. Rudyard—who has a weird collection of old keys, nails, pottery scraps and chunks of stone—rushed and packed all the treasured trash in paper bags and cans. Victoria, having nothing to pack, occupied herself in dashing frantically back and forth between her brothers, snatching treasures from each one's hoard and carrying them to Tanya, shrieking gleefully "Pack this fo' me"…incurring thereby explosions of wrath from the respective rightful owners of the loot.

Yes packing was a big job. Had we paused to think we might have been staggered at the problem. But we did not pause to think. That is usually the better way, anyhow, when tackling a job of this kind. While Tanya packed I carried, back-load after back-load down the long winding trail of Ghost Mountain. The burros were out at pasture, far away. But I did not regret not having them. For packing up the mountain they did nobly. But it was always hard for them to transport loads down. The trail was too steep. A man can do better, as a burden carrier, than an animal, on precipitous trails—as the carriers of mountainous China and of other sections have demonstrated. I used my own shoulders and made sometimes six round trips each day. There was a lot of stuff to move. And an amazing amount of books. The books were the heaviest. For some of the articles that were too large to be carried by back-pack we made a sort of litter, with two long poles. Tanya took one end and I the other, while Rider stayed atop the mountain to look after Rudyard and Victoria. A long, hard job, the carrying. But eventually it was all finished.

Came then the equally staggering job of transportation. How was this carefully selected mass of essential property to be moved? The old car could not begin to hold it. We cast eyes on an old two-wheel trailer which we had discarded years ago. Yes, perhaps it could be fixed. Its tires had been left on the wheels. For over six years they had been standing flat and bleaching in the desert sun. Dubiously we brought the pump and pumped them up. Astoundingly they seemed to hold. We went over the old trailer with a monkey wrench and tightened up bolts in desert-shrunken timbers. Then we began to load.

There was far too much—even by the most dangerous overloading of car and trailer—to be transported in one trip. We saw that we would have to make two. But to where? Our destination was unknown—still is. What should we do?

We solved the problem by hauling a first load away to a distant desert point where we stored it; solving also another problem, that of our two pet goats. We could not leave them behind at Yaquitepec, unattended. And we did not want to divide our family by having someone stay behind to look after them—fire hazards this summer having been much worse than usual in our desert mountain region. So we took Conchita and Juanita along, building them a tiny pen on an overhanging extension of the trailer. And, after many days, having stored our load, we brought them back with us. For there was no one at the other end to look after them either.

And when we had come to the foot of Ghost Mountain again we had cause for thankfulness that we had not left any of our little family at home. For around our land the desert was an inferno of smoke and flame. Roaring over desert ridges, seemingly barren, an ocean of flame was tossing to the sky. Smoke hung over everything in a terrifying pall. A huge mountain not far from Yaquitepec was a seeming volcano of rolling smoke and soaring flame. For a week it burned. Perhaps the first time within centuries that fire had ravaged it. And when the last coals were dead it was a blackened, lifeless mass. But the flame-furies spared Yaquitepec. By a miracle our goods were safe.

So we loaded the last load—an even more staggering one than the first had been. And we put Conchita and Juanita back into their tiny pen on the trailer. And we climbed into the old car, with Rudyard sandwiched into a little niche all his own, among the books and boxes, and set out. Slowly, down the rough stretch of home trail, between the creosotes and mescals and yuccas we lurched our laboring outfit and with bated breath turned down the treacherous sandy wash for the last time. On its further edge we paused and looked back. Ghost Mountain shimmered in the sunlight. Lonely. And somewhere behind its rim rocks we knew the little house stood. Silent. Lonely too.

Our eyes were misted a little. There was a tight clutch at our hearts and a little sob in our throats as we waved a last farewell. Then we went on, heading down the road, our heavily loaded trailer creaking behind us.

To where? Not yet do we know. But we know as surely as we knew that evening, when the sun sank in a glory of crimson and gold behind the hills and the grey, silent nighthawks began to flit above the desert creosotes, that it is to a greater, better location. For Life moves onward. And though the old is behind there is always the new ahead…new vistas, new experiences, new promise and new hope. Perhaps Rider is right—perhaps it will be very soon that we shall come upon the place that is to be our new desert home. When we come to it we shall know it. But for now we go on through desert dawns and starlight—seeking. Perhaps by next month we may be able to tell you of something found.

Desert Refuge 16
(November 1942)

THE SEARCH goes on. Not yet have we topped the rise—which is always just ahead—and seen before us the new home which we set out from Yaquitepec to find. But somewhere behind dim horizons it lies waiting. More and more certain we are of this.

With every mile, as our old car and creaking, heavy laden trailer lurch through the dust of desert ruts, our hopes burn brighter and conviction strengthens. Rider and Rudyard are constantly making plans—plans as real and definite as though they were already well established upon the new location which lies at the end of the rainbow. Victoria plans with them. She is very anxious to be part and parcel of everything and as she cannot quite figure out what it is all about she plays safe by echoing all Rudyard's assertions.

Rudyard (after much weighty thought) solemnly declared, "I'm going to plant radishes in the north end of my new garden—near the rocks." Victoria instantly repeated, "An' I'm doin' plan' wadishes in norf end of *my* darden too—near wocks." She is always very definite. And if Rider teases her, as he sometimes does, arguing mischievously that the *south* end of her garden would be by far the better place for the radishes, she wheels on him furiously. "No! No! *Norf* end! Jus' like Wudyard." Often there is hot argument and Tanya has to pour oil upon the troubled waters. For Rider overbubbles with a spirit of teasing fun—and little Victoria has an explosive temper.

And so we move on—seeking, looking eagerly forward to each new day and treasuring to the full each day's new experiences. After all it is the quest that gives joy as well as the finding. Especially have we found this true in our wasteland search. For to no one does the desert open its heart as widely as it does to those who go gypsying through its by-ways and solitudes; to those who, each night, spread their blankets upon its breast, beneath the stars.

Did we think that we, desert dwellers now of many a year, knew all the beauty and mystery and fascination of the unpeopled spaces? Childish illusion! The desert laughed at us—and in mocking laughter spread for us each day new scenes of weird enchantment and fantastic color.

Pictures! Pictures—and, alas, the color tubes and brushes are packed deep in the trailer load and fast tied beneath a score of lashings of rope and wire. And there is no time to tarry and paint pictures, anyhow. Through the creosotes the trail winds on.

California—the wasteland filmed with dust. Through the ocotillos and the ironwoods the dull glint of uncouth steel monsters lunge in awesome lines of battle maneuver down the sandy washes and across the rocky slopes; sun-wink upon the binoculars of grimly intent officers, perched upon turrets and the vantage points of observation stations; the roar of motorcycles, demon-hooded messengers hurtling by into the din and haze-filmed air. Roar and thunder upon the highway; the pavement shaking to the resistless rush of mile upon mile of mighty cannon-leering tanks. Grim raw hills backed against a hard sky like the dead mountains of a dream. A sign, cringing by the roadside, "Watch out for cattle." But there were no cattle. Here is only the gathering might of War.

And over and around it all the metallic sky, the far, hard, thirsty reaches, the inscrutable mystery of the desert.

We had passed far by and out into the emptiness of sunlit space when they hove in sight—a last, isolated detachment of armor-plated monsters. We had paused to one side of the road to wrestle with a blown-out tire and from the north they came suddenly upon us, an awesome line of grim things that might have been unthinkable giants from another world. As they heaved over the swell of the rise ahead and came charging down the highway one could but know fear. Dust and stones flew in a storm from beneath their clanging tread. The sun was behind them. Wrapped in sun-glared dust as in a cloud of fire, they roared headlong upon us.

And then, suddenly, as our ears deafened and our eyes blurred and we gathered for a leap to safety, the line swerved. Almost upon us the swaying monsters lurched aside and went bucking into the soft earth of the roadside. In the reeling turret of the foremost, a grim helmeted figure waved a sudden arm and in a storm of flying stones the line of thundering steel terrors ground to a shuddering halt. Were we in trouble? inquired a clear-eyed, clean-cut, efficient being from Mars. Did we need any help?

And we told him no—we would be fixed up directly. It was only a tire.

And we thanked him. And he grinned and said you never knew…maybe he'd need help himself some day. And he waved a signalling arm again to the long line of halted demon, and they woke to roaring life. And in a moment were off, lunging and thundering down the highway—a grim nightmare of leering cannon and pounding steel. And they faded away into the dust and were gone.

And soon we were gone, too, chugging along the long road on our mended tire. And we were silent. But it was the silence of hearts that were warm and full. Because, for just a moment back there, we had been permitted, across the savage frown of armor-plate and the ready muzzles of guns, to look deep into the clear eyes of America—the *real* America. And we had seen something there, something far deeper than windy words or hysterical flag waving.

Adiós, clear-eyed man of Mars, whoever you may be. Drive on—atop thy bucking tons of flame-spewing steel, drive on to Destiny, to Victory and to Safe Return. Good luck go with you. The future is secure. Storms may come and bitter winds must blow. But neither from without nor from within shall the torch be quenched; clear-eyed and resolute the real America moves on to great and greater dawns.

Nevada and a cold wash of sunset, a vast sweep of desert valley. Wind-carved mountains tumbled against a crimson sky. A lone jackrabbit kicking clean heels in flight across the road. Nevada State Line. "A debt free State welcomes you." Grey road winding on and on into the dusk.

"Where shall we camp tonight, Daddy?" Rider asked presently. "How about that place ahead? It looks pretty good."

It was good—a wide clear space beside the road, well free of any bushes that might serve as attraction for snakes and other wildlife prowlers of the dark. And when we had pulled in and halted and untangled our cramped limbs from the car we unstrapped the bedding from the car roof and spread our blankets upon the stony earth.

But before we could eat supper and stretch out to rest, there were the goats to be fed and attended to. Conchita and Juanita are philosophic about this trip. They are resigned, by now, to their tiny pen on the back end of the trailer and they load and unload with something of the skill of trained circus animals. Not always is their lot a happy one. For sometimes there are desert sections whereon it is almost impossible to find anything edible—even for a goat. This first night in Nevada, however, was a happier camp spot and we were able to gather for them great bunches of sweet, dry desert grass.

Long into the night, after we had crept into our bed and lay gazing up at the stars, we could hear their steady, contented munching. It was a soothing sound. There is,

Tanya and the children by the trailer en route to Utah. The goats are in the trailer.

somehow, a peculiar, primitive satisfaction in the close proximity of domestic animals. Something which seems to link one closer with Nature and the Great Spirit of all Life.

Nevada is a grand state; the spirit of a wide freedom seems to dwell in its vast desert spaces and amidst its weirdly beautiful mountains. But we did not find our home-spot there, despite our trekkings into old mining camps and into far canyons. Despite also the whole-hearted efforts of good friends in Las Vegas. Our closest lead came from a lady in a picturesque little mining town who, after considerable pondering, opined that a certain "Horse Thief Canyon" might suit us. But the name seemed to suggest that residents should be gifted with special qualifications, and we doubted if we were eligible. So, regretfully, we turned away.

The children found their first desert tortoise in Nevada. A lively little wanderer detected in the act of plodding across a road and promptly christened "Tiny Tim." A tortoise, however though it does carry vague associations with water, is most certainly *not* a spring.

We doctored the weak places in our tires with bandagings of friction tape and wandered down to Lake Mead—there to be delivered, with military pomp and escort and between the ready rifles of watchful sentries, into the arms of Arizona.

And it was in Arizona that Betty joined us. Betty is a true child of the wanderlust and wide open spaces. We had expected her coming…but by some unaccountable mistake in calculation, not nearly so soon. So, when we pulled to a camp spot one evening and found her, an innocent-eyed, lop-eared mite in the trailer pen with Conchita, her mother gooing and cooing over her, we were about the most thunderstruck collection of voyagers that you could have found in all the western desert. About the only really self-possessed individual at the moment was Betty herself. She stood there upon her tiny wobbly legs and blatted at us with all the vigor of her diminutive lungs. Victoria stared in amazement and said "O-ooo! Baby doat!"

That broke the spell. Rudyard shrieked: "Oh Mother—Daddy! See the little goat! Look there—look at the little goat!" (as if we were not already staring at it with all our eyes). "Oh! Oh! That's my goat!" He danced around.

Spoke up Rider, the official goat expert and field manager of the family. His words were very deliberate and final. "Oh yes?" he said. "Well that's my goat! Who do you think looks after them, anyway? And I'm going to call her Betty. I've always wanted to call something Betty!"

So that was that! And after we had bedded down Conchita and her new daughter with fresh grass and had hustled Juanita out of the pen to spend the night in grumbling protest hitched to the trailer wheel, we went to bed and to sleep. And in the morning went on our way happily. Betty is still with us. She is a lively and pert little rascal by now. And Rider has secret dreams of some time getting to be a "Goat Baron"—or something.

Cactus and the wind. A roadrunner scudding down a lonely road. Yuccas lifting savage bayonets against the sky; black shadows lurking in the clefts of sunshine-blazed buttes. White sand glaring in dry washes—and in the shady dimness of mesquite thickets the eternal whisper of wandering breezes that seem to sing the romance of long forgotten things. Arizona!

And Arizona brought to us our first real spring. It was deep in the heart of a grim butte. Mighty boulders—monstrous as the far-away boulders of Yaquitepec—towered in a titan pile. It was as though, in the sparkling yucca-staked desert, some careless giant had dumped a wheelbarrow load and had wandered on. Bees hummed round the footslopes and silence and the sleepy sunlight brooded amidst the rocks. And when you had gone in through the gap in an old fence of ocotillo and had passed under the whispering shade of an ancient pomegranate tree and tangle of grape vines—a fence erected and trees planted by the hands of someone long since gone away

into the silence—you came to the spring, hid deep under the overhang of a huge rock. A dark, tiny pool of cool soft water, grateful as nectar of the gods to a thirsty wayfarer.

There were caverns back in the boulders and we found bits of pottery. The Indians had been there in the long ago. Long, long even before the white man who had built the fence and planted the pomegranate tree and the grapevines. But they, like he, also had been gathered to the silence. The old fence cast shadows and the pomegranate tree rustled its leaves in dreams. Somehow the stillness was very hushed and heavy.

And the voices in our hearts cried "No. No! This is not the place. You must go on." So we turned away into the open desert. The old tires still limp out the miles and the song of the sunlit winds croon a far call.

Yes, we must go on.

Desert Refuge 17
(December 1942)

WE CAME upon the deserted station by chance. When one wanders nomad-like through the wasteland reaches lured ever onward in a search for distant springs, many things happen by "chance"—of which, of course, there is no such thing.

We saw it from a great way off, glinting white in the vast stretch of the desert like a tiny pearl dropped upon the rough weave of a gray-green carpet. As we drew closer we saw that it had a tower. A white tower with windows. Lifted there in the silence, above the endless tangle of sun-glinted creosote bushes, the lonely building might have been an old Spanish mission.

But it wasn't. It was just a deserted filling station. "Texaco," proclaimed a swaying sun-blistered sign. As we came to a halt a loose sheet of roofing iron, stirred by a puff of passing breeze, banged mournfully.

"It looks haunted," Rider said, sniffing hopefully as he climbed out of his seat. "Do you suppose there would be any really truly ghosts here, Daddy?"

"Ufff! Ghostesses!" Rudyard wrinkled his pudgy nose. "Too hot for ghostesses! I wanna dwink."

"Give…me…one…dhost." Suddenly alert under the impression that eatables were under discussion Victoria shrilled, "Give—me—one—two—three—dhosts." Expectantly, pronouncing each word in the painstakingly "correct" way that she has, she held out her hands.

"I'm afraid they don't come quite in that way, precious," Tanya told her. "Not good to eat. Cold. Clammy. You wouldn't like them."

"Oah," Victoria said. She looked quite disappointed. The loose roof iron banged again and somewhere in the house a door creaked on rusty hinges.

We pulled open the unlatched screen door and went inside. The five revolving chairs of the deserted lunch counter, tilted drunkenly upon their pivots, seemed to leer at us. Torn signs and ragged remnants of old Christmas decorations hung from empty shelves. Across the floor lay a long heavy ladder. From an open-doored adjoining room another ladder led upward through a trap door to the floor of the tower. A dead bird lay there in the dust. From the staring windows the eye ranged out over a shimmer of yucca-studded distance that merged into the lift of dry, tumbled mountains. A vast land of empty silence. And across it, glinting in the sun like a taut stretched wire, lay the thin hard line of 66—coming out of the far nowhere, vanishing into the heat-blurred loneliness ahead. Nothing stirred upon it. At that moment there was not a car in sight.

Presently from Rudyard, scouting afoot in the eagerness of exploration, came an excited yell. He came headlong on twinkling feet. "A spwing!" he gasped. "I found a spwing. I found a whole lakeful of spwings! Quick! Quick!"

It *was* water. But it wasn't quite either a spring or a lake. When we had hurried to the spot, goaded on by frenzied urgings, we found a big, muddy puddle, bordered with cattle tracks. A thin ramble of bermuda grass trailed on the soggy margin and in one corner clear water bubbled up out of the earth. "See!" Rudyard shrieked triumphantly, pointing. "A spwing! A flowing spwing! An' I found it."

Rider, whose pet hobby it is to shatter illusions, narrowed his eyes in a desert squint. He squatted by the bubbling fountain and grubbed with his fingers in the mud. "Flowing spring, nothing!" he announced loftily. "This is just a break in a pipe line."

"It isn't not! It's a spwing! My spwing! I found…."

"It's a pipe line."

"It's *not*!"

"It *is*!"

Battle and loud tumult, in the midst of which Victoria, shouting "'Ping! 'Ping!" and more intent on waving her arms than on her footing, tripped in a cow track and fell with a plop into the muddiest part of the puddle. Her lusty yells put an end to the argument. And when she had been rescued and dried off and peace once more had been restored, we investigated the mysterious pipe line further. It came from away off somewhere in the jagged mountains. Here and there, scarring the distant slopes, the line

of its route was visible. Evidently the water it carried came from a real spring and had been the station's source of supply. And it was good water. Poking and exploring about the buildings presently we found the shut-off valve—and faucets that previously had yielded only gasps of air came to life with silver trickles. No there wasn't much force. The break in the line diverted most of the flow into the cattle pool. But there was enough.

We camped at the lone white-walled station for several days, fixing worn tires, tightening bolts—doing many little overhaul and refitting jobs in preparation for another stretch of the trail ahead. We tethered the goats on the scanty patches of bermuda grass and other little pockets of available forage. Tanya built an outdoor fireplace of stones, unloaded from the trailer the big iron kettle that we had hauled from Yaquitepec, and busied herself with the concocting of many a savory "hunter's stew."

The children played in the wavering light-flecked shade of the several trees that had been planted about the building, amusing themselves by filling and refilling with water the long dry earth basins about the roots. They watered too the fragrant cluster of mint which surprisingly still thrived in the hard soil beneath one of the front windows. Cattle came down to the muddy pool at regular intervals to drink and to regard us curiously. Doves cut the morning air with whistling wings on their way to water. And at night coyotes, which were very bold, yammered at us angrily.

When the desert thunder showers drove down upon us, which they did more than once, we would snatch up everything spoilable and bolt to the shelter of the big front room. Here in security, while the desert wind roared and the thunder boomed and the loose iron sheets slam-banged upon the roof, we would sit and watch through the many-paned windows the rolling wall of dust, and the blinding whip-flicks of the lightning come charging across the desert like the mad rush of an assaulting army. There is a thrill to the hard sound of savage desert rain upon a metal roof. But in these headlong storms, brief as they were, we were glad to be under shelter.

Full days. Days of new experiences. For automatically, by the very fact of our being there, fate had cast about our shoulders the double mantle of property guardians and service station operators. It was inescapable. For it was seldom that 66 was as deserted as it had been on the occasion of our arrival. Usually it shuttled with life. Cars and trucks came whirring dustily out of the north and out of the south and quite a percentage of them stopped. The gas pumps of the station long ago had been removed. Its main sign had been blown down by the wind. Old car cushions and the litter from camps of many wayfarers strewed the approaches and the space beneath the wide porch roof. It would have seemed that anyone with half an eye would have realized 10 blocks away that the place was closed to business. But still the callers came, swerving their cars in to come to an expectant halt beside the wrecked cement base where once the gas pumps had stood.

Some came for gas and honked loudly at the gaping emptiness for service. Some came for lunches and betook themselves haughtily off when we came hastening to tell them that they had made a mistake.

Mourning dove

But most came for water. There was an old tub under the front porch, and a cracked enamel saucepan and a bent water pipe from which the faucet had been removed. The pipe yawned dry and thirsty when we first came. But after we had discovered the secret of the control valve at the back of the building we found that it could be made to spill forth water. After that we kept the tub full and the saucepan beside it for a dipper.

Rider appointed himself Chief of the Waterworks and after a short time we all became so adept that we usually could tell 200 yards away which cars were going to swerve in and stop. Then one or other of us would call, "Water, Rider." And, away behind the building, he would turn his precious valve. As the car slowed to a stop a thin silver stream would begin mysteriously to fountain from the pipe and splash into the tub. When the canteens or the radiator had been filled we, going about our own duties in the rear of the house where we had parked our car, would give Rider the high sign and just as mysteriously the water fountain out front would stop. Often it would shut off its splashing before the departing callers had climbed back into their car. Since none of us went out front to talk to them unless they really wanted information this sudden magical appearance and disappearance of the water ought to have been a bit puzzling to our visitors. But most of them accepted it as a matter of course. Or perhaps they concluded it was some automatic labor saving device, installed especially for their benefit. Which, after all, perhaps it was.

But not all travelers were unobservant, or heedless or scornful. Our few days' pause in that desert "house by the side of the road" where for a space we tried in a small way to "be a friend to man" was an experience never to be forgotten. For 66 soon ceased to be a highway; it became an artery of life. A throbbing artery in the body of a nation through which pulsed the very life blood of America. Comedy, tragedy, gladness and tears, joy and despair.

Day after day, hour after hour came the cars and the faces. Whirling out of nowhere, vanishing into emptiness. Old faces, young faces. Hard faces, simple faces. The faces of sinner and saint, of gangster and priest. Faces as different as the cars which bore them. Cars whose glittering lines and unworn tires seemed to shriek a heartless scorn at the misery of less fortunate humanity; cars whose tires, and the very rims upon which those tires had been mounted, had long since gone, so that they floundered by at a snail's pace, thudding their way onward on battered, revolving hunks of metal—spokeless, angular—any shape but round.

Voices in the night of children, voices to awaken you as you drowse in your blankets beneath the stars. Weary voices, sleepy voices—"Do we stop here tonight, Daddy?" The dark loom of a halted truck, the whimpering complaint of a pet dog. The hoarse anxious voice of a man speaking in low tones to reassure a couple of sleepy half-scared kids. They had limped to a halt and the battery was dead. They couldn't start the heavy loaded truck again. Headed for California. But they got off in the morning. All of us strained and pushed. And levered with a length of old pipe. The ground sloped a bit and the truck rolled and caught from the generator. They chugged away into the morning sunlight. The pup whimpered and wagged his tail and the two little boys waved. Out into the distance—down 66.

We left our deserted desert station at last and chugged onward ourselves. We were both glad and sorrowful to go. It had been so vital a spot—such a window upon life. But there was yet a spring to be discovered, a homespot that would fill the requirements we had set out to find. There were springs back in the mountains, it is true. But none of them were for us. We loaded car and trailer again and jumped the goats once more into their tiny pen. Once more on the open road for the desert ahead.

And we said good-bye to the roadrunner. The afternoon of our last day the children gave him a farewell party, tossing him bits of bread and desert-made cake, which he accepted gravely, cocking his head, bright eyed, and swallowing with a queer gobbling gulp. He was in many respects a remarkable roadrunner. Suspicious, the first day that he came trotting in from the desert to investigate us, he soon gained confidence and would come ambling up, carrying his long tail in that odd, wind blown fashion that roadrunners sometimes affect. He liked the shade of the car. And tidbits from the cook pot.

The last night of our stay at the old station we sat around the flickering light of a mesquite-wood fire. And Rider got the sudden notion to dig out from amidst the car load where it lay handy, the old photo album filled with pictures of the little, now far away, home at Yaquitepec. He thumbed through it slowly, and more slowly. Presently he stopped and sat gazing wistfully a long while.

"Daddy," he said suddenly, "couldn't you please send *this* picture to be published sometime?"

"Why?" I asked, bending closer in the dim dance of the fire flames to see the print at which he was pointing. "What's particular about that one. It's one of the old ones. What do you want that one for?"

"Because...Well, just because I—I like it," he said huskily.

It was a picture of Rhett and Scarlett taken on the last day he had seen them—the day he had helped lead them away through the desert canyons to pasture.

Desert Refuge 18

(January 1943)

IT WAS Victoria who first saw the little river as we came coasting down the flanks of the Utah mountains in the warm glow of a desert noon. "Watah!" she shrilled, pointing, "Too much watah, muvver! Big ocean."

"A wiver—a real wiver," Rudyard shrieked, his own eyes electrified, almost at the same instant, by the silver glint among the cottonwoods. "A wiver—the Mississippi wiver! Oh Daddy, can we go in and swim?"

"That's not the Mississippi," Rider said crushingly. "That's just a creek. It looks cool, though," he added. "And there might be tadpoles in it. If we could just stop a bit...."

So we stopped a bit, halting our sputtering old car under the whispering shade of a giant cottonwood, a pebble's toss from the rippling water. Dragon flies darted back and forth along the course of the little brook. And in the background, far beyond the belt of green cottonwoods and willows, cliffs of red sandstone glowed warm against the blue bowl of the sky. There was a dense patch of sunflowers on the opposite side of the road and Tanya, who mixes practicality with poetry, began to gather armfuls of the tender stalks and broad leaves for the goats. In the middle distance, across the hard knees of the hills, wound the tree-marked line of an irrigation ditch.

But our trio of youngsters waited not on a contemplation of scenery. Their entry into the state of Utah had been marked by the discovery of more fresh water—in one piece—than they had beheld in many weary leagues. And the day was warm. Shedding garments in a manner to suggest the trailing tails of comets Rider and Rudyard were already racing down the sloping bank. With wild yells of delight they flung themselves splashing into the shallow stream.

Victoria followed more slowly. Feminine caution asserted itself in the manner in which she poked gingerly at the ripples with her toes. A long while she studied the rippling streamlet, resisting—and even howling lustily—when we tried to urge her into it. "Too much watah," she said at length. And that was final. She picked herself a nice, cool, high and dry rock in the shade of a clump of young willows and sat down, for all the world like some staid old dowager at the seashore. All she needed was a piece of knitting.

But the boys splashed and rolled joyfully, chasing each other and exploring all the hollows and deep pools for tadpoles. Birds slipped softly through the thickets, and the over-arching branches of the trees patterned the singing water with shadows of smoky gold. A deep peace and content reigned there in that little tree-crowded dell and it was hard to realize that it too was as much a part of the desert as the ranks on ranks of bristling Joshua trees through which we had passed but a few miles back—a liquid note of softness and peace amidst the war chant of a barbaric symphony. But then, that is the desert. And in these startling contrasts lies its charm.

We went on at last—down the valley skirting the flanks of the glowing ruby cliffs. And the irrigation ditch, symbol of the toil and courage of Mormon pioneers, marched with us, till the rolling slopes opened and broke in a checkerboard pattern of green and silver where fields on fields of lush alfalfa mingled with the winding stream of the Virgin River. Thus we came to Utah.

It was Sunday. A Sabbath hush brooded the mellow sunlight that wrapped the old high-roofed Mormon houses. Along the grass-grown lanes primly dressed little girls walked decorously beneath the shade of the tall Lombardy poplars. The stores were all closed. Over the valley into which the Mormon pioneers had transported their wagons, piece by piece on their shoulders across the grim lava ridges, hung the drowsy benediction of peace.

But we were desert hungry and we halted presently before a big two-story farmhouse, whose time-stained adobes, warm-tinted with the weatherings of more than four-score years, would have stirred any artist to rapture. Water gurgled in the canal that bordered the vine smothered fence and by the gate that opened on a tree shaded lawn there was a sign that proclaimed "Goldfish for sale." An ancient rustic rocker sagged contentedly beside the porch steps and hard by the lift of the old brick walls spread the leaves of clustering fig trees. We bought grapes there, buying them from a sun-browned country boy, who went out into the vineyard and gathered them while we waited. Desert grapes. There was a spice and tang and freshness to them which only desert sun and air can give.

And then, chugging on through the drowse of that Sunday afternoon, we came upon the Little House. It stood close by the highway, sheltering timidly from the traffic behind a little patch of weed-grown lawn There was a mulberry tree and a grape arbor, and from somewhere among the low shrubs came the murmur of water trickling from an open faucet. Some of the windows of the Little House were broken and a silence hung over it—a silence that was wistful and friendly and appealing. We stopped the car and tiptoed across the neglected lawn to investigate.

The Little House was empty—empty and deserted save for Tibbets the cat. We did not know that her name was Tibbets then, but that was the name we gave her later. "Meow," said Tibbets sociably. She rubbed against our legs and purred. Tibbets was very thin. By actions that were as plain as words she welcomed us. "My people have gone away," Tibbets said. "But this is my home. Will you not come and live with me?"

And the Little House seemed to say the same thing. Delightedly, craving rest after weary travel, we explored about it, peeking in at the gaping windows, pausing to admire the yellow-gold bunches of grapes that hung in the little arbor. Victoria hugged the lean Tibbets in two chubby arms and Rider and Rudyard, scouting, reported that the water trickling from the faucet on the lawn came from a real spring…"away off somewhere at the foot of the hill." "Let's stay here, Mother," suggested Rider a bit enviously, "just for a little while, anyway…a month maybe. It's so quiet and beautiful."

"But we can't just stay," Tanya objected. "Someone owns it. You can't move into other people's property."

"Well, it's a nice place," Rudyard put in, "P'waps we could find out whose it is. We ought to inwestigate." He wrinkled his pudgy nose.

And the upshot of the matter was that we did "inwestigate." And in the town we found a charming, gracious lady, herself a daughter of one of the sterling pioneers who had first broken trails into the valley. "Why of course you can move in," she said when we had talked with her. "The house is my married daughter's and she is living now in Salt Lake City. She'd be happy to have someone there." And she waved us on our way with smiles that were as wholesome as the desert sunshine.

And so, happily, we came back to the Little House and to Tibbets the cat. And we unloaded the weary goats and set them to grazing upon good grass. And we swept the rooms and unpacked some possessions and watered the lawn and settled ourselves to a brief period of rest. Only Rider and Rudyard and Victoria refused to rest. They were too busy exploring. There was a spring back under the edge of the hill. Two springs. And there were cattails and bamboos and dark mysterious caves. And they built dams in the warm, red earth and filled them again and again with water…lots of water. "You 'member, Daddy," Rudyard said one day, "when we left Yaquitepec I wanted twelve whole gallons of water. Well, I fink now that I have had it."

And, judging from the mud with which the three rascals had plastered themselves, I thought so too.

There is fascination in Utah. Fascination and mystery—desert mystery that seems to sit oddly sometimes with the visible sights of ordered fields and irrigation and Mormon industry. An old land this, and strange. Along the ridges the black lava rocks tell a weird and terrible story of an Age of Fire; in the mountains the erosion sculptured cliffs tell an equally terrifying tale of an Age of Water. And the ground underfoot, even amidst the smiling gardens along the rivers, holds strange things. Arrowheads, pottery, beads—even such mysteries as charred fragments of wood and of human bone completely encased in incrustations from the waters of ancient lakes.

It has been pleasant and busy in the Little House—pleasant in the quiet peace that reigns here in this little valley beneath Utah's desert skies, and busy with many a side trip into adjacent territory in search of a permanent tarrying place. For the Little House and its springs never can be ours completely. We must find our own desert homespot. And that has not been yet.

But the passing days, as they have drifted one by one like falling leaves towards winter, have been happy. Tibbets the cat has grown fat and sleek and the goats drowse away the hours in good pasture. Rider, Rudyard and Victoria, sun-tinted and water satisfied are already going into mysterious conferences regarding the approach of Christmas. Speculating sometimes anxiously on old Santa's chances

Mule deer

this year of getting his sleigh and reindeer teams through the war-torn skies. Quiet days. And an occasional spice of adventure too. As, for instance when the lone, grey timber wolf came down out of the rocks in broad daylight and tried to carry off Betty, Rider's pet baby goat, and was scared off just in the nick of time. Rider, who first glimpsed the marauder, is not yet entirely convinced that it really was a wolf—claiming that timber wolves ought to be extinct in a civilized section. Well, that may be. But there is no argument as to his size. If he wasn't a wolf he was the most awesomely big coyote any of us have ever seen.

Yes, it has been happy here in this sheltered valley of the desert. But the day before yesterday, out of the north, the Pilgrim came down the road. He was driving a pair of big white burros attached to a covered wagon. In the wagon itself, among the pots and pans and blankets, snuggled a tiny black baby burro, while its mother, of the same color, trotted along behind.

A strange man, the Pilgrim—a man of rocks and specimens and ancient arrowheads and the atmosphere of the lone wastelands. The light of mystery was in his eyes—the mystery of far, lonely mountains and desolate desert reaches. A Pilgrim of the forgotten trails.

The Pilgrim came to a halt beside the Little House. And presently, as we talked, he looked at us fixedly. "What are you doing here?" he demanded. "This is not the place. Go on. Go on."

A strange man. He might have been a Spirit of the Wastelands. But he camped that day near the Little House and in the evening shared a simple meal with us. The grave, sincere philosophy that ran through all his talk and his tales of far places might have been almost terrifying to the uninitiated. But we had dwelt long in the lonely places ourselves and we knew that he spoke truth. We parted in the starglow. And in the morning when we went to look for him he had vanished. Wagon, burros—all had vanished somewhere into the far maze of dim trails. Rider and Rudyard, startled, solemnly affirmed that he had been a ghost. But there were wagon tracks and burro tracks upon the sandy earth, and they headed away—away into the distance. Ghosts usually do not leave tracks. So perhaps he was just what he said he was, a Pilgrim. He had delivered his message and departed.

So now we do not know. Shall we follow into the far reaches—head for the region he spoke of—or shall we stay on, waiting till the chill days of winter, tempering into spring, make travel easier. Not yet are we quite certain. But in a few days we shall know.

Desert Refuge 19
(February 1943)

IT IS a good while now since the Pilgrim, with his covered wagon and burros, vanished down the lone desert trails. And we are still here in the Little House under the Utah stars. Here we shall remain a while. For at the last minute we decided to put off our onward trek until the milder weather of Spring. Not that we have forgotten the Pilgrim's message, nor his tales of buried Indian cities. But the high mountain passes are chill now with snow. The search must wait awhile.

And the delay, though we chafe against it at times with an impatience to be on the trail once more, has brought no dull moments. There has been so much to do— and, in this new section of the great desert wonderland, so much to see. Plans or no plans Time will not stand still. Already it has swept us past another Christmas and into the wide highway of a new year.

It was a happy Christmas. And even though in a war torn world the word "happy" may seem out of place, the deeper significance of Christmas is such that the festival should be a happy one. Even in the midst of sorrow and battle and sudden death. For what is Christmas but a token, a sacred reminder a testimony to Immortality—to a Life and Hope that rise triumphant over death? It matters not where you celebrate Christmas—in a mansion, on a battlefield, or under the lee of a creosote bush on a lone desert. Its inner sacred meaning is the same.

But Rider, Rudyard and Victoria still view Christmas from the very personal angle of Santa Claus. Doggedly, all through these past few months, they have refused to be impressed by our numerous gloomy warnings that the old Saint would have a difficult time getting through this year. What with the bombs and the airplane-crowded skies and the gas rationing and the shortage of sugar, we warned them, he might be prevented from making his annual round entirely.

"Sandy Klaws," announced Rudyard with lofty authority, "—is majick! It would take more than the worst-est war to stop him. I just *know* he's gonna come. An' I'm gonna hang up my stocking just like always."

"An' I donna hang up *my* 'tocking, dust like a'ways, tew!" shrilled Victoria, faithfully echoing, as is her custom, the words of her hero. "Sanda Caws is maddick!"

Rider refused even to be drawn into the discussion. When Rider knows that a thing is so, then it is so. Why waste time arguing the matter. These tiresome oldsters, with their wavering faith! In due course, matter of factly, he hung up his stocking with the rest.

And the calm faith of all three of them was justified. Of course! For on Christmas morning there hung the three stockings, stuffed full. Shamefacedly we had to admit, amidst triumphant laughter at our expense, that we didn't know a thing about Santa Claus. He really was magic, we acknowledged.

Christmas always makes one a little misty eyed with its renewal of the ties of friendship and remembrance. So many friends, new friends and old. Friends whose cheery greetings came in person, and friends whose hearty letters and cards came winging in from every quarter of the compass, across many a weary league of desert and of mountains. And how shall we answer, we who so sadly lack the magic of old Santa Claus whereby he annihilates distance and who would, if he could, leap nimbly down the chimneys and grasp the hands of every one of his well-wishers. That is what we would like to do. But we cannot. We are tied to the feeble substitute of mere words. Dear friends, our thanks. To you, each and every one of you both near and far, our sincerest thanks and our heartiest New Year's wishes. Your cheery cards and letters all will be acknowledged in time. Alas how slow we are sometimes. Some of you must have lost all faith in us as correspondents. But it is not from indifference that our letter writing lags. Often sheer time lack blocks the task. These last months upon desert trails have been busy ones.

Snow whips often, these days, against the mountain peaks. And the winds that come galloping down across the foothills into this sheltered desert valley sometimes have a real bite in them. But the little tin stove which this year must take the place of the Yaquitepec fireplace does its duty nobly. We miss the dry mescal butts which on Ghost Mountain made the fires roar with their tossing fountains of flame. But there is other fuel in plenty and our "fuel gathering expeditions" of Yaquitepec merely have been transplanted to Utah. Dead mesquite and cottonwood and rabbit bush. It all goes to swell the pile in the back yard which each morning is crusted everywhere with thick crystals of frost—a lacy tangle of sparkling white sticks and branches through which the little white-crowned sparrows hop chillily, hunting for their breakfast.

Winter and warmth make a happy combination. The little stove rears red and there is usually a big iron pot bubbling upon it. A combination to induce story-telling. And it often does. The other morning, busy about our various tasks, we were suddenly aware that—down by the stove—Rudyard was regaling Victoria with a lecture on—of all things—the city of New York.

"...an' it's the biggust city in the world. An' down on the corner of Fourth Street there's a tree-menjus building, six feet high. An'...."

A loud, sarcastic sniff, from the region of the table where Rider was plowing through his daily dose of arithmetic—with one ear cocked for outside diversion—at this point disconcerted the lecturer, causing him to hastily amend his statement:

"I mean th' t'menjus building is a'most one hundred an *twenty* feet high," he declared loudly. "An' the peepul...."

The sniffing from the listening arithmetician here lifted to a wild horse laugh, against which no amount of self-importance could stand. Flustered, Rudyard leaped to his feet: "C'mon," he ordered gruffly, grabbing the enthralled Victoria by the hand and starting for the door. "C'mon outside. I got some bizness derangements to 'tend to."

And on the outside step, in the sunshine, where the lee of the wall sheltered them from the wind, the thrilling travelogue was run to a peaceful conclusion, with Victoria, breathless and goggle-eyed, hanging on every word. We couldn't hear much, even with the window stealthily opened. But we did get fragments of amazing statements. As, for instance, that: "In Noo York all the ground is full of submawine twains, jus' packed full of peepul. An' all day they go—Bizzzzz! Right between your feet." And "All the emptiness is used up, so there isn't any more room to build houses. But the peepul don't mind. They live all lots of hundreds together in little compartments, very happy and demented."

Yesterday, because the afternoon was so sunny and pleasant, we sidetracked a score of pressing tasks and all went up to the old reservoir. The reservoir is part of the domain of the Little House too. Some distance away and under the toe of a ridge it is a favorite spot with Rider, Rudyard and Victoria. Its weedy bottom, partly silted in, is now a thicket of water-grass and reeds. Cottonwood trees stand sentinel along the embankment and cast fantastic reflections in the shallow, marshy water that is the haunt of frogs and all manner of diminutive swamp creatures. Birds flit to and fro over the reeds and cottontail rabbits hop through the low, brushy thickets that have grown up along the neglected fences. From the summit of the embankment you can look away off across the valley and the desert ridges to where far fantastic cliffs of blue and white and pink and lavender hang phantom-like against the sky rim. Mysterious mountains—they draw and hold the imagination. For behind them lies some of the wildest, most alluring lands on all the earth—the vast sweep of the Painted Desert and the Indian country.

The fever of "exploration" drew Rider and Rudyard away from the reservoir after a while. And Victoria clamored so hard to go with them that we all tramped back among the stony ridges, investigating the gullies and peeking hopefully into every small cave. Black lava and red sandstone here take the place of the Ghost Mountain granite boulders. And as wind and rain can carve sandstone much more easily than granite the supply of tiny caves was quite satisfying. But not so their contents. The ancient people lived all over this country. They were here in numbers in the dim period subsequent to the "fire age." And there is ground for belief that they were here even before the volcanic eruptions. But the mills of Time, which slowly grind all earthly things to dust, had not spared many traces A couple of fragments of very old pottery—undecorated—were all that even the sharp eyes of Rider and Rudyard were able to discover for their "museums."

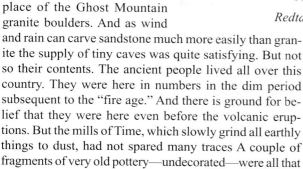

Redtailed hawk

We obviously had wandered into a poor relic district. But farther back, in the canyons and on the rocky mesas overlooking the Virgin River, we had been told there were petroglyphs and old village sites and a wealth of shattered pots.

Up a little sandy wash that was patterned with the crisscross trails of the small furry folk of the desert, we presently came upon several willow trees, lifting above a bordering thicket of rabbit bush. Somehow the sight of a willow tree always evokes thoughts of basket making. And our glimpse of these proved no exception. They were promptly raided for a supply of long pliant shoots, which Rider volunteered to pack home. There has been little enough time for basket making lately. But it is a craft which, like pottery and weaving, gets into one's blood. Once practiced its lure persists, and fingers are always itching to be at it again.

It is a healthy sign, and also a significant one, that interest in the primitive arts is growing. There are far too few people who realize the "escape" that handiwork of this sort provides. To nerves raw-edged and shattered by machine "civilization" there is nothing more soothing than the moulding of a clay pot or the weaving of a basket or a blanket. The nerves relax. As fingers fashion the moist clay or weave the threads or pliant straws, Time and Life seem to slip back into their rightful place. One seems to live again in an honest simple primitive world of homely virtues and peace. It is an inexpensive means of temporary "escape" too, as well as a fascinating one. Some sort

of clay is almost everywhere, for the digging. And almost everywhere one can obtain some sort of natural material from which to weave baskets or rugs. Try it sometime. You may be surprised at the enjoyment you get from it. And it is not outside the bounds of possibility that skill thus gained may, some time or other, be extremely valuable to you.

We wearied of exploring and tramping at last and sat down to rest upon a high sandstone ledge. From our vantage point we could look far out across the sere, foreground slopes and deep down into the valley of the Virgin River. In the sunlight the river was a thread of flashing silver, winding amidst the patterned green of Mormon farms.

It is evening now. And as I sit here on the embankment of the old reservoir, the typewriter balanced on my knees, my back against a gnarled old cottonwood, all the world seems very still and hushed. The sun has gone down behind the red sandstone ridges and a thin haze of storm, perhaps a warning of heavy weather to come, films the southern sky. Twilight is reaching into the canyons along the Virgin River, glooming them with phantom draperies of blue. Across the sparse brown grass of the slope below me there is a patch of color moving. It is Rider in his little red and blue blanket going to bring in the grazing goats for the night. The faint, musical tinkle of their bells comes drowsily across the silence. Silence and Peace and the Mountains.

Yes, the mountains. For, away on the horizon, hardening to a rose-tinted indigo in the lifting shadow of night, stand the great buttressed mountains that are the gateway the Great Spirit reared to guard the land of the Navajo—a simple, nomadic people, very close to the earth. And somehow, this evening, as I watch the eerie shadows deepen amidst the far distant crags and battlements, I am thinking of the words of an old Navajo, spoken many, many years ago:

"This is our land. It was our fathers." We were here before the white man came. We will be here long after he has vanished away."

The words of an old, old man of the desert. And spoken in bitterness. Just how much truth do they hold?

Sometimes I wonder.

Desert Refuge 20
(March 1943)

THE necklace lay upon the table. In the wintry desert sunlight that fell across it from the window it shone with a strange mellowed, yellow glow. Something like old ivory; yet different, more mysterious. Our friend, the archaeologist who had brought it, touched the beads lovingly.

"Basket Maker," he said. "At least 2,000 years old. Perhaps much more. Observe this pendant! Note the workmanship."

With the absorption of the specialist his fingers strayed here and there, touching individual beads, pointing out the carefully drilled string holes, calling attention under the lens, to a mass of fascinating detail that would have escaped anyone but an expert.

"We were examining a room in an old Pueblo village," he explained. "And somehow I wasn't satisfied. I had a feeling—call it a hunch if you want to. I began to dig deeper. And away down below the level of the first floor we came upon...."

You could see it all as he spoke. The grey sweep of the desert and its backing of tumbled mountains. The hard, dry, dusty earth with the traces of old walls. The yawning excavation in the ancient floor—a shaft that went not only into the depths of earth but also the depths of time. From the records of one ancient vanished race into the records of another, still more ancient. And there in the bottom of the shaft, grey with the dust of forgotten things, you saw the body. And the little heap of beads that, before the string had decayed, had been the necklace. And the water jar. And the cooking pot.

Knees drawn to chest the woman lay upon her side, her face turned upward. The water jar, deliberately punctured in two places, was under one arm. The cooking pot by the other. The grey bones of the body, laid to its rest in the forgotten centuries, were crumbling to soft dust in the touch of the outer air. And there in the grey dust lay the necklace. A little pile of beads and their semi-transparent pendant—lying where they had trickled down like tears

when the slow-march of the years had finally snapped the string that had bound them about a dusky throat.

Our friend went on to tell us about that ancient house located less than two miles from where we now lived. It had been under the floor of another dwelling whose builders had not in the least suspected what lay below their homesite. He told us of the posts and beams, whose fire charred sockets were eloquent of tragedy. He told us of the strata of sand and soil which the slow trowel of Time

Marshal grinding wheat on a rock. It was unsatisfactory because of gravel and it required too much sifting. They began using a hand mill.

had spread above the ruin. Strata which told of the changing courses of rivers, of the drifting banks of desert dust.

But we scarcely heard him. We were looking at the necklace lying there yellowed and mysterious in the glow of the winter sunshine. It was a talisman. Before its mellowed gleam 20 centuries rolled aside and fled. And it seemed to us that in the bright glow of other days we could see again the desert and the mountains and the gleaming silver of the river. And the little houses among the cornfields. And the smoke of the cooking fires. And we heard again the voices of men and women and the laughter of children and the steady thudding of grinding stones, pounding out meal.

And the necklace was moving to and fro, clasped about a slender dusky throat that was vibrant with life and with song. She must have been beautiful, that ancient wearer of the necklace. For, even after the lapse of 20 centuries, her teeth, as our friend had told us, with a touch of scientific awe, had gleamed in the dusk of that opened burial pit like a cluster of dazzling pearls.

Gruesome? No, it wasn't gruesome. If you could have sat there as we did, gazing at that old necklace gleaming mellowly in the sunshine, and if you could have sensed, as we did, the things that lay back in the soft dusk of the Time mists, you would have found nothing gruesome about it. Quite the contrary. For somehow that old necklace and the pictures it brought back out of the dead years was a song of glory. A message of Faith and Hope and Immortality.

* * *

Rudyard has his dog. Ever since Rudyard could walk and talk he has dreamed of some day having a dog. Now the dream is realized. For the other day, out of the north—just as the Pilgrim came—there came another wanderer. But this time it was a four-footed wanderer. We called her Bonny.

Bonny is of uncertain ancestry. But mostly shepherd. What story of other homes and other days lies behind her gentle brown eyes we cannot tell. Without collar or mark she came up the dusty path along the adobe wall and adopted us. She was weary and hungry and very footsore. The children rushed to hunt up a plate of scraps for her, which she gulped eagerly. "Maybe," said Rider, speculatively, "she fell out of some car or truck. Someone must own her."

But Rudyard wasn't bothering about questions of ownership or anything else. He just flung his arms around Bonny's shaggy head and hugged it to his heart. "My dawg. My dawg—my always-wanted-dawg," he kept saying huskily. For an hour or more, as she lay stretched on a sack, resting in a sunny angle of the wall, he sat beside her, holding her head and stroking it tenderly. Bonny likes Rudyard.

Bonny is now a firmly established member of the household. The boys hunted up a big box to serve as a kennel and Victoria toddled around collecting old sacks to lay in it for a bed. Now we have a watchdog. In her kennel Bonny curls up every night with just the tip of her sensitive nose visible in the starlight. And no intruder, either two-footed or four-footed, goes unchallenged.

There is only one jarring note in the new order of things. Tibbets, the cat, has moved out and left us.

Tibbets does not like dogs. Bonny tried her best to make friends with her. But Tibbets would have none of it. She drew aside her skirts with great dignity, spat twice—and departed across country. Rider still has hopes that Tibbets will return, as indeed we all have. Tibbets was Rider's special pet.

* * *

Wood gathering is an important job these chilly days, just as it was at Yaquitepec. Fortunately there is a good deal of dead brush and larger growth to be found in the little canyons and in the watercourses. And quite a bit of dry, burnable material in the thicket around the old reservoir. On pleasant days the youngsters make excursions and come home well loaded with kindling. And once in a while we take the car and trailer and haul in a mountain of varied fuel.

On the last of such expeditions we felt convinced that we had accumulated enough to last over the winter. But the bulk of it was willow logs which vanish in the stove almost as fast as our Ghost Mountain mescal butts did. So, soon we will have to make another foray. The boys don't mind, though. Not yet have they outgrown the novelty of this new location, and every trip is an adventure.

The cottonwoods lift bleak, bare branches against the sunset, and the edges of the mesas are iron-hard and grim against the chill dawns. But so far we cannot complain about the winter weather of this new section of the desert. Far to the north of Ghost Mountain though it is, the climate is surprisingly like the one we have been used to. Perhaps even a little milder. For there is less wind. The roaring gales that used to leap upon Yaquitepec with a fury that sometimes seemed to make the entire mountain tremble to its core, are absent here. Sometimes we miss them.

You grow to love the wind. The roar and thunder of it—the elemental force. A storm has a strange power over the human spirit, a sense of buoyant stimulation queerly tempered with fear. For none of us have yet become so "civilized" that we have outgrown our primitive awe of the elements. We sometimes think that we have. But that is only a pretense—a thin veneer of artificial shelters of glass and brick that we hide behind. Deep at heart the human being still quails at the heavy rumble of the thunder and at the blinding slash of the lightning—even as did his ancestor who cowered from the tempest in the darkest recess of a drafty cave. Fortunately, in spite of all our frills and trimmings, we are still creatures of the earth. And there is hope and comfort in that.

* * *

Playing outside the other day Rudyard pulled up an oddly shaped stone that was half buried in the earth.

Memory of similar shaped stones away back on Ghost Mountain prompted him to trot inside and show us his find. Sure enough it was a grinding stone such as the Indian women use in rubbing out corn. Evidently it had had considerable use before it had dropped from the last dusky hand to be buried in the desert dust. How old?

We could not tell. But we dusted it off and wiped the clinging earth from the crevices—and put it to work again at its old job. Another link across the mists of Time, in the chain that binds all humanity and all Life together. The dusky fingers lay down the tool, and the white fingers pick it up, to go on with the work. Not the first time that we have turned old things to our hands in the wilderness. Tanya, who still remembers long busy hours in the fevered offices of Wall Street, smiles sometimes at the queer changes the marching years have brought her.

We made a batch of pinole with the old grinder. The whole family, even Victoria, gathered round to shell the corn. We had bought it in the ear. Corn that had been raised back in the hills, perhaps—who knows—upon the self-same land as that from which the Indian owners of the grinding stone had drawn supplies. The gleaming ears were yellow and red, and the fat kernels, as we stripped them from the cobs, seemed literally bursting with the health and bounty of the good earth. Victoria chose easy ears and did not get off many kernels, because she stopped to admire each one carefully before she dropped it into the dish with the others. "I don' wan' to hurt them, muwer," she explained laboriously. "They are so boo-tiful."

You parch corn to make pinole. And when we had enough shelled we dumped it into a big iron kettle and set it over the fire, stirring it constantly with a wooden spoon so that it would toast evenly without burning. When it was toasted to a fragrant, brown crispness we took the pot off and spread the hot corn grains out to cool. Then, with the ancient grinding stone we rubbed them to meal on an improvised metate.

A long job, but worth it. You can eat pinole "as is" or you can eat it with a little sugar and milk. Any way it is delicious. There are various kinds of it. Some pinole is a mixture of different varieties of toasted grains. The old desert Indians went to a lot of trouble in collecting tiny seeds. Many of them seeds of grasses and not much bigger than dust grains.

* * *

Agave

A while ago, choosing good weather, we made a dash down into Arizona to investigate a possible location close to the Grand Canyon. The trip proved a failure as far as helping our problem of a new homesite. But it was rich in reward in other ways, for we brought back unforgettable memory pictures of a vast and lonely and beautiful land. Vivid, thrilling memories of Zion National Park, of the Navajo Bridge, of the quaint little town of Kanab of a host of other high spots in a mighty untamed world of solitude and color.

But most of all we brought back memories of the Navajo and the section of their reservation through which we passed. Not perhaps so much memories of sights—though there are picturesque enough things, and to spare, to be seen in Navajo land. But the things that clung to us were memories of sensation. For, somehow, in the land of the Navajo there is a strange sensation of Freedom—the old natural freedom which has vanished from most of the rest of the earth. It is not a complete freedom, it is true. The shadow of restraint hovers ever in the background. But still there is a great measure of Freedom there—the proud freedom of a land and of human beings who hold "Progress" and its insiduous fetters in scorn. Freedom is a fierce and precious thing. To some, self-satisfied in ease, it is a thing of small moment. But to those who love it as the wild things love it, it is more precious than the breath of life itself.

The Navajo dwell upon no sainted pedestal. God knows that they, in common with all of us, have faults enough to balance their virtues. But they love Freedom. They love it with all the passionate fierceness of the desert. And their love of it—does something to their territory. A mysterious something. As you pass through that land you can feel it. The wind blows a little fresher there. The sunshine is a little brighter. The faint subtle scent of the junipers, clinging along the sandstone cliffs is a little more fragrant than elsewhere. The smoke of the hogan fires rises towards the desert sky like the fume of a thousand altars, lifted in praise to the Great Spirit.

Freedom—those of us who hold in our hearts and veins that longing and that fire would rather tread a thousand times the hard trails and eat the lean fare of the wilderness than round out fatted years beneath the yoke of "Progress."

Desert Refuge 21
(April 1943)

CRACKLE of burning wood in the grey light of dawn—the aromatic tang of smoke lifting like incense in the chill morning air. Before the sun climbs above the ridge to eastward there is still the glitter of hoar frost upon the stems of dry grass and upon the black piles of fallen brushwood. Rudyard and Victoria have figured out a theory of their own to account for hoar frost. To them the sparkling crystals are "frozen moonlight"—a fanciful notion which despite error has much to be said for it.

A wood fire is a subject which easily arouses enthusiasm—nor is this reaction dependent upon chilly mornings. Cold or heat, dawnlight or dark the red flicker of fire flames through dry wood calls forth a mysterious "something" in the heart of every man who is not an utter clod. Perhaps this is because campfires and freedom have been so closely linked together in man's history, ever since he clambered above the groping intelligence of the brutes. The campfire in the cave, the campfire in the forest, upon the barren mountaintop, in the lone reaches of the desert—around those raw, leaping flames have always gathered the pioneers, the rebels, the defiant souls who would not wear the collar and chain of an ordered life fashioned by mass-minds.

Wood fires have solid, practical virtues about them too. There is more health to food cooked over wood flame. No other heat, no matter how "modern" and highly endorsed or chromium plated can begin to approach wood in its virtues of healthful and flavorful cooking. Maybe your scientists will scoff loudly at this. No matter. Let them continue to tinker with their gadgets and switches. But for a wholesome, satisfying meal, literally bursting with goodness and with every last particle of flavor brought out to perfection, we barbarians of the wasteland will vote for wood every time.

There is a logical explanation for this, for the thing is most certainly not "imagination." The reason is deep buried in laws of which we know little. Fundamentally it is a matter of vibration. Each different substance gives out a vibration that is peculiarly its own. There is a subtle difference in the quality of the heat given out by different fuels and heating methods. These different vibrations act upon the food. And thus, directly, upon the health of the eater.

In these days, modern housewives have brought about an avalanche of "refined" cooking methods—at who shall say what staggering costs in health. Even the devitalized "staff of life" limping in pallid spinelessness, as though ashamed of its spurious art-tan complexion, is only the hollow ghost of those husky bouncing loaves of crusty healthfulness which came from the bread baking ovens of our grandmothers. You found ash flakes on the under side of those loaves very often. And occasionally an honest black fragment of charcoal. But when you bit into a slice from one of those loaves there was flavor and health; you were eating real food.

Sometimes, since we left Yaquitepec, I have been sorry that we ever built the tiny little mud oven that was our first homemaking work. We set it up in the midst of the rocks and mescals in the wilderness of the mountaintop—carrying the water to make the mud for it up the mountain on our backs and tramping its adobe floor level with our bare feet. Its low, flattish dome was reared of juniper branches thickly covered with clay.

A little oven, but efficient. We baked bread in it and we cooked savory stews in black iron pots before the heat of its open door. Around it we built our home. Yet now, sometimes I am sorry that we ever made it. For the thing has become uncanny—we must have built into it something more than we knew. Often in the hushed watches of the night, while the stars twinkle and the night wind whispers softly to itself among the creosote bushes, that little old mud oven reached out across the long, lonely leagues and tugs insistently at heart strings.

* * *

Bluebirds driving in a gusty whirl of color past the grey poles of the old corral—cottonwoods bright and sparkling in a glory of new leaf. Along the fence in the lee of a piled mass of last year's tumbleweeds, Betty, Rider's special pet goat, is rummaging happily for fresh green grass. Yes spring is here. The deep, throbbing heart of the earth pours out new life and hope and the world of the desert rouses to begin another year.

Rider is setting type. The composing stick is crude and home made and he has to handle it warily to avoid spilling out the letters as he reaches about the type case picking out A's and E's and T's with painstaking precision. Rider sets type quite well and seldom makes mistakes. With a natural aptitude for anything mechanical requiring care he has taken to printing like a duck to water.

Rudyard prints too—with weird wooden type of his own construction, sawed with much puffing and nose wrinkling from odd scraps of old wooden boxes. Rudyard's type—and the printed creations they turn out—are like nothing ever seen in earth or sky or sea. But he is very proud of his work. His ambition at the moment is to "print the most remarkablest book in all the world." Somehow we have a conviction that it will be just that.

Our desert printshop has grown slowly. About like mescals and chollas grow—almost imperceptibly over a long period. Our first printing press was homemade. It was fashioned of wood and iron scraps and held together by homemade bolts.

For its design we studied, by the aid of a magnifying glass, the engraving of an ancient printing press which was on the postage stamp issued to commemorate the three hundredth anniversary of printing in America. All things considered our modified copy wasn't a bad press, even though it did function by means of a screw taken from a discarded piano stool, and with a hand lever that once had been a wheel-cap wrench in the good old horse and buggy days.

To hold the type we made a chase out of wood, a remarkable contraption of our own invention that was more efficient than handsome. Our first experimental type was cut with a jackknife from scraps of old boards and old boxes found around the house. This and some illustrative wood-cuts, fashioned from similar discarded bits of wood, enabled us to really start printing. We didn't even have a hand-roller in the early days, but used a homemade leather buffer—quite in the approved style of Gutenberg with which to ink our type and cuts.

In such manner we started in upon our career of "Printers and Binders." We graduated to linoleum-cut type and blocks after a while. And later still to what Rudyard calls some "really, truly" type. We got our first big thrill when we "published" our first book. This was a microscopic volume containing just three stanzas selected from an inspired narrative poem that had been written by a scientist friend in Colorado.

The original poem, a remarkable work of genius, dealing with the massacre of the cliff dwellers by the Navajo on Fifty Mile Mountain, contained in its entirety 57 stanzas. But that number appalled us. Anyway our type volume wouldn't have begun to take care of it. So we compromised on three stanzas (all we had type for). After printing, not forgetting a neat little notice of the publication date and the fact that it was produced by "The Yaquitepec Press," we rummaged our odds-and-ends stores and bound the work in scraps of art paper and imitation leather.

It was strictly a "limited edition." For only two copies of the book ever were printed and only one ever bound. But of that one bound copy we were rather foolishly proud. The author was proud of it too—a fact which speaks volumes for the loyalty of friendship. He hadn't known, when he sent us the poem to read, that he was submitting it to a "publisher." So when the tiny little volume fell out of his mail one morning he was both astonished and delighted. He treasured that little book with inordinate pride, up to the day of his untimely death. And I have no doubt that somewhere, among the mass of brilliant scientific data which was left unfinished by his passing, that little volume still reposes in ordered, and listed, security.

So our desert printing has, in a fashion, already acquired a background and an honorable history. Equipment is a bit better now. The old wooden press has been superceded by a tiny modern one that works by a hand lever. And the type supply is a bit more adequate. A long, long way from where our dreams have set it in the future. But still, like the desert plants, it slowly grows. Already, in comparison, it has come quite a way. The sunlight falls through the window and across the type cases. And amidst the clicking of my machine, as I write these words, I can hear the low sound of Rider's voice as he whispers, half to himself, the words of the "copy" he is setting up.

* * *

…I had just written the sentence above when suddenly something happened. Nothing that you could see, nothing that you could feel. The sunlight still beat warmly through the window and beyond, to the north, the hard rocks of the barren ridge still glistened amidst their thin tufting of creosote bushes. There hadn't been a sound or a flicker out of ordinary. Everything was seemingly the same as it had been a dozen seconds before.

But it wasn't. *Something* had happened. A bubbling flood of thought had ceased as suddenly as though a valve had been closed. I could not write another word. I sat there baffled and puzzled, staring out into the sunshine. Thought was dead. And presently, in the hush, I became aware of another thing. Rider's whispering to himself and the click of the type as he assembled the letters together was growing slower. Soon the faint sounds ceased altogether. A bit sheepishly he laid aside the task and yawned. "Think I'll go out and see what Rudyard's doing," he said lamely. He drifted out of the door. Work was at an end. I sat for another 20 minutes vainly trying to understand what had happened to myself. Then I too gave up. There was wood to chop, anyway. At least I could do that. I put away the typewriter.

That night there was a sudden freak storm. The temperature tumbled. Savage winds roared with bitter cold. All the next day we hugged around the stove. Then came night and peace. And this morning the sun came up bright and smiling as though nothing had happened. The whole desert world was back to normal. And thought had returned. Also unasked, Rider went back to his typesetting.

All of which signifies—what?

Well, it signifies a good deal. Not as an isolated instance—that way you might dismiss it without particular notice, the way we do so many things. But this, for us, was not an isolated instance. It was just one more link in a chain of similar "mysterious" happenings. Happenings which reveal startlingly the effect which environment and natural happenings exert upon man and other living creatures. There is nothing new about this effect upon thought, activity, health and life, which storms and atmospheric changes bring. Savages and wild creatures react to these influences instinctively, without question. But there is something new to the acceptance of these facts by "civilized" man who, while he realizes that he gets wet if it rains and gets hot if the sun is too warm, scoffs utterly at all the more subtle influences of what for the sake of simplicity we may call atmospheric changes.

Yet these subtle influences, which of course go much deeper than mere barometric indications and pressure areas, have a wide reach and an influence that hardly is guessed at. The nervous organism of a living thing, *if it is living a natural life close to nature*, is more sensitive than any instrument. Birds are sensitive to coming changes long before any signs are apparent to the eye or the duller senses. The animals of the forests and the deserts and the savage also have this inner prompting.

Almost everything has it that is in intimate contact with the earth. All except civilized man. Civilized man is so insulated in his houses, his paved cities, his shoes and his insulating armor of clothes that he is immune to natural vibrations. At best they reach him only feebly and imperfectly. Yet how many battles have been lost, how many nations have fallen, how many races and civilizations have wilted and withered because of some subtle, temporary or permanent change in the invisible environment.

But man does not give much thought to his invisible surroundings or to nature while he dwells in fat valleys or in cities. It is mostly in lean wildernesses, in the vast hush of deserts or in the savage wind-howled mountains of lands like Tibet, that his thoughts turn outward, away from himself and to a contemplation of the unguessed miracles of the Great Spirit that surround him on every hand. It was the wise men of the deserts of old Chaldea who learned to unravel the mysteries of shining night skies. It was the wise men of the deserts who saw also the Strange Star in the East—and followed it.

Desert Refuge 22
(May 1943)

THIS is the time of year when, upon Ghost Mountain, the hardy mescals thrust lofty flower shoots toward the desert sky. This year will be the first of many that the mescal season has not meant a great deal to us. For the period was always looked forward to. Not alone for the yellow glory of the blooms, which transformed the desert into a garden of tossing gold, but also because of the wholesome, candy-like food which roast mescal hearts provided us.

Perhaps, more than any other thing, the mescals and the ancient mescal hearths, where the old-time Indians roasted the toothsome delicacy long before our day, expressed the spirit of Ghost Mountain. In that rock bound solitude of hushed desert peace, where silence reigns and where the warm, faint breeze, laden with the spicy tang of creosotes and of junipers, drifts down sunlit slopes, the lone, deserted old mescal hearths are like shrines left by a forgotten people. One can sit beside the ancient, fire-blackened stones and dream, weaving a tapestry of fancy back through the long dead years of a simple, primitive world that has crumbled and vanished, even as have the brown hands that once tended the ancient roasting hearths.

But the desert is the desert. Minor features may vary with locality, but the mysterious, inscrutable spirit of it remains the same. Right here, where we are at present, we have no mescals. But there are other things to compensate, and the song of the desert has lost nothing of its charm because of the one missing note.

To console us for our lost century plants we have new strange ridges of fantastic black lava, new cliffs of wind-sculptured sandstone that glow pink and vermilion in the changing light, new ranks of aromatic sage brush to scent the wandering winds. "It takes hold of you, this country," said a friend who had drifted in from away beyond Kayenta. "I came out, in the first place, for just a couple of weeks. But I haven't got back yet."

"How long ago was that?" we asked him, for he didn't look like a recent arrival.

"Quite a bit over 40 years," he answered, his face crinkling in a grin. "Guess maybe I'll decide to stay. I wouldn't know how to live anywhere else now. The desert sort of gets into your blood."

It has been raining for almost a week. Spring rain. The sort that always makes your fingers itch to be working in the moist earth. In the desert especially. Because somehow every primitive and fundamental urge of man and nature seems to be intensified in the desert. Nature's spur of adversity working to goad life towards more strenuous efforts. It is this combination which has developed the defensive armor of desert plants; which has made desert animals so tough and resourceful, which made the desert Indian more than a match for his rivals of more favored localities.

This particular storm was a surprise. We had not expected it. We had planned a trip to investigate a possible new home location of which we had heard. All arrangements had been made and we were ready for an early morning start. Rider and Rudyard had gone to bed all keyed up with the sense of impending adventure, impatient for morning. And we all awoke to the steady drip of rain. Drip! Drip! A depressing, monotonous trickling. Adventure faded. In the glum light of the open door we could see away across shadowy ridges wrapped in chill half light that was a blend of fog and retreating night.

"O-oh," Rudyard said. And there was the ultimate of dejection in his voice. "Won't we be able to go, Daddy?"

Answer wasn't necessary. He knew well enough. Rider scrambled from the bed covers and drew back the curtains—the same curtains that we had hauled all the way from Yaquitepec—and peered out. "No," he said gloomily, "we're not going today. And probably not tomorrow either."

The desert was a world of dripping grey, through which the nearer rocky ridges shouldered like ghosts. The creosotes and the mesquites and the grey hunched sage brushes stood about bedraggled and dripping like dejected chickens in a barnyard. The sky was roofed with a canopy of weeping cloud which rifted every once in a while to reveal long, sinister streamers of denser, sodden vapor hurrying in from the southeast.

Desert cottontail rabbit

Drip! Drip! Drip! The water trickled from the house eaves and the cat, outside the screen door, mewed querulously to be let in. Betty, the little goat, stamped and fidgeted in her hutch, near the porch. And Bonny, the dog, snuffed and scratched noisily for fleas in her improvised kennel. No, there would be no excursion today.

The storm brought unexpected compensations. For, after breakfast, to console the boys for their lost trip, I led an expedition out across the gully to get yucca leaves for basket weaving.

A wet trip. Rudyard had thoughtfully suggested that Victoria come too, arguing that the more hands the more yucca leaves would be brought home. But Tanya, after one glance at the downpour (which Rudyard had assured her was "almost stopping") declined the kind invitation on Victoria's behalf. A duck, she said, might make the trip. But as for Victoria—

Victoria howled. "I wanna go! I wanna go! I am, too, a duck! I wanna...." Rain shut down in a curtain and blotted the lamentations. Rider, Rudyard and I floundered

off into the sloshy greyness. There was a wind rising and as we crossed the gully it lifted in a whirling gust, driving the rain in chill sheets before it. Rudyard, half blinded, lost his footing, sat down heavily in the slick mud and shot like a toboggan to the bottom, half scaring to death a tiny cottontail that had been sheltering under an old mesquite stump. As the rabbit fled away into the mist and Rudyard picked himself up, sputtering, Rider voiced a triumphant shout.

"You've found clay!" he yelled, pointing to the deep, muddy track of Rudyard's descent. "Look, you've found clay. Now we can make some pots."

It proved to be true. Eagerly, his mishap forgotten, Rudyard clawed muddy fingers into the red, gooey streak that his fall had laid bare. It was clay all right. Not a very good clay—too much sand in it. But clay nevertheless. "You go on for the yucca leaves," Rudyard ordered. "I'll stay here an' dig out a whole armful. I want to make a tremenjus pot."

We left him squatting in the rain—a little brown ball of mud, with two muddy little hands, busily quarrying more mud. When Rider and I got back, lugging bundles of green yucca leaves, he had a great pile of the sticky stuff all ready. Happy and muddy and as soaked to the skin as any trio of all but drowned desert rats, we plodded homeward with our loot.

* * *

There are disadvantages in the use of green yucca leaves for basket making. Chiefly because they shrink and change shape as they dry. The right way is to season the leaves first. Or if you need an especially pliable material, to prepare them as fiber and spin them into cordage. However, the green leaves are pleasant to work with. And if you make reasonable allowances for what you may expect in drying you can get quite serviceable results. We wanted to make baskets and to experiment with fashioning yucca sandals, which was the footgear the ancient Indians of these parts habitually wore. We decided to use the green leaves for both, even though cordage, for sandals, is almost a necessity. Still, it would do no harm to experiment.

Results were better even than we had hoped. For basket stakes there were enough willow twigs already in the house, left-overs from a previous handicraft session. And there were even several short lengths of yucca cord, that we had made some time before—just in case we happened to need them. Rider elected to make himself a hanging basket—"that would maybe do to hang up a potted cactus in." I decided to experiment with the sandals and Rudyard settled, with the big store of clay, to the fashioning of "tremenjus pot."

Work, if it be something in which one is really interested is the finest means of "escape" which life holds. We were soon so absorbed in our jobs that we forgot all about the rain, which poured from the eaves, and we did not hear the trumpeting of the wind, which skirled drearily through the cottonwoods. The little tin stove, around which earlier in the morning Tanya had set pans of bread to rise, threw out a cheery warmth. Thomas, the yellow cat—he who had taken the place of Tibbets, who never returned—sprawled on the floor and dreamed. Victoria got out her dolls, propped them in a row against the wall and started in to teach them to read—from an old magazine held upside down.

A cheerful, companionable half-silence settled over everything—quiet which was patterned by the soft rustle of busy fingers weaving yucca leaves and-by a low, intense series of agitated puffs and grunts as Rudyard laboriously rolled out lengths of moist clay and coiled them down with much squinting and nose wrinkling, on his great pot. Tanya came and softly took away her loaves after a while, and soon the warm odor of baking bread drifted through the house. Victoria with her pet doll clutched tight in her arms had gone to sleep beside the cat. Peace reigned—and industry. The weavers wove on.

Suddenly there was a hideous yell—a shriek so unexpected and startling that I jumped as though from an electric shock. Rider fell over backwards from his stool. The cat leaped for safety. Victoria woke, squalling in terror, and from the adjoining room Tanya came in a frantic rush. The air was suddenly hazy with whirling yucca stalks and hurtling pieces of mud. The space around the stove had, in a twinkling, become a tornado. And in the center of it all, when our shocked nerves had snapped back and our startled eyes would once more function, we beheld Rudyard, yelling like a mad Indian, leaping up and down furiously upon a shapeless mound of mud and hurling fragments of wet clay right and left against the wall. The "tremenjus pot"—which for a long while had been teetering perilously like the Tower of Pisa—*had fallen in.*

Pandemonium raged. Capable writers in such a crisis are wont to sigh tactfully, "Let us draw a veil…." But this was something over which no veil would have had any power. We would have needed a tarpaulin and several blankets. Rudyard has a slated future which lies along musical and art lines. And he has all the temperament. When things go wrong he tears his hair like any opera singer.

And this time he was tearing it with gooey, muddy fingers. And yelling at the top of his lungs. His dream had fallen; his heart was broken. The wonderful pot! It had collapsed in horrid ruin. And so much toilsome effort! And nose wrinkling! And laborious puffing! Gone! All gone into a shapeless mess. It was more than human nature could bear. And he didn't intend to bear it. Savagely, yelling incoherent weird words, he leaped up and down upon the wreck of his masterpiece, tearing his hair and pounding the squashy clay into the floorboards.

It ended after a while. After we had all made a concerted attack upon the artist and had practically gagged and hog-tied him and carried him off to be pacified by honey and new bread and many bribes—which included immunity from his task of helping with the dishes that evening. But the party was broken up and the weaving was at an end for that day. After we had cleaned up the mess of clay and collected the scattered yucca stalks it was time to light the evening lamp. It was still raining outside.

And it was raining the next day. And the next. But the battered clay was pressed again into service on a smaller pot and the yucca leaves held out. It is still raining. But you can see ragged breaks in the clouds over the mountains. Tomorrow there will be sun—the dazzling desert sunshine that always has a diamond sparkle after a rain. And the deep blue of the sky will be dotted by tumbled masses of billowy vapor dispersing like scattering fleets of white sailed ships towards the wire-sharp rim of the distant horizon. The storm is about over. And the yucca sandals are finished. And the hanging basket. AND the pot.

Desert Refuge 23
(June 1943)

ON THE road again, the blue bowl of the desert sky for a roof and a fringing rim of far blue mountains everywhere upon the horizon. The old Ford puffs and chugs and the heavily loaded trailer creaks and sways as it trundles along behind. It is good to be on the trail again, even though a scrupulous care in the conservation of gas and rubber has shorn our voyaging down to absolute necessity. But the miles that unroll now beneath the wheels are really those that we stored up during the winter, when for the greater part of the time the car was laid up and we used our legs instead. It was a long rest—or it seemed so, to our impatience. Now it is good to be once more on the move.

The children are all excitement. To them all things new are an adventure. And their eyes are constantly searching the horizon. But there is a tinge of wistful remembering threading through their eager chatter. Those were happy days in the Little House. And under the cottonwoods among the bushy thickets of the old reservoir.

Rudyard still thinks of the frog that had his home in a grass-grown cow-track at the base of a gnarled rabbit bush. A friendly jewel-eyed little fellow, that frog. Half concealed by the grass blades in his little retreat he would sit and watch us with his deep, shining eyes until Rudyard would tickle him gently with a grass stem. Then *flip!* he would be gone, a tiny mottled green body making great hops towards the reedy water. But next day he would be back again in the cow track.

After a few times we got the notion that he really expected us. And enjoyed it all as a great game. Now that we come no more he probably will sit and muse about all the strange meaning of his adventures. And he will tell the story to his children. And it will be handed down from generation to generation. And become frog mythology. And bespectacled frog scientists, in the days to come will prove that it was all just a wild dream about something that never really happened. Just as our own learned men can prove to you, in short order, that there is positively nothing at all in old legends and fairy tales and in the strange dim stories handed down from generation to generation by all primitive peoples.

Shimmers of warm air ripple mysteriously across the great sweep of the land that falls away in broad glowing reaches from where I sit, until it fades into dim, pastel distance. The weird Joshua that reaches above me throws a pattern of fantastic shadow sharp as though cut from jet. Overhead a buzzard wheels in high effortless circles. And the hard, glowing mountains that march across the horizon are those of Nevada. Silence lies over all. And peace. The faint, almost inaudible stirring of the little threads of desert wind that steal through the creosotes might be the soft footfalls of the Great Spirit, walking through the wilderness as in the beginning of the world.

It is a hushed dreamy place, this noonday lunch spot. Tanya is feeding sun-bleached greasewood sticks to a little fire over which a skillet frizzles. And between times she

Rider and Rudyard—budding artists.

is scribbling a poem with a stub of pencil upon the back of an old envelope. Rider, Rudyard and Victoria have carried a piece of old canvas to the shade of a wide spreading creosote bush and are stretched upon it in drowsy content, the two younger ones scuffing happy fingers in the warm desert earth as they pile twigs and bits of stone together in play houses and fences and corrals. Rider, a bit apart, is experimenting, thoughtfully, with the braiding and weaving possibilities of yucca leaves.

A happy desert trio, these young hopefuls. And beginning more and more to take hold upon life. When they heard me bewailing the fact that a suitable photograph would be unobtainable for this month's article they promptly went into a mysterious huddle. From which emerged, some time later, the three sketch layout which this time does duty for a photo. Rider, with the mature wisdom of nine years contented himself with one sketch. But Rudyard, perhaps feeling that he must, in some way, even up his disadvantage of being only five, decided to put in two.

Victoria had a hand in the pie also. But the boys, knowing her "Impressionistic" style of drawing, foxily talked her into putting her masterpiece upon a separate sheet—which alas, failed to get by the art critic.

* * *

The wheels have rolled onward. The camp spot this evening is far different from our resting place of noon. The Joshua trees have gone. In their place the creosotes stud a flatter, lower land that is greying in the mists of a lonely twilight. Wind stirs bleakly through the bushes and the supper fire skirls ragged streamers of orange flame. The bed blankets are spread in a clear open space as far as possible from any bushes. For he who seeks the shelter of greasewood or other desert growths for his bed is likely to attract unwelcome bedfellows. Not that the presence of a warmth-seeking sidewinder is to be expected. But it is something to be cautious about. And scorpions, too, are more apt to be lurking about the base of bushes where they den in the mouse or chipmunk burrows. A bed well in the open is the prudent thing. And a little healthy desert wind hurts no one.

Certainly it does not seem to be hurting Rider, Rudyard or Victoria. For they are at their nightly acrobatics, turning swift somersaults from one end of the spread blanket to the other. Sometimes all three of them, in line, go whirling heels over head, clear down the whole length of blanket covered earth and back again. Like these nimble tumble-bugs they go so fast that all you can see is a blur of flying brown arms and legs and revolving bodies. And the evening air vibrates with wild shrieks of joy—punctuated by an occasional "Ouch!" as one or the other overshoots the blanket padding and rolls off onto the pebble littered earth.

But such mishaps only serve to add spice to the game. They never seem to grow tired and each night the circus has to be terminated almost by force. Victoria is just as much a somersault fan as the boys. Perhaps more so. She has tried very hard to teach her rag doll "Georgine" to turn somersaults. But so far with only partial success.

It has grown darker. Night is folding down like a shadowy blanket. Tanya has just thrown a fresh armful of dry sticks upon the fire and now sits silent, lost in thought, gazing deep into the red heart of the blaze. The wind has gone down a little and above the luminous drift of the fire smoke, clear stars are winking. I have moved closer to the leaping flames. Not for warmth but because without their ruddy light upon the page I can no longer see to write. Out of the darkness and into the circle of glow about my feet comes ambling a huge old pinacate beetle, dignified, investigative, for all the world like some frock-coated old professor out for his evening stroll. His shiny black body glistens in the firelight as he pokes about, waddling around pebbles, thrusting a curious nose under fallen twigs. Gently I touch him with a slender stick. And instantly he stands upon his head and freezes, his pointed rear end upreared like the menacing muzzle of a siege gun.

Curious fellows these pinacates. And widely distributed. Scorpions are said to abhor them. For very practical reasons. For it is asserted that the pinacate is capable of discharging a cloud of gas that is death to scorpions. I have it on the solemn authority of an old-timer that if you place a pinacate beetle and a scorpion together in an empty glass fruit jar the scorpion will speedily succumb. Whether this be true or not I cannot say, for I have never tried the experiment. There is grief enough among the ranks of our "younger brothers" of creation without humans having to add to it.

Desert Refuge 24
(July 1943)

ON THE trail—somewhere in the desert. This is written in the shade of a cottonwood tree that lifts a crest of green into a crystalline sparkle of morning sunlight. Carpenter bees drone in the belt of shadow and the stir of a faint breeze trails wisps of smoke from the dying breakfast fire across my feet.

The tangy aroma of dry burning creosote sticks. Some people don't like it. The greasewood—or creosote bush—has had hard things said about it. Even grizzled old prospectors have been known to display an amazing vocabulary of explosive words over the presence of a few accidental creosote leaves in the coffee brew.

Yet the creosote, to those who love the desert for what it really is, is a shrub both respected and admired. It fills a place in desert scenery for which no other growth can substitute. To us, those sections of the wasteland where the creosote does not thrive carry a sense of incompleteness. Poets have sung wistfully of longings for the sight of pine trees, for glimpses of ferny dells, of cravings for the sight of clambering roses. I never have known such heart tugs. But I have been often acutely homesick for the sight of creosote bushes.

I can remember arousing the wrath—and I believe pity—of a good eastern friend, by dividing the map of the United States into two sections, or rather, two regions of climate range. The pink shaded portions—all the area in which creosote bushes could exist—were the "abode of the blest." Everything outside was a howling wilderness—unfit for human habitation. That was a good many years ago, and passing time has mellowed the edge from youthful intolerance. I no longer draw maps to hurt the feelings of those whose tastes differ. Yet I still think that the creosote bush is emblematic. Its range defines the boundaries of a "homeland" outside of which I am heavy hearted. And I still think that a creosote bush in full bloom in the desert spring is one of the most beautiful shrubs in the world.

Out of the picture galleries of memory I can call up many beautiful recollections of blooming creosotes. But one such picture always will stand out sharp above the rest. It was on the occasion when I was trekking home to Yaquitepec with the two burros, Rhett and Scarlett, whom I had brought from Paul Wilhelm's Thousand Palms Oasis, away over beyond Indio. It was near the end of the trip. We had come a long way that day and we were tired. My two faithful four-footed friends, seasoned though they were, were stumbling. And I was footsore and unutterably weary.

As we plodded up the grade, winding up from the desert land into the lower reaches of Sentenac Canyon, the sun was setting. Blue shadows were gathering against the towering steeps ahead and the canyons and gullies were eerie chasms of indigo. Across the mountain crests the last shafts of the sun struck through the rising evening greyness like the level beams of searchlights stabbing through mist. And there, by the side of the road, as we started up into the gathering dimness of the pass, stood a great creosote bush in all the magnificence of late full bloom. It was in the direct path of a shaft of sunlight that fell upon it from a gap in the westward mountains and covered it with glory. Against the background of the blinding rays that flooded it and flung it into a tracery of delicate silhouette, it stood as an ethereal thing, a thing wrought not from plant fibers but from flashing precious metals. Drenched in a glove of gold and silver from its myriad yellow flowers and tufty white seed globes, its maze of interlaced slender branches and glittering green leaves lifted against the sun-flare in a brilliance that was almost blinding. The thing was breath-taking. We all stopped. Perhaps the burros stopped because they were tired and because I had stopped. I do not know. But I know that it was not because of weariness that I halted. The action was involuntary. I felt as though, for a flash, I had *seen something*. Such flashes bring one very close to God.

We went on presently. Winding up into the velvet dimness of the pass where owls had begun to hoot to each other from wall to wall across the rocky canyon sides. Night rolled down from the peaks as we plodded on. But somehow I didn't feel half as weary as I had before. And, from whatever reason, even the burros were stepping more briskly. Just a creosote bush against the sunset. Sometimes I wonder how long man will seek his assurance of immortality in musty books and in gloomy temples of man-reared stone, when the evidence surrounds him on every hand, in every vista of wonder and of beauty which the world of the outdoors holds.

* * *

The sun is climbing across the sky. The shadow of the cottonwood under which I sit has begun to break up

into a filigree pattern through which, on the warm earth, ants scurry exploringly. Heat waves dance and shimmer along the distant ridges. And through the still air the voices of Rider, Rudyard and Victoria rise sharp and clear as they prowl around the camp, seeking treasures and adventure among the rocks and bushes and mesquites. For them this home-search could go on indefinitely. Their eyes and hopes are always fixed on far and new horizons. They do not want to stop searching. It is too gloriously exciting. Yet we have a feeling that the goal—and the decision—is not now so far off. Perhaps we too shall miss the thrill of seeking through the desert and following new trails when we cast anchor. But there will be compensations. It is good to root down for a while and weave a thatch above one's head and call it "home."

Yet there is joy to seeking. Joys and surprises that spring up unexpectedly to cheer hard trails as though with a magic bloom of flowers. If there is one thing more than another which has heartened us, since we set out on the trail from Yaquitepec, it has been the realization of the great invisible bond of friendliness which binds all desert dwellers and desert lovers into one solid fraternity. A cheerful clan, eager and warm-hearted and friendly.

Never has it failed that when disappointment struck at us, or when trails ahead looked bleak, desert friends always were on hand to lift the gloom, either by personal word or by letters or even by telegram. "Do not be disappointed. It is always darkest before dawn," wired a good friend from Nevada who learned of our unexpected set-backs. "There just must be—and is—a right location somewhere for you and yours," writes another friend from California. "I'm going right along with you, in fancy. And I know that soon you're going to have a glorious find," says another in New York state.

And so it goes…New Mexico and Oregon and Arizona and Utah—and from every other state and section of the desert country and country that is not desert—everywhere where desert lovers dwell—have come crowding messages of friendship and cheer. We are lugging around with us a bulging sack of unanswered mail, over which we sweat nightly in the accusations of conscience that we get it answered so slowly.

Would not even the chill heart of a stone image be thrilled and quickened by the magnificent backing of such a clan of friends?

How can one lie beneath the soft glow of the desert stars at night without feeling these loyal friends, in spirit, at one's side? How can one listen to the desert night wind whispering around the shadows of the swaying tent—a tent which was itself a friendship gift shipped to us from a dear friend in Pasadena, California, whom we have never met but whose letter reveals her as a true initiate of the deepest philosophy of the desert silences—how can one lie and hearken to these soft whisperings of the wasteland wind without seeming to hear in them the actual, cheering speech of this assemblage of friends, both near and far, whose hearts are with us? It is a feeling that does something to you, this strange mystic sense of brotherhood.

* * *

There is the sound of grinding. Out by the car, where the little hand grain mill is attached by wing-nut bolts to its "on the trail" position on the running board, Tanya is grinding flour from the hard small-grained red wheat that was raised in the fields of Juab County, Utah. Victoria has gone to sleep on a blanket, stretched beside me in the shade of the cottonwood.

In another section of shadow Rudyard, his pudgy nose wrinkled in desperate concentration and a stub of pencil clutched in his little fist, is trying to transfer a bit of desert scenery to paper. Near him Rider, squatting upon the warm earth and tracing designs with a bit of stick in the dust, is trying to figure out how one could invent a new type of speedometer, which would record distance by a complicated system of knotted strings and revolving drums.

Away off among the bushes, thinking himself secure from observation in the black blot of shadow at the base of a creosote, a roadrunner dozes. Hush holds the desert. With a stab of heartache for those who would long to be back within the tranquility of its sunlit borders—and for the present cannot come—one recalls the Navajo prayer:

"That it may be peaceful before me; that it may be peaceful behind me. All is peace. All is peace."

Desert Refuge 25
(August 1943)

PATTERNED on the lonely wind-sifted sand dunes of the desert the "little people" leave the record of their wanderings. Mice, lizards, beetles; leisurely, slow-pacing tarantulas, furtive, suspicious centipedes and black-coated, meditative pinacates—upon the soft surface of the sand their varied tiny tracks cross and crisscross in a maze of trails that tell tangled stories of exploration and of search.

When we think back upon the windings of our own desert trail, since the day when we set out from Yaquitepec, we are reminded again of the bond of kinship which binds all dwellers of the earth into one brotherhood. For if we were to take a pen and some red ink and trace back all the windings and turnings of our course, from its beginning until now, the resultant pattern would be a fair duplicate of the involved amblings of some meditative old pinacate beetle wandering over the dunes in search of food and a better dwelling place. Back and forth, in and out. Crossing and recrossing. Here a long pause. There a hasty scurry past some uninviting section. Here a bit of luck; there some delaying mishap. Between our own search and the search of the serious old beetle there is little difference. The record of the one is written in tiny tracks upon the sand. The record of the other in wheel tracks which, in the vast spread of the universe, are just as tiny.

We have been stalled for many days. And the reason and the trouble can be told in one word—tires. There is a limit to the endurance of tires, even when you coddle them and baby them and swaddle them in artificial wrappings and lavish upon them a hundred times more tenderness than Uncle Sam ever imagined, even in his most inspired moments.

The limit of our tires was reached and passed long ago. But we shut our eyes and minds to it. And for a long time it seemed the tires ran on will-power alone. But even that would not last forever. There came a day when our long suffering chariot sighed softly, looked at us reproachfully from out of her two desert bleared headlight eyes and sank wearily down under the shadow of the red sandstone cliffs of Utah. Evening came up across the desert on silent feet and the bats began to flitter forth from their caves. It was time indeed to "re-tire."

"Be of good cheer," said Uncle Sam's efficient but sympathetic representatives when they had delved fully into the matter. "Behold, here is a magic paper. With it you may go out into the marts of trade. And by virtue of the words that are written thereon the kings and princes of commerce will unbar the gates; the merchants will unlock the innermost strong boxes. They will draw forth two tires and will sell them to thee to replace those two which are now as ragged fragments. Behold, I, Uncle Sam, have so decreed. So fear not."

So we took the magic paper in great joy. And we fared forth into the marts of the silversmiths and the goldsmiths and the diamond buyers and the sellers of tires.

And the first merchant to whom we presented the magic paper said, "Ah yes. Be seated just a moment while I descend to the strong room and speak with the guards and unfasten the locks. I will bring you your two tires." And he went away smiling with the happiness of one who has made a sale.

And he was gone a long time. And returned without smiles. "Alas," he said, and his voice was choked, "I have not the size! I have not the size. It is an old size—and rare."

And he wept and wrung his hands together and handed us back the magic paper. And in sorrow he watched us depart. For his heart was heavy.

So we hastened away to other merchants. And to others. And still unto others. And with all the story was the same. Cunning jewels, yes. Peacocks and rubies and spices; all the silks and perfumes of the Indies—even a thrice sacred five pound sack of sugar could we have. But tires, in the 450-21 size? Alas and alas! These things were a dream. Even the old men did not remember ever having seen one.

So we became alarmed. And we sent swift messengers by the talking wires to the East. To the West. To the farthest corners of the land. And the replies came back with sobs and tears. All of the 450-21s were extinct. None had been seen in the land for more than a thousand years. So we sat by the mesquite bushes, under the red cliffs of Utah and mourned.

Then, into our grief, as we sat in the cold ashes of the campfire, there came a mysterious messenger bearing a scroll written by a great magician whose castle we once had visited in the ancient city of Kings, which is called also Kingman, and is in the State of Arizona.

And when we had read the scroll we leaped to our feet and shouted. And we exclaimed for joy. And we clapped our hands and summoned 20 swift runners and 10 riders of fast camels. And we loaded them with silks and spices and jewels and camphor wood and oil and incense and all manner of wealth, yea even to five times a king's ransom. And we commanded and said, "Speed quickly. Haste thou. Pause not until you have reached the castle of W.J. Tarr, which is south of the railroad tracks of Kingman, Arizona. Deliver to him all this wealth. But return not without the two slightly used 450-21 tires of which he speaks in this scroll. Rush now! Hurry. Beat it—lest, unhappily he selleth the tires before thou gettest there. Scoot!" And the messengers departed running.

So that, dear desert friends, is that. And as far as matters have gone at present. Will we get our tires? *Quién sabe?*...for we have heard no word yet from our messengers. But we think we have a good chance. There are very few things that our Kingman friend cannot supply for cars of every known vintage. The accumulation of long years of wrecking and classifying and storing. His is in truth a magic castle. So if he hasn't sold the tires in the meantime...

Next month you shall know.

But there is a silver lining to every dark cloud. And often the lining is more important than the cloud itself. The seeming disasters of life are in many cases really its stepping stones to better things. The majority of people, who can look back calmly over a course of years, will be ready to admit that this is true. Therefore, convinced as we are that no circumstance of existence is due to "blind chance" we are not worried overmuch by our enforced waiting. For one thing it is no more than a fresh demonstration of the truth that the farther human beings get from nature and the ability to support themselves by their own efforts the more helpless they are against misfortune.

* * *

The special glory of the desert land of southern Utah is its coloring. The whole landscape swims in a sea of color that is so vivid it often is unbelievable. Vermilion and purple and rose and lavender, jutting minarets of ruby red against a far, tumbled background of ridges that are shadowy violet and pink and grey and fleecy lacings of white. Sometimes the scintillating color vibrations are so intense that you begin to doubt your eyes. Your ears seem to ring with the quivering waves of rainbow hue that sweep back and forth between the fantastic, glowing cliffs.

What a priceless world of enchantment is this varied Desert Empire which we Americans are privileged to enjoy. Too few of us are aware of it or really appreciate it. Like children our eyes and ears are susceptible to the tawdry blandishments of far foreign places. It has not dawned upon us that the richest offerings of the world are within our own borders.

But what I really started out to explain was that the "silver lining" to the dark cloud of our enforced halt has been really worthwhile. Our camp spot is pleasant, with high, rustling cottonwood trees that cast welcome shade along the edge of a tule-grown hollow. Among the dark green of the crowding rushes, innumerable white flowers of the deer-tongue gleam in the sunlight like a scatter of newly fallen snowflakes. Bees drone around the blossoms of the mesquites. Stray hummingbirds, intent upon their business, whizz past like feathered bullets.

Sardonic ravens live hereabouts. "Wauk! Wauk!" they cry, as they flop heavily overhead eyeing our stranded car. "Walk yourself!" Rider and Rudyard shout back angrily. Little Victoria dances in the warm dust and shakes her tiny fist furiously at the sable jokesters. "You walk youselfs!" she shrills. But the ravens only chuckle throatily and flop on towards the vermilion cliffs.

There is a pool of water here too. A pool big enough for the boys to go voyaging upon a crazy raft. Sometimes they take Victoria and her doll Georgine for passengers and go poling along the reedy shoreline of their tiny lake, a joyous bunch of bare skinned, sun-browned little savages whose happy laughter swerves the dipping swallows and startles the dozing bullfrogs from their hideouts amid the water grass. The towering red sandstone cliffs glow warmly in the sun and the still surface of the pool mirrors their reflections and the drift of the lazy white clouds across the blue Utah sky. I don't think that Rider, Rudyard or Victoria are very worried about the tire situation. I have a sneaking suspicion that it wouldn't bother them much if the tires never appeared.

An old land of ancient memories—sometimes drowsy in the sun, sometimes yelling with a fury of wind and storm. You climb back into the canyons and you find here and there little walls of rock built to block crevices between boulders—little bulwarks that were man's effort to keep the driving wind from his rude camp spots. On the mesas there are mounds where you may dig up age-blackened pots and a few crumbling bones. Around the old waterholes are chips of obsidian and broken arrow points.

How long has man wandered and lived and made his dwelling amongst the red cliffs of this desert land? Perhaps the wind could tell— the old desert wind that goes about sweeping industriously with its ancient broom of the fled and fleeting seasons. Blotting tracks, blotting graves, blotting peoples and civilizations. The wind talks to itself. But mostly at night and amongst the cliffs and caves.

Rudyard (left) and Victoria at the mouth of the cave that was the source for the little spring.

There are springs up under the cliffs and along the gullies and canyons too. Springs that many men have known in the past and which perhaps will continue to quench the thirst of many a weary desert wanderer long after our present day pomp and civilization have followed that of our predecessors beneath the blanket of dust. Not yet have Rider, Rudyard and Victoria forgotten the days at Yaquitepec when water was an infinitely precious, hoarded thing. The sight of a spring, be it big or little, is still to them a thrill. Something to be exclaimed over— the miracle of real water welling up from the earth.

We came upon such a spring a few days back, when we were actually following the advice of the ravens to "wauk, wauk." We had walked. We had tramped out across the sunlit desert and circled back through the mesquites and creosotes into a long, sandy wash that drew down from the red sandstone ramparts to the north. Tamarisk trees grew thickly in the wash bottom together with a scattering of willows. The banks were a tangle of thick rabbitbrush, varied with an occasional mesquite or a big bunchy cholla.

The day was hot. Beyond the sultry vegetation of the creek bed the red cliffs rose as a thirsty glowing backdrop on a stage setting of shimmering dryness. The banks of the gully drew together as we pushed onward, their steep sides crowned with a savage capping of black lava rock in which, here and there, were eerie caves.

And then suddenly, there was water under our feet— real sparkling, cold water that came welling up out of the sand to chill, gratefully, our earth-scorched bare toes. "Spring!" Rudyard shouted, "Another spring! Look, Daddy!"

We all looked across the glinting stretch of sand, following his pointing finger. There, spilling down the opposite bank in a little cascade, came the thin stream of water which was soaking the sand on which we stood. But it did not originate there. For, when we had climbed the bank and traced the tiny rivulet back through the thick brush, we came at last to a shallow cave, brush screened, under a steep bluff. Within, patterned by sunlight and shadow was a shallow pool into which, with tinkling music, a thousand drips and trickles from the wet rocks fell splashing.

Outside the sun blazed. Inside, within that cool grotto, were cathedral dimness and the liquid music of fairy harps. The contrast was startling. Perhaps only in the desert can one see—and really appreciate—such contrasts. Small wonder that the old writers of the scriptures—themselves dwellers in a dry and thirsty land—alluded so often and so feelingly to the shadows of great rocks and to the music made by running water.

Desert Refuge 26
(September 1943)

THE MUSICAL *tonk, tonk* of bells across the desert silence. A wilderness frayed little burro train jogging out from between the creosotes and mesquites. Six well loaded pack burros and a couple of riders on wiry horses. One of them a slim girl in faded Levis and a bright red shirt; her companion a tanned young Arizonan, sitting his mount with the careless ease of a lifetime spent in the saddle. A sheep outfit headed into rough country where they could not take a wagon.

The slim girl was the boss' wife. And as we watched, the boss himself appeared, high up on the crest of a nearby rocky butte. He shouted and waved his hat to the riders below and they swung off, heading in the direction he indicated. From beyond the butte the dust of the moving herd smoked against the sky in a thirsty brown cloud.

We knew a little of the outfit. For the boss himself had talked with us the day before as he had been scouting ahead to pick the trail. They were from the Arizona Strip—that vast lonely empire that lies between the north rim of the Grand Canyon and the Utah line. Rugged desert people—product and part of the land where they lived. Weather tanned and reliant; totally unconscious of their picturesque blending with their desert setting. The slim girl in the red shirt was beautiful and she rode with an easy grace that suggested the slender branches of creosotes swaying in the wind. The burros trotted and bounced their packs and the bells tonked and the boss, from his lofty perch, yelled and pointed some more. Then they were gone, fading away into the dun distance and the dusty haze of the moving sheep. The red shirt of the girl vanished last, a brave moving spot of color dwindling and swaying away into the hot dust.

* * *

But did our tires arrive? They did. Our good friend in Arizona did not fail us. Glinting with all the haughty grace which only suddenly precious rubber can assume, our new tires, mounted and rearing to run, now reflect the desert sunshine with a radiance that is positively dazzling. The old car, heaved up from her slumped despondency, quivers with a joyous eagerness that waits only the word to go.

But sometimes one makes haste slowly. And our present tardiness recalls a story told me several years ago by Laurence M. Huey, of the San Diego Natural History Museum. It was while he was on one of his scientific expeditions into the little known parts of Baja California that one day he and his party met a Mexican family, moving with all their possessions across the desert, headed for a new home in distant Mexicali. Even the family cow was part of the caravan. But she was a leisurely creature and objected to desert travel in hot weather. Both the señor and the worthy señora were annoyed. "We make haste so slowly," they complained. "But what is to do? Can one leave behind a perfectly good *vaca* just because she will not hurry. She is of value." But they were irritated.

Three days later the San Diego expedition met up with this selfsame Mexican family again. Camped at a waterhole. The cow had vanished. But draped over poles and stretched riatas and the limbs of mesquite bushes was an astonishing array of jerky, drying in the torrid sun.

"Ah yes," the señora explained, sighing. "Poor Carmencita. She became more lazy. And when we reached this water she would not leave it. And so my Juan, he decided—" She shrugged her ample shoulders and spread her hands in an expressive gesture of resignation. "But the *carne seca* will be good. Señor," she added, brightening, as she indicated the drying meat. "Now we can carry Carmencita with us upon the burro and make much better speed. We have lost nothing."

Which is a parallel to our own experience. For here, in this sunny little Utah valley, where the industry of the Mormon pioneers has planted the desert with little irrigated fields of fertility, fruit flourishes. And a good friend presented us with a huge quantity of delicious apricots. Apricots are somewhat like the manna of bible days. Subject to spoiling. And the amount of ripe apricots that even Rider, Rudyard and Victoria can get away with is limited. So, like the owners of Carmencita, we found a happy way out of the problem. We sat us down to "jerk" our apricots. In other words we split them open and spread them out on improvised racks to dry in the hot desert sunshine.

With astonishingly satisfactory results. Unless you have tried it you have no idea how swiftly the brilliant sun and dry air of the desert can dehydrate fruit. Three or four days, and before you know it your orange gold spread of nectar-filled sweetness has toasted up to an array of toothsome chewy morsels of a deliciousness that can only be realized through personal experience. The sunshine does something to the fruit—something which no system of artificial drying can do.

Now the apricots are about jerked—I mean dried. And soon they can be loaded, like Carmencita, and go along with us. Preserving food by drying has many advantages. Not the least being storage space. We used to do a great deal of drying on Ghost Mountain. There, however, we had to take more precautions against our animal friends. There are not nearly the number of mice and

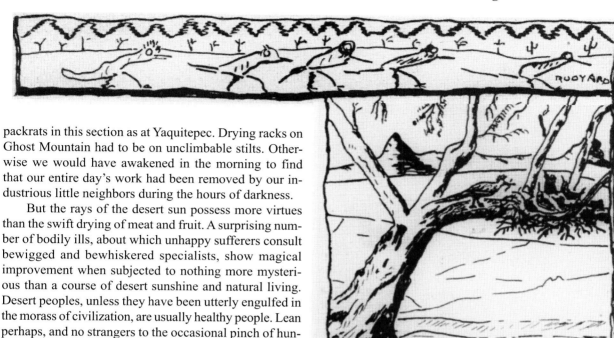

DESERT ROADRUNNERS
BY RIDER + RUDYARD, AGED 9 & 5

packrats in this section as at Yaquitepec. Drying racks on Ghost Mountain had to be on unclimbable stilts. Otherwise we would have awakened in the morning to find that our entire day's work had been removed by our industrious little neighbors during the hours of darkness.

But the rays of the desert sun possess more virtues than the swift drying of meat and fruit. A surprising number of bodily ills, about which unhappy sufferers consult bewigged and bewhiskered specialists, show magical improvement when subjected to nothing more mysterious than a course of desert sunshine and natural living. Desert peoples, unless they have been utterly engulfed in the morass of civilization, are usually healthy people. Lean perhaps, and no strangers to the occasional pinch of hunger, they are nevertheless wiry and reliant and possessed of a fierce vitality which has enabled them time and again to sweep down and overthrow the dwellers of more "fertile" sections.

The sun long has had complete charge of the health of our own family. And does his job so well we seldom think about him from a health sense. Until something goes wrong. Such as a headache. Headaches are unnatural. No one should have a headache. And whenever we do get one we know perfectly well that it is our own fault. Fortunately they are sufficiently rare to make us a little proud of our diet habits. But on those occasions when we err, and nature tells us so, we promptly remember Dr. Sun, and carry the case direct to him.

The other day having strayed unwisely down the alley of some alluring "civilized" food, and having awakened with a throbbing head, I went to a convenient spot and stretched out upon the hot earth. There were no rocks big enough or handy enough. But the clayey soil was scorching enough, and soon I began to feel the tingling, driving sunrays chasing the pain waves out along my spine and out through my head and toes.

Rider and Rudyard had come along too. They never neglect any opportunity that promises interest or a chance for exploration. They brought along a shovel with the idea that it would be interesting to find out how far, in this locality, one might have to sink a well for water.

While I toasted they dug. They dug for quite a while without finding anything more interesting than a few fragments of charcoal that might or might not have been relics of some prehistoric Indian campfire. "Pouff!" said

Rudyard at last. "It is too hot. And I think the water is deeper down here than it is at Yaquitepec." He scrambled out of the shallow trench and hot footed it for the shade of a high bank. Rider followed him.

Then we heard a mysterious "*Carrook.*" A weird, throaty sound. It seemed to come from somewhere in a nearby shallow draw where thorn trees grew. And where, far beyond, the mountains swam in the heat like savage patterns sewn upon smoky gauze. "*Carrook.*" A pause. "*Carrook.*"

"A frog!" Rudyard whispered excitedly. "A bull frog!"

"Huff!" Rider scoffed. "What would a bull frog be doing here—unless he had an asbestos suit. What is it, Daddy?"

But I didn't know either. The headache was about gone. And I was as curious as the youngsters. Cautiously we set out to track down the mysterious sound. "*Carrook...Carrook....*" The thing faded from us uncannily and elusively.

Then Rider suddenly spotted the roadrunner, an inconspicuous brown shadow, dodging furtively through the stunted bushes up a hot slope, and a moment later Rudyard's sharp eyes discovered the nest in a thorn tree. "*Carrook*"...the source of the sound was now unmistakable. But it was new to us. The roadrunner's vocabulary is extensive, and extended by flagrant mimicry. But we hadn't heard one dispensing that throaty croak before. We didn't bother the dodging mother bird as she slipped away up the slope. We were too interested in the nest.

It was like most roadrunners' nests. On a limb not too far off the ground. But it was exceptionally well defended. The parent birds must have spent much time in choosing their locality. No war-wise commander could have bettered the array of spiky defense which hemmed their rough nest of sticks on every side. It wasn't a hard tree to get up into—if it hadn't been for the thorns. But they were the vilest, spikiest, most vicious thorns we ever had seen. They jabbed and tore and stabbed at us along every inch of progress. When we finally did work high enough to get a glimpse into the nest it was at the cost of much shed blood. Some of the thorns drove deep in and broke off, and had to be dug out with pain and language, hours later.

There were five husky young roadrunners in the nest. Almost fully feathered. Hunched down, camouflaged by the patterns of their feathers against the mottled background of the nest, they regarded us with suspicious hostile eyes. There is something lizardlike and reptilian about a young roadrunner. If you ever should entertain any doubts as to the descent of birds from lizards a few minutes' study of young roadrunners in the nest would do much to dissipate them. And the bird has much more inherent savagery in it than you would suppose. At least in youth. The swagger and droll comedy affected by the adult birds are characteristics which come later.

Suddenly, to our consternation, one of the nestlings, with a low squawk of rage, or fear, hurled himself from the nest. To land with a thud upon the hot ground below. Captured promptly by Rider and thus saved from a blind staggering dash to death in the hot desert, it nevertheless threw us into a panic, for fear that the entire brood might follow its example. We withdrew hastily, blaming ourselves for our curiosity. But the question now was what to do with the prisoner. To attempt to put him back in the nest, by hand, might result in a general exodus of scared birds. This we dared not risk. It was a tough problem.

We solved the matter by taking "Snapper," as the boys named him, back to camp. There he was lavished with love and attention until next day, in a specially built nest all his own, in a specially built cage. But he would not eat. He snapped and chattered his bill at us. And pecked savagely. And glared and refused to be sociable.

It was with relief that we lugged him back to the nest the next day, by which time we judged the other young birds would have recovered in some measure from their fright. We returned him artfully. We tied a long strip of soft cloth to the end of a pole and wrapping the strip round and round Snapper's feet, with the end loosely secured, we hoisted him ignominiously by the legs up and over his nest. There, by a little jiggling and jerking we managed to shake the end of the wound cloth strip free. It unrolled and let Snapper fall into his nest. The other young birds never stirred.

Desert Refuge 27
(October 1943)

IT WAS early morning in the little town of Mesquite Nevada. As I entered the cafe to get a cup of coffee his was the first face I saw. He sat at the counter snatching an early breakfast. It was obvious that he was one of the passengers on the bus parked at the curb outside. We never had set eyes on each other before. But he hailed me with the enthusiasm of an old friend. "Come? sit here," he said affably, indicating an empty stool at his side. "Have a cup of coffee on me! Have breakfast with me as my guest!...Come. Come on. Please," he urged, as I hesitated. "This is my treat. Really. I want you."

His face was alight with enthusiasm and a sort of boyish eagerness that was compelling and would take no refusal. As I slid into the seat beside him he patted me genially on the back. "I'm feeling facetious, this morning," he said, grinning in explanation of his joviality. "For once in my life I'm thoroughly happy. I'm on a trip—on a vacation. The first one I've had in a long time. And I'm just going to enjoy myself in my own way. What'll you have?"

"Just the coffee," I told him. "I've been driving all night. Got to keep awake."

He nodded. "But something with it," he urged. "Some of these crullers…Something…."

"Well, a couple of donuts, maybe," I conceded.

"Donuts. Donuts. Make it donuts with the coffee, too" he waved the order genially after the demure little Mormon girl as she departed. They did not understand him, these grave, wholesome little desert misses who waited upon the cafe customers. But I did. We grinned at each other as old friends. His eyes roved over me appreciatively. "You fit this country—the desert," he said frankly.

I had been on a long hard scouting trip, alone. Tanya and the youngsters had been left safely established in a camp by a waterhole and now I was on my way back to them. The journey had been tough and hot and sleepless—and punctuated with more tire trouble than I cared to remember. I wasn't feeling particularly picturesque. Nor did I care, at the moment, whether I "fitted the country" or not. I ran appraising fingers over a ten day bristle of beard and grinned at him wryly.

"But that is nothing!" He waved the matter aside with a dismissing gesture. "It is the spirit that counts. The fitness. And you are particularly part of this desert scenery somehow. Look! Isn't it strange that we should meet! Here am I—sixty-six years of age—and released for a few days for care-free vacation in this desert that I love. And we encounter each other. Ah, this wonderful desert. You know, in the writings of George Wharton James…his Indian blankets…baskets….Perhaps you knew him?"

Yes I had known him. "And Charles F. Lummis? You member him too, maybe?" I suggested.

His face lit like a lamp. "Knew him well. Ah…the old days. You remember on the Los Angeles Times…."

We were off. The puzzled and a little scandalized young lady brought the coffee and the donuts. But they went untasted as did my friend's breakfast. What are such things as breakfast and coffee when two kindred souls bump into each other like voyaging ships in the midst of the loneliness of a vast ocean. Such an eager comparing of notes. Such a digging and rummaging in the precious memories of fled days. Was this Mesquite, Nevada? Or wasn't it? We had forgotten.

The passengers had all trooped out to their places in the waiting bus. The driver, seated apart at a little table writing up his notes and accounts, was the last to go. He swept his papers into his leather satchel and buckled it. As he passed the lunch counter on his way out he tapped my friend upon the shoulder. "We're leaving," he warned. "Better hurry!"

And my companion woke, as from a dream. He hadn't touched his breakfast. There it lay in the platter before him. A crisp salad, fried potatoes—an assembled appetizing combination of different foods. But all, fortunately, things that could be transported. Frantically he signaled to the little waitress and she came hurrying with waxed paper and a big paper sack. She swept the food together and packed it expertly in a jiffy. The bus outside tooted impatiently and my friend snatched the sack. "Your name," he cried breathlessly, lingering an instant with outstretched hand. "I don't even know your name."

I told him. In that hectic instant of parting, while the bus horn blew angry

Creosote bush

blasts, I mentioned the *Desert Magazine*. "Why—why of course!" he cried delightedly. "The *Desert Magazine*! I take it. Couldn't do without…."

He bolted through the door and was gone, plunging headlong for his seat just as the bus was backing out. The heavy motors roared and the dust skirled in the roadway. Then silence slipped down from the mountaintops again and he and his fellow passengers were just a memory, a fleeting blur whirring out along the desert highway on their way to Salt Lake City.

Mechanically I began to munch my donuts and drink my coffee. On the other side of the counter the demure little miss who had eyed us both askance passed, and paused.

"I think," she said disapprovingly, "that he had had a glass of beer."

"Maybe," I said. "And maybe not. There's such a thing as the intoxication of desert freedom. Did you ever spend long years a captive in the city?"

"No," she answered severely. "I never did."

And she went away hastily. "Two of a kind," her glance and actions said, more plainly than words. But I wasn't particularly worried over her reaction just then. For it had all at once dawned on me that I didn't know my new-found friend's name. In the whirlwind rush of parting I hadn't asked him. The realization was a dampening blow. And as I finished my coffee and went out again into the morning glint of the Nevada sunshine it was with a sense of loss. For I would like to know my friend's name and address. Perhaps, if this meets his eye, he will drop me a postcard. I hope so.

* * *

Rider and Rudyard have a new job to add to their already full list of occupations. It is tortoise herding. And if this sounds a little out of the ordinary—even in a world where strange trades flourish—you are to be informed that Don Antonio and Grandpa Tortoise, both vigorous representatives of the desert tortoise clan, have joined our establishment and travel right along with us.

And, being independent minded, as most desert dwellers are, neither Grandpa Tortoise nor Don Antonio take kindly to being whisked hither and yon in a smelly automobile. So to compensate, when on the road, the children take them on hikes at every camp spot and stopping place where time and conditions permit, herding them carefully through the cactus and creosotes and picking out for them the choice areas of pasture.

And Don Antonio and Grandpa appreciate these rambles. They are very tame and well used to the family. Their habits of ducking back into their bullet-proof vests on our approach have long since given place to an air of careless friendship and they stroll amiably around with us, sniffing for tidbits among the dry sticks and munching at grass tufts and choice morsels of dust and gravel. A desert tortoise's taste in the matter of food is peculiar. He will turn up a scandalized nose at the choicest of greenstuff and go eagerly after morsels which would discourage even a burro.

Grotesque and comically lovable creatures, their speed is something to marvel over. A short period of observation of their ungainly but persistent gait is sufficient to give anyone a new appreciation of the "Hare and Tortoise" fable. And they are adepts at concealment. It is with risk that you remove your eyes from them for a single instant. For in that moment they are likely to duck into some cavity beneath a stone or a cactus and vanish utterly from sight—with your chances of locating them again slightly less than nil.

We sometimes think it must be very annoying to Grandpa and his partner, after they have indulged in a terrific burst of two-mile-an-hour speed towards the distant mountains, to be picked up and carried back to the starting point again. Sometimes, when they have tried to climb into impossible situations, up steep banks, and have rolled down and landed upside down, they give audible sighs of relief and gratitude when we turn them right side up again. Not that they particularly need this service—for the belief that a tortoise can't turn over when on its back is a fiction, as far as desert tortoises are concerned. But the turning process is hard and involves a terrific lot of effort and straining with out-thrust head and legs, which they are grateful to be spared. It is interesting to watch an overturned turtle right himself, though. And sometimes it takes a long time. But he usually manages to do it. It is very possible that should he have the bad luck to find himself bottom side up in some depression or bowl-like hollow he would be unable to turn. But so far we have never found our pets in this fix. Ordinarily brother tortoise can take care of himself.

But he doesn't stand heat well. Like the rattlesnake he seems to have the peculiarity that the very desert sun upon which he thrives will prove his undoing if he gets too much of it, without adequate shelter. Ignorance of this fact caused us the loss of our first tortoise pet, Tiny Tim. The children babied him and fussed with him. He had a special traveling box, well ventilated and bedded with grass and leaves. That was the trouble. It was too warm. There was no deep, cool burrow to which he could retire. And one morning, after a particularly hot desert run of the day before, we found Tiny Tim dead. The children's grief was beyond consolation for a long while. Tiny Tim was buried with many tears in a desert grave among the creosotes near the jagged peaks of the Turtle Mountains.

It gets hot on some of the desert reaches in summer. But the heat of different sections has very different qualities and reacts upon the human system in very different ways. Vegetation, or its absence, seems to play an important part in this. As do altitude, soil composition, nearness to mountains and to big bodies of water, and a number of other factors, many of them seemingly unrelated. The invisible "river channels" and "drifts" of the overlying atmosphere have tremendous influence on desert climates, being responsible for numerous climatic pockets and zones in the wasteland empire. And man himself, at times, with his works, steps in to upset the finely adjusted balance of the great "machine." There is little doubt that the assembling of a vast body of water as has been done at Lake Mead, has tipped the scales of climate strikingly. Especially in the former route and frequency of summer thunder showers. There are skeptics who scoff at this. But you don't have to go far to find abundant support from old-timers as to facts. Nature-balance is delicately adjusted. It is swayable by far less obvious things than the tremendous evaporation from man-made lakes.

But there are other more simple deductions to be culled from desert summers. One of the most striking is that hot drinks are in their final effect, more cooling to the system than are chilly ones. It is not to be denied that the appeal of iced liquids on a sweltering day is very strong. And against them a hot cup of tea or coffee or a drink from a sun heated canteen doesn't pack much attraction. Yet the warm drink induces a profuse perspiration which sluices through the entire body and results in a much longer period of comfort. Besides being much more healthful than the shock of a chilly draught. The old Spaniards spoke with considerable knowledge when they wrote: "*En la sierra fria, agua fria. En sierra caliente, agua caliente.*" Which, in free translation, signifies that cold drinks are best for cold countries, hot ones for hot climates.

So don't worry if your summer draught from the canteen in the desert resembles a drink from the boiler of a locomotive. You'll have the satisfaction of knowing that it is more healthful than a cold glassful of tinkling ice water. And at least it won't be an insult to the intelligence, such as are the wanly cool swigs from the waterbags of paraffin-dipped canvas which some brilliantly inventive minds have lately placed upon the market. Some of us old-timers who know what a *real* waterbag is, and the evaporative principle upon which it chills its contents, can only contemplate these new paraffined inventions with sadness and disgust, muttering the while into our desert scorched beards, "Ain't science *wonderful.*"

✳ ⋔ 🌵

Desert Refuge 28
(November 1943)

ACROSS the dim trail, between a bristling cholla and a bunch of withered mescal stalks, stretched a slender cable of gleaming silver. From its center swung a tiny bell of white silk—a fairy bell swaying gently in the faint stirring of the desert air. A good omen. There in the silence and the warm glow of the late afternoon sunshine it seemed to be ringing a glad welcome. Carefully we turned from the path and stepped around it to avoid injuring the work of the little desert spider whose home it was.

A hush held all the desert. On the horizon the mountains rose up warm and glowing like the rim of a golden bowl—a golden bowl filled with a wine of silence spiced with the fragrance of creosotes and junipers and sage. The whole world was so still one walked as in a dream. We did not speak. No one—not even the irrepressible Victoria—wanted to break that hushed peace. The click and clatter of occasional stones rolling from beneath our feet sounded startlingly loud.

The trail wound up the mountainside, cresting ridges and doubling back across tiny plateaus. Soon we were clambering among frowning boulders—clambering and panting, for we had grown out of practice with steep trails. An inquisitive chipmunk eyed us from a rock top as we rested a moment. Then with a saucy flirt of his tail scuttled for safety. There were junipers here, and bisnagas and the bristling bayonets of rank on rank of guarding mescals. We went on more slowly. For we knew we were drawing near to something.

"I see the roof!" Rudyard shouted all at once. "Look, Daddy! The roof an' the chimney an'—"

"—An' the 'ittle bird house!" Victoria shrilled in a sudden wild excitement that periled her perch upon my shoulder. "The 'ittle bird house in the twee. It's still there!"

"Yes," Rider said. "That's the roof. And the bird house." He drew a deep, quick breath. "Yaquitepec," he said softly. He darted away, ostensibly to see if his special cistern had any water in it. Rider's feelings are deep and sensitive. But he likes to hide them.

And so, through the junipers and the tall swaying mescal stalks, on that warm, still desert afternoon, we came HOME. Home to Yaquitepec—and to the end of our long trail of wandering and of search. The quest was over. The dream place had been found. Nor does it lessen the satisfaction that we found our ideal on the very spot from which we had set out. Rather it adds to the importance of the search and to the solid joy of the final discovery.

It was not a noisy or exuberant homecoming. The hearts of all of us were too full for demonstration. For a long while we did not enter the house. We just sat under the ramada and rested. And drank in the far vast blue-distance of the desert extending east from the foot of the mountain, far below. Everything was still. Hushed and peaceful and sunny. Even the faint stirring of a drowsy breeze along the edge of the western cliff seemed immeasurably far away. And in the midst of the deep, solemn peace the little house, hemmed by its toy like junipers and clutter of giant boulders seemed to hold out invisible welcoming arms to us.

It might have been but yesterday that we had gone. So little had changed. As we began to move about, treading on tip-toe as though reluctant to break the hush, it almost seemed that our whole wandering trail of the past months had been a dream. With a sort of wonder we picked up familiar objects, resting still where we had laid them down on the last day of our going. Save that there were weathered patterns beneath them and faint outlines where the drifting days and infrequent storms had traced their imprints, we might have placed them there just a few minutes before.

There had been visitors to the little house in our absence. But they had been kindly visitors and desert friends. They had disturbed little. Some of the old toys that had been scattered beneath the ramada were arranged in ordered ranks which plainly told that some of the visitors to the little house had been children. And along the edge of the terrace someone had arranged some of our colored rock specimens in a way that bespoke not only artistic appreciation but also loving interest. Several panes of glass had been shattered in one of the front windows. But that evidently had been a prank of the wind.

We went inside after awhile. The front door, which someone had managed to unfasten, was held shut by a prop and several rocks. This loving service, together with the securing of the unfastened front window and the barricading of a loose rear shutter, had been the work of the artist, Thomas Crocker, at the time when he had climbed Ghost Mountain to transfer Yaquitepec to canvas. On the table lay a wide thin piece of clean white board, evidently part of the side of an apple box. It had been headed, in pencil, "Great Register" and upon it several Yaquitepec visitors had inscribed their names. To this improvised visitors' book Mr. Crocker also had added a few lines of friendly appeal to subsequent callers to keep doors and windows securely fastened.

We had expected to find rats' nests and a wild litter of cholla scraps and mescal pods which these industrious little rascals generally haul in to empty houses. But even the rats seemed to have realized that we eventually would return. There was no trace of their activities. On the shelves where we had left them, a few trinkets still stood in orderly array. A couple of pictures hung on the walls. Silence and a thin filming of desert dust.

The house contained but one native tenant...a big, philosophic "Tittums 'pider" (Victoria's rendering of Tarantula spider) who sat beside the fireplace regarding our intrusion with a stoical indifference which wasn't in the slightest ruffled when we carefully herded it into an old can and carried it out to a place of safety among the rocks.

Tanya began to open windows and dust tables and chairs—multitude of little preliminary tasks towards the job of reestablishment. With the beginning of such first tasks something of the unreality vanished. We began to realize that we actually were home once more. With full hearts and a happiness greater than anything we had known since the day of our leaving, we all turned to the big job ahead of us.

And it was a big job. Every pound of our personal possessions, which we so laboriously had carried down Ghost Mountain when we had gone away, had to be re-carried up the trail. That was going to be a strenuous job. But it was not particularly this task which gave us concern. Our chief anxiety was the old question of water. That was vital. Hastily we took stock of the situation.

It turned out to be considerably better than we had anticipated. The carefully corked five gallon bottle which, from sheer force of desert habit, we had left in the house on our departure had not been molested. And the regular inside water barrel still contained about 10 gallons of pure liquid. We went out to inspect the cisterns.

Evidently a heavy thundershower had passed across Ghost Mountain about a week or ten days previous to our homecoming. Evidences of the brief downpour were visible in cut channels in the gravel and in the mud stains in now dry catch holes. Also the overflow pool, to which the roof guttering had been connected, was still about a quarter full of water. It wasn't good water because the open cemented pool had become cluttered up with trash during our absence. Still it was water.

Our main drinking water cistern was dry, except for a slime crusted puddle in which a defunct centipede reposed peacefully amidst a litter of other "animalitos." Another smaller cistern likewise was bone dry. The same

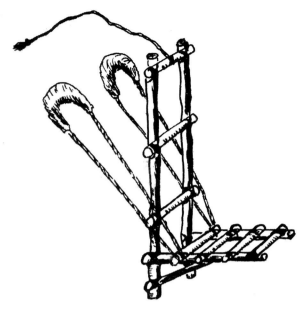

Marshal's carrying chair or pack board made from mescal stalks and fiber used to carry supplies up the steep trail to Yaquitepec. Note padded shoulder straps and top hand-hold rope (see p. 49). Sketch by Marshal South.

was true of a couple of other containers. But to our great joy a carefully covered tank still retained, bug-free and pure, the 60 gallons or so of water which we had left in it. This store, with the water in the house, gave us a head start on the water question of about 75 gallons. We suddenly felt our chief worry evaporate.

There still was much to be done. On that first trip up the mountain we had been unable to bring much in the way of supplies. So Rider and I hurried down the long descent to the car and trailer. Here we hastily collected a few blankets and essentials and started up the mountain again, taking note, on the way up of several stout mescal stalks which, on the morrow, could be pressed into service for the making of a "carrying-chair."

Dusk was closing in by the time we returned. Tanya had the lantern lit and a sketchy camp supper on the table—to which we did more than justice. Weary and gloriously happy we all turned in to drowse contentedly towards slumber, lulled by the song of the old, well-remembered desert wind, harping across the cliff edge and the rooftop.

"Towards" slumber, I said. For suddenly, in the still night, there was a crash. Bam! Wham! Clatter-te-clatter-te-clomp! Bam! Slam! Tanya sat up with a startled jerk. Rudyard said "Ouff?" in a scared, inquiring voice. From the depths of her covers Victoria snuffled and yawned: "That is onwy thee owd pack wat. He comed home to his house on thee woof," she observed sleepily. Of course. Temporarily we had forgotten the old packrat who has his dwelling up in a little pocket under an overhanging roof-cave.

Next day, having fashioned a pack chair from mescal poles and fiber, we settled to the job of carrying in real earnest. A big job. It isn't finished yet. But there is joy in the labor. When you have swung around the circle, and finally proved that your heart lies in the location you started from, the satisfaction of the knowledge far outweighs any physical toil.

For, in summing up, there is for us but one Yaquitepec. No other place, no other scene, in all the desert empire we have traversed, can compete with it. We saw solitudes and beauty. We found wells and waterholes. We gladdened our hearts beside the silver trickles of springs singing their cool song beneath the glowing lift of desert cliffs. But we found no peace and no contentment like the peace and tranquility that wraps around the little home that perches on our bald mountain summit. Yaquitepec!

The granite crest shoulders back the driving winds. The ravens wing above it and the savage chollas crouch in the spaces between the tumbled rocks. It is barren and sun scorched and storm harried. And there is no water. But—it is HOME.

Desert Refuge 29
(December 1943)

A BIG whiptail lizard moves slinkily across the noon-glinted stretch of white gravel before the house. In the shadows of the gnarled old juniper tree, where the sifting sunlight makes fretted patterns of gold upon the bluish-brown mosaic of fallen ripe berries, Rudyard and Victoria sit close together, intently turning the pages of an old picture book.

There is a sense of hush and stillness over everything, despite the restless stirrings of a wandering little desert breeze that harps a low sleepy song of solitude with its swaying of an open window. Tanya and Rider are away off down the trail somewhere, doing their daily part in the water carrying program, a task in which we all share. Above the somnolent lullaby of the rasping, wind-swaying window hook, lifts the occasional hushed murmur of voices from the two engrossed youngsters under the juniper tree. The peace of the desert lies over everything like a crystal

bowl. Ghost Mountain and all of the vast stretch of the shimmering wastelands beyond are a-drowse in the sun.

But in all the wide-flung desert sky there is no hint of rain. And rain we need desperately. All the desert needs it. Even the chollas and the mescals are beginning to look a bit discouraged. Cleaned and new tarred our empty cisterns wait. But in vain. The days march past on brassy feet. Dry, fine, thirsty dust is upon the creosotes and upon the yuccas and each sunset the dispirited clumps of beavertail seem to shrink a little smaller within their wrinkling skins. Still it does not rain.

Oddly enough dry conditions do not seem to have had a depressing effect upon our bird visitors during the past nesting season. Rather the reverse. For the first time in our records, all of the little houses we had provided were used, even the oldest and least pretentious ones. There had been such a demand for quarters that some of the late comers had had to construct hogans and wickiups for themselves. This they had done in the precarious summits of junipers and under the sagging bundles of mescal poles that span our ramada. It must have been an interesting colony. Evidently we missed something by not being at home.

Judging by the varied types of building material used in different nests, several new varieties of birds had joined the usual crowd. Our old friends the olive-sided flycatchers, who have a permanent lease upon the little red-roofed house in the juniper by the cisterns, had been back, of course. And the desert sparrows. And the canyon wrens had occupied every one of the hollowed mescal butts tucked away in the shadowy places. And the house of the purple finches had been lived in too, as had the domiciles of all the other old-timers.

But we could not figure out what little desert sprite had resided in the diminutive bungalow way up on the summit of the pole above the ramada. Nor could we determine the builders of the new wickiups. Birds are as definite as humans in their architectural designs. But, as we made the rounds, cleaning out the nest boxes and getting things ship-shape for next season, we could not decide who the newcomers had been. Maybe they'll come back next year. Anyway we're glad that while we were away adventuring on far trails, our little house here among the swaying mescal blooms had its loneliness cheered by the constant bustlings and twitterings of a glad company of feathered friends.

Life at Yaquitepec is back almost to normal. Not quite, for there is much arranging and contriving and even new construction to be done before we can thoroughly drop back into a smooth course. We had feared there might be a few wistful regrets over the memories of frogs and minnows and waving green cattails and the murmurous gurgle of running springs. But not a bit of it. The children have enjoyed their wanderings. They have known what it is to have water in abundance. They have expanded their horizons and have added to memory's storehouse scores of localities which before were just names on the map. I think Victoria neatly sums up the feelings of all three: "Twips," says Victoria, "are pwetty good. But it is good-er to get back home to Yak-a-pek. I LIKE Yak-a-pek."

* * *

Ghost Mountain juniper berries are good and ripe. In fact the crop is about over—a fact to be noted with regret by the coyotes who by moonlight and starlight have come trotting up our precipitous trails to enjoy them. Coyotes at this season of the year seem to make juniper berries their chief article of diet. When you get them just right, the berries are good. A bit woody, but sweet and tasty, with a flavor reminiscent of St. John's bread.

The Indians appreciated them and ate them not only "as is" but also ground into meal and baked into little cakes. The tiny little hard, filbert-like kernel—the part you discard—has a diminutive, meaty interior which the chipmunks like. But one almost needs to be a chipmunk to get the benefit of the morsels. They are so tiny you never get a proper taste of them, however patient you are.

To the furry little rock dwellers, though, the size is just about right. From the open doorway of my writing house among the rocks I often have watched some little grey rascal, his tiny white-trimmed brush of a tail arched pertly over his back, squatting on the summit of a branch-shaded boulder, enjoying a hearty meal of juniper-berry kernels, scampering back and forth to help himself to the berries from the heavily laden branches, cracking the kernels expertly and letting the empty shell halves tumble down into the rock crevices below him. It is all very simple. But when you try to crack a juniper berry kernel yourself all you get is a smashed whiff of something which is just tantalizingly good enough to urge you to repeat the experiment again and again. And always with discouraging results.

Packrats like juniper berries too. They work over-time to lay in a generous supply for winter. The big rat, who for so long has made his home under an overhang-ing eave of our roof, is no exception. He is a far-seeing thrifty individual. A few days ago he decided that his roof storehouses were inadequate. So he came down into the house, taking advantage of a hole where, during our ab-sence, a chunk of mud plaster had fallen out. He is a big handsome rat with an expensive-looking waistcoat of cream-colored fur. An old tenant of ours of several years' standing, we felt rather benignly disposed towards him.

So, although we saw him flitting to and fro and hurrying importantly along shadowy wall bases in the lamplight we took no "steps." It was true that on several occasions we heard mysterious noises in the dead of night that linked themselves with our flitting visitor But we dismissed the matter tolerantly.

Thus, in our role of gullible Simple Simons we drift-ed along, suspecting nothing. Not even when Tanya began to worry over the disappearance of her pet table knife—the one with the red handle. Or when Rider com-plained that a plaster mould, in which he made clay ducks, was missing. Or when Rudyard accused Victoria of hav-ing taken, and lost, a little red metal toy auto, on which he set great store—an accusation which she vociferously denied, entering a counter complaint that "Rudggy" had "tooked my wed an' green pencils."

Then one night came the grand finale. We had gone to bed in peace and good fellowship with all the world. Only to be torn from slumber around about the witching hour of midnight by a ghastly hubbub. Tumbling from our covers, to the accompaniment of Rider's startled ex-clamations, Rudyard's shouted questions and Victoria's lusty yells, we were aware of an awful noise proceeding from the gloom-shrouded north archway, the one that leads into the unfinished room. Right now the archway, tempo-rarily walled about by a lath and tar-paper cubby hole, serves as a sort of storage space. It was from the depths of this cavern of shadow that the racket proceeded...ham-mering and beating and grinding and creaking and the chilly jangling of chains. "A mounting lion," Rudyard puffed breathlessly, scrambling at our heels as we snatched the dim-burning night lantern from its hook and dashed towards the scene of commotion. "A mounting lion! He's escaped into the house an' he's dewouring someone. He's cwunching up bones!" (Rudyard is noted for his exces-sively cheerful imaginings.)

But it wasn't a mountain lion. It was our old friend the packrat. In the flickering lantern-light, as we peered among the piled trunks and boxes inside the archway, all we could see was a glittering litter of smashed glass, a tumble of overturned tin cans and a wild scatter of spilled nails, screws and small bolts, in the midst of which con-fusion, jerking back and forth upon the surface of a big flat slab of rock, like a dumpy tugboat buffeted by a chop-py sea, moved a battered old graniteware pot, upside down. Bang! Crash! Skreek, clatter! It would advance and re-treat. And go sideways, lifting every once in a while and clanking back upon the stone as though all the jumping beans in Mexico had taken refuge beneath it. The thing seemed possessed.

"Ha! The rat!" Rider said, his sleepy tones hold-ing something of the melodrama of Sherlock Holmes of

Baker Street. "He's been on the shelf and he's upset that tipsy carton of glass jars and nails and things. And the old pot has fallen down on him. He's under it."

And he was. All we saw of him, as we gingerly lifted the pot was a flash of expensive fur waistcoat—a whizzing pale streak that hurtled away into the shadows. To be followed later by a bamming plunk as his scrambling body hit the iron roof outside. He was gone.

But he left the evidence of his misdeeds behind him. For there at the foot of a big pile of earth which he had burrowed out from beneath the flat rock slab, lay Tanya's red handled knife, Rider's duck mould, Rudyard's tiny toy auto and Victoria's pencils, together with a varied collection of other trifles we hadn't missed. And under the stone, strategically disposed in a half dozen little nooks and corners amidst the piled boxes about it, were heaps and heaps of carefully gathered juniper berries. You'd never have dreamed that one rat could have lugged in so many berries in such a few days. In the morning, when we came to clear things up, we took out five tomato cans full of them.

After which, heartlessly, we took a little of our precious water and mixed it with some good desert clay into a thick mud. And we plugged the hole up under the beam. We believe in conservation and in industry. But there are limits.

Now, nightly, we hear our friend of the expensive fur waistcoat wandering disconsolately up and down on the roof outside the plugged hole. He does not enjoy being relegated to the region of outer darkness. His feelings, I imagine, are akin to those of humans who, every once in a while, are rudely awakened by Fate to a startled realization that they cannot forever trample insolently on the toes of God.

Desert Refuge 30
(January 1944)

OUR desert world marches on through fall and toward winter. Already the gusty storm gods have

Rudyard's drawing of a packrat.

made preliminary attacks upon Ghost Mountain, and the cliff-edge junipers have breasted their windy clamor with threshing, defiant branches. But the heavy weather, if there is to be any this winter, is not yet.

This may be an exceptionally severe winter, as has been predicted, or it may be quite the reverse. But we can take no chances. Every spare moment these days, Tanya and the two boys trail off across the ridges and return carrying high piled baskets of dead mescal butts and sagging shoulder-loads of their tall, dry flower stalks. And on every possible occasion Rider and I fare forth with ropes and pack boards to those distant sections of the mountain where dead juniper wood still may be found.

There are compensations, though, which far outweigh the labor involved. There is a fountain of health in vigorous outdoor exercise that far exceeds the virtues of any nostrum dispensed in bottles or capsules. Especially when such exercise can be taken without the body-choking impediment of clothing. Work and sweat are healthy honest things. And when free beings labor with their own hands to supply their own simple wants there is no slavery even in the hardest toil.

There is another joy to fuel gathering too. For it is on these expeditions that we come very close to the heart of the desert. And the heart of the desert is deep and full of constant surprises. No matter how much you think you know a particular locality you discover something new each time you visit it. Maybe not a dinosaur's egg or the lost Pegleg mine. But something which will thrill you. For instance the carefully concealed bird's nest in the summit of the old storm-gnarled juniper.

We had passed that spot a score of times and each time had admired the old tree, its tints of green, its sturdy ruggedness and the fantastic shapes into which the winds of hundreds of years had twisted its branches. We had even loitered beside it, picking and munching sweet dry juniper berries from it and peering about the limbs and trunks for bits of exuded, amber-colored gum.

But we never had seen the bird's nest. And it had been there all the time. It was left for Rudyard, who has a positive genius for finding things, from lost pins to desert snails, to make the discovery. He announced the find one day with a startled shout that brought us running. It was a beautifully constructed last season's nest of a cactus wren. It was the first cactus wren's nest that we had seen in a juniper. Its camouflage was perfect. Even after we had touched it and admired it we could step back a pace or two and completely lose it again. It was this fact that particularly intrigued us. Before a bit of art like that human efforts at camouflage are clumsy.

Most of the Ghost Mountain days still are balmy and delightful despite the official season of the year. Delicate little white butterflies with brown and black wing decorations hover here and there above the *ramarillo* [rabbit-brush] bushes. Nimble lizards stalk flies upon the warm surface of sun-bleached granite boulders. Curtsying rock wrens hop from point to point on the stern welter of jumbled stone that surrounds the house. And their sisters, the canyon wrens, give us occasional trills of sweet song as they perch upon the topmost twigs of junipers or flit, like tiny shadows, from tree to tree. Ghost Mountain always has been, to a certain extent, an "island." Many quirks and variations of climate are exclusively its own.

But "if winter comes" so also comes Christmas. We were reminded of this important fact when an earnest, eager-faced deputation came this morning to remind us that it was about time we were giving some thought to bringing in the Christmas tree. "You know, Daddy," said the spokesman, "last year we were on the trail. It wasn't a really-truly Christmas. But now that we're home again— and you remember, that tree just down from the top of the ridge?"

Yes, I remembered the tree. It was only a few days after we had returned to Yaquitepec that they had picked it out—looking forward, even then, to the most wonderful day of the year. It was a big, sprawly tree, possessing several large symmetrical branches which, as Victoria cannily observed, "thee twee won't, not never, miss."

Yaquitepec Christmas trees never entail the destruction of a living juniper. The children, trained conservationists, would be horrified at such a thought. But we build our festal "trees" from branches selected from trees that won't miss them, binding them together with concealed lashings until the finished product does duty as a complete tree.

We think Santa Claus doesn't mind this. And we are certain that the scheme is beneficial to our clan of Ghost Mountain junipers—many of which were here before Columbus started the prows of plunder towards the New World. Perhaps "composite" trees may even claim something, too, in the way of symbology. For the evergreen Christmas tree symbolizes everlasting life. And surely everlasting life is composite, built up of many conditions and experiences.

So in a few days we will go down and get the "tree." We will plant it in the old, weathered oaken tub which has done duty for several Christmases. And we will haul out the little box of carefully saved trimmings and decorations, which each year emerge from their obscurity, and we will trim it, with the silver star of Hope upon its topmost twig.

If Tanya and I, as we trim it, are conscious of the black shadow of sorrow which war has spread over the world, we will not let such thoughts dim the joy of those whose eager young fingers assist us. Sorrow comes early enough to everyone.

Gladly, if it were in our power, would we send forth the light of our Christmas candles and the message of the Star into all the world, to cheer and comfort the aching hearts of those of every creed and nation, that they might, in realization of their common brotherhood, cease their childish battlings and brutalities in the broad bond of an understanding peace. But this we cannot do. We shall strive therefore to build peace and understanding and joy and hope in those young lives which the Great Spirit has placed in our immediate keeping.

Our desert turtles have gone to sleep. Wearying of chewing up bunch grass and specially raised young wheat shoots and in taking long rambles over rocks—during which they often had to be rescued from upended tumbles upon their backs—they finally hunted themselves a nice warm spot under some old sacking, and pulled the bedclothes over their heads for the duration of the cold season. Along with bears and certain other creatures they are able to hibernate. Not an unhandy gift at times. But we miss them. Somehow they always had about them an air of profound wisdom. But perhaps it was just plain stupidity.

* * *

One of several new projects which have been added to the regular work since we returned to Yaquitepec is the building of a storage house. We have needed this for a long time. Now the job is well under way. For a construction plan, we hit upon a combination of the Navajo hogan and the ancient pit dwelling, a scheme which offers the maximum construction returns for the minimum of invested labor.

In a convenient earth hillock we started to dig a pit with a connecting entrance open cut. As the earth was loosened and dug up we mixed it with water, trampled and worked the mud thoroughly with our bare feet, as in the primitive preparation of earth for adobe bricks, then built the mud handful by handful up around the edges of the circular pit as mud walls. In this way the building progresses two ways at once—upwards and downwards.

This type of wall isn't quite as strong as one made of sunbaked adobe bricks, nor is it nearly as substantial as one made of damp earth rammed between wooden forms (which is the strongest of all earthen construction). But it is a method used in all arid countries. And the walls so built last surprisingly well. Some at Yaquitepec have stood ten years exposed to the elements with comparatively little damage.

* * *

We have added a little California fox to our list of Yaquitepec animal friends. A shy graceful little fellow who comes in the early twilight and in the moonlight to forage for tidbits of food upon the leveled earth terraces near the ramada. Yesterday evening he did not come, and the children, who look forward to his visits, were disappointed. "Somefing may have eated him up," Victoria said uneasily. She went to bed greatly worried.

About midnight I awoke. Unable to sleep I arose noiselessly, took a chair and went and sat by the window. There was a bright moon and its glow brimmed the bowl of the world in a luminous white mist of ghostly silence through which the savage granite ridges with their dotting of tumbled boulders and shadowy junipers lay against the sky like the unreal mountains in a dream. Black shadows of jutting beams made ebony patterns upon the outside walls of the house, each little hollow in the rough

Cactus wren

adobe a dark dimple in the white light, like hammer marks left by a silversmith in a beaten bowl. It was very still. The moonlight held everything in a flood of mystery, and through it, in the immensity of the sky, the stars gleamed upon a ghostly world of utter hush that might have been quite lifeless—a desert of hammered silver upon a planet dead and forgotten.

And then it was that I saw the fox. He came out of the shelter of a *ramarillo* [rabbitbrush] bush and paused a moment upon the white surface of a granite boulder. His large ears were thrust forward, listening, his handsome, fluffy tail brush low, held with a grace that seemed to soften and accentuate every line of his slenderly fashioned body. His searching eyes were for a moment a flash of twin diamonds in the moonlight, and every hair of his coat seemed touched with frosted silver. Soundlessly like some desert wraith, he stepped down daintily upon the terrace, picked up the few scraps that had been laid there on an old plate for him and slipped away into the bushes with such swift, shadowy grace that it was an instant before I quite realized he was gone.

The moonlight beat down and the silence held everything in its cloak of phantom mystery. After awhile I went back to bed, feeling infinitely richer for my midnight session of window gazing. And in the morning I was able to make Victoria very happy with the knowledge that her little friend was quite safe and that no one had "eated him up."

* * *

Tanya is busily grinding flour. Rudyard has his nose wrinkled over a new sketch. Victoria is on the bed, an old dictionary held upside down in her hands, as she wrestles with the job of giving her doll, Barbara, what she calls "an eju-kashun." And Rider, with little screws and bolts and odds and ends and bits of tin and wood, is working with another of the mechanical inventions on which he spends every minute of his spare time. Rider is seemingly headed for the field of invention and engineering. But I am going to drag him away from his beloved bolts and screws presently. For we have to pack home some more loads of juniper wood from away off across the southern ridges.

Desert Refuge 31
(February 1944)

STORM and the roar of storm. Wind thundering up the mountain and shouting through the threshing junipers with the deafening tumult of ten thousand titan harps. Through the yuccas and the creosotes and the ocotillos of the desert lowlands rush a hundred screaming eddies which flail the branches and strike yelling discord from myriad whistling thorn spines. Against the ragged grey rim of the distant sierras moves a sullen sea of cloud. The towering masses of it, like the packed ranks of an advancing army of giants, press upon the peaks and spill avalanches of driving squall into the canyon deeps. Through rifts in the slow-moving, ominous pall, rare shafts of the discouraged sun flicker like ghostly searchlights, the grey gleam of them laced with the steel stitching of driving rain.

And over all the wind. The wind is a living thing. It seems to shake the mountain with its gusty thunderings. The low sprawled *ramarillo* [rabbitbrush] bushes and the stocky shapes of the ephedras cringe and flatten to the blast. Whooping maelstroms scream and clamor among the giant boulders. The little house at Yaquitepec seems to hunch down more solidly upon its foundations as it braces itself against the maniac fury that roars above its roof.

"Do you think, Daddy," asks Rudyard, cocking a speculative eye at quivering beams, "that the roof will blow off?"

But we do not think the roof will blow off. That humming sheeting of iron overhead is held down not by nails but by long screws. Nails would have failed long ago. Nails are a poor thing to use anywhere in the savage climate of the desert. But these screws have ridden out many a storm and will ride out many another. Reassured, Rudyard goes back to his cushion on the hearthstones before the big fireplace where Rider and Victoria are. In the ruddy glow of the flames that leap from blazing mescal butts the three of them sit, a graduated row of squatting Buddhas. The firelight turns the smooth skin of their naked sun-tinted bodies to bronze and fills their eyes with mysterious lights of dreaming.

But these winter storms that at intervals come charging down upon Ghost Mountain and our desert usually are short lived. Even the most savage of them, when to the trumpeting of the wind is added the iron-chill fusillade of driving sleet and hail. When the fury of the tempest has died and the sun comes out again in a sea of glory, every indrawn breath of the keen fresh air makes one rejoice and tingle in the sheer pleasure of being alive.

Snow comes to Ghost Mountain too, in winter. Sometimes the fall is heavy, sometimes only a flurry. But in every case it is something to delight in, with junipers and rocks and mescals and gaunt *chollas* decked in a coating of fairy ermine. Eager little faces line along inside the windows, noses flattened to the glass, despite the cold. Intent eyes are held fascinated by the drifting, fleecy curtain that veils the mountaintop as in the fluttering dance of myriad white moths. Our three desert-bred youngsters make no secret of the fact that they love winter—its storms and all. And we do too. But all of us are equally enthusiastic over spring and summer and fall. To us the desert climate is as near perfection as one could find anywhere on earth.

Christmas has come and gone. Its slow approach was productive of many small fingerprints upon the calendar and many worried puckerings of childish brows. Now it has been taken down, wrapped in tender thoughts and tied with a golden string and laid away in the great storehouse of memory. The tree has been taken down too, and its silver star put back into the little box to wait for next year. But not the gleam of it. We didn't put *that* away. The bright gleam of it is in our hearts.

It was a good Christmas. Not yet have all the cards and gifts and letters of friendship which lay beneath our tree on Christmas morning been personally acknowledged. But they will be. And, in the meantime, dear friends, our thanks and every sincere New Year's wish.

* * *

The ancient Romans, judging by accounts of their doings, were always building arches and walls. And it seems to us that in this respect we are like them. Not so much in the matter of arches, though we have built a few (arches are convenient in doorway construction where the scarcity of wood makes the use of lintels impossible). But in wall building we feel that we are close runners-up of Caesar and his industrious legions.

It seems that we always are building walls. Even though there are few completed walls to show for the labor. Lack of water makes construction progress by unbelievably slow degrees. We add a bit to this one and a bit to that, as the water supply permits. Once, in a particularly long rainless period, we built an entire archway and partition wall with just the mud made each day from less than a quart of water saved from kitchen and cooking operations. Now that it's finished and whitewashed we sometimes find it hard to believe the handful-by-handful way in which it was built.

But not all our walls go up quite so slowly. A section, almost two feet thick and built of granite blocks set in mud mortar, on the southwest end of the house, made faster progress, notwithstanding the fact that a lot of the water for mud mixing had to be hauled. Of this recent bit of construction, which enables us to straighten out a long-standing, inconvenient "jiggle" in the south room, we are somewhat childishly proud. Especially in these storm periods, when we listen to the wind snarling and raging impotently at the outer face of the barrier. Elemental satisfaction perhaps. But deep rooted. Only a little while ago we noticed Rudyard and Victoria standing with their backs to it and all their senses keyed to the beat of the tempest on the other side. They explained that they were doing that "just to feel solid an' comfortable." Which gives one some glimmer of insight into what must have been the triumphant feelings of primitive man when he first discovered how to construct dwellings that would defy the elements.

This recent wall building had an unexpected side issue which threw light upon another method of construction—that of making walls from moist earth rammed between forms. "Rammed earth" is a very old building device. It dates back at least to the times of the ancient Romans, who used it a great deal in the construction of watch-towers and forts. It is suited to a wide range of climate, but especially to dry areas like the desert. When we first began the building of Yaquitepec we experimented with it, but gave it up in favor of adobe bricks and mud. These aren't so strong, but are less work. Also we lacked the solid planking of which to build the forms.

But we did make several foundation sections by this method. In our recent building operations we ran against one of these fragments of wall which had been laid down in accord with an early plan of the house. One which long ago had been abandoned. The bit of time-seasoned "ramming"—over ten years old—was in the way of present construction and had to be removed.

And we learned from it. That little fragment of wall about eighteen inches high, a foot wide and about a foot long, provided one of the toughest problems we had tack-

Pottery, baskets, blankets, and statuary made by the Souths.

led in a considerable time. It would not yield to tools. Crowbars and pickaxes struck sparks of fire from the mass, and bounced back at us. Dust and slivers came away. It was like battering at concrete.

Yes, "rammed-earth" is tough. We did manage to get rid of our unwanted bit of it, finally. But only because it was such a small section. Had it been of considerable area the story would have been different. However, we now can give an "unsolicited testimonial" to rammed earth construction. If you have any building to do, and are interested in this type of work, it might pay you to investigate. It's cheap and durable. The government publishes (or used to publish) a booklet of clear instructions. And I believe the University of California, at Berkeley, does also.

* * *

Pottery making hasn't got back into swing yet, at Yaquitepec. Since our return there has been much to do, and we have had little time. However, unable to keep "itching fingers" entirely away from the satisfying feel of moist clay we did make a few hasty pieces—things we needed. We were penalized for our haste by almost total failure. Not in the drying or in the decorating, but in the firing. This is always a tricky operation. And in our impatience we neglected to shelter the ware from the too-fierce heat of the flames—something accomplished in primitive methods by propping up little strategic barricades of sections of old broken pots. So most of the stuff cracked. All that came from the fire intact was one plate and one cup and a little bowl. "More haste, less speed." Anyway we have chilly satisfaction in the knowledge that our predecessors, the old desert Indians, often must have felt as we did. Judging by the amount of sherds, in different sections, the mortality among their pots must have been high. Higher, perhaps, than our own.

Still, though this last venture was largely a failure, we do have the one plate and the cup and the little bowl. And that is *something*. And we do not forget the joy that we had in fashioning the pieces from the moist clay, and in decorating them. For the chief reward lies in creation. In the striving toward a goal, rather than in the somewhat static satisfaction of a height attained. This is, or should be, the case with all work. It is particularly true of handicrafts.

For there is, about those arts which depend directly upon the hands, a fascination which is unique. Handmade things have a "soul" which machine manufactured objects lack. There is, too, in such primitive home industries as spinning, weaving, pottery making and the construction of furniture, a restful close-to-nature feeling which is soothing to jangled nerves. If I ever were to direct the affairs of a colony or community I would insist that every article of domestic use, wherever possible, should be made by hand. It is by hand work that the artisan, under natural, non-commercial conditions, develops not alone his skill at his craft but himself as well. The old days, to which so many tired moderns look back with longing, hold bright pages of sincere and honest crafts and of artisans who worked for love of their work and not alone for money.

* * *

Grey shadows lean heavier upon the blusterings of the wind, and the day wanes. With the long iron poker Rider beats the dying mescal butts to a new life in a whirling tempest of sparks. There is a tinny rattle as Tanya drags out the sheet of flattened coal-oil can and sets it in place on its grid above the coals. There will be hot whole-wheat tortillas tonight, cheered with a great steaming brew of squaw tea. Tortillas toasted to toothsome savoriness upon the flattened strip of thin metal that once surrounded five gallons of kerosene. Primitive? Yes, but practical. Not upon any of the gadgets of your finest electric ranges can you cook tortillas so satisfactorily. But of course not everyone yearns to cook tortillas. The tortilla is a primitive thing, the friend and mainstay of primitive peoples and those "semibarbarians" who prefer deserts and waste places for their habitations. Yet the tortilla is not without sterling virtues. No less an authority than that prince of desert explorers, Carl Lumholtz, has written enthusiastically of the tortilla—and of the flattened kerosene can.

Desert Refuge 32
(March 1944)

THIS IS the time of year when our Ghost Mountain climate is temperamental. One day you may shiver in a howling windstorm. And the next be shedding wraps and blankets to bask in a flood of dazzling sunshine as tingling and kindly as that of early summer. Only yesterday we were all hugging the big open fireplace, feeding mescal butts and husky chunks of juniper wood to the leaping flames. Today, in a hushed warm stillness more perfect than any day in June, the youngsters have lugged out the old cement mixing trough, launched it on the pool, and gone canoeing—using fire shovels for paddles.

But the winter storms were good to Yaquitepec this year. All the cisterns and catch pools were filled to overflowing. The rains fell and fell until we, so long in need of water, began to feel anxiety. There were ominous damp patches here and there on the inside of the walls. Big sections of exposed construction outside slumped and slid off in ruin. We began to know the fear which every primitive dweller of the desert has when rainstorms of long duration assault his adobe. Would the adobe hold? We had uneasy thoughts of finding ourselves in the plight of the mud house dwellers of Egypt who, when unprecedented Nile floods lick at their foundations, frequently find themselves groveling in a heap of gooey mud—surmounted by a collapsed roof. Adobe construction, unless plaster or cement protected, does have weak points.

But our fears were groundless. Our good stout walls, although scarred outside a little and marred in places by falls and slides, stood up nobly. And after the rain had cleared away and a few mild days had dried the earth we repaired the weak spots and took away all traces of storm from our interior finish by a good heavy coat of whitewash.

Lime whitewash is an excellent thing. Whitewash and adobe have the same affinity as bread and butter. They go together. If properly applied there is a great deal of protection for exterior walls in whitewash alone. There are various mixtures. One of the best we have run across consists of 25 pounds of hydrated lime dissolved in 10 gallons of hot water, to which is added six pounds of salt, three ounces of ground alum and about a pint of syrup-thick common boiled glue. The glue, salt, alum combination makes this whitewash stick extremely well.

If you don't have all the ingredients you can get along with just the lime and salt. In such case increase the salt amount heavily. We have found that the latter mixture makes a very durable coat, if applied thickly, about the consistency of cream.

This is a durable coat, even for other things, as Victoria discovered. She was extremely interested in our whitewashing. Wrapped in what she calls her "bath-a-robe" she stalked about among the pails and homemade mescal brushes with a great deal of dignity and importance, tendering all sorts of advice. "You forgotted the ben-zoated-ob-soda," she said, sniffing at the little tub of mixed whitewash. Like her two brothers Victoria takes keen delight in launching shafts of sarcasm at this commercial food preservative.

"You don' incorporate benzoate of soda in whitewash," Rudyard assured her with dignity. "It's only used for pweserving mummies an' in foods for sick people."

Victoria sniffed. She drew her bath-a-robe closer about her. "Now you've forgotted another place," she said to me severely, as I teetered precariously on a chair with my brush. "Uppa there, by thee window. You are getting awfuey careless."

The outside door opened suddenly. Rider came in lugging a spiny mescal butt for the fire. "Gangway!" he cried warningly. "Look out for the spikes!"

What happened then we don't quite know. We *think* Victoria stepped back suddenly. At any rate one moment she was standing on the floor wrapped in her three years of importance—and her bath-a-robe. The next instant she had vanished in a white geyser from which a pair of diminutive heels and a shock of blond curls stuck upward at an acute angle. There was an ear-splitting shriek which, as I toppled from my chair and Rider dropped his spikey burden, brought Tanya rushing from the next room. "*Victoria* where are you?" she gasped.

"She pwecipitated herself into the whitewash," Rudyard sputtered, groping to clear his face and body from the wave of white splashes that had struck him. "She's *wasted* all of it."

We fished Victoria from the tub. There wasn't any lime in her eyes and none had a chance to get into her mouth because she was yelling so lustily. But otherwise she was well-coated, and the bath-a-robe was a mess. It took a good deal of warm water and much sponging down before the open fire before she looked human again. Also it cost Rider a necklace of threaded juniper berries and Rudyard three snail shells as presents to her majesty before she would consent to stop yelling. After which she curled up contentedly in bed with her doll and went to sleep. While Tanya laundered the bath-a-robe and Rudyard and I mixed more whitewash. Yes, it has good covering qualities. And it does *stick.*

There are other angles to Yaquitepec rains besides repairing damages and whitewashing. No one who dwells in the desert will ever quite get over the thrill of seeing new life unfold after a steady downpour has brought moisture again to a long parched earth. No matter how accustomed we may become to seeing this miracle year after year there is always something mysterious about it. This season, in particular, the change was startling, for the dry spell had been long and hard.

When we came back to the mountain the bunch grass all appeared dead. The mescals were shrunken. Famished rats had made cruel inroads on even the struggling chollas—in some instances stripping them almost completely of their fleshy bark. In long walks we could find nothing of those showy succulents known popularly as "hen and chickens" except seemingly blackened corpses, wedged in the crevices of the rocks. It appeared that Ghost Mountain could never "come back."

Then came the rains. A few days after the first storm had subsided we went out to some of the farther ridges to collect fuel. The change in all the country was a shock. Everywhere there was a sense of slumbering life having suddenly awakened. Under the lee of almost every big rock delicate little desert ferns had unfolded their green fronds. Mosses and lichens glinted among the stones underfoot. Thin blades of grass were thrusting through the sticks and gravel of every sheltered patch. All the cacti, especially the beavertails, looked plump and swollen and alive with new strength. And in all the rock crevices where the blackened shapes of the lamented "hen and chickens" had mouldered, tiny leaf edges groped towards the sunlight. It was a sort of mass resurrection. We came home with our load of firewood feeling strangely happy. Also we had seen a snail. Maybe it doesn't seem very important, the sighting of a snail. But on Ghost Mountain the discovery and observation of a live desert snail is an event. There must be numbers of them on the mountain, for their whitened shells are fairly plentiful and Rider has collected them for years. But no matter how you search you almost never see a living specimen. The only ones we ever have found have been discovered immediately after rains Then at rare intervals, you will find one trailing its dainty form across the damp rocks. Delicate and striking little creatures these desert snails. Although of the same family as the common garden snail, it resembles it no more than a slender songbird resembles a fat barnyard hen. These Ghost Mountain snails are jet black with fine, racehorse lines. And their delicate shells are, in life, beautifully shaded with markings of brown. These brown markings do not last long after the creature has died. They soon fade. Almost all the empty shells that Rider and Rudyard discover are a bleached, desert white. Always it is a shock to discover a snail in the savage surroundings of the desert. Like finding a fur seal somewhere in the jungles of the equator. But then, there is the equal shock of the desert tortoise. And once we found a tiny tree toad under a rock, right on the heat seared crest of Ghost Mountain.

* * *

The Yaquitepec mail sack, when it gets in, is usually well filled, these days. And that is something to rejoice over. For if there is one thing more than any other which makes life worthwhile on our mountaintop it is to receive letters from good friends. They are good friends too. For they uncomplainingly stand the test of waiting scandalous periods for often the briefest of replies. Somehow they seem to know that all their letters are carefully treasured, even if sheer pressure of circumstances often force just hastily scribbled postcards in return.

Mail day is always a big day, and it is a family affair. Everyone gathers round, as for a tribal council. Rider perches himself on a chair and Victoria stands on a bench, in order to see better. Rudyard usually squats precariously on the extreme edge of the table top, his little heels partly overhanging space and his whole, intent, compactly bunched body giving the impression that each instant he is going to topple backwards to disaster. But he never does. He and Victoria appoint themselves Masters of Ceremonies. They direct the order in which the mail shall be opened. And if their rulings ever are ignored pandemonium breaks loose, with all the shoutings and gesticulations of a regiment of excited organ grinders.

All letters are read aloud, attentively listened to and commented on. Sometimes we have to go back and re-read special paragraphs. The Board is very thorough and gets a great deal of joy and excitement out of its widely spaced mail day "meetings."

Most letters are from kindred souls—often far distant—whom we may never meet, but who also feel the restless urge towards freedom and simplicity of living which is today tugging at the hearts of so many of the human race. Once in a while we get letters of censure—frank scoldings from good folks who declare that we are very wrong to have "deserted civilization." They say that we are deliberately erecting stumbling blocks in the path of progress. And when sometimes I answer and ask innocently *what* "Civilization?" And *what* "Progress?" they become very angry and their replies sound as though, while writing them, they had been jumping up and down like our enraged pocket mice do when they are squabbling over grains of corn. Some correspondents are greatly worried about the "Futures" of our youngsters. And one expressed grave concern for their health "separated as you are from all properly prepared commercial foods," she wrote, "are you sure that they are getting enough vitamins?"

That one was a poser. It brought the Board up with a short turn. Victoria wrinkled her nose: "Wita-mines? Witermins?" she puzzled, puffing out her plump little cheeks. "Do you qwite wealize what she means?"

"Of course!" Rudyard pounded on the table with his fist like Tarzan calling for order in a council of gorillas. "Of *course!* Vitamins are all the goodness which is carefully extwacted fwom food so that it can be pwoperly *enwiched* later on. Are you so absolutely ignorwant?" He glared at Rider who was chuckling like a cheshire cat.

So that was that! We forwarded on Rudyard's definition to our correspondent, telling her also that we did not know about the vitamins on Ghost Mountain. That there *might* be a few, lurking in the farther rock caves which we had never thoroughly explored. But we did not think the children would come to any harm from them, as they were all thoroughly aware of the necessity of giving a wide berth to all dangerous looking creatures. We have not heard from her since.

Yaquitepec wears winter white. Rider (left) and Rudyard choose a site for their snowman.

Yes, mail days on Ghost Mountain are happy days. Despite "Civilization" and "vitamins" and "Progress"— even the irate correspondent who told me that "after the war" the "new, mechanized civilization will be a thing surpassing our wildest dreams of liberty and ease"—we get along very well.

If it be our personal conviction that what "Civilization" needs is not more softness and ease but more simplicity and nearness to the earth and fundamental things, at least we are not alone.

Desert Refuge 33
(April 1944)

WE HAD thought wistfully that spring was hiding just beyond our mountain crest. But, as Rudyard puts it pithily, "Ewidently we thought a lie." For instead of the glad-eyed Indian maiden with flowers in her hair, it was fierce old War Chief, Winter, with his glittering arrows and shaking white plumes who leaped upon us from ambush beyond the rim rocks. Savage his war whoop and savage also his hundreds upon hundreds of fierce braves who came racing at his heels upon their crowding horses of cloud. The junipers whistled and bowed to the charge. The whirring arrows of ice shivered and splintered upon our walls and low-hunched roof. Long and bitter was the attack—while we, who had dreamed of spring, crouched before the red leaping flames of our great fireplace. Yes, evidently we had "thought a lie."

But hard on the heels of the storm furies came the snow fairies. And there was reward. Our trio of youngsters love snow and they greeted the glittering world with shouts of delight. Somehow, under a blanket of snow, Ghost Mountain is breath-taking. Perhaps because of the startling contrast to its usual vivid sun-soaked coloring. In their foreign trimmings of ermine the mescals and chollas and bisnagas and ocotillos assume a fairy-like unreality, like growths in an enchanted world. In the crisp white blanket that covers rocks and gravelly earth the tiny tracks of birds and the scribbly scurrying of mice are like the footprints of elves. And over all, the sparkle of the desert sun and the cloudless arch of a turquoise sky.

"But it goes so quickly," the children lament, as they race excitedly through the shallow drifts and pelt each other with fluffy snowballs. "Oh look! It's melting *so* fast!"

Their regret is genuine. Their unclothed bodies glow with the healthy exposure to sun and crisp air. It is only when bare feet and eager fingers become too chilled for comfort that they make brief dashes back into the house to warm up. But only brief ones. Snow-time is too precious to be wasted indoors.

Besides, snow and ice mean the possibility of homemade ice cream. And that most delicious of all treats— honey poured over a bowlful of snow. Then, too, there are snowmen to make. And snow to bring in, in pots, and melt over the fire—just to see how the Eskimos do it. Yes, snow is popular at Yaquitepec when it does come. "When I grow up," says Rudyard, carried away by temporary enthusiasm, "I am going to the North Pole to live."

But the snow fairies have gone now and have taken their magic with them. Once more the sun-sprites and the laughing brown elves of the wasteland hold sway. Grass is greener and taller. The sun stands higher in the sky.

And it is warmer. For this year at least Chief Winter has made his last big raid.

"But when summah comes how will you bake thee beans and thee bread?" inquires Victoria, pausing long enough in a rapid-fire recitation of the alphabet to ask the anxious question. "Because if we doant have great big fires we woant have such lots of hot coals to bury thee bean pot in at night. And there woant be any more baked beans." She looked doleful. Baked beans, seasoned just so, are Victoria's especial weakness.

"You don't have to have roaring fires in order to bake beans, ignorwamus," said Rudyard impatiently. "Beans can be baked in—in mul-ti-tu-din-ous ways." He drew a deep breath after the effort of the word. "They bake beans even in Boston," he added as an afterthought.

"But somehow they don't taste as good," Tanya said. "There's always a *something* about our winter-baked beans."

And it is true. For the bean is a temperamental entity, despite its humble station. Its possibilities are too little appreciated. For, like the toothsome mescal heart, the bean requires long slow cooking. By a wood fire, of course. The quality of the heat vibrations given out by various fuels and heat-making methods are very different.

So in this matter, as in many others, a little back-tracking from modern illusions is in order. Back to the pit ovens of the savage. Or to the old-fashioned bean hole. Provide yourself with a cast-iron pot or Dutch oven, with a close-fitting iron lid. And, having measured into it the desired quantity of beans, pinto beans or any other variety you favor—fill it generously with water. To this add seasonings, a matter for individual preference. For this is where the art of cookery comes in.

Chili—the inner pulp scraped from whole well-steamed Mexican red chilies, if you can get it—takes first place. Then garlic—not just a whiff, but a generous helping of chopped garlic cloves. The garlic is one of the most healthful things provided by Nature, a system purifier and a potent agent for the relief of high blood pressure, as well as being the possessor of many other sound virtues. Then put in your tomatoes—be generous with these too. Then salt, and any other seasonings and herbs that your personal tastes and experience dictate.

If you are a vegetarian you will find that you have ample scope among natural herbs and seasonings to prepare a bean pot that will be second to none. But if you are not a vegetarian you may like to add some diced bacon or some salt pork. And a goodly measure of beef fat rendered from suet will add body and flavor. And finally, when you have performed all these rites (good cooks have first to be born, then perfected by a lifetime of devotion) you hie you away to your pit oven, a homely gadgetless hole in the ground in which a good fire has been blazing for an hour or so. And there, scraping aside or lifting out, with a shovel, the glowing coals and hot ashes, you bury your tightly covered and water-filled bean pot in the hot mass. Cover it up with coals and ashes and finally heap the earth over it. Then you go happily away and forget it for 12 or 16 hours or so—longer if you want to. And then—

But why anticipate the gates of paradise? He who with a healthy outdoor appetite has not experienced the thrill of digging up a properly prepared bean pot and lifting its lid, he who has not sniffed its delicate odor of indescribable allure, has not really lived. Empires have fallen and thrones been overturned for much less. (Oh yes, we know that some cooks put molasses in bean pots. To desecrate real beans, especially the Mexican *frijole* bean, with molasses should be a matter for a 'dobe wall and a firing squad at sunrise.)

But it is not only perfectly cooked beans that are a product of our big winter fires. There is bread too. Not summer bread, but winter bread. For in winter Yaquitepec thrives upon a special variety of hard bread—a bread very different from the pale blown-up product, a loaf of which Mayor La Guardia once crushed together in his hands as he made the angry denunciation that the people were being fed wind. For our winter bread at Yaquitepec is made without yeast or leavening agent of any kind. It contains simply flour, salt and water. Positively nothing else. Kneaded together in a rather moist dough, the loaf filling a big cast-iron Dutch oven about two-thirds full, it is set upon the hot ember-cleared floor of the fireplace at night. And around it—very close but not touching—the glowing coals and hot ashes are arranged in a high, encircling bank. For bread, we do not use the tight-fitting pot cover. Instead the loaf is covered by a loose iron plate which rests irregularly upon the rim of the pot and lets the steam from the baking mass escape. Also we provide for better circulation of heat by keeping open, doughnut style, a round hole in the center of the loaf, by means of a collapsible tin tube, fashioned from an empty tin can.

With the ring of embers arranged about our great loaf, and with a few chunks of burning wood upon its flat iron lid, we go blissfully to bed. In the morning our loaf is done. Solid? Yes, it is solid. But it also is remarkably healthful and sustaining. Especially since it is made from homeground, unrobbed whole grain flour, mostly in a combination of one-third wheat and two-thirds rye. The critic who once said, scathingly, that for many years the public had developed the fashion of demanding harder and harder butter upon softer and softer bread, would have no cause for complaint with this.

* * *

The one gap in the otherwise perfect wasteland view which unrolls from before our windows has been filled. Perhaps it wasn't really a gap except in our imaginations, but it bothered us. We felt there ought to be yuccas growing in that particular spot. And there weren't any. A long while the lack has irked us. The natural thing, of course, was to move some yuccas to the spot. But yuccas, even though they look so coy and disport themselves in the grass skirts of hula girls, are in reality very serious things, and as hefty as lead elephants. So for a good many winter-spring seasons we have dodged the issue. This year, however, we decided to do something about it.

There are plenty of yuccas on our personal Ghost Mountain domain. But we wanted particular ones to fit the particular need. So Rider and Rudyard were sent out as scouts. They were gone a long while, but finally returned to report that finding the right kind of yuccas wasn't nearly as easy as it might seem. However, they believed they had located a pair. But they were not on the summit of the mountain. They were down at the foot of it.

This was discouraging. But remembering that the mesa-top Pueblo Indians of New Mexico used to stage races up their precipitous trails, carrying sheep upon their shoulders, Tanya and I decided that we ought to be able

A scene from the frieze that Marshal painted on the walls of the Julian Library.

to carry up yuccas, one at a time, on a sort of ambulance stretcher slung between us. So the following day, guided by our scouts, we went down the trail carrying a pick and shovel, some coils of rope and two long, supposedly strong, poles of "civilized" wood from which to fashion the carrying stretcher. Finally, out on the lowland, Rider stopped and pointed:

"Those are the yuccas," he said. "Those two on the outside edge of the bunch."

"And I found them," Rudyard hastened to add. He puffed up with importance. Then, sensing something from the expression of our faces, "Don't you think they are awfu'y decowative?"

"Well, yes," Tanya admitted. "They are *that,* it is true. But...."

"An' they're young an' wigorous," Rudyard hurried on in breathless persuasiveness. "They can pwobably be twansplanted to unparalleled adwantage. And...Why, what are you laughing at?"

"I don't quite know," Tanya choked. "But perhaps it's because I'm afraid that these young yuccas of yours may be *too* young. This one here can't be more than 300 years old. And the other not a day over 250."

"And neither of them weigh over a ton and a half—if as much," I pointed out.

"Well, suppose," said Rider, grinning mischievously, "you try to locate some. We ran all over the map. And these were the best we could find. All the little ones are too small. You said you wanted 'artistic' yuccas."

"I know. I know," Tanya said consolingly. "We'll all look."

So we all looked. Up and down and in and out. We disturbed several jackrabbits and one coyote. We found all manner of things that we weren't looking for—dim, long-abandoned mescal roasting hearths, weathered sherds [shards] of ancient pottery, swarms of bees in hollows under rocks. But no "artistic" yuccas—that is, none that we could carry. Hope went down. So also did the sun, dropping lower and lower in the desert sky.

And then, just as we were on the point of abandoning the quest, we located a couple of suitable specimens—at least they were the best we could hope to find. They were a long way from our trail. But we dug them up—an easy matter, since the earth was still loose and moist from the recent rains. With much haste we constructed a stretcher from our ropes and poles. Loading one specimen we

Yucca

started for home. A few steps and the poles—the only ones of their kind in all our district—broke.

"And now what?" Tanya asked, surveying the wreckage.

"Nuffing," said Rudyard glumly, "just nuffing! I am afwaid we are utterly fwustwated."

"Frustrated nothing!" Rider snapped. "Let's get some mescal poles."

So we ranged the surroundings and brought back several of the toughest looking, long, dead flower stalks of mescals that we could find. We tied them together with fibers and re-made our carrying stretcher from them.

With Tanya and me bearing the prone yucca between us, we climbed the trail. Just as the sun was setting we planted our burden in the hole which we previously had prepared for it and watered it generously. And next day we went down and brought up its mate and planted that too.

So now there are two yuccas growing, where no yucca grew before. At last we are satisfied. For they are, as Rudyard says, quite an "acksquisition" to the landscape.

Desert Refuge 34
(May 1944)

THE flower legions of Ghost Mountain stand firm against the sullen gods of storm. And the smiling-faced little warriors of the new order, who brandish no lances and launch no arrows, are winning out in every direction. Some have been laid low in the last vengeful charges of a reluctantly retreating winter. But for every one that has fallen, with bruised and trampled petals, ten thousand others have leaped up to take their places in the ranks. Down the washes and up the footslopes, along the ridges and across the shoulders of the hills march the glowing blossoms of triumph.

White and yellow and scarlet and blue, close-packed, confident, irresistible—once again the annual battle between death and bitterness and life and beauty has been fought out on Ghost Mountain. And once again—as it always will be—new life leaps up triumphant. Desert spring—spring *anywhere*—always is something to deeply stir the heart. Why then is it that man glooms himself with doubt? And persists in grubbing for his assurance of immortality only in musty books? It is written everywhere. Across the earth and across the stars.

* * *

Victoria has her new shoes. Thick, felted soles of cloth, after the Chinese pattern. A gay bit of heavy woven stuff, in designs of red, yellow and blue, for the uppers. There were no shoe stamps expended in supplying Victoria's shoes. I doubt that a whole bushel basketful of stamps would procure a pair like them. They would undoubtedly, though, produce severe lectures from that class of shoe "experts" who assure us that if the human foot is not confined suitably and "supported" it will spread and the arches will break down.

But Ghost Mountain fortunately is far from the haunts of "experts." And Victoria, as she parades up and down admiring her new footgear, knows nothing of their balderdash. Like the other dwellers at Yaquitepec—where even sandals are worn only occasionally, and life is lived almost entirely barefooted—she has high arches that are tough as steel springs. "See my new shoes," she keeps saying. "Doant you think they are *very* pretty?"

"You are getting werry wain," Rudyard sniffed reprovingly. "I am weally sorry that Daddy fabwicated them for you. Your chawacter is in danger of getting stucked-up by affluence. Those moccasins are only for going to town in, wemember."

"They're not mock-a-wins!" Victoria shrilled indignantly. "They're *sooes!*" She appealed to Rider.

"They're moccasins," Rider asserted with finality. "And what's wrong with moccasins? You're trying to give yourself airs. You're a little aristocrat."

Victoria burst into tears and fled into the house.

"Rider called me a little whiskit-krat!" she sobbed. "I'm not a whiskit-krat! I'm not. I'm *not!*" She flung herself into Tanya's arms, weeping wildly.

But later, the storm subsided, she sat in her chair munching a rye-flour tortilla thickly spread with desert honey. She put her head on one side and wiggled her toes. "Anyway I like my new mocca-sooes," she said, giggling as she regarded her gay little feet. "Doant you think I look awf'y *pretty* in them?"

* * *

Spring days are happy days on Ghost Mountain. Storms still charge against us at intervals. But notwithstanding these periodic set-backs, each day seems brighter than the one before it. Soft footed and singing to itself the warm desert wind wanders up the sunny washes and through the swaying junipers. The tiny yellow and white daisies nod to each other as they carpet the gravelly earth between the clumps of budding mescals. The scarlet banners of the low growing mimulus wave welcome to the droning bees.

"The snakes are out, children," warns Tanya. "You must be on the watch." It is a warning often repeated. For when one lives bare-bodied and barefooted in the midst of a wilderness, sharp eyes and caution are a necessity, especially in spring and summer. Rattlesnakes are as a rule peaceable. But they are temperamental. Vigilance and sharp eyes always should be in the make-up of hikers in snake territory. In this connection the civilized boot and shoe have their definite drawbacks as well as virtues. For while high boots or stout puttees afford protection against a striking snake, on the other hand they encourage a heedless, blundering progress. The eyes of the hiker are relieved of the necessity of constantly watching where his foot will be set down. And, as Nature always discards that which is not used, the attention of eye and mind thus dispensed with is lost. And the keenness of the senses is thereby dulled. The eyes and the attention of the Indian had, of necessity, to be everywhere at once. That is why old-time Indians were masters of the wilderness, attuned to many of its mysteries. The eyes and thoughts of civilized man are too often anywhere but on the thing that he is doing.

We are good to our Ghost Mountain rattlesnakes—as far as lies within our power. We dislike to kill them; we feel that we have no right to. The earth is a realm of tooth and claw, of life preying upon life. But that does not alter the truth that only through mercy can man hope to climb. And it is also true that the wild creatures speedily recognize you as a friend or killer. They know too if you are an eater of meat. The old stories of Saint Francis of Assisi and the beautiful tales that Rudyard Kipling wove concerning the bonds between man and his furred and feathered relatives, are not myths.

And so, unless they are quartered close to the house (a rattlesnake does not range far from his home spot) we leave our rattlers strictly alone. We have come upon them dozing contentedly in the shadows of boulders or in the cool of mountain caves. And we have looked at them and they have looked at us. And we have parted in peace. There is something starkly grim about rattlesnakes. You cannot meet them and look into their eyes in a spirit of frivolity. They know their power. They know also how to mind their own business. A commendable virtue.

Our Ghost Mountain rattlesnakes give no warning rattles. Nor do they, until molested, show fight. They just lie quietly, as though expecting to be let alone. It is only when they are convinced that harm is coming to them that they whirr their danger signal and go into fighting pose. This isn't very helpful, of course, if they are blundered into. For a rattler can strike just as surely from an uncoiled pose as from a coiled one. But it indicates that they have been disturbed very little.

We have encountered rattlesnakes in other sections—sections more accessible and man-haunted than this—and almost without exception they showed fight on sight. Which would seem to demonstrate that a snake can lose confidence in the human race. This is true not only of the snakes. The actions of all persecuted animal life testify to the same fact. Hates and fears are born a long way back—far longer than the mere span of one lifetime. That is why past wrongs, either against animals or fellow humans, cannot be atoned for all at once.

The best known remedy for rattlesnake bite? Cut and suck! Enlarge each fang puncture with a small, fairly deep cut from a very sharp knife. Cut lengthwise of the limb so as not to run the risk of severing important tendons. Keep up the sucking process, with as few rests as possible, for several hours. Even the venom of the tropical Bushmaster is said to be conquerable by this procedure. Learn the proper course to take in case of snakebite *first*. Don't wait until after being struck.

* * *

Due to winter fuel gathering and the demands of several new projects which absorbed almost every instant of available time, there hasn't been leisure for much recreational handiwork at Yaquitepec of late. However, we recently finished a bottlenecked grass basket, made by the system of coiling and sewing that is so useful for many materials, including pine needles. There is a fascination about basket making. Once you have started one you can't leave it alone. You can make a basket out of almost anything. Grass, willow splints, corn husks, mesquite twigs, yucca leaves—the materials are legion. Perhaps the greatest charm of the work is that each different material has a temperament all its own, which requires the application of different kinks and methods that are discoverable only by patience and experiment.

You can, for instance, make beautiful baskets out of the green, round-stemmed swamp reeds, often called tules, which are so abundant around desert soakages. They are satiny and pliant when growing, yet if you weave the basket from the tractable, easily coiled green reeds, you will find next day that the work which looked so handsome when you sewed the coils firmly into place, has shrunk amazingly. All your stitches are loose and the whole affair is an impossible, wobbly wreck. And if you try drying it first, it will break in your hands like so many sticks of thin brittle glass.

Most basket materials have to be soaked in water. But there is a trick by which you can work the tules without wetting. And the scheme is to roll up carefully the freshly gathered reeds into neat symmetrical coils, of varying diameters that will approximate the dimensions of the different stages of your planned basket. Hang the coils away. And in a few days, when they are thoroughly dry, take them down and begin work on your basket, selecting a sufficient number of strands, to form the thickness of your basket coil, from the bundle that has the most nearly corresponding curvature. You will find that, dried in the coiled form, they will accommodate themselves to quite a range of size changes before snapping. And you can cinch the coils together, as you sew round and round and build up your basket, with a stitch of good tight tension which you can feel assured will not loosen. A desert fiber is the ideal material with which to sew a desert basket. But raffia, sold so much for basket making, will do equally well. And raffia does have a satisfactory primitive look.

* * *

Hummingbirds whirring like living jewels about the tall, gently swaying dry yellow stalks of last year's mescals. The warm wind freshening a little as it draws steadily up from the distance of haze-veiled mountains. And faintly upon the breath of it, as I sit here among the rocks and junipers finishing this, there comes the voice of Rudyard, proclaiming after the manner of the prophets of old: "Flee from the cities! Live in the desert! Eat nothing civilized! Eat juniper berries and other wild stuff! Flee from the cities!"

Stirred by this startling piece of oratory I climb upon a rock and stare. Away back, by the house, I can just see him. He stands upon a boulder, his red and blue seldom-used mantle draped across his shoulders, his right arm upraised in an attitude suggestive of Elijah denouncing some sinful king.

"Flee from the cities!" he declaims, shaking his fist dramatically. And, faintly, blended with his exhortation, comes the breathless shouting of Victoria, his constant understudy and fervid convert:

"Fee fwom thee cities! Live in thee desert! Eat juniper bewwies an' ower wild tuff! Fee from..."

Wind sings through the junipers and blots the shouting of the "prophets." And I come back to my seat chuckling. Fiercely fervent little sons and daughters of the desert are these hardy little sun-sprites of Yaquitepec. And perhaps there is wisdom in their childish oratory.

Desert Refuge 35
(June 1944)

THROUGH the east window the ragged mass of an unfinished wall bulks like ebony against the pale dawn light. Except for the vibrant blundering notes of the big carpenter bees about the eaves troughs, Ghost Mountain is wrapped in a cloak of silence as absolute as though it was the first morning of the world.

Soon the sun will be up. Already the jagged rocks along the eastern ridge, where the mountain crest plunges into the shadowy lowlands, are beginning to glow pink. Lone, dead mescal poles are gaunt against the sky. Between the bulk of giant boulders the silhouettes of gnarled junipers are an edging of black lace. Rider is already awake, lying quiet and thoughtful in his covers, awaiting the arrival of the goldfish.

Every morning, just as the sun looms above the horizon, the goldfish make their magical appearance, swimming gracefully down the length of an old smoke-tinted ceiling beam. First, along the dark length of the stretching timber that is their promenade appear the shimmering waves of a pale golden sea. Then, suddenly, in the midst of it, there are the goldfish. A long line of them. Flashing, ruddy-gold fellows of assorted sizes, all headed south. Their appearance and the ceremony of counting them, marks the official beginning of a Yaquitepec day. Rudyard and Victoria always wake up to take part in this tally of the magic fish, and always are baffled. Because, no matter how many times they count them, they never can arrive at the same number twice. "Twenty-two," says Rudyard. "No, seventeen," declares Victoria. And they are both wrong—or maybe both right. For when Rider, the countmaster, makes the check, there are but eighteen. And as he goes over his count to verify it, there perhaps will be fifteen. Or nineteen. Magic is in the goldfish, that changes their number, from second to second, with the rapid lift of the sun. Sometimes we think that those people whose houses are so well constructed that there are no spaces beneath the corrugations of roofing iron through which the sun can paint glowing goldfish upon beams are missing a lot of fun.

*   *   *

Mescal roasting was hurried this year. We really ought to have done more of it, for the children love the brown, delicious, natural sweet. But there have been so many other tasks, and days have been so crowded, that we found it hard to use the necessary time.

Those days that we did manage to spare were picnics indeed. For we drift now through that enchanted period of spring when the rock crest of Ghost Mountain is vibrant with the crystal notes of orioles and canyon wrens, and all the white, gravelly stretches are gay with a carpet of desert flowers. To set forth in the early dawn, armed with shovels and digging bars, and bearing food for a day's outing, is sheer delight. There is a tang to the air, and a wide sense of freedom that belongs not to this age but to another, when man was not so enmeshed in miseries of his own devising. Bare feet fall softly upon whispering gravel. From the junipers, as one brushes past their dark green branches exhales an aromatic fragrance. In the stillness we imagine we see, just ahead, the shadowy shapes of those simple hearted children of the desert whose dusky feet traced out these ancient trails between mescal hearth and mescal hearth in the long vanished years.

Mescal roasting is a family affair. Tanya and I find and bring in the sprouting plants that are ready for the baking. Rider helps dig the pit and fetches stones to line it. Rudyard and Victoria trot hither and thither, lugging in fuel. They cease their labors occasionally to hunt for snail shells or to admire the tiny thickets of desert ferns that grow in cool sheltered niches at the base of giant boulders.

It must have been like this in the old days, which only the silent rocks and ancient junipers remember. Then, as now, the orioles flung their liquid notes along the slopes. The blossoms of the desert pea bush crowded the space between the boulders with gay bouquets of dazzling yellow. The bodies of those who moved to and fro at their tasks were innocent of clothes. The old days and the simple dwellers of the desert are gone. "They killed them all off," an old Mexican woman once said to us sorrowfully. "They killed off all those poor people. But, *gracias a Dios,* maybe the padres at least saved their souls."

Mescal roasting is strenuous work. There is the pit to be dug. And afterwards it has to be roughly lined with stones. On these old hearths, where the earth is permanently black from the scorch of unnumbered ancient fires, the digging usually is not so hard as it would be in fresh ground. Also there are plenty of fire blackened stones that have been used and re-used numberless times in the past. This lessens the labor somewhat. But still the work requires considerable effort.

The dimensions of the pit can be governed by ambition—and the size of the proposed baking. About three feet across and from 18 inches to two feet deep in the center, when stone lined, is the average size of the pits we make. The stone lining is hasty and crude—just sizeable rocks laid together in a pavement over the bottom and up the sloping sides to the rim.

Digging in these old hearths always gives us a vivid sense of their antiquity. The blackened earth extends downward to great depths. Their age must be measured by many centuries.

About the hardest part of the proceedings is gathering the mescal hearts. The sprouting plants first must be found and suitable ones always are widely scattered. You have to catch them in just the right stage. If the flower shoot is not high enough you lose a great deal in content. If it is too high the succulent juice pulp has begun to transfer itself to the upbuilding of the stalk. The ideal stage is when the sprout is up about 15 to 18 inches. At this period maximum plumpness—as far as roasting purposes are concerned—has been attained by the hearts.

Your plant located, the next task is to remove the central heart so that it can be roasted. This means taking practically the whole plant, with the exception of the extreme woody root, and divesting it of leaves. The old-timers did this by means of chisel-pointed hardwood digging sticks. With these they wrenched out the swelled heart and its attached sprout and pried off the surrounding dagger-pointed leaves. We still use the wooden sticks on occasion. But we have found that a light iron digging bar, although it is heavier, is more effective. It is sometimes quite a struggle to get off all of the stubborn leaves. When this is accomplished, you have a whitish-green club, something like a grotesque animal foot. This is the heart, the forerunner of your subsequent delicacy.

When a sufficient number of hearts have been collected, we lop off the extreme, spine-armed tip of the sprout and arrange them, thick end inwards, around the circumference of the roasting pit upon a low coping of good sized stones, built around the rim for that purpose. Then you proceed to pile the fuel in a great heap all around, covering coping stones and hearts alike. For this purpose any handy dry fuel will do. Usually we use the old dead butts and stalks of mescals themselves, intermixed with occasional dead branches of juniper, if there are any around. Apparently, from the comparative rarity of charcoal in the old fire hearths, this was the course followed by the ancients. Dead mescal butts provide intense heat, but leave almost no charcoal as compared with wood.

When the fire is lighted it must be kept well fed and blazing hotly for from a half to three quarters of an hour. Mescal hearts are stubborn things and can stand lots of heat. The blaze blackens them and makes hot the rim of rocks upon which they lie, heating also the lining of stones in the pit. Coals and blazing fragments fall into the pit and add to its temperature. It is a hot job and long mescal poles come in handy for stirring and arranging the blazing fuel.

At the end of half an hour or so the fire is allowed to die down. When it has dwindled to a mass of glowing embers, through which scorched mescal hearts and blackened rim rocks smoke hotly, you go around the edge of the pit, with a pole or a long handled shovel, and tumble scorched hearts, hot stones and embers all together into the pit. Then the rest of the hot ashes are piled in a mound

Roasting mescal—ink sketch by Marshal South.

above them. And over all a thick, heaped covering of earth. Then you go on to the same round of proceedings at the next roasting pit. Or you go home. The job is done.

And you leave your mescals cooking in their primitive oven for *two days.* At the end of the second day you go back and open up the pits. Things will have cooled down by then so they easily can be handled. The hearts that you take out won't look very inviting. They will be charred and earth plastered, and the shoots will be limp, brown sticky things. But don't throw them away. Carry them home tenderly and with reverence. For beneath the scorched, charred envelope lies something more delicious than many a famed delicacy of civilization.

Take a knife or a hatchet and carefully trim off the outer crusting, and the prize lies before you. Brown and golden and rich! Something like a roasted yam, yet holding also an indescribable tang of pineapple and of mango. Roast mescal! In all the desert there is nothing quite like it. And it must be tasted to be appreciated. It will keep, too, if you slice it and dry it for future use. But we at Yaquitepec seldom get this far. Our enthusiastic youngsters believe in living in the present, and the golden brown stuff doesn't keep very well with us. It tastes too good.

* * *

Our desert tortoises are awake again. All through the cold months they slumbered, hidden away in dark corners behind trunks and boxes in the house. Well sheltered in their hide-outs they were oblivious of the icy blasts that roared above Ghost Mountain. That is, two of them passed the winter in this orthodox fashion. The third—General Machado, our latest acquisition and by far the biggest of the three—scorned the protective folds of the covering which we had laid over him. He vanished at the beginning of winter, and we could not find him.

Then one day, Rider, poking about in the dark hinterland of the storeroom with a flashlight, came hurrying out with the sorrowful news that General Machado was dead. "Frozen, poor thing," Rider said dolefully, shivering at the icy wind howling about the house. "Come, see for yourselves."

So we went and saw for ourselves. There, six inches from the floor, in a dark corner, wedged between the wall and the leg of an old cupboard, was General Machado, stiff and stark. Cold and rigid, his legs dangling out of his shell, and already mouldy looking, he hung there like a dead stiff coyote across the top of a barb wire fence.

We could not reach him without moving a quantity of piled boxes and stored stuff. His appearance, in the wan beam of the flashlight, told us that we couldn't do any good if we did reach him. It was too cold to undertake the job, anyway. And besides we hadn't much heart for it. Somehow the sight of our poor pet hanging there lifeless, as upon a gibbet, cast a gloom over us. Several times during the winter when we really ought to have moved stuff in that corner to get at things we wanted, we invented excuses.

With the coming of spring, the other two awoke. They came down the aisle between the trunks and stores looking for green grass. "We ought to get that other dead tortoise out of the corner," Tanya said reluctantly. "The weather is warming. It's not healthy."

No one wanted the job. But it had to be done. So Rider brought the long iron fire rod with the hook at the end of it and Rudyard fetched the flashlight. "See if you can hook him out," I said glumly, trying to decide whether

Desert tortoise

we would bury him or keep his shell as a memento. "Be careful though. He's probably pretty smelly."

The youngsters grubbed in the corner, on hands and knees. There came a sudden exclamation. "*He's not here!*" Rider's voice was startled.

Flashlight in hand Rudyard backed out from under a table. His eyes were wide. "Someone has spiwited him away!" he said hoarsely.

"Oaha!" Victoria cried breathlessly. "I know! The angels! They came and tooked him!" She bolted to Tanya to impart this amazing news.

But it wasn't the angels. For that afternoon, after we had hunted unsuccessfully for General Machado's body, we met him coming down the aisle, calm and distinguished looking. He had an air about him. An air of authority, such as any really worthwhile general ought to have. "Out of my way," he seemed to say haughtily. "Can't you see I am in a hurry. I have to rejoin my command."

So we restored him to his command. And they welcomed him with sour looks. For they do not like General Machado. Nor do we, now. Well, not much. For we feel, somehow, that he has been guilty of dying under false pretenses.

* * *

Quail calling from the ridges. "*Chouk!*" And again: "*Chouk!*" The bustling flutter of the purple finches who are putting the finishing touches to their nest in the tiny house atop the high pole at the center of the ramada. The sun has dipped far to the west now, and the shadow of the house roof reaches out to the chunky little squaw-tea bush that stands in the center of the white gravel court. Along the rocks of the terrace nod the blue-flecked chia sage blooms, and the desert four-o'clocks are just opening their white flowers. On the slope, beyond the little flat through which the foot trail winds, a clump of desert paintbrush flames a splash of scarlet.

Desert Refuge 36
(July 1944)

ANDY for so long the friendly little sprite of Yaquitepec, has passed on. Andy was a white-footed desert mouse of more than ordinary intelligence—which is saying a good deal, for the white-footed mice are an intelligent and lovable tribe. But Andy was exceptional, even among his own people.

His beginnings are shrouded in mystery—even his name. For we yet don't quite know how we came to call him Andy. He must have been with us for some time before we noticed him for the twilight shadows of Yaquitepec are full of soft-moving little people, and one mouse looks very much like another. By the time we had begun to recognize Andy as an individual he long since had adopted us as his friends.

To trust the human race usually is a fatal error for the creatures of the wild. But Andy seemed to have decided that the roof beams of Yaquitepec covered the Lodge of Brotherhood. So he boldly put behind him all the teachings of his forefathers and took us whole-heartedly into his life.

He made himself a member of the household. Someone to be looked for and to be sharply missed on those rare occasions when he failed to appear. With the first twilight shadows, and often long before the lamps were lighted, he would be with us. Coming from we knew not where and scurrying back and forth between the legs of the table and chairs, like a busy little brown-grey elf, in his search for crumbs. We learned in the course of time that Andy was set apart from other mice by a distinguishing brand—a tiny nick on one of his soft gnome-like ears. An ancient battle record, probably. It was Andy's brand.

Not that we needed the identifying mark. For we soon came to know Andy through his special mannerisms. He had a confident gait and poise. While his tribe-folks slipped softly by along wall ledges or peered at us with bright beady eyes from the corners of shelves or cupboards, Andy would come boldly down, running nimbly across the perpendicular faces of adobe walls and slipping confidently about between our bare feet, as he hunted for dropped bits of bread or fragments of piñon nuts. Sometimes he ran over our feet. And on occasion would use them as look-out stations upon which to perch while he scanned the surrounding terrain. On such occasions we would say, "Andy, *please!* This is my foot—not a watch-post!" And we would jiggle our toes a little, and he would hop down. But not in fear. He had made friends with the "gods" and he knew that they would do him no harm. He knew, too, that manna frequently came down from "heaven" in the shape of various special tidbits—even whole piñons. These he would accept with perfect politeness, taking each one delicately from between the offering fingers and squatting dark-eyed and trustful upon his haunches while he nibbled the morsel to the last fragment.

Nor was his range confined to the floor. He explored the whole house, hunting into every odd corner in his search for edible items of interest. We never knew him, however, to be guilty of doing any damage. His was a simple little soul and he asked nothing save the crumbs and left-overs. One of his favorite ranges was upon the

Marshal wearing handmade clothing.

big flat top of the fireplace. There, among the jumbled collection of "treasures" that Rider, Rudyard and Victoria collect, he often would discover chia seeds grains of Indian corn, sweet juniper berries or fragments of old tortillas. Whenever he made such a find he would carry his prize triumphantly to a favorite spot at the extreme northwest corner of the fireplace top. There he would squat down gravely and, holding the morsel daintily in his forepaws, would proceed to enjoy his meal.

Andy did not live under our roof. He had a little personal wickiup outside somewhere among the rocks and mescals and cactus, to which he departed when he grew tired of adventuring. He had his own particular pop-hole near the summit of one of our unfinished walls, which he used for his goings and comings. But some nights he stayed in the house a long while.

Often Tanya, whose habit it is to get up at midnight and write poetry in the silence while all the rest of the household is wrapped in slumber, had him for attentive companion. Out of the shadows he would come, climbing nimbly up a table leg and appearing above the far edge of the long table top. Here he would pause a moment, as though to give polite notice of his presence. Then he would come pattering down the length of the table and would choose a vantage point, usually upon a book, where he could be within a foot of Tanya's moving pencil. There, in the lamp glow he would squat, silent and attentive, his large delicate ears and sensitive nose twitching with intense interest, as his bright eyes followed the movements of her hand at its writing. Sometimes Tanya would speak to him softly and his nose and ears would move as though in answer. But he sat on unafraid; undisturbed even by the movements and rustle of the paper when she turned pages. After a long while he would get down from his perch and silently go away. Perhaps he too was a poet. Who shall say? The great pianist Paderewsky had a similiar experience with a tiny spider which came regularly to listen to his playing.

Now Andy of the bright eyes and trustful heart is dead. No more will he perch upon our toes. Or nibble juniper berries upon the corner of the fireplace. Or come in the silence to worship the mystery of the moving pencil in the lamplight.

Andy died in battle. Never will we know the whole story of Andy's ending, any more than we will know the details of his beginning. All we know is that, going out one morning, we found in the bottom of a dry shallow water cistern, upon which we were making repairs, five white-footed mice. Three of them were huddled, heads together, in a little grey ball in one corner. Two others lay out in the center of the cistern floor, mangled and dead. And one of the dead mice was Andy.

The sides of the cistern were smooth plastered, and once in it the five had been unable to escape. But how did all of them manage to tumble in together? And just what sort of a bitter struggle had been waged there in the night darkness? The battle had been savage, as the blood, spattered plentifully all over the plastered floor, bore witness, and as the chewed feet and tails of the dead combatants attested. The three trembling and fear-numbed survivors gave us no clue. One of them was badly wounded. And when we had lifted them gently out of their prison and turned them loose beneath the shelter of a spreading juniper they vanished into the cover of the rocks and grass, carrying their secret with them.

* * *

Every once in a while, one or other of our correspondents, mistaking the reasons which inspire our love of the desert and our revolt against Civilization, see fit to chide us, more or less good-naturedly. Alluding to our ideas of clothing and of food and to our disdain of many of the gadgets of progress they accuse us of "aping the Indians." To which we often reply that the charge is no insult. That on the contrary if some members of our population would "Indian the ape" much good would accrue.

Not all of our well-wishers quite understand the barb in this retort. Those who do, however, and whose "come-back" letters recall that heroine of Kipling's who "spread her anger hot as fire through six thin foreign sheets, and more" are very definite.

We grow a little annoyed sometimes at the aspersions often cast upon the original inhabitants of this great land which our nation has appropriated for its own. Although the Indian was no paragon of all the virtues, as some would have us believe, neither was he the inferior and ignorant savage, as too many regard him.

The American Indian is a human being fashioned of the same clay as we all are. He is our blood-brother, as are all other members of the human race, irrespective of creed, nationality or color. And just as no one man can gather all the treasures of the earth into his own satchel, so is it impossible for any one nation or race to be the possessor of every good quality and virtue. The wise man seeks for pearls of beauty and understanding in every quarter. And having found such treasures is rejoiced, counting it of no moment whether they came from the mussels of a river or from the oysters of a tropic sea. In many ways the philosophy of the Indian and his simple natural way of life were much superior to those stilted fetishes before which our vaunted civilization bows. It is all a matter of balance and choice and of common sense. I have no sympathy with "mass" thought. Brains were given the individual to think with. In this regard the actions of many people reflect the lament expressed in Kipling's ballad, "The worst we took with sweat and toil. The best we left behind."

The Indian, particularly the desert Indian, was the embodiment of nature's freedom. In these days of permits and forms and of cluttering of every action of speech and motion by a multiplicity of civilization-engendered rules, the Indian stands out as a bright light in the darkness. We like to remember sometimes the tang of the winds that come down over the red cliffs of the Navajo reservation. A spurious tang. For there is in the very nature of a "reservation" little of freedom. Still there is something free in the breath of that vast silent land and the feel that comes to one from contact with its dark-skinned resolute people. There is a sense of fundamental things, of beginnings. In silence and great spaces was liberty born. Always has the flame of it burned brightest in the hearts of silent peoples, tending their flocks beneath the desert stars.

* * *

Summer, the magic weaver, favors now the bright trails of Ghost Mountain and its surrounding desert. Already, among the junipers and the tall blossoming stalks of the mescals, she has set up her loom. The warp is stretched. Brightly dyed skeins of color lie ready to her hand, and already she has begun the weaving of that magic blanket which each year gathers into one perfect whole all the freedom and fascination of the wilderness.

Watch now, as the design grows under the nimble brown fingers. Mystery and Symbology, Sunlight and Shadow. Foreground and dim purple distance. Hope and Fear. All of man's longings and frailties, his hazy future and his mysterious past.

See! Here is a friendly thread of brown, an inquisitive racer snake, gliding like a painted shadow between the dry stems of the dead buckwheat bushes. And over here is sharp contrast, a splash of brilliant scarlet woven from the flame tips of the ocotillos and the ruby berries of the wolf bushes. Look, too, at this broad band of yellow, more dazzling than all the useless gold of all the world. It is fashioned from the honey-laden blooms of league upon league of tall, gently swaying mescals. The shimmer that dances about it is wrought of the jeweled wings of myriad honey-bribed bees.

Over here, again, is an odd patch—a queer design of a drowsy little horned toad [horned lizard] asleep on the top of a rounded grinding stone, a stone which perhaps has not been disturbed since it last was touched by the hands of an Indian woman half a thousand years ago. And see this other pattern—this triangle of indigo shadow! This is Silence—the silence of a deep canyon whose secrets of

Horned lizard

the past no man ever shall unlock. And what is this— these zigzag threads that pass beside it? Ah, that is a forgotten trail, the trail into the purple distance down which perhaps the Indian woman went, from her last task of grinding, and her four brown desert children with her, and the stalwart desert brave who was her mate down, down and on into the dim distance.

And what is this shimmering design where the threads cross and mingle so bewilderingly? That? Why, that is Mystery, the mystery of the desert. For, do you not see, the pattern is not finished. Nor will it ever be finished. For here the roads end—and begin. Here Progress halts and its tinsel trappings crumble. For here dwell the old gods of the desert who keep the portal, and scatter the dust over the tracks of the passers—and over their bones. The Spaniard lies here—under the dust. And here lie also those who went before the Spaniard. And those who went before *those*, also. The sands shift and shimmer. The mirages swim. The fingers of Summer, the weaver, fly faster and faster, blending the threads, wearing the pattern of the blanket. But that bit—the pattern of Mystery—never shall be finished. Mystery belongs to the gods of the desert—and to Eternity.

Desert Refuge 37
(August 1944)

IT ONCE had been a prosperous village. But it was abandoned now. Under the desert sun it lay bleak and melancholy. Around the edges of the hard trampled area that once had been vibrant with the goings and comings of busy life there still were strewn evidences of industry. Great piles of earth and rocks, excavated from underground kivas and dumped by the excavators; huge deposits of household waste and village trash that had been likewise carried to the edge of the settlement and there thrown in ridges. The old dim trails that led out into the desert land to the north and to the west still were visible. But nothing moved upon them. Only the lonely wind stirred the bunch grass and sang a low dirge of silence—and of death.

Suddenly we saw the shrunken, motionless bodies huddled upon the earth. And in the same instant we glimpsed the monster. An ugly, uncouth thing, bulking gigantic as he bent horribly over the twisted corpse of his latest victim, he stood over by one of the village refuse heaps. At sight of him we stopped *dead* in our tracks.

Perhaps one would think it absurd to be affected by the sight of an assassin bug or to be disturbed by his brutal slaughter of the last survivors of a once teeming colony of harvester ants. Especially when all over the earth men are slaughtering and maiming their fellow men by every brutal method devised by science.

Yet death is death. And be it of solar system, world, man, ant or microbe, it is an event of solemnity to the victim. So the sight of that rapacious, blood-sucking brute and the twisted shapes of his ant victims, as we saw them that desert afternoon, affected us strangely. It was as though we, as gods, looked down upon a devastated city of humanity. Somehow there was a feeling of horror about it, recalling some of those odd tales that the Navajo tell—of how the cliff dwellers originally chose their precipitous dwelling sites so that they might be safe from the monsters that roved the earth in the misty dawn of time.

We stooped closer to investigate. We had known that colony of harvester ants in its prime, and had seen it many times when the tiny trails that led to it were thick with hurrying inhabitants bearing home their burdens of herbs and seeds. We had watched the builders staggering out of the big tunnel entrance carrying rock grains which, relatively speaking, we ourselves could not have stirred. We had watched the busy workers come from the underground threshing floors with their loads of husks and waste to dump upon the trash piles.

Now all was silent. Nothing but a few dead bodies—and a hideous, long-beaked creature sucking the blood from a still limp body. The tribe was extinct.

This was our first experience with assassin bugs in connection with ants. The desert ant, especially the large black one, is a fighter not to be despised. Speaking from painful experience we would prefer to be stung by an ordinary scorpion or a bee than to be bitten by one of these ant warriors. Yet here was evidence that they were prey to something stronger and much more gruesomely savage.

How long that particular bug had haunted the village we had no means of knowing. It did not seem—and still

does not seem—possible that he could have been responsible for the destruction of the colony. For while there were a lot of huddled sun dried little corpses strewn around, which obviously were those of his victims, still there were not nearly enough to represent the ants which had occupied the place. Perhaps some other destruction had fallen upon the town. Or perhaps, after the slaughterer had taken up his abode in the vicinity, the colony had abandoned the place. At any rate the monster had had an orgy of gruesome killing, liquidating the last survivors and stragglers.

He was an ugly fellow—if judged by the horror that his nature inspired. Otherwise I suppose he was handsome enough in his markings of red and brown. For, in actuality, there is nothing created by the Great Spirit which we—who judge only by our own prejudices—have a right to call ugly. He was full of courage and intelligence, too. For when Rider picked a dry stalk of bunch grass and pried him away from the body of his last victim, he went grudgingly, backing off and facing this thing which he could not fight, with every show of rage. He refused to be routed, always backing away, or walking sideways, with a truculent gait that had in it nothing of cowardice. We hated him because of his brutal slaughtering and blood sucking of industrious little beings that have much in their activities that is akin to our own scurryings. But we conceded the monster his right to live and to fulfill that place in the scheme of things which the infinite wisdom of the Great Spirit has appointed. For, in the balance of this imperfect physical existence, the destroyer is as important as the upbuilder—a fact which many people fail to realize. We went away finally and left the monster still haunting the village ruins.

Ants always repay study. Perhaps, if you reason deeply enough, the lesson to be learned from them is a broader and more ominous one than the glorifying of industry. But aside from this, their actions provide plenty of food for thought. My friend A.R. Wellington, who used to live at Ocotillo, and who is deeply interested in nature, believes that the central nest sends out impulses like radio waves, for the guidance of the roving individuals who are afield. Whether this is so or not could not be definitely asserted without considerable investigation.

From my own observation, I am convinced that something of the kind is true. The way in which ants locate food, in seemingly inaccessible and unlikely places, is puzzling. And watching colonies which were closing up their citadels at evening time or against inclement weather, I have observed "signal" ants mount to high points close to the main entrance and, facing this way and that, apparently send out "calls"—the effect of which was to make the last stragglers, far down the trails, redouble their speed towards home in a surprising manner. The Ant People move and exist in a separate world and undoubtedly are largely unaware of our existence.

* * *

Rider, who always is investigating, has discovered a new world—one containing more thrills than that found by Columbus. With a small lens, which he salvaged from an old camera view-finder, thrown out as useless, he has begun to explore the mysteries of those regions which lie just beyond the range of the unaided eye. He is fascinated by the results even from his low-power magnifier. Tiny flowers and herbs, that one ordinarily would pass without noticing, reveal unexpected beauties that are breathtaking. A wealth of tiny life exists in the desert. And it is for the most part unknown. Many worlds has the Great Spirit set, one within the other and each complete within itself. Yet men close their eyes to all save the affairs of greed and hate.

Crack! Crack!...Crunch. Nibble. Nibble. A mouse? Oh no! Just Victoria at her favorite occupation of eating piñon nuts. Always, it seems, Victoria is nibbling piñon nuts. She is more industrious than a squirrel or a packrat. In the early morning, after she wakes, you hear her little fingers scuffling through the bowl of nuts, hunting for the largest ones. In the hot afternoons, when the yellow mustard flowers along the outside wall are drowsy in the sun and all the far desert lowlands shimmer in the dancing mirage, you hear her tiny white teeth crunching down happily upon her favorite delicacy. In the evening, when the lamp is lit and the mice steal out of the shadows and the night wind skirls above the lone roof of Yaquitepec, she still is nibbling. "You should weally exercise some disqwession," Rudyard admonishes her often. "If you don't you are going to upset your eqwilibrium an' be twansformed into a twee squirrel."

But Victoria just giggles. And goes on nibbling nuts.

Nor is she alone in her liking for the toothsome little brown morsels—though she easily heads the list as a star consumer. All the Yaquitepecos have a weakness for piñons. After an evening session the table, with its litter of empty shells, looks as though a troop of chipmunks had banqueted there.

The ideal way to crack piñones is with your teeth—at which Victoria is expert. But each one of us has developed, in addition, a side method which is called into play for variation. Tanya uses an old pair of pliers that harks back to the days of the Model T Ford. Rider cracks his adroitly by the aid of an ancient cannon ball (a feat no one else can duplicate). Rudyard is fond of a particular bit of wind-rounded stone that came from the vicinity of the Salton Sea. As for myself I have found nothing, for

speed and efficiency, which will compare with a long-bladed, ancient knife—used back down and hammer wise.

The piñon nut is not as popular as its virtues give it a right to be. Many people find its small size makes it too tedious to be bothered with. Yet it probably is the most healthful of all our nuts. A natural product, a true food of the wilderness, its goodness has not been "legislated" out of it by cultivation and "selection" over a long period of time. My first acquaintance with the piñon nut dates from a day in Mexico, when to the great scandal of aristocratic friends, I took a long railroad journey, third class, among the lovable Mexican Indians, who in those days patronized third class travel exclusively. My seatfellow, Don José, a kindly leather-faced old son of the desert, had a great red bandanna, knotted cornerwise, full of the little brown nuts, to which he promptly introduced me. And for many a league, while babies squalled and fighting cocks gawked and stalked among the seats and the panting little locomotive hauled us south through the dust of Sonora, we munched piñon nuts and exchanged friendship and homely bits of desert philosophy.

Which brings us to the name, Yaquitepec. Many friends have asked its derivation. And how to pronounce it.

It is a word compounded from two others. Yaqui—the name of that tribe of fiercely freedom-loving Indians who live in Sonora, and Tepec, the Aztec word meaning hill. As, for example, Chapultepec—grasshopper hill. Thus Yaquitepec means simply Yaqui hill, or hill of the Yaqui. And it is pronounced YAKeete-PECK. Not Ya-KEE-tepeck, as so many mistakenly suppose. Ghost Mountain is quite a considerable jumble of rocks, in its own right, and Yaquitepec is the name we have chosen to designate our house and its immediate surroundings. As for Ghost Mountain itself, the name is self explanatory. This is an ancient bit of the desert. And an ancient mountain whose weathered boulders are steeped in the sense of half forgotten things.

* * *

The new cistern isn't finished yet, and the outside catch-pool long has been dry. Cement work does not readily proceed without water with which to mix the materials. And we dare not use any of the precious store in the drinking tanks—which already are going down at an alarming rate. So we wait for some summer thundershower to give us surplus water. Years ago, before Boulder Dam was finished, we could count on one or two—sometimes three—good rainstorms in the summer. But now that the blue surface of Lake Mead has upset the desert moisture balance and the thunderstorm cycles have altered accordingly, we never are sure that we will get anything. But we shall continue to hope that the Thunder Birds will flap at least one good shower our way before the summer passes.

* * *

And now I have come back, after carrying the mescal beetle outside. I barely had struck the period in the paragraph above when loud shouts from Rudyard and Victoria proclaimed that another long-time resident of our mescal beams had forsaken the old home and decided to go forth into the world. So I had to go and rescue it from the confining bounds of the house and set it free in the outer air. Gay and handsome fellows, these mescal beetles. Members of the numerous long-horn family they look very smart in their dull red wing cases and long slender feelers. All winter, in the grub state, they have been boring and nibbling channels through the lengths of the mescal poles which we have stored, to season, across our ceiling beams. Fat and industrious though they are at this stage, they are very helpless, and several times during the winter we had the job of assisting back into their tunnels, individuals who had tumbled out and landed upon the floor.

And now that these helpless grubs have gone through a death change and have risen as winged beings, they come forth as into a new heaven. An inch and a half long, some of them, with feelers often a full half inch or more longer than their bodies, they cannot understand why screens and walls prevent their reaching the wide world. And they fuss and buzz about until turned loose in outer space. The Indians knew this class of beetles too. In the grub stage, carefully fried in grease, they make excellent eating. Carl Lumholtz, that price of desert explorers, having enthusiastically gotten away with two heaped platefuls served him by his Indian hosts, declared (before he knew what they were) that they were delicious, tasting something like roasted peanuts.

Desert Refuge 38
(September 1944)

BESIDE the weathered fence of dry mescal stalks, set upon end, General Machado, the largest of our trio of desert tortoises, slumbers in the shade. And beyond him, a half dozen paces away among the rocks, a big brown squirrel perches adroitly in the spreading crown of a flowering agave. His long fluffy tail hangs down as,

with both front paws, he busily crams his mouth with the fleshy golden blooms.

But General Machado is interested neither in agave flowers nor in squirrels. He has outlived, and will outlive, many generations of them. Head extended upon the sand and flippers sprawled in limp ease, he dreams on. Life for desert tortoises is an unhurried thing. Their normal span of existence is very long. Is there a reliable formula for estimating a tortoise's age? We have never heard of one. But Rider, whose mind runs to the figuring out of the answers to scientific puzzles, has advanced the interesting theory that the concentric ridges or markings of the horny plates of the shell stand in the same relation to the creature's age as do the growth rings of a tree.

The theory sounds well founded, for the little regular ridges, which are characteristic of each plate, all follow the shape of the plate exactly, but in a regular area increase, from the center outwards. Exactly as do tree rings. That these markings represent growth rings is certain. The only point—and one that could be determined only by careful observation over a considerable period of years—is just what space of time does each ridge or ring represent. Does a tortoise add one expansion ridge a year to each plate, or several? Or does it take more than one year to add a ridge? Rider figures on settling this point in the course of a half dozen years or so. But perhaps some naturalist already has the answer.

* * *

This year the canyon wrens have been particularly numerous. Which is strange, for the nesting season was so severe, with cold and high winds, that the wrens passed up most of our ready-made nest boxes. Their sense told them that in times of stress it always is safer to be in close contact with the earth. So they picked embattled little hideouts among the mescal clumps, where the stormy winds howled impotently above their heads. Some of these nests are remarkably well concealed.

One nest was in the hollow of a decayed mescal butt that had been for many years overgrown by new plants. Access to the cavity was obtained through a narrow chink between two big fleshy leaves. Somehow the wrens had discovered this fortified little cavern, and had constructed within it a tiny nest. When we located it, it was well packed with very food-conscious, halfgrown nestlings, who gaped at us with eager expectancy.

There must have been several well concealed wren nests close about the house. Because, later, the friendly concourse of young families, flitting through the trees and bushes in the wake of proud parents, was quite large. The canyon wren usually is reputed to be a shy bird. But we have never found them so. Curiosity and not shyness always has been the chief characteristic of our Ya-quitepec canyon wrens. Several times, when packing loads up the mountain trail, one of these pert brown mites has followed me for a long distance, slipping from branch to branch and rock to rock, getting ever closer. Sometimes they even have alighted on the shoulder-pack itself, examining it with bright investigative eyes.

* * *

Yesterday we had another visitor. The genial brown racer snake who has lived somewhere close around the house for several years, paid us a call. Each year he seems a little longer and bigger. But his disposition hasn't changed. He is a friendly, slightly mischievous humorist with a facility for turning up in the most unexpected places. This time it was on a shelf of a storage alcove. Rider, who had gone to get a pair of tin snips out of a tool box, ran face foremost full against the snake's exploring nose. It was a bit dark in the alcove and contact with that inquisitive snout was rather startling. Rider came out of the archway with a yell, dropping the tin snips. The snake seemed to enjoy the joke. For when we got there he had his head cocked a bit on one side, his long slender body still extended a foot over the edge of the shelf. And you could have sworn that there was a mischievous twinkle in his eye. Rider had been so startled that he forgot his manners. He grabbed the fly-spray gun…"You—" he gasped breathlessly. "You *would* do that, huh! *I'll* show you!" And the next instant the smirking jokester found himself enveloped in a cloud of fly spray, as Rider worked the gun furiously.

The snake was offended. He whirled and darted for an exit so fast that, although I grabbed for him, intending to carry him outside, I missed my aim. In the semi-gloom he was just a brown whizz. "Ooah! He's goned through the mouse hole!" Victoria shrieked delightedly. "Look! He's twaveling to the outside!"

He was indeed. And when we dashed out and around the house he was still traveling. We caught a flash of a flirt of slender tail flicking like a whiplash through the *ramarillo* [rabbitbrush] bushes. Rider shook the spray gun after it wrathfully: "And don't you come back," he shouted, "or you'll get more of the same medicine!"

But he did come back. The same afternoon, he poked his head out of a crevice of the terrace wall, near the water olla. Rider saw him and grinned. "You can come out," he said graciously. I forgive you. But *don't* do it again."

Whether his words were understood or not, the snake did come out. Sliding leisurely across the hot sunlit

Rider (left) practices use of bow and arrow while Rudyard observes.

gravel he went off into a mescal clump, probably in search of mice.

* * *

Yesterday brought another scare. A bigger and more general one. The threat of fire.

Now fire in the desert may sound improbable to anyone who pictures a desert as being a barren expanse of rock and sand dune. But a comparatively small portion of the western American desert is of this variety. Most of it is what Dr. Hornaday has aptly termed an arboreal desert. That is, a dry area that supports a good sprinkling of arid zone bushes and dwarf trees. Our Ghost Mountain district is of this variety. Although fires are very different from those that range in heavily wooded sections they are something not to be laughed at.

Almost all desert plants are highly resinous. Many of them need only the slightest encouragement to burn briskly even when green. And when dried to tinder by the heat of the desert summer they are a food upon which fire feeds with ravenous fury. Especially in a high wind—and somehow there almost always is a high wind whenever a desert fire starts. Once the flames get under way the blazing fragments, swept aloft by the heat and driven by the wind, spread deadly brands over an ever increasing area. A desert fire can be a terrifying thing.

Yesterday evening, Rider came hurrying with the information that we had a fire "right in our back yard." The alarming news brought everyone running. From the rim rocks of Ghost Mountain we stared off across the desert at the ominous lift of yellow and steel-gray smoke. It wasn't a big fire, as yet. But it really was in our "back yard." It was less than four miles away. It was on the far side of a great sugar-loaf butte, so that we could not determine exactly where it was, or what was the extent of the blaze. If we had been able to see details perhaps it would have been less terrifying. As it was we could see only the sinister billowing smoke rising from behind the hill. The wind was strong, and setting directly towards us. Four miles seemed a very short distance.

"It will go up the side of that ridge fast," Rider speculated. "And it will come down this side of it very slow, as all fires do when they're traveling down hill. But when it hits the flat country…."

He didn't finish the sentence. It wasn't necessary. We were all thinking of that. And of the dense growth of yuccas and creosotes that sprinkled the lowlands in patches. We began mentally to count the number of dry sandy washes that crossed those four miles, like defense fronts between us and the enemy. We hoped that they might prove at least partial firebreaks.

"There's a good chance that, even at the very worst, Ghost Mountain won't burn much," Tanya said her eyes roving affectionately over our tumbled mass of wind scoured boulders. "Granite doesn't offer much encouragement for flames. And our sprinkling of junipers and *ramarillo* [rabbitbrush] bushes isn't very heavy. We're a bit different here from the lowland country. But still…."

We continued to watch. The smoke seemed to be increasing. The wind was freshening.

It was near sunset. And presently the red disc went down behind the distant wall of western mountains. Behind us a great moon almost full, floated upward from the badlands and mingled its flood of silver with the dying, ruddy light of day. Dimness crowded the canyons and the lee of the hills as the shadows of night crept from their hiding places. A coyote broke the stillness with a far off chilling wail.

And beyond the butte, four miles away, the grim cloud of yellow grey still hung against the twilight. It was neither bigger nor smaller.

"I don't think it's coming, right away," Rudyard said, grimacing with the intense effort of trying to stare a hole

through the distant butte. "And, in the meantime, can't we go in and have our story-book reading?"

"I think we might," Tanya agreed. "We can't stand here all night."

I elected myself as the first to do sentry duty and settled down in a nice sheltered crevice of the rim rocks. But just as all the others moved off, Rider turned back. "If it gets worse," he said, "please give me ample warning. I want to have time to put the three tortoises in a safe place. They've a right to their lives. And I've got to take care of them."

But the fire threat came to nothing. After a long vigil—merging in the end to regular excursions far into the night, from the house to the lookout point on the cliff edge—all trace of smoke faded. The moon-washed desert dreamed through the night hours in peace.

Just as most of the perils and sorrows of life drift, after a period, into the limbo of forgotten things, so passed a period of very real anxiety. It left behind it, as its most acute memory, not the recollection of fear but of comedy—a comedy provided by the antics of a little, grey desert mouse.

This little rascal, whom I first noticed on one of my midnight trips through the house on my way to the lookout, was intent on getting some of the sweetness from the edge of a big iron pot of desert honey which we had that day melted to separate from the comb. The pot, now cool, hung from a hook and chain over the stove. From the nearest wall ledge to the pot lid was quite a long mouse jump. But the little grey busybody had made it. As I came past with a lamp in my hand, my first sight was of a grey tail and a pair of plump hindquarters balanced on the far edge of the pot lid.

Its attitude, as it leaned over with its head away below the rim while it nibbled at remnants of boiled-over honey and wax was irresistibly suggestive of some portly dowager on her knees with a garden trowel before a pet flower bed. The temptation to give the bending little gnome a prod with a forefinger was too strong to be passed up. But almost in the same bounce with which it sprang away from pot to wall ledge it turned and bounced right back. Flinging me a glance of plain annoyance it turned its plump little back on me and bending over, again fell to nibbling.

Again I prodded. And again it jumped. If a mouse can snort it certainly did. And its beady eyes sparkled both daggers and contempt. Back it came again like the rebound of a rubber ball. Insulting human meddler! Over it leaned, farther than ever. Its tiny teeth nibbled lustily.

Anxious to see just how far things would go I kept up the comedy. So did the mouse. But I tired quicker than it did. By the time I had given it a dozen prods, and it had made as many leaps and returns, I decided that I had other and more pressing things to attend to. So I hoisted the pot away up on its chain—far out of the jumping range of even an enterprising mouse—and departed. The last sight I had of my persistent little friend was a rotund grey shape ambling off disgustedly across the top of the fireplace in search of new and easier pastures.

After the night, came the new dawn, with the shadows of apprehension forgotten in the yellow glint of the bunch grass against the rising sun on the mountain slopes. With the gold fountains of the tall mescal blooms swaying against the sparkling sky and the morning air shot through, as by fairy shuttles by the darting flight of myriad bees and beetles swarming about the flower banners. Long, trailing spider webs glint like drifting wires of silver, and the junipers and the grey rocks loom sunlit and solid above the distant haze of the lowlands.

☀ ⋔ 🌵

Desert Refuge 39
(October 1944)

THE BIG ocotillo on the southwest slope of Ghost Mountain finally blew down, and a few days ago Rider and I went down to bring it home. For many months it had been slowly drying and getting more and more shaky in the winds. So when a last gale put an end to the drama, we went as quickly as possible in order to secure the wood before beetles and borers and all the other agents of decay could get ahead of us.

We like ocotillo wood for many reasons besides its excellent burning qualities. The thicker portions of the spiny wands, when peeled of their leathery armor of bark and spikes, make smooth white poles that are handy for a multitude of uses around a primitive establishment such as Yaquitepec. Also, when properly seasoned, the wood is tempting for carving purposes. It is not entirely satisfactory for this as it is a bit brittle and short grained, with an annoying habit of chipping off when the design calls for fine details. But it is nice to work with nevertheless. And one can achieve quite satisfactory and ornamental bottle stoppers and knife handles and such nick-nacks from it. Rider and Rudyard, by means of boring and whittling, often make themselves whistles from the white wood—whistles which, as silence shatterers, are entirely too satisfactory.

It was quite a job lugging the fallen old monarch up over the tumbled boulders to a spot where we could

divide it into sections for carrying. But the job was completed finally and all the good wood peeled and put up under the roof to season. The bark and spines and all the small sections went into the fuel baskets for immediate burning. Although dead ocotillos make marvelous fuel we have to be more careful in handling it than any other. The reason for this is that the spines are so distributed that no matter how small a fragment of broken stalk lies on the ground there always will be one or more spikes pointing upwards—like those devilish spiked iron devices which were used in early warfare for hindering the movements of infantry and cavalry. Yaquitepec is a barefoot establishment, and although our feet are toughened, the upturned ocotillo thorn is damaging. So ocotillo fuel always is burned first—and with scrupulous watchfulness that no fragment escape.

There are thorns AND thorns. Those of the much talked about cholla—like a great many other things of exaggerated reputation—are probably the least dangerous. We don't worry about ordinary chollas. The staghorn, which is the kind most widely spread over Ghost Mountain, isn't half as bad as it is painted. The youngsters get spiked and pincushioned with them constantly—and yank the adhering sections from their feet by means of two stones, used pincer-wise, and go on as though nothing had happened. The silver cholla—*bigelovii*—is different. That we do treat with respect. It has a nasty disposition. And if it doesn't actually *jump* at you, as it is fabled to do, it nevertheless is bad medicine. So we give it a wide berth. Fortunately those sections of Ghost Mountain which we range constantly are not over supplied with Bigelow's cholla.

The two types of spines which do call for constant watchfulness are those of the mescal (the agave) and the beavertail. Oddly enough these are at opposite ends of the thorn scale—those of the mescals being vicious, needle-sharp daggers from an inch and a half to two inches or more long, and those of the beavertail cactus being so small that one needs a magnifying glass to see them. If you run hard into the stiletto-shaped weapons of the mescal, with any portion of your anatomy, you are in for trouble. The thorn, like a slender jade dagger, almost invariably breaks off deep in the wound in such a way that it often defies extraction.

On the other hand if you have an argument with the fuzzy brown spine fluff of a beavertail it may be hours, sometimes days, before you will get rid of the last of the intensely irritating, microscopic little stickers. The points of nearly all desert thorns seem to carry a poison particularly adapted to make punctured flesh ache. Perhaps, in this respect, the handsome Mojave yucca—the Spanish Bayonet—can claim highest honors. Yes, there are thorns

AND thorns. But what true desert dweller would trade any one of them for fairest flowers or tenderest ferns of rain-drifted forests?

* * *

The cisterns are dropping lower and lower. Last season, just a few days before we returned to Yaquitepec from our year-long desert search, a heavy downpour passed over Ghost Mountain and we had hoped the anniversary of that shower would bring another. But so far we have been disappointed. There have been not even any promising showings of thunderstorm formations, despite the fact that Victoria faithfully stares off at the dark line of the horizon each night, looking for them. Several times fitful, distant flashes have brought her running to us with the breathless information that there was certain to "be a wain tonight" because "the distances are jus' full of lightling." But so far the lightning has been an empty promise.

A good many things now wait upon the rain. Walls and cistern building, as well as the replenishment of domestic water supply. Wool that needs washing before it can be carded and spun. A new garden frame. One acquires a high valuation of water when its supply is limited. It is true that our storage capacity steadily increases. But so also does our consumption of the precious fluid. As our little clan grows there are more and more demands upon the cisterns. And on summer days it is astonishing how quickly a big olla of water, swinging in the breeze to cool, can be emptied. Yes, we need rain.

* * *

Last night about midnight, I got up and went into the house to see how the pots were drying. Tanya had made a couple of large ones during the afternoon and had set them to harden on the inside table. There is always a thrilling uncertainty about the drying of handmade desert pottery. Clay is temperamental. Seemingly perfect ollas and bowls, fashioned with care, and a joy to behold when wet, on drying will develop mysterious cracks which utterly ruin them. On the other hand a pot flung together in a hurry to serve some pressing need will astonish us by drying out as a perfect and flawless creation.

A brief inspection, by lantern light, of Tanya's handicraft convinced me that the drying process was not proceeding rapidly enough—there was danger ahead. So I carried the two jars outside and placed them in an angle of an unfinished wall where the free sweep of the desert wind would hasten their setting. The stars burned with crystal clearness. Through the broken thatch of the ramada the moon made patterns of ghostly light. Wind marched against the mountain with a steady roar, rocketing upward from the protecting edge of the cliff and hurtling past overhead with the rushing sound of an invisible torrent. Stray gusts of it, swooping downward, came charging around the house, slatting loose thatch and drawing weird music from an insecurely fastened sheet of roofing iron.

After I had settled the pots safely in their new position the mystery of the night held me. So, instead of returning to bed, I picked myself a nice comfortable vantage point upon the top of the outdoor work bench, squatting there, Indian fashion, in the moon-fretted shadow of the ramada, while the wind spirits trampled ceaselessly overhead and the moonlight wove blankets of jet and silver in the swaying branches of the junipers.

There is something about the feel of a moonlit desert night which calls to unfathomed deeps within the heart; which stirs vague memories of long forgotten things. Small wonder that from desert lands and from their nomadic peoples, forced to solitude and the tending of flocks under sunlight and starlight, have come to us so much that is worthwhile. For it is by meditation that man increases his understanding. Times, and conditions of liberty and progress, have little to do with it. There have been as great minds and as great philosophers in all ages. Contentment, happiness and understanding come from within—not from one's surroundings.

* * *

Victoria's hair is long enough now to be easily braided. And a proud little miss she is with her new style of hairdressing. Busy and merry the whole day long, Victoria grows fast. She loves to work and always is hunting new duties. She gathers dry sticks among the bushes and rocks and trots tirelessly on twinkling feet to heap her loads in the fuel basket by the stove. One of her regular jobs is to guard the outside water barrel against bees whenever it has to be uncovered for filling ollas and house crocks.

Bees, both tame and wild, are water-thirsty in the summer desert. The tiniest opening serves as entrance to barrel or tank. Victoria's job is to stand by the barrel and whenever a bucketful is removed, to carefully shoo off the snooping bees and replace the cloth cover. Then, upon tiptoe, and with both little arms flung around the cloth to hold it down in the playful wind gusts she stands guard until we return for the next bucket. Victoria is proud of this job. She usually sighs with regret when it is over and the cloth covers of the barrels have been securely tied down into place.

All the openings of water barrels and tanks on Ghost Mountain are cloth covered. No other scheme works. Ordinary lids will not serve. For here we have to make our containers tight not only against small animals, lizards and bees, but also against ants which can get through almost anything. A time saving trick for keeping a cloth securely bound down over a barrel top is to use one of those long coiled springs usually employed to pull screen doors shut, as a section of the tie cord. Then, when once you have the cord adjusted tight, you don't have to untie it each time. Simply stretch the spring a bit and slip it off. A stout rubber band cut from a section of old auto tube will serve equally well, but doesn't last long in the desert heat, as compared with a spring.

* * *

Last Sunday afternoon I dug out an old copy of the *National Geographic* magazine from the bookcase and read the youngsters an account of the excavations at the old Indian settlement of Pueblo Bonito in New Mexico. They are tremendously interested in such things. Not only because their own desert existence approaches very closely the life led by the ancients, but also because on their recent long trek they became familiar with the type of country in which these old-time Indian communities had their setting. So while the big scaly lizards waddled over the sun-scorched boulders and the heat waves danced across the distance of the thirsty lowlands, the three of them lay on a blanket beside me in the shade, listening with eager ears as the words on the printed page rolled back the sands and mystery from a chapter of desert life that was closed a thousand years ago.

To understand the story of ancient Pueblo Bonito, one must be familiar by personal experience with conditions which are similar. It was this knowledge which made my young audience so appreciative. They studied everything from a practical angle. All pictures were scrutinized with extreme care. The construction of ancient buildings and underground kivas was commented upon. Shapes and decorations of old pottery received careful attention.

Unhampered by modern fetishes or by the molds unconsciously imposed by association with mass thought, our youngsters have free rein to weigh and appraise the good points and the bad of both primitive and modern worlds. Armed also with an understanding of time, not as a make-believe span to be measured by clock-ticks or by the ephemeral duration of human life, but as a state which exists, they can better appreciate the significance of the rise and decay of communities and empires. It is life that counts, and the way it is lived, whether it be in Pueblo Bonito or at Yaquitepec. And as they roll out a bit of clay for a coil to build a pot with, or pound a mescal leaf to obtain a few strands of fiber, our youngsters get a great thrill out of the knowledge of that shadowy, but very real bond, which binds the present to the past.

Primitive methods, though, occasionally bring their moments of comedy. As yesterday when Rudyard, having decided that he would make a little wooden bowl by the process of burning out the center of a mesquite block by means of a coal and a blowpipe, tried to teach the art to Victoria.

"You just blow it slightly," he said, handing her the little tube. "Just enough to keep the coal burning steadily. Blow just *slightly*—you understand."

So Victoria took the tube and blew "slightly." Victoria has a good pair of desert-grown lungs. The coal hopped from its charred hollow like a shot from a catapult and struck Rudyard squarely upon the tip of his nose. Rudyard has an explosive temper and there are times when he forgets chivalry. This was one of them. He made a pass at Victoria and hit her. And she promptly hit him back. They both are good scrappers. So for a time, before the "storm troopers" could be rushed to the spot, the uproar was considerable. Later on, however, when quiet had been restored and the two combatants had been sent outside with a piece of cake each, we heard them talking over the matter.

"You know I said you were jus' to blow it slightly," Rudyard explained, between munches.

"But I did, Ruggie, I did," Victoria protested. "I browed it all the slightly I could. Really I couldn't have browed it any more *slightlier.*"

Desert Refuge 40
(November 1944)

TO THE southeast, where the dim reaches of desert horizon veil the Rio Colorado, white, puffy clouds of vapor are forming in the morning sky. Again the Thunderbird is at his task of herding the storm heads together. Will he be successful this time or will the unwilling rain spirits again elude him and scatter into nothingness—as they have done so often these past months? *Quién sabe?* But we cling always to hope, so long as a single cloud lingers on the skyline. The dry spell has been a long one.

"Nuh! no rain," says my cheerfully pessimistic desert friend in whose veins runs the blood of those who possessed this wilderness of sun and thorn before the white man came. "Nuh. No rain. Old Man angry with us." He flashes white teeth and grins as he gestures towards the sky. A mellowed old-timer of the desert, neither heat nor cold nor rain nor the lack of it ever upset his good humor.

But I catch in his remark a significant reflection of something which I have heard often before. Something which was put into crisp Spanish by a vigorous old Mexican lady—the last of an early California family. "In the old days, señor, things were better. There was more rain. We had many more springs. But the good Dios became angry because of the cruelties that were done the Indians. He began to take away the waters."

The sun mounts in the sky. And the shadow of the great rock, beneath the overhang of which I have set up my tiny typewriter table is shrinking swiftly. Soon I will have to move. But not just yet. It is still cool here, hunched close to the lift of the ancient, weathered granite.

Beyond the rim of sheltering cool the sun beats upon a dazzling world of jagged butte and shimmering wash and the grey endless leagues of immensity. Underfoot, where little wandering wind wisps from the desert come also to seek the shadow, the quartz gravel is crisp and white. In deep clefts and hollows that the winds of ages have carved in the stone, cling tiny shy desert plants and diminutive ferns. Stiff, gray-green agaves rim the approaches with their bayonet spines. Nearby, under the shade of a gnarled jojoba bush, a bright-eyed lizard basks. And over all, the dome of the sky, like an inverted turquoise bowl, shuts down upon the silence. "The shadow of a great rock in a weary land."

Well, again the Thunderbird has had no luck with his roundup. The scatter of little puffy thunderheads have broken away from him and bolted, like a bunch of wild desert cattle, into the immensity of space. The only cloud visible in the whole circle of my desert world is the little film of smoke which hangs above the crude kiln among the boulders and junipers where Rider is firing our latest batch of pottery.

From where I sit I just can see his lithe sun-tanned figure as he moves about, now stooping to break up with his axe the dry mescal butts; now carefully thrusting with a long pole fresh fuel into the fire hole. It is a job in which carefulness and judgment must combine. For the right heat must be attained, and at the same time the fuel not be wasted. Fuel, unless one commits the unpardonable crime of destroying scenery, is none too plentiful in the desert. Especially on Ghost Mountain, where the demands of household cooking and winter warmth have always to be met.

So it was really the fuel—or rather, the need to conserve it—which led us to do our pottery baking in a kiln. Formerly we had used the Indian method of these regions, which is simplicity itself: Merely the piling of brush over the assembled pieces and setting fire to it—keeping the bonfire going briskly until the pots are baked.

But this system devours fuel. I always flinch, mentally, when I recall how many dry yucca trunks and good mescal butts are needed to fire a sizable batch of pots. So finally, we resorted to a kiln. The present one, for we have built several, increasingly larger, as our needs and ambitions expand—is a hastily constructed crude affair. But it does the work. And the saving in wood is startling.

Pottery, one of the most ancient of arts, has like weaving always been closely bound up with man's existence. And its broken sherds, scattered everywhere about the earth, provide a fascinating record of his history, extending far back along age-dim trails from which no other record has survived. Pottery has this strange quality. Though one of the most fragile of creations it is, in fragmentary form, one of the most enduring. The shaft of the spear will rot and the blade of the sword will corrode and vanish into the earth along with the bones of its maker.

Rider firing pottery in the Yaquitepec kiln. With a long pole he thrusts fresh fuel into the file hole. Sketch by Marshal South.

But bits of painted and burned clay, shaped by the loving fingers of the potter, will endure to tell their story throughout all the changes and convulsions of thousands of years. Whether it be from a pit dug in the ruins of the forgotten Hurrian city of Nuzi, or whether it be a roadside cutting in Smyrna, or the grave of a Cliff Dweller, or from a deep shaft through the strata in the Valley of Mexico, fragments of an ancient art constantly are coming to light to attest man's presence and his residence upon earth for greater spans than are covered by any written or conjectured history.

Pots! How vast has been the number of them. How deep about the earth is the litter of their shattered shapes and the dust of the buried cities in which they were fashioned?

And the broken sherds [shards] tell another story too, as well as that of their mere making. For they tell not only the tale of the rise and fall of races and civilizations, they tell also of the flowering and decline of the best fundamental qualities in the character of their makers. If you want to see the unfolding of art and the genuine yearning in men's souls toward the higher things of life you must go back to the primitive handmade pots, fashioned from the plastic clay with no tools save the skilful fingers of the maker.

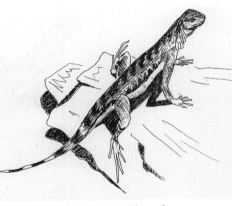

Zebra-tailed lizard

Into these pots, after they had passed the first crude era of stark necessity, went the souls of the makers. Into them went a deep, sincere craving for grace and for the beautiful. Crude, if you will, but fashioned with fingers that delighted in their work, and decorated in designs that were generally, as in the case of the ancient Cliff Dwellers, reverent prayers in symbol form, the ancient handmade pot and jar stand supreme as things of soul and grace. Later came the potter's wheel—the dawning of the mechanical method of production. And soul and grace and meaning slowly pass from the clay shapes. Like their owners and their buyers—for soon, in his march of progress, man became too busy and too proud to make his own pots. The jugs and the vases and the bowls become elegant and haughty and ornate and mechanically perfect—and soulless.

But there seems no way of checking the weary cycle. For even today the simple child of nature, unaware of the true worth that he has created in his handiwork, and following, as do his civilized brothers, that deadly will-o-the-wisp "some easier way," soon abandons his beautiful clay jars and ollas for the white man's empty coal oil can. Which is of course hopeless. You can't do much with a coal oil can as regards art and grace and soul. You can't, with decency, inscribe reverent prayers on it. And even if you decorate it with verses and ditties from Omar Khayyam and play sweet songs to it upon a flute you can't do much. It takes more than verses and the piping of an altruistic ditty to disguise the ulterior motives in a coal oil can—even if you pipe it in Persian.

Nevertheless there should be, by those who care, a return to the simple worth of honest handicraft wares. There should be more home weavers and more home potters. Especially potters. And most especially desert potters. For somehow the arid Southwest, with its mysterious history of the past; with its sand-drifted abandoned cities and its wealth of relics from the fingers of long dead potters whose skill and grace of form never have been excelled, seems peculiarly the region for those whose craving for self-expressive things leads them back to the fashioning of moist clay.

Primitive pottery is not difficult. Its scope for individual exploration and adventure is vast. But its fundamental steps are not hard to master. Unfortunately technical books can't tell you much about it. Their writers have forgotten the simple things and have passed on to those rarified realms of higher learning where you purchase the clay and use prepared glaze and turn the kiln switch—and bolt number 897 comes merrily down the assembly line on "perfect job" number 25704.

But there is another way—the way of the Indian who sat long ago in the shade of his cliff house and put his dream of beauty and his reverence for his Creator into the thing he built with his fingers from the plastic earth. We of Yaquitepec haven't learned yet, by a long way, all there is to know of that ancient Indian's art. But we have discovered a little. Enough to begin with. And it always has been our dream someday to assemble those few crude facts together into a little booklet for the benefit of those who, like ourselves, long to create things with their own hands. Maybe when the rain comes, and the cisterns are finished we will get around to writing it. Again, *quién sabe?*

𝒟𝑒𝑠𝑒𝑟𝑡 𝓡𝑒𝑓𝑢𝑔𝑒 41
(December 1944)

ON SEPTEMBER 27 the first flock of wild geese passed over Ghost Mountain, going south. It was early on a bright sunny morning, and our thoughts were on anything but portents of winter, when suddenly Rudyard, who had been working on one of the upper terraces, came bolting into the house: "Geese," he gasped breathlessly, "wild geese going south! Quick!"

We all ran out to look, headed by Victoria who in her haste tripped sprawling over the threshold, but was too excited to lament the mishap. Yes, there they were. Against the turquoise sheen of the sky the geese stretched—a dark, irregular line of big, steadily flying birds, in a formation that was more like a great bent bow than a V. Above them, in the blue depths, there floated a long narrow ribbon of thin white cloud that might have been a canopy, held there in farewell by the sorrowful handmaidens of departing summer. Below them, flashing like a mighty shield of polished silver in the blue-grey mystery of the desert leagues, lay Laguna Salada in Mexico, like a course marker by which to steer. The great wings beat steadily, tirelessly.

Down through the silence of the desert sky their cries came to us. There is something poignant about the calling of wild geese. Something which one cannot quite define, yet something primitive and deep which stirs the soul like a hand upon harp strings. It was Ernest Thompson Seton, I believe, who in one of his books tells the story of an Indian who, confined in a white man's prison for some trivial offense, suffered all his trials with stoical resignation, but died of a broken heart when the calls of the passing wild geese drifted down to him through his prison walls. The story well may be true, for there is never a year that we hear the calling of the passing honkers without a lump rising in our throats and a tightening of our heartstrings. But perhaps it is because in the mighty symphony of creation each creature has been given some special note, the wild goose being entrusted with the call which will most stir the hearts of those to whom freedom is the most precious thing in life.

* * *

Yesterday was the day of the Great Tortoise Race. This Festal Occasion and Spectacular Contest long had been planned to decide once and for all the Yaquitepec speed championship for desert tortoises. The thunderous clamor of the excited crowds has died away. The dust has settled over the course. The judges have almost forgotten

Rider (left) and Rudyard with Mojave— one of their desert tortoises.

the abuse heaped upon them and, save for the chewings and scufflings of the victorious racers, still happily browsing among their "prizes" of cabbage leaves, things have returned almost to normal.

The race was the outgrowth of a long-standing argument between Rider, Rudyard and Victoria as to the merits of their favorite tortoises. Our tortoises are nicely graduated in size—their dimensions corresponding, in proportion, to those of their respective owners. Rivalry therefore is rather keen. Victoria who claims Doña Antonia, the smallest, is always shrill in her assertion that Doña is the smartest, swiftest and most intelligent tortoise the desert has ever produced. Claims which Rider and Rudyard, owners respectively of General Machado and Juana Maria Better Than Nothing, hotly deny.

"Why don't you have a race?" Tanya suggested once, jokingly. "That would prove everything."

The idea, somewhat to our dismay, was instantly adopted. "A race! Why of course! A race!" There ensued a hubbub of plans.

"But there'll have to be pwizes," Victoria declared shrilly. "Doña Antonia isn't going to run herself all out of breff winning for nothing."

"The winner shall be banqueted upon cabbage leaves," I decided. "Nothing less. So we'll have to postpone this contest until we get some."

They agreed to that—and I drew a crafty sigh of relief. I couldn't spare the time at the moment to supervise a tortoise race. But there came a day when cabbage leaves were at hand. Excuses and hedging were unavailing. So we pushed work aside and went out to stage the tortoise race.

The course had been selected long in advance—a fairly narrow strip of gravel between banks of rocks and clumps of mescal, which it was hoped would more or less confine the attention of the contestants to their purpose. Also a few broad and general rules had been agreed upon. For instance, the owner of each entry would be allowed to excite his racing animal to fresh bursts of speed by dangling before its nose choice bits of rattlesnake weed or other dainties. Also a certain amount of yelling, arm waving, endearing entreaty, and what not—within reason—were to be acceptable to the judges. The owners lined up their steeds, the starter slammed a tin can against a rock, in lieu of a pistol shot, and the race was on.

Surely never since Ghost Mountain was upheaved from chaos has there sounded amidst its rocks such a pandemonium of human laughter, yells and cat-calls. A chronicle of every detail of the ensuing 15 minutes would I fear make little sense even to us. We had expected something dull and wearisome, we found ourselves engulfed in madness.

Possessed by some unusual demon—possibly it was a sensing of the importance of the test—our turtles started out running in grim earnest. They plodded and sprawled in a sort of breathless turtle-haste. Jaws tightly clenched, necks outthrust and swaying from side to side, they waddled on as though the Evil One bedeviled them with a pitchfork. Up rocks and through cactus clumps they puffed, sliding down steep slopes and landing upon their backs in hollows—from which they had to be rescued by shrieking incoherent owners. The trouble was that they all persisted in going in different directions. "Turn round! Turn round and go the other way," Tanya kept shouting, quoting from a movie burlesque of a horse race we once had seen.

At the end of 15 minutes—invoking the time limit—we declared the race well and truly won. By measurements and calculations, and taking into account the tribulations and misadventures of each of the breathlessly plodding contestants, we decided that each and every one of them had come in first and were therefore all entitled to the first prize, a heaping portion of cabbage and lettuce leaves. Thus ended the first—and probably the last—Yaquitepec Tortoise Derby. Once is enough.

But our pets soon will be too sleepy for races, anyway. Long before this appears in print they will be dreaming the placid tortoise dreams of their hibernation period, safely tucked away in a warm corner of the house. For quite a while the instinct has been moving in them to prepare. And each day, now, when they are taken out to amble over the little juniper studded flat, to browse and nibble among the bushes and dry grass, they return to a certain bush beneath which, in the soft earth, they have begun to dig holes.

* * *

When we first came to Ghost Mountain and began to trace out, from guide stone to guide stone, the ancient pathways of long forgotten feet, it was not long before we came upon abundant traces of the Bighorn sheep. Their abandoned bedding places were in the shelter of overhanging rocks. Their whitened bones lay beneath gnarled junipers, in the silence of little glades. Their weathered horns blackened in the desert sun upon boulders where Indian hunters had placed them for trail markers. There were no living sheep, for the Bighorn had gone, previous to our coming. Just as the Indians had gone, before the Bighorn. In the old days dusky savage and mountain sheep had shared this crest together. But the Indian had gone first. Now, too, the reign of the Bighorn was ended. The few survivors had faded away somewhere into those further reaches of the desert, where, despite game laws, the binoculars and bullets of stealthy "sportsmen" still pursued them.

But we never quite gave up the hope that some day we would encounter living specimens of these beautiful, freedom loving animals of the wastelands who, like the buffalo, have been swept almost to extinction by the white man's insatiable blood lust. For a while we even had serious plans of re-establishing the Bighorns upon Ghost Mountain—of building for them artificial catch-pools in the

Bighorn sheep

rocky canyons to trap storm water for their modest drinking needs. But this dream we were forced to abandon. Consultation with competent authorities established the fact that raising of mountain sheep, even under the most careful protective measures, is almost impossible. Furthermore we could not get any specimens of Bighorn, either young or old, with which to start our herd.

Years passed, and although we continued to search every ridge and crest on every desert tramp, we never saw sign of a living Bighorn. That there were some of them still alive and not far from Ghost Mountain, we now knew, for desert friends who had seen the tracks and occasionally glimpsed one of the little band, had told us. But we ourselves had no success in the matter. The buzzards wheeled and the shadows of drifting clouds wrought a thousand phantom shapes among the mirages and the buttes. But the Bighorn were gone.

Then suddenly, not a dozen days ago, as the whole family of us, out on an excursion, made our way down a dry desert valley some miles from Ghost Mountain, something big sped through the creosote bushes ahead. "A deer! A deer!" cried Rudyard, pointing excitedly.

But it wasn't a deer. As the dark body broke from the fringe of brush and leaped upon the lower rocks of a precipitous hillside not 30 yards distant, we saw that it was a great ram, a magnificent Nelson [Peninsula] Bighorn. Victoria caught her breath in a little gasp of admiration. "Oooo!" she exclaimed softly, "one of the cheeps!"

It was a monarch among sheep. In that flash instant in which poised upon a boulder, he glanced back at us before starting upward; he was a sight to stop the heartbeat. The desert sun beat upon his great, dark horns and lifted head and shimmered his slaty brown sides and prominent white rump patch with a glow of fire. A split second—arrested motion cast in gleaming metal—he halted, appraising us. Then he started up, bounding swiftly up the almost perpendicular ridge with a sure footed skill that gave a deceptive illusion of leisurely ease.

Up and up and up. Until presently he reached the crest. Here, silhouetted against the hard blue of the sky, the tall sharp line of a dry mescal pole rising beside him like a lifted standard he paused again. Silence held the desert—and us—as for perhaps 20 seconds he stood outlined against space: A creature of freedom, gazing out across the rocks and ranges of his homeland in whose beetling cliffs and hidden canyons still some trace of dwindling freedom lingers. Then he was gone. The skyline was empty, and our hearts came back slowly to normal beating.

Desert Refuge 42
(January 1945)

THE SUN has moved far south into the lowlands and the long string of "goldfish" which announce his rising each morning, are back in their places upon the smoke-blackened ceiling beam. The goldfish, which are fish-like splashes of golden light caused by the sunbeams striking through under the edges of badly fitted corrugated iron roofing, abandon us in the summer. For then the sun is too far north and the angle of the light is not right. But every winter they return, varying in number from 10 to 22 as the sun moves. They serve as alarm clocks. For, on those rare occasions when we happen to drowse beyond sunrise, we are bound to be aroused by the solemn chanting of Rudyard and Victoria as they count the long line: "One, two, three, four…."

Yes, the goldfish are out, and it is high time to get up! Another desert day has begun.

But the winter-moving sun brings us, this year, more than a line of brilliant little fish to thrill the sense of beauty. For, on these mornings, as it lifts above the silhouetted summit of the juniper tree and pours his flooding beams in through our east window, it brings us what Tanya calls "The Treasure of Kings"—a great, tall jar of flashing gold, as dazzling as any that ever were the pride of Aztec emperors. Fashioned by Tanya during the long days of summer and as big as one of the huge oil jars that figure in the ancient phantasy of the Forty Thieves, it sits now, against the wall, upon the summit of a green chest, waiting for the day when it will be taken out and baked in an open fire—for it is too big for our primitive kiln.

A homely thing. A thing of mud—of unfired clay. Yet now, each morning as the sun rises, it flames to a thing of glory. Humble enough, through all the day, set there against the drab background of a mud wall as unfinished as itself, it nevertheless leaps each dawn from the shadows to stand forth as a glowing golden urn over whose beauty we have not yet ceased to marvel.

Mud! Mud turned to gold at the touch of a sunbeam. Just a trick of the light. A simple thing, one to smile about and to forget. But somehow the thing has become our daily miracle—a flashing symbol of the manner in which human clay, touched by the rays of the Great Spirit, can suddenly flame forth to unguessed heights of glory. And perhaps Tanya may be right when she calls her pet *olla*, "The Treasure of Kings." For the true treasure of kings lies in understanding.

Tanya polishes her "golden" olla.

* * *

The wind gods that herald the approach of winter, prowl now about Ghost Mountain. And often in the night rush upon it with shoutings, roaring through the cliff-edge junipers and flinging quartz gravel upon our iron roof like clattering bursts of buckshot. Several times in the dark we have arisen and by flickering light, gone out to sweep eaves troughs and to prepare for threatening showers. False alarms, most of these midnight scurryings. But we have had two tiny rains. From one we caught 25 gallons and from another 15. Not much, but enough to be a heartening promise. The rain will be along later. Perhaps before these lines see print we will again be contentedly drawing from newly filled cisterns.

But if our recent catch of drinking water was limited, the showers at least provided a welcome diversion for our trio of young Yaquitepecos. Water has been for so long a jealously guarded, non-wasteable commodity, that to use it for play purposes has been out of the question.

But the two storms, light as they were, fell not only upon our roof, but also upon the private baths of Rider and Rudyard—tiny reservoirs built carefully of cement in strategic points among the granite boulders. Therefore, after the showers, there was much excitement and rushing to and fro with tin cans and bottles to collect the precious liquid and store it before it could evaporate. There were hasty dashings, with Victoria trailing along in the rear of the procession, slopping water from her own tiny bucket and shrieking in breathless excitement. What an orgy of "mudding"—until the water gave out.

Rider and Rudyard build model 'dobe houses, situated cliff-dweller fashion in crevices of rocks. But Victoria builds cisterns. Her cisterns are constructed by the simple method of heaping up a mound of mud and patting it nice and smooth on top. After which the whole family is summoned to admire the work of art. "A vewwy *fine* cistern," says Victoria, contentedly eyeing her own work. "An' after I get it smoothed out some more—"

Oh the mud that one happy, barefoot youngster can acquire! But mud is healthful—that is, *clean* mud. Humans would be better off physically if they came more often in contact with it and with the earth. The Indian knew this. But, being a savage, he has been outvoted.

There is an end to mudding when the water gives out. And there wasn't much this time. The builders now have gone back to the regular daily round of lessons and of fuel gathering and of helping set and distribute type—and the score and one other daily duties. That is, the two boys have. Victoria has gone back to the job of raising Susie and Barbara, which, outside of her light daily allotment of reading and writing, provide her with worries enough.

Victoria decided some time ago that her dolls needed sun treatments. They should bask each day in the healing rays of the desert sun. "Only thing, they haven't got a truly bed," she lamented. "They are 'fraid to sleep right on the ground. They are 'fraid of—of *mice*." And she wrinkled up her nose and giggled as she said it. For mice happen to be Victoria's chief delight.

So it came about that, taking the hint, Rider and I, in secret, constructed a "truly bed" of just the right size to accommodate Susie and Barbara—and even, if necessity called, the somewhat dilapidated Peter Rabbit also. We flatter ourselves that the bed was, in its way, somewhat of a work of art, being fashioned of nicely trimmed dry mescal shoots, lashed and fitted together with not a nail in all its fastenings. And the bed "spring" was of interlaced fiber also, after the manner of the old style rawhide laced beds. Bringing this contraption home by stealth we hid it. And when Victoria's birthday came round a few days later, we presented the bed to her, with fitting speeches.

Victoria sits beside her invalids in the sunshine and holds converse with them in encouraging tones. And the bright eyed young collared lizard whose habitat is on the window screen, cocks his head and wonders what it's all about.

Quite a little desert sprite, that collared lizard. It has been so long since he took up his residence in the vicinity of the window screen that we have come to look upon him as part of the scenery. And we miss him when he happens to be away for a while. A mighty hunter of flies, he has learned that his favorite game always hangs round window screens. Through long practice he has developed a technique which seldom fails. Observing an alighted fly contentedly cleaning its forelegs together in the sunlight he begins to creep cautiously toward it. Stealthily he executes a wide, circling approach. Then, with a lightning rush, he dashes upon the over-confident insect from behind. You cannot see what happens to the fly. But you can see the satisfied hunter going off, smacking his lips. The number of flies that he consumes in a day must do no little toward keeping the balance of nature adjusted.

Remarkably intelligent these harmless reptiles. The small fly-lizards, the most numerous, can spot their quarry at long distances. Often I have seen a fly alight to sun itself upon a granite boulder in a section where there apparently were no enemies. And then, from a distance, I have noted the cautious approach of one of the beady-eyed little lizards. You can see his tiny eyes fixed intently on his prey. Nimbly he slides down the sides of intervening boulders. Swiftly he darts across open spaces, taking advantage of every scrap of cover. With deadly purpose, keeping out of sight as far as possible, he begins to climb the stone whereon the fly rests. Sometimes, from its thousand eyes, the fly glimpses him, and makes off. But more often than not it leaves the rock tucked away inside of Mr. Lizard. I even have seen these lizards leap several inches from the ground and capture flies upon the wind. A feat comparable to that of a bare handed human catching flying birds.

…And, just to even matters, before I could finish this the rain gods, possibly having read what I wrote in the first part, decided to come in good earnest. In full ceremonial costume heavy laden with water jars, they swooped down upon Ghost Mountain, shouting their songs and whirling their headdresses and sounding rattles.

How the water splashed from their ollas! And how the wind gods yelled in accompanying chorus. What sudden scurryings to and fro on our part—adjusting rain spouts and dragging dry fuel to shelter. The falling water made a deafening tumult on our iron roof. Mud fell from the plastering over the windows, for a leak suddenly developed in the concrete eaves trough and spilled an overflow along the wall top and the front of the house. The first fire of the season roared merrily in the big fireplace and three happy little Yaquitepecos toasted hands and toes in the cheerful warmth. And while water plunged into the empty cisterns, whirling snowflakes sheeted the distant mountains in white.

Rain! and WATER! And the far sight of snow. Yes, perhaps, as we expected, it will be a cold winter. But today the sun is shining again and the mudders are busy at their building. The lizard is back at his fly-catching. And it is such a gloriously warm and clean-washed world that it might well be a perfect day in spring.

"But it really isn't spring," Rudyard and Victoria object, as I voice the thought. "It's really *almost* Christmas!" "And don't forget," Victoria adds, looking up, muddy faced and muddy handed from her vigorous patting of wet adobe, "that *vewwy* soon we all have to go and bring home the Christmas tree."

✳ ꟽ ⟱

Desert Refuge 43
(February 1945)

A CLEAN desert wind whips from the east, driving in from the far distance where the Sierra de los Cocopahs stretch a dim rampart of goblin blue across the horizon. The low hunched junipers of Ghost Mountain sigh chillily to the gusts, and the eddying smoke from Yaquitepec's one tall chimney trails to leeward like that of a steamship bucking a head wind.

But the desert sun, low hung upon its southern course, shines from a cloudless sky. The whole vast, tumbled panorama of wasteland wilderness—of jagged peak and saw-tooth ridge and writhing lowland wash—glows in crystal light. Yes, it is winter. But this is just one of those wide, clear, bracing brisk days that gives desert winter its special charm.

There are however pools of summer warmth—little sheltered nooks where, screened from the drive of the wind, the sun beats down in a drowse of lazy warmth. One of these protected little patches is in the lee of the house. And here, assembled in tribal council, Rider, Rudyard and Victoria are living over again all the exciting events of Christmas. The sun glows on their sun-tanned bodies and the long, slender fingers of the gnarled little squaw-tea bush beside them make shadow patterns upon the white gravel as they talk. I am out of earshot of all but the wind-drifted blur of their voices. But I can guess well enough at the words. For old Santa and a host of desert friends, whose camp fires now send flickering greetings even from the other side of the world, made this a memorable Christmas at Yaquitepec.

Friends and friendship are soul-stirring things. And it is always at this season of the year that we reflect sadly on the madness and stupidity which set one human being against the other in bitter enmity, when instead they could so easily share the unlimited blessings of the Great Spirit in friendship and fellowship. Linked as we are in the bonds of understanding with such a host of desert friends, the greater number of whom we have never seen, it is doubly hard for us to contemplate the spectacle of a world gone mad and wading savagely through seas of blood toward a common destruction. Human beings, all. No matter of what race or creed or color. Fashioned of the same clay, in the same mould. Pursuing the selfsame cycles of existence, with the same needs, the same joys, the same sorrows and the same loves and fears. And in place of the extended hand of friendship, each to each, there is the blow, the word of insult, greed, treachery and the sword.

* * *

Yaquitepec days are busy ones in winter. Which does not infer that summertime is not packed full of tasks also. But in winter the shortened hours of daylight give less time for work. Yaquitepec is essentially primitive. And the lengthening of the work day by means of artificial light is neither practiced nor desired. When the sun rises work begins; when it sets activities have to be suspended. This is the natural way of life, and the healthy way of life. But in an age of electric illumination man has largely forgotten this truth, and pays a sad reckoning in physical ailments, including that in injured eyesight, in consequence. The keen eye of the unspoiled savage is proverbial. Just how much of that keenness may be traced to the fact that he does not assault his sensitive eye nerves with any artificial light stronger than the yellow glow of torch or fire?

But short days make more crowded work hours. And to this is always added the winter job of keeping the fireplace fed with fuel. No small task in a region where fuel is scanty.

The bulk of our heating comes from the mescal—that marvelous desert plant of one thousand and one uses. Mescal butts, when of last season's flowering and thoroughly dry, are unsurpassed for heat and a brilliance and fury of burning. Natural oil and alcohol in the substance of the plant results in an almost incandescent flame, and the spreading, spiny butt, as it dies down into a glowing shape of coals, like a huge flower fashioned from illumined glass, is a thing of beauty which no crackling log can even approach. But the heat and the glow are short lived. Not so short lived as the twists of straw which the pioneers on the plains were forced to depend upon. But nevertheless short enough.

The amount of butts which a fire will consume on a chill winter day is staggering. All these butts have to be carried for considerable distances down, or up, the slopes of the mountain. And each butt, with its long dry flower stalk, is generally a hefty load. The collecting of great heaps of this fuel, as reserve against the sudden descent of snowstorms, is something which Tanya and the two boys generally undertake. It involves considerable walking and mountaineering. It is not likely that the inhabitants of Yaquitepec will ever need to lay out a golf course in order to enjoy the benefits of physical exercise.

There are other fuel products of the mescal, however, besides the comparatively new, dry butts. The remains of dead plants also are excellent burning material. Though, being rotted down and closely matted, they are inclined to smoulder and smoke. The dry flower stalks too, cut into handy lengths, make excellent, though short lived, stove fuel. But it is the ancient roots—the dark, almost petrified core of very old dead mescals—which give the longest burning, though not large, fires. These old cores are almost the equal of mesquite wood. They are hard and very difficult to get lighted. Once burning however, they will form a glowing mass, very much like that of hard coal. Such a little fire will glow and smoulder for hours on a cold winter night You have to crouch close to it, Indian fashion. But that is in keeping too, with good sense—and with the desert.

We never cease to marvel at the mescal. What the bamboo is to the Oriental so is the mescal to the dweller of those sections where it flourishes. So many of the basic wants of primitive man are supplied by this one plant that it is difficult to speak of it without an excess of enthusiasm. Not only does it supply fuel after its life span is ended. But during its existence it is capable of furnishing footwear, cordage, clothing, food, drink, sugar, alcohol, vinegar, paper, soap—and a host of other products. The Aztecs were fully aware of the many excellent qualities of the plant. And the Mexican variety of it, which is much larger than the native growths of Ghost Mountain, was called upon to supply a large proportion of domestic needs. There is even a record, in Aztec history, of the spiky thorns of the plant being used to punish unruly boys, who were jabbed—let us hope more or less tenderly—with them.

There is no single growth on Ghost Mountain upon which we are as dependent as upon the savage dagger-pointed mescals. If a sandal strap breaks when we are on a tramp we turn to the nearest mescal clump for repairs. The tip of a long, fleshy stiletto-pointed leaf bent over and stripped down yields a natural needle with a length of tough threads already attached. If we need a longer or a stouter thread, all that is necessary is to sever a big leaf close to its base and pound the pulpy flesh with a rock until the fibers are loosened and can be combed out and separated by the hand. Then a quick arrangement of strands and a few twists, or even just by braiding—and your cord or rope is made. At one time we always used rawhide or leather for sandal straps. Now we use mescal fiber. It is easier to get.

If a brush is needed to sweep about the fireplace, or a broom needed for the floor, or a big paintbrush for applying asphaltum to a water cistern, or a tiny brush for decorating pottery—again we turn to the mescals. You can make brushes from the fibers as artistically as you have leisure for. Or you can just pound the edges of the big dry leaves on a stone and use them "as is." You can tie them in bunches, with their own fiber, and build up as big a brush as you need. And in the case of a broom you use a length of dry mescal stalk for a handle.

If curtain poles are needed, or legs for light tables, or if there is a light fence to be built, or if rustic shelves are required, or napkin rings, or boxes for small objects—for all of these, and for many more needs, the mescal is our first thought. And in the springtime, when the plants begin to send up their new shoots, there is the toothsome, pumpkin-yam sweetness of the roasted mescal hearts. Here on Ghost Mountain we have not even begun to tap the resources of this desert friend of man. And it is with malicious satisfaction that we hug to our bosoms the knowledge that the hand of Commercialism is not likely to reach for the mescals in these regions, despite their many virtues. There are not enough mescals growing wild to feed the greedy maw of a factory. Exploitation must go farther afield…to the regular agave plantations…for its cordage. The Great Spirit of the desert planned a jest for all the despoilers of its useful plant life. They grow too slowly and there are not enough of any of them in any given area to make any schemes of greed profitable. This applies to the Yuccas and to the Ocotillos and to the Mescals alike—as many impractical, and often fatly subsidized, concerns have discovered to their chagrin.

* * *

Clumps of short velvet-green grass spread spots of color along the bases of the boulders and in the shelter of squaw-tea and buckwheat bushes. The rains that drift in across the western wall of the sierras have washed everything clean and the quartz gravel sparkles in the sunlight like a strewing of crushed marble. The three tortoises are sound asleep, tucked up for their winter hibernation within the shelter of the house. Rider's three stalks of corn are

all dead and yellowed. But we harvested five tiny ears from them. Not bad (at least so Rider thinks), considering they were nourished on water saved in spoonfuls from domestic uses, and upon occasional bottlefuls brought home on water hauling trips. Onions now have the limelight, for we have a little patch of them, the gift of a friend, growing bravely on our smallest garden terrace. At night they are covered up tenderly with gunny sacks, for the spears of the frost and ice stain violently sometimes in the hours of darkness. And often the water in the outdoor catch-pool is frozen over.

Practically all of the lizards have gone into hiding. And the squirrels who used to come for scraps on the terraces appear no more. Little white-crowned sparrows hop demurely about under the house windows or pose, watchful for crumbs, under the shelter of the junipers. The *ramarillos*—a species of rubber brush [rabbitbrush]—have their grey green coats trimmed with a woolly sprinkle of dingy-white dead blossoms, amidst which, here and there, late lingering blossoms prick out little dabs of yellow. The cottonwoods of the lowlands all have shed their leaves. The creosotes are sere, and the mesquites and the catsclaws are stark and chill.

Yes, it is winter. But what a winter. And what a land. You must live in it to love it. And you must love it to live in it. For localities, like people, have souls. And their full charm and confidence is given only to those who love them.

And here, in this jagged desolation of tumbled rock and waterless wash, and dim blue distances, the spirit of the land is very real. How many shall turn back the pages of the long vanished years and read its history? How many shall even guess at the secrets which are crooned by its night winds, whispering about the old rocks and about the fire-blackened stones of long deserted hearths?

Desert Refuge 44
(March 1945)

IT WAS on a cold evening that we first noticed Chitka. Outside in the sable twilight a raw wind yelled across the desert, trampling up the ridges of Ghost Mountain and threshing the tall, dead poles of last year's mescals this way and that against the hesitant stars. Inside the house the red flames from a piled cone of dry agave butts swirled in the big fireplace and the kerosene lamp, turned low, filled the kitchen with comfortable shadows. Supper was over and the table cleared. The curtain over the archway had been pulled into place to keep out the chilly draughts and we had all settled cosily on the floor before the blaze to enjoy the warmth. And there, suddenly was Chitka.

As silently and mysteriously as a fragment of shadow he came into the fireglow and paused, right among us. His long tail with its tufted tip lay on the warm flagstones. His tiny, wistful eyes peered into the mystery of the dancing flames as if fascinated. "Oooah!" said Victoria, drawing a soft breath. "The ghost of our Andy mouse has come back."

"Shish!" Rudyard whispered, "You'll fwighten it."

But the tiny grey shape was gone, and so swiftly that we did not see its going. "There!" Rudyard chided angrily. "I told you! You've fwightened the life out of him!"

"But I don't think so." Victoria said confidently. "He knows us. It's Andy. He didn't like staying dead. He wanted to get back to us. So he jus' got himself re-borned. He's not afwaid of us." She wrinkled up her pudgy nose, peering here and there into the shadows.

"If it's Andy," said Rider, "he's changed his nationality. Andy, you may remember, was a white-footed mouse. This one is a spiny pocket mouse."

"Which wouldn't necessawily make any diffwence," snorted Rudyard, bristling instantly against this implication of superiority. "Don't you wealize that there is such a thing as pwogwession? If you don't, I'm sowwy for you. Anyway his name isn't Andy now. It's Chitka."

"Ho!" said Rider with heavy drama. "Ho! So that's it. How do you know?"

"Because!" Rudyard said stubbornly."

"Stop it!" Tanya said sharply, suddenly alive to the gathering tension. "Rudyard, put down that weapon. And Rider, you don't have to be so critical. I will not have any argument here. If Rudyard says the name is Chitka, then it shall be Chitka."

"And a vewwy good name, too, I fink," Victoria wrinkled her nose at Rider in a triumphant grimace. "You were twying to stir up a wow," she added sweetly.

But there was no row. For just about that time Chitka came back. Came back and sat down companionably on a warm bit of hearthstone just at the side of the fireplace. He was a cute little fellow. But somehow he seemed a trifle wistful and lonely. We wondered how he had gotten into the house. The white footed mice go and come at pleasure, utilizing the many holes up under the roof beams, which Yaquitepec's hit and miss construction affords them. But the pocket mice are different. Of the aristocracy, they are retiring and perfect mannered. They mind their own business and do not go skittering up walls and through cracks like a pack of brigands. It was strange that Chitka had come into the house. And stranger still that he stayed.

But stay he did. And become more and more a part of the family circle. We came half-way to believing Victoria's theory that he was the reincarnated spirit of our old friend Andy, who, months before had met death in battle against overwhelming odds in the bottom of a dry water cistern. At any rate Chitka was one of us. Every evening he was part of the circle about the fire. Like a little grey elf he came and went between our feet pausing to blink into the fire and then slipping away to hunt for crumbs beneath the table.

We never saw him in the daytime. And his hideout was a mystery. One morning, however, Victoria, up early, discovered a hollow in the earth in a chink between two irregular hearth stones. "Chitka is digging himself a hole," she reported.

But there didn't seem to be much of a hole. Just a little hollow place. Rudyard filled it up with some fresh earth. But next morning it had been cleaned out. We pushed exploratory fingers into the depression. But it was only about an inch and a half deep. Just a play hole, we concluded. A mouse was entitled to some amusement. So we forgot about the matter. Chitka came and went happily in the evenings. But he was having his troubles too. For one night we noticed that he had lost at least half of his tail. The slender tip and the graceful paintbrush tuft had been nipped off. Evidently the battling mantle of Andy had fallen upon him also.

At length there came a morning when, clearing the ashes out of the fireplace, I noticed that there was a lot of earth among them. Mice tunneling under the wall, I concluded. Trying maybe to get into the storehouse. I had forgotten about Chitka. By way of investigation I rooted up a big flagstone in front of the fireplace.

There was Chitka's home. Even as the stone heaved up, exposing its guarded secret to the pitiless light of day, I realized what I had done. And it needed not the anguished exclamations of Rudyard and Victoria to whelm me with swift contrition. This was Chitka's home. This was the house he had been building so long and so industriously beneath the big flagstone. This was the meaning of that little hollow—the tiny doorway which each morning, before daybreak, he so artfully plugged up with earth. This was the meaning of the mysterious accumulation of earth in the fireplace. Chitka's home. A home built with love and with forethought and with patience and with art—for the cup-shaped nest which, like a four poster bed, occupied the center of the spacious little chamber, was composed of gaily colored tissue paper which had once been the wrapping of Christmas packages. Here was his spacious hall. His bed. His living room and his adjoining store chambers. Here also was Chitka himself frantic, dazed by the sudden inflood of light to his secret dwelling. From a side store chamber his eyes peered at us, his whiskered nose twitched nervously. "Oh Daddy, cover him up again. Don't fwighten him!" Rudyard cried. "Please! Quick! Poor Chitka!"

So we carefully replaced the roof of Chitka's underground palace. We set the flagstones back into their places as before, being sure to leave the chink between them so that the artful little doorway would still serve its purpose. And we went out and got fresh earth and filled the gaps between the stones as neatly as we could. The doorway was still open. We did not dare to pour earth down that for fear of filling up all Chitka's underground domain. But it did not remain open long. For even as we worked Victoria clapped her hands joyfully. "He's still there," she exclaimed, "I see his nose peeping out."

But she didn't see it again. For the next moment, in place of the nose, there came from below a little surge of loose earth. And then another, and another. The doorway chink was filled and once more took on its innocent look. Away downstairs Chitka was busy with nose and paws stuffing up his passageway.

So Chitka—whom Victoria still insists is Andy, in new guise—dwells on in his little house beneath the hearthstones of the gods. Nightly he comes forth to gather his share of crumbs and tidbits and to marvel at the astounding miracle of the fire. He has become tamer than before, and more sociable. It may be that his little heart has taken new courage and his philosophy of life has been established more fully. For did he not pass unscathed through the Great Disaster—through the day when the

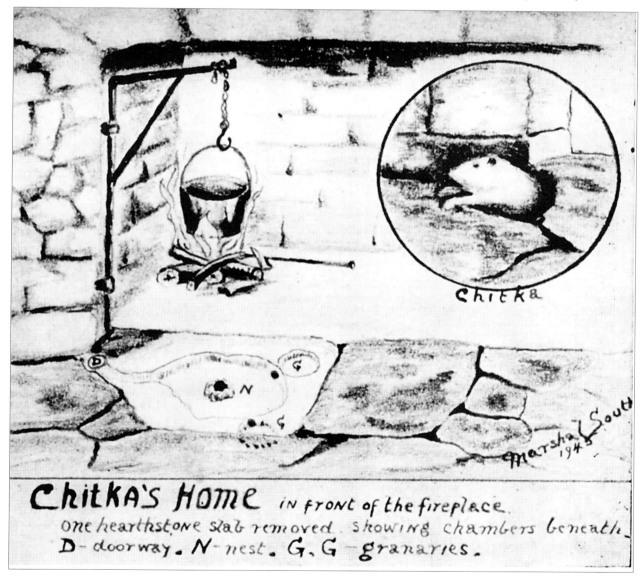

Chitka

Marshal South 1945

Chitka's Home in front of the fireplace.
one hearthstone slab removed. showing chambers beneath.
D - doorway. N - nest. G, G - granaries.

solid earth was torn asunder and the great light shone and the voices spoke in thunder. Through all this has he passed. And he lives, and even the gaudy bed of Christmas paper remains unharmed. What mouse could ask more proof of the miraculous or of the fact that life is lived in the shadow of unguessed powers of mercy and understanding.

The pocket mice are a lovable breed. There are a good many varieties of them. And it has always seemed to me they are among the most attractive of the many different types of creatures which make the desert their home. Though fairly numerous in some localities they are not as numerous as the white-footed mice. They are generally more shy. And even in those districts where they are plentiful their cautious habits are such that one can dwell in a locality for a long time without being aware of their presence.

When first we came to Ghost Mountain there were quite a number of them resident about the place where we built our house. And, perhaps due to the fact that Ghost Mountain was an unspoiled wilderness, they were remarkably confident and trustful. Every evening they would come about the tent and the first unfinished shack, skipping nimbly here and there in their odd, nervous manner of movement, as they searched for scraps and scattered grains of wheat and corn that had been dropped at our meal grinding. With their long tufted tails, their excited long jumps and their amusing manner of stuffing their cheek pockets with the loot they found around our campfire, they always provided us with evening entertainment.

Deliberately we set out to win their confidence. And, after a while, they trusted us completely. They would come and take wheat grains from our hands, stuffing their cheeks greedily until they would hold no more. Then off they would run and cache the load in hastily dug holes and hiding places and come racing back for more. Often they forgot these little treasure troves, which next season's rain would reveal in the shape of green shoots of thickly clustered wheat. They became so tame that, with a little coaxing, they would run up on our shoulders. I think that much of the charm of those first months on Ghost Mountain was due to the antics and gentle trustfulness of these little desert sprites.

That grand old scientist the late Frank Stephens of San Diego, once had a pocket mouse as a pet. It stayed with him contentedly for five years. And during all that time, and up to its death, it consistently refused to drink water. Nor would it eat green food or roots of any kind. Its favorite food was dry grain—wheat or barley. And its home was a small box with an inch or so of sand in the bottom, which Mr. Stephens kept in a perfectly dry place in the corner of the hall. He provided it with some cotton, of which the mouse fashioned itself a snug, ball-shaped nest. How the little creature could exist on dry food

without moisture Mr. Stephens confessed was a mystery to him. Yet the fact stands. It would not drink.

Enough, though, for the present, about desert mice. All this talk about pets, however, brings back to mind several loose ends which might have been floating around a long while untied. These are matters which concern Rhett and Scarlett, the two burros and Juanita and Conchita and Betty, the goats. All of these good animal friends, who were at one time part of our household here at Ghost Mountain, have aroused much interest. And this seems a good time to answer the many letters of inquiry that have come to us concerning their fate.

Well, Rhett and Scarlett have been retired to a sort of earthly burro paradise on the desert edge estate of good friends who played the part of good Samaritans to the burros during our absence. Their mission in life is now purely decorative. And in place of the bleak cholla cacti of Ghost Mountain—which I have seen them eating without either false teeth or gloves—they now feast upon watermelons and other choice garden tidbits. When we returned from our ramblings our friends met us. "We have your wandering burros" they said. "They were loose in the scenery, so we offered them temporary hospitality. When do you wish to take them?"

"Keep them," we answered. "Keep them. From henceforth they are yours. Your springs are a more dependable source of water than our cisterns." Yes, Rhett and Scarlett have cast anchor in a snug harbor.

To a snug harbor also came Juanita and Conchita, the two Ghost Mountain goats, and Betty, Conchita's daughter. We found for them a good home in Utah where, under the shadow of the red sandstone cliffs, they now dine upon alfalfa hay and rolled barley, and look back, as upon some fearsome nightmare, at the memory of their many weeks of bumping over desert roads in the narrow confines of a tiny trailer. So they, too, are provided for.

So now, at last, all the loose ends are tied, and the questions answered. And I find, as I look up, that the day has waned. A chill mist veil has wafted in across the low sun and the rocks and junipers are turning blue with the promise of a grey evening. The little lizard who has hung around my typewriter for most of the afternoon, speculating on the chances of stray flies, has decided to call it a day, and has gone home.

And I think I shall follow his example. But there is a cheerful thought to end on. For soon, now—not so very far ahead in the future—the wild geese will be winging north again over Yaquitepec. Soon—soon again—it will be spring.

Desert Refuge 45
(April 1945)

*W*ELL the wild geese have gone north again, winging their course in dawnlight and starlight and through storm above the low roof of Yaquitepec. The glorious Spirit of Spring reaches out in new life and promise across the desert. In the earth and in the air the wave of energy stirs in root and in leaf and in darting insect. And this morning, as I went out in the early dawn to carry a can of ashes to the dump, the first hummingbird of the season whirred about my head, darting by to light, a tiny jewel of feathered green, upon the summit of a nearby juniper. Yes the spring is here.

And we are ready enough to greet it. The winter on Ghost Mountain was cold. Not as grimly cold as previous signs had led us to expect. But quite cold enough. The youngsters, who are always wishing for snow, were gratified. And had about all they wanted of snow-and-honey desserts. For a long while a big snowman, of which Rider was the chief designer, kept guard by the yuccas in front of the house, his black eyes formed of juniper charcoal, peering fixedly through the wan sunlight and through the ghostly radiance of the moon. But the snowman is gone. And though the children swept up his eyes and buttons and personal adornments dolefully, their elders shed no tear at his passing. Snow, especially desert snow, is beautiful. But there is the bite of iron hidden beneath its ermine. The warm winds of spring are more gracious.

Yet we have affection enough for winter. For Ghost Mountain winters have a generous sprinkling of joy and are always fragrant with happy memories when they are laid away, one by one, in the treasure chest of the years. Memories of cheerful roaring fires. Of the strong harping of the gales, driving across the roof in the starlight. Of stories told around the warm mound of snapping embers. Of memory pictures woven by the fire glow upon bare, healthy, happy young bodies against the tapestry of the dark. Of the cracking of piñon nuts. Of the rustly scurryings of inquisitive mice.

And there are always the memories of sunny interludes, too. For winter never endures too long in one stretch. Always it is broken in irregular fragments, between which the gods of storm go on vacations—sunning themselves in indolence amid the drowsy peace of desert canyons. Such respites are not long. But while they last they are perfect. And, upon one pretext or another, we generally manage to take advantage of them.

Tanya viewing the light snowfall on Ghost Mountain.

It was during one of these sunny recesses that we discovered "The Cave of Memories."

The name sounds romantic. But Rudyard, who broods over forgotten cities and spends his time, at odd moments, scribbling weird bits in "The Book of Tilpan," insists that that is its name. So The Cave of Memories it has become.

Of course we didn't set out to find the cave. Not having the least idea that it was there. What we really went out for was to scout for more dead juniper trees to help with the fuel supply. This break of wonderful weather, we said, was a golden opportunity which we really could not afford to miss. So we pushed daily duties aside and, having made solemn proclamation (after the manner of Governors and other exalted personages) that this was "Go-Search-for-Juniper-Day" and therefore a complete holiday, we packed a lunch and taking the crowbar—to uproot dead stumps with—and the necessary carrying ropes, we set out.

The summit of Ghost Mountain is a savage wilderness of rock. Upthrust in a shattered mass from the parent crust of earth by mighty forces, the riven granite has been ground and weathered by the slow march of thousands of desert years. It is hard going between these monstrous boulders, fortified by their footing of jumbled stones and massed bayonets of mescal thorns and cholla. Each step must be taken with judgment, for a false one may lead to serious disaster. Under such conditions any burden soon makes itself felt. It was not long, therefore, on our excursion, before we found a pretext to abandon the heavy iron bar. It would be better to do our scouting first, we said, and come back for it when we had located the dead trees.

So, having thus thrown dust in the eyes of our accusing consciences, we cached the bar at the foot of a big wind sculptured boulder, beneath the shadow of which lay the blackened stones of an ancient roasting hearth, and went merrily on our way.

We felt better without the bar. Because we knew, in our guilty hearts, that we hadn't really come out looking for juniper, anyway. We had really come out for a holiday. And now that we were freed of the heaviness of that bit of iron, dragging at our spirits with the dead weight of a New England conscience, the day seemed brighter everywhere.

You don't choose definite directions when you are on an exploring trip such as ours. You just keep moving, leaving the direction to chance—which is always sure to lead you into something worthwhile. So we just tramped and scrambled along. Stopping often to peer into mysterious hollows under leaning boulders; to examine weird bits of cactus growth, or just to look out over the vast immensity of the distant desert that rolled away from beneath our mountain in all the fantastic shades and mysterious allure of an unknown land never before trodden by the foot of man. That it had been trodden we knew only too well. But it lay so weird and silent and distance-shrouded that even the knowledge could not destroy the illusion. The desert, of all the different regions of the earth, has the strongest personality. Man and his works cannot break it. Always, in the background, lies the Spirit of the land, watching, brooding. Waiting the day when she can sweep clear the stage of thread-like trails and human gopherings. Man always overestimates himself. The old gods always have the last word.

We came to a rim, presently, among the rocks, and found ourselves looking downward into a rugged canyon that we had never seen before. It was drier here, seemingly, and the heaped boulders looked thirstier. They were blackened and reddened under the wheeling suns of unguessed centuries. The scatter of junipers through which we had been passing seemed here to pause, as though sight of the thirsty depths had checked their ranks. One or two—as though adventurous scouts—had gone down. We could see their dull green shapes clinging here and there to the scorching rock tumble below. But the main body had halted, appalled. A dry wind came out of the depths and the slopes that fell away from our feet were a thirsty yellow-white sheen of the vicious *bigelovii*—the

cruelest cactus of the desert. Truly it seemed we had stumbled upon the Canyon of Desolation.

But youth takes small stock in appearances, being swayed only by the luring spell of adventure. Rider and Rudyard were already skipping nimbly down the rocks and we had little choice but to follow them. I turned over the water canteen to Tanya and picked up Victoria. Victoria can hold her own with the boys under normal conditions. But her little legs are as yet too short for scrambling jumps among boulders the size of young houses. We started downwards.

We went down the canyon a long way. And it was quite warm in the lower depths, for the sun, slanting directly into the gash, struck savage reflections from the thirsty rocks. The several juniper trees which we had seen from the top and which had looked so diminutive and toy-like proved to be gnarled and husky specimens, undoubtedly centuries old. Now that we saw closer where they grew the wonder was not that there were so few of them. The miracle was that there were any at all. These must indeed have been daring spirits, seeking adversity for its own sake.

Our two wild Indian guides, whose lithe naked bodies had been flitting like shadows down the canyon ahead of us, paused finally and exhibited signs of excitement. From their beckonings and gesticulations and faint, distance hushed shouts, we gathered that they had reached the end of something. For which our aching muscles were not sorry. We saw them sitting down presently, upon the top of a huge flat rock, talking together and pointing down the gorge, which, beyond them fell away and away into shimmering distance until it merged with the misty blues and violets of the far lowlands.

And we soon found why. For a few minutes later, rounding a great boulder and sliding down a short wind polished rock incline, we found ourselves in a tiny, crater-like basin, rimmed with mighty and terrifying rocks and carpeted with as beautiful a floor of gritty white sand as ever gleamed on the beach of any South Sea island paradise. It was warm here and silent and altogether delightful. We set Victoria on her feet. And with a cry of joy at the feel of the smooth sand she sped off like a twinkling brown sprite to join her brothers.

Only to be halted by wild yells. Hair flying and arms waving, Rudyard came sprinting back towards us. "You all take care!" he panted. "That's the place where it jumps off into nuffink. It's 15,000 feet deep over there. Or—or maybe a bit less!" He was out of breath.

"Whenever there's a heavy enough storm" Rider said speculatively, "there must be a waterfall here."

"An' there might be a spwing!" Victoria exclaimed, struck with the sudden idea. "Daddy, you should go home at once an' bwing a shovel an' try digging, down there at the bottom."

"Some other day, sweetheart," Tanya said softly. "Anyway we probably can find other places that might be nicer to dig in. Ufff! Just to think of going *over* there! How about some lunch?"

So we ate our lunch way back from the rim, in the drowsy shade of a vast rock, the dazzling white shimmer of the oatmeal-coarse sand ringing about our feet. A lone buzzard wheeled far up in the blue arch overhead, and here and there, on the steep scorched slopes that rose up around us, the savage clumps of Bigelow's cholla sparkled a brassy yellow glare of glistening spines.

And it was while we sat resting there, our eyes roving idly over the pressing desolation, that we saw suddenly the huge barrel cactus, the shadowy hollow and the little wall of stones.

"Looks like a cave up there," Rider said, pointing. "See. There by that big cactus, under that overhanging rock." "And a stone wall!" Rudyard gasped, excitedly. "Quick! Quick!" He fled away, an unfinished piece of bread in his hand, Rider sprinting at his heels.

It was a cave all right. A cave which, when we had clambered up to it, urged on by the frantic goadings of Victoria, who weeping with disappointment at not being able to get there as swiftly as her brothers, proved to extend back some little distance under the great rock. Like all the other caves of the Ghost Mountain region it was formed through the leaning together of a group of giant rocks. Such caves are usually not very big. But this one was larger than most. And undoubtedly it had been lived in. For, in addition to the low breast wall that had been built up before the entrance, all the cracks and crannies of the cave proper, where the irregular shapes of the rocks came together, had been carefully built up and plugged with fragments of stone. Storms and the march of years had dislodged many of the smaller pieces, so that now the sunlight struck through chinks and draught holes. But in its prime the little rock dwelling evidently had been quite weather tight and snug.

Yes, undoubtedly, this cave had been lived in. But that had been a long, long while ago. No one was living here now—or was there? Absurd. What a question to ask, with the evidence of utter abandonment so plain on every hand. But there is a solemn hush about such places. A "something" which, as we stood there in the utter silence of the canyon, did not make the queer thought seem so absurd. It was easy enough in that solemn hush to imagine anything. The weight of the past was over us all at once. The boisterous excitement of the children had gone out of them. They were all at once very quiet. As we moved about, peering and exploring cautiously in the dimness, we spoke in whispers.

There wasn't much in the cave. The "old people" were very poor, as regards earthly possessions. A broken olla. A couple of rubbing stones—one of them a very graceful one of the roller type fashioned from grey granite. A few sticks of ocotillo wood and several hunks of age-worn juniper. A thin scattering of charcoal fragments and several smudged areas on walls and roof where ancient cooking fires had left their trace—these, and a deep worn mortar hole in a flat boulder beside the cave entrance, were all the mute testimony which the cave contained.

Not much. Yet, as we stood there, looking out over the vast, wide sunlit sweep of glistening boulders, that swept away in desolation down the far course of the canyon until it opened out into the further vastness of the mysterious lowland desert, we could not shake off the odd feeling with which the cave inspired us. "I fink," said Victoria softly, "that there are ghostesses here." She looked around her expectantly. Victoria is deeply interested in "ghostesses." They hold no terrors for her any more than they do for the other two youngsters.

"Whoever used the grinding hole, used it a long time ago," Tanya reflected, half to herself. "See how that big barrel cactus crowds above it. No one could possibly use the hole now for grinding. That cactus must have grown since." We all looked at the cactus and were silent. This was a giant. Bisnaga grows very slowly.

Rudyard went back into the cave. "You know" he said, when he came out, "there's a funny heap of dirt and charcoal bits and piled rocks in the back of this cave. Do you s'pose that whoever lived here...."

"Maybe," Tanya said, not waiting for him to finish. "Maybe. I shouldn't wonder. It feels like it. And anyway, if they *are* buried there, I don't think we ought to stop here any longer. Anyway there's a feeling here as though someone resents our presence. Let's go. It's their cave. Let's leave it to its dreams and memories."

"The Cave of Memories," Rudyard said solemnly, as we went down the slope. "I shall call it by that name. It is like the things I write about in the Book of Tilpan."

So we went home. Climbing out of that silent canyon we threaded our way back across the summit of Ghost Mountain. And we retrieved the iron bar from where we had cached it. And we reached home just at sunset, when the long shadows of the mountains were thrusting purple fingers into the twilight mystery of the desert.

𝒟𝑒𝓈𝑒𝓇𝓉 𝑅𝑒𝒻𝓊𝑔𝑒 46
(May 1945)

𝒴AQUITEPEC was just getting nicely into an early spring. The first desert daisies were winking at the sun. The first orange-colored flowers of the mallow were dancing like brilliant butterflies on branching stalks. Here and there among the tumbled boulders the scarlet trumpets of the penstemons were lifted to the warm wandering breezes. Quail called from the ridges. Lizards basked upon the stones. And the whole wilderness summit of Ghost Mountain basked in a golden glory of sunshine that was drowsy with the drone of bees.

Then came the storm. Hard upon a morning of dazzling sunshine it came, driving a rush of dark clouds across the summits of the western mountains. By midday the world was drear and sullen, and by nightfall icy rain was driving in a howling wind. All the next day the cold and the fury increased. The iron roof roared to the hammering of the deluge. The water swirled in the run-off gutters and the churning wind gusts fell upon the house with such fury that one particularly violent one, corkscrewing down the chimney, toppled a blazing mescal butt out of the fireplace and sent it rolling down into the midst of our young Yaquitepecos as they crouched about the fire. Everyone escaped except Victoria, who did not jump quickly enough and in consequence got several bad burns on the legs. We had reason then to be thankful for the Yaquitepec mode of life. Had she been hampered with inflammable clothing the outcome might have been much worse.

And that night came the snow, falling like a ghostly winding sheet across the shivering shoulders of spring.

Rider (left) and Rudyard shoveling snow.

We woke to a white world. To a silence and stillness. To the end of the storm—and to wild, youthful shouts of delight. "Snow! Snow again! Oh Mother, where is the big bowl? So we can have snow ice cream for breakfast. Oh quick, *quick*! The sun's shining! It's *melting!*"

"Huh, melting is it?" observed the long disillusioned family elder, muffled deep in his blanket and conscious of chilly fingers and toes. "Melting, did you say? Well, I certainly *hope* so. Too much is plenty. And anyone who can be so crazy about...."

But they do not stay to hear. Bare feet. Bare bodies. Victoria's little legs twinkling and her "bath-a-robe"—held to her person only by one pin at the neck—streaming behind her like a flag. Out the door. Over the rocks. Leaping like chipmunks from icy boulder to icy boulder. Snatching up handful after handful of the precious white, powdery stuff—"Snow!... Snow!..."

The cisterns are full now. The storm brought just enough rain to make up what they lacked. And again the sun is shining and the bees hum and the flowers lift their heads.

* * *

Chitka, the spiny pocket mouse, has severed his connection with Yaquitepec—by request. Chitka was one of the most lovable of pets. And we had had dreams of having him with us as a permanent member of the household. But Chitka, despite his many virtues, had one fault. He was too progressive. A miner by trade, he insisted on pushing his particular talent beyond the bounds of all reason. The region of the fireplace, where we had joyfully allowed him to establish himself, soon grew too small for his ambitions. He longed for fresh worlds to conquer. And emboldened and fortified by the fat living which we showered upon him, he set out to conquer all the foundations of Yaquitepec. He began to drive ambitious tunnels.

For a long time we did not know what Chitka was up to. Occasionally we saw piles of fresh earth in the fireplace. And indulgently carried them away with the ashes. Chitka, we assumed, was enlarging his palace beneath the hearthstones.

But one evening Chitka bobbed out of the earth in an entirely new quarter, a long way from his home grounds, in a disquieting region. There is one mouse-proof room at Yaquitepec which we use as a storehouse. Whole grains and foods are stored there, for Yaquitepec is a long, long way from the corner grocery. We keep a "mouse detector" on the floor of this room. It is a simple device which consists of a dish of squash seeds. Yaquitepec mice are very fond of squash seeds, and whenever by any infrequent chance a mouse gets into the storeroom he makes a bee line for the squash seed dish. And leaves evidence of his feasting in nibbled fragments—which evidence results in our turning out full force to evict the intruder and plug up whatever chink or cranny has served him for an entrance.

But all those mice had been white-footed mice. Not underground engineers, as was Chitka. Our hearts chilled as we visioned an unending battle against an underground attack. The foundations of our storeroom riddled by tunnels. Chitka opening up lanes to the outer world of his brothers and sisters, who in the dead of night, while we slept, would rise from the bowels of the earth and carry off our supplies. The amount of grain that even a single pocket mouse can remove in one night is startling. Small wonder that we became alarmed. We had no data on the speed with which Chitka could dig tunnels. But we did know that a tiny mole has been known to tunnel 75 yards between sundown and sunup. Chitka might not be a mole, but he had demonstrated his ability to travel fast and far by the underground route. Unless we were willing to put concrete over the entire floor of the storeroom we were at his mercy. Therefore, Chitka, we decided, would have to move.

So we fashioned a nice box for Chitka. With a sleeping compartment and ventilation holes and a cunning little door, closed by a slide. And we stored it with grain and with enough wool and scraps to make any mouse an elegant nest. Then, one evening we led a train of grain inside the box and when Chitka had ambled in, collecting it in his cheek pouches, we shut the door.

He didn't care for the new arrangement. But we felt considerably relieved at having him under lock and key. And a few days later, when we felt that he had settled in his new home (he had built himself a nice wooly nest) we carried the box out onto the flat, quite a distance from the house, sunk it half-way in the ground and constructed an earth tunnel to it. Then we opened the slide door and went away feeling virtuous.

But the next morning Chitka was no longer in his house. The nest where he was wont to sleep was empty. "Somefing has tookened him away?" Victoria said, sniffing tearfully. "Some thiefs in the night?"

That night, after supper, Chitka bobbed up cheerfully in the firelight. He walked around our feet, sat down on the edge of the hearthstone, cleaned his whiskers with his paws, then with a sarcastic flirt of his stumpy tail, betook himself down into his diggings. Next morning Chitka had a new pop-hole, still nearer the storeroom.

We caught Chitka again. He was easy to catch. And we kept him in durance vile for several days—time which he passed in industrious nibbling at the inside woodwork of his box (yes, pocket mice *do* try to gnaw their way out of confinement, previous testimony to the contrary). Then again we took Chitka out into the wide wide world. This time we carried him far up the ridge of Ghost Mountain. Finding him a nice homeland amid some juniper trees and rocks, we took him out of his box, gave him a last gentle stroking and bade him a sorrowful farewell.

* * *

Rudyard, our seven-year-old, whose bubbling enjoyment of life extends over a wide field, chiefly artistic and literary, has found himself a new hobby. This is setting his own stories in type. Squatting on a bench, a much too big composing stick in his hand and a case of twelve point type before him, he makes up the story as he goes along, combining the tasks of author and typesetter into one operation. For long stretches he squats thus at his task, his face deep furrowed with concentration, the soft "tick, tick" of the type, as he slips them into place, broken at intervals by such worried questions as, "Mother, how do you spell 'obnoxious.'" Or, "How many esses are there in 'possession'?" When the words are long there usually is a frantic wail, "Stop!...Stop!...Give it to me in *parts.*" Then, as he gets it, section by section, he jams the type into place, letter by letter, with a sort of grim triumphant determination. With his interest and knowledge of printing whetted by a good deal of previous service as "assistant foreman" in our Yaquitepec printing jobs, he makes an astonishingly good job of his typesetting, a proof of a couple of booklet size pages usually revealing no more errors than I would have made myself. And though the spectacle of Rudyard, when he tugs at the lever of our hand operated press always reminds me of that bronze group in San Francisco in which muscular, all but nude artisans cling their straining weight to the giant lever of a metal punching press, yet I feel a thrill of pride as I see him puff and haul. Good friends write me sometimes, in worried vein, "But what will be the future of your children?" Well, I am not worrying.

And at the present moment, far from worrying, I am all puffed up. And why? Well, because I am the proud possessor of something, the like of which no other individual on earth possesses. It came about that I had a birthday. Such things to me are of no great moment. But my young "braves"—and "brave-ess"—think otherwise. So on each of these occasions I am loaded with a multitude of gifts, laboriously constructed bit by bit for months beforehand. Among the gifts on this occasion were notebooks, carefully made up and sewn together by Victoria. A bright shiny dime and a collection of manuscripts and pictures from Rudyard. And from Rider a varied assembly of mechanical marvels, ranging from an instrument for detecting the direction of the wind to hand beaten metal bowls in which to burn incense and an improved device designed to do away with the necessity for drying ink with blotting paper. But somewhere down the line of the long collection I came upon a contraption which puzzled me. It was a block of wood, upon which a pivoted, hammer-shaped weight behaved in a queer and mysterious manner that was fascinating. "Rider," said I, vastly interested, "now just what—what in the sam hill is *this?*"

"Oh—that," he said a bit impatiently. "Oh, that's merely an automatic paper weight. You just slip the papers under the pivoted hammer—and there you are. See!"

He turned back to the wind detector, and went on explaining how it worked and how I could adjust it.

But my head was in a whirl—for I was the owner of the only automatic paper weight in all the world!

Desert Refuge 47
(June 1945)

BUTTERFLIES are drifting across the ridges of Ghost Mountain like skirling eddies of gaily painted snowflakes. Where do they come from, so suddenly and mysteriously, these dainty little sprites that are drifting and tumbling everywhere upon the desert wind? Most of them are a reddish tortoise-shell. But there are all sizes and colors, down to the very tiny fragile-looking ones that flutter the bushes with their yellows, whites and pale blues. Rudyard has his nose buried deep in reference books. But it is a hopeless job. As well attempt to classify sunbeams from a crude lithographed chart as to identify all these fragile desert fairies by consulting pictures and descriptions.

Yaquitepec is richer by a new desert relic. A grey inconspicuous fragment, but one that is a treasured link in the chain that binds Ghost Mountain to the misty past. It arrived the other day in a howling windstorm, tucked away in one of the baskets of fuel which Tanya, Rider and Rudyard had laboriously boosted up over the gale-whipped boulders of the southern ridges. When they reached the house Rider picked a queer, irregular fragment of grey, termite-nibbled, flat, ancient wood out of his burden and presented it for inspection. "Now," he demanded, "what is that?"

I turned it over in my hands. It was light and weathered—and very old. The desert sun had sapped all the weight and strength out of it. About 11 inches long, at its longest projecting point, it had a width, in the broadest portion, of about seven inches. Sun, storms and termites had wrought havoc upon it. Yet at one end there still was a trace of human handiwork in the shape of a quite apparent tapering in thickness, and there were unmistakable signs of wear from vigorous use. Although tattered and worn and ghostly, the ancient fragment, to my eyes, fairly shouted its identity. "That, my son" said I, with all the impressiveness I could muster, "is a portion of the blade of an ancient Indian mescal roasting shovel."

They all gathered around eagerly. It is seldom, in these days, with two lively sons and a remarkably active and critical young daughter, that I have much chance to pose as the "expert" on anything. So I seized upon my one golden moment. With befitting dignity I expounded upon the probable age of the shovel. Of how it undoubtedly had been broken while in use by some too ambitious wielder in the dim days when Ghost Mountain was ranged by dusky Americans who had no inkling of the coming of the white invader. It made a good lecture, and probably a fairly correct one. For the fragment undoubtedly was very old. With the resultant enthusiasm we all made a pilgrimage to the spot, not so far from the house, where the fragment had been discovered. This was close by an ancient mescal roasting hearth. One so old that it was all overgrown with tall ocotillos and a generous sprinkling of cholla cactus. From the site we could look far down the mountain to where, in the distant valley, there once had stood a populous Indian village. Standing there, with the evidence of the old mescal hearth at our feet and with the grey fragment of the ancient shovel in our hands, it was not hard to slip back into the past. Into the dim days when the drifting, shy ghosts that now haunt the caves and ridges of Ghost Mountain were not ghosts, but lusty flesh and blood.

Our fragment of Indian shovel is the only evidence of these tools which we have discovered on Ghost Mountain itself. There have been digging sticks—which are companion implements to the shovels in mescal roasting—but so far no complete shovels. There may be a dozen perfect specimens lying hidden away in crannies under the rocks within sight of the house. Indian relics, like gold, are where you find them.

And in case you should happen upon any of these relics of old mescal roasts while prowling in the desert, it is well to know that the complete, unbroken shovels are of varying sizes, but usually are about two feet long, from the tip of the handle to the tip of the blade. In shape they are something like a crude canoe paddle, though with a squarish tip. The width of the blade is eight inches, more or less. And the implement is all in one piece, the round, stick-like handle being simply a trimmed down continuation of the blade part. Evidently they were fashioned, with infinite labor, out of flat slabs of wood split from trees, perhaps obtained in the mountain canyons. The best place to look for them, as for the mescal digging sticks, is in crannies under boulders that are not too far from the ancient roasting hearth sites.

* * *

Tortoise herding again has become one of the daily occupations of our young Yaquitepecos. For all our desert tortoises woke up promptly, as though by an alarm clock, on the first calendar day of spring. And they brought with them healthy appetites. Victoria, who loves to feed them tidbits, finds the task an exciting one. All of our pets have varying tastes. I have heard of desert tortoises who, in civilization, became so high toned that they would eat nothing but rose petals. Ours are not yet quite so educated—being by no means exposed to the perils of civilization. They do, however, fluctuate between filaree prickly bush, rattlesnake weed, ancient corn husks and old and weathered fragments of packing cartons.

* * *

Rudyard, tucked away yesterday in a sunny hollow among the boulders, day-dreaming to the steady harping of the wind as he roved meditative eyes over the landscape, discovered a hummingbird's nest—sighting it as it swayed to and fro, a tiny camouflaged grey dot, on a branch of juniper. It was last season's, of course. But we never had seen it before, notwithstanding the fact that it was so close to the house that we could have dropped a lariat loop around it from our back window. How perfect is the art by which the creatures of the wild conceal their habitations. Rudyard, who long has had a burning desire to find one of these nests, was thrilled over his discovery. This morning he has gone with sketchbook and pencil to make a pictorial record of it. We have hopes that last year's experience may influence the tiny jeweled builder to make another nest in the vicinity this season.

Chances are good. For our bird world has been very active around Yaquitepec since the weather warmed. And we are glad that, despite other pressing chores, we managed to get up several new bird houses in time for spring. One of them, Rider fashioned from chicken wire and

A mescal roasting hearth on Ghost Mountain. Sketch by Marshal South.

cement. Covering the wire framework with a cement stucco and painting the roof a cheerful red, above white-washed walls. Set on lengths of old iron pipe—to block the evil designs of squirrels and other climbers—these houses drew excited comment from our feathered friends. There was much rivalry over the question as to "who was to have which." So far, however, there have been no real fights. And our chief worry is that the Flycatchers, who always arrive much later, may be greeted with rows of "No Vacancy" signs, for the "housing situation is acute." Even the Guard House—the little sentry box, fashioned from a mescal butt, thatched with wide leaves and set upon one end of the last warning sign that protects the Yaquitepec trail—was taken early. The sharp-eyed little sentry of our outpost is already on the job.

* * *

Yaquitepec's contact with the outside world, maintained by the many welcome letters that come drifting in, is a happy one. Yet, every once in a while, real problems come along by the same route. These are in the form of queries from correspondents who feel deeply the urge to break loose from a machine patterned world and to strike out for themselves in "some unspoiled field" that will be "close to nature."

This is a natural and healthy desire. And one that is a bright gleam upon the drab curtain of lock-step civilization. But these questions are always almost impossible to answer with any degree of satisfaction to the questioner. The reason is that every problem of this kind is different. It all depends upon the circumstances and upon the qualifications of the particular individual. It is a question, too, of values. Of what one values most—freedom and independence; or money, comforts and gadgets. That anyone who really wants to, can break away from civilized props and carve out his own life in "the great open spaces" has been proved many times. But the unknowable factor in each case is just how sincerely does the dissatisfied individual want to change his lot. Many think that they do—and really don't. Deep in their hearts they would be horrified to face the prospect of throwing overboard almost every one of the advantages to which they have been accustomed, and to engage in a life of hardship and scanty monetary reward. Few can stand the test.

Yet it is to those few that America—that the whole human race—owes its vital life spark. It was men and women who had ideals greater than money and comfort who won the West. Barehanded, friendless, moneyless and alone, the man who has a vision of freedom and of self reliance will go forth against all adversity and against the gibes of his fellows. This is the breed that builds empires, that blazes the broad trail that others, the weaker, the more timid and the more crafty, follow. Not in money does the pioneer take his reward. He takes it in something infinitely finer—in freedom, in the satisfaction of being his own man, no chattel dependent upon the whims of another. It is to these freedom-loving souls who will not march docilely in the ordered ranks to the piping of those who would sway them, that all freedom owes its life. They are the bearers of the sacred fire. When any nation has succeeded in crushing out these independent souls—in bludgeoning them down with the rest into the conventional mould—then that nation is dead. Dead as are the nations of the ants, whose every ant hill—held up so often as an example of industry by uncomprehending philosophers—is a ghastly illustration of universal slavery and frozen progress, born of the crushing of individuality.

This then, is the answer to those who query. Balance your values. Make your choice, without illusion and with eyes open to what lies ahead. And if it be that in you stirs that spark of divine fire which must have freedom or perish, then fare forth with an untroubled heart. And the blessing of all the gods go with you. For the world has need of you.

* * *

More than once, from wanderers whose chief happiness it is to explore old desert trails, gleaning a treasure of chips and sherds of ancient pots, has come the query, "Why the almost universal round shape, or modification of the round shape, for the Indian olla? Didn't they know how to make other shapes?"

Yes, they did. But there is a good reason, in fact several good reasons for the globe design. In the first place, using a crude native clay, with a high degree of shrinkage, there was much less danger of cracking during drying and firing with round shapes than with those having sharp angles. A clay "bubble," which is really what an olla is, shrinks inward upon itself in an even manner. Strains and stresses, which are very pronounced in flat-bottomed pots with straight sides, are largely avoided.

This was one good reason. Another was that a round pot, upset, will not crash. It will just roll without damage to itself. An important factor when one considers the extremely fragile nature of Indian fired pottery. There is, however, another excellent reason for the shape. A round cooking pot, used in camp cookery, as the Indian used his, has great advantages. By means of scraping a very small hollow in the earth it can be set up to stand firmly. And, with the fire built around it, no stones or other raising devices are needed; the bulge of the pot gives it full heat. Further, when liquid and solids are cooking together, as in the case of mushes or stews, there is much less danger of burning. The solid matter which may settle and pack to the bottom is in a relatively cool zone—the portion of the pot in the earth hollow. The main heat is concentrated around the bulge of the pot, higher up, where the contents are likely to be most liquid and freer moving.

* * *

Winds slatter across the roof of Yaquitepec and make desert music through the chinks. This desert music of the wind is something which has a grip upon the heart that is peculiarly its own. All true desert wanderers and dwellers know it. It is inseparable from lone spaces and isolated, sun-blistered desert shacks. Mournful? Maybe— but not to those who understand it. *Chittery-squeak…chittery-squeak… Whooo sh ssh… Urrr urr rrr...* Miles and miles of creosotes and lonely dim buttes, blurry in the rush of the wind. The wan sunlight of late afternoon striking in spots of round light through nail holes in walls and in roof and lacing bars of dust-speckled gold through silent interiors. Ashes in the fireplace, hiding in the shadows. Blackened pots and skillets upon the stove. And beyond the windows the long, long leagues of the desert greying into dim distances in the rush of the sobbing, never ceasing wind.

Desert Refuge 48
(July 1945)

THE SUN sparkled upon the mountain. Against the gleam of the desert sky, flecked by a few lacy veils of white that had been flung aside by the waking dawn, the first blooms of the ocotillos swung in splashes of scarlet. Through the swaying junipers the desert wind walked, talking to itself and crooning snatches of forgotten songs as it plucked at the harp strings of the wire grass. "Come with me," whispered the wind. "Come with me and I will show you something. Come."

And the tall dry shoots of the mescals swayed together in approval and the new blooms of the buckwheat nodded their heads: "Yes, go," they counseled. "It is too beautiful a day to stay at home. And perhaps you will find something. Go!"

So we took a canteen of water and a little package of food and shut the door of Yaquitepec behind us and set out upon the heels of the wind, which had wandered away down the ridges and was calling to us from between the

rocks. The white sun-warmed gravel and the sloping surfaces of the granite rocks were pleasant beneath bare feet. High overhead in the clean blue of the sky a giant airplane forged westward, shattering the silence with the jarring din of its four motors. But on a swaying wand of ocotillo on a ridge beside us an oriole perched unconcernedly and poured forth a trill of liquid music.

We tramped on, following the wanderings of the wind and the glad notes of the orioles and the waving banners of the ocotillos. The desert had settled to its glowing pattern of forenoon gold. The yuccas threw pools of jetty shade. Upon the ridges the black trunks of great bigelow chollas stood like savage sentinels each crowned in a sun-flamed mop of bristling spines. In the far clefts and canyons lurked weird deeps of purple shadow and across the patches of white gravel between the mescal clumps startled whiptail lizards streaked from before our feet. Sunshine and vast space and an unspoiled wilderness of rock and thorn and glowing earth.

We had started without destination. But after a while, as we wandered on, pausing often to pick up fragments of stone or to admire some new desert growth or to peer into the nests of cactus wrens, we became aware that we were following an old trail. There were only dim traces of it here and there, but it was a trail for several times Rudyard picked up chips of weathered pottery. And once, by a boulder overgrown in a tangle of chollas, we came upon a place where someone long ago had dropped an earthen jar—an accident attested to by several large sherds, including one that had formed part of the lip. The fragments were worn with age. How many desert suns, we wondered, had risen and set since the dim day when that jar had slipped from the brown fingers that had been carrying it?

We made no attempt to follow the trail traces. It would have been useless, they were so old and dim and infrequent. The desert, especially in the vicinity of Ghost Mountain, is full of these phantom footpaths, that seem to begin nowhere and to end in the same baffling manner. We came out presently upon the thin thread of a tiny dry wash. And there, just up the opposite slope, among a scatter of creosotes and huge boulders stood "House Forgotten."

It wasn't much of a house—not after the manner of those mysterious ruins left by the cliff-dwellers. Even when it had been occupied, it could never have been anything more than a rather crude shelter. But to someone, or some family, it had been home. And to any home, however crude, there always is an aura of sentiment. In the age-old stillness of the desert which shimmered around us in the hot glare of noon, we approached it in hushed excitement.

The front wall, crudely piled of rough dry stone, had slipped and collapsed. But as we made our way up the dim trail, we could see signs enough that the house had served as a human shelter for quite a long time. Pottery fragments were abundant; the pathway, though dim and age worn, had seen plenty of traffic in its time, and the big rocks that had been rolled in to fill gaps or to reinforce the wall spoke plainly of a great deal of expended energy. Like all such places it had its atmosphere—its feel of the past. And while the "feel" of this old, forgotten dwelling was different and less haunted than that of the isolated little cave which we had discovered in the hills, it nevertheless was very definite. In the silence of the desert noon the past hung over it heavily.

There was no roof to the dwelling. In the beginning the reason for its construction had been a low, overhanging projection of rock, before the ready-made shelter of which the original builders had reared the loose-stone wall. Probably the space between the edge of the ledge and the summit of this wall had been spanned at one time by yucca trunks and thatch, as is suggested by remains that we have found in other places. But of this roofing no trace save a short and very ancient fragment of yucca trunk—which may or may not have formed part of the original beaming—remained. Upon the drifted earth within the house, where a litter of packrat sticks and thorns lay thickly collected, the noon sun beat down unobstructed. Only under the overhang of the natural rock was there a ribbon of shade. And here, in places, the scorch of ancient fires still showed on the cave-like wall and roof.

As the first hush of awed strangeness gradually passed from us we went to exploring. In the other cave—the lonely little cavern of the canyon—there had been every reason to feel that the crude little shelter was also a tomb. Here however there was no such insinuation. So in the sunshine and silence, stepping cautiously (for packrats have a genius for collecting the most villainous thorn clusters) we spread out to see what we could find.

On top of the overhanging ledge, that had served partly as a roof, there was a mortar hole worn into the rock. And here, evidently, members of the family had done some of their pounding of mesquite beans and other seeds. Down the slope a little distance from the house there was another mortar hole. But this had been made in softer rock and passing years had almost weathered it away. Near the house we found an ancient fragment of bone, too weathered for identification, but probably a piece from some slain mountain sheep. And inside the house, in crannies under the overhang of the rock Tanya discovered some large pottery sherds. By the side of the wall, at a point where, when the roof had been in place, had been the entrance to the dwelling, lay a nicely rounded stone used

in the preparation of roasted mescal and fibers. How long it had lain there, carefully set down by its last user, we could not guess.

But our greatest finds were in the line of pottery. Not in size—for all fragments were relatively small—but in significance. For, at this site, were types of pottery which we never before had found. Wandering back and forth over the slopes in front of the house both Rider and Rudyard picked up chips of a red clay earthenware which had been carefully coated and polished with a white clay finish. This had been laid on and worked before firing. And the white glaze polish had formed a perfect bond with the body material, a finish which the passage of all the succeeding years had been unable to mar. This was a find important enough, of itself. But Victoria, grubbing about cautiously among the packrat spine litter on the house floor, discovered a very thin fragment that evidently had been part of the upper side of a small bowl. This was beautifully fashioned—as thin as any modern chinaware— and though obviously handmade was almost as symmetrical as though thrown on a potter's wheel. Around the rim of the bowl—or rather that portion of it which the fragment represented—had been painted a band of white. A small streak of white still showing on another edge of the sherd showed also that the white design had been carried to other sections of the bowl.

The discovery of this white polished, and also the decorated ware, produced a good deal of excitement. The ancient Indians of this section did not decorate their pots. And except for some small scratched designs, found once upon a fragment of a storage olla, we never before had encountered any attempt to beautify pottery. The find set House Forgotten in a class by itself. For while it is probable that the dwellers of this little desert home did not make the pots themselves—the ware in both instances being of different body clay to that of pots fashioned locally—still it is obvious that they must have obtained the ware either by trade or from visiting friends.

We are not "diggers." We have little sympathy with those whose hands in curiosity pry into graves and tear up the ruins of abandoned dwelling places. So we did no trenching and turning of the earth, either in the sun drenched floor of House Forgotten or in its vicinity. We did search for the spring which we surmise existed somewhere close by. But the surface of the earth changes with the years. And faults in the subterranean rocks close. The desert spring from which the dwellers of House Forgotten filled their treasured white polished olla no longer exists.

It was late when we left, for after we had done our exploring and picked up our pottery fragments and hunted for springs and eaten our lunch there was still a sketch to make. And after that a good deal of sitting around on vantage points, soaking in the silence and the shimmering stretches of desert view.

The canteen was lighter on the homeward march. Which was an advantage. But not much had been gained by the emptying of the food sack. For Rudyard and Rider promptly annexed it as a collecting bag in which to carry home all manner of specimens—stones and odd sticks and seed pods and pottery chips and skeleton sections of ancient Bigelow cholla trunks. Victoria, too, added industriously to the collection, pattering here and there in search of treasures. On one of these side excursions she was thrilled to discover in a low bush the perfectly concealed nest of a pair of desert

A Marshal South watercolor sketch of an old Indian ruin they discovered.

sparrows. In the beautifully woven little home reposed three tiny white eggs, from which—having permitted us only the hastiest of glances—Victoria shooed us all away. "Hurry," she said. "Let's all go away quick so the spawwows can come back. I don't want them fwightened."

The desert was waking to the cool of the evening. Under the buttes and out from the deep gorges the shadow dancers were already shaking their sable mantles. A long way off an investigative coyote lifted his quavering note. The ravens were flopping homeward, flying heavily and commenting upon our progress with sardonic "wauks." A stubby tailed rock python, his glassy-blue metallic length half out from the protection of a mescal clump watched us as we passed and flickered a speculative tongue. Down a tiny, well worn chipmunk trail, an old brown tarantula moved, while from beneath a gnarled juniper a soft-eyed little antelope squirrel sat up from its meal of berries and squatted erect upon its haunches, watching like a friendly elf in a fur coat, the procession of queer two-legged beings that tramped past.

Our friend the wind overtook us. He was coming back to spend the night wandering on the ridges and playing his harp among the rocks and junipers.

"Well," said the wind, "didn't I promise to show you something?" And he laughed. "You know," said the wind, "someday someone is going to discover the ruins of *your* house. And find bits of your pottery. And they are going to speculate learnedly upon it and decide that you were creatures of a very primitive order. But that you did have

just the rudiments of the intelligence which has come to its full flower in *them*."

And so we came back over the last ridge. And skirted around the edge of the ancient mescal hearth which is on the little flat. And there stretched on a cord between two boulders was Rudyard's sign which says "This is the town of Tilpan"—the sign which guards that mysterious retreat where he and Victoria toil mightily, constructing pit dwellings and piling up walls of rock. The sign swung in the wind, which was already beginning to chant and to harp upon the mountain. And as we went on and came around the corner of the last juniper and into sight of the little low-hunched house of Yaquitepec, we saw that in our absence the Flycatchers had moved into the tiny red-roofed home in the summit of the gnarled tree near the water cistern. They were just tidying up after a busy day of carrying nest material.

"Te-quip" and "Tee-churrr" they said in greeting. Then they flew off into the sunset.

So we opened the door of our own house and Tanya lit the supper fire and the two boys and Victoria dumped their sack of specimens upon the floor and eagerly began to go through them. I went out to take a final look around and make all snug for what promised to be a windy night.

For across the western mountains, the wild harpings of the wind already were calling in weird cloud shapes—grey monsters of mist born of the damp spume of the waves which roll their thousands of leagues and their sullen depths above the sunken continent of Mu and all its cities. Grey cloud shapes of mystery which, through the night, would go charging eastward toward the shores of that other ocean which rolls its billows above the vanished glories of Atlantis.

As I barred the shutters and tied down the covers of the water barrels, I knew that the wind was right. Someday, someone will come and speculate and search amidst the ruins of Yaquitepec. And will exclaim over the pottery chips and the few thin relics of another House Forgotten.

Desert Refuge 49
(August 1945)

IN THE early dawn Yaquitepec belongs to the birds and the desert bees. Not the honey bees. But the great, black, bumbling carpenter bees. These big handsome fellows who bore and chisel catacomb-like homes for themselves in the soft pith of dead mescal stalks, come out in the early morning to buzz and boom all along the eaves of Yaquitepec. There is a peculiarly comforting drowsy peace to the sound. Something that speaks of the wilderness and freedom. When one has just awakened from sleep and is considering, in a detached sort of way, the prospect of getting up and beginning the work of the day, the deep booming drone of these giant bees is soothing music.

We often have wondered at the regular rite which they perform of seeking and bumbling and bumping all around the eaves before sunup. They are persistent about it. And it is not just one round of the house—it is many. There cannot be anything very attractive about roofing iron. And certainly it is not edible. We have suspected that during the night tiny specks of moisture may condense on the undersides of the iron sheets, where they project over into the eaves troughs. Perhaps that is what the bees are after. But if so they are sharper sighted than we, for repeated examinations have failed to disclose any traces of dampness. Nevertheless we are still inclined to the notion that water is what the bees are after.

And why not? In portions of the African desert, where there are great daily temperature changes, moisture will collect in the deep interiors of loosely-piled rock cairns. In fact in some sections specially constructed water towers—very thick walled buildings—are fashioned to take advantage of this very circumstance. In these towers, whose walls are pierced with many small openings to admit the heated air, there are arranged a maze of slanting pieces of slate, upon which the warm air condenses and forms drops of water. It is the steady dripping from the slanting slates—collected in a hollow in the floor and led off in a stone gutter—which furnishes the steady trickle of water which the water tower provides. Not much of a supply in comparison to the great labor of construction involved. But water is water in any desert.

There is not much mystery surrounding the morning twittering of the birds around our eaves. These little bright eyed dwellers of the wasteland are inspired by several reasons. In the nesting season it is frankly a business one. For there are many desirable scraps and threads to be found around and among the house walls. Yaquitepec is proud of the distinction—which it shares with all true desert establishments—of being compounded of a great variety of building materials. And, in addition, as there always is some portion under construction the harvest of mescal fiber, fragments of cloth, frayed rope scraps and trailing sections of gunny sack, is fine for nest-builders. On their quest, bird couples flit and flutter along the wall tops, twittering and tugging at ends and fibers with great good will.

The birds—who are fresh air advocates themselves—thoroughly approve of our house construction, and sometimes come in to look it over better. The most recent of these self-appointed inspectors was a tiny canyon wren that hopped in through a hole up near the summit of the west wall two days ago. The sun was just lifting above the eastern ridge of the mountain and in the level golden shafts that struck in through windows and smaller openings our tiny visitor found plenty to occupy its curiosity. If it was scandalized that we were not yet out of bed it at least kept its feelings to itself. After perching for awhile on the suspended length of mesquite wood that does duty as a chandelier over the table, it proceeded to a flitting examination of the house. Pictures, clay ollas, typewriters, water jars, baskets and benches—each in turn was selected as a perching place—while, with much head cocking, our diminutive long-billed brown sprite studied attentively every detail of this mysterious realm that it had penetrated. Apparently satisfied with its adventure, it flew through the archway into the next room and attempted to hop out through the window. Then it encountered a mystery as baffling as the fourth dimension is to humanity. The window was shut. Against the glass pane—as against some supernatural barrier through which it could see but not pass—it fluttered and beat wildly.

Rudyard, Victoria and Rider scrambled out of bed and dashed to its aid. But as is often the case with fear-crazed humans, it misunderstood their motives. There was a whirl of brown feathers and a fleeting rush—and the wren had disappeared. We all searched for it. We suspected that it had darted into the other room and was now hidden in some dim corner up above the mescal poles which are laid for seasoning along the ceiling beams. But our search was unavailing. We had just given it up when the wren again was at the windowpane. This time with the aid of a wide cloth scarf it was captured, conducted gently to the opened door, and liberated. It flew into a low thicket of squaw-tea bushes and vanished. The adventure was over, but it provided the children with a topic of conversation and speculation which kept their minds busy for some time.

Little things? Of course. But all of that adventure which we call life is built up of little things. And perhaps if time could be found in this frantic rush of progress for more attention to little things the big things might be simplified. It is one of the happy necessities of life at Yaquitepec that every incident, however trivial, calls forth attention and thought. Particularly in the matter of desert plant and animal life, by which they are surrounded, are the interests of our youngsters held and drawn forth. The birds, the squirrels, the lizards and the pinacate bugs—all are to them part of the family. And incidents befalling these little brothers of the wild are taken with a deep seriousness and sympathy.

There was, for instance, the tragedy which befell the homemaking dreams of the cheerful little pair of desert sparrows, who had decided to build their nest in a low cholla that grew among a clump of mescal plants just back of the house. Rudyard discovered this skilfully hidden little home when it was almost completed. Thereafter the busy little birds, as they flew back and forth bringing in fibers and grasses, were under almost constant though cautious observation by one or other of our youngsters. Interest reached its climax when the little nest had become the cosy container of three tiny white eggs. Victoria went about in a state of constant anxiety and watchfulness for fear that the squirrels would discover the little house and rob it of its precious treasure. The day when the eggs would hatch was looked forward to eagerly.

But the eggs never hatched. What it was we never will know. A hawk, perhaps. At any rate the nest suddenly was left desolate. Days passed. And weeks. And the three tiny white eggs lay there lonely beneath the glare of the desert sun and under the shine of the desert stars. For a long while Rudyard, in whom hope dies hard, clung to the scant comfort that maybe the sparrows were off on a temporary excursion and would return. But slowly, with the steady passing of the long days, even his hope died. Finally he set a time limit. "I shall wait just a month," he announced sorrowfully. "If they don't come back by that time I will know that something has happened. And I'll take the nest and eggs into the house and keep them. Just

to remember. It isn't any good leaving them out to be finally torn up by the wind and rats."

He was suspiciously close to tears. For Rudyard is tenderhearted. By the end of the month, time had softened the sorrow. Gravely he went out and brought in the little deserted home and its three tiny white unfulfilled promises. It hangs now, from a slender wire, just below the deserted nest of a weaver bird, almost within hand reach of where I sit typing.

* * *

A correspondent demands to know "just what do you get out of separating yourself from civilization and walling up yourself and family in a desert solitude?" He is puzzled. He cannot understand why it is that we are willing to turn aside from the brassy parade of progress, or to deny ourselves electric lights and the priceless privilege of radio music sponsored by Purfumed Soap.

Well, since he is not alone in his disapproval of our having dared to turn aside from the Grand March, I shall answer his question.

In the first place we get freedom. Freedom of mind and freedom of body. In this sunlit desolation of rock and thorn, where the sun beats down through an unending march of days and the desert silence which broods among the boulders and ocotillos is broken only by the harpings of the wind, we can spread freely the net of our minds to gather those priceless, fundamental stirrings of the infinite which are most easily come by when one is close to nature. Our thoughts are our own—to weigh, to digest, to evaluate. No coloring lens or distorting mirror—either of the printed word or the shouted aerial tirade—can stir our judgment, or influence it. What we think we think ourselves. That which we value we can develop. That which we hold to be trivial and unworthy we can escape. By dawnlight or starlight or in the glare of noon we are spared the constant effort of thrusting aside a ceaseless stream of ready-made thought, which sponsored by every diverse "interest" under the sun, beats constantly upon the eyes, ears and brain of the marcher in Progress' proud parade. Thus, quite unassisted, we can do our own thinking more easily. Not that it is impossible to think, even in the clamor of a boiler factory. But the process is more efficient and more pleasant in the wasteland solitudes where silence is stirred only by the desert wind.

And, even as it grants us freedom of mind, so does the desert grant us freedom of body. Here, far in the friendly shelter of our sun-seared rocks we need bow no knee to any sacred cow set up by the gods of fashion or of convention. Nature, the Great Mother, who with wise and loving hands directed the costumes and the health of our dusky Indian predecessors upon these wild slopes, extends her kindly care over us in similar fashion. When the snow falls or the bitter winds roar we can, if we feel so inclined, wrap ourselves in the warm folds of a blanket. When the sun shines and the warm breezes bring the glad tang of bodily comfort over the ridges we can discard our blanket. And there are none to say us Yea or Nay. From the cramping bondage of shoes our feet likewise have escaped. If, in the winter, the ground is frozen, or if, in summer, the rocks and gravel are too hot for comfort, we can—and do—wear a simple sandal such as the Yaquis wear. But for the most part we can go barefoot. And this without "scandal" or exposing ourselves to the "pity" of our neighbors, or the kindly "advice" of interested medicos.

Thus, on both counts of mind and body, do we secure a freedom which is denied those who cannot bring themselves to forsake the hollow bribes of progress. And with the gaining of this freedom we gain also something else. The boon of natural health.

Further, our "unnatural turning aside" has brought us peace and contentment. It has brought us to the state of consciousness where each day is a separate jewel to be lived and enjoyed for itself. Where each hour is a living thing, filled with the singing joy of fundamental life. Of the whispered mysteries of the drifting wind, of the glad notes of the birds, of the glinting sparkle of sunshine gold upon rocky pinnacle or upon swaying thorn. It has given us a deep kinship and understanding with all nature, the abiding sense of the oneness of all things, a clearer perception of the glory of the Great Spirit, as much in the jeweled eye of the desert lizard as in the majesty of the desert dawn.

Therefore, as through hour and day and month and year, we pursue our way upon this Pilgrimage of Life, finding joy in simple things—in the sun-cast mottled shadows of the clouds creeping in patterns across the tawny flanks of barren mountains, in the webs of purple mystery which sunset wraps about the lowland wastes, and in the long grey fingers of the fog which, at seasons, loom ghostly in the passes of the western sierras—we are content. We have found peace. Has my accusing correspondent also found it?

☀ ᛗ ⚶
𝒟esert 𝑅efuge 50
(September 1945)

THE carpenter bee, who lives somewhere in the headrail of our outdoor bed, is an early riser. When the first streaks of dawn begin to whiten the rocky ridges to the eastward we hear him begin to stir. The bed head rail, which is fashioned from dry mescal poles, has a neat round hole near one end, which is our little friend's doorway. From this he has run his tunnels far back along the soft pith of the pole's interior. How, in his dark retreat, he knows when it is dawn, we cannot guess. But know he does. Regularly each morning, at the same time, we hear him stir and begin to come down the long length of his hidden passage, uttering querulous complaint at every step, much like some grouchy rheumatic old farmer, stirred from a warm bed on a cold winter's morning, to go down to the barn and feed the stock.

This is the time of the year when the fierce arrows of summer sun beat upon the iron roof of Yaquitepec. Ghost Mountain is hot, and the children scan the horizon anxiously for any thunderclouds that may hold the promise of rain. Towering and weird are these mighty water-bearers of the sky, with the hot brassy rays of the sun reflecting blindingly from their mighty battlements and casting caverns of awesome shadow in their titan clefts and canyons. Squatting in the shade Rudyard and Victoria were watching a particularly imposing thunderhead. "It may come here," Rudyard suggested. "It is very near."

Victoria wrinkled her nose, as she squinted, desert fashion against the sun-glare: "I don't fink so," she said pessimistically. "It may be near. But I fink it is altogether near too far." Which proved later to be excellent judgment, despite the fact that Victoria is as fond as a lawyer of making her remarks complicated.

Yes, we wish it would rain. But there is health in heat and in sunshine, notwithstanding the discomfort which is inseparable from desert midsummer. The dry heat of the desert is charged with benefit for the human body. Humanity gets far too little of the sun—that is, civilized humanity. The unspoiled savage was, and is, different. But civilized man has turned his face to the darkness, in more ways than one. You may read articles and listen to discourses which seek to prove that sunlight should be taken in cautious doses, that too much of it is a positive danger. All of which sounds very official. But the exponents of these theories make a very poor showing in actual health. About ninety per cent of the people I know are afraid of the sun, afraid to expose their skins to it, saying that they will burn. Which they do. But most of them are sick in some way or another.

* * *

Rider, whose mathematical mind runs to investigation, lately has been bitten by the "perpetual motion" bug. He frequently is to be observed, these hot days, sitting at the bench under the ramada deeply absorbed in some device whose underlying purpose is to produce continual and costless power. The latest is a steel ball designed to run around a circular tilting trackway, the momentum of the ball to produce power by the constant, alternating up and down movement of the track. So far this device has not been any more successful than its predecessors. But Rider is not discouraged. And though the scoffers have been poking fun at "perpetual motion"—just as they did at the idea of the airplane there is not much basis for their jibes. Perpetual motion—so far as human existence is concerned—is everywhere in the universe around us. It remains only to harness some of these perpetual powers.

But summer, notwithstanding sunshine and health and the opportunities for invention, also has its tragedies. The other day Rudyard, scouting around in a park of bottles and containers (in which, when it rains Rider stores a supply of water for his own projects) discovered one bottle that was uncorked. The stopper had somehow fallen out and the bottle, an ordinary quart vinegar bottle, had lost about half of its contents by evaporation. A mass of grey feathers and an almost unrecognizable drowned shape floated in the remaining water which the bottle contained. Upon breaking the bottle we discovered that the remains were those of a little canyon wren. Though how it had managed to come there we could not imagine. Canyon wrens are small bodied, but the neck of a vinegar bottle is even smaller. That the bird could have forced itself through so tiny an opening seemed impossible, especially as the bottle had been standing in an upright position. The only explanation seemed to lie in the possibility that the feathered mite, in its inquisitive prowlings, had spied the uncorked bottle and, possibly intrigued by the dead flies—of which there were several floating in the water, had forced itself head first down through the bottle neck. Once inside its doom was sealed. For not only did it fall into the water, but the perpendicular smooth sides of the glass, sloping in to a dome over its head, gave it no hope of foothold for climbing. It must have perished miserably.

* * *

Old Mojave, the latest addition to our Yaquitepec tortoise herd, has begun to change his snoozing place. The sun has moved—and so has the shadow which, up to now, he has enjoyed. So he is plodding off to find another cool spot. Desert tortoises ordinarily dig themselves deep burrows under bushes or rocks. But the conditions at Yaquitepec don't admit of any satisfactory efforts in that line. So we have to provide artificial shelter. Mojave, however, is a distinct character in his own right. He likes to rove around and to suit himself. He is very domestic. And nothing pleases him so much as to prowl about the house

where, at night, he has his own special sleeping box. In daytime, however, he snoozes in the shade outside. Or, if it gets too hot, returns to the house where he has a retreat deep under a cupboard or type case. Early morning and late evenings is tortoise time. It is then that these strange and queerly lovable desert creatures like to roam and feed.

* * *

It was said by one of the ancient philosophers that "The proper study of mankind is man." But I think that this advice should be amplified to include the whole of animate creation. For certainly man may learn a great deal by intelligently studying his "younger brothers" of fur and feather and all their many classes of relatives. Not studying them in the sense of knowing their Latin names, or their exact measurements. But by seeing the world—their world—as far as possible, through their eyes. In this way much may be learned of their "human" reactions to various situations. Also the varying degrees of intelligence possessed by not only different classes of creatures, but by different individuals of the same class. Study of this sort will do much to rid man of the exalted mythology of greatness which he has woven about himself. The Indian, before his liberties and his soul were destroyed by his ignorant white conquerors, knew much of this lore. To him the creatures of the desert and of the forests were not just "animals." They were younger brothers, about whom a vast store of knowledge and understanding were accumulated. Something that today is thrust aside by those who stampede along in the mad scramble for the baubles of "civilization." The Indian knew better. But then the Indian was part of the natural picture. And he had the advantage of being unhampered by books. Books are all very well in their place. But they are a menace if overdone.

But the Book of Nature—the same one that the Indian studied so successfully—still is available free to all. And the Desert Edition of it, whose pages we on Ghost Mountain ruffle through every day by the aid of wind and sunshine, always provides interesting items and food for thought.

There was, for instance, the chapter written by our pair of flycatchers and the brown racer snake. A chapter of tragedy. But one nevertheless which contained many side lights on bird and snake intelligence.

This pair of flycatchers nested very late this year. They were a long time deciding on their nest box. Also they took their time about building. Finally the job was complete and the eggs laid. The female took up the task of hatching them. A few hot days passed. Frequently in the afternoons she would come and sit in the nest box opening, cooling off.

It was on one of these hot afternoons that a wild outcry arose from the children. Rider had seen a long "something" hanging out of the nest box—a shape at which the frantic bird, hovering near the entrance, was wildly pecking. "There's something in the flycatcher house" was the wild shout that brought Tanya and me running.

It was the young brown racer snake who has spent all his life around Yaquitepec. He is now about 30 inches long and full of misguided humor. His lithe tail hung out of the nest box, which is situated in the summit of a gnarled juniper tree. And as I came rushing up and grabbed him, he withdrew a startled head and a mouth full of nest feathers. He looked innocently astonished.

The poor flycatcher was swooping and fluttering around in frantic terror. So tumbling his snakeship unceremoniously on his head among the branches—from which he hastily scooted—I wrenched open the nest box door and felt in the deep little nest pocket. There were still two eggs left. We secured the door of the box again and went quickly away to give the terrified bird a chance to return. The snake, we felt, having had some ungentle handling and a scare, would not be likely to return.

Marshal South's sketch of figurines he whittled out of mescal pith, which is easy to carve because it is light and soft, but the finished product is fragile and breaks easily.

It took the flycatcher a long time to calm herself. We would have worried about the eggs chilling had it not been such warm weather. She hovered around and around the nest and peered at it from vantage points on the branches for so long that we grew tired of watching and went about our work. And then we heard again a frantic twittering and crying. And again we dashed, out.

It was the snake again. He hung half out of the box as before. This time I was really angry. Without ceremony I yanked him forth and sent him whirling out over the mescals and rubber bushes. I distinctly remember how stiffly he went round and round in the air. Just like a stiff stick. And, luckily for him he landed in a springy rubberbush a considerable distance away. Rider, racing to the spot, advised that he was making off across country at top speed.

He had managed to get another egg. That left a solitary one. We decided to move the nest box. We sawed it from its wooden pole support and remounted it atop a long length of steel pipe, which we set up in a crack of some great boulders some ten feet from its original treetop site. We feared that this was the end of the flycatchers' homemaking. It didn't seem possible that they would ever come back after this. And they didn't.

But the snake did. Incredible as it may seem that slim brown piece of rascality came back for the third time, looking for the last egg. Shortly after we had finished the job of establishing the nest box upon its steel pole, I discovered him sprawled out along the branches in the juniper tree. He was looking at the severed end of the nest box pole in a puzzled sort of way. He conveyed the impression of one who, having imbibed too freely, is "seeing things" or, in this case, *not* seeing them.

I shook my finger at him and gave him a wrathful lecture. But you can't get really angry with a racer snake. They are so full of humor. He just looked at me with his peculiarly expressive eyes. He seemed to wink. Then he slid swiftly away.

"Why didn't you kill him?" a friend asked us later. He couldn't understand why we hadn't swatted the robber. But things aren't managed that way at Yaquitepec. We do not shed the blood of our brothers—it is only the ignorant who resort to killing as a solution to problems. Gaining thereby not a solution but an intensification of the trouble. The command "Thou shalt not kill" is a very real plank of our religion. There was a time once on Ghost Mountain, when—through ignorance and a fear for what baby footsteps might blunder into—we backslid on our convictions as far as rattlesnakes were concerned. But we have repented of our failure and our error. And the rattlers now rest, with all our other brothers, under the seal of peace. For we have seen what this upsetting of the balance of nature does, even in the short period when we were guilty of it. For the squirrels and the packrats of Yaquitepec have increased alarmingly. And the native vegetation suffers. He who is wise will leave the balance alone.

Desert Refuge 51
(October 1945)

ACROSS this page as I write lies the sun-fretted shadow of an old tree, veteran of many a desert storm. Around its gnarled roots flows a thin silver ribbon of water. Bees cluster thirstily along the edges of the little rivulet and the sound of their continuous hum lends an added note of drowsiness to the long dun leagues of sun-steeped desert that sweep away and away into the hot haze of distance.

On a tiny slope of green, where the trickling of the little water run gives nourishment to some hardy grass, Rider is busy riding herd on the grazings of the four tortoises, while near by, Rudyard and Victoria are investigating a nimble red racer snake who has poked his inquisitive nose under a pile of dry wood in search of mice. An easy biscuit toss to my right a friendly roadrunner meditates in the shadow of an overhanging rock. And a few yards to the left of him a sentinel quail keeps his vigil upon the summit of a bush. There are towering thunderheads massed along the southern horizon, and it is hot. For this is summer. But this is not Ghost Mountain, nor Yaquitepec.

For the hand of War reached out and cast its shadow over Yaquitepec—as it did over hundreds of thousands of acres of surrounding desert wilderness. "Naval Air-to-Air Gunnery Range...the Secretary of the Navy...pursuant to authority of an Act of Congress...extremely hazardous to you...your removal from your present location is considered to be necessary." ...and so forth.

We were for the moment stunned. Like a bolt out of the blue the blow had fallen. We had had not even the remotest forewarning of its approach. And here we were, to be dispossessed and thrown out "for the duration." It was a staggering blow. And worse because it was hurry...hurry! Shooting was shortly to commence. Ominous red and white signs appeared suddenly upon the roads. All traffic was to be stopped. "Naval Gunnery Range" ...Already in imagination we seemed to hear the chatter of machine guns above our beloved mountain. To see the wheeling, diving planes. To watch the raging devastation of the brush fires which are almost always caused in such maneuver areas. Our hearts chilled and ached at the thought of the fate of our ancient junipers, of all the little wild denizens of the mountain, of all the tangle of primitive desert vegetation, unmolested since the days of the vanished Indians.

And where were we to go? We did not know. Nor had we the time nor the cash to go exploring. Frantic haste was the keynote. We must get out right away. The guns were impatient to bark. Good friends, whose kindness will be long remembered, made suggestions and whole-hearted offers. But the whole world was black and had crashed about our ears. Victoria, with the battered-faced "Susie" hugged tight in her arms, sat upon the edge of the bed and wept.

And then, in the dead of a moonlit night, the spirit of the Old West came speeding across the desert. Insistent hails and the signalling bark of a six-shooter drifting up from the lowlands across the rim rocks of Ghost Mountain roused us from troubled sleep. From the cliff edge we blinked answer with a flashlight. And hurrying down the long precipitous foot trail we were met by the Grand Old Spirit of the West—two of them, to be exact—in the persons of a well-known westerner and his wife. They had heard of our plight and made a long night trip across the desert to offer, at considerable inconvenience to themselves, a wasteland retreat tucked away in the solitudes of desert buttes and foothills. Here, in much the same isolation and freedom as that of Ghost Mountain, we could stay until the guns had ceased to bark and we were free to return home.

And so, once again, as it so often does, the magic wand of true friendly fellowship turned darkness into light. Plans swiftly were made, and all hands at Yaquitepec fell to the toilsome, back-breaking task of carrying down the mountain such possessions as we would need in our exile. There was a discouraging quantity of them, for life at Yaquitepec has many angles which must somehow carry on despite uprootings. How many trips we made up and down that long climbing trail I do not know. No matter how ambitious one may be there is a limit to physical strength and to the amount which can be packed at one time upon one's shoulders. Everyone toiled, lugging burdens. Even Victoria, who each time picked her way down the trail with the rest of us, her arms heavy burdened. The Navy had promised to send a truck and a work party to help us. But by the time the great powerful monster with its attendant jeep and cheerful work party arrived at the foot of Ghost Mountain, we had already carried down the bulk of our effects. Only a couple of trips up the mountain by our new gang of willing helpers, to bring down such stuff as we had found difficult to manage alone, were needed. Then, with the big truck loaded almost to capacity, we rolled away from Ghost Mountain into the shimmering desert. Life at Yaquitepec—for the duration—was over.

So, for a space, in our new desert home there is a new life, with new scenes. Our young Yaquitepecos, who uproot more easily than their oldsters, have the solace of new sights and new "adventures" to offset their spells of wistful longings for the old haunts. There is the trickling water of the spring to splash in and to exclaim over and to dam into pools with rocks and mud and sticks. Pools which soon are inhabited by fascinating little black tadpoles which lie like miniature ocean sting-rays on the sand at the bottom of the clear water. There are new friends to be made with the quail and with the roadrunners and with the jackrabbits and the snakes and with the little black and white flycatcher who sits all day upon a tree twig above a tiny water pool and waxes fat upon venturesome yellow butterflies and gauzy winged gnats.

The youngsters have made a garden too, irrigating it carefully with buckets of water carried from the pool. The possibility of this combination of seeds with water and soil is not without its effect. And this morning Rudyard, after meditating awhile upon the miracle of a melon seed that had sprouted in his own particular plot, wandered off to the typewriter and upon a torn fragment of paper napkin—the first bit of paper that he found handy—produced the following:

> *The Melon.*
> *It comes up.*
> *Its leaves are folded together.*
> *It slowly opens them to great life*
> *And its coming future.*

(At seven years of age Rudyard has not yet definitely decided whether his life work is to be that of an author, an artist or a poet.)

Yesterday we went up to the source of the spring which supplies water to the house. It lies up under the toe of encircling rocky ridges, and that characteristic atmosphere of primeval peace which is the special attribute of mountain solitudes lay over it like a healing benediction from the Great Unseen. All places, like all human beings, creatures and objects, have their own aura or atmosphere. A surrounding area of given-off vibrations which are just as real and distinct as the area of light rays emitted by a lamp or candle. There are dwelling houses that are sinister and others that are joyous. You can sense the spirit of them the moment you set eyes upon them. And the uplift or depression of them falls upon you heavily as soon as you cross the threshold. There are places where the birds sing and all the spirit of gladness seems to reign. There are others that you instinctively flee from, pursued by uneasy dread which you cannot put into words. The roar of his soul-destroying machines has made civilized man less sensitive to these primitive vibrations, even to the point of incredulity and scoffing. Primitive peoples who live close to the soil and to nature do not mock at such vibrations. Nor do animals—who are closer, physically, to fundamental sources.

One did not need, however, to be possessed of any exceptional "sensitiveness" to appreciate the peaceful atmosphere of the little mountain rimmed bowl where our spring came bubbling its limpid waters up through a cleft in the earth. A single glance around was enough to attest the fact that the peace and soothing quiet which wrapped the place had endured through centuries. On one side of a little meadow of green, kept verdant by the seeping waters of the spring, rose an inviting thicket of mesquite trees. While on the other, through tangles of wild plum bushes, weathered boulders and the cream-and-rust blooms of crowding buckwheat, the land heaved upward steeply, between ranks of yuccas, to the mystery of narrow canyons, dim with deep shadows and tangled greenery.

Indians had been here. Traces of them lay all about, despite the many years that had drifted by since their passing. Time covers swiftly the relics of its vanished children. Yet the storm worn guide stones and the ancient weathered metates, lying lone in the silence, told a mute story that was eloquent with the mystery of dead and vanished days. For how long had this little haven amid the hills, warmed by the desert sun and made softly musical by the breeze in the mesquites and the murmur of its bubbling water, been the gathering spot of the dusky children of the desert, before the European invader, greedy-hearted and intolerant, came marching up across the wastelands? For how many centuries had the little crystal spring at our feet been flowing? And for how many generations had the desert people gathered here to rest and to gossip and to grind the beans of the mesquite into sweet flour? The desert and the mountains are silent. The whitened stones of the metates give no answer.

There were luxuriant patches of tuna cactus along the rocky gullies. And its pink fruit, almost ripe, clustered temptingly amidst the bristling spines. So this little desert Eden provided its old-time guests with fruit also. Even to this last detail it was perfect. Were they sad to lose it—those departed ones whose abandoned grinding stones lie wistful in the silence? One suspects so. For, even though the trails of the Happy Hunting Ground be pleasant, it is difficult to imagine anything more pleasant than sitting in the cool shade of a mesquite, beside a bubbling spring, on a hot desert day and eating the delicious juicy fruit of the tuna cactus. There are some things that are not exceeded.

For the fruit of the tuna is something that is not sufficiently appreciated by modern residents of the Southwest. Perhaps it is because of tediousness in the picking and preparation. Our generation is not given to the taking of trouble. It prefers something that can be taken in rush order. Yet in Mexico and in other countries where the tuna (or mission cactus) flourishes or has been introduced, it is more popular. Not only are the fresh ripe fruits—rubbed clean of their growth of defensive spicules—readily obtainable in the markets, but in addition, considerable trouble is taken to prepare syrups, jellies and preserves from the crop.

Queso de tuna, or Tuna Cheese is a delicacy highly esteemed in Indian and Latin America. This thick, toothsome sweetmeat is prepared by boiling the carefully skinned ripe fruit for long periods until the syrup has been evaporated to a jelly-like semisolid. Primitive methods of manufacture are generally used, the fruits being peeled by hand and the numerous hard seeds separated from the pulp by means of a homemade contrivance (often fashioned from a large tin can or drum) whereby a revolving wooden paddle wheel forces the soft pulp of the fruit through perforations in the metal cylinder which are too small to allow the passage of the seeds. Thus seeds and pulp are separated. The juicy product is then boiled in ollas over wood fires until it assumes the required thick consistency.

Desert Refuge 52
(November 1945)

BREAKING a long run of years when thunder-showers avoided Ghost Mountain, this summer has brought electric storms and rain in plenty. It is a little jest of Fate that this, the one summer when we would have been able to sit under our own roof, to listen to the trample of the driving rain and to oversee the white weltering rush of water down the eaves troughs and into the cisterns—instead of laboriously haul it—that we should be exiles from Yaquitepec. Only in imagination can we hear the storms gust and thunder about the little mountaintop house and see all their bounty of water running to waste into the greedy heat of the desert sun, and to the bees and to the wandering coyotes.

Here, with a spring that pours its crystal flow night and day beneath the shadow of alamo [cottonwood] trees, we have no cause to worry over water. Still there is a deep, primitive fascination and joy in the streaking jets of silver that come slanting down from the driving cloud banks; there is a stirring, tempestuous thrill in the crash of thunder and the furious blasts of desert wind. To watch one of these summer tempests come driving in across the wastelands, fringed with flickering lances of electric fire and tossing a billow of dust and twigs and flying leaves

from before the sheeting spume of a wall of roaring rain, is no small thing. It is then that one knows the thankfulness of having some shelter to draw back into for refuge. Even if it be but a cave or some screened hollow among the boulders.

The desert is especially beautiful during a summer of frequent rains. It is then that all the leagues of wasteland snatch out once more all the hidden finery of the past spring. And with improvements, as though each thorny desert plant and bush and tree had been thinking over, with regret, all the things it had meant to do in spring, and had forgotten to do. So now in joyous gladness they hasten to make the most of this new holiday. Out come new leaves and new blossoms. And if the supply of blooms cannot succeed in creating a second spring, the supply of leafy green more than makes up for their lack. The ever optimistic ocotillos deck themselves hastily in their coolest, brightest greens. The desert gourds race out wreaths of leafy runners. New leaves crowd thick upon the mesquites and the palo verdes. Across every dry lake and hollow spreads a tender emerald carpet of filaree and low growing clover. And miles and miles of sombre grey galleta grass bursts to glad life in myriad spears of sparkling green. Everywhere the bees hum and the lizards dart and the hummingbirds whirr amid the creosotes and the yuccas. Spring again! And beneath the glowing beat of the desert sun the moist warm earth sends up a heady incense of praise to the turquoise sky. Even the stars look brighter and fresh washed.

* * *

Yesterday Rudyard discovered an exceptionally big rattlesnake dozing, comfortably coiled, in the shadow of a rock about a dozen paces from the house. We all went out to take a look at it. But by the time we got there our visitor had decided that he had rested enough and it was time to hunt supper. He had unrolled himself and was trailing leisurely along beneath the catsclaw bushes, flowing over the hard earth in a steady motion that seemed effortless. The nine horn-shiny rattles of his tail were held high and clear of the ground with the grace of a house cat, and his slender tongue flickered and darted with a constancy and speed that suggested the illusive play of lightning. He saw us coming and checked an instant. But concluding that our intentions were peaceful he continued on his leisurely way, his sensitive nose and grim-looking triangular head searching this way and that for the easiest passage through the catsclaw thicket.

There is a desert myth which says that the roadrunner, if it finds a sleeping rattlesnake, will gather joints of cholla cactus and build a fence around the slumbering reptile, which upon waking finds itself imprisoned behind a thorny barricade from which it is unable to escape. So it perishes miserably. It makes a nice story. But anyone who ever has watched a rattlesnake sliding easily and gracefully through, around and over all sorts of villainous spines, knows just how much the yarn is worth. It is on a par with the old "hair rope" fetish—which may bring peace of mind to the credulous who religiously stretch the hair riatas around their bed rolls.

We watched our roving rattler for a long while. He did not resent our presence unless we got too close. Then he would increase his speed slightly and sheer out of the way. Obviously he was looking for something to eat. And the way that he kept poking his nose into likely corners and crevices was strongly suggestive of a busy old farm lady peering into the barn hay for eggs. Victoria kept telling him that there were a lot of nice fat gophers in the garden. But he took no notice.

There are a lot of gophers in our present location, due to the presence of the water, which provides a certain amount of dainty and regular greenstuff. When we first arrived and laid out a hasty garden the resident gophers whooped with delight. They ran tunnels from all directions to the enchanted spot. They popped out of mysterious holes and nibbled the multiplier onions. They chewed down the beans. Driving ambitious galleries with devilish skill they devoured the roots and kernels of sprouting corn. They came out of caverns and devastated our tiny patch of alfalfa. It was a gopher holiday. Something had to be done. And still the "peace" had to be kept. Finally deportation was decided upon. The offenders were to be captured and transported to new and distant diggings where they might continue to enjoy life without endangering any of our treasured greenstuff.

The scheme had one serious drawback. How do you catch a desert gopher to deport him? It looked like the old flaw in the ambitious plan to bell the cat.

But we did begin to catch and deport gophers. And the queer part of it was that the gophers themselves did most of the hard work.

It came about in this way. Our little garden is a slope of small terraces. And, to reach it, the little furry engineers have to drive their tunnels upward at a rather steep angle. Also the stream by which we irrigate is about the flow of an inch-and-a-half pipe—which just about matches the inside diameter of a gopher hole. These two facts work perfectly together. There is lots of water. And when we irrigate and the banked-up terraces get flooded the loosely plugged gopher holes give way. Down goes a Niagara of nice cold spring water into the steeply sloping retreat of Mr. Gopher. And, in nine cases out of ten, out he comes flustered and gasping, from some lower pop-hole. In this disorganized state he is easily picked up on a shovel and

dumped into a wire cage, to be transported away down the gully to some far removed damp spot where he no more will trouble our lush green shoots of Argentine corn. Since we have put our plan into operation we have "exiled" a number of energetic little plunderers. And, strange as it may seem, the remainder now seem to recognize that the little garden spot is "forbidden ground."

At any rate the corn grows on unmolested. The onions are no longer nibbled. And the tiny patch of alfalfa—what is left of it—is quite gopherless. In addition we are the richer for a better knowledge and a closer acquaintance with these hard-working, valorous little gnomes, who by their unwanted industry, draw down upon their heads the almost undiluted anathemas of every gardener.

For they really don't deserve it. They are a problem, it is true—to humans. But so are humans—to all other creatures. The gopher has many points to his credit. He has boundless energy and tremendous courage. For every bite he gets he works hard. He is as much entitled to existence upon this planet as is any other creature, two legged or four legged. And the work that he does in soil improvement is such that it entitles him to considerably more than the vengeance and curses which are his usual lot. Not often does the average person—especially if he be a gardener whose pet vegetables or plants have been spoiled—stop to consider the benefits which accrue to the soil through the gopher's indefatigable tunneling. But no less authorities than hard-headed scientific societies and agricultural departments of the U.S.A. have acknowledged his beneficial services. Like the earthworm he is a very necessary factor in soil preparation. He is part of the "balance"—just as much as the universally abused "house-fly" is part of the balance. It is approved sport to "swat the fly." But more good would be accomplished by removing the cause for the fly's existence.

* * *

The San Ignacio dam (the name is Rudyard's invention and the dam is Rider's) is now complete. Both the boys toiled mightily in its construction, lugging rocks down the hillside and grubbing with hoes and shovels in the bottom of the little draw. It now flashes a gleaming sheet of 20 or more square yards of water to the desert sun, and is highly thought of by the population of tadpoles that have taken up their residence therein. The water gurgling over the spillway makes soothing sounds, especially when you lie listening to it in the night. It provides, moreover, an incentive for all sorts of interesting experiments with waterwheels and such devices. The miniature lake has begun to attract the attention of other desert dwellers also. Some drawn doubtless by love of the artistic, and others from more practical motives. As I got out of bed the other morning, I observed a heron departing hastily from the "lake" shore. Rudyard, who is sold on the decorative appearance of herons, is convinced that it came to admire the beauty of the water in the dawn-light, and perhaps to gaze at its own handsome reflection. Privately, however, I share with Rider the firm conviction that Rudyard's pet tadpoles had more to do with the heron's appreciative interest.

Nor is San Ignacio dam the only new feature of our present dwelling site. We have also a "Boot Hill"—or maybe it more correctly should be termed "Bootless Hill." This morning, hearing a sound of industrious hammering, I went around the corner of the house to investigate. There, in a shady patch beneath the cottonwoods, sat Victoria, squatting on her heels before a number of squares of white paper which, by the aid of a singlejack and a lot of four inch spikes, she was industriously nailing to the ground.

"Victoria!" I gasped. "My best nails. What *are* you doing?"

"I don' care," said Victoria defiantly. "I am just se-cewering down my gravestones. Rudyard is getting weedy to blow the Last Twump. An' I don' want all these things wising from the dead. So I'm nailing them down in their gwaves."

Startled, I peered closer. Staring up at me from the nearest square of paper, inscribed in wobbly pencil scrawl was the legend:

> *Hennery Jonathan Small*
> *Pinacate Bug*
> *Buried Here August 3, 1945.*
> *Died of Heart Trubble*
> *May His sole rest in peace.*

There were others too: *Tom Jones Jackson Wasp—Died of Newralgia. Bill Bee—Died of Wreumaticks. Jones Moth—Died of working hard.* And several others. All had their paper "gravestones" securely spiked down over their graves. "I just won't have 'em wising an' wessurwecting," Victoria said definitely. "I've had too much trouble already burying 'em."

I went in search of Rudyard. He was discovered hiding in a corner, a large tin funnel—Gabriel's Horn, presumably—clutched menacingly in his hand.

"Rudyard," I said, "you shall not 'Trump.'"

"Aw, I was just teasing her," he defended. "She wouldn't help me wheel rocks. An' so—"

"Nevertheless," I said firmly, "Curfew—I mean Trump—shall not blow tonight. Give me that funnel."

I took it from him and went back to Victoria. "The Day of Resurrection has been, for the moment, averted," I announced. "You can now give me the singlejack and the rest of the nails."

She handed them over obediently, dusted her hands and with a sigh of relief scrambled to her feet. "Thank you," she said, "for stopping him. You see I've had a lot of work burying them. And a lot more getting Rudyard to help me write the gravestones. I didn't want it all Trumped Up and ressurwected. It's such a happy cemetwery. Don't you think so?"

I said I thought it was. At any rate I had saved some of my nails.

Desert Refuge 53
(December 1945)

$\mathcal{T}$HERE still are a few blossoms left on the Palo Verde tree, over which the desert bees croon all day a dreamy lullaby; still a few fallen petals to fleck the warm shadow-fretted earth beneath it with glints of gold. One of the most graceful and beautiful trees of the desert, a Palo Verde is always a joy to look upon. Perhaps the Smoke tree is more mysterious in its phantom robes of haze and its foot-carpet of fallen indigo blossoms. But the graceful Palo Verde when in full bloom is a thing of glory.

Our own Palo Verde is a particularly graceful one. Standing in comradely fashion close by the corner of the house its branches in the forenoon cast just the right amount of sun-sprinkled shadow to make a perfect writing location. By night they lift a screen of delicate tracery through which, as we lie in our outdoor beds, we can watch the soft glow of the low-hung western stars, like the tiny crystal lamps of angels, hung there among the branches. As the long, slender leaves of the Palo Verde sway in pencillings of jet, the star-lamps among them flash and twinkle.

By morning and evening demure little cottontail rabbits come to feed close around our beds, and as we sit at breakfast under the big cottonwood tree there generally are four or five of them nibbling their own breakfast from a damp grass-covered patch not far from the table. Their interest in us is frank and friendly. Their big eyes follow our every move, full of a curiosity which has nothing of fear in it. And at almost any time of the day we can go out and find one or two of them contentedly dozing in the shadows of the catsclaws beside the pathway.

Squirrels are here too. Not the soft-furred, bushy-tailed grey tree-flitters of the mountains but the hardy, white collared ground squirrels. The ground squirrel seems capable of existing anywhere. Though how he manages to survive in some sections of the desert is a mystery. It is reported that they go deep under ground and pass some of the hottest months in a state of suspended animation much akin to hibernation, but bob up again the minute weather or food conditions become the least bit favorable. Canny and foxy little rascals; expert and saucy and venturesome as bad boys, they will turn everything to their advantage. And they're as nimble as jungle monkeys. I have watched them daintily picking their way up the slender, thorn-spiked, swaying wands of blooming ocotillos. They go with extreme care, but with sure-footed certainty. When they have reached the very tip of a branch they will hitch themselves into as comfortable a position as they can and squat there, feasting upon the scarlet ocotillo flowers. A brightly colored lunch, but one not as fantastic as it might seem. Ocotillo buds and flowers formed a part of the diet of the desert Indians.

But the squirrel's resourcefulness touches its highest point in his conquest of the flowering mescal. The mescal, or desert agave, is tough to handle at any time. Its bristling, needle-pointed spines are ever ready to break off in a wound. But when the mescal sends up its lofty flower shoot it becomes a tougher nut to crack. All the plant's energies are bent to the purpose of protecting those precious buds and seed pods—the final desperately triumphal culmination of perhaps 20 long years of a grim fight for life in blistering desert heat and drought. In one last magnificent life-burst the embattled plant flings aloft its slender, towering flower-pole, smooth as glass, and defended at regular intervals with thin malignant leaves, each armed with a peculiarly keen, penetrating spike. Up and up. When the flowers finally break out in a golden fountain from the summit of this swaying, needle-defended flagpole—itself rising from the very center of a bristle of bayonets—one might feel reasonably satisfied that the plant had achieved its purpose—that its precious seed pods would HAVE to be let alone. The task of molesting them might well dismay any animal.

But it doesn't dismay the desert squirrel. The squirrel technique has long been perfected. It is simplicity itself—the little rodents simply jump. They amble along until they find a particularly fine mescal, whose towering shoot is well laden with bulging green seed pods. Then, judging their distance carefully, they make a bold leap, right over the summits of the bunched, bayonet base-leaves, and grab a smooth place in the central flower shoot with their claws. Then, carefully and steadily, avoiding each needle-armed leaf and digging their sharp

Tanya puts finishing touches on a pair of moccasins.

claws into the glassy-smooth, but comparatively soft, open spaces of the flower shoot they go up—much like a South Sea Islander climbs a coconut tree. When they reach the summit they settle themselves comfortably in a crotch of the spreading pod stalks and go contentedly to feeding—dropping a rain of discarded fragments from their quickly moving little jaws.

Having finished his meal, the squirrel descends, picking his way down the tall pole head first with the same care and confidence as when he came up. When he gets to the right spot near the base of the shoot he makes another expert flying leap, away out over the lances of the base, and lands safely on some rock or clear patch of earth. Then he goes home to sleep. That is all there is to it. Perfectly simple.

* * *

In the dark mysterious corner by the north wall, where the old corrugated iron is piled, lives the Spotted Skunk.

And a cute little fellow he is. We don't see a great deal of him because he is of retiring disposition and minds his own business. But occasionally when we need to move some old boxes or some of the iron sheets, there he is, usually curled up comfortably in a neat little hideout and eyeing us with an inquiring, "Now what's the meaning of all this disturbance?" expression. He does most of his rambling around by night. And in the starlit quiet we often hear the bump and thud of his busy little feet as he noses and pokes and prowls about on his own business. Time was when we had the usual desert-dweller's dread of the Spotted Skunk, as a carrier of hydrophobia—an unpleasant habit of which more than one scientist has accused him. But we are not letting a little thing like that cause any misunderstanding between us and our little spotted brother of the night. He is a good friendly fellow.

Animals are like humans, even to the changes in their dispositions and activities, which changed locations give. For instance packrats look much alike no matter where you may chance to run into them. But they have "national" or to be more exact, "locational" differences of temperament. Our Yaquitepec packrats were mild and steady-going, not given to temperamental outbursts or excesses. They "packed" and "appropriated" and "walked off" with things in moderation, it is true. But in a strictly respectable manner. They knew the courtesies, and never transgressed the bounds of etiquette.

Not so the packrats of our present abode. These packrats are progressive. They are afflicted with the same spirit which produces Booster clubs and schemes for embellishing Mudville with a five million dollar chromium-plated Town Hall. At Yaquitepec our rats dragged a few sticks across the roof at night, then went to the checker-players club or to the sewing circle. *These* rats rush madly back and forth the whole night through. They bang cans. They throw hunks of wood in and out of boxes. They charge, with hollow-sounding feet, across iron roofs. They lug nails—by pounds—from their receptacles, and drop them into the depths of empty honey cans… "Tunk!" and again "Tunk!" all through the night. They carry in Palo Verde seeds and store them carefully—tall nicely hulled—in pottery jugs. They carry away small tools and pencils. They carry off kindling. They even are guilty of storing up munitions of war. For I have come across a nice cache composed of live cartridges of all calibers, from 30-30 down to .22 shorts.

Another ingenious rat party, working from aloft, carried trash and dumped it down a stovepipe which projected only a short distance above the roof, so much of it that they almost filled the six inch pipe from floor to summit. A circumstance which I did not discover until, needing a fire in that heater, I found the chimney plugged up—and had to disconnect the entire length of lofty smokestack to clean it.

There is one old fellow who lives in the outer porch where we keep the shovels and the tools. He was in residence when we came here. And though we had to disturb his home in order to accommodate some extra goods of our own, he very promptly rebuilt it with a grand collection of rat treasures. We respect his feelings. But he has no regard for ours. The other evening Victoria brought in several big armfuls of nice long dry cottonwood sticks for stove kindling. She set them down in a neat pile on the porch by the kitchen door. In the morning they had vanished. Summoned by Victoria's loud lamentations we hurried to investigate. Search brought the solution. Mr. Rat had them. He had lugged them all over to his nest behind the picks and shovels. The conical heap of his nest was neatly thatched with them. The white-barked sticks laid over it with painstaking care gave the nest the appearance of the dwelling of some African pigmy. We hadn't the heart to despoil the robber. We just let him keep them. Victoria trudged out and brought in some more for the stove.

So thanks to the activities of our numerous brothers of the wild, we do not lack for entertainment. Entertainment that is at least more full of thought-food than any provided by the average movie. Our days are full. And there always is a host of held-over jobs waiting to absorb any spare moments from regular tasks. These held-over jobs pile up and finally crowd in, in the order of their importance until they no longer can be ignored.

We are faced now with the periodic task of bringing our footwear up to date. Materials will wear out. And little feet will grow. So once in a while all the sandals have to be "revamped"—replacements made, straps and cords renewed and new soles cut to take the place of those that have been outgrown. Usually everything is outgrown. It seldom or never is worn out, for foot protection is rarely needed around home. We prefer bare feet.

But for those times, as on visits to town, when some sort of a shoe is desirable, we keep on hand sandals and other primitive styles of footwear. We have tried out a great number of designs. For it is not until you actually begin to handle the matter personally that you realize what a difficult thing it is to devise a satisfactory foot protector. One might say that it is an impossibility for man. And one returns again and again in admiration to the natural foot. You cannot improve upon it. You can "protect" it and "encase" it. But in so doing you always hamper it and injure it. The only way to secure foot health is to go without shoes entirely.

Desert Refuge 54
(January 1946)

IT WAS on one of our infrequent trips to "civilization" that Rider saw the bottle. It lay in the partial concealment of a clump of dry desert grass at the base of a cluster of vicious cholla. Over it, in the slanting rays of the sun, a wiry mesquite tree cast a lacy pattern of shadow. Between the spots of sunlight and shade, as our car movement altered their position, the bottle flashed gleams of fire like some gigantic diamond.

"A bottle!" Rider shouted excitedly. "A most beautiful bottle! Stop! Stop!"

So we stopped. And he and Rudyard, with Victoria at their heels, spilled from our ancient conveyance and went racing away among the creosote bushes.

They came trailing back, exclaiming and chattering excitedly. Rider was carrying the bottle. "Look," he said, holding it up. "It's slender and graceful. We might make something out of it."

So the bottle, which once had held in its heart the glowing vintage of Virginia Dare, went home with us and was carried carefully up the precipitous trail to the summit of Ghost Mountain.

"Now, what are you going to do with it?" I asked. "It can't just lie around here. You've got to find a use for it or we'll have to banish it to the dump."

All three of them went into a huddle. "We might make a vinegar cruet out of it," Rudyard suggested finally. He wrinkled his nose and squinted fiercely at the bottle from various angles.

So a vinegar cruet it was to be. We took stock of our resources—and of the bottle—and fell to work.

The first thing was to disguise and embellish the bottle mouth, which, though it had spilled forth in its heyday the poetry of joy-producing amber drops, was nevertheless woefully prosaic in its utilitarian screw top. Beauty must weave some sort of a spell over this eye-sore. We invoked the desert goddess of Necessity—who, as everyone knows is the mother of Invention. And she did not fail us. In a surprisingly short time the job was done and the bottle, haughty now with a brand new top and lip of homemade plastic, derived chiefly from the useful catsclaw, was laid aside to await the fashioning of its handle.

We hunted around quite a while before we found a piece of wood to suit us. Finally we hit upon a long-seasoned section of desert growth that had lain for years in dry storage awaiting the possibility of just such a

need. This was a bit of catsclaw wood also. Very, very old and rich and red. It was quite a job to saw it down and cut out a piece of heart-wood that was suitable for our purpose. But at last the task was done. And the new handle, shaped, rubbed down and polished, was ready for attaching. This we contrived by the aid of a couple of bands of scrap sheet copper, discovered among the odds and ends in the storeroom. Hammered down, polished, fitted and riveted, these did the job nicely. Our bottle had by now begun to take on all the airs of elegance.

But we still needed a stopper. "A splendiferous stopper," according to the specifications of Victoria, whose ambitions now were fired to the point that she demanded I should make one representing "flittering angels." However I did not feel, at the moment, quite equal to this order—and anyhow I was a little vague in my mind as to what a "flittering angel" might look like. So I compromised by whittling a nice white section of ocotillo wood into the shape of a little figure seated upon a stump. This, after some persuasive sales talk, Victoria accepted, and it was installed as a stopper—the completing item of our salvaged and glorified bottle. Thus, with desert scraps and odds and end, Rudyard's vision of the vinegar cruet came into actuality. It has been a good vinegar cruet. And if the

Ghost Mountain craft work—a bowl and vinegar cruet.
A watercolor by Marshal South.

liquid which now glows in its crystal heart has at all soured its disposition, it at least says nothing and gives no sign.

"But the dish," says Rudyard, peering over my shoulder at what I have written. "Haven't you forgotten to tell about the dish?"

I was coming to that. But the dish isn't important. I put it together with the bottle because I thought that the bottle, by itself, looked austere and lonely. And the little dish has an entirely different disposition, calculated to keep anything in good humor. For one thing its inside, where the tracery of engraving is, is a cheerful tartar red. And the outside of it—the part you can't see in the picture—is a rich walnut color. What do you suppose the little dish is made of? No, you'd never guess. It's fashioned from the creosote bush. The desert is a good mother. She will give you almost anything if you stay there long enough and have patience to try to understand and love the things which she holds in her heart.

* * *

We are still in exile. And now the winds roar down among the bleak foothills and wrench savagely at the high-sloped roof of our little dwelling place. Sometimes we tremble for the fastenings of that roof—fearing for the safety of our little friends the cheerful skunk family who live up under it in the mysterious recesses of the attic.

We doubt, however, if the skunks ever give the wind a thought. In the very height of storms they gaily prance up and down along the board ceiling which stretches above our heads and hides their activities from our view. Weird, these tramplings. One would think that darksome ghosts paced to and fro or played tag up there among the shadows and cobwebs of the beams. Sometimes the big pack-rat who lives out in the porch, among the picks and shovels and tools, pauses in his busy stacking and shifting of sticks and nails and seems to listen to the "ghost dancers" overhead. But they don't hold his interest long. He still has a great quantity of nails and spikes to move and pile. And as he does not yet seem quite sure where they ought to go, and is always changing his piles, it probably will take him a long while to finish the job.

* * *

Away back in the hills from where our little dwelling dreams beside its splashing spring there is a gorge where the shadows of the slopes and mighty rocks crowd close upon the ribbon of growth that winds down from the higher levels toward the sun-glared whiteness of the desert floor. It is cool here, even in the hot days of summer. A cool, branch-shadowed silence that is broken only by the soft singing of the wind as it goes wandering down toward the lowlands. There is a murmur of trickling water too, if you go up high enough. And places where the grass grows and the willows arch and wild grapes hang in thickets over tiny waterfalls whose music is like that of a silver flute to those whose days have known mostly the glare of sere rocks and the scorch of waterless sand.

So, perhaps, it is not surprising that as often as it can be managed and when the weather is favorable, we gather a little food into a basket or carrying sack and tramp off up the ravine to spend a day listening to the whispered stories of the wind and those marvelous tales of fantasy and imagination which only a little brook, on its way to lose itself in the desert sands, is capable of telling.

The children love these excursions. For one thing the holiday usually represents for them the successful outcome of many days of eloquent argument for a one day vacation from lessons. And for another, the outing offers all sorts of adventurous possibilities—from the discovery of coon and coyote tracks in the trail dust to the chance that good fortune will put them in the way of an undiscovered Indian cache or some arrowheads or attractive pottery sherds.

Then, too, there is always the chance of meeting again the Hermit Horse.

Now the Hermit Horse is an institution around these parts. It was not long after we had been deposited by the U.S. Navy in our little "St. Helena" (maybe Napoleon would have been more contented in the desert) that we first met him (the horse, not Napoleon). He was wandering over the landscape with a peculiarly independent air which all free things have. It was something not quite natural in a man-dominated horse.

But he saw us and made off. "Ha," exclaimed Rudyard, reacting to a generous priming of Buffalo hunts and George Catlin stories, "—See! See! A wild horse!"

But the rest of us knew better. There were too many signs of past years of enslavement about that vanishing brown splash among the bushes to admit of any such romantic explanation. "He's hiding out," Rider observed shrewdly. "He's run away and he's come to the desert, like we did, to find freedom."

And so it proved. For after many days we came to know the Hermit Horse very well. Yes, he had run away—that we soon came to know by close observation. For it was not long before the Hermit Horse accepted us as friends or at least as part of his domain. There is not much, even to a suspicious horse, to suggest civilized cruelty and saddle-and-bridle slavery in the sight of naked sun-browned figures slipping silently through the bushes. And not much in the sight of the tracks of bare feet in the trail dust to suggest the toilsome hauling of heavy loads. So the Hermit Horse—with his pitiful sway back and the white marks of ancient saddle sores—accepted us. Sometimes when we rounded a sudden bend of the trail we would meet him, almost face to face. On such occasions both the Hermit and ourselves would stop abruptly. And he would survey us for a moment or so from his soft, deep brown eyes. Then quickly and quietly he would step aside and vanish like a shadow among the brush tangles. He trod softly. He moved with the stealth and skill of a deer. More than once we offered him handfuls of grain. But he would have none of them. Memory of slave days was still too fresh. He respected us, but he was taking no chances.

There were wild grapes still upon the vines in the deep canyon when we made our last excursion. Not many, to be sure, for the birds had feasted for a long while on the fruit. But still the few that remained were sweet and wholesome and made a nice dessert to our simple meal. There is this about wild grapes—as about all other wild fruits and food. They are like the true children of nature in that they have little artificial polish but a great deal of sterling worth. The particular complaint that the wild grape is nearly all seeds and skin, with but little juice, is true. But on the other hand the "civilized" grape is a blown up product of pulp and water in which real nourishment and food value has all but vanished. The wild product has the strength of the earth in it. Harder to eat, yes. But there is infinitely more health and strength in it than in its glorified relation. Sadly one is forced to the conclusion that show and real worth no more consort together than do comfort and health.

Now the wind is rising and there is a hint of snow in the air. "But that," cry our three merry hearted youngsters, dancing expectantly, "only means that Christmas is coming."

Desert Refuge 55
(February 1946)

CHRISTMAS is over and the Book of Record has turned another page. The weary old Chief of 1945 has surrendered his staff of office to his successor. The new Chief, lusty in his youth, sits in council. The hearths are new swept and new fires kindled. Upon the house tops and upon the tops of the mountains the scouts and the new watchers take their places, scanning the horizon. What will the New Year hold?

Our cheerful youngsters, together with the packrats and the jackrabbits and the sociable family of spotted skunks in the attic—and all the rest of the carefree desert family—are not unduly concerned about the future. The memories of Christmas and of Santa Claus are still too vivid with them. And though Rider, as befits his mature age of almost 12, belongs to the "initiates," a fellow-keeper of the Great Secret, that fact, and his consequent deeper knowledge of the old Saint's private affairs, does nothing to spoil his enjoyment of the season. Perhaps it adds to it. Sometimes we think so—catching often a quizzical twinkle in his eye. Secrets do give one a feeling of importance.

This Christmas makes the second one which the youngsters have spent away from their beloved Yaquitepec. And, as in Utah, they indulged in some needless pre-Christmas worry as to whether the old Saint would know where to find them when he came to the little Ghost Mountain home and found it empty. However they now are satisfied that he is a pretty good "locater" for he dropped around to our present abode of exile with no trouble at all.

Nor was old Santa alone in his skill. All up and down the friendship trails which radiate through the desert to all parts and sections of this great land, a host of grand and loving friends sent in their gifts and greetings and heartfelt wishes.

* * *

There is an inquisitive wasp drumming around my ear. Now it is only occasionally that we see a lone wasp. Once they were here in great numbers. Industrious fellows, building their multiple-cell nests in every handy spot—on overhead beams, from the tops of outside window frames, from the inside slope of outhouse roofs. Like grotesque upside-down bouquets these nests were hanging by their single slender stalk from their supports and with the bright colors of the always busy wasps further heightening the flower effect. Paper-nest wasps, these. Their nests are constructed of an ingeniously fabricated paper, handmade or rather mouth-made—from vegetable materials.

Having experimented a little with paper making ourselves we were willing to grant to the wasps high honors for their ability. But when, in the fall, they began to move into our sleeping quarters, our high regard for them began to warp a little. What it was that attracted them I don't know. Maybe it was some peculiarly delightful aroma in the waterproofing substance in a big piece of tarpaulin with which we covered our blankets. Whatever the cause, they formed the daily habit of congregation around our outside beds. And in the evening, when we retired, we always would have to dislodge two or three hundred of them from snug berths in the deep folds of the canvas. Sometimes they managed to get through crevices in the under-tucking and penetrated to the bed itself. Where, on more than one occasion, being lain on, they became annoyed and retaliated by jabbing their red-hot daggers into us. This was bad enough. But when the victim happened to be Victoria it was worse. Victoria can yell loudly and continuously. On occasions when she and the wasps had arguments we lost hours of sleep.

* * *

which he had seen in some ancient dwelling. He opined that the man who had built it had been too lazy to cut fuel. Of course all his hearers laughed. But it was one of those laughs which come out of the windy depths of nothing. For I doubt that any of them ever had to rub shoulders with natural living. If they had, they never would have laughed. It is true that the reason for making a fireplace ample may be to avoid the cutting of fuel. And the underlying reason may be "laziness." Yet it is a peculiar sort of laziness. It is the "laziness" of intelligence; the laziness which is the driving force of all labor-saving

Santa Claus finds Yaquitepec closed by the U.S. Navy

There is a good little heating stove in our present refuge. On chilly days it dispenses a comfortable warmth. But the children miss the great roaring fires of dry mescal butts which cheered the winter days on Ghost Mountain. Moreover, this heater, being a unit of the march of progress has to have its wood cut for it. It must be just so. A piece a little too long is haughtily rejected. And whoever happens to have the job of keeping the fire burning must go out into the chilly darkness and cut the offending piece of fuel shorter.

I remember once listening in while an "eminent person" was humorously discussing a great, open fireplace

progress. It is the same laziness which impels a man to put the weight of a load upon wheels instead of dragging it by sheer brute strength along the ground.

It is the "laziness" of primitive intelligence. Which, in its beginnings, is a marvelous thing. When it goes for a certain length of time along its path and becomes "civilized" and set into patterns then it often becomes changed from intelligence into foolishness. As witness the complicated and stupid things which almost every "educated" "developed" person does every day of his life. Just because it is custom. Just because everyone else does them that way. Just because it is the fashion. When one pauses to reflect, sometimes, on the amount of human energy—and tears—expended in order to make the Laws of Nature conform to the Notions of Man, one does not wonder why the old Greeks thought that the gods, on their perch in the heavens, were continually in roars of laughter at sight of the human comedy below them.

And this thought, in a way, brings me to a discussion of the question, often asked by friends and acquaintances: "What are you going to do with your children?"

It is a personal question. And it is one which I hotly resent or else deeply appreciate—according to the motive and the disposition of the questioner. For, after all, despite the customs of an era in which everyone seems to think that he has been especially appointed by Divine Providence to act as his brother's keeper it is nobody's business—except mine and my children's. Provided always that we do not go out of our way to infringe upon the rights of others. Something which we have no intention of doing. "Peace," said that great Mexican, Benito Juarez, "is respect for the rights of others." An immortal sentence. This would be a world much pleasanter to live in if it were taken more to heart.

But to return to the immediate question—a question which, at the moment, I feel disposed to answer in part—what do I intend, or plan, for my children's future? Did I, in the first place, go to the desert in a huff, there to glower and snarl and crunch bones among the peaks—there to raise a breed of befeathered, painted savages? Or did I run out on civilization because I was incapable of measuring up to its intellect—bringing forth, in my wild retreat, descendants who will be ignorant, timid weaklings? Was there "method in my madness" or was it all just an accident? In short, to be definite, and to frame the question in the agonized words of some of my questioners: "Why, oh why, did you do it?"

And to that definite question I shall make an equally definite answer. *I did it to break the mould.* I did it, and am doing it, with the deliberate intention not only of freeing myself from the shackles of a system of existence which is drugged and paralyzed with error and convention, but to give opportunity to several other souls to grow up in an atmosphere and an environment in which they would not be afraid to think for themselves. In which they could face, clear eyed and clear brained the fundamental realities of life.

A mould is a terrible thing. Whether it be human thought or melted iron, the moment you pour it into a mould you kill its individuality. The pot which the Zuni Indian makes by hand, singly, is a thing of soul and beauty. Let a commercial organization get hold of that pot and make a plaster mould of it and start to turn out cast moulded pots from it, in wholesale numbers—even though they are cast of the same clay as that from which the original was fashioned—and you get things not of soul and beauty but of soulless, uninteresting mediocrity…I had almost said of horror. The life, the individuality, everything worthwhile in the original pot is gone.

So also with human beings. The moment civilization is firmly established it begins to cast them in moulds, to crush them, to hedge them around, to prohibit their individual thinking. Their ways are ordered for them. Their thinking is done for them. They are afraid to accept any idea that is at variance with the mob. They are victims of the mould. And it is a mould more difficult to break than any mould made of steel.

But, in the case of my "desert experiment"—as some have called it—I have broken the mould. For myself absolutely. For my children almost definitely. I say "almost" because there are two of them still who have not yet had enough years of freedom to enable their mental outlook to stand alone. Rudyard and Victoria are young. If they were dragged back now into the "factory" it might be that their early training would not be strong enough quite to resist the corroding influence of the "acid." Rider, however, is free. For though in later years he may perhaps elect to associate himself with civilization it will have no power over his free thought. Neither now nor then will he accept any condition or statement without challenge—without subjecting it to personal analysis. Names to him mean nothing. But truth means everything.

And do I have plans for the future? Yes, very definite plans. They go forward slowly, but definitely, from day to day. Those plans aim at the establishment of a center of handicraft, art, publishing and industry. Yes, a family center, if you will. Or if you choose, call it a clan center. A cooperative, personal body as self-supporting as were the ancient monasteries (which, in their day were the guardians of most of the worthwhile things of their age). Food will be raised. All necessities needed will be products of home handicraft. It is my hope that in this my children will find outlet for the immediate home use of their several talents. And that when they become old enough they will marry and settle at home.

This is the hope. There is no compulsion. The world is wide. If they have other plans they are free to follow them. But at present, from the interest they show in printing, art work, mechanics, agricultural study and philosophy, the outlook is bright.

Desert Refuge 56
(March 1946)

THESE are the days when storm gods make excursions to the desert. Over the summits of the western mountains they come trooping with their grey blankets, to throw shadows over the sun and to wrap all the creosote lowlands with swirled curtains of wind-whipped rain.

The wind roars and dead leaves of the cottonwoods fly in the blast. All the trees about our little spring, save only one lone tamarisk, are under bare poles, their gaunt skeleton branches gesturing impotently at the yelling gales. The wind is strong here. More strong and savage even than it was on Ghost Mountain. Sticks and small stones fly before it. Buckets and washtubs are picked up and flung far into the catsclaw thickets. Beehives are overset and heavy wooden wheelbarrows caught up and hurled crashing. But the house roof holds. And the rock walls defy the blasts.

At night we can lie listening to the wind coming down the canyons with the noise of ten thousand horsemen leading the charge of the rumbling chariots of the storm. Across the desert stillness the din of the oncoming fury holds a sense of fear which all foreknowledge will not quite still. It is as though you listened to the resistless advance of some terrible, mysterious host of ghostly riders, whirling down upon you out of the black darkness of the mountain canyons. The skeleton trees, dim-seen against the stars, seem to shiver. Louder and louder grows the wild thunder of the approaching gale, until with a shuddering boom, like that of a mighty breaker bursting upon a rock bound shore, it rolls over house and trees and goes thundering on and away into the black darkness of the eastern lowlands. The house shakes to its foundations. The trees whip and scream. Rain hammers like buckshot upon the iron roof and the whole night yells to a fierce, maniac fury of never-ceasing wind. Only the stars to eastward gleam on in silent, untroubled peace.

But storms bring with them their ultimate reward. For beneath every bush and in the lee of every sheltering stone, new green life is pushing up through the desert soil. The steady drip of the rains has wakened seeds from slumber. Rider's magnifying glasses have plenty of work in the examination of the varied host of tiny shoots and leaves that come pressing up through the hard earth.

It is not all "rain-dances" and "storm-dances." Many, and increasingly long, are the periods when the sun god rules. Then the wind, softened and gentled to a drowsy zephyr, stirs and murmurs among the mesquites and sings through the willows of the canyons. The lizards come out to bask upon the stones. And all the wild things come out of hiding.

Such a day is today. The whole world is wrapped in peace and sun. The damp, fragrant earth is drying out and I have brought a table and my typewriter out into a level space on an old abandoned road.

And I am not alone. For, hardly had I begun typing on the first sheet, when a bright-eyed young cottontail rabbit hopped softly out of the buckwheat bushes. From a distance of about four feet from my chair be studied me intently—a soft, vibrant ball of grey fur, topped with a sensitive, twitching nose, a pair of wide, dark eyes and two alertly cocked ears.

Having satisfied his curiosity, he presently moved off, nibbling his way leisurely from green shoot to green shoot, until he had disappeared in a catsclaw clump. It was not long, however, before his place was taken by a roadrunner. This comic-opera brigand of the desert bird world, whose lugubrious croaks I had heard for some time from various directions in the surrounding bushes, slipped stealthily out of cover almost under my feet, and, pausing with cocked head, subjected me to much the same appraising scrutiny as had the rabbit. Then with a brief jerk of his long beak and a flirt of his trailing tail, he sidled across the clearing with that exaggerated, professional conspirator manner which roadrunners affect, peeked into a small cholla—on the false scent of a lizard—and moved off. For some time after I could observe him energetically panning out the surrounding territory in search of snacks, peering into bushes and cocking his head hopefully around the lee of rocks.

Despite his buffoonery and the protection which he enjoys, the roadrunner is not altogether a blameless character. Strictly speaking he is a bird of prey. Let him be seemingly dozing peacefully upon a stump or rock, and let some tiny feathered songster of the desert lift its notes, and instantly your dozing kindly jester will be sharply awake. In a grim, sinister silence he starts immediately for the spot from which the song came—covering the ground in a swift, ungainly, hunched run which gives you a distinctly unpleasant sensation. Generally by the time he gets there, the little singer will have sensed its danger and flown off. But sometimes it is taken by surprise. It is true that the roadrunner eats scorpions and a variety of such creatures. Also there are fictional stories about the way it traps and destroys rattlesnakes. But it does other things as well. There is a dark and hidden page to its activities. Its destruction of young quail is said to be considerable.

But due to the inherent savagery of human nature, there is a deadly peril, even to the showing of kindness. Sometimes, with aching hearts, we ask ourselves if it would not be better to chase our cottontail friends away. To throw stones at our jackrabbits and to drive our roadrunners away with sticks. For the next passerby on these desert trails is likely to be one who neither knows nor regards the Great Law. And those very creatures which we love and have called our friends, will become victims through the trust which they have acquired in their contacts with us.

"Oh boy! Say! See that rabbit? Sittin' right there! C'd almost touch him! Gee—whatta shot!" *Bang!*

"An' lookit that bird. I c'd almost hit him with a stick. Quick—gimme the gun!" *Bang!*

And twitching grey balls of bloodstained fur and ripped feathers, stretched upon the desert earth, seem to cry pitiful accusation at those who taught them to have trust in anything in human shape.

* * *

A few days ago we stumbled upon the ancient dwelling site of the People of the Vanished Water. The sun threw long shadows across the mesa. The thick growth of desert mesquite and underbrush in the narrow, precipitous little canyon was heavy with a weird silence. And the little brook which once had run in its depths had vanished, like many another spring, below the desert sand.

To Rudyard is due the credit of finding the campsite. For it was he who first noticed the fallen walls of crudely piled rock. And he who found the first of the numerous pottery fragments. But it was Rider who first found the low rock-walled cave beneath the giant boulder. After that we carefully began to examine the locality. We found the old worn rubbing stones. And the mortar hole, and the smooth-rubbed places on the granite rocks where seeds and beans had been rubbed into meal. Also we found the old trail, now heavily overgrown and blocked by thorn branches, which led down from the cave entrance into the depths of the shadowy canyon. That was where they must have dipped their water—there beneath the whispering shade of mesquites and sumacs—from the little rill that has vanished.

It is always hard to judge, after the lapse of long stretches of desert years, what a camp or dwelling site must have been in its prime The primitive people were not given to elaborate buildings. And desert seasons are hard. Shelters of brush rot and blow away, leaving no trace. The flimsy roofs of thatch which may have covered primitively walled enclosures dissolve and disappear. Even the walls of piled dry stone topple and slip down, bit by bit, under the pounding of the rains and the winds. Then the bushes grow up. The catsclaws push in their thorny clumps and the buckwheats invade the dust-silted enclosures. Little remains to tell the story. It is the old rubbing stones

Entrance to the cave dwelling of the People of the Vanished Water. Sketch by Marshal South.

and the worn places on the rocks and the wide scatter of broken pottery that tell most of the tale.

Good caves are a rarity in this section of the desert. Usually those places which are termed "caves" are little more than hollows, either under or between boulders. The cave dwelling of The People of the Vanished Water was one of this kind. A mere shelter beneath the overhang of a tremendous boulder. It was low, and not much, as caves go. But the people who had lived there had gone to a lot of trouble to make it a snug dwelling. With an industry and effort, which can properly be appreciated only by someone who has had a lot of rocks to move, they had walled it around, closing the open sides and leaving only a low narrow doorway by which to enter. Some of the rocks they had piled were big and heavy, and doubtless were intended to act as supports in case the great overhanging rock ever tipped and crushed down. Wind and weather and the passage of years had rolled a great quantity of the smaller stone chinkings out of the walls and left them ruinous and draughty.

But in its prime the shelter must have been comparatively snug. There was a dense blackening of smoke and scorch on the north side of the wall and upon the cave roof at the same spot. Here, evidently, had been the chief fire site. However, scorch discolorations, from numerous fires, were scattered all over the underside of the roof. The cave was low, and washings of rain and the accumulations of packrats had silted it up until now it is not easy to get into. Even in the best of times it must have been impossible to stand erect there. But as a sleeping place and a place in which to huddle comfortably around a tiny fire when the desert storms howled it must have been very serviceable.

We made no attempt to "dig." We never do. Perhaps we are peculiar in this respect. We often have been called sharply to task by those who consider our lack of "scientific enthusiasm" as something culpable. But we are not greatly disturbed at such criticism. Let the dead past bury its dead. What is there to be gained by a ghoulish grubbing in the dust of things once sacred to human hearts? Here once dwelt our brothers and sisters. That is enough. May peace be upon their memory.

It is not the dead bones and relics about ancient dwellings which intrigue us. It is the memories. The bones and the relics are sad and dead. But the memories, if you are attuned to them, are very much alive. Wistful perhaps, and tinged with melancholy. But very real and very human. There is a long enthralling story in all of these old, old dwelling sites. One has only to tread softly and reverently and let the shades of the dead years retell it.

We left the place of The People of the Vanished Water— just as we have gone away and left other ruins of bygone days. But first, along the old overgrown trail, we made our way into the depths of the canyon and we stood upon the banks of the little brook that is now no more. It was a hard passage down that trail. For the mesquite thorns were thick-clustered and sharp. Undoubtedly ours were the first naked bodies to make that passage in many a long year. But it was worth the toil and the scratches. For, standing there in the silent shadows, with the desert wind whispering softly through the branches high overhead, we knew that we were not alone. That not anyone is ever alone. That the whole universe—the past and the present—is held firmly together like beads upon a string. A string that is the love and the infinite mercy of the Great Spirit. And in that realization there is a secure and an abiding Peace.

Desert Refuge 57
(April 1946)

THE DESERT wind that came drifting down from the summit of Ghost Mountain had the fresh, tangy scent of junipers in it, and the spice of creosotes and of sage. There is nothing stronger than a familiar fragrance to rouse trooping ghosts of memory and we who were wandering near our old haunts, stopped as we emerged from a thicket of mesquites and lifted our faces to the wind, sniffing eagerly.

Then we saw them—Rhett and Scarlett, our two faithful burros, who, by every right and circumstance should have been miles and miles away, safe behind cattle-guards and barbed wire, in the pastures of those friends of ours

who have given them a good home ever since we came back from Utah. What were they doing here?

The moment they sighted them, the children led a headlong race in their direction. "Rhett an' Scarlett!" Rudyard shouted excitedly. "Whett an' Scarwett!" Victoria shrilled. With Rider well in the lead the trio went racing out across the herbage-yellowed surface of the dry lake toward the lone mesquite tree, beneath which our two old-time companions stood placidly watching us.

It was a touching reunion, with much hugging and patting and endearing words on the one hand—and nuzzling and snuffing and twitching of long ears on the other. They very obviously remembered us and were as glad at the meeting as we. Gracefully, and with all the old-time satisfaction, both Rhett and Scarlett accepted bits of tortilla and munched them contentedly, while the wind stirred the thin, winter-yellowed dry grass and the swaying branches of the mesquite tree sifted a pattern of sunlight and shadow over the dark, shaggy hides. A roadrunner, in pursuit of a bug, skittered across the flat, and to the east the rim rocks of Ghost Mountain thrust harsh against the sky. It was like old times.

Rhett and Scarlett are growing old. Rhett's dark shoulders are more heavily frosted with silver; his grizzled head lifts a bit more wearily in greeting. Much of Scarlett's self-importance has ebbed away, and she stumbles more as she moves about.

There was a lump in our throats when we said farewell to our two old friends and left them there in the

Rhett and Scarlett, the devoted pair of burros, unexpectedly re-entered the life of the South family. Sketch by Marshal South.

silence of the desert, standing together in the thin shadows of the mesquite tree. There was nothing we could do for them. They know the desert and the trails, the waterholes and the gaps in the fences, better than we do. They are desert-wise. And while strength lasts they can fend for themselves. From the summit of a rise we waved them a distant good-bye. Then the tops of the creosote bushes closed in, and they were gone.

It took us a long while to quite recover our spirits. For in Rhett and Scarlett—their wanderings, the mystery of their origin and in their unshakable devotion to each other—there is something singularly touching. They are of the desert, freedom is in their blood and they will be no man's slaves. When they tire of work or of confining pastures they will pick up and leave.

Out of the mystery of the desert they came one day to Paul Wilhelm at his Thousand Palms oasis. They adopted him and used his place as a base from which to take long and short excursions into the wilderness. Sometimes they would be gone for three or four weeks. Then they would nonchalantly show up again and rest around for a while in the shadows of the palms before starting on another excursion. When we decided to try out burros on Ghost Mountain, Paul, who expected shortly to go in the army, got in touch with me and I trekked Rhett and Scarlett through the 120 mile trip down into the Ghost Mountain territory.

Some time later, when we left on our long search for a possible new Yaquitepec—one with a water spring—Rhett and Scarlett were taken to the ranch of a friend, there to await the success or failure of our exploring journey.

But they did not "stay put." They used their vacation to get thoroughly familiar with the surrounding territory. This done, they made themselves at home in it. Thenceforth they possessed the land. They knew its waterholes and its trails and secret retreats. They have wandered at will over it ever since.

Undoubtedly they are happy. And they are always together. Theirs is a great love story, a burroland epic of constancy and devotion. Out of the desert they came-together. And into the dust of the desert they will in all probability vanish together.

* * *

A correspondent who recently has realized a long-held ambition to own a desert homesite, sends me an entertaining description of her efforts to restore a badly shattered Indian olla, found on one of her exploring trips.

The "resurrection" of this particular pot—one of several whose fragments were found jumbled together—is a record of patience and of genuine desert understanding which it does one good to read. For it takes real love and interest to bring back to life, fragment by fragment, the shape that the dusky potter created in the dim, unrecorded past. Having done a little of such work myself I can testify that there is infinitely more of a thrill to it than to the piercing together of any "picture puzzle." And it takes much more skill and patience. Always there will be those heartrending gaps—the bare spots in the pierced together structure for which the fragments simply can not be found.

But it is just those difficulties that challenge the determination of the re-builder. In this case my correspondent actually went out in the desert and obtained raw clay, of similar texture to the pot upon which she was working, and from this shaped new pieces to fill the gaps in the old olla. These new sections she baked in her home fireplace, then fitted and cemented them into position. I think this is a faithful thoroughness that calls for high praise.

Ollas—genuine and complete ones—are becoming harder and harder to find. About the only way left to get one is to follow the trouble-beset path of carefully collecting the fragments of smashed ones and sticking them together. Nor, I assure you, is there any sense of owning something inferior when you exhibit a "stuck-up" pot. On the contrary it somehow seems much more valuable than an uncracked one. For memory of the toil—and the thrill—of fitting a heap of bewildering clay sherds together until they finally emerge as a graceful pot always will remain in the mind. Somehow it seems to enhance the value of the relic enormously. At one time it was somewhat of a problem to get a good tough cement with which to stick the bits together. But there are now on the market excellent cements, so the novice who embarks on the fascinating job of pot restoring need have no worries on the adhesive score.

All in all I can recommend the careful collection and re-assembling of Indian potsherds to anyone who is in search of a new hobby. Experiments soon will provide knowledge and skill. There are, for instance, several ways of filling in the gaps caused by missing pieces, which, though not as genuine and correct as actually shaping and baking new clay sections, nevertheless serve very well and are simpler to accomplish. One of these methods is to stick a cardboard or stout paper backing behind the hole, on the inside of the pot. Then the vacant space is carefully filled in with plaster of paris, which when it sets is artistically scraped and sandpapered down to exactly conform to the contour of the pot. After this, by the application of the right shade of a bit of oil color, carefully rubbed in by the tip of the finger, a very presentable repair can be made. A little portland cement, mixed with a small quantity of fine sand, will work as well as the plaster of paris and may be tinted in the same way. Often it is a good idea to give the entire pot, when restored, a color rub of suitable thin flat tint. Only experiment and the consideration of the needs of each particular piece can provide the key to success.

*   *   *

New buds and blooms are opening everywhere as the desert moves forward into another spring. The blazing fires of the chill evenings grow less and less necessary and the stove has lost much of its attraction. The chessboard, however, still retains its popularity. The game has found favor with the youngsters and they spend much of their leisure in thoughtfully moving Pawns and Knights and Bishops into strategic positions and gleefully crying "check!" whenever they have the enemy King bottled up. Through the long winter evenings and on the stormy days when rain and howling gales kept them all confined to the house our young trio developed considerable aptitude as chess players. Especially Victoria, our five-year-old. She has taken to the game like a duck to water and asks no odds from anyone. Wrinkling her little nose thoughtfully over every move she wages a skillful, strategic battle and usually comes out winner, both with her brothers and grown-ups.

An ancient game, chess. But then, everything in the world is "ancient"—or "new"; whichever term you prefer to use. For, actually, there is nothing that is either new or old. All the ingredients which are juggled together in this whirling sphere that is our home have, as far as we are concerned, always been. They do not change. But successive individuals, races and civilizations, get a thrill out of re-assembling the parts of the fundamental jig-saw puzzle in patterns which they believe are "new."

*   *   *

Nature is expert in hiding "yesterday" beneath "today." Not far from where we have our present abode there are ancient stone houses. No, not Indian houses—pioneer houses. They are roofless. The walls are very thick. Built by infinite labor from rough rocks, fitted together dry, without mud or mortar. Heavy bushes grow now inside the spaces that once were rooms. And the dust and sand have silted up into great mounds that cover deep all traces of human occupancy. Who built those houses? As it happens, from inquiry among old-timers, I think I know. But it is a story that is already becoming dim. And the period, from the time those houses were lived in to the present, does not span much more than 70 years. What would you expect then, in seven hundred years? Or seven thousand?

When we first came out to the wilderness of Ghost Mountain we used to pass, on a section of desert trail that was close to the highway, a neat little wooden house. It was empty, and had been so for some time. We remember it because, once, having had occasion to visit it, we were able to release a desert sparrow which had become trapped in the abandoned garage.

Just a few years ago—five or six—that little house was pulled down and carted away. And we marvel now, each time we pass the spot. For the desert has blotted every sign of where it once stood. Of all that cozy little home, which once throbbed with human hopes and fears and joys, nothing now remains save a vivid picture in our own minds—a memory of dusty sunlight and the flutterings of a tiny bird. The desert has blotted it and it has gone. You would cheerfully testify that no house ever had stood there since the beginning of the world.

Desert Refuge 58
(May 1946)

WARM DAYS and the drift of drowsy wandering winds along shimmering dry washes fringed by yuccas and creosotes and the bright green of stunted catsclaw. All the desert sleeps in the sun, wrapped in a veil of turquoise and shadowy indigo that is flecked here and there with the gleam of flowers. Forgotten are all the bleak days and the thin whining winds. The hummingbirds are back. The eager sap that pulses in the new flower shoots of the mescals lifts their tall green wands higher and higher toward the cloudless sky.

Every spring we marvel at the mescals. The fact that we have watched their sprouting over a stretch of many years does not lessen the thrill. If anything time has increased it. For now we know many things about mescal of which in the beginning we were ignorant. The mescal—the agave or century plant—is a remarkable organism. It has so many virtues it is in a class by itself. It has been our chief standby so long that whenever we find ourselves in a district in which the mescals do not flourish, we feel more than a little inconvenienced. When sandal cords break on tramping trips, we have been accustomed to make repairs simply by stripping a length of stout fibers—furnished with an excellent attached natural needle—from the nearest mescal. So, when there are no mescals, it is disconcerting. Also they would be missed for light building poles, for brushes of many varieties and a host of other purposes for which the mescal stands ready to supply the primitive desert dweller.

There are several varieties of mescals. The one which bristles the landscape on Ghost Mountain and vicinity is the Desert Agave. Not a large plant, as sizes go, but the area over which it grows in our neighborhood, is the largest, for its variety, in the United States. One of the most appealing things about our agaves is their food value. For, roasted in the proper manner, the young flower shoots and hearts are delicious. But there are two other angles of interest, which always have impressed us.

First, is the tenacity with which the plant clings to life. Against its efforts to flower and produce seeds, thereby guaranteeing the continuance of the life-cycle of its species, every force of the desert seems to be arrayed. Its enemies display cunning of a high order in outwitting the defense of needle-sharp spines. It is one of the tragic sights of the wastelands to see a majestic flower stalk, the sole supreme effort of perhaps 20 years of growth-fight against heat and drouth, cut down just before the breaking out of its flower buds, by the industrious gnawings of some sweet-toothed rat or squirrel.

I have seen stalks that have been gnawed through to all but a mere wisp of outer rind continue the fight. Unable to stand, and fallen by their own weight, they somehow hang onto life. They turn back, and up, upon themselves, forming grotesque figure-eights and other weird knots, until they can lift their summits once more toward the sun. From the contorted ruin of what once was a proud, lusty stalk, they finally fling forth their banner of yellow flowers.

They will do more than this. I have seen stalks whose budding tips have been completely severed, send out from the edges of the ragged stump fresh flower buds in a queer, struggling ring. And those buds, handicapped and stunted though they were, came to successful flowers and seeds. Sometimes the plant, seemingly in a frenzy of desperation, accomplishes things that are little short of miracles.

The other characteristic of the mescal plant which always has struck us forcibly is that, in its life-cycle, it typifies the civilizations which man, from time to time, builds. They start feebly. For a long period there is little sign of growth or expansion. Then, bit by bit, they become larger, better organized. Defended behind the ramparts of spears they come finally to lusty power. Then, in one wild burst of effort they fling forth to the world a final flowering of glory. After which they swiftly die. Worms gnaw at their hearts. They crash into oblivion, and their decaying bones form the soil from which arise their successors.

* * *

The little grey desert fox, who for some time has done us the honor to include our domicile in his regular circuit, came again last night to see what pickings were to be found. In the still night hours I was aroused by the stealthy clinking of metal. Looking through the window I saw our visitor in the moonlight, industriously going through a collection of tin cans that had been assembled for removal to our dump. Though he looked my way and I am certain he knew he was being watched, he betrayed no concern.

He was very systematic, going through each can as though it were a single problem. Several cans which had held milk came in for special effort. He seemed very fond of milk. Though the cans had been opened in the usual manner, by punching two small holes in the tops, he up-ended them so that he could catch in his tongue the few drops of liquid which they still contained. Sometimes a can would slip from his paws and go rolling away. At such times he would bound gracefully after it—a soft, soundless grey wraith, almost invisible even in the moonlight. After a while he would come back, appearing to be licking his lips, and start pawing for another can. When he had been through the whole bunch and was satisfied that this stopping place held nothing further for the night, he lifted his head, gave a final glance at my window, and trotted away.

Marshal among a cluster of tall mescal shoots almost ready to flower. The ring of rocks beside him is an ancient mescal roasting hearth.

He was a quiet, fascinating little fellow, reminding one more of a shadow than a creature of flesh and blood. It is impossible to imagine him raising a racket like our friends the packrats. Or fussing about with self-important swaggerings like the little spotted skunk who has condescended to adopt us. "Jimmy," as he is called, has lots of assurance but not good manners. He was making such a disturbance prancing around in the porch the other night I went out with a bit of food as a bribe. For some reason he was offended at my appearance. After glowering at me from his temporary vantage point upon the lid of a water barrel, he retired into a crevice behind a cupboard, scuffling and scratching vigorously. But he could not resist the bribe. After I had called him several times he came out in his best masked-bandit manner, sniffed the tidbit, grabbed it from my fingers and retired to his hideout. As a rule, though, Jimmy is very sociable almost too much so. When we meet him on evenings in the porch he scampers around our bare ankles like an amiable kitten, the beautiful plume of his tail giving him a background like a cascade.

Our porch, which is Jimmy's stamping ground, is an outrage to the neat and orderly arrangement of any refined person. In it—in addition to screen-wire coolers for food—we keep miscellaneous piles of sticks and dead branches and bits of dry cactus intended for fuel and an assortment of old boxes, mud nests of mason wasps, chairs and benches, picks, rakes, axes, crowbars, wood saws, lanterns and water barrels. In addition there is, in one corner, a large packrat's nest, with all the trimmings of sticks and junk which are so dear to a packrat's heart. The overflow from the nest, consisting mostly of dead, dry cottonwood leaves, spills artistically over a great deal of the porch floor in a formation which geologists refer to as a perfect alluvial fan. We never have the heart to hurt our friend's feelings by sweeping it out. Besides, what's the use? He would only lug it back.

There are two other packrats' nests on the porch. One is up under the eaves—a sort of penthouse dwelling. The other is on the lid of a water barrel. To this one the builder has added tin cans and odds and ends of the children's discarded playthings. At one time Jimmy the skunk used to come into the porch and stamp around among the litter of dry leaves, making a rustly, scattery sound, and scare the daylights out of the packrats, who barred themselves up in the innermost rooms of their fortress and swore venomously at him. (And if you think a packrat cannot swear you are in for a terrible shock sometime.) But lately the family has lived together more peacefully. Jimmy takes fewer malicious leaps into the leaf heaps. And the rats swear in a softer voice.

Oh yes, there is another packrat living in the porch. He's the fellow who must have been reading about the hanging gardens of Babylon. At any rate he has his nest inside an old saucepan which hangs, top in, from a nail in the wall. There is just room, between the top edge of the pan and the wall, for an active rat to wriggle in. The "nest," just like that of a very neat bird, is constructed entirely of ropeyarn…Yes, we like the general arrangement of our back porch. And we wouldn't want it any other way. Of course, other people might react differently.

* * *

A friend stopped me some time back, on one of my periodic visits to "civilization," and asked me if I were really happy living out in the desert. "Don't you ever feel," she said, "that you and your family are *missing* something?"

"Yes," I agreed. "I think we are. Transportation strikes, for instance. And newspaper scare heads. And jazz. And nervous prostration. And other things."

"No," she said. "I didn't mean that. But isn't there anything you'd like?"

And I said yes to that too. But when I started to tell her several of the things I'd like—especially things I'd like to see done—she stopped me again.

"Oh, but that's politics. I didn't mean that either. What I meant was Happiness. Opportunity. Money. Couldn't you do better for yourself somewhere else?"

And to that I had to say no. Of course I couldn't say it so briefly. I had to explain that it was all a matter of viewpoint. That, as far as I was concerned, I had found Happiness and Opportunity. And that, as to money, it depended upon the value which you place upon money—whether you command it or it commands you. And that there can be more enjoyment derived from spending a nickel or a quarter, if you spend it with a contented heart, than can be obtained by many a man who reckons his income and his spending by thousands of dollars—being harassed the whole time by the devils of worry and uncertainty. I pointed out that times hadn't changed so much from that period in which was written: "Better a meal of herbs, where love is, than a fatted ox and hatred withal." We had quite a long talk. And my friend went away feeling, I think, that sympathy for my "underprivileged lot" was entirely wasted.

* * *

Rudyard is shouting loudly for assistance. The perpetual motion machine which he has invented from some old cogs, springs and rubber bands, has stopped. This is a fearsome invention, which, as the advertisements say, "must be seen to be appreciated." Briefly the idea is that if one rubber band revolves the flywheel half a revolution, and you have another rubber band and some springs and cogs adjusted so that they will take over and revolve the wheel the rest of the way, so that it will engage with the tension of the first rubber band again, then why in tunket won't the wheel keep on going round and round *ad infinitum*?

I'm sure I don't know. But it won't. And that is what Rudyard is so mad about. He demands the services of a "specialist."

Desert Refuge 59
(June 1946)

CRESTS of the mountains are veiled in grey banks of smoking cloud. Upon the sheet-iron roof of the little house is the tinny drum of falling rain. Rains hang on late this year, perhaps to make up for their tardy arrival. As the children sit by the window, watching the dim shower squalls chasing each other through the distant miles of lowland creosotes it is hard to realize that yesterday the sky was cloudless; the hot sun beat down with electric life and our four desert tortoises—carefully herded by Victoria—ambled among catsclaw bushes in leisurely search for tasty young filaree leaves.

There is a homely satisfaction in having our queer tortoise pets as members of the household once more. At first glance there would not seem to be much in their gnarled, leathery exteriors to excite affection. But when you come to know them, there is something strangely lovable about these slow-moving inoffensive creatures. They ask so little of life or of attention that, as pets, they are in a class by themselves. We believe the keeping of any kind of pet—if it be a wild creature in captivity—is wrong. But in the case of these tortoises, so long as several are kept together, for company, and they are given water and sufficient range and proper food, it is probable that they do not suffer much by the curtailment of their liberty.

Unfortunately, little as they need, they frequently suffer at the hands of careless or forgetful owners. They need enough range so that they can pick up tidbits and earthy substances which their peculiar organisms demand. They need enough green and dry food. And they need water. It is an illusion among many people that because desert tortoises make their home in arid lands they never drink. They do drink. And quite a lot. After heavy rains they drink eagerly and deeply from puddles. Like the camel they seem to have the ability to store moisture within their bodies and these reserves see them over long dry spells. But tortoises kept in restricted range, should have water

available at all times. Sometimes they will not touch it for long stretches. Then suddenly they will drink thirstily.

Apart from food, water and reasonable range, desert tortoises need little except a cozy place in which to enjoy a long winter sleep. If they have a suitable outside enclosure in which they can dig holes for themselves in a well drained bank they will do their own housing. But even this needs some supervision, as sometimes they are guilty of bad judgment and run tunnels on a level that the flood waters will fill. We gather up our tortoises, when they become drowsy with the approach of their hibernation period, and stow them away in the house, in roomy boxes in which is a layer of warm dry earth. Over them we tuck old blankets or anything which will serve to insulate and protect them, taking care that they have enough air for breathing.

Tortoises in the depth of sleep usually are relaxed—not tightly drawn up in the shell, as many suppose. For this reason they need roomy sleeping boxes, where they have space to stretch their neck and legs. The date of the beginning of hibernation will vary with individuals. Last year Mojave, our largest, began his snooze November 13 and did not wake up until the 27th of March. The other three went to sleep the 6th of November and began to stir again April 3. It is bad for a tortoise to be artificially awakened. So never be impatient. Undoubtedly their long resting periods, deliberate physical movements and extremely placid habits are responsible for the normally long lives which these creatures enjoy. Mankind could read here a valuable lesson. The popular craze of "Faster! Faster!" has certain disagreeable and inevitable results.

* * *

Hummingbirds are on the prowl, seeking good nesting material these days. The whirr of their wings as they hang poised before any wind-weathered tuft of fiber or old cloth or wool which the wind may have hung on post or bush is music in the still, sunny days. The little sprites will grasp drifting threads in their slender beaks and, backing away—under power—endeavor to drag the desired bit loose. Sometimes, when the particular thread is too firmly attached, they will have a long tugging battle. But they are persistent and will not relinquish their desires until thoroughly convinced that it will not come free. Their nests are models of design and camouflage. But, even when you know where to look, you seldom will find an old nest. Other birds, particularly purple finches, have discovered that a discarded hummer's nest is a grand treasure trove of the choicest building materials, and they will carry away every scrap of it to build their own.

We are going to miss our Yaquitepec bird colony this year. We have not put up any nest boxes at our present

Hummingbird

location. Nevertheless, we do have bird lodgers. There are birds building up under the roof. And a trustful little canyon wren has long considered herself owner of the porch. Quail roost nightly in the cottonwoods over the little lake which Rider and Rudyard built. And robins and juncos and flycatchers do pretty much as they like along the paths and in the doorways.

* * *

Uncle Sam has relinquished the gunnery range area which surrounds Ghost Mountain, so Yaquitepec is in no further danger of being liquidated by machine gun slugs. We are free to return home, but we have not yet decided when we will be able to do so. For there are other problems besides that which has been solved by the removal of war activity. For one thing the water situation is not promising. Our cisterns have suffered by our absence. And, since it is impossible to leave the roof run-off connected to the tanks when we are not in residence—because trash and impurities collect in the guttering if it is not kept clean—we have lost most of our seasonal supply of water. There are other things to be done too—little repairs to be made and improvements arranged for. Despite our own frequent visits and the good cooperation of friends, wind and storm have left their traces on the little house. Right now, therefore, we are circulating back and forth between the two places. Meanwhile a whole new set of desert plans are building.

* * *

The Candles of God, as the Mexicans call the blooming flower-stalks of *Yucca whipplei*, lift in glory upon the hillsides. We did not have any of these at Yaquitepec. There evidently was some condition in the Ghost Mountain region which was not suitable to their growth—just as here, neither mescal nor juniper are to be found. These tall, white flower fountains of the Whipple yucca are quite a change from the defiant golden banners of mescals. But they are equally glorious in a different way. It has been interesting, too, to make the acquaintance of this yucca, which has a host of useful qualities all its own. Like the mescal it dies after flowering, in which respect it differs from its relatives the Joshua tree (*Yucca brevifolia*) and the Mojave yucca (*Yucca Mohavensis*). The dead flower shoot of the *whipplei* is stouter and, for primitive purposes, in some ways more useful than that of the mescal. And its leaves are more adaptable for basketry than are those of the Mojave yucca.

But it requires the pressure of enforced close-to-earth existence to reveal all the virtues and properties of natural things.

These warm sunny days when flowers sway to the passing of desert breezes and the air quivers to the drone of bees, butterflies drift past in increasing numbers. The other day Rudyard, lying upon a blanket on a sunny slope and contemplating their wafting flight, was moved to inscribe the following:

THE BUTTERFLY

*A butterfly. A flower floating
in the air. A little spark of
animal life-wave is the butterfly.*

*The wind blows it along, like a
flower cut off its stem.
How innocent a little thing.*

But Rudyard's literary output is not confined to poetic philosophy. Here is another sample, from a jumbled collection of scribblings entitled, "Adventures of Gilbert"—

Gilbert was speeding along in his new car. Suddenly a call of "Stop, you demon!" caught his ear. He slowed down.

A body of armed men stepped out of the bushes. The man at the head rode on a horse. He shouted again: "Stop, you demon!"

Gilbert knew better than to stop. He put the car in high gear and left the body of armed men behind. Presently a shot was fired at his car, but the man who shot missed.

Gilbert drove about half a mile when he sighted his Mexican friend riding on a horse. As he passed him he yelled: "Rebels! Bandits!" and went on.

Gilbert was in Mexico when this occurred.

This highly edifying piece of literature has been set in type by the author who, when the spirit moves him, hunches himself over a type case, somewhere out under the shade of a tree and, composing stick in hand, sets up his copy, scowling fiercely while he selects his type and his spaces and his periods. Someday, when he has enough of these thrillers set up in type, Rudyard plans to "publish" a book. But it goes slowly. Staggering along under the weighty burden of his eight years Rudyard steers a vacillating course between "bloody murder" literature and tender poetry.

*   *   *

The rain that ushered in the morning has stopped. Through the cloud banks that stoop sluggishly away across the desert until their grey bellies mist the piñons on the distant mountain crest, scattered shafts of sunlight strike down upon a wet and fragrant world. Out on the front porch, hanging from a beam that spans two pillars, Rider's sack of drying "coyote melons" (desert gourds) sways back and forth, tracing a blotch of moving, lumpy shadow across the glistening surface of the wet cement floor. Thoroughly dry and with a coat of hard varnish over their decorated or undecorated rinds, these coyote gourds make attractive bits of color about the house.

Time was when gourds—not of the "coyote" variety, but the larger sort—were important items as water containers and carriers. They have been displaced, as have so many other things, by the gadgets of progress. But they have their seasons of mocking laughter still. For when you drop your beautiful crystal glass water jug or bottle it promptly shatters to fragments—whereas the homely gourd merely grins and rolls away intact. Not a matter of much moment, certainly—if you are protected by the shapely arm of civilization. But if you are on the desert in midsummer with no other water available, it may mean much.

It is in this respect that the Apache water bottle of basketwork, calked with desert resin, has the advantage of the haughty canteen. The canteen like so many other "conveniences" is all right so long as you are close to the artificial sources that produced it. But if it springs a leak or gets a hole rusted in it, and you have not the facilities to solder it, you are at its mercy. Your temporary repairs—be they plugs of cloth or of wood—will go out on you when you happen to forget them. ALWAYS at the worst possible time. The primitive old wickerwork water bottle, on the other hand, was light; it would not break easily; if it developed a leak it could be easily repaired by native materials, always at hand.

Desert Refuge 60
(July 1946)

THE DESERT sparkles in the sharp morning light. In the east, where the sun is an hour high above the dim tumble of distant mountains, a thin blue haze veils the lowlands. Against the background of its far mystery the barren buttes that crowd the foreground of our footslope valley stand harsh and savage in the sunglow. The light spills dizzily from the precipices of their titan boulders. In the vast clefts of the rocks are blue caves. Here and there, clinging thirstily in fissures of the age-scorched stone, are sparse shapes of cactus and wiry thorn.

Our little house is muffled in a drowsy silence. The blanket of peace and quiet is made even more complete by the multitude of tiny sounds woven through it—the almost inaudible rustle of cottonwood leaves, the drone of bees, the distant calling of quail, the metallic whir of the wings of an inquisitive hummingbird as he hangs suspended above my head, an occasional murmuring from the far end of the porch where Rider, Rudyard and Victoria are deep in their lessons. All these faint sounds, and a host more, contrive to add to the spell of solitude and silence.

Cottontail rabbits nibble at the grass which grows in the shelter of catsclaw bushes; on the brown ribbon of roadway near the front steps a pair of quail are sauntering about, picking up trifles, and the two desert phoebes, whose mud walled nest up under the porch eaves is almost complete, are chirping and whispering to each other as they fly in with tufts and streamers of nest-lining material—streamers which often are several times as long as themselves. Our whole little desert world seems happy, and it promises to be a good day, even for the gophers. For the big red racer snake who was poking a speculative nose among their earth mounds and tunnel openings last evening became annoyed at Rudyard's scientific interest in his movements and lit off cross-country in a red flash.

The days are warm now—warm with that elusive, satisfying quality which makes desert sunshine superior to that of any other region on earth. Daily the sun gathers strength and the children, who take the tortoises out of their pen for a period of free grazing every afternoon, have taken to carrying an old umbrella so as to provide a movable oasis of shade into which their slow-moving pets can retire for a cool-off any time they feel the need of it. These tortoise herdings are not the joyous occasions that they used to be, up until a few days ago, and the young herders, as they superintend the nibblings and meanderings of General and Doña and Juana Maria, are oftener closer to tears than to smiles. For they cannot forget Mojave. Wherever they go, up the sandy wash or across the slope or among the thin shadows of the catsclaw bushes, Mojave's ghost moves with them—lumbering, lovable, good-humored wraith that plods on and on, dragging a ghostly tether chain—a poignant shadow of memories that blurs in a welling dash of tears.

For Mojave is dead. The largest, most intelligent and most lovable of all our tortoise quartet, he came to a tragic death just a few days ago. It was a Sunday morning and Rider had carried him out of the house, where he had spent the night in his padded box, and tethered him by his long, light chain to his accustomed stake in the garden. It was Mojave's regular stamping ground. He used to graze and nibble and amble all over it, retiring when it got too sunny to the shelter of a big box half dug into a bank of earth. Mojave always had been contented in that location and never had any trouble.

But this day something went wrong. For some reason, contrary to his usual habit, Mojave decided to walk round and round his tether stake. And he did it at close range, so that when he tired of his new trick and wanted to get to his shady box he just couldn't make it. He had wrapped the chain around the stake and it wouldn't pull free.

Imagination is a terrible thing—especially when it is imagination made accurate by previous knowledge of facts and conditions. All of us would give a great deal if we were not able to reconstruct so clearly in our minds our poor old pet's frenzied strainings and pawings and tuggings in his efforts to reach that life-saving shade, just a few inches beyond his reach. Rider was busy with some chores about the house that morning. He did not make his usual frequent trips to see how his pet was getting along. When he did come Mojave was dead. He had been dead maybe an hour—perhaps less, for this was well before noon, and it was not a particularly hot morning.

For a long while the children wouldn't believe that their pet was gone. They soaked him in water. They gave him salt pack applications. But to no avail.

We buried Mojave the next morning, prying out for him a deep hole among the rocks of a sunny slope. The children cushioned his last resting place with piles of green grass and fragrant wildflowers that tucked him in like a blanket. Then we filled in the grave and went away.

* * *

Yesterday we went up the canyon for fuel. Fuel gathering is one of the continual diversions which is fortunately imposed by primitive living. I use the word "fortunately" because it is one of the sad qualities in man that unless he is impelled by necessity he will neglect many things which are vital to his well-being. Nature is a wise mother. She knows this tendency in her children toward those habits of indolence and inactivity which invariably end in degeneration. So, upon those who dwell close to her bosom, she enforces activity. Wild creatures and primitive humans have to keep hustling—have to keep both their wits and their bodies at keen edge by constant exertion. This is a law laid down by Nature which man never yet has succeeded in circumventing. He deludes himself with the idea that he has done so. But Nature

always comes back with the last laugh. And by the use of his every device to escape physical exertion, his whole physical being suffers and degenerates. The automobile, which makes it so much easier to ride than to walk, enfeebles his legs and every organ of his system. His lighting systems—which are so much "easier" than torches or campfires—ruin his eyes.

So the necessity, forced upon us, to collect and carry home fuel is an excellent thing. And though, like all other animate creatures, we sometimes complain of making the effort, we invariably return from these excursions invigorated both in body and mind. For any task or any experience reacts upon us precisely in accordance with the mental attitude we bring to it. I have known people who, upon their first view of the Grand Canyon, have declared that they would not give 15 cents for the whole region (and perhaps, to them, their valuation was correct). On the other hand, there have been many individuals who have gained for themselves both ennoblement of soul and imperishable fame while languishing in a prison cell. "Disadvantages" nearly always are stepping-stones to greater development, if we have the wit to appreciate them. It is the "advantages" which are deadly.

Fuel changes with location. And the materials which we feed to our fires are different here from those which we packed home over the rocks of Ghost Mountain. There our reliance was upon the dry butts of dead mescal plants and upon the dead wood of gnarled, windblown junipers. Here we have neither of these but in their place a variety of wood, sticks and stumps which range from the smoky, swift-burning stems of dead buckwheat bushes to the hard, long lasting wood of the desert mesquite. There is not much of the mesquite, however. For the clump of trees from which we gather it is small. The mesquite which is in many ways a wonder tree has been ruthlessly destroyed by the white man so that now, to cut down a living tree, is nothing short of a crime.

There are other growths, however, which contribute to the baskets and bundles of fuel which we carry home

Quail

upon our shoulders. There are the stumps and dry branches of the wild apricot, the wood of dead sumac, the tall dry stems of the Whipple yucca. All of this makes good burning. Often though, it is with great reluctance that we consign big chunks of naturally seasoned wild apricot to the flames. Some of this wood is so beautifully grained and colored it seems especially intended for the fashioning of artistic trifles. One cannot however save every stick of firewood for "art" work. And besides our time for such occupation is limited. Many of the desert growths produce beautiful wood. It is small in size, but it well repays carving or polishing. It isn't necessary to destroy living growths to obtain specimens. The very best pieces are those that have died naturally and seasoned on the tree or bush. The dead flower stalks of the Whipple yucca have little staying power as fuel, being somewhat like the twisted straw and grass which the early pioneers had to burn on the plains. But they do give an intense quick heat while they last. These tall dead stalks, whether erect or blown down by winds, are popular as dwelling places with various little desert creatures, who take advantage of the hard outer surface and soft, easily gnawed interior, to construct themselves cosy homes. One particularly big stalk with a huge base bulb which we carried home proved, on being broken up, to contain a mouse dwelling, neatly and cunningly constructed in the hollowed-out interior of the butt and reached by a long passage down the inside of the stem. A couple of startled mice scampered from their ruined domicile as the trunk split under our axe blows. Since this incident we carefully examine every yucca stalk before bringing it home. Our little desert brothers have to work too hard on their house building to have their homes unnecessarily destroyed.

Thus it is that fuel gathering always adds to our desert knowledge, besides contributing to our well being through healthy physical exercise. Yesterday we saw a deer flitting like a shadow through the underbrush of the canyon, and Rider came home with a collection of gay new flower blooms as well as his wood load. In addition we brought back with us pleasant recollections of a meeting with a friendly racer snake; a pause to examine a contented little horned toad [horned lizard], lazily sunning himself upon a boulder; and the discovery of a broken Indian metate at the edge of the mesquite clump.

There was a mysterious scratching and tapping in the house when we came back and opened the door and it took us some time to determine that the strange noise came from the stovepipe. This, on being disconnected, released a panting and startled crested flycatcher which, after a brief rest on the corner of the table to get its breath, flew gratefully through the door to freedom. The bird must have been making venturesome exploration of the stovepipe opening on the crest of the roof, and, having gone too far down, was unable to use its wings to fly out. Thus it had slipped and fluttered down the long stove pipe to the stove damper. Fortunately the stove and pipe were quite cold.

* * *

The palo verde tree glistens with the sheen of new green leaves and tiny globes of forming flower buds. Before this is printed it will be a glory of yellow blossoms, a brilliance of color responsible for the poetic name of *lluvia de oro*, which is Spanish for "shower of gold." And a shower of gold it truly is when in full flower. The beans too, which follow the flowers, are good to eat, either boiled while green or pounded into a meal after maturity.

Last summer an industrious mouse stored a huge quantity of these beans under the safety of an old overturned deep graniteware pie dish that lay beneath the tree. It was a granary to which the owner made periodic trips for food, obtaining access each time by digging down under the edge of the dish and afterwards plugging up the tunnel with earth. A canny packrat, at the same time, brought a pint of the carefully cleaned beans into the house. These he stored in one of our small pottery jugs that was standing on an open shelf. He brought in beans enough to completely fill the jug. Afterwards, bit by bit, as he needed them, they disappeared.

* * *

It is afternoon. Cactus flowers flame upon the rocky ridges and across the grey line of the buckwheat bushes the sides of a close-crowding mountain shimmer hotly in a blur of thin brush and glaring rock. Flattened, alert, upon sunny stones bright eyed lizards watch for unwary flies. And upon a blanket in the cool shadow of the house wall, Victoria picks her way carefully through a little book entitled *The Dancing Goat*. Beside her Rudyard plows steadily through a story in the *Saturday Evening Post*. The regular afternoon reading session is in full swing.

And so, fulfilling its promise of the morning, another desert day draws, in peace, to its close. There are some who will try to tell you that life is grim and earnest and a most serious matter. Do not believe them. Life, whether in sunshine or in passing shower, is a glad song of Eternity, sung to the music of the spheres. All that matters is how you accept it. For, like a mirror, it will return to you in full measure just what you give it—either in scowls or in smiles.

Desert Refuge 61
(August 1946)

THE DESERT wind comes rustling up the wash and the shadows of the swaying junipers are cool. The morning sun is an hour high above the summit of Ghost Mountain and the huge storm-scarred granite boulders that rim its crest are already arrayed in harsh contrasts of glare and shadow against the blue background of the sky. From where I sit, among the yuccas and junipers at the foot of the precipitous ascent, those boulders look a long way up, and the knowledge that every pound of the jumbled collection of household possessions that surrounds me has to be shoulder-packed up the steep trail and beyond that frowning rampart does not make them seem closer. There are times when Ghost Mountain does appear savagely high.

But there is no help for it. For, like the mail, which we are told always "must go through," all these possessions and "household gods" of Yaquitepec must go up. And there is no other way but to carry them.

For the exile is over. We are once more upon our own *tierra*. Had circumstances been just right this might have been accomplished some weeks earlier. But there were difficulties, chiefly those of water, which had to be ironed out first and these occasioned some delay. Yesterday, however, Uncle Sam's highly efficient Navy, having been given the "all clear" sign, swooped down upon our temporary abode with two huge trucks and a detachment of eager Navy men who whisked up our chattels and charged them thunderously back across the abandoned gunnery range to the very foot of Ghost Mountain.

Our return to our old haunts was not lacking in certain elements of the melodramatic. For as the truck column, accompanied by a grey vicious-looking little tractor and various other cars came winding and crashing in through the narrow yucca-bordered road, it had all the earmarks of an invading task force. There were cameras, including movie cameras, lined up by a group of friends who had assembled in the desert to welcome us home. Never since the first coming of the Spaniards had there been such excitement in the Ghost Mountain country. The jackrabbits promptly lit out for distant parts. The roadrunners fluttered and fled. The chipmunks took to their deepest

Jackrabbit

holes and even the lizards had urgent business elsewhere. Such a riot and hubbub. It was a vastly different arrival from the day, now over 15 years ago, when we had driven a weary, limping old Ford into the shelter of a clump of junipers and had set out to climb an unknown mountain, carrying as our burdens a can of pineapple and an axe. It was true that the axe—the selfsame axe—did come back this time with us again. And also, by strange coincidence, there came a can of pineapple—for one of our good friends, coming out to welcome us home, had brought it as a gift. But for the rest, things were very different.

There might have been even more excitement to our homecoming, if naval plans had materialized. For, by inspiration, and at much trouble, they had sent along the vicious-looking little war-dog tractor, aforesaid. It was the idea that the "cat" would romp up our mountain dragging behind it a sled upon which our effects were to be piled. This plan however never got beyond the theoretical stage. For, while a war "cat" can go almost any place on any normal mountain, the slopes of Ghost Mountain more than qualify up to Sherman's famous remark about war. They have deceptive stretches on them—that look very nice from the bottom. And then they switch off into picturesque bumps and ridges that are—well, just what Sherman said. Nothing but a thoroughly organized military force, equipped with bulldozers, high explosives and all the men and machinery of difficult roadmaking could break a path to the summit.

So the idea of tractoring our possessions up to the little house that stands upon the crest was abandoned.

Not without some slight friction and bitterness. For the "master of ceremonies" was very anxious to try his tractor—which he had provided, at some trouble, for the occasion. He professed solicitude for the Navy boys—fearing that some of them might physically collapse, from sunstroke or other causes if they were subjected to the strain of carrying our goods up the hill. The tractor, even if it succeeded in getting only part way up, was in his opinion the only way out.

So, as he was so determined and as I was equally determined not to have the vegetation of the lower slopes of Ghost Mountain scarred and destroyed by ineffectual tractor flounderings—to say nothing of having the "cat" driver exposed to the very real danger of having his machine roll down the mountain on top of him—the whole affair ended in deadlock. The jackrabbits and other denizens were robbed of a violently exciting exhibition of tractor crashings. And the Navy boys—who were not themselves worrying about "sunstrokes"—were disappointed in not being able to get up to see Yaquitepec. They were a fine bunch of young men whom it was a pleasure to meet. They would have galloped up the hill with at least the major part of our possessions and treated it as an adventure. We want to express to all of them who made up the work party— petty officers, truck drivers, supervisors and men—our deep appreciation and thanks. Had it not been for the unfortunate tractor fiasco, the move back home to Yaquitepec would have been one grand adventure.

So the trucks rolled away and the "captains and the kings" departed. And the disgruntled tractor betook itself off and left us and our effects at the foot of the mountain. At least we were mighty glad to get this far back. The stuff will go up. The three youngsters and our two selves will handle it. Fortunately there is no one to worry about our "sunstrokes" or our chances of physical collapse. Anyhow exercise never did harm anyone very much, provided they are sensible about it.

However, when the Navy had sailed away, we wasted little time in contemplation of our jumbled pile of goods. The day was still young, and was not this a gay occasion of rejoicing? Had not a bunch of loyal, dear friends journeyed far out into the desert to welcome us home with their good words, their recording cameras and their kindly gifts? What is life made for if not for joy and friendship? So away we all went, welcoming committee and all, up the trail to the summit of Ghost Mountain.

It was an enjoyable climb. The day was warm, but not too warm. And the wind that came in from the westward across the crests of the distant mountains brought the faint tang of the distant sea with it. Mescals were blooming, tossing their great fountains of yellow flowers against the sparkle of the sky. The aromatic scent of junipers was in the air and below us, as we went up, the whole wide sweep of the desert and its outcropping of sere mountains and rocky buttes seemed to unroll like a vast, silent map. Away off, beyond a stretch of gray-green creosotes, a pillar of red dust, marching across the dun surface of a dry lake, marked the fading retreat of the great vehicles of war that had brought no sound. The desert was utterly quiet.

Storm and neglect had wrought damages to the little house during our long absence. But already it seemed to be waking from its doze of waiting. The windows, which Tanya had cleaned on a hasty previous visit, winked a cheerful welcome to us. And the white gravel, still neat and orderly with the marks of Rudyard's raking, on the same occasion, seemed waiting to be patterned by eager young footsteps. Purple finches, contentedly rearing their broods in our weathered bird houses, winged off

to vantage points on house beams and nearby ocotillos and watched our arrival with bright-eyed confidence. The old black scaly lizard whose usual station is upon a warm boulder just above the clump of beaver-tail cactus, roused himself from his sunning just long enough to peer at us curiously, then subsided again into drowsy content. Away off to the eastward, where the phantom shadows of the old sea still fill the dry gulfs and lagoons of the weird badlands with a ghostly simulation of blue water, the mountains and thirsty buttes slept in an elusive haze of pink and purple. Silence and utter peace.

There was to be still another happy note to our homecoming. For when we had come down the mountain again to see our house-warming party of friends off to their homes, we found an efficient-looking jeep parked beside the other cars and we met Dan Taylor of Imperial who, as an official part of our home-bringing, had come up across the long, thirsty Carrizo trail to see that all arrangements went off smoothly. But he had been delayed, rendering assistance to a party trapped in the sand along the route, so he had been unable to reach Ghost Mountain until after the moving detail had departed. It was our first meeting with Mr. Taylor. But it might have been the ten-thousand-and-first. For there are some people whom you know at first sight. They speak your language. We fell upon each other as old-timers. We knew, it seemed, the same people. We had roved the same sections of the desert. We shared the same ideas. It wasn't a dry "official" meeting. It was a reunion. Such things happen sometimes when you meet *real* human beings. They are meetings to be remembered.

So the day ended on a high note of happiness and deep appreciation. Deep appreciation for that most precious thing—friendship. For in all life there is no treasure which anyone can collect that can compare with friends. Gold and silver and precious gems are baubles—bits of metal and—glass on the order of the useless trinkets that jackdaws and packrats hoard. And paper money is an illusion founded on the fickle faith of governments. But friendship is something woven of the same substance as mercy and love and kindness and the glory of the Great Spirit. It is something which strengthens and sustains the soul. It is like a draught of fresh, cool water come upon suddenly amidst the burning sands of a weary desert. Friends! No one can measure real "wealth" by any other standard.

And thus we were thinking as, with full hearts, we climbed back along the trail that led to the summit of Ghost Mountain. We were thinking of Mr. and Mrs. Hatheway (who in their collection of home-welcoming gifts had included that oddly symbolic can of pineapple) and we were thinking of Mrs. Alice Blanc who, with them, had made photographic records of our homecoming. We were thinking of Mrs. Myrtle Botts who, no matter how her many duties pressed her, has never been too busy, over a long period of years, to give help to the many friends we have referred to her for directions as to how to reach Yaquitepec. We were thinking of Mr. Phillips and of Mr. Taylor and of "Chuck" Holtzer, and of the many, many others, near and far, whose very names alone would make a list much too long for the pages of *Desert*. We were thinking of Ad. [Adeline] and Bill Mushet, of the picturesque Banner Queen Rancho, with whom it has been our privilege to sit around many a campfire beneath the desert stars. And we were thinking too of Lena and Everett Campbell, of Vallecito, in whose hearts burns undimmed the spirit of the Old West, and whose hands were quick to reach out and provide us with a haven of refuge when the Navy evicted us from Ghost Mountain. Of all these good friends and many more we were thinking as we slowly climbed the old trail and watched the pink flush of sunset touch the giant rocks that stand guard over Yaquitepec.

The sun is drifting down in the sky and the leaves of the old juniper, beneath whose low-crowding branches I have wedged my improvised typewriter table, are making shadow patterns on the paper. Reading back over what I have written it seems to me that this month's record is rather a personal one. But after all it is events and personalities that count. And this homecoming is a vital thing in which one's own feelings and the friendship, help and personalities of others are all inextricably bound together. So you can't write about it with dry formality. Sometimes I think that this would be a better world to live in if there were a lot less formality and convention and set forms and rules, and we all realized and acted as though we were all human beings together and could see ourselves as we actually are—all interdependent. All part of one great plan—as much connected together and part of each other as are the individual atoms in a pail of water. It's only when you pry them apart and separate them into diverse drops that you spoil the harmony.

I can hear voices coming down the trail. My industrious family—while I have been sitting here at the foot of the mountain—among the piled clutter of boxes, packages and bundles—have been making trip after trip, packing the most necessary articles up hill to the house. The typewriters are still down here, so as it was easier to bring myself down to the typewriter than to bring the typewriter up to the mountaintop, I have written this month's article in the "lowlands." But next month's ought to have the tang of the clouds in it, as my writing machines will be "topside" by then.

Desert Refuge 62
(September 1946)

THE WILDERNESS of tumbled boulders, which is the summit of Ghost Mountain, gleams in the sun. The desert is utterly still. Not even one of the vagrant little winds which are almost constantly tip-toeing amidst the mescals and the junipers is stirring. The ramada casts a rectangle of shade which is as sharp as though it were a section of black paper, cut out and laid upon the white quartz gravel. In its cool shadow Rudyard and Victoria squat like little Indian statues, watching the three desert tortoises who are gathered, heads almost touching, about a bit of green upon which they are eagerly munching. This is, for the tortoises, a great occasion. For they are feasting upon lettuce—something which is as dear to their leathery hearts as the most exotic dish would be to an epicure. They do not often get it. But yesterday I went in to town for supplies and, under orders from Rider, who spends a good deal of his savings in buying tidbits for his queer pets, brought out a supply of lettuce sufficient to last them for some days. Our tortoises are, alas, softening under the influence of—to them—civilization. When we first adopted them they would not even look at such things as melon rinds, cabbage leaves or even lettuce. They preferred to munch hardy desert fare like rattlesnake weed, galleta grass, bunch grass and the tasty twigs of dry and spiny bushes. But the system-weakening insidiousness of easy living has left its mark upon them…as it does upon everyone. Shame to relate they lately have been seen contentedly eating corn meal mush, apple parings, bread and many other trimmings from the outskirts of "Progress." Then they discovered lettuce. And, like the Indian with alcohol, it has gone to their heads. They have no resistance. Lettuce days are the days when all other food is absolutely ignored.

Well, I suppose they are entitled to some pleasures in life. A desert tortoise has few dissipations and does not even seem to get any thrill out of politics or shivers about atomic bombs. They have been terribly spoiled since Mojave died. For Rider was so heartbroken at the tragic fate of the big tortoise that he fusses and worries constantly over the remaining three. On very hot days they get damped down at regular intervals with precious water. And on chilly or stormy nights they are carried tenderly to comfortable quarters within the house. All these attentions, however, Rider feels were amply repaid the other day when Juana Maria Better Than Nothing contributed two very fine eggs to the tortoise establishment.

This was a momentous occasion and one that was not lightly come by. For Juana Maria spent a long while making up her mind—and changed it many times after making it up. She spent several days digging trial nests, all of which, after almost deciding, she discarded. Finally, while out on the flat before the house, during one of the periods when she and the others were being herded on pasture, she found the ideal spot beneath a goatnut bush. Here she excavated a little pit approximately eight inches deep and deposited therein two pinkish white eggs about the size of large bantam eggs. This done she carefully filled in the pit and spent a lot of time making an artful camouflage of the spot where it had been dug. When her labors were completed all the earth, dry twigs and fallen leaves had been replaced so expertly that it was absolutely impossible to see that they had ever been disturbed. Then, contentedly, well satisfied that she had done a good job, Juana Maria ambled off to rejoin her companions—and Rider, Rudyard and Victoria, who had watched the proceedings with breathless interest, carefully dug up the precious eggs and installed them safely in a screen-covered box of earth to hatch. When—and if—the tiny tortoises emerge to the light of day they can count on a hearty and affectionate welcome.

* * *

We are still far from settled. In fact it often seems that we have not yet even begun to start our settling. Almost all of our possessions still are scattered over the landscape, sketchily housed against possible thundershowers by scraps of canvas, old roofing iron, tar paper and anything which might serve to turn storm water. Many of them are uncovered, for there is not enough cover material to go around. Still, bit by bit, they are going up the mountain. It promises to be a long task. And, while it lasts, many other activities have to be suspended. Mail is backing up, unanswered, into a pile of terrifying proportions. We hope our good friends understand.

Meanwhile we are excavating for a dugout that may serve as a temporary storage place for some of the more spoilable things. The boys are working on this with a will. A short time ago they were thrilled by thinking they had struck water. Their picks and shovels broke through into a pocket of very damp sand, between banks of soft limestone rock. "Water!" shouted Rudyard. "Look, we must be close to water! A spring!" And the shovels flew and the sand flew.

But the wet sand petered out and the gritty limestone grinned thirstily under the desert sun. The boys were disappointed, but not entirely discouraged. There might be water nearby, or deeper, they argue. And this hope lends energy and a fascination to the digging.

Nest of a desert sparrow in a low Bigelow cholla cactus growing among desert agaves, or mescals. Watercolor by Marshal South.

* * *

Day before yesterday they passed another definite desert milestone by their introduction to dynamite—an intriguing compound which they never previously had seen. It was a fascinating experience to them to drill the hole, spoon out the rock dust, cut the fuse and crimp on the cap. The business of cutting a stick of Giant Powder in half (we have to use very light charges because of nearness to many breakable objects) and adjusting cap and fuse to it and tamping it down likewise was thrilling. When the little blast went off and scattered a rain of falling gravel over the juniper tree behind which we had taken shelter their satisfaction was complete.

One bit of practical demonstration is worth years of theory. They never had seen Giant Powder used before. Yet when the gravel had ceased pattering they scurried back to the hole and like old miners criticized the way the shot had been handled. It had been wrongly placed—of course. The hole should have been drilled so—and so. It should have been better tamped. And the fuse could, with advantage, have been just a bit shorter—or longer. Anyway they were one more lap along the desert trail and a new page of knowledge has been opened.

* * *

The season on Ghost Mountain is late this year. When we came back the purple finches still were fussing with their broods. And a short time after our return we were astonished to see a crested flycatcher carrying nest material into the little red roofed cement bird house that stands among the junipers down in front of the house. This is much later than usual for the flycatchers who, in the section we moved from, were already well in the midst of their home-making season. There are cactus wrens, too, that are equally busy. A cactus wren usually prefers a nice bristling Silver Cholla to nest in. But they are not too particular. Down at the mountain foot, close to our temporary camp, there is one that is working hard to complete an elaborate nest that is perched among the bayonet leaves of a tall yucca. The cactus wren, however, like some of the other wrens, has a tendency towards making play houses and sleeping nests. Birds and animals, in this respect, are much like humans. They play and enjoy themselves by doing apparently aimless and silly things. And each creature is just a little different from its fellows. It has been said that "The proper study of mankind is man." But that should be amended a little. The proper study of mankind is all of animate—and inanimate creation. One cannot understand man without observing and studying also the animals and birds and insects. And one cannot understand birds animals or insects properly unless he first understands something of the reactions of the human family. The whole of creation is one great brotherhood—all beads upon the one string.

It has been said also that "One touch of Nature makes the whole world kin." And this also is true. For it is the fundamentals which establish brotherhood and understanding. Somehow this is particularly noticeable in the appeal of the desert. The desert is fundamental. It is like the ocean in this respect. But the desert is more accessible. There is, deep within the heart of every human being, a yearning to get back to the peace of the Infinite which is found only in a close association with nature. It is the call of silence. Of the peace of wide stretching, uninhabited land. The call of the wind, of the stars and the glowing sun of the solitudes. That is why the desert appeals. It holds within its heart the balm which a tired, civilization harassed, humanity craves. So it is not astonishing that more and more people turn to the desert. It is a turning toward "home."

And from all parts they come. And from far places. Thus came Jade to Yaquitepec. Jade is a gemstone of mystery. Subtle. Full of strange lights and shadows. Revered of Chinese Emperors and the joy of a long line of skilled craftsmen and fashioners whose shadowy ranks stretch back and back beyond the lost horizons of forgotten time.

But the Jade who came drifting mysteriously through the creosotes of the desert was not a cold stone. We never had seen her before, and her car came unheralded and almost silently from between the junipers and the yuccas. Yet when the door swung open and she sprang lightly out with glad words of greeting and introduction she was one of the family. There are some people whom you know at first glance. You have known them a lifetime—have known them for many lifetimes. And there are others whom you will never get to know—not even if you live side by side with them for a lifetime; for many lifetimes.

Jade is an interpretive dancer. She was a lithe flame in the sun and she moved between the cactus and the crowding mescals as pliantly and as surely as the desert wind. The footlights of many countries have seen Jade turn the bodily grace of the dance into sheer poetry. But she came back to the desert. "I love it," she said "I've always loved it. And I'd heard of you and your mountain. And I knew we'd be friends. I just had to come."

We spent a long, happy day talking to Jade. She climbed the mountain—barefoot to get the thrill of the earth. And she sat under our ramada and gazed off into the dim distances where the haze and the heat devils weave mystery across the lowlands. She told us of far places, and—what was more important—of deep dreams and longings. "I was in Panama," she said—and as she told of it you could see the Isthmus in all its characteristic glare of patterned color and tropic heat—"and so many times I would shut my eyes and see again the picture of just one bit of desert up here that I knew. It was as though I were standing there—watching the sunrise touch the ridges; watching the silver of the moon upon the lonely buttes. And I wanted again the peace of it all. I just had to come back."

Jade went away with the sunset. She had far to go and a heavy list of appointments. But she will be back. They all come back. The desert calls them. It is tired children, weary of noise and foolish gaming, who turn homeward in the quiet dusk towards Peace and Mother.

* * *

It has not rained so far, though the possibility of thundershowers keeps us ever on the alert for the safety of our unprotected goods. We need rain, though. Precious water ran to waste last season because we were not here to attend to the cleaning of the eaves gutters. You cannot be too careful in the collection of cistern water. Any trash or impurities which may find their way into the tanks speedily renders the water unfit to drink. For this reason, unless we are at home, the catchment system usually is disconnected. So our reserve supply is of the slenderest and water hauling is a regular order of the day. We bring it to the foot of the mountain and store it in barrels, carefully covered against ants and bees. Then each day the "water gang"—which consists of the whole household—descends the rocky foot-trail and loads up on the precious fluid, each, from the youngest to the oldest, carrying his (or her) capacity in filled water jars or canteens. It is a procession and a pilgrimage. But it is easier than it used to be in the old days when there were but two of us to do the carrying. How like the Pueblos and their burdens of filled water ollas we become. But is it strange? Like conditions will produce like results, customs and actions. After all we all are products of the land. And thought, and morals, and behavior are but products of geography.

While we were away the Yaquitepec packrats which previously had been extraordinarily well behaved, developed new—albeit quite normal—lines of thought. They went "packrattish" in a big way and carried spikes and nails and bolts all around the interior of the empty house. Taking them from their rightful places and building of them platforms and pyramids—and just plain junk heaps—in other places. The effect was good, in the main. But we heartlessly levelled these edifices. Even with all due consideration to one's fellow house tenants one does have to have a little free space and some rights.

And, did you ask if our three sun-tanned youngsters are shedding any tears over the flowing rivulet of water which they left behind them when they moved back to Ghost Mountain? Not a bit of it! That is over and passed. They had it—and they enjoyed it. Now they are back home. And home is home, whether the water bubbles from a sparkling spring in uncounted hundreds of gallons, or comes laboriously up a scorching rock trail in two quart lots. Perhaps they, with their desert upbringing, have acquired something of the dry-land natures of the desert lizards and the cheerful little horned toads [horned lizards].

Desert Refuge 63
(October 1946)

*A*SILENCE holds the desert. It weighs down upon the tops of the mountains, and in the sharp sunlight, the thin dark shadows of the tall mescal poles seem to lie across it like bars of steel. Far off the tawny flanks of the buttes are pencilled with scribblings of white where the outcroppings of quartz and granite reefs shimmer in the heat. There are a few bees exploring hopefully in the illusion that they may find a leak in the tightly covered water barrel. In the tremendous hush their tiny murmurings are suggestive of querulous humanity, shouting its puny complaints amidst the awful silence of God.

Few individuals understand the tangible quality of silence, for silence has been all but banished from the modern world. In its place has come a muffled medley of ten thousand jarring undertones which beat so ceaselessly upon dulled nerves that they are accepted as quietude. "Ah, how silent," says the confirmed city-dweller. But the thing which he refers to is not silence. It merely is the muted mutterings of unceasing noise.

For silence is a real thing, a fundamental and a healing thing. I have had long-time denizens of civilization come out and stand upon the bald, wind-polished boulders of my mountaintop and complain that the desert silence hurt their ears; that it made them ring and pain with the very intensity of it. It frightened them. They were in somewhat the same case as a diver coming up into outer air from the previous pressure of ocean depths. They felt as though they were going to fly apart. Their long crushed-in nerves had nothing to lean against. The primeval silence of the desert made them suddenly afraid.

I have known the feeling and I can sympathize. Particularly do I remember one occasion, many years ago, when I had to go from Douglas, Arizona, down into Sonora, Mexico. Douglas is not a noisy place. And in those years, despite the presence at that time of a considerable military encampment, due to border unrest, we always looked upon it as a quiet little city.

But we soon were to find that the Douglas silence was of the synthetic variety. For as my companion and I drifted down into Sonora—first on the railroad to Nacozari, then in a weird and rickety old Ford—the desert rose up and wrapped its cloak around us. We did not notice it so much at Nacozari, for there the pulse of a mining town, even though beating in the leisurely harmony which belongs to all things Mexican, served somewhat to hold back the hush. But when we had left Nacozari behind us and had begun to bump and jounce south in our flivver along dusty Sonora trails, the thing really took hold of us and we began to understand how badly our ears had been abused.

The first night out of Nacozari we slept at Moctezuma. Moctezuma is—or was, in those days—one of the little dream towns of sunshine and shadows and crumbling 'dobe walls and drowsy burros which are the particular jewels of the Mexican desert. If you will trace down on the map you will find it marked below Cumpas. Moctezuma is no boom town or recent village. There is an old church there which lays claim to almost four centuries of service. Its facade is elaborately carved and the carvings are deeply scored by time. The great church doors are studded with huge iron bosses, and behind them the hushed shadowy interior of the great building is filled with peace—and ghosts.

And SILENCE. For in Moctezuma we really made the acquaintance of silence. Most Mexican desert towns are silent. But Moctezuma was super-silent. For it was dead. Revolution had killed it. War had closed all the surrounding mines and ruined the adjacent ranches. Political revenge had pitted its walls with the bullets of firing squads. The few inhabitants who remained moved slowly, their feet making no sound in the dust. When they spoke their voices were hushed. In the silence of the desert Moctezuma lay wrapped in the greater silence of death.

That night after supper—a silent meal served in the silence of a great room of a great house that had been looted and despoiled and had sunk into the silence of despair—my friend and I sat upon a silent, crumbling balcony where, through holes in the rotting floor boards we could look down into the blackness of a silent, deserted street. In the silence our locally made cigarettes of home-grown tobacco, that had been sold to us by a silent Mexican in a silent store, winked lonely points of fire against the massive adobe walls that backed us. Together, our chairs braced gingerly to avoid crashing through the mouldering floor boards, we sat without speaking, watching the moon come up behind a weird range of ragged hills. Its silver touched the dome of the old church and woke it to a poignant, phantom beauty. The long, silver rays fell into the black caverns of empty streets and filled them with gibbering ghosts. Somewhere, a block away, a starving burro was nosing about in the shadows, seeking for some shreds of dry corn leaves. In the awful stillness the sound of its snuffing and munching was like the rustling of age-bleached bones.

SILENCE! That night when we went to sleep we both had terrible nightmares. Yes, silence, when you are unaccustomed to it, can be a very real and painful thing. Sometimes it gets up and hits you right between the eyes.

* * *

Rains march around us these days. "Around" is the right word. For, with the exception of one light shower, from which we collected possibly 15 gallons of water, the rainfall upon Ghost Mountain this summer has consisted of a thin scattering of drops not sufficient to lay the dust. But sometimes as close as a mile-and-a-half away the thundershowers have dumped literally tons of water. From our thirsty cliffs, we have watched the marching curtains of steely-gray rain blotting in a watery spume over buttes and badlands, filling dry lakes and hurling muddy torrents down blistered washes. But the circling storms have not touched Yaquitepec.

There are few things more spectacular and impressive than a thunderstorm in the desert. Thunderstorms in mid-ocean—especially if seen from a small boat—are awe inspiring. But they lack the weird element of suggestive mystery which only a desert setting of harsh, fantastic mountains and dim, lonely leagues of greasewood and yucca, can give. Somehow these tremendous manifestations of Nature's power—of piled, terrific cloud; of eye-blinding electric flares, ripping the sky from zenith to horizon—convey more than anything else a sense of man's insignificance. The all-blotting thunder is the voice of God; the smoking onrush of the charging rain is the irresistible advance of the armies of the Last Judgment. No one who dwells in desert solitudes and watches the yearly marching and counter-marching of these great electric storms, ever would doubt the existence of a Great Spirit. No humble savage of the wastelands or the mountains ever has such doubts.

We have had several lightning-started fires this summer. None of them has been serious. The most alarming one—quite close to the base of Ghost Mountain—was squelched by a combined attack, with shovels and axes, by the Yaquitepec household, reinforced by a nervy and efficient young lady guest who happened to be visiting us. It was only a small blaze. The lightning had slashed into a dry juniper and a bed of dead, tindery mescal, but until it was put out, it occasioned plenty of apprehension. The wind happened to be just right to bring the blaze, once it had taken hold, right up the slopes of Ghost Mountain. There are some who think that the desert will not burn. But we have seen too many of these racing, wind-driven conflagrations to have any such comforting illusions.

* * *

Yaquitepec has a door bell now. The blame is Rudyard's. He dabbles in most things, including electricity. And the brilliant idea that the house was incomplete without a push-button by the door was his alone. It is somewhat of a shock. You come out of the silence, in the midst of nowhere, and there, on the desert-scorched planking—as incongruous as an alarm clock ticking on the tomb of Eternal Silence—is the nice shiny push button. Who uses it? Who can use it—here? Well, Señor Rudyard uses It. He rings himself in and he rings himself out. The tinny clatter of the little bell wakes the doze of the shadows away back in the house. And Rudyard is mightily content. For the rest, the bell provides some entertainment for the two pet mice who stir from their drowsing and stare curiously at the clattering, vibrant thing. They seem to think that the bell was installed especially for their pleasure.

They are a source of a great deal of fun, those mice. They are not natives of Ghost Mountain. They are from away over by the little house near the bubbling spring. Just prior to our recent return, after Ghost Mountain was declared no longer part of a navy gunnery range, Rider found them, crouching and shivering beneath an old sack on the porch. They obviously were orphan babies and the three children promptly adopted them and set about saving their lives. Not any too hopefully. For this was the second "adoption." The first had been a case of three baby packrats, whose mother had succumbed to an argument with a snake. But the packrat babies were too young. In spite of loving care and ministrations of milk by means of a medicine dropper, they all departed for a happier sphere. Victoria opined that these two mice would "up and die" too. But she was mistaken.

They lived and throve. Soon they were chasing each other in high spirits round and round their tiny cage. Soon after we returned to Ghost Mountain they outgrew it, and Rider toiled mightily fashioning another—with all the improvements. It has a ladder and a feeding platform and a swing and an attached bedroom. Also a teeter-totter—this last the contribution of Rudyard.

The mice really have great times. There has been no attempt to teach them tricks. But they have developed a surprising variety of tricks and games of their own. One of the most spectacular of these is the "back handspring." They will take a short run along the surface of their feed platform, then throw themselves upward and back, just touching the top and far side of the cage in their dizzy circuit, exactly like an aviator looping the loop in a plane. Over and over. They are so fast and expert that it makes one dizzy to watch them. Yaquitepec does not go in for pets much. Here, with freedom all about, there is a deep-rooted family antipathy towards depriving anything of its liberty. But the two orphan mice are an exception. They obviously are not having a bad time.

So, for the present, what with mice and tortoises and electric door bells, Yaquitepec rocks along in contented fashion. And—oh yes—the stamp collection. I had almost forgotten that we had a stamp fanatic in the family. Where he became infected with the germ I do not know. But Rider has caught the disease badly. Stamps! Stamps! The jargon about special issues, about perforations and whatnot. Being of a dull and unimaginative mind, I frequently suggest that the stamps might be used, if carefully pasted together, to paper the walls. But Rider snorts. He is going to search the four corners of the globe—and of the U.S.A. His is going to be the finest, most complete collection of stamps that ever was. "Why, don't you know how valuable stamps are? Now once there was a collector who...." But what's the use. Anyway he's getting a lot of pleasure out of it.

* * *

There is a beautiful, metallic-looking little rock python tucked up in a crevice under a rock on the terrace by the house. All the youngsters are up examining it and trying to reach in gentle fingers to stroke its satiny scales. These little harmless snakes are beautiful, and as gentle as they are pretty. There is not the faintest suggestion of anything sinister about them. And it is hard to see how even a person who dislikes snakes could fail to be captivated by their inoffensive grace and good nature. But, with the snake subject—as in most other things in life—ignorance is the chief cause for hostility.

Desert Refuge 64
(November 1946)

THE AMERICAN desert is a big place and its dim mystery-haunted leagues sometimes seem limitless. Yet it is astonishing how closely knit and interwoven its affairs are. In this respect it is like Africa which, especially in its more primitive sections is so crossed and crisscrossed with native grapevine lines of gossip and communication that the hasty, ill advised words which you thought you said in confidence and secrecy at one end of the country are likely to rise up and shout at you—with many colorful additions—at the continent's other extremity. You can't get away with anything—not for long anyway.

And you can't, indefinitely, get away with anything in the desert. Even burros can't. And burros can be awfully foxy sometimes.

These reflections are the result of a letter which came to me the other day from Mrs. C.L. Wood of Long Beach, California. As I slit it open out fell two photographs which caused me to sit up suddenly. For there, looking up at me from the table top, were the unmistakable, long-earned countenances of our old-time pets and faithful burden bearers Rhett and Scarlett.

There wasn't any mistake. You could pick out the disarmingly innocent appearing faces of those two desert nomads from among a million others at first glance. But what startled me was that they were in unfamiliar surroundings. They appeared to be in the possession of other owners. There was a suggestion of strangeness and mystery about the whole matter. Eagerly I turned to the letter.

And there was the whole story. The good old desert "intelligence system" finally opened a dark chapter of mystery in the lives of Rhett and Scarlett.

For you may remember that there always has been a mystery around Rhett and Scarlett. They had no beginning. They just happened. Out of the thirsty shimmer of the desert mirages they came trudging one day to the shade and water of Paul Wilhelm's Thousand Palms oasis. They were weary and the rustle of the palm fronds and the trickle of the little stream sang sweet music to their ears. They stayed on and they adopted Paul—or he adopted them. They settled down and became part of Paul's idyllic establishment. Every once in a while they would go off on rambles. Sometimes they stayed away for three weeks or a month. But they always came back—sometimes under their own power and sometimes having to be rescued by Paul from foolish predicaments into which they had maneuvered themselves. Paul's oasis to them was home.

Then the war came. Paul expected to be called into the army. He was worried for the future of his long-eared pets. He learned that we, on Ghost Mountain, were trying to find a couple of burros in the hope that they would solve our burden-packing problems. Through the *Desert Magazine,* Paul got in touch with me. He said we could have Rhett and Scarlett in return for giving them a good home. Randall Henderson, *Desert's* editor, made the long trip out to Ghost Mountain to drive me over to Thousand Palms. Here I took over the burros from Paul and trekked them back over the 120 miles of road which separates Thousand Palms from Ghost Mountain.

It took Rhett and Scarlett quite a while to accustom themselves to Ghost Mountain. It was a different country and there were no palms and no running water. For a long time they were homesick. They did like Rider, Rudyard and Victoria though, and the children fussed over them so much that finally they gave up pining over vanished days and settled down as part of our little family.

But they were no good for packing burdens. The savage rocks of Ghost Mountain were a little too much even for burro patience. Some parts of the grade were altogether too steep. We soon discovered that we could pack stuff on our own shoulders with less grief than we could wrestle with the job of loading and unloading—and coaxing—our patient, panting little friends. We retired Rhett and Scarlett from the active list. Thenceforth their function became purely decorative. They didn't protest at this and they and the children got along very happily.

Then came the event of our long trip through Utah, Nevada, Arizona and New Mexico in search of another "Ghost Mountain"—one with permanent water. We couldn't take Rhett and Scarlett along. So we took them down to Everett and Lena Campbell's property on the desert and turned them loose on the cattle range near some flowing springs.

Rhett and Scarlett had a good time there. But they were a little lonesome. Going back and forth to the springs for water with just their own company didn't appeal to them. So they invented the practice of waiting around the waterhole until a small bunch of cattle had collected. Then they would calmly round up the obliging cows and steers and herd them along to the feeding grounds. Thus they satisfied their craving for companionship. When they

Marshal with Rider and Rudyard.
Photo courtesy of Jim Manner.

wanted another drink they would take the cattle back to the waterhole with them.

It was a good game and one which they carried on for some time, as Everett Campbell told me, with amusement, after we came back. But after a while they tired of that also. The desert was wide. They were freeborn spirits. Why should they stop in one place? They decided to drift. They said goodbye to the Campbell ranch and vanished.

Then, after long wanderings, we ourselves came back from our unsuccessful search. Water or no water, there was only one Ghost Mountain in the whole desert. We were glad to come home.

At Banner, on our way home with the first load of household effects, the first person we met was Bill Mushet of Banner Queen ranch. We hardly had exchanged two dozen words when Bill said, confidentially, "Say, do you know I've got something of yours— "He was going to say more, but at that moment I happened to glance up and I saw the "Something." On the other side of the fence were Rhett and Scarlett eating watermelon. They wore smirking grins of contentment on their deceptive countenances.

"We found them wandering in the desert," Bill explained. "They needed water. So I just brought them home and the boys—" The boys, Mike and Buzz, emerged from the house just at that moment. Anxiety was written all over their faces. (I learned afterwards that they had been frantically going through their joint savings with the idea of making me an offer for the burros on the spot—anything to avoid losing their new pets.) But they didn't have to say anything. I could see it in their eyes. Especially in Buzz's eyes. So I just looked at Buzz and I looked at the two graceless watermelon munchers—and I thought of the hard, hot rocks on Ghost Mountain and the scanty pickings of squaw-tea and cholla. Then I looked at Bill. "You keep 'em," I said. "From now on this is their home. They belong to Mike and Buzz. But for the love-of-pete don't feed them all the time on watermelon. They'll ruin you."

"Oh no, we won't," agreed Buzz happily. "Mostly we give them apples and peaches and oranges and green corn—just stuff like that."

And so that is how Rhett and Scarlett came to have a new home at the Banner Queen. Except when wanderlust grips them and they go off on a ramble. But they come back. They know a soft snap when they find it.

And now for the secret page which the letter and photographs have revealed.

Rhett and Scarlett are not Rhett and Scarlett at all. They are Jake and Stubbie. They are runaways. They are escapees from the Lost Angel mine, away out in the desert north of Indio. Once, in 1937, they were peaceful burden bearers, packing ore down the desert trail from the mine. But they tired of a steady job and security. So, after a year of ordered ways, they abandoned their post and lit out for the open desert. There was not reason for their going, save the call of the wild. They had had a good job with an abundance of hay, oats and wild feed, and they had been the pampered pets of the miners. But freedom and love of the open range is in their blood. They just had to go. As Mrs. Wood says in her letter, "We could never catch up with them, and we decided that they loved the freedom of the desert as much as we did."

So now we know a little more of Rhett and Scarlett (they have worn the names Paul gave them so long now that Jake and Stubbie might as well be laid aside). They are characters in their own right, and perhaps have earned a niche peculiarly their own among the famous of burroland. And, inasmuch as it was through seeing their

portraits in *Desert Magazine* that their former owners, the Wood's, recognized them, perhaps there may by other readers of *Desert* who, seeing these pictures, can trace back the Rhett and Scarlett history a little further. They are old—too old to have to shoulder the burden of work any longer—and undoubtedly there are long unrecorded years of their existence, prior to their sojourn at the Lost Angel mine which might be of interest.

*   *   *

A while ago I made an excursion down into the big canyon where, years ago, we found the huge ancient olla in the cave. I was curious to see if I could locate the cave again, for it is not easy to do so and I had failed on a previous attempt. Individuals who are not familiar with the desert always find it hard to understand why so many prospects and mines are "lost." They argue that if you could locate a place once there is nothing in the world to prevent your going right back to it. But it doesn't always work out that way. Old-timers who know their desert understand this and will never argue over the reason mines are lost. But it is hard to convince other people that the desert can play tricks.

The canyon of the olla is a sizable place. It is a giant slash between harsh thirsty hills. At the bottom of it there is a thin, scribbled line of white which is the bleached sand that wind and water have spread along the channel scoured by rare storms. It is very quiet, down there in the bottom, and there is always a thin wind that comes stealing up out of the lowlands to sway the green branches of the stunted catsclaws across the glass-smooth surface of the age-polished rocks. Sometimes you see a silent bird, flitting like a shadow through the bushes. And sometimes, on the clean carpet of sand, you will see the imprint of a coyote's foot. But these traces of the presence of life are few. High above, tremendous, fantastic boulders teeter terrifyingly along the precipitous rim. Black clefts and pools of shadow pattern their immensity. Mostly the canyon of the olla is the haunt of silence and the sun.

I spent the best part of three hours in the canyon. But I did not find the cave. Three hours is not a long time, but it is a considerable period when you devote it to locating one little spot of whose position you are absolutely certain. I would have guaranteed that I could find that cave. I could have drawn you a map of it and I would have been willing to make a bet on my ability to go right there. But when I tried I failed. Yet the cave is no myth. It is no dream wrought up of hardship and thirst. A very sizable olla came out of that cave. We hefted it out ourselves. And the olla was no dream either. It is still in existence. But the cave has vanished.

Of course there are explanations. There are people who will try to tell you that giant, side wall boulders slip;

that they cover up openings that previously existed. This may be true to a limited extent. Perhaps once in a thousand times this explanation will be the correct one. But I am convinced that such a thing rarely happens. It is more probable that we shall find the correct answer in the confusing sameness of the desert and the hypnotic effect which this quality has upon the sense of the searcher. Distances are vast and deceptive. Objects which appear near in reality are far off, while landmarks that are seemingly at a distance sometimes are relatively close. There is a sameness, even to the very diversity of rocks, clefts, ridges and buttes. And in this maze the eyes of the searcher and his sense of direction alike are led astray. It is not "inefficiency," for seasoned desert dwellers are repeatedly subject to the same failure. It simply is a peculiar quality of the desert. Most of the "lost" mines really are lost. They are not myths. And every once in a while some newcomer to the district—sometimes a tenderfoot—stumbles upon one of them and proves the old tale to have been the truth.

* * *

The pet population of Yaquitepec has increased. For the two "back-handspringing" mice suddenly decided to set up housekeeping and greatly to the joy of Rider, Rudyard and Victoria, presented the world with quadruplets. For a while there was a great fluttering of excitement caused by fears that the proud father might harm his diminutive offspring, so another cage was hastily provided for him. Poor little father greymouse, however, pined so much and was so obviously unhappy at being separated from his mate and family that the children feared he might die of a broken heart. He was accordingly restored to the old home—to his own joy and the joy of Mrs. Mouse and her babies. The little family is getting along famously. But there is a shadow in the offing. A shadow cast by arithmetic.

Because, having done a little figuring, I am disturbed as to just where this mouse multiplication business is going to end.

Desert Refuge 65
(December 1946)

THE MOUNTAINS seemed to be floating in the mists of evening, their summits ruby-red in the rays of the setting sun, their skirts dim in a swift-rising tide of purple mystery. The sky was sunset-gilded and the whole lone sweep of the land somber with the shadows of a brooding Earth. Such a picture was the desert the other

evening as we sped down from the rocky escarpments of the mountains toward the lone, windwhispered playas that pattern the dry bed of the Vanished Sea.

This trip was my friend Crocker's idea—Thomas Crocker, the artist, who can capture upon canvas imperishable color records of both human personality and desert mystery. It was his idea entirely. Like all true artists Tom is temperamental. Also unpredictable. One can never quite figure what he will do next. In this case it was quite late in the evening when, out of a clear sky, Tom suddenly said: "Ah, what a beautiful sunset. I can actually feel the soft touch of the wind as it comes up across the ripples of the Salton Sea. Quick, let us go down to Brawley and have dinner at the Planters Hotel."

And in less than five minutes we were off. I tell you Tom is like that, sometimes. So, in sincerity, I warn you, if you value your peace of mind do not have anything to do with artists—especially artists who are real geniuses. You can never tell what they are going to do. In the midst of getting a camp meal—the coffee pot just coming to a boil and the food all but cooked—they are likely to say, "Ah! Just look! That light effect—that bit of desert over there! Magnificent! Quick! Quick!...Out of the way."

And before you can say "Jack Robinson" or "Hot potatoes" they have upset all your pots and camp gear and are sitting right there at an easel in the midst of the wreckage painting away for dear life. You have to be a thoroughly experienced optimist if ever you go wandering around with an artistic genius—particularly one who specializes in desert landscapes and portraiture.

Well, anyway, with barely time for me to grab my zarape, and no time at all to wash my face (there wasn't much water around, anyway) we were off. Crocker owns a sort of Flying Carpet—one of those mechanical contraptions on wheels whose smooth purring and effortless rush often make us wonder if the puffing, boiling and wheezing old Model A, which is the mainstay of Yaquitepec, is really an automobile or just a collection of busted ironworks, held together with binder-twine and hay-wire. I don't know the make of Crocker's car—which is probably just as well, as it would only make all the other car manufacturers jealous if I mentioned it—but anyway it does get over the ground. As we eased out from among the creosote bushes, Tom glanced at his watch and said: "Splendid. We shall arrive at the Planters exactly right for dinner"—just as casually as though we were only going to step across the street, instead of heading out on a journey that in the old ox-team days would have entailed weeks of struggle and hardship.

A run down over the long leagues which separate the mountain country from the desert lowlands always is impressive at sunset and twilight—even if you do take it in company with an artist, who is always urging you to squint your eyes so that you can get the full value of the "mass effect" of scenic gems and color arrangements. Mystery lives in the desert. And there is no section of desert that I know, upon the North American continent, that holds more allure and mystery than that area which contains and surrounds the bed of the old Vanished Sea, which men today call the Imperial Valley. Perhaps this is because the old sea is not yet entirely "dead" nor "vanished." For from the desert foothills and from the summit of Ghost Mountain you can still see it, nights and mornings whenever the light happens to be right. It lies—or rather the "ghost" of it lies—just where it always lay in those past ages before the sun sucked it dry. From the mountaintops you can see it plainly, rolling blue in its old bed—covering the towns and the highways and the cultivated fields deep beneath its heaving blue shadow. The old islands still lift above it, as they did in the old days; the old gulfs and lagoons still border its margin with blue, mysterious patterns. Fancy? No, I do not think so. I have taken men who did not know the country to the summit of Ghost Mountain. And have said simply to them "Look."

And they have stared, and marvelled. And have sworn that they could see even the tide-rips between the rocky islands of the lowland ocean. Nor, after they had been told the truth, would they believe that they had been staring only at the ghosts of waves that have vanished these many centuries.

So cushioned in ease we sped on down the ribbon of concrete into the purple dusk. Mountains, ghostly and fantastic and unreal as shapes from another world, floated up at us out of the darkness, revolved and drifted away. Distant lights winked at us out of indigo gulfs like the far gleam of phantom watch-fires or the flickering torches of disembodied spirits treading again a maze of long-forgotten trails. The wind came out of the lowlands and whispered across the white, dry playas rustling the pale fragments of age-dry sea shells in its passage and muttering to itself around the rocky headlands of dry and long forgotten coves. The moon came up, full and awe-inspiring in its lonely majesty, and flung a mantle of beaten silver across a desolation of naked jet. Far off, unreal and spectral in the unearthly moongleam, an aviation beacon swung slowly like a brandished sword. The man-made lights of Brawley were a necklace of earth-spilled stars.

Barrel cactus

It had been a long time since last I had had dinner at the Planters Hotel. And I was prepared to be disappointed—for the flood tides of what passes for progress have a habit of blotting out so many things of worthwhile and sentimental value. But my fears were groundless. I knew that the moment I entered the spacious lobby—the moment I had grasped the welcoming hand of Dave Foster, the genial manager.

There are quite a few paintings bearing the signature of Thomas Crocker hanging in the lobby of the Planters Hotel. And after I had made the rounds of these and we had enjoyed a good dinner, we went out in the patio and sat under the palms in the night and listened to the faint, outer noises of Brawley—and talked philosophy and art. Being interested in the painting of a ceiling upon which I had vague ambitions to depict colorful cupids bearing wreaths of roses—I felt at the moment well qualified to discuss art. Also I had ulterior notions that I might entrap the master artist into giving me a few tips. But Tom utterly refused to be lured into the realm of anything so sentimental as cupids. His special genius lies along the lines of portrait painting.

Yaquitepec was chilly beneath the stars when I arrived home—at two o'clock in the morning. At that I narrowly avoided a most picturesque climax to a really picturesque evening. For, feeling sentimental as I drifted in over the trail, I was humming to myself a few bars of one of Kipling's melodies. I learned later that Rider, believing the music to proceed from an advancing pack of timber wolves, was just taking down the rifle. Fortunately, however, he has good eyesight and, as I stepped out of the shadows of a juniper near the house, he was able to perceive his error.

Speaking of, Rider recalls that he is, at the present moment, wandering around Ghost Mountain with a plaster cast on his left arm, which was broken in an encounter with a bicycle, which he was endeavoring to rope and break to the saddle. Whether the bicycle threw him and rolled on him, or whether it kicked him as he was roping it, we have never been able quite to determine—and his own ideas on the subject are hazy. But due to skillful medical setting and the healing effects of desert air and sunshine it is doing very nicely and will probably soon be as good as new.

* * *

The population of Yaquitepec again has increased. This time the newcomer is a baby desert tortoise. For, after a little over eleven weeks of waiting, one of the two eggs which Juana Maria Better Than Nothing laid so carefully beneath the shade of a goatnut bush (and which we subsequently removed to the house for better protection) hatched out into a fascinating, toy-like little creature. This fragile looking little elf, a perfect edition in miniature of its elders, captivated the attention of the entire family. No larger than a silver dollar when hatched, it seemed almost impossible that so tiny a creature could survive the hardships of desert life and develop into the rugged, sun-leathered tortoises which we knew. Yet we knew well enough that Mother Nature thoroughly understands her business, and we gathered both satisfaction and amazement in observing how thoroughly the new baby arrival seemed to understand the business of life.

It has been said that "The proper study of mankind is man." But this is not altogether true. For just as much, if not more, can be learned about life from an intelligent study of all the rest of animate and inanimate creation. If men would pause a little more to reflect upon the daily lessons which Nature spreads before them there would be fewer puzzles and doubts upon subjects connected with immortality.

For instance here was a tiny spark of life, no more than a few hours emerged into light of day. Yet it understood its business perfectly. Worried that it did not seem to want to eat, the children got the notion that perhaps it would like to drink. So a tiny, shallow pan was provided and filled with water. But our new arrival ignored it completely. However, a little while later, while Rider was adding some fresh water to the dish, he accidentally spilled some on the sand close to the seemingly dozing baby. Instantly it galvanized into life, thrusting its tiny head eagerly into the damp gravel and tilting its body forward to the highest upward reach of its hind legs, in the peculiar, characteristic kneeling pose which adult desert tortoises adopt when they are drinking from rain puddles. The action was so typical that it was startling. Here was a spark of supposedly "new" life. But it was an old hand at all the old rules and mannerisms. The artificial drinking pan it ignored. That was strange. But the splash of water upon desert sand was perfectly familiar. It was something to think about. So, taking the cue, we splashed more water on the sand and, bit by bit, coaxed our new-born to an understanding of the unfamiliar tin pan. From which, having become accustomed to it, he drank deeply. There were other hints that our new arrival was by no means new to this world and its problems. It had a confidence that could come from nothing less than previous experience.

Of course, if you want to, and have nothing else to do, you can explain away all these things in a perfectly logical manner. But we have long since ceased to worry too much over science or logic. Both of those bespectacled by-paths of human existence can be terribly overdone. "One touch of Nature"—as we have been told—"makes the whole world kin." And it is equally true that one startling demonstration of previous existence, as was provided by our baby tortoise's reaction to what it thought was a desert shower, will explode a lot of the musty, man-created theories that are found in books.

Good fortune—like bad—seldom comes in single doses. And this chronicle would be woefully incomplete if it neglected to mention also the joyous arrival of "Monica."

Monica is another tortoise. A native of Palm Springs, California, by birth—and of Santa Fe, New Mexico, by adoption and many years of residence, Monica came to Ghost Mountain through the kindness of H. Cady Wells, of Santa Fe, who was Monica's affectionate guardian.

A crisis had developed in Monica's many years of protected existence. It was necessary that a new home and protector be found. And, by correspondence, Monica's guardian inquired if we would undertake the charge. Would we? The children were wild with enthusiasm. An immediate letter of acceptance was dispatched. And, presently, from the historic and glamorous atmosphere of Old Santa Fe, Monica headed westward upon the racing wheels of a transcontinental Flyer. Not as a humble desert tortoise did Monica return to her birthplace. She was preceded, surrounded and accompanied by telegrams, air-mail letters—and a barrage of succulent lettuce. For there was much to arrange. Ghost Mountain is a place difficult of access even to express shipments, and our friend, H. Cady Wells, like an experienced general, was leaving nothing to chance. And nothing *did* happen by chance. So well laid were plans and so efficiently were connections arranged that Monica arrived at Ghost Mountain in high spirits, without the slightest hitch—and with still one lettuce left. The children welcomed her with open-armed joy—almost at midnight. And she was conducted to a warm sleeping place in the royal suite—for they insist that a tortoise over whom so much trouble has been taken and who has lived so long under the protection of so much loving care must be of royal birth. And maybe it is so. For Monica is a wonderful and a most lovable tortoise. The biggest, by far, of all our tortoise family. We hope that Monica will like her new home— she ought to, if the care and affection of three happy youngsters has anything to do with it.

PART FOUR—DESERT TRAILS

Desert Trails 1
(August 1947)

[Comments from Editor Randall Henderson in announcing a new series of stories from Marshal South]

...You may not agree with Marshal's philosophy of life in every detail—but you must respect them as honest opinions from a man who lives what he believes. This world would be a dull place if we all had the same ideas.

*M*Y FRIEND Bob Crawford had told me about the Elephant tree which grows on a steep sidehill within sight of the campground at Mountain Palm Springs Canyon in California's San Diego County.

Elephant trees are not especially rare or remarkable—except to people who have not seen them. Their habitat is always the desert and they are a common species in

The swollen branches of the elephant tree.
Photo courtesy of Lowell Lindsay.

Sonora and Lower California. Occasionally they are found in the foothills along the western edge of the Colorado Desert, and there is a lovely natural park containing several hundred of them in the Borrego area south of Highway 78 at Ocotillo. (*Desert*, Nov. '37)

And so I had driven my aged jalopy out to the secluded cove at Mountain Palm Springs to spend a night on the good earth and look for the Elephant tree.

Next morning, not long after the sun had blazed into a clear sky to make hot patterns across Carrizo Wash, I found it. It took a little scrambling and some searching. But after I had located it, I was astonished that I had not seen it from the first. It is visible a quarter of a mile away, north of the improvised fireplace at the campground where the road ends.

It isn't a big tree as trees usually are reckoned. Below the border it is said to grow occasionally to a height of 30 feet. But the specimens to be found in the arid region of the United States rarely exceed 15 feet. The one growing on the rocky slope at Mountain Palm Springs is about eight feet high, with a branch spread equal in diameter to its height.

Scientifically, Elephant trees belong to the *Burseraceae,* the Torchwood family, from which division of plants the aromatic product known as frankincense—often mentioned in religious writings in connection with myrrh—is obtained. The copal, which is burned as incense by various tribes of American Indians in religious ceremonies, is a product of the Elephant tree, the resinous properties of which are very marked. The tree is

260

credited with having a blood-like juice, or red sap, in the bark at certain seasons. But curiosity in this respect should be sternly repressed. For anyone who wanders round with a hatchet gashing Elephant trees to see them "bleed" is a type of human who does not belong in the desert or any place else.

Like many others—before I had seen my first Elephant tree—I was curious as to the reason of the name. But after you have studied the growth, the designation is readily understandable. The swollen, tapering branches suggest very strongly the trunks and the general characteristics of elephants. Although an equally apt definition might have been "Octopus" tree—because the smooth, tapering, writhing limbs suggest equally well a sprawling marine monster, upside down and waving its tentacles toward the desert sky. The tree, in many ways, carries a resemblance to some weird growth from the ocean depths. The tips of the branches are reddish brown, giving the tree, when seen from a distance, the appearance of a brown blur on the desert or rocky slope. The rest of the bark, however, which clothes the limbs and low trunk, is a mixture of white, whitish-yellow and green. This coloration is due to the construction of the bark, the outer layers of which are white. These, peeling off in thin sheets, expose inner layers that are green. The bark layers below are thick and red.

There were only a few leaves on this Elephant tree when I visited it in late May. But the crevices of the rocks surrounding it were thick with a rust red deposit of fallen dead ones. The leaves on the tree are an almost perfect reproduction, in miniature, of the frond of a date palm. But they are very tiny "fronds." The tree does not assume its full dress of leaves until after the flowers appear, which usually is sometime in June. The fruit, a tiny berry about the size of a pea, which turns from green to dark reddish-brown as it matures, ripens along in October.

The wood of the Elephant tree is hard, close-grained and yellow. In places across the Mexican border the trees are reported to be so numerous they are used for firewood. But it is my sincere hope that my brothers of the desert who may come after me to view the tree whose location I have revealed, will refrain from any clipping of souvenirs. The guardian spirits of the desert—and especially of Mountain Palm Springs—will not look with approval on such vandalism. You may not be superstitious and you may laugh it off. But it won't help you. I have

California fan palm

enough of the redman in me to be wholesomely convinced as to the fate of people who work thoughtless mischief.

The day was still young when I got through checking up on the Elephant tree—not even forgetting the delicate remains of a tiny nest which some trustful little desert bird had built in a fork of the aromatic brown twigs. The hot beat of the sun upon bare skin and the low croon of a warm, gentle wind coming down the canyon were too strong a lure to be resisted. I kicked off my sandals, dumped them into my dunnage sack and started happily, barefoot, up the wash.

The crunch of the warm, yielding sand underfoot was electric. And I was glad to discover that a sojourn in civilization hadn't tendered the soles of my feet too much. Civilization—which is a badly used word—does things to you. Especially to your feet. The construction of the human foot is perfect, for ease of movement and for health—if it is only let alone. The moment you fetter it and tie it up and "protect" it, you start trouble—corns and fallen arches and shortened tendons, and a whole host of similar ills from which foot specialists wax fat. Even a light sandal—though it is the least harmful of all footwear—is bad for the foot. Feet were meant to be worn bare. But humanity—which values form, convention and elegance more than health—has never ceased arguing with God on that subject. So far humans have lost every round.

Several canyons radiate from Mountain Palm Springs—like the diverging fingers of a hand. And all of them are worth exploring. Some of the palms have been trimmed by fire but there are others still in natural full dress of brown, dead leaf skirts without which, to me, a desert palm never looks just right. In a clump of these unspoiled queens of the wasteland solitudes, grouped as if for worship in a cathedral-like rock-walled pocket of the canyon, I sat down to rest.

It was quiet there. Quiet with a peace which is encountered, I think, only in such desert sanctuaries. The silence, save for the faint rustle of the wind in the fronds of the palms, was complete. And the wind rustle didn't detract from the silence. Rather it added to it.

I lay there quite a while, soaking up the sunshine and the magnetic strength of the warm earth. I lay perfectly still, and I thought I was alone. But I wasn't. For presently a pair of doves dropped out of emptiness and lit not five feet away. They were utterly unconcerned, merely cocking their heads at me once or twice, in appraisal, and then going quietly about their business of searching and picking for food among the grass stems of the damp spots near the roots of the palms, following each other back and forth and across-ways, in the methodical manner of stepping which doves have.

I was enjoying their company, and their confidence, when I saw another visitor. It was a red-diamond rattlesnake. It came gliding past like a shadow through the dry weeds not six inches from my extended bare foot. He looked at me too. But it was only a glance of languid interest, and I watched him until he slid from sight beneath a big rock on the other side of the glade. Whether the doves saw him or not I do not know. But neither snake nor doves took the slightest notice of each other. There was a truce in the glade—and Peace. Even the representative of that greatest enemy of all living things—man— who lay there, was tolerated and respected. Perhaps because he wore few clothes. And that is a strange and significant thing. For it has been my observation that the unclad human body is accepted by the creatures of the wild as friendly, in most cases. Whereas they will flee in fear from a human arrayed in the unsightly, choking collection of rags which most of us worship as clothing.

The doves flew away after a bit, and once more I thought I was alone. But no. From up the canyon there came a soft click and shuffle, and the clatter of a stone rolling down a slope. From around the brown skirts of a palm there stepped into view a little grey burro. He was obviously young. But also, obviously, he was wild. No galling fetters of human service had ever circled that wiry little body or dimmed with weariness those big, bright eyes. He stopped when he glimpsed me. Stopped dead. His whole body stiffened as though a powerful spring in it suddenly had gone taut and poised. He sniffed, and his nostrils twitched wide. What was this two-legged thing that lay there on the dry grass?

But I lay quiet, scarcely breathing. For a long minute our eyes held, each to each. Then, once again, the passport of natural bare skin won. My little visitor lowered his tautly raised head. His big ears twitched in a flick that might have been a friendly salutation. Unconcernedly he continued on his way, threading between the palms and disappearing from view around the angle of the canyon. I lay listening until the crunch and click of his daintily picking little hoofs faded away into nothingness.

Evening shadows were closing down across the desert when I woke the foothill silence with the stuttering exhaust of the old car and headed away from Mountain Palm Springs on the back trail. All the wastelands were greying with the loneliness of night, and far across the wash the gaunt flanks of the Fish Creek Mountains, pitted with vast, hobgoblin shadows, stood up stark and mysterious as a painted scene from Grimm's Fairy Tales. The road beneath the speeding car tires was lonely and sandy and white in the gloom. It was a very different and much more traveled trail than the one over which I had come when I had last visited Mountain Palms. And, for a space, that thought, and the realization that everywhere the desert was being furrowed by new trails, brought me sadness.

But it was only a temporary sadness. For I remembered suddenly that all the hills and washes were patterned with far older tails. Trails that in their day were well traveled, even though they were traversed only by bare or by crudely sandaled feet. And those trails today are dim— ghost threads that, in the loneliness, are crumbling to oblivion amidst the mists of dying memories and the dwindling glow of romance.

So, also, will these new, raw, modern trails pass— and the hurrying makers of them. And in the years to come the desert will cover them with its mantle, and forget. The feet come. The feet go. But the desert remains.

Desert Trails 2
(October 1947)

*J*udging by the height of the morning sun it must have been about ten o'clock when I came around the corner of the low rock, where the squaws had done their grinding, and entered the old campground.

It hadn't changed much. Several years had elapsed since I had last seen it. But despite progress and automobiles—including now the insatiable ramblings of jeeps— the Spirit of the Desert holds pretty tenaciously to its own. It was that veteran prospector, Charlie McCloud, I believe, who drove the first car through the creosotes and into this old Indian campsite many years ago. Many people have followed the tracks that Mac made. All the storage ollas that once were cached among the rocks on the mountainside have gone. Also most of the smashed pottery fragments that at one time littered the ground among the huge boulders that dot the camp area. But the lash of hard summer thundershowers still uncovers shiny black fragments of obsidian that fell from the hands of ancient arrowmakers. And, once in a while, with great luck, you will find a perfect arrowhead.

The deep-worn mortar holes in the rocks, however, defy the hands of both Time and souvenir hunters. And the sloping, polished rock, down which I have always liked to imagine the youngsters sliding, is still there. Maybe the ghosts slide down it yet, on moonlight desert nights. I know that I would, if I were a ghost. It is tempting. But then, of course, some people don't believe in ghosts.

There was an empty pop bottle on the flat rock beside the biggest mortar hole. And, before I sat down to fix the thong of my rawhide sandal, I gingerly took it away and hid it deep under some debris behind a boulder. Empty pop bottles are, I suppose, perfectly all right in their way. And in the centuries to come—when Time will have blotted our present age and all its works—some scientist will probably dig them up and exclaim over them. But at present, somehow, in the desert—and especially in silent lonely places that have a more or less sacred feel to them—pop bottles jar me. I once took a friend who was an archaeologist to one of the undisturbed, forgotten old desert campsites. He could pick up the old grinding stones, laid there by fingers long since turned to dust, and describe the women who had last used them.

I didn't try that with the pop bottle. I didn't want to. Somehow my imagination is too vivid.

I spent a few minutes sitting on the grinding rock and fixing my sandal. The knot through the sole, under the big toe, had worn off, and I had to slide the thong forward through the loops and re-knot it. A Yaqui sandal, if it is properly made, is one of the simplest things in the world to mend—and also the most comfortable to wear. But you have to get used to them—both as to feel and as to looks. Most feet—and people—are too civilized to countenance them.

It was warm, sitting there in the sun. But not too warm. A friend, when I had set forth on my expedition, told me that I was slightly crazy to go on walking trips in the desert in July. And when I told him that I liked the desert heat and that, as far as I was concerned, it never really got too warm, he retorted that that was because I had lived there too long and had gotten all dried up and cracked "like all the rest of those desert rats."

For which I thanked him—and then made a few edged remarks about the enervating heat of his allegedly cool pine-clad mountains. My friend and I understand each other very well.

I finished my sandal repair, shouldered my light pack and canteen and started up the canyon. I would have enjoyed basking longer amidst the sunlit hush and peace of the old boulder-pillared campground, but some slight twinge of conscience goaded me on. After all I had supposedly come out to look for a spring, hadn't I? I ought, therefore, to make some effort to find it—even though I didn't expect to. Rider and I had searched for this same spring very thoroughly years before. And had just about convinced ourselves that it was a myth. But my credulity

—in the matter of springs—is colossal. And I had heard a new rumor. I really didn't believe it. But the excuse it gave to go searching was too strong to be resisted. So here I was.

The canyon was familiar ground. Years before—before we had settled on Ghost Mountain—we had penetrated its depths and had been halted, suddenly breathless with something like incredulous awe, at the spot where, through a gap between the tumbled walls of savage rock, all the mystery of the blue and purple badlands—leagues distant and far below—had burst abruptly upon our vision. The same view, today, halted me again. And for a long while I stared at it with the same fascination. Some places hold us with shadowy chains. We know not why, but they are home. They belong to us.

This view out over the distance phantomed reaches of the Vanished Sea—which is now Imperial Valley—has always held me. Whether it be from the summit of Ghost Mountain or from any other vantage point the effect is always the same. I can forget the towns and the highways and the cultivated fields and the irrigation canals that I know are there, hidden by the haze of distance. I do not see them or sense them. I can see only the sea—the sea that is there no longer. In the changing light its ghostly waves heave and the tide-rips make grey riffles around its rocky headlands.

I spent several hours exploring the lower reaches of the canyon. That is to say I employed my time in clambering up over and between titanic boulders the size of houses, that lay jumbled in the mountain gash like heapings of marbles some giant schoolboy had flung into a ditch.

The ravines which rare floods and the windstorms of ages have worn in the flanks of these desert mountains are fearsome places which, if not haunted by demons, hobgoblins and malignant spirits, as they sometimes seem to be, are at least under the spell of an awful desolation and thirst. The sides of the mountains, as you work down into the drier fringes of the lowlands, become increasingly barren and more sun-blasted. Bare, heat-blackened rocks cling ominously to the slopes and ridges in positions which appear to defy the laws of gravity. At any moment, it seems, they might turn loose and fall thundering into the canyon depths. And many of them have so fallen—the inferno of stone monsters, which choke the gorge depths, is testimony to that.

Between these grim masses are chinks and dark crevices through which, by squirming, an active human can sometimes make his way. But it is a cautious business. For always there are dark holes underfoot that yawn into blacker and more mysterious depths. The winds of thousands of years have howled through these rocks and scoured them in places to the slippery polish of ice. To lose footing and go plunging down into one of these subterranean death-traps would be all too easy.

Of course there wasn't any spring. At least I didn't find it. Sometimes I think that old-timers—especially when they have passed a certain age—are a little unreliable. Not intentionally. But they get their geography mixed and superimpose Arizona, Utah, New Mexico and California locations one upon the other. So that the resultant picture is a bit fuzzy. I hunted in vain for the "three big boulders, leaning together" with a dead juniper tree "just about a hundred yards to the east." Maybe it's there. And maybe not. Anyway I abandoned the search and began to make my way back along the ridges toward the old Indian trail that runs to Vallecito.

It's a rough trail and poorly marked. But I had traveled it several times before. Just as I reached the first old Indian trailmarker, however, I was surprised to meet a mountain sheep. We almost ran into each other as I turned the corner of a clump of rocks. For an instant he stopped, startled. Then with a bound he swung aside and fled nimbly up the precipitous slope, skipping from boulder to boulder as only a mountain sheep can. He was a big ram and I felt pretty certain he was the same one that I had seen two years back on the other side of Pinyon Peak. Meeting him here seemed to lend color to the possibility that there might be a spring in the vicinity after all. But it is slim evidence. Mountain sheep range a long way from water. In fact in the Pinacate Mountains, in Mexico, south of the Arizona border, they are reputed to get along without water entirely— possibly subsisting on the moisture contained in the bisnaga cacti.

The day was edging toward twilight when I broke free from the cluttered desolation of rocky ridges and headed across the ocotillo-staked desert toward the old Vallecito stage station. I had sudden evening company, too. For, happening to glance aloft, I was aware of a streaming flight of buzzards passing above me, headed for the sunset tinted heights of the distant southwestern sierras. There must have been hundreds of them. They flew slowly, in an irregular, streaming formation, like a cloud of ominous warplanes. What the reason is for these buzzard migrations I do not know. They are not a regular occurrence. It is only at long intervals, in this particular desert section, that all the wandering birds that are usually so solitary congregate. Only a few times during our long residence on Ghost Mountain have we seen such mass flights. And they are not always in the same direction. If they were more regular, they would be more explainable.

The old stage station was deserted, and in the dusk the shadows lay heavily across the lonely tule marshes which border it. I spread my single light blanket on the ground beside one of the adobe pillars and, after a long drink at the pump—which now makes the waters of the spring accessible—I stretched out to watch the bats flittering around the treetops and to look for the diamond points of the stars as they appeared one by one through the growing velvet of the night. Far away beyond the tule marshes a coyote yammered and the sound quavered lonesomely across the whispering dark.

* * *

Desert trailing, on foot, has many advantages—provided you know something of your territory. The desert is no place for foolhardy stunts or for the taking of long chances as to water—especially in summer. But, with reasonable caution, there is much to recommend walking. Walking, in these days of automobiles and frantic haste, is almost a lost art, it is true. And that is a pity. Because in no other way can you gain such an intimate acquaintance with any region. Walking is cheap and healthful and to all those who are outdoor-minded I would most heartily recommend it. Carry a notebook—and a sketchbook too, if possible. They will add to your fun. But—and this is a serious warning as regards the desert—be sure you know something about your territory before you start. Don't try to cross long, unknown stretches of waterless country. There are plenty of easy trips.

TIME!

Here, in the silence and the heat,
*   where Time steals past on slippered feet,*
They, who before possessed this land,
*   have left their trace on every hand—*
A shattered jar, a lonely grave, old campsites
*   where the greasewoods wave—*
Trails, dimmed by years and sandstorm's blast—
*   these left as record "They who passed."*

Who owns the land? Beneath the sun,
*   in blots of indigo and dun,*
The shadows of the clouds move by,
*   beneath the arch of turquoise sky.*
Sunlight and shade in patterned change
*   across the wasteland's endless range—*
Time—on soft feet. And who shall find,
*   the records we shall leave behind?*

Desert Trails 3
(December 1947)

Now there is virtue in Water, and in the Sun, and in the healing essence of many sorts of Herbs. But if a man be sick the chief Healing lies within his own Soul.

OF ALL the trails that wind down into the desert there is none more sought, or more important, than the trail to Health. The Indians knew this. And ever since my few notes on the healing water of Agua Caliente springs appeared in the pages of *Desert* (July '47), it has been made very clear to me that upon at least one subject—that of the quest for health and healing—the Indian and his white brother are one.

For I have had many letters from sufferers who, in the account of the curative qualities of these natural springs, caught a gleam of new hope. And it is the eagerness and earnestness of these many inquirers which leads me to believe that a few words regarding the desert as a mecca for health seekers may not be amiss.

To a great number of individuals, the desert has been—and is—a magic region as regards health restoration. That point has been settled long ago. And the great army of men and women who have come into its domain suffering from lung troubles and other body weaknesses and have gone away, or remained, completely cured, constitutes living and uncontrovertible evidence as to the virtues of the dry air, sunshine and abundant peace of the wastelands.

This much is undisputed. But we must also recognize the truth that a great many who have come to the dry lands seeking relief have gone away disappointed. Not for them has the sun and the wandering wind among the greasewoods brought renewed health and vigor. Disappointed, disillusioned and often embittered they have turned their backs upon the Spirit of the Silence and gone away in sorrow—sometimes in anger. "The desert," they say bitterly, "is a fake—like all the other fakes." And, hopelessly, they return to their own places; their "remedies"—and their despair.

Yet the desert is no "fake." From the beginning it has held out welcoming arms and hope to the sick and weary of every race and color and creed. And the vast majority of them have not been disappointed. Why, then, does it fail a few?

Here is an important question. And perhaps we shall find the answer to it if we go back a little into fundamental things. Into the fundamentals of the world of Nature—and especially of human nature.

In the first place the desert is essentially a primitive region. Its characteristics, perhaps more than any other of the earth's varied localities, precludes frills and pampering advantages. It is true that by the expenditure of great labor, time and money, you may succeed in dressing up and improving small portions of the desert. But the portions so treated cease immediately to be desert. They become resorts—or, at the best, artificial oases. And neither of these is desert.

True desert is a raw untamed region, and it belongs by right to a hardy, primitive people. Generally they have been noted for their health and hardiness. And they are, in the main, fierce fighters. The people, like their desert, are fundamental and primitive.

Like attracts like. The music of Nature can tolerate no discords. Unless there be harmony there will be destruction. The harping thunder of the sea must find its answer in the heart of the sailor—else he will be a poor sailor. And the soft music of the winds which sing down through the long sunlit washes of the desert, or murmur amidst the desolate moonlit rocks, must strike a deep answering chord in the heart of the dweller of the desert—else he will be no part of it. He will be an intruder and a discord—and as such will be thrust, unsatisfied and unaccepted, from its borders.

For you cannot mix the fundamental and the true with the superficial and the false.

And it is for this reason, I think, that so many who come to the desert expecting great things, go away chagrined and disappointed.

The fault is theirs—not the desert's. For, to get benefit from the desert—or from any environment you must be in tune with it. You must come with an eager open heart. You must really love the desert or it will not love you. And loving you not, it will not heal you.

Now this, I think, is something which a vast number of human beings fail utterly to understand. Enmeshed in a man-made web of artificiality they have lost touch with fundamentals. The truths of Nature—the harmonies and vibrations of real Nature—are so utterly foreign to them that they dismiss them as fantastic or as silly superstition. Their ears are too close to the tinny blare of radio propaganda and the trivialities of social custom. To them life has become a business of price and money. If you can meet the price and you lay down the money required, then you can demand the return—be it a gilded gadget or bodily healing.

But in the desert—in fundamental Nature—matters are not arranged in this fashion at all. In Nature there must be harmony, and faith and acceptance and humbleness—and love. And without these are all hope and seeking vain.

The Indian knows this. All primitive races know it. But the white man has forgotten.

Thus it is that many of those who come to the desert with ailments fail to be cured.

They hear of some spring or of some particular locality which has helped others, and they decide to go there—just as they would decide to purchase some new cure-all in a bottle. They think that if they merely drink the water, or take the baths or live awhile at the prescribed altitude, that the reward of new health must certainly be theirs.

And they are woefully disappointed. Because they, many of them, come to the desert despising it. They are frightened by its vastness and roughness. They chafe bitterly against its disadvantages. They grumble unceasingly against its heat and its loneliness, its limited supplies, its lack of entertainment. Unwillingly, complainingly, they stay—enduring, their every moment a martyrdom. And finally, unhelped, disappointed, they sputter home on roaring motors, happy to escape. The desert is a fake.

But the fake and the failure is not in the desert. It is in themselves. A seed will find no roothold on stubborn rock—nor can healing be accomplished if the heart is not in tune with Nature.

For the desert does heal—provided you are of a nature that loves the desert. Just as the mountains will heal—if you love the mountains. The answer is in you.

When I first came to the desert, climbing the precipitous steeps of the old Indian trail that wound up over the last 1,200 feet to the little plateau where we built Yaquitepec, it was with the shadow of a weak heart hanging over me. But I did not let these ominous warnings worry me. Apart from the desire to find escape from a top-heavy and worry-burdened existence was another desire, equally strong. And that was to get back close to the earth. To get in tune once more with the healing rhythm of Nature. To me the desert held out its arms, not only as a haven of Peace but also of Healing.

But, and I think this is most important, I loved the desert. Its vast sunlit spaces, shimmering away into the grey mystery of distant horizons, called to my heart. It was, in some mysterious fashion home. I loved its disadvantages. I accepted its hardships. The stones that bruised my bare feet, and the cholla thorns that scarred and stabbed my bare skin, were to me, friends. Savage and primitive friends, if you will—but nevertheless beloved. I panted in the heat—and rejoiced in it. I shivered in the cold—and found it good.

And the desert repaid my confidence and trust and affection. Little by little, at first, but afterwards with increasing confidence, I was packing heavier and heavier burdens up that 1,200 foot rise which lay between the limit of wheeled transportation and our mountain-crest home. As nerves and bodily strength grew better the doubtful heart grew better. Until there were few burdens that

baffled me. Regularly I used to carry up that precipitous trail, sections of which were just stepping from rock to rock, hundred pound sacks of grain, potatoes, cement and other supplies. And I have never been very husky. Never in my life has my weight exceeded 140 pounds.

Nor was my own case an exception. As the desert can heal, so also can it keep well. Our three children, raised from infancy on primitive food and amidst the so-called hardships of the desert mountaintop, never, up to the time they moved from the desert, had or needed—with but one single exception—the services of a doctor. And the sole exception can hardly be counted. It was an accident. Coming up the trail one night Rider, then about eight years old, tripped and fell head foremost into a bed of mescals (agaves) . The accident probably would never have happened but for the fact that his hands—and attention—were busy in carrying tenderly some little playthings, which a good friend had sent to him. Anyway he fell. When we hauled him out we found that several of the savage mescal spines, woody and needle sharp, had driven through the skin and flesh of the top of his head and broken off. They were lodged between the flesh and the bone of the skull.

After an unsuccessful attempt to cut these out myself—an attempt which failed not because of the lack of nerve on Rider's part, but my own, we took him in to a doctor. In a few minutes with a local anaesthetic, the barbs were removed. And that was that. The incident was closed. It wasn't something which you could hold against the desert's healing power. But it was the only time in all the years at Yaquitepec that a doctor's services were needed.

So I think I am right in saying that the desert will, in most cases, heal you—if you go to it, accepting it and expecting to be healed—and obeying the rules of Nature.

For there are rules. And the rules are that you must get close to the earth—and to the sun and to the air and to the general peace of the wilderness. Leave your civilization and its false notions behind. Become a denizen. Perhaps this sounds fantastic to you. But there is magic in it.

If possible go somewhere where you need not be burdened with too many clothes. Give the sun and the air a chance. If you can't go barefoot, then wear the lightest and flimsiest of sandals. Lie around in the sun. Loaf in the shade. Take long prowls through the canyons and up the washes at daylight and in the evenings. Rough it. Cook and eat in primitive fashion. And throw away as many of your fancy camping gadgets as you can. They keep you from the feel of the earth. A little sand in your food won't hurt you…nor will a creosote leaf or two in your tea or coffee. (The creosote is a reputedly valuable desert remedy, anyway.)

And above all let the peace and silence of the desert seep into your soul. Forget the world—and business. It will be there— all too much of it—when you get back. Forget money. If you are spartan-like and really primitive a little money will go a long way on the desert—at an isolated camp-spot.

And, observing these conditions, it is my belief that the desert will cure a great number of ailments, either with or without natural mineral springs. There are virtues—great virtues in mineral water baths. But there are also greater virtues in getting back close to Nature and relaxing.

But the greatest virtue of all lies in your own soul. If you go in confidence, accepting, believing—feeling glad to be back again in tune with the earth, the chances are that the earth will respond and will cure you. Be it desert— or any other earth.

So there you have the sum and substance of my personal belief. Can you get relief—can you get cured at Agua Caliente springs?

Yes, I think so—if you play the game and obey the rules. But then, I think also that you can get cured at innumerable other places in the desert. It's just up to you.

Desert Trails 4
(January 1948)

What profit the whirr of Wheel,
The roar of Wings, the clang of Steel—
If, from a world in these arrayed,
The builders turn away, dismayed,
Weary and sick of mind.

FOG WAS spilling over the mountain rampart to the southwest. Under the beat of the noon sun it was very white and dazzling, and as it lapped over and fell in snowy cascades into the hollows and canyon heads that scored the desert side of the sierra, it was irresistibly suggestive of a mighty table cloth. Just the same sort of a "cloth" as Nature, from time to time, spreads across the flat-topped, mountain massif which guards the entrance of Table Bay, South Africa. My friend, the Railroad Executive, who knew South Africa, drew my attention to the similarity. And I was glad to find someone else who had noticed it. For a few minutes, while we compared notes, he forgot his prospecting and collecting of pottery sherds.

But it is a long way from South Africa to the desert section of southeastern San Diego County, California. Not only in actual distance, but also—as it happened—in elapsed time. My friend said presently that he liked the slopes of Ghost Mountain better than those of Table Mountain, anyway.

And he climbed up the ridge again. His partner was calling him. His partner thought he had found a cave where, perhaps, the old Indians had buried something.

So I sat on my rock and looked out over the lowlands. The desert, in contrast to the cold cap of dazzling white fog that crowned the distant mountains, was brilliant and sunny and warm. There had been a recent rain and despite the lateness of the season, many of the ocotillos had put on a dress of vivid green leaves. Ocotillos are temperamental, anyway. But I was a little surprised to note, away up the slope, a tall mescal shoot crowned with a banner of yellow flowers. It just wasn't right. It was far too late for flowering mescals. But there it was. There was no argument. I could take it or leave it.

I was turning over in my mind what I could best do to entertain my friend. He and his companion had only this one day to spare for my section of the desert, and they were eager to make the most of it. It was some years since they had been able to get away from the east on a vacation. And their hunger for things deserty was almost tragic. I was only mildly interested in the excited shouts from up the slope. I had been all over that territory and I knew well enough that there were no Indian relics buried in caves up there. But the reference to buried things had made me wonder if perhaps I ought to take these two enthusiastic tenderfeet down to the site of old Paul Sentenac's house, on the knoll at the entrance of Sentenac Canyon. Legend had woven a lot of stories about things buried there. Treasure, for instance. Lots of people had dug. But none of them had ever seriously disturbed either the legend—or the treasure itself. "Maybe," I said to myself, "I ought to take them there. People always like to dig for something. And, anyway it's good exercise."

My two friends came scrambling down the stony slope. The Railroad Executive—whose name I won't tell you, because you might know him—was carrying something else in his hands besides his prospector's pick. "It wasn't really a cave," he said.

"And I don't think that there's anything hidden there. But we found this among the rocks."

He held up a fairly large pottery fragment. It was the almost perfect mouth of a clay olla. All the sides had been broken away, leaving the ring of the lip complete except for just one small broken section. "It must have been a big olla," my friend said. "It's too bad there wasn't more of it left. But we couldn't find another fragment. What do you make of it?"

I told him that his find had once formed part of a narrow-necked storage olla. "Probably one that they used to store pinyon [piñon] nuts in," I said. "It doesn't follow that its original location was up there in those rocks. Some youngster-may have been playing with this piece and dropped it. Indian kids are much the same as other small fry when it comes to lugging around junk."

"Where would they get the pinyon nuts—here?" he asked, glancing around dubiously. "I don't see any source."

"Plenty, up there on that mountain to the north," I told him, pointing. "That's why it's called 'Pinyon Peak.' The old-time Indians had food caches scattered around in strategic places all over this desert."

My friend and his companion had seated themselves beside me. The companion wore dark sun glasses that somehow gave him a mysterious look. He was a Banker in his home sphere. But here he was just a little boy. He and the Executive pawed over the old olla neck like a couple of excited kids.

"I'll bet," said the Executive, "that it must take a lot of skill and art to make a thing like this—by hand." He caressed it lovingly.

"Not nearly so much education and skill as it takes in the railroad business," I said.

The Executive snorted:

"To h—with education—and railroads, too!" he snapped explosively. "Sometimes I wish there weren't such things as railroads. Sometimes I wish they'd never been invented. We were all better off, I think, when we drove horses—or when we just walked. At least man wasn't any more cruel than he is now. And life was slower—and easier to bear. Do you know that sometimes—" he looked at me with almost savage earnestness, "—sometimes I wish they'd hurry up and drop those atom bombs and wipe out this whole civilized-mess—and give the world a fresh, primitive start again. It needs it."

"That's telling 'em, George!" the Banker said. He chuckled nervously. But his dark glasses nodded a vigorous approval.

"This," I said, "is not the first time I've heard those sentiments. But, coming from you two—"

"But I mean it," said the Executive, earnestly. "I'm not joking. The thing is in a mess—the whole world. We're drifting. We're on the wrong track. The lights are all against us and there's wreck and chaos ahead. Money! Money! —Politics! Greed! See here; I'm worth quite a bit—so far as money goes. But what good does it do me? It has me by the throat. I can't quit. I've got to stay with it—and sink. Where's the real profit in all this mess?"

The Banker lit his pipe: "'What does it profit a man,'" he quoted softly, "'if he gain the whole world and lose his own soul.'"

Though small and crude, to the inexperienced potter this olla was a masterpiece. Sketch by Marshal South.

"Exactly," the Executive agreed. He drew a deep breath. "Do you know," he said soberly, "I'd give a year's income if only I were primitive enough, and skillful enough, and close-to-earth enough to be able to make one of these things with my own bare hands—like a human being." He fingered the old bit of baked clay wistfully.

A sudden idea struck me. It was an illuminating flash. This would be better—much better—than grubbing for mythical treasure on old Paul Sentenac's homesite. "Come on, then," I said, getting up off my rock. "Your ambition is about to be realized—and it won't cost you a year's income, either. Only some time—and a little gasoline." I started toward their car, which we had parked near a juniper clump.

"Just what do you mean?" the Executive demanded, hurrying after me. "Have you gone crazy?"

"Not a bit of it," I told him cheerfully. "But you are going to make an olla. Let's get going. We haven' too much time."

We got going. Between breaths, as I gave hasty route directions, I managed to do some sketchy explaining. Not much, for the trail was rough. But, for a raw hand at desert driving, the Executive handled his car pretty well. We went up an old canyon where the age-blackened boulders, big as houses, clung precariously along the sky rim. There had been an old foot trail through here once. And once upon a time an Indian encampment. But I turned a deaf ear to the suggestion that we stop and explore for relics. There was a short little Army shovel in the car, and when they had parked where I told them to, I took it and started out to look over the ground.

Yes, the clay deposit was still there—as I had remembered it from almost ten years back. While the Executive lugged over the five gallon can of emergency water and an old gunnysack and the Banker hunted around for a handy shaped stone to pound with, I cleared away the overlaying stones and dirt and dug a small hole down into the clay bed. It was good honest desert clay. Red and satisfying and full of enough sand and impurities to make it interesting. It was the sort of clay I like to work with. I have never had any luck with the civilized and refined varieties.

We scooped the clay lumps out onto the gunnysack and pounded them to powder with the rock. Then we mixed the clay powder with water and worked and kneaded it to the right consistency. We got a skillet out of the car and, having filled it with fine sand from the little dry wash in the bottom of the canyon, we spread the gunnysack over it—making a hollow place in the center to act as a support for our projected clay pot.

By this time the Executive was all steamed up with excitement. And the Banker had become so eager that he had actually taken off his dark glasses—in order that he could watch better. I shaped out a little saucer-like disc of wet clay for the bottom of our proposed creation, laid it in the hollow in the sack covered skillet, and told the Executive how to go to work.

And he caught on. Surprisingly, into those fingers that for years hadn't done anything more strenuous than push call bells and sign checks, there came an eager skill. Oh, it was clumsy, of course. I had to help him a lot at the beginning. But the latent ability was there. By the time we were getting toward the end of the job he was doing most of the work himself—and was mighty proud of it.

It wasn't much of an olla. It was small and it was crude. But we were working not only against inexperience but also against time. For the sun was going down fast. By the time it was finished and had dried a bit the canyon was deep in the gloom of late evening. The Executive wouldn't hear of abandoning his masterpiece—although I told him that it was far too new and wet to stand transportation. He packed it as a mother might pack a baby, in the carton which had held the lunch supplies. I think he wrapped expensive items of personal clothing around it. He had faith, he said, that he would get it back east all in one piece.

And his faith was justified. By some astounding miracle the pot, crude and clumsy as it was, survived. It didn't even crack in drying. We took along a package of clay from the canyon and, before we parted, I carefully explained to the Executive how he could polish his pot,

Indian fashion, with wet clay slip and a smooth pebble. I didn't think these directions would ever be necessary, as I would have been willing to wager almost anything that when he got it home his pot would be just nice crumbly fragments. But Fate ruled otherwise.

There must have been a charm over that pot. Because it survived not only the polishing process but also the firing. For my friend wrote me later that he had made a kiln out of an old iron barrel and had "cooked" the pot himself, in a secluded corner of the garden of his country estate. He was very proud—and insistent—in impressing upon me that he had done every bit of the work with his own hands. I understand that this momentous olla is now in a glass case and constitutes a sort of shrine to which my friend proudly leads his most intimate friends…"I done it!…I done it! With my own hands I done it!"

All of which chronicle quite apart from the fact that both the Executive and the Banker have now gotten themselves kilns and have embarked whole-heartedly in the fascinating hobby of pottery making—may, or may not, have a moral. It is just a little incident, wherein the lure of the desert and the urge of the primitive have been instrumental in providing an escape valve for a couple of human beings, wearied and nerve-raw from the circumstances in which their lives are cast. But, somehow, I think that this little episode had particular significance. For it goes to show how deep-rooted—and universal—is the weariness which has come upon a world which, supposedly, is enjoying the blessings of a superior civilization.

Mankind is tired. Something is wrong with the picture. They have feasted upon the Dead Sea fruit of progress and mechanical gadgets. And the core of it all is ashes. Gadgets and noise and show and television and music that comes out of the thin air are poor food for the soul if the price in heartache and tears and shattered nerves is too high. Mankind everywhere is today seeking an escape from the monster which they themselves built. They seek peace, and quiet lives and old-fashioned pleasures and virtues. And the right to do things for themselves—with their own hands.

And that is the reason why more and more soul-sick human beings are turning each year to the healing peace of the deserts and the forests and the mountains—and to the relief of wearied nerves by means of personal expression through handicrafts. It is a good sign. And one to rejoice over. For in this direction— and in this only—lies the salvation of our present progress-mad age.

Desert Trails 5

(March 1948)

"Come! Come!" they said, "'Tis time to up and do—
Too long have you sat dreaming in the noon.
See!—'Progress' beckons! See!—the golden heights!
Haste! Haste!—for Fortune passeth over soon!"

So he, who sat in peace, forsook his hearth.
His bow and quiver left he by the spring.
His feathers and his beads he laid aside—
And for them took the Chain and Iron Ring.

And after many days—all spent and worn—
A fettered slave, he sank to earth and grieved—
"Lo, I have traded Freedom for the Rod,
And Stars for Bubbles. I have been deceived!"

YAQUI WELL sleeps in the sun and the desert silence. On the gleaming surface of its crystal water, which lies like a tiny scrap of shattered mirror in the hot sand, dance the reflected images of ironwood trees and ragged bushes and the towering lift of crowding mountain ridges whose gaunt brown flanks, streaked and spotted with patches of alkali-gray and riven by the savage scars of cloudbursts, brood over the narrow dry wash like the Spirit of Thirst over a whitened bone.

Springs in the desert are generally much more than just waterholes. By virtue of their vital importance they acquire an aura— an atmosphere that is like a human personality. Woven from the very fibres of Life and Death and Joy and Despair and the bitterest dregs of desert tragedy, the spirit that is a part of each watering place is strikingly individual—and very real. Yaqui Well, for all the sunlit peace of its setting and the dreamy whisper of the lazy wind through the branches of its ironwoods, hugs to its crystal heart grim secrets. Secrets which are part of the legend of Pegleg Smith and of the tragic fate of many others who headed out into the wastelands in search of his lost mine.

A couple of days ago I went down into the desert to renew my acquaintance with Yaqui Well. It isn't hard to reach now, for a paved highway, No. 78, passes almost within a biscuit toss of it, and now there is even a bus connection. For the recently instituted service of the Mountain Stage Lines between Julian and Brawley will set you down right at the sleepy little turnoff road which leads from pavement down through the chollas and ocotillos to the well. It is only 18 miles from Julian. A distance that means nothing now. But in the old days the roads were different.

But neither the proximity of pavement, the convenience of bus service nor the nearby loom of powerlines, which now march through the Narrows, have shattered the old-time atmosphere of Yaqui Well. The desert has absorbed these intrusions. The ocean of silence has welled up and engulfed them. A few steps down the dry dirt road and the desert wraps you around with its friendly blanket. You are as much in the solitude of the wastelands as though you were a thousand leagues from modern Progress.

Smoke trees stalk like grey ghosts down the harsh gravel of the bush-grown wash. And creosote bushes and burroweed compete for place with the bristling heads of the Bigelow chollas. Ocotillos writhe their spiny wands towards the sun and cast a basket-work of ragged shadows from which little groups of drowsing quail scurry off, startled, at advancing footsteps. It is very quiet. And over all brood the mountain ridges. The ironwood trees are inviting havens of shade against the sere glare of the sun-scorched slopes.

I had come down by the stage line. And I was glad of it. Because now, as I made my way along the trail toward the well, I was afoot. And for absorbing the spirit of the desert—or any other region—there is no mode of progress to compare with foot travel. There is a soul-comforting satisfaction about it which outweighs a thousandfold any of the dubious advantages which mechanical transportation has conferred. As a people—thanks to gasoline—we have almost lost the art of walking. And with it, I think, we have lost also something else.

The well hadn't changed much during the long span of years which had elapsed since I had last seen it. It is true that a few alterations had been made. A small concrete container topped with an arrangement of iron pipe made the water more accessible for cattle, but otherwise "improvement" had touched the place lightly. I reflected that the weedy basin which had held the water of my previous memory had perhaps been more picturesque. But I did not feel like quarrelling with the cattlemen just because of that. Anyway there were no cattle in sight. Though around the trough and in the muddy, grass-grown overflow, their tracks were everywhere apparent.

Yaqui Well isn't really a well. It is a seep or spring— probably an uprise from the underground flow that moves down from the high mountains, along the underground channels deep beneath the hot sands of the wash. A trickle of this, diverted perhaps by some subterranean rock ridge, rises to the surface like a leak from some buried water main. This is Yaqui Well.

Perhaps, in the beginning of human record, the spring was dug out as a well or basin to receive the up-bubbling water. Mayhap the Yaqui Indian, after whom the spot is named, was the first to do this. But it is not likely—because this spring must have been well known to the desert Indians for a long span of time prior to his advent. The Yaqui moved in and established himself about the year 1880. He came up from Sonora, Mexico, and married an Indian girl of a tribe dwelling in Grapevine Canyon. It is possible it was from her he learned of the spring. At any rate the place has been known for him ever since.

The Yaqui's bequest to those who came later includes something more than the name of a spring. Reliable report says that from the spring, as a starting point, he had a secret trail which led out toward the sun in the desert badlands where there lay a fabulously rich deposit of gold. Whether this gold deposit was the same as the one found by Pegleg Smith cannot of course be certain. But local evidence and accumulated stories point to this connection. At any rate the Yaqui went after gold whenever he had need of it. It is possible he derived his information about this mine from the same source from which he had learned about the spring—that is, from his Indian wife. Later he was killed in a brawl and the secret died with him. His widow never would reveal to anyone else the trail he had used.

There is good reason to suppose, however, that another character, well known around Julian and Banner in the early mining days, also got on the right trail to the elusive gold, which Pegleg Smith made famous. This was Jim Green. "Nigger Jim," as he was called, came into the limelight as an unassuming hotel porter around the gold camp hotels. Later he became exceedingly rich, and then mysteriously disappeared. The source of his wealth was said to be reached by a secret trail in the vicinity of Yaqui Well. No one ever succeeded in following Nigger Jim to his mine. But at least once he stated positively that Yaqui Well was the last water to be had on the route which led to it. Nigger Jim Green was a close mouthed individual. Like so many others, he faded from the stage in a haze of mystery.

One could go on indefinitely weaving the web of story and legend which Time has built up around Yaqui Well as around the hub of a wheel. That grand old-timer, Charlie McCloud of Julian—who perhaps came closer than anyone else to unravelling the secret of the lost Pegleg—knew all the stories and could tell them by the hour. The only personal story that I can contribute to the collection—and it is a second-hand tale at that—is the account given me by an old prospector who declared that on one of his trips he came up with an Indian woman near the Narrows. It was nightfall and drizzling with rain to boot. But in the gloom he could just make out that the woman was dragging something which looked like the body of a man. She told him that this was her man, who had died recently.

She was taking him into one of the canyons to bury him. Pointing to the burros she asked for help, promising that if the white man would help her she would repay him with gold.

More out of sympathy than with any hope of reward the prospector agreed. The body was loaded on one of the burros and the woman led the way up a small side canyon. After a long journey through pitch blackness and almost impassable country the woman stopped at what appeared to be an ancient burial ground. Together they scooped a shallow hole in which the body was placed and covered with stones.

Then, bidding the white man wait, the woman vanished into the darkness. Rain had begun to fall and so swiftly did she disappear that it was impossible to determine which way she had gone, much less follow her. The prospector had no choice but to wait.

He waited a long time. After what seemed several hours she reappeared suddenly like a ghost at his elbow. "Come," she said. She turned and led the way back, following with an uncanny sense of direction the circuitous route by which they had come. Not until they reached the point where the other two burros had remained tethered did the woman speak again. Then she thrust a bundle into his hand. "This for pay," she said—and she was gone into the night. Rain soaked, disgruntled and stumbling in the inky dark the prospector finally located a spot to camp. Later when he opened the package the woman had given him his bodily discomfort and ill humor vanished. It contained several small nuggets of almost pure gold.

But his high hopes went for nothing. The rain had ceased by morning. But although he spent a week in the vicinity he was never able to discover where the woman had obtained the specimens. He could not even find the spot where they had buried the dead Indian. One more skein of mystery had looped itself around the ghost-haunted borders of Yaqui Well.

Ghosts are reputed to haunt the waterhole. Perhaps this belief comes from the fact that actual Indian burial grounds are in the vicinity. Charlie McCloud was responsible for a well authenticated story of an Indian who, wandering through one of these old burial places, picked up an ancient clay pot of queer design. He carried it home to his camp near Julian. That night the spirit of an old-time Indian witch doctor appeared to him with such fierce threats that the terrified bowl-snatcher got out of his blankets and, though it was midnight, started back to the desert. Nor did he rest until he had laid the ominous little bit of pottery back in the place he found it.

So much for legend and mystery. The fact remains, that despite its weird links with the past, Yaqui Well today is a peaceful and inviting spot. Giant ironwood trees close to the spring make alluring camping places. And though the desert moon can weave shades of wandering ghosts among the smoke trees and the calls of plover can, in the eerie stillness, simulate the complaints of disembodied spirits, there is peace. The desert silence lies over the old waterhole like a benediction. The world and its foolish bickering seems very far away. Under the soft blaze of the stars the wind whispers to itself as it wanders in the wash. The ocotillos sway darkly against the gloom of the ridges, and afar off, the coyotes lift their mournful voices amidst the tumbled rocks. Daylight or dawn or dark or in the hot stillness of noon there are many places in this weary world that are less attractive than Yaqui Well.

I am going back there again.

Desert Trails 6
(April 1948)

He who seeks for that upon which the Ancient People have placed a curse, follows a trail to death.
—Old Indian saying.

THE DESERT region which was once the bed of the ancient upper reaches of the Vermilion Sea—now known as the Gulf of California—is a weird and fascinating area. Civilization and progress, though they have pressed upon it roads and canals, have not destroyed its mystery.

The early Spaniards who toiled across these scorching wastes brought back fantastic tales of mirages and phantom ships. And you can, if you are lucky enough to find the right desert rats, still hear weird tales. Particularly is this true of the so-called badlands—the desolate section of eroded clay hills which lie upon the desert like a vast goblin relief map, the haunt of all the devils of desolation and of burning thirst. I have heard some strange tales of these badlands and have seen some queer things found in them from old iron cooking utensils, of curious design, to arrowheads, bits of Spanish armor and stone age axe heads.

My own contribution to this legendary material is strange enough, and thoroughly in keeping with the atmosphere of the region. Until a few months ago I could not have told the story. Now, however, the man whom it chiefly concerns, the last of an old Mexican family, is dead. There is no longer any reason for silence.

This is the tale of a lost mine. But the mine is not in the desert badlands. It is in Mexico. And it is still lost.

The location of "*La mina del tortuga de oro*"—the mine of the golden tortoise —is probably lost forever.

The story begins in the city of Guadalajara, which is the capital of the Mexican state of Jalisco. Years ago when Don Porfirio Diaz was president of Mexico and Don Miguel Ahumada was *gobernador* of Jalisco, I was in Guadalajara. And while there I made the acquaintance and became the fast friend of a brilliant young Mexican of high family whom we will call Fernando Suarez—because that is a name which does not even faintly resemble his real one.

One afternoon as we sat on a bench in the Guadalajara plaza, watching the Mexican army officers and important looking civilians who drifted in and out of the doorway of the *Palacio de gobierno*, Fernando Suarez told me the story of a lost mine. At the time, I had the feeling that he was mixing fact with fiction. But I have since changed my mind.

According to Suarez the ancestors of his family had come over to Mexico at the time of the Conquest. And, like most Spaniards who had a nose for Aztec gold and the source of its supply, they had been interested in mines. One of the mines which Suarez' ancestors had located—or rather had persuaded the Indians to reveal—was *la mina del tortuga de oro*—the mine of the tortoise of gold. He said it was very rich, and sacred to the Indians. It was located somewhere in the mountains in the region which is now the Mexican state of Michoacan. "For many, many years," Suarez continued, "my ancestors had in their possession the little gold tortoise from which the mine took its name. It was of very ancient Indian workmanship and not pretty to look upon. In fact it is—how shall we say— 'the bad luck.'"

The Suarez family never actually had worked the mine, although through Indian channels they had received considerable gold from its ledges. Its location was given on a piece of parchment which they had acquired from unrevealed sources.

Finally, when members of the family set out to locate the source of the gold they found the directions confusing. They tried many times, but always failed, and eventually the parchment was lost. But the ugly little gold tortoise (the *tortuga*) that seemed to embody the bad luck—or maybe the Indian curse, as Suarez said meditatively— stayed merrily on with the family. Suarez had often seen it in his youth. "It always," he said, "seemed to leer at me. It was an ugly thing, even though made of gold."

The family fell upon evil days. Eventually Suarez' father, who was a government official, was given a post in Baja California and the family moved to residence close to the United States border. The little gold tortoise went along. Accompanying them was an uncle, a brother of

Suarez' father. "He was," said Fernando feelingly, "a devil of the first class, with neither conscience nor regard for God or man. A thorough scoundrel." This uncle, Ramon, had the habit of going over, with painstaking care, all the old family records and documents—of which there were many. "This," said Suarez, "was the only work that he ever did in his whole worthless life." He made no secret of the fact that he was trying to unravel the clue to the lost mine. But by that time it was not seriously regarded. The years had dimmed its lure, and the family was wearied and crushed by troubles.

One day Uncle Ramon disappeared. And with him the gold tortoise. He left a sarcastic note saying he had discovered the clue to the lost mine—a map on a bit of parchment pasted between the leaves of an ancient book—and that he was going to be rich. Also that all his relatives could go to the devil. They wouldn't see him any more.

Which was the actual truth. They never did. Uncle Ramon apparently vanished from the earth. For long it was supposed that he had gone to Michoacan, where legend said the mine was located. But all inquiries failed to bring any trace of him—or of the golden tortoise. "The Indian curse of bad luck," said Suarez, dramatically, "undoubtedly dissolved him into the incomparable dust of hell."

So ended the story that was told me in the sunny plaza of Guadalajara. Some time later, after I had left Mexico, my friend Fernando Suarez, choosing his allegiance unluckily among the many factions of Mexico's revolutionary days, was shot against an adobe wall in a sleepy little town in Sonora, a hundred miles south of the U.S. border. I mourned him sincerely. He had been a dear friend and he was a brave man. I often wondered what had become of his little son, Pablo, whom I had known as a bright, eager boy.

The years passed, with their trail of lights and shadows—joys and troubles. Long years.

And then, one day, nine months ago, in the little town of Julian, California, a bright, athletic man walked in the door. I knew he was a Mexican. And in that same glance, before even he uttered a word, I wondered where I had seen him before. There was a something…

He greeted me by name and held out his hand. "I have read your articles for a long time," he said, smiling. "I know you. You knew my father."

Coyote

"Pablo!" I exclaimed, startled. "Impossible! Can it be that you are really…."

"But yes," he said, gripping my hand hard. "It is true. I am Pablo—the little boy whom you knew so long ago in Guadalajara. And I have things of importance for your ear alone. Where can we talk?"

We found a place to talk. And he talked swiftly and convincingly. That evening I left Julian with him in his car. It was an expensive one and powerful. Apparently he was not a poor man. But he told me frankly that the things I saw and judged by were about all. His finances were all but exhausted.

We camped that night in a desolate section on the edge of the desert badlands. If I am vague it is because I wish to be. This thing is now over and done. I will be no party to subsequent searchings. Hunters could find nothing. But they might possibly find death. The badlands are still bad.

We started walking in the early dawn—when the light was still ghostly and mysterious and the stars were still faint slivers of diamonds in a grey sky. Across the forbidding tangle of sculptured clay hills that lay before us Pablo Suarez extended a dramatic, pointing arm: "Uncle Ramon came here," he said. "He did not go to Michoacan. He was a scoundrel—and he feared to go too soon to the mine. But there were other scoundrels whom he feared also. All my life I have sought the clues. And I found them. Now we shall soon see if they are true."

We walked—scrambling and toiling on through a goblin land of eroded desolation. Dawn came and the sun. The badlands are not a pleasant place for walking exercise—especially when the sun warms up. Somehow those weird hills and ridges of glaring clay, carved and sculptured by ages of wind and rain grow upon you with a feeling of awful loneliness. They are devoid of life almost. Here and there, there may be a scraggly scrap of burroweed or a lone tuft of desert holly. But over all is death and barrenness. We had brought canteens of water and Pablo Suarez carried a small light shovel.

By what particular landmarks Pablo steered I do not know. But early in our tramp I discovered that he was steering a course —and a very precise one. He had told me casually that he was, by profession, an engineer and a surveyor. And I now thoroughly believed him. His clues and information apparently were very definite. He never faltered. Almost he seemed to be using a sixth sense. At one point, towards evening, we cut across a curved section of what was plainly a very ancient trail. There were some pieces of broken pottery to one side of it. And just where it vanished into nothingness on the edge of a scoured out storm channel there was a greyed piece of wood, set like a post, in the side of a clay bank. It was very old and weathered and there was a rusted bit of metal driven into it. It might have been an old knife blade.

Pablo Suarez, however paid no attention to the trail. He was evidently short cutting. He could walk faster than I could and he seemed all muscles and nerves, like a bloodhound on a hot scent. By nightfall we came upon the almost unrecognizable foundation traces of what had once been a little hut. It was in the desolation of a dreary gully. "This," said Suarez, wearily, "is the place. But first we must sleep."

By the first streaks of dawn the following morning he selected a place near what had evidently been the old chimney and began to dig with his little shovel. The thing is uncanny, but he struck the old metal box exactly. It was badly rusted and the lid crumbled in his hands as he lifted it from the hole. Inside was a modelled representation of a tortoise done in the ancient Aztec style. It was about the size of a small saucer and very heavy. With it was a packet, evidently papers or parchment, wrapped in fabric that had been soaked in either wax or asphaltum.

"Well," said Pablo Suarez briefly, "we seem to have succeeded. Let us go."

It was late that night when we got back to the car. We were very weary. But neither of us had any inclination to camp. We started back toward civilization.

Early the next morning Pablo "If I find the mine, you also, friend of my father, will be rich. But if I find only death, then write of me this story. It will make for you a good article and I would so wish it. It would be good to tell of the bad luck of this evil little *tortuga* of gold, no?"

He shook my hand and departed.

Six months ago he was slain by Indian bandits in the mountains of Michoacan. So I have told here the story.

Desert Trails 7
(May 1948)

The cities perish. And the "learning" goes.
  Empires depart and darkness comes again.
But, trodden in the dust by naked toes,
  The fragments of old urns and pots remain.

And in their testimony, lone and mute,
  Declare the riddle of the marching stars—
Bare feet, and clay, and singing minstrel's lute,
  Rise ever from the dust. Life knows no bars.

THE morning sun was high and bright over the desert as we headed our jeep up the steadily mounting slopes toward the upper end of California's Borrego Valley. Tints of rose and turquoise and that mysterious ashy grey which is so hard to define clung to the slopes and battlements of the towering Santa Rosas. And upon a heaving brown shoulder of the mountains, as though sculptured there by the chisels of a long-vanished race of giants, the weird, white figure of "The water boy" [Anza's Angel] trudged his monstrous, burden-laden march along the foothills. Just as he has done, mayhap, for the last five million years.

The road was good and our little car made good time. Jeeps are so efficient one can almost forgive them for the way they slaughtered up the desert scenery in war days. And, though my resentment dies hard, still, in spite of myself, I could not help a feeling of admiration for the sturdy little mechanical contraption that was presently racing us without effort through the green marching ranks of the ocotillos toward the De Anza Ranch.

The De Anza Ranch, which comprises the property homesteaded in the canyon mouth many years ago by "Doc" Beatty, flashed us a cheery greeting from its picturesque white walls as we wound down over the bluff and through the scatter of old buildings which were, for long, Doc's headquarters. The spirit of the desert by-trails began to close in with the crowding approach of gaunt mountain flanks and the rush of lonely canyon waters flowing down over a rutty, stony roadbed that was, for much of its length, nothing but the floor of Coyote Creek.

There was a good deal of water in the creek and our jeep carried a considerable load of camp equipment in addition to our party of six. Nevertheless, piloted by Mrs. Alma Loux, its owner, it made good time, splashing through stretches of foaming water and shouldering nonchalantly out of cavernous holes that would, in the old days of less versatile cars, inevitably have spelled disaster. One of the pioneer homesteaders of Borrego Valley, Mrs. Loux possesses an inexhaustible fund of desert legend and regional information. Her anecdotes of the early days, together with the many stops which Mrs. Myrtle Botts, head of the Julian Annual Wildflower show, insisted on making to investigate floral possibilities, put wings under the passage of time—despite the road difficulties. Shortly before noon we plunged our chariot down a break-neck bank, forged across a broad wash of white, deep sand and broke out into the wide brush-grown mouth of Indian Canyon, a tributary of Coyote Creek.

The day was perfect and there was a wine-like fragrance to the gentle wind that stirred through the mellow sunshine. Monster yellow and brown boulders, reminiscent of Ghost Mountain, clung in teetering awesomeness to the abrupt lift of the nearby ridges. Against a sky that was flecked by tufts of white cloud, the mountaintops, in breath-taking precipices of ragged, uptilted strata, bared savage fangs above the deeps of rock-choked canyons. Across the wide wash a lone palm lifted its trunk and tangled crest against the hillside like some sullen Papuan sentinel. And beyond it—beyond the clutter of mighty rocks and the green of sycamore trees which marked the confluence of Sheep and Cougar Canyons—a green headed cluster of at least a dozen more palms bulked in the distant shadows above a ledge.

The whole world was hushed, and wrapped in a silent peace that seemed as though you could almost reach out and touch it. But we were not alone. Along the sides of the canyon lay spots of reddish-brown color—the tents of a party of state employes engaged in the business of rooting out and destroying infected wild grape vines. But the landscape had swallowed the workers. The stillness gave no clue. We knew that they were up the canyons somewhere. But they might as well have been on some other planet for any hint of their existence. No sound of voice or echo of blow came down on the faint wind. Even when we saw them—much later—filing down a trail between the bushes, they seemed more like ghosts of the old-time Indians than living men. Silently they passed, and were gone. The hush of the desert mountains had laid its magic upon them. They were men in a dream. We also were caught up in the same fantasy. It was as though we had stepped out of the world.

But those silent canyons, cutting deep into the shadows of the San Ysidro Mountains, held a lure for us that was stronger than dreaming. One of the old-time residents of Borrego Valley, whose early-day hobby had been the exploring of its most solitary corners, had told us a story of a wild goose which, many years ago had been shot as it winged with its companions overhead. Falling, the bird had plunged among a clump of boulders, upon the top of which was a heap of brush, looking, at first glance, something like the huge abandoned nest of an eagle. Curious however, as he investigated where the goose had fallen, our informant had poked with his gun barrel amongst the heap of brush and dead branches. His probing struck sudden resistance in the center of the pile. Further investigation revealed the fact that the heap concealed a perfect and very finely decorated olla. It was almost full of ashes. Ashes which experts declared subsequently were those of some highly venerated Indian chief.

Mortero holes mark ancient Indian grinding areas. Photo courtesy of Lowell Lindsay.

Decorated ollas are rare in this section of the desert. So rare that it has sometimes been asserted that the early Indians never made them. It is declared that the few specimens that have been found were importations from a long way away, or even from south of the Mexican border. This last argument is, however, open to doubt. I have found occasional decorated fragments. And I am of the opinion that, on occasion, some rare pot maker did indulge in art flights. Usually the decorations are crude. But occasionally one finds markings which measure up to a very high standard. At any rate this story of the decorated olla had fired a craving to investigate the region. There were other stories too, equally, if not more, intriguing. But these, for the scope of this narrative, must wait.

So there we were—practically on the scene of the great discovery. Were there other ollas here? So many years had passed since that wild goose fell. Besides, suddenly, all the mountains and canyons roundabout seemed very vast. Ollas are little things. And the dusky, old-time makers were experts at hiding them.

Said Sterling Loux, our mechanic—who, by virtue of his uncanny skill with tools and also because he had once been part of a previous expedition into these parts, had accompanied us: "I'm just sure this is the place my brother and I came last year! See that rock....Well, now I remember! That's the place where we found a cave! And in the cave...."

His eyes were shining. And he was breathless with excitement—and all the importance of his ten, very-wide-awake years. He ran on, words tumbling over each other as he pointed out landmarks. But presently he began to falter. The solemn mountains grinned down on him. They seemed to wink sardonically. In the end Sterling wilted and gave up. "I'm not so sure," he said. "Maybe this isn't the place. Still, that rock...."

In the end the silence laughed at us. Our mechanic and guide admitted defeat. We split up our party and went our ways—up into hushed canyons amidst grey rocks and the murmur of cold gurgling crystal water. Old pottery cracked beneath our feet. Sherds. Big and little. Sometimes the almost perfect necks of old ollas. Traces of old camp fires. Old guide stones piled beside the weather-dim trails. Silence and the rustle of sycamore trees. The papery whisper of solemn palms.

No, we did not find any more painted ollas. We did not find any old sweat houses or decorated burial caves. But we had the feeling that all those things—somehow—mysteriously—were there. We sensed the spirits of the Old People among the rocks.

But we did find a fragment of gaily decorated pottery. A very tiny fragment. The lines of color were firm and bright and clear. No crude daubing hand had drawn those lines. It was like a star of hope to us. But, search as we would, we found no more.

In late afternoon we came back to our pre-arranged meeting point. And in the shelter of a mighty boulder, where undoubtedly the Old People had camped many times before, we lit our fire and cooked our meal. The wind had risen a bit and the fire tossed and flared. Squatting around the blaze one could not help reflecting on the cyclic path which man treads. He rises from the state of the open fire and his bare hands in the wilderness. He progresses and he toils and he schemes. And he collects gadgets and worries and pays income taxes. And, this being done, his soul craves, more than anything else, to return once more to the open fire—and his bare hands against the wilderness.

And this is the reason that so many people nowadays, who have been "blessed" with riches and this world's gee-gaws, will flock out eagerly to dude ranches and to resorts where, for fantastic sums per day, they can go back once more to at least a feeling of the primitive.

Verily the human being is a strange animal. Not yet, even dimly, does he begin to understand himself or the true value of life.

Desert Trails 8
(June 1948)

*"Feet of the Desert Wind, so softly shod
That on the dunes no trace your passing leaves,
Where are the Towns and Roads and all the Gear
Of centuries fled, o'er which the starlight grieves?*

*Is this the end—that in the silting sand,
Soft as the snow, which spreads its winding sheet,
Man and his works are doomed to pass and go,
Down blotted trails, lost to forgotten feet?"*

*Thus asked I. And the Silence made reply:
"Not so. Be not dismayed by 'loss' or 'strife.'
Dust covers up the old. But, like the seed
The 'old' springs up to 'new,' in deathless Life."*

WRAPPED around by Silence and the sun, old Borrego Spring broods on a mysterious past. For the ancient desert watering place Time does not exist. The clock has stopped.

All Nature has a sublime indifference to those hectic scurryings and mound-buildings which mankind imposes upon the face of the earth. The winds blow through the forests and the leaves fall and cover man's works. The sands of the desert drift and engulf them also. Man scratches in the earth like a lizard. And like the traces left by the lizard his marks are soon gone. Silence rolls in like a wave to blot the sound of his bickerings.

Particularly is this true of the desert. The desert is inscrutable—and wise. And of everlasting patience. The old spirits stand aside with an enigmatical smile until the shouters and noisemakers have gone. Then the old spirits of the land come back. This they have done at the old Borrego Spring.

An ancient Indian watering place of importance long before the advent of the white man, the springs today are probably more lonely and deserted than they have been for centuries. And this is surprising. For, not many miles away, Progress is again in the land. Human ants rush to and fro with much business and clamor. But the old springs sleep and smile in their dreams. The wind makes wire-thin harp notes through the mesquites. The dry reeds rustle in the stirring air and the hot desert sun casts ebony patterns from the spindling creosote bushes upon the bleak surface of the flood-flats. There are a few traces of broken clay pots as record of the Indians, and a few rotting timbers that tell of the one-time presence of the white man. The rest is loneliness—and Peace.

Though only a few miles eastward from the present activity center of Borrego Valley, the location of the old springs is today unknown to a great many people. In fact the original spring is not only little known but has in reality ceased to exist. The desert has buried it and planted arrowweeds and a sprinkling of crowding brush to cover its grave. But the springs themselves, like the immortal soul that dwells in man, still live. For, across the wash, a scant half mile away, the underground flow which fed the ancient Indian waterholes, rises to new life in a different setting. The springs have died—yet they still live.

The ancient history of the springs—and it must have been an interesting one, for Borrego Valley was a popular territory with the Indian people—is hidden in mystery. We may build theories about it by studying the contours of the surrounding country and by noting the many fragments of old Indian pottery which strew the region. Old burial grounds were not uncommon in the district. And the sand dunes and the desert ridges still yield abundant evidences of old and populous encampments. The background of desert mountains that rise to the north and northeast holds a rich atmosphere of legend to this day. There are tales of pre-Spanish gold mines which the Indians worked.

The ancient history of the springs can never be written, though it affords a limitless playground for a deductive imagination. But, coming down to the time of the white man's record, we find that the waterhole, in the beginning of civilized penetration, was known as "Nigger Springs"—this because "Nigger Jim" Green, well known around Julian and Banner in the early gold boom days, once made his residence there. Jim, whom reputable legend has connected with the lost Pegleg mine, was a mysterious character whom Time has buried, appropriately enough, in an even deeper mystery. His residence at the springs is, by now, an all but forgotten fact.

About the first white claim made to the springs was established by that well-known desert character, John McCain, who homesteaded the spot and built a cabin, the tattered, weatherworn remnants of which are today visible beside the ancient mesquite tree which marks the spot of the old spring. There are not many of these derelict timbers remaining, for the desert has done a thorough job of erasing the traces of the old cabin. But the few sticks and fragments lying amidst the crowding brush speak as eloquently of the transitory nature of all man's works as do the crumbling bricks of Babylon.

The era of McCain's homestead was in the days when the original spring was in existence. About 35 years ago earthquake shocks and floods obliterated this first, ancient spring. The same floods also cut off the shoulder of a nearby ridge, exposing a forgotten Indian burial ground

Myrtle Botts (right) and friend sample the water at Borrego Spring.

of great antiquity. Nearly all traces of this, however, have been wiped out by the elements and by souvenir hunters.

Neither floods nor earthquakes, however, sufficed to quench the Spirit of the spring. The life giving waters rose again through a new opening half a mile away, across the wash. This new uprise is, today, the Borrego Spring location. It is just a small "ojo," or eye—a grass-rimmed hollow filled with water which is a welcome enough sight in the sere austerity of the desert. The shoulder of a ridge rises behind it, and to one side there is a dense thicket of mesquites. Sunlight plays through the thorn trees and the silence, that is the soul of the desert, presses down heavily with a sense of peace. Most of these desert waterholes are ghostly—if you are sensitive to such things. And by this I do not mean anything terrifying or repellent, for desert ghosts are rarely that. But it is in such places that one comes to a deeper understanding and a sensing of Life. And of undercurrents which are not apparent to the usual flow of existence, but which are nevertheless very real and vital.

I spent some time wandering around the site of the springs—both the old spring and the "new," or resurrected one. No two desert places are alike, and there was an atmosphere to old Borrego Spring that was peculiarly its own. Back of the new spring, on the shoulder of the ridge, was an old metal road sign marking the trace of an abandoned dirt road to Brawley and El Centro. The traces of the old wheel tracks have all but vanished in the pressing ranks of the stunted desert bushes, and the old sign stands up gaunt and lonely and bullet scarred—another signpost of mystery. It is a government one. For it antedates the era when the Auto Club of Southern California placed markers on the desert roads. Somehow it intrigued me by its desolate loneliness… Signpost on the road to nowhere. Guardian of forgotten trails.

The huge, gaunt mesquite tree beside which the McCain cabin once stood at the site of the old spring, had a funeral look. Its black limbs, even in the brilliant sunshine, seemed to give a somber cast to the few rotting timbers that remained of the old house. It might have formed an appropriate roost for buzzards. And the rustle of the wind through the ranks of the dead canegrass that marked the site of the obliterated waterhole was like the mutterings of dusky spirits, jealous of the white man's intrusion in their old haunts. But in spite of the loneliness of the place, the harsh glint of the high sun on the white sand of the wash made a brilliant foreground to an alluring desert picture that was backed by the glow and shadow-deeps of distant mountains.

Salt grass and dead tules crowded about the sand buried grave of the spring from which both Nigger Jim and John McCain got their water. And clump grass and yerba mansa helped out with a pattern that held a compelling fascination in spite of its loneliness. It is significant that the old spring, despite its burial, still shows signs of life. The sands have covered it. But the evidence of moisture indicates that with a little digging in the right place it could doubtless be restored. However, with the new waterhole just across the wash, there is really no need to wake the sleeper.

Which calls to mind that this vanishing of springs is quite a common occurrence. In the case of the Borrego Spring there was a simultaneous new opening. But in the majority of cases when a spring disappears it stays lost. Old-time Indians have repeatedly told me that in the early days there were many more waterholes than there are at present. One old lady went so far as to assert solemnly that the good *Dios* was so mad at the cruelty which the Spaniards inflicted upon the Indians He deliberately dried up the springs as a punishment. Making allowance for some slight wishful thinking—and he would be a rash person who would assert that the theory is all wild imagination—there is also the very practical explanation that the Indians themselves deliberately lost numbers of springs as a means of causing discomfort to their white tormentors. These old-time Indians preserved, for a long while, accurate memories of the spots where the springs had been covered in. And, in case of their own journeyings, could go from hidden waterhole to hidden waterhole, across otherwise impassable stretches of desert. Carefully, each time, after slaking their thirst, they buried the precious water. So that the pursuing white man, and the foolhardy traveler, taking the same route generally left their bones to bleach in the wilderness—often within just a few feet of covered water. Particularly was this true in some of the stretches of Baja California. I have had well authenticated stories told me of Indian guides who

held the secrets of these buried life savers. Of course not all the lost springs were due to man's actions. Frequently earthquakes and floods, as in the case of old Borrego Spring, wiped them out of existence.

Any story of Borrego Spring would be incomplete without some mention of Bob Campbell. Bob was an old-timer of the region. And, being possessed of a generous proportion of Indian blood, he was perhaps particularly fitted to sense the romance and the mystery of the locality. Bob was reputed to know the location of more than one lost Indian mine. But the strain of blood from the Old People was an effective lock upon his tongue. He would not talk. What he knew—and there is reason to believe that he did know—he kept to himself. And perhaps wisely. Only the ignorant scoff at spirits and curses and the mysterious vengeance of the departed. I have seen a little of this myself. And I am not ashamed to say that I, also, am superstitious—if that is the word you want to use.

There is evidence however that Bob Campbell had a sense of humor that was not above taking advantage of the later-day white invaders. East of old Borrego Springs there is a sinister dark-colored rocky mountain which, probably in some connection from the old Indian past, is called to this day Ghost Hill [Borrego Mountain]. (This is not the Ghost Mountain of Yaquitepec, which lies a long way to the southwest of it.) The possibility is that old burial grounds on the hill were responsible for the belief that it was the prowling ground of disembodied Indian spirits. Natives firmly believed that ghosts, carrying torches prowled the slopes and eerie canyons at night time. Stories of lights moving on the hill during midnight hours are frequent.

At any rate Bob Campbell did nothing to dampen the interest in such tales. On the contrary he spread them. There are stories that he would frequently take out parties of the half-way credulous to view these night displays. And, having led them out into the desert in the darkness, below the old spring, Bob would manage to slip away from his confused charges. Very soon they did see lights—ghostly lights moving through the bushes and among the rocks. It was very impressive—for Bob was smart and knew how to do a good job. Perhaps he acquired merit from the ghosts of the Old People for thus hoodwinking the white interlopers in the ancient lands. At any rate the ghost seekers saw lights. And they were willing to swear to it. Ghost Hill had maintained—and it still does maintain—its shivery reputation.

Desert Trails 9

(July 1948)

Within a cave he sat. And, in the gloom,
Fashioned by flint and fire a murderous club,
Which, when 'twas done, he sallied, naked, forth,
To spill his neighbor's blood upon the ground,
That he alone might rule, and own the earth...
  "Lord, strengthen Thou my hands that I may slay!
  "Power! Give me power—more power! My cause is just.
  "Oh God of Battle and of Glory—Hear!"
    (His cave is empty now. And in the Spring,
    Above his bones, and ruins, wild birds sing.)

Rimmed by high towers of glass and gleaming steel,
He sat and pondered, lean and cold of eye.
And at his touch the lightnings flared and burned
And ghastly things of Steel, with mighty wings,
Sped high above the world—to give him power...
  "Lord, strengthen Thou my hands that I may slay!
  "And blast ten million lives at just one blow!
  "Oh God of Battle and of Glory—Hear!"
    (His towers shall perish, and the sea waves roll
    O'er him who "gained the earth"—
    and lost his soul.)

LIGHT grew in the east. On silver sandals, from the dusky dimness that was the distant line of the Rio Colorado, dawn came stealing across the desert. Coyote Peak stood up cool and blue and phantom-like against the faint flush of the approaching sunrise. Far away, to the south, in the hazed reaches of the ancient river as it pushed towards the gulf, there lifted a dim column of smoke.

The desert was silent with the electric hush of expectancy—the old, old, ever-new miracle of a new day. Around the stony little open space where I had spread my bedroll the night before, tall mescal stalks, a-bloom in their full glory of yellow flowers, stood against the cool wash of the dawn like banners of gold. Already wild bees and a myriad of nectar-loving insects were gathering to the feast.

As the light brightened and the red ball of the sun rose out of the phantom mists of the eastern horizon like the fantastic dome of some Arabian mosque, I saw that all the ridge slopes around me were laced with a delicate weaving of

Sidewinder

gleaming silver lines—long, trailing streamers of spider-web. In the glint of the sunrise they streamed and waved from every mescal stalk, way up and down the slope as far as the eye could reach. Fairy cables trailing in the softly stirring air like slipped mooring lines of a myriad dream ships that had set sail with the dawn. A hooded oriole came in a flash of color from across the ridge and perched on the stalk of a mescal flower almost over my head.

And it was then that I saw the olla neck. I had not noticed it the night before. It had been late when I had spread my bedroll. And I had been weary. But now, suddenly, just as the bird lit on the swaying flower, my eyes flashed to it. Was there some connection? Some strange interrelation of spirit-stirrings or magnetic currents about which we know so little? Who shall say? At any rate there the fragment lay. It was just under the shelter of a plump and bristling mescal plant and almost within reach of my hand. I scrambled out of my blankets and picked it up.

There is always something about primitive pottery that has a particular fascination. It is a feeling that is deep and fundamental. After all, despite our advance along the road which is supposed to lead upwards from barbarism we have none of us come very far. Our heartstrings are still very closely interwoven with open fires and arrowheads and earthen pots. The bond between man and clay is still strong. It is a bond which, on this earth at least, can never be broken. The body of man is created of the dust of the earth—and so is the body of the pot.

Sitting on my blankets in the sunrise I examined my find. It was an olla neck—perfect, as far as the neck part went. And there was a bit of the side of the pot, about six inches long and three wide, in its widest part, still attached to one side. The rest of the vessel was missing. I searched among the mescals and found several other small pieces. But they were all tiny. The majority of the fragments which must have been strewn around when the pot broke had vanished.

A delicate and graceful pot. Smaller necked than most that I had seen. And very well made. The old Indian potters never used a wheel—which is perhaps why their pottery has so much soul. A wheel—the first step up the ladder of separation which leads from the soulful feel of handcraft to the soulless hardness of machine craft—destroys something in pottery. It is like all other mechanical inventions.

I sat a long time in the sunlight looking at my bit of handformed, baked clay. It was all at once more than just a bit of broken water bottle. It was a link. A timber in a vast bridge of souls that seemed to span, suddenly, all the tremendous stretch of space between the sunrise and my lonely hillside. The fingers that had made this fragment had been part of the vast human pattern of brotherhood of which I myself was a portion. The shadowy touch of them seemed to reach across the centuries. Almost under my own fingers I could feel the moist yield of the wet clay. In a breath, it seemed, my whole desert hillside was alive—peopled with an invisible unbroken procession of life. And was not raucous, jarring, trampling and shouldering life. It was a comforting, steady, all-enfolding ocean.

How many people are there who are interested in pottery? In primitive pottery sherds? The number is very great I imagine. Almost all desert-lovers are. It is a fundamental feeling. It is like following back along an old and well remembered trail.

And the trail has an endless fascination. Always, as one prospects for the traces left in the desert by its early dwellers, new angles and surprising discoveries are turning up. They do not have to be epochal or things that will shake the scientific world. There is just as much thrill in the simple finds (and probably just as much importance—when it comes right down to it.). Imagination is often a much more reliable guide than science when delving into the past. Imagination speeds ahead—and senses. Science lags behind, poking in the dust and arguing over trifles. Science usually leans over backwards in a desperate effort to escape accepting a perfectly obvious fact. It is a painful life to be really scientific.

So, if you are independent enough to throw science and its dark glasses out of the window, you can have a lot of fun and acquire a very worthwhile understanding of human nature by collecting—and speculating over—the traces of primitive man which you will find almost everywhere in the desert. Human history, in this land which we today call America, stretches back to vast periods of romance and antiquity. The waves of human migration—the crest and ebb—the development and decline, form one of the most fascinating studies which it is possible to engage in. If you are not already familiar with the works of Churchward on the lost continent of Mu, you will find these books vastly interesting reading. Science is, grudgingly, being forced finally to consider this long known and very obvious evidence. [James Churchward, *The Lost Continent of Mu, Sacred Symbols of Mu, Cosmic Forces of Mu*, and *Children of Mu*]

Even though you do not have the luck to find many—or any—perfect ollas or pots, you will most certainly discover a wealth of sherds. The desert is strewn with such an accumulation of these fragments that it provides much food for thought. Not only as to the density of previous Indian populations but also as to the duration of man's residence there. Most of these fragments are run of the mill—commonplace. But one never knows when something startling and thought provoking is going to turn up. Not only in pottery scraps but also in other evidence.

There was, for instance, the bit of old blue-and-white patterned plate—a looted piece perhaps from some burned wagon train. This provocative fragment, of which I have given here an illustration, was discovered down on the edge of the badlands of the Colorado Desert. It is, of course, white man's pottery. But from it the dusky new owners—and perhaps also the murderers of some family of westward pushing emigrants—had endeavored to chip an arrowhead. Unacquainted with such hard pottery, and doubtless deceived by the glassy glaze into thinking that the material was akin to obsidian, they had tried to make an arrowhead from their prize. And had failed… What a story there may be behind this old fragment. He would be dull indeed who could not derive a thrill from trying to reconstruct it.

Then there are the occasional bits of painted pottery which will appear from time to time. These are always full of absorbing interest. Generally the potters of the southern California desert tribes did not decorate their ware. So when you find a bit that has painted lines you instantly start a train of speculation. Did it come from the pueblo tribes, part of trade exchange? Did it come from Mexico? Or did it perhaps come from Asia in one of the ancient migrations? Then there is Mu always looming in the background. Did some potter of the ancient, vanished continent originally fashion the pot whose remnant lies in your hand? Each possibility opens almost endless avenues of speculation. Clay, one of the most primitive of things, is also one of the most indestructible after it has been fired. It lasts and bears record. All the iron and steel and the fancy towers of a vainglorious civilization crumble to rust and dust. But the pot that came from Mu may still survive. Fundamentals last. The further you get away from them the more perishable you become.

Or—and this is another fascinating scope for guesswork— the decorated bit you may happen to find may be a strictly local product. There were local potters who did decorate. There were only a few of them, it is true. But some did. Often this decoration consisted of inscribed lines, traced on the wet clay with a sharp stick or a thorn. But some of it was genuine painting. I have a friend who once found a fragment of highly glazed pottery in the litter of an ancient desert Indian camp. Was this glazing an accident? Was it local make or an import? Unfortunately there was just a scrap of the pot—just one. Questions like this are baffling. Sometimes it seems that fate enjoys beclouding the record.

Then also there was the olla found in a cave not very far from Ghost Mountain. Upon the side of that olla was a crude design of a man on a horse, with (as the discoverer told me) his feet pointing backwards instead of forwards. Was this a clumsy quirk of the potter artist—and primitive people seem to delight in such quirks—or was it an impression of an early Spanish horseman wearing the huge spurs which the Latins frequently affect? Here we have room for more speculation. This pot, however, dates itself. It was fashioned well within white-man's times.

The same however cannot be said of the bit of pottery picked up near the entrance to Sentenac Canyon. This bit is undoubtedly very old. The illustration which I have drawn cannot show the crude texture of the clay or its color. But this bit shows the clear trace of some sort of an impressed design. Most designs are drawn crudely with a thorn. This one has been pressed in by some die or tool. It suggests the branching rays of a sun—or was it part of the arms and Legs of a crude human figure? There is not enough of the design to answer these questions—and not another fragment of the pot.

What also of the tiny pipe bowl, found buried in an old Indian campsite, also on the edge of the Colorado badlands? This relic is most probably not desert Indian. This little pipe bowl has evidence of glaze. It was obviously made in a mould of some sort, and was intended to be attached to a stem fashioned either from a quill or a reed. With it, at the same site, were found several small saucers, possibly used to contain face paint or for the materials of some witch doctor. Was this pipe bowl Chinese or Mexican? Or is it much older—or more modern? You can speculate.

Of undoubted antiquity however was the ancient stone axe—or hammer—head, discovered in 1937 by Robert Garmire, one of the earliest settlers in Imperial Valley. This relic, of which a sketch is here given, was dug up from a depth of many feet underground, in an excavation of the All-American canal, on the east side of Pilot Knob. Mr. Garmire, who was then—and still is—connected with the California division of highways, happened to be on the spot when the relic was uncovered, and it is still in his possession. How did it get where it was found? What sort of a man was it who dropped this primitive weapon? And how came the very obvious mark of a tube-drill on the side of the stone? More speculations. But they are a lure that beckons ever onward. Once a person starts down this trail of discovery and speculation there is no turning back.

So, if you are not already a student of the great book of the past, whose torn fragments are littered so generously over the desert, I recommend that you get started. It

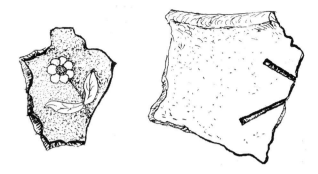

Indians had attempted to chip an arrowhead from a broken white man's glazed pottery (left). An Indian shard (right) with a design pattern. Sketch by Marshal South.

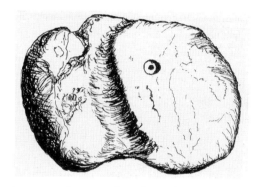

Ancient stone hammer found at Pilot Knob. The dark eye is a drill hole. Sketch by Marshal South.

is fascinating. Also, broken pots, if enough fragments are found together, can be glued together and restored. Also, one can graduate to the actual making of pottery. There is a fascination in that, too, as I can testify—having done it.

Desert Trails 10
(August 1948)

ABOUT 13 miles down from the mountain town of Julian, California, State Highway 78 shoulders its way into the high and barren desert ridges which form the entrance to Sentenac Canyon. And right by the canyon entrance thrust out Gibraltar fashion amidst the green ocean of tules which parallel the road, there stands a rocky promontory. Upon the top of this boulder-piled headland old Paul Sentenac once had his home.

Paul was an emigrant from France. And, in the 80's, he had a goat ranch at the mouth of the canyon which now bears his name. His stock ranged the surrounding foothills and desert playas and doubtless grew fat on the lush herbage of the tule marshes which are fed from the waters of the San Felipe Creek.

Old Paul was a rugged character about whom many picturesque stories still are told. The imagination of the tellers has colored these tales and with the passage of time they have drifted into the province of legend. You may hear many yarns about Paul. And, as would be expected, nearly all the versions hint that he had a cache of treasure. This is quite in keeping with desert tradition, because almost everyone who has become an old-timer or an outstanding character on the desert, is popularly believed to have dug holes and buried away a mysterious cache. Some did, it is true. But not many. However, the tale-tellers must have their fling at mystery. Someday, undoubtedly, eager diggers will go prodding and gophering about my old home at Yaquitepec on Ghost Mountain. I wish them luck. There was and is wealth on Ghost Mountain—but not the kind you can put in holes in the ground.

But it was not with old Paul's legendary treasures or with the details of his picturesque life that we were concerned on the bright desert day when I parked my car in an alcove in the mesquites alongside the highway and made my way on foot across the marshes. I wanted to see his homesite. I had never visited it and had a craving to view at first hand what might be left of this former citadel of a salty emigrant from France.

White faced Herefords of the San Felipe Ranch herds dotted the green of the tule marshes with generous splashes of red. Some of them didn't look too friendly, so I detoured to a deserted section before invading their realm.

Water in the desert country has an enhanced significance. And the gurgle of the San Felipe Creek as it swirled about my ankles as I floundered through the tangle of reeds was pleasant. There was much watercress growing among the tules, and, in spite of my water-sloshed shoes, I delayed a little while to gather and nibble some of this tangy herb packed with vital energy which science calls vitamins. The Herefords, browsing afar, watched with suspicious interest, and I reflected that in some respects the dumb animal has an advantage over the self-important human. Animals can rustle their food with a minimum of fuss—and they get all the good out of it. Whereas the lords of creation cannot enjoy a meal without the employment of a host of gadgets.

The first trace of man's abode as I made my way out of a thicket of mesquites and started up the rocky slope was the remains of an old post and brush corral. In her unhurried indifference to man Nature is very thorough. Winds wipe out footprints and storms dissolve walls. And the endless drift of the mellow days consigns, in the end, the mightiest sweat-reared human works to oblivion. As time is measured in human affairs not many years had gone past since that old corral was in active use. Now it was a few forlorn heaps of blackened sticks lost among the desert bushes. But it served to whet my interest.

Sherds of old Indian pottery were scattered on the boulder strewn slope above. The dusky dwellers of the desert had appreciated the strategic importance of the site long before Paul had pre-empted it. Pottery is a "book" which reveals many secrets of the lives of prehistoric tribesmen. "Man," says the sage, "was created from the dust of the earth." And, following the example of his own Creator, man himself created his pots from the same material. But the pots survive the physical forms of their makers. And give foothold for the imagination.

Standing there on the slope with a scatter of earth-brown olla fragments spread out before me it was not hard to reconstruct the past. The same silent mountains had rimmed the horizon. The sky had been the same blue. And the far reaches of the desert had swum in the same haunting elusive haze of distance and mystery. There had been no cattle in the marshes. Nor had there been the

The ruins of Paul Sentenac's cabin. Sketch by Marshal South.

ribbon of concrete highway with its shuttles of speeding cars. But it was somehow easy to forget these later details. Brown feet were again on the slopes. And healthy free naked bodies at work or play about the old camps. One seemed to hear voices in a strange primitive tongue. But perhaps it was just the wind, coming up the canyon and stirring through the creosotes.

One may wonder just what dream was in old Paul Sentenac's mind when he settled here and built his castle. For castle it was —at least in the making. The desert has a way of sapping dreams. And more often than not heroic plans wilt bit by bit— even during the sweaty labor of them—until the final result is another monument to futility.

At any rate Paul began his dream on a heroic scale. Massive retaining walls of laboriously piled boulders and powder-cracked rocks bear witness to his toil—and to the play of a directing imagination. The mortarless walls are falling. Storms and vandals have overthrown many of the granite blocks. But enough remains to show that the Frenchman who chose this as his desert homesite had ambitions far beyond the rearing of a mere desert shack. Perhaps he had in mind one of the old feudal castles of his far-away homeland. It may be, that in the back of his mind, banners floated from the summits of towers that were pierced with narrow slits through which bowmen could launch their barbed shafts. Perhaps mailed knights trod the courtyards and made a brave show upon the lofty battlements. Who knows? At any rate the beginnings of a dream are still there. But it is a crumbled dream. How full the world is of them.

Let no one think that there was ever any magnificence about Paul Sentenac's residence—even in its heyday. It was probably quite humble—even the scanty remains of the old stone cabin attest that. Perhaps, to a casual visitor, there would appear to be little of interest in the tumbled rocks and the remnants of the old retaining walls. But if one looks deeper, there is a better key to the nature of the builder than is obvious on the surface. Paul had something. One must have something of the poet or the artist or the dreamer to build his home upon a hilltop. Most men build theirs in holes and hollows. It is easier.

Creosotes and cactus grew among the old foundation walls and cluttered the road which once led around the brow of the rocky bluff. There were a few fragments of shattered dishes. A few old nails. Bits of rusty iron and the usual scatter of old tin cans. There weren't many relics. The place has been thoroughly combed over during the years that have elapsed since Paul died. Among the rocks, though, weather-bleached among scraps of obsidian from ancient Indian arrowheads and cheek-by-jowl with sherds of shattered olla, we picked up an old-time pocket lighter. Upon its embossed copper side was engraved the date of its manufacture—the year 1900. Not much of an antique, but still almost half a century.

Treasure hunters and seekers after Indian relics have contributed in no small measure to the wrecking of Paul's old home. The myth of buried wealth has been responsible for many trial holes sunk within the enclosure of the old walls. Such mining operations bring speedy ruin to any building. And today there isn't much standing that will give any clue to what the house looked like. There are the remains of a small fireplace—with, of course, a treasure hole gaping in the earth not far from it—and a couple of angles of foundation wall. Paul used some old Indian stones in his building. Some of the walls were, on that account, wrecked by relic hunters to extract rubbing stones and metates. The seekers have made a thorough job of it. Nothing now remains to tempt further effort.

None of the stories I have been able to gather about Paul throw much light upon the manner of individual he was. Since it is so hard to judge those among whom we are thrown in daily contact, how shall we form opinions of a man about whom the vague threads of gossip and misunderstanding have been woven for many years since his death? Some say that he was a hard man. Others that he had a wealth of likable qualities. We do know that after his death a brother came out from France to settle up the estate.

But what matter? Human life is a fleeting thing. And after all it is not the physical that counts; nor the success or failure of earthly affairs. The thing which is enduring is something which cannot be seen, touched or measured by material standards. It is the spirit of a man. His ideas— the inner light or urge by which he moves. Such a hidden light burns in every man and woman regardless of the valuation either for good or evil which the world places upon them. And as surely as he lives each will in some manner in life, betray something of that secret inner nature that is the real self. In the ruins of his desert castle, Paul Sentenac has left his monument and his epitaph. He was one who dreamed dreams. He had something of the divine fire of the poet. The tumbled stones of his hilltop Gibraltar prove it.

With my companions I ate lunch in a shady cove formed by the spreading trunk and branches of an ancient mesquite tree about half-a-mile from Paul's homesite. In backward glance, through the lacy pattern of leaves and branches, the old castle site lost none of its romance. The warm sunshine of the desert beat down in the silence, and the rocks and ridges and the dim reaches of the desert quivered in the heat waves. The wind drew up from the lower reaches of the canyon in lazy wide spaced drifts that rustled the leaves over our heads and threw a shimmer of sun patterns over the brown twig-strewn soft earth upon which we sat.

Where the old tree grew had once been an ancient Indian burial ground. All around the surrounding area it was possible to pick up pieces of fire-blackened ollas, and according to reports, more than one cache of human remains had been dug up and removed within a few paces of where we sat. But the rustle of the leaves in the gnarled old tree whispered only of peace and forgetfulness and of something better and beyond and more satisfying even than the bright silent sunshine of the desert.

We ate our lunch with peace and contentment in our hearts. It mattered not to us that beside the lunch basket, in the changing pattern of sunlight and shadow, there lay a scatter of tiny fire-scorched bony fragments. We knew they were ancient fragments of human bone. But peace was upon them also. They were part of a mighty pattern that is free from fear. It is the pattern of Eternity.

[Many people believed the stone house was built by Paul Sentenac. In actuality, it was built by Paul's brother Pierre. Paul had a wood cabin but moved into Pierre's stone house when his brother died in 1905 and lived in it for many years. He later sold his Sentenac Canyon property in 1925.]

Desert Trails 11
(December 1948)

[Comments from Editor Randall Henderson]

This story from Marshal South came to the Desert Magazine *editorial desk in late summer and was in the composing room awaiting publication when word came on October 23 that the author had died the previous evening. Marshal has been a regular contributor to* Desert *for more than eight years—and there are many readers who will share with our staff a deep sense of loss in his passing. He will be remembered as one who has disclosed new beauty and understanding to those of us who have followed him along the desert trails and we are sorry, very sorry that his earthly trail has ended.*

WILL the old Indian emerald mine in the Santa Rosa Mountains bordering Borrego Valley ever again be re-opened and worked?

That is a question which I have asked myself many times, particularly during the last few days. Probably the answer is "NO!" But *quién sabe?* Perhaps I attach too much importance to the words of old Pablo Martinez. And anyway, I have been accused of being superstitious. But you shall form your own conclusions.

This old Indian mine truly belongs to the class of lost treasure. But it is lost only because I doubt if it is within the power—or at least the profitable power of white men to recover it. It is one of those things which Nature has taken back unto itself.

Comparatively few people, I think, have ever heard of this old gem mine. The legend is not as well known as that of the Pegleg or the Lost Arch and other will-o-the-wisps which have taken such hold upon the imagination of Southwesterners. Nevertheless the emerald mine perhaps more rightly deserved a first place than any of these. Emeralds—good emeralds—are rare. And there are comparatively few emerald mines in the world. This one—the one in the Santa Rosas—is, judging by the claims of legend, probably the only one of its kind in the United States.

The story of the old mine has always fascinated me. Perhaps because it was so very difficult to learn anything definite about it. Yet I have never had any real doubts as to its existence. Several individuals have tried to find it. And some have come very near. One who put his hands—or rather feet—closest to the location was the late Bob Campbell, old-time resident of Borrego Valley. Bob—who had a generous proportion of Indian blood in his veins—almost found the mine. On the last lap of his search, something stronger than hope of wealth deterred him. "I am afraid," he said simply. "I cannot go on. The spirits of the old people do not want this mine discovered. I must go back."

His companion protested and argued. But Bob was obdurate. He turned back. The search was abandoned. The old mine, which legend says had been worked from the earliest times by the desert Indians, who had a trade route for the gems down into Mexico and beyond, was again left in its shroud of mystery.

So, through a number of years, the thought of this mysterious Indian gem deposit has held my interest. Several times I have been on the point of setting out to hunt for it. But always something intervened. Recently, however, the opportunity came. In company with Robert Thompson, a South American mining engineer, I went in search of the mine.

We were not alone. For Thompson, who came from the southern republics several months ago on an extended vacation, had found somewhere an ancient Indian Pablo Martinez. Pablo who was very old and hailed originally from Hermosillo, Sonora, averred that his great grandfather had been one of the workers in the emerald mine.

Stories concerning it had been handed down, he stated, from father to son. Some of these stories, to which I listened, obviously were fantasy based on a slender thread of truth. But there were others that sounded convincing.

Thompson knows emeralds—the Republic of Colombia, where he operates extensively, produces many of the worthwhile emeralds of the world. Also he knows Indian psychology. We set out on our trip with high hopes.

There wasn't anything particularly mysterious about the initial part of our trip. We wound down through Borrego Valley and across Clark Dry Lake. The base for our search was to be Rockhouse Canyon, as it had been for Bob Campbell and the various others who had preceeded us. We took the car as far as we could, parked it and made camp for the night. The next morning with canteens and light packs the three of us set out on foot.

Rockhouse Canyon and the site of the Rock House deserve some mention in their own right, for they are interesting spots with an imagination-stirring atmosphere all their own. But I cannot spare space, at this time, to devote to them. Our quest lay beyond, among the precipitous slopes and barren ridges. Without delay we struck off into the savage, upended terrain.

We were not traveling entirely blind, for by diligent sifting of all the reports which I had been able to unearth, I had some idea as to where to head in. Old Pablo began from the first to justify our rosy hopes. Either he had actually absorbed a lot of information from family legends or else he was acting under some sort of an uncanny inherited sixth sense. At any rate he seemed to know his business. He led off oddly in the manner of a man who knows just where he is going. He was astonishingly wiry despite his years—scrambling up over rocks and ledges with the agility of a mountain goat. From time to time he would pick out old Indian trail signs that neither Thompson nor I would have noticed. We began to feel curiously elated. The grip of a strange excitement mounted in us.

Nevertheless it wasn't going to be as easy as all that. As the rugged tangle of the mountain increased we began to realize this. Desert mountains are heartbreaking,

especially under a hot sun. Everything was thirsty and barren and the glare hurt the eyes. Doubling up gullies and floundering across interminable ridges began to confuse us. We were tired and our nerves were getting jittery. Pablo lost his agility and began to lag well in the rear. As the day wore on he became either confused or sullenly unwilling. "A ridge with rock formation on it that looks like a castle" had been part of the vague information. But all the rocks looked like castles. The upthrust of weird boulder-shapes against the skyline was bewildering.

We made a camp at dark in a lonely depression between desolate ridges. I, for one, had the feeling that we had circled aimlessly. We were all depressed. At least Thompson and I were. Pablo said nothing.

Marshal South's sketch of where the emerald mine is probably found—below tons of rock.

The stars were points of yellow fire against black velvet. And the thin wind that came down from between the ridges was lone and chill. I fell asleep listening to Thompson telling a yarn about searching for an emerald mine in the Andes. I didn't hear it very well. I was disheartened.

I slept badly. It seemed to me, in my dreams, that the lonely canyons about us were peopled by a myriad of ghosts. Brown ghosts. Unfriendly ghosts. Several times I awoke in a cold sweat. Pablo was restless too. Only Thompson seemed to be sleeping soundly. He is a practical man and has little use for spirits.

We aroused to a chill and cheerless start well before sunup. We had a cold breakfast. Our enthusiasm of the day before had all evaporated.

And then, all at once, and not a hundred yards from the spot where we had camped, we came upon the Indian trail sign which marked the terminus of Bob Campbell's attempt. I recognized it at once, from what had been told me. Two big brown rocks, set one upon the other, with a smaller white stone on top. And off to one side a couple of

Mountain lion

tall boulders leaning together at the tops like an inverted V. I gave a shout of triumph that brought Thompson running. Even Pablo brightened up. His old enthusiasm returned. He began to jabber excitedly in Spanish.

After that things began to go better. It was as though we had turned some sort of corner. I don't know what it was. But I think it was principally Pablo. He had changed. He shuffled around a bit, scanning the ridges against the skyline. Then he started off at his old wild-goat lope—and in a direction totally different to that which common sense would have dictated for us. "Look now for *un cabeza del lobo,*" he grunted. "Way up. On top."

But it was not on top of a ridge that we eventually found "a head of the wolf." It was way down in the bottom of a steep gully. It was a mere chance that caused Thompson to glance at the fallen rock mass. But as he did he gave a yell of excitement.

"There's your wolf head," he shouted. "Look down there! Wrong end up!"

It didn't take two looks to prove he was right. The outline of a wolf's head was unmistakable on the rugged mass, even in its upside down position and with the clutter of fallen stones that lay piled around it.

Thompson's practiced eye was sizing up the opposite slope. "Earthquake," he said briefly. "The old boy was right. It has been on the top of the ridge. But a heavy earth shock must have toppled pled it. And there, if I'm not badly mistaken, is your mine. Goodbye emeralds!"

He was pointing. And following his leveled finger my heart sank. An earth shock, and a heavy one, had done it, without doubt. All the slope opposite was a cascade of smashed rock and jumbled boulders. The old emerald mine, if it had been, as Pablo had averred, below the wolf's head was now hopelessly buried beneath millions of tons of rock and earth.

And as we stood there, stunned by the realization, we were aware of old Pablo, skipping and scrambling up over the fearsome slide like a malevolent billy goat. About half-way up he sat down and pointed to the rocks at his feet: "*Aquí!*" he shouted down to us, "*Aquí,* señores! Here is where was *la mina.* But make not the false expectations. The emeralds are still here. But they are not for the white man. This is a curse from the old people. The mine will never be worked again except that it be by the *indios.*"

There was a sort of wild, fierce triumph in his cracked voice. At that moment he looked less like a wizened old man than some spirit of his people, gloating at our disappointment. But just then we were both too dejected to pay much attention.

We spent most of the rest of that day searching the vicinity. We uncovered evidence enough that here, in all probability, had been the ancient mine. We found pottery sherds in plenty, and fire traces of old camps. In one place, where the sliding rocks had swept aside its earth covering, we found an old burial—an ancient grave. And amidst the bits of age-weathered human bone something sparkled like a bit of green glass touched with flame. Thompson pounced on it. "Emerald," he exclaimed breathlessly, "—and of first quality! Look!" He shoved it at me, along with his pocket lens.

Yes, it was an emerald all right. Small but fine. And in the hollow where the bones lay we found also bits of pale green mineral—beryl, the substance emeralds are found in. We had found the site of the lost emerald mine of the Santa Rosas. The decision was inescapable.

But much good it did us. Here was the mine—"Here," as old Pablo said, pointing downwards. But hundreds of thousands—perhaps millions—of tons of rock lay above the primitive workings. Where would come the machinery and the money to heave aside all this disheartening, monstrous overlay? And in the end, perhaps, draw only a blank. Another disappointment.

"For you never can tell about an emerald mine," Thompson said. "Emeralds go in 'pockets.' And the old-timers may, after all, have worked it out. You never can tell."

Yes, you never can tell. Nor will anyone now, I think, ever tell. Well, we had the fun of finding the lost emerald mine of the Santa Rosas. But the irony of it is that it is still lost.

PART FIVE—
MISCELLANEOUS ARTICLES

Mescal Roast
(December 1939)

FOLLOWING an age-dimmed trail through the clear, hushed dawn of an April morning, we reach our destination at length—an ancient circle of fire scorched stones. It is about 12 feet in diameter. Within it, in the center of the level patch of flame blackened earth which it encloses, there is another roughly ranged ring of rocks. This inner ring is perhaps three feet across. An old, old mescal roasting hearth. How many Indian feasts, in the dim past, have its fire-smudged stones witnessed? Who now shall say? But we have used it also ourselves many times. We are no strangers to its delectable product.

The sun is up by now and we set swiftly to work. Eagerly our five-year-old runs to a great boulder and, with a wary eye for possible lurking rattlesnakes, drags from a dim recess beneath it two ancient digging sticks. It was there, long ago, that we found them. They are heavy and weathered with age. But they are still serviceable. For us, as for the aboriginal brown hands which placed them in their hiding place, they win toothsome banquets.

Tanya is hunting for fuel—her efforts curtailed somewhat by the task of caring for the youngest "tribal member" who is too small as yet to be given free rein in a world of bristling thorns. But that does not prevent him from giving advice. There is an oriole trilling away off on the summit of a tall, dead mescal stalk. About the scarlet flowers of the swaying ocotillos, hummingbirds flash. Over to the left, against the tumbled boulders at the foot of the ridge a bulky bisnaga flings back the sunrays from a glowing crown of yellow blossoms.

Meanwhile our five-year-old and I have scooped a shallow depression in the loose earth in the center of the smaller stone circle. We have brought stones from the outer ring and laid them in the depression. And finally we have brought in the rest of the stones from the outer ring and built them as a sort of coping around the edge of this circular hearth, leaving spaces between them where we are to lay the mescal hearts.

Now for the hearts themselves. These, in spite of this year's abundance, take some finding. For they must be just in the right stage of growth. They are best when the big, new shoot is first beginning to thrust upwards. With our digging sticks—when we have found a mescal plant in this stage—we wrench out the shoot and core of the plant. Then we strike off the top of the shoot and trim the leaves. For this job—for once sacrificing sentiment to utility—we use a modern hatchet. The resultant product, a clean bud about 15 inches in length and eight or 10 inches thick at the butt end, is laid in one of the spaces left between the stones piled as a rough coping around the hearth.

When we have filled the openings left in our ring of stones, stones alternating with buds, we are ready for the fire. Over our little circular hearth and its surrounding

Mescal or agave (agave deserti).
Photo courtesy of Lowell Lindsay.

ring of stones and mescal butts, fuel is piled thickly. Principally this fuel consists of the dry stalks and dead plants of the last season's mescals. But all sorts of handy dry brushwood and sticks are pressed into service. It has to be a rather big fire and the more material in it that will produce hot coals the better.

Usually the fire is kept up for about half an hour or so, the embers falling in on the shallow stone-lined pit. When it has burned down and the stones are hot the fire-charred mescal buds and the hot coping stones among which they have lain are tumbled into the shallow hearth-pit and over the hot heap earth is piled generously.

This, for the present, completes the process. If there is time—and there usually is—we will move on to the next old roasting hearth and repeat the process. And to the next. Weary—for the work is hard—we tramp homeward through the desert dusk along the ancient trails.

From 36 to 48 hours later we are making the rounds again, opening our pits, raking aside the rocks and levelling out the heaped earth. Queer things these charred, limp butts appear as we rake them out of the ashy sand.

Queer, strange looking things! Yes, but when the charred outer covering is removed and the golden-brown interior mass, sweet as molasses and resembling somewhat a cross between a baked sweet potato and a delectable slice of pumpkin pie, comes into view then is all expended labor amply rewarded.

Tasty and delicious! A flavor all its own! Delectable when fresh and even more so when sun dried—in which state it will keep for long periods—the heart of the mescal makes ample amends at the last for its long life of savage, dagger-armed viciousness.

"*A-mooch*" some of the California Indians called the mescal. Botanists call it *Agave*. But what is a name? Wending homeward with our burdens of rich, tasty sweet, our hearts are happy. The "old people" who made these ancient trails and fire-hearths were wise in their generation. Hail to the Mescal!

☀ ᴍ 🌵

Campbells of Vallecito Desert

(December 1939)

ONE DAY a party of motorists stopped at the ranch home of Lena and Everett Campbell in the Vallecito

Desert of Southern California and jubilantly announced they had discovered a white ocotillo. "And we marked the place so we could come back and get it later," they boasted.

Now white ocotillo, for the information of those who do not know, is exceedingly rare in the desert Southwest. There are millions of ocotillos with red blossoms, but those with white flowers are almost as hard to find as legendary lost gold mines. Except when they are in blossom the red and white flowering plants look exactly alike.

It was not news to the Campbells that a white ocotillo grew on the desert a few miles from their ranch house. They had discovered it years before, and guarded the secret of its location carefully. To them it was almost a sacred shrine—and the thought that the rarest plant in their desert garden had been found by people so thoughtless as to suggest removing it, was depressing indeed.

They said nothing, but the next day Mr. and Mrs. Campbell rode down the valley to visit their pet shrub. Sure enough, a stone marker had been erected beside the white flowering ocotillo.

Carefully, stone by stone, they moved the marker to another ocotillo, a similar one of the common red variety some distance away. And then they smoothed the sand to hide their footprints.

Several weeks later, after the flowering season had passed, they visited the spot again. Someone had been there with a truck and dug the marked ocotillo out of the ground and removed it, roots and all. But the white ocotillo was safe.

Everett and Lena Campbell are that kind of people. The desert is their home. They know about the struggle for existence in the land of little water. They have been through it themselves.

Located in one of the wildest and most colorful sections of the desert—a region steeped in the atmosphere of the old overland stage days—they fit their surroundings perfectly. True pioneers of the old West, they and their ranch home nestling in a green oasis at the foot of savage desert mountains have become a legend and a landmark.

A well-graded road leads over the hills to the Campbell ranch. Dynamite and tractors have torn out the side of the mountain and provided easy access to their little oasis. But it was not that way when they came to Vallecito Valley. In the early days Everett Campbell and his wife and daughter followed a winding, narrow, perilous grade, a rocky trail gouged out of the side of a precipitous slope.

There is a history to that old grade. Cars have gone over the brink of it, crashing down into the rocks.

It was on that grade that Lena Campbell, one wild, snowing winter night, driving home with her husband from

Julian, where she had taken him to get a broken leg set, saw car tracks in the snow—*car tracks that went over the edge into space.* She stopped her car and set the brakes and chocked the wheels with stones as an extra precaution. Then she climbed over the edge and down through the dark, over boulders and cholla. There was a wrecked machine down there, and an old neighbor dead beneath it. Lena Campbell took her injured husband home, and when she had settled him in bed, drove back alone up that grade through the wind and storm all the way to Julian to notify the coroner. "The trail *did* look awfully narrow, that night," she admits. "But of course I had to go. There wasn't anyone else."

And it was over that grade and the lonely road beyond, that for a long period Everett Campbell's young daughter, Orva, used to bounce in a ramshackle old Ford, on her daily trips to school.

The ranch house lies under the lift of the barren mountains, a scant quarter of a mile from the thread of road where, on dark desert nights, if you are imaginative, you can hear the ghostly teams and creaking coaches of the old Butterfield stage go by again on the wind. The house today is big and rambling and western, with Navajo rugs, Indian baskets and deerskin stools keeping company with oil paintings and massive, carefully selected modern furniture.

The original house the Campbells built years ago, when they cleared the creosote and mescal of the virgin desert for its foundations, has been added to several times since. But the great cottonwoods which shadow it with rustling green are the same trees Lena Campbell and her pioneer father, the late George McCain, planted back in the ranch's beginnings. There is grass beneath those trees and cool shadows. And as you pass up the wide path, bordered with Indian mortars and relics and weird desert rocks, you catch the pleasant sound of running water.

There is peace and welcome here—the peace and welcome atmosphere of all that was best in the old West of 50 years ago. Sunlight strikes patterns across the big screened porch, and the gracious lady who comes with smiling welcome to greet you is part of the gracious atmosphere. Gunfighters and senators, cowboys and

Lena and Everett Campbell.

governors, famous artists and weary desert derelicts—all have known the peace of the Campbell ranch porch and the hearty straightforwardness of an old-time western welcome. "You can't judge a man by his clothes or his pocketbook," Everett Campbell says bluntly. "You've got to treat him according to what he really is—and if he needs help."

"…if he needs help." There, in those words perhaps, as in no others, you have the key to the Everett Campbells. They are no "easy marks"—no one who has fought the desert for the years that the Campbells have is likely to be an easy mark for schemers. But you will not hear of a case or a time when genuine misfortune ever called in vain for aid at this western ranch. It may be an Army flier, driven to a forced landing in the desert wastes; it may be a starving "bum" who has lost his way. To one, as to the other, goes the helping hand in the unfaltering code. It is a strict code and just. For 20 years Everett Campbell carried a sheriff's star; he carries a star today. And if need be, the eyes that are swift to soften with sympathy at real misfortune, can grow hard as steel.

But these are sidelights. The business of the Campbells is cattle raising. It is a romantic enough job, even in hard actuality. But it is also hard work. Everett and Lena have not been afraid of work. Their ranch is a monument to their industry.

It all looks simple perhaps. The casual visitor, unaccustomed to the desert, is apt to take a great many things for granted. As he drives past the big, tree-shaded reservoir on his way down to the ranch house he may admire the cool glint of the water, ruffled perhaps by the hasty flight of the wild ducks that find there a protected refuge. But he cannot know the amount of courage and hard work that went into the bringing of that water there. It comes from Mason Valley—brought from the other side of the mountain in a line of ditch and by a pipe line that Everett Campbell built.

It cost them $10,000 to put that 10-inch pipe and its constantly flowing stream into that big earth reservoir. In addition there was the hard work. "Packing the cement up the side of the mountain was one of the hard jobs of building that ditch," Everett Campbell told me once when he was in a reminiscent mood. "For a long while we packed it up on our backs. Then we got a burro. After that it went a bit easier."

What water means in the desert and what it will do, is demonstrated in the lush alfalfa fields, dotted with sleek, grazing cattle, below the reservoir.

There are no stores to run to. The Campbells have had to rely on their own efforts and be their own mechanics. If ironwork is needed or if machinery breaks Everett Campbell rolls up his sleeves and lights up the forge in the smith shop.

A broken wheel on an automobile would dismay most women. Not so Lena Campbell. It happened one day when she and her daughter, Orva, were driving to town. They were going to a party. That was in the days of the old road. In the fierce, heat-reflecting Box Canyon section they had the bad luck to become trapped in the deep sand of a wash. That might have been bad enough, but in their maneuvering to get out of the sand one of the front wheels crumpled. "We had just lurched free from the sand, too, when it broke," Lena Campbell said as she told the story casually. "It was too bad."

"But what did you do?" I asked. I had lively recollections of that lonely, scorching stretch of the old road.

"Oh, of course we had to fix it. We just jacked up the wheel and put it together and lashed a couple of tough pieces of ocotillo on with wire to strengthen the broken spokes. It wobbled. But it took us back to the ranch."

"And the party was off," I condoled.

"Oh no," she said. "We weren't going to miss *that*. Orva had set her heart on it. We just piled out of the car and grabbed the little ranch work truck and started for town. We startled Everett I guess. He was riding in from the range when we rushed by him on the truck. We hadn't time to stop and explain. We just waved. But we were at the party on time."

Everett Campbell is an expert horseman. Today however, he doesn't go out of his way to break wild horses just for the love of it, as he once did. A man of exceptional knowledge and wide reading, he keeps abreast of all that is going on in the world, and especially in the cattle business. He brought Brahma bulls out to the desert and developed a cross with the Hereford that produces a hardy breed of cattle of superior beef quality.

The Campbell cattle brand is the swastika—the sign that was ancient long before the Indian association with it. Campbell smiles about that. "My friends come out here sometimes and look at my cattle brand and think I stole the idea from Hitler," he chuckles. "Why, I was branding my cattle that way years before I ever heard of Hitler. The swastika is one of the most ancient symbols in the world. It's pretty near as old as human history, I guess."

Through his efforts the big ranch is now a game refuge, under the protection of the fish and game commission. Here many state-raised game birds have been liberated for the purpose of breeding and of re-stocking other areas. In the soft desert evenings when the jagged mountain peaks are rosy in the glow of the sinking sun and shadows lie across the valley, it is a pleasant sight to see the quail, with their broods, drifting into water.

And Everett Campbell has been a conservationist in other things. It was he who saved from destruction by vandals the ancient timbers of the old Vallecito stage station, during the years when the historic ruin was at the mercy of "treasure" hunters and the unscrupulous. It was natural, therefore, that when the county of San Diego decided to take steps to restore the landmark they chose Everett Campbell to supervise the work. The old stage station, as it stands today restored in every faithful detail, is a permanent monument to Everett Campbell's ability and to his sincere interest in his desert and its history.

Everett Campbell was born at Las Animas, Bent County, Colorado, May 11, 1886, and most of his youth was spent in that state. A lover of the outdoors from the first, he crossed the plains with the last of the great trail herds and at 18 was holding down the difficult job of foreman of cattle outfits. Educated as a chemist, the lure of the outdoors drew him back into the cattle and stock business. A project of shipping horses from Colorado to San Diego resulted in his settling in the southland. Here, in 1905, on Las Viejas Ranch, one of the properties of the late George McCain, he met and married Miss Lena McCain. The young couple subsequently moved to Imperial Valley where Everett Campbell spent five years with the Imperial Irrigation District. He returned to San Diego in 1914 to become associated with Arthur W. Savage in the San Diego plant of the Savage tire company.

The lure of the outdoors was not to be denied however; the stock business was in Everett Campbell's blood. Some years previously, while on a trip with George McCain, he had been impressed with the Vallecito section. There, at one point, was the possibility of developing water. It was a dream which persisted in his mind—a dream which his wife shared also. The idea eventually grew so strong that contrary to the advice of his business associates, Campbell resigned his position as supervising chemist at the Savage tire plant, and embarked upon the hazardous occupation of desert cattle ranching. On the 17th of March, 1916, the Campbells settled in their present location and broke ground for their home.

It is not all work on the Campbell Ranch. Of late years out of the rewards of industry, Everett Campbell and his wife have been able to find time for interest in other things. Of course their main "interest" is in their sturdy, five-year-old grandson, Rodney, whom Orva brings often now on visits to the old home ranch so that he can "look over the cattle business" and play cowboy about the big corrals. But, for matters outside the family circle, lodge work has drawn the Campbells to a great extent. Everett Campbell is one of the best known Shriners in San Diego County, and this year Lena Campbell, as worthy matron, presides over the destinies of the Santa Maria Chapter of the Order of the Eastern Star at Ramona.

It was my privilege to be present and see Lena Campbell installed in that office. As we sat there during that impressive ceremony, I could not help wondering just how many there were in that gathering who realized that the gracious lady who took the gavel of office and made her clear, straightforward speech of acceptance, and her husband, the bronzed erect man in evening clothes with a white carnation in his buttonhole, were really what they *were?* To me they are something more than good American citizens. They are symbols—living symbols of an American ideal and an American era that has no parallel in all the world.

They are the kind of people who are preserving the American ideals—just as they are protecting that exquisite white ocotillo which grows down the valley below their ranch.

Home on the Rim of the Desert
(April 1947)

[Comments from Editor Randall Henderson]

Banner Queen was once a roaring gold camp. But the rich ores pinched out and the camp had long been abandoned when Bill and Adeline Mushet rediscovered the rambling home where the mine superintendent had lived. It was a lovely setting high up on the edge of the desert. And now they have restored the building with its old-fashioned balconies—and have found contentment in operating it as a cattle and guest ranch.

WHEN the late Charles F. Lummis, picturesque author and individualist of the Southwest, was building with his own hands his romantic home in the Arroyo Seco, Los Angeles, he had for spectator and self-appointed helper, a thoughtful little boy of twelve years who was tremendously interested in the building of walls, the fashioning of adobe bricks—and in each item of Indian handicraft in the Lummis collection.

The little boy's father was one of Lummis' closest friends. And with this passport, as well as that of his own eager interest in everything of the West, the Indian and the desert, it is not surprising that the bond of friendship which grew up between the boy and the celebrated author-builder was very close.

That little boy was William Mushet. And the fruits of that friendship with Lummis when the boy grew older, were a succession of construction jobs, all of them flavored with the picturesque. The very first of these was connected with the making and placing of adobe bricks in the construction of the "Casa Adobe," an annex of the Southwest Museum.

That was the beginning of a colorful career of building and contracting. The word colorful is used deliberately. For, as Bill Mushet says today: "There are just two ways to do a thing. Either you can love it and put art into it, or you can figure it as just a job to be done—and make grim drudgery out of it. And I don't care if you are building a palace or a hog pen. The same truth applies."

And color and imagination and genuine love of the work in hand went into all of Bill's construction jobs. He prospered and made money. On the side—for his own amusement and his own home—he fashioned furniture and gadgets and bits of art work, each of them with the distinctive flavor of the pioneer West and the Indian desert country that is part of his nature.

Bill was fortunate. For when he married Adeline the team was complete. Adeline, or Ad, as she is known to all her acquaintances, was an artist in her own right. She sketched, painted, hammered upon silver, wove and wrought batik, and had a flair for interior decoration. Soon the Mushet home resembled a museum of handicraft. The job of adequately housing the collection became increasingly complex. All this time Bill was working and building and making money.

"But I wasn't satisfied," Bill says, "and Ad wasn't satisfied either. The thing was empty. There was something we wanted and hadn't got. Money isn't everything. You can't feed your soul on it. Besides, the youngsters were desperately important. We wanted to give them the best possible foundation in life."

Finally, Bill closed up his contracting business and Ad shut the door of her gift shop. They took their car and headed inland, away from the creamy surf of the California beaches. They headed toward the desert.

It was a long search. "We traveled all over the Southwest," Ad says, smiling reminiscently. "We hunted all sorts of sections and couldn't find a thing that suited the ideal we had in mind. We were discouraged when we turned homeward. It just didn't seem that the place we wanted existed anywhere on earth."

But it was on the homeward trip that they found it. Right in the desert foothills of their own backyard—in southern California. It was the old story of the man who searched for diamonds —when they lay, all the time, within arm's reach of his own back porch.

Bill and Ad had found their dream place. And it was in San Diego County, on the rim of that enchanting desert of the ancient Cahuilla Indians [Banner is in Kumeyaay territory; the Cahuilla lived just to the north]. Leaving Julian the road tips downward along safe and easy grades through the wind-harped music of the pines towards the long, mysterious vistas and mirage ghosted buttes that are the desert wonderland. It is a great land; a mighty and mysterious land which no modern intrusion of man—neither concrete highway nor droning airplane—has been able to rob of its charm and mystery. There it lies, shimmering in the sun; each turn of the road opens it up in new vistas of breath-taking beauty.

And, inset like a jewel on the inner edge of the mountain uplift that forms the rim of the great bowl, you will find Bill and Ad's haven. It nestles among the desert foothills, its green trees and cool trickling rills of water glistening in the sun. You can't miss it, for it is only six miles down the grade from Julian, and just a short distance beyond the ghost-remnants of the once roaring mining camp of Banner. Banner was a booming camp in its day, when the golden flood that poured from its mines drew hard-fisted miners and adventurers from all parts of the nation. But the winding-sheet of the silently drifting years has covered it. And today, the old townsite, almost utterly denuded of its once crowding buildings, sleeps in the shadow of its oaks and sycamores. Only the name remains. Banner! It is significant.

The Banner Queen ranch has captured and still holds much of the flavor and romance of the old-time mining days—and of the days long, long before the miners ever

came. In the gravels of the creek there is still gold, and beneath the broad spreading oaks there are worn mortar holes. Holes that were made who shall say how far back in the dim past by patient Indian women, grinding their acorns and mesquite beans. Somehow, beneath the oaks and the sycamores and beside the trickle of the little creek,

The Mushet family (from left: Mike, Buzz, Adeline, and Bill) and the Banner Queen Ranch. Photos courtesy of Buzz and Dorothy Mushet.

there dreams a land of yesterday—a colorful atmosphere of the past which the genuinely western ranch maintained by Bill and Ad does nothing to disturb. Rather it adds to the charm. For with the happy gift which both of them possess, they have succeeded in wedding the past to the present in a picture that is both restful and fascinating. And then, too, there is Leandro.

Leandro—Leandro Woods, to give him his full name—is an institution at the Banner Queen Ranch. Leandro is one of those rarest of rare things, a genuine old-timer of the frontier. Romance—in boots —walks with Leandro. Just to see him roll a cigarette—to see him swing into his saddle—to see him wheel his horse amidst the dust and excitement of a roundup—is to catch a genuine part of the days on the border—the days that are almost gone. Leandro's eyes are almost always cheery, with a glint of genuine good fellowship. But there are slumbering lights in them. Once in a while they can flash hard. Then you can see another Leandro. A Leandro who once swung racing coaches across the dusty deserts of Sonora and whose eyes could glint hard along the barrel of a blazing six-gun. Because he is so good natured and nearly always joking, many people do not see the real Leandro. He is an old-timer of the Julian district and *muy hombre*. Leandro can, if he will, tell you many a tale of the old days, the old days of Banner, and of Julian—and of the Mexican border.

Bill's business is cattle ranching. But he still amuses himself by making original and artistic furniture for the rooms and cabins of his big ranch house. And Adeline still beats upon silver and indulges her talents for painting and interior decorating. Indeed I suspect that they get more satisfaction out of these pursuits than they do from the colorful business of the ranch itself.

Bill and Ad now take a few guests at their comfortable ranch house, where Jerry, Ad's sister, assists with the management. "I didn't have to do it," Bill told me, "but somehow I felt so darn selfish, locking up all this peace and sunshine for just ourselves. It didn't seem right. So I decided to make the experiment. It's worked out well and we're very happy over it."

Perhaps the reason why Bill's guest experiment has worked out so well is that neither he nor Ad look on their paying guests as guests. To them they are friends — and real friends at that. Guests may come to Bill and Ad as strangers. But they cannot remain so. There is something about the genuine warmth of welcome, something about the flavor of western hospitality which exists in the great ranch house living room, with its hand carved furniture and great ceiling beams, that banishes all feeling of aloofness and substitutes the warmth of a friendly handclasp.

"It's a pretty good world," Bill said to me not long ago. "Pretty good if you go after the good things in it. Only some people haven't sense enough to know what the good things are. Maybe I wouldn't have known either if it hadn't been for the things I learned from my Dad, and from old man Lummis. But anyway I'm glad I had sense enough to cut away from the grind and throat-cutting and to head out here. I didn't know just exactly what I was looking for when I closed up my business and started out to search. But anyway I found it. Found it right here."

He fell silent, leaning back in his old rawhide chair and staring out across the railings of the ranch house porch. The sun was setting and a maze of purple shadows were weaving mystery through all the tumble of mountains and ridges and far desert washes. You could almost see the Past there—hazy and mysterious as a half-veiled picture. And with it the Present— which is no less alluring. A nighthawk went by like a shadow, brushing the ranch house eaves with a faint rustle of ghostly wings. And presently Adeline came out and stood silently, the turquoise and silver of her Navajo bracelets gleaming mysteriously in the shadows. The pinks and blues of the far reaches deepened and darkened and faded and the peace of night drifted in to fill the great, mountain-rimmed bowl.

Yes. Bill and Ad have found something. They have found it on the rim of the desert.

[Banner Queen is now owned by Buzz (Gary) and Dorothy Mushet. It is no longer a guest ranch. It is now the Banner Queen Trading Post Gallery, which sells art and gifts, and is open Friday through Sunday from 1 to 5 p.m.]

Healing Waters of Agua Caliente

(July 1947)

[Comments from Editor Randall Henderson]

To the Mexicans who first explored the Southwest, every spring where warm water comes from the ground was agua caliente. *In Spanish the words mean warm water. Today there are many Agua Calientes on the map— and one of them is located in San Diego County, California, where Americans seeking health come to bathe in its mineralized waters. So far, this Agua Caliente has resisted all efforts of those who would commercialize it— and Marshal South has written a vivid account of life in a community where there is cooperative democracy, without admission fees or profit.*

*T*HE INDIANS have gone now, and so have the bighorn sheep. But in the hushed peace, where the desert wind rustles the mesquites and stirs the tall ranks of the arrowweeds, the hot and cold springs of Agua Caliente still spill forth their healing waters across the sunlit sands.

It was on a day in late April that I went back to Agua Caliente, in San Diego County, California. I had not seen it for many years. But this day, all at once, the urge of it was upon me. Perhaps it was the throbbing stir of the new springtime. Or perhaps it was the haunting voice of the wasteland calling. Or perhaps I was just curious. "Agua Caliente has changed," some people had told me. I wanted to see for myself.

Scarlet Buglers winked their gay flowers along the footslopes of the sierras, and as my old car wound its way out into the desert, along the roadside there were lively scurryings of quail. The mesquites were vivid green jewels in their new leafage, and here and there in the brown-gray monotone of the silent, stretching land, the Spanish bayonets were exploding in fountains of creamy-white bloom. Sunlight, sharp and dazzling, beat upon the harsh flanks of the tawny hills, and the canyons that lay beyond the low crests of the rolling fore-slopes were mysterious in a thin haze that was as blue and metallic as the fume from hot artillery. Warm quiet lay over all the world. There was a faint stir of wind, but it was hushed and meditative. Away to the southeast a towering thunderhead, rising above the dim distance of Mexico, was a mighty carving of ivory, posed against the vivid blue of an inverted turquoise bowl.

Ocotillos flaunted their crimson flags along the ledges of Box Canyon. And in the lower reaches of Mason Valley the tall green spears of the mescals already were flaming to gold. It was lower here, and warmer. Blossoms were further advanced. The mesquites were showy with feathery tassels and the canary-yellow flowers of the creosotes were already well interspersed with the silver spheres of developed seed pods. The car radiator boiled lustily, demanding frequent stops for refilling from the battery of five gallon cans which I always carry. The radiator, like all the rest of the car, is old and temperamental. It has been that way so long that I would not feel quite at ease if it were to reform.

Past Vallecito—the sleepy brown adobe of the restored old Overland stage station brooding its memories against the green of the tule marshes—and along a winding road that followed a wash and then lunged between sere ranks of savage Bigelow cholla. And then, suddenly, three-and-a-half miles beyond Vallecito, a battered metal sign: "Agua Caliente Springs!" I swung into the side trail and threaded between the thrust of thirsty foothills.

And, abruptly, there was green—the soft friendly green of clustering mesquites and catsclaws. And there was the sway of arrowweeds, and the shadows of little gullies and canyons and the sunlit glare of grotesque formations of white, chalky earth. There was the brown blur of tents and the flash of the sun upon the metal sheathing of parked trailers. Agua Caliente—Hot Water. Yes, since last I had seen it, the place had changed.

But changed for the better. Somehow I knew, even before I had parked the car and climbed out. You sense those things. All places have an atmosphere of their own—either for good or ill. And there certainly wasn't anything ill about my first impression of Agua Caliente. It was decidedly friendly, and refreshing and different. I was at home—and very happy about it. Because I had come prepared to find—well, never mind what I had come prepared to find. As long as the world rolls, I suppose, there will be a certain class of people who will spread malicious and unfounded reports. They would spread them about Heaven itself—and have, in fact, done so. But it is nice, sometimes, to explode their fabrications.

Figures were moving among the trees. From the quiet, unobtrusive assurance of their actions they might very well have been a part of the long dead days that are past. These people were not Indians, though. They were modern Americans. There was no sound of voices or camp activity or clamor. Peace moved with the wind through the sunlit green of the mesquites and the catsclaws. And the rugged strength of the backing, everlasting mountains lay like a benediction over the little cove. The old spirits of the desert had not been dispossessed. They still ruled. You forgot the glint and the shapes of the city-built trailers. They had been transmuted.

The two fig trees were still there—and the two pepper trees. By whose hands they had been planted I do not know. But they are lusty trees now. They fitted the landscape too, and were part of the picture with the native vegetation. But the little cabin which in former years had stood near them, had vanished as though it had never been. Torn down and hauled away to the last board and nail by other desert dwellers perhaps. Or perhaps burned. Anyway it was gone.

There was a box lettered "U.S. Mail" nailed to a post. And near it a neat sign which directed me to the "City Hall." There were other signs too, very neat and orderly, which gave the names of established residents and indicated their campsites. Some of the citizens of Agua Caliente have been there a long while.

Civic office, title and honor—all of it purely complimentary and unofficial—gravitate naturally, in Agua Caliente, to the residents of longest standing. I therefore set out in search of Mrs. D.J. MacDonald, who, by virtue of residence seniority, now holds the office of "mayor." I was not unmindful of the fact that I had been promised the keys of the city should I ever happen to come to Agua Caliente.

I found the mayor in an attractive "office"—which was a cozy, tree-shaded trailer, tucked away in a peaceful camp-spot. She was reading a book of philosophy. But this was laid aside in order that proper official attention might be given to my stated mission. The promise of the keys of the city was recalled. But diligent search failed to locate them. It was concluded that the last person to be so honored had pocketed the keys and forgotten to return them. Only one of the keys was any good, anyway. That was the key of an old Yale lock—which had been lost. The other two keys were of the kind used to open coffee cans. We concluded to do without the keys. But the mayor graciously consented to act as my guide and escort in a tour of the city. The squad of motorcycle cops were away on vacation, and the "official" city car was laid up for repairs. The mayor suggested, apologetically, that we walk—pointing out, as a happy afterthought, that only a burro, or a pedestrian, could navigate the narrow trails anyway.

Agua Caliente is unique. I know of no other place in the desert—or in all the West, for that matter—just like it. As a natural health resort it has a long and honorable history, stretching further back into the mists of the past than we can ever hope to penetrate. For how many years—or centuries—these healing springs, both hot and cold, have welled from the earth and spilled their precious waters across the glinting desert sands, no man can tell. But the Indians knew of and appreciated the waters and the locality. For long it had been their custom to bring their sick there for healing. In those days the bighorn sheep were plentiful in the neighborhood and the dusky dwellers of the wastelands and the nearby mountains used the springs not only as a sanatorium but also as a hunting base.

Perhaps, of any man now living, Bob McCain, that grand, picturesque and fiercely individual western cattleman, whose stock have ranged the surrounding desert for decades, could tell you the most of Agua Caliente's past history. Frank Stephens of the San Diego Museum, could have told you too—and dear old Charlie McCloud. But Frank is dead now. And Charlie also has gone on the final prospecting trip across the sunset ridges. The history of Agua Caliente wavers towards the confusing shadows.

But what matter? The waters are still there. And so is the sun and the peace and the song of the wind through the mesquites. If you want history the gentle ghosts can tell it to you. You can find them anywhere in the desert if you will lie in your blankets in the still of the starlight and listen for their whispering voices.

Cures? Well, one could tell many stories of well-authenticated cures which the waters of Agua Caliente have wrought. But the mayor, as we made our rounds of the pools and bathtubs, scattered through the mesquites and arrowweeds, was insistent on restraint in this matter of the healing powers of Agua Caliente's water. "Please be cautious," she urged. "We would not want to misrepresent or to give any erroneous impressions. Our waters here are healing. They confer great benefits and they work wonderful improvements, it is true. But the word cure is very wide and positive. I would not wish anyone to build too much hope, and be disappointed."

I agreed with the mayor. She is like that—the soul of sincerity and integrity. But, even as I agreed with everything she said, I studied her a little as she stood against a tall thicket of arrowweeds on the margin of a limpid, rock-lined pool. And I could not help remembering, as I noted the healthy desert tan of her cheeks and the clearness of her level eyes, that a year ago, when she had come to Agua Caliente, a sufferer from arthritis, she could barely walk or move and couldn't use her hands. She had been in a bad way—much worse, as she admits herself, than many other sufferers who had resigned themselves to the prospect of spending the rest of their earthly spans in wheel chairs. But she hadn't fancied an exit of that sort. She had no taste for wheel chairs. So she came to Agua Caliente instead. And she has done reasonably well.

Less conservative was my old friend Joe Edwards of Julian. I hadn't expected to find Joe at Agua Caliente, but as I rounded the corner of a trail there he was, hailing me from his seat at the foot of a mesquite. "Cures?" said Joe, as we sat in the shade. "Now let me tell you about cures. Especially of rheumatic fever! Just look at my son, will you?"

I looked at the fine young man, who had just then come up. Bare skinned to the waist he was the picture of sun-tanned, healthy vitality. "The springs did it," said Joe with deep feeling. "Why, do you know that boy lay in bed for five months dying with rheumatic fever. We'd about despaired of being able to do anything for him. Then we brought him down here—last year. Up to now, off and on, he's been here between seven and eight months. The springs did it."

Yes, the springs had done it. The springs—and the sun and the desert. I talked to young Joe Edwards. He is almost 19 now—supple and tanned as an Indian, and good to look at. He showed me his own tub where he takes his mineral water baths and sun baths. Like all the other tubs and bathing facilities which the campers at Agua Caliente have installed—by their own labor and at their own expense—it was scrupulously clean. The clear, crystaline warm water bubbled in through a pipe, and there was also an ingeniously devised shower. The bath-house was roofless and the warm desert sun beat in with electric health. Outside the wind came down the flanks of the mountains and across the mesquites in a gentle rustle that was somehow full of peace and healing and abundant promise. I sincerely believe that it would be hard to stay sick at Agua Caliente. There is a something there.

And it is that very something which the present residents of Agua Caliente—campers, all of them—are especially anxious to hold and to protect. They don't want the springs commercialized. For they realize that the minute this happens the something will be killed. The virtue will be gone—and these free healing desert hot springs will be lost, for all time, to the very people who need them most.

And they face a very real danger. For all down through the record there have been attempts to grab Agua Caliente. To commercialize it—to exploit it as a profit enterprise. There are such plans in the offing right now. Fostered by interested parties, all kinds of rumors are in circulation regarding Agua Caliente. The place, you will be told, needs supervision and control—meaning that it should be made to pay a profit to someone. To a great many warped minds it is nothing short of a scandal that there should be a desert spot where the general public can go freely and, without cost or fee, enjoy the waters of healing which the Great Spirit designed for the benefit of all his children.

Thus the undercover agitation for the control of the springs—for the erection there of some sort of a charge sanatorium. It is the old story. Many attempts have been made to tie up the area. Men have tried to homestead it—working in secret agreement with commercial interests. Other men have dug holes in the ground and endeavored to hold the territory as a mining claim. There have been all kinds of subterfuges.

But uncannily, every one of these schemes has failed. Misfortune—and death—have been the weapons which the Guardian Spirits of these healing waters have wielded against every designing individual. And with deadly effect. For no scheme—or schemer—however suave and plausible, has ever succeeded. The miners have been broken, and thwarted and frustrated. The homesteaders have pulled out in disgust—or have died. Strangely, grimly, the Spirits of the springs guard their own.

But the citizens of Agua Caliente today, are nevertheless keyed to watchfulness and are fired with a resolution to uphold their freedom—and the freedom of the waters. With a regular population of about 20 campers (the number fluctuates), the springs run themselves as an ideal, mutual-interest community. It is a reversion to the old Indian system. A community which functions after the manner of those of the Hopis—the peaceful ones. The present organization (or absence of organization) of the Agua Caliente community is unique. It is a model of order, neatness, contentment—and cleanliness. Nowhere will you find more orderly, spick-and-span camps. Every camper seems to take pride in his campsite. There is no evidence of trash or litter. Many of the campers have tiny gardens in which a few gay flowers nod bravely to the desert sun. Peace and fellowship walk the trails through the arrowweeds and mesquites. Those individuals who are fond of dreaming of the brotherhood of man and of the idyllic life might study the pattern of this unique little community with interest. The average stay of resident campers—other than transients—is about three or four months. There are cold springs as well as warm ones. For the use of the warm, healing waters, the campers have erected several free community bath-houses (one tub each). I visited these bath-houses and found them scrupulously clean. There is nothing pretentious about them. But the work that has been done, with the available materials, has been well done. The temperature of the warm water is about 100 degrees as it issues from the springs. The supply is a little limited, and with the installation of more tubs the temperature tends to diminish. At the present time, due to this, the temperature in most tubs runs about 92 degrees F. The water is said to contain sulphur and iron. But I have no analysis to consult at this time. However, such technical details are of small moment. The important point is that there is healing virtue in Agua Caliente water and in its sunshine and dry air. It is a combination which is of great benefit in cases of arthritis, rheumatic fever and sinus troubles. The springs are about 38 miles from Julian, California, and best reached over State Highway 78, which connects with a good graded road that turns off at Scissors Crossing—12 miles from Julian—and goes to the springs by way of the old Overland stage station of Vallecito. The springs are three-and-a-half miles beyond Vallecito.

As a final word, I would say to interested readers: Don't go to Agua Caliente unless you are a real desert lover and are serious. It is distinctly no place for whoopee parties of the merely curious. The community is not at all like that—and its dwellers resent such atmosphere.

If however, you are a genuine lover of the desert, and the freedom of the great open spaces where peace and freedom and health still walk—and if you are genuinely in search of healing—the unique community of Agua Caliente will welcome you with sincere human brotherhood. Their desert is precious to them. And so are their healing waters. Let's hope they will always remain free!

Tracks of the Overland Stage
(November 1947)

There's a valley I know in the wastelands
*   Where, down through the greasewood and sage,*
Like a dim, ghostly thread from the years that have fled,
*   Stretch the tracks of the Overland Stage.*

Lone, ghostly and dim in the starlight;
*   Grey, desolate and pale in the dawn,*
Blurred by heat-waves at noon—still o'er mesa and dune
*   Wind the tracks of the wheels that have gone.*

Old coaches whose wheels long have mouldered,
*   Old stage-teams whose hoofs long are dust;*
Still, faint and age-greyed, wind the old wheel-ruts made
*   By tires long since crumbled to rust.*

And down where the silence lies deepest—
*   Like a lone, crumbling bead on a thread—*
In the mesquite-grown sands the old stage-station stands,
*   Hushed with memories—and ghosts of the dead.*

The desert rays wake not its brooding.
*   But oft 'neath the star-powdered sky,*
Round the walls on dark nights there move dim, ghostly lights,
*   As once more the old stages sweep by.*

And again, across dune, wash and mesa,
*   As the dead years turn back on their page,*
Pass the dim, racing teams from a ghost-world of dreams,
*   Down the tracks of the Overland Stage.*

The ruins of the Vallecito stage station before restoration.

Sequel to Ghost Mountain

(April 1949)

[Comments from Editor Randall Henderson]

During their long sojourn on the mountain, many friends who became interested in the Souths through Desert Magazine, *were concerned about the children. They wondered if Rider, Rudyard and Victoria, taught only by their mother and living apart from other humans, would later be able to adjust themselves to the complexities of the outside world.*

Two years have passed since Tanya and the children moved to San Diego to establish a new home—and now that question of adjustment can be answered. Desert's *editor recently asked Tanya about their life and progress in the big city. Here is her answer.*

LATE yesterday afternoon, Victoria came running breathless to say that Rudyard had been beset by three boys who were beating him up, and threatening to rob him of his prized lawn-mowing job. In instant response Rider and I fled to his rescue. We met him coming home alone, with a smug little grin.

"What happened?"

"N-nothing."

It took much persuasion to make him tell. "Well, after I knocked two of them down, the third boy turned chicken."

Do you think Rudyard can manage to tote along in this civilization? I do! He is brilliant! Eleven last Christmas, he has three major subjects above grade in his sixth grade report. He reads voraciously of adult works—never fiction, unless that has a direct, informative bearing on his absorbing specialties, engines and airplanes. At that he gladly leaves his reading for a game of baseball. He pridefully retained his title as captain of the school baseball team for a long time. He is nurse monitor and sells the *Los Angeles* Sunday *Times* every Saturday morning. You'd love him!

You'd love them all! You'd never recognize our flame-topped Rider! The boy has shot up, and I know many a man of smaller stature. He is his mother's great pride, a freshman at high school,

and we celebrated his fifteenth birthday recently. He has given up the Boy Scouts, for he is mature, impatient of the slow passage of time. Life holds bright vistas for him, if his dreams become realities. However, he is doing well at school. The teachers, during "open house" assure me he is a fine student and good boy. They like him. He has definite ideas regarding a livelihood, but they are original, I cannot reveal them.

Victoria is beautiful! Her reports deserve framing! She does everything excellently! She is shy, reserved, a lady!—class secretary and head of the "Lost and Found." She too is above grade in reading, for she is constantly reading library books. She is eight now, in the third grade, and has learned to ride a bicycle. She still plays chess, monopoly or cards, while listening to the radio. Her furious skating has given place to jumping the rope.

We have pleasant comfort in a light, airy four-room apartment on the summit of a steep hill. Our pooch, the frisky Ginger, is a definite personality in our household, and the four large tortoises are now waking up from their long sleep. I passed a Civil Service examination. To date, I am tapping typewriter keys. God has been very bountiful with love and mercy, and the fruits thereof.

Adiós, good friends, and warmest regards!

—Tanya South

The Souths in Carlsbad in 1947.
From left: Tanya, Victoria, Rider, and Rudyard.

APPENDIX 1

MARSHAL SOUTH'S PUBLISHED AND UNPUBLISHED WORKS (not in *Desert Magazine*)

[Editor's note: This list is not complete. In all likelihood there are more poems, articles, and short stories to be discovered. If a reader should find something by Marshal South that is not on the list or finds more information about an incomplete current listing, please forward that information to Diana Lindsay at Sunbelt Publications, P.O. Box 191126, San Diego, CA 92020.]

<u>POETRY</u>

1906 (December 7) *Port Augusta Dispatch*, "A Horrible Catastrophe"

1907 (February 1) *Port Augusta Dispatch*, "The Coming of the Yellow Man"

1907 (June 21) *Port Augusta Dispatch*, "Which May Be Felt"

1907 (June 28) *Port Augusta Dispatch*, A response to his poem of June 21 from Walking Man nee Pedestrian [a probable pseudonym]

1907 (July 12) *Port Augusta Dispatch*, "Which May be Felt," dedicated to Walking Man nee Pedestrian "on his departure from Port Augusta" [Marshal's farewell to the city in which he hints of being all the previous respondents to "Which May Be Felt": A.B.C., Non Itchia, Walking Man, and Pedestrian]

1912 (May 7) *Los Angeles Tribune*, "Intervention"

1913 (December 20) *Los Angeles Times Illustrated Weekly*, "The Lights of Vera Cruz"

1914 (February 28) *Los Angeles Times Illustrated Weekly*, "The Song of the Sea"

1914 (April 25) *Los Angeles Times Illustrated Weekly*, "Dreams"

1914 (April 30) *Los Angeles Daily Times*, "The Ancient Truth" [note at bottom—Oceanside, April 25, 1914]

1914 (May 2) *Oceanside Blade*, "Lines Inspired By a Public Fountain"

1914 (September 12) *Los Angeles Times Illustrated Weekly*, "Red War"

1914 (September 26) *Los Angeles Times Illustrated Weekly*, "Finis" [also published in the *Oceanside Blade* on October 3, 1914]

1914 (October 31) *Los Angeles Times Illustrated Weekly*, "The Fall of the Gods" [also published in the *Oceanside Blade* on November 7, 1914]

1914 (November 14) *Los Angeles Times Illustrated Weekly*, "The Mystery" [also published in the *Oceanside Blade* on November 21, 1914]

1914 (November 15) *Los Angeles Sunday Times*, "The Emden" [note at bottom—Oceanside, November 11, 1914]

1914 (November 24) *Los Angeles Tribune*, "Farewell, 'Bobs' (The Passing of Field Marshal Lord Roberts, November 14, 1914)"

1915 (January 7) *Los Angeles Daily Times*, "Beware!" [also published in the *Oceanside Blade*, January 23, 1915]

1915 (January 30) *Los Angeles Daily Times*, "The Protest of the Dead" [also published in the *Oceanside Blade* in two parts on January 25 and February 6, 1915]

1915 (May 2) *Los Angeles Sunday Times*, "The Shadow" [note on bottom—Oceanside, April 20, 1915]

1915 (June 26) *Los Angeles Times Illustrated Weekly*, "The Sea Wind"

1915 (July 26) *San Diego Sun*, "Welcome" [for Theodore Roosevelt's arrival in San Diego]

1915 (August 21) *Los Angeles Daily Times*, "The Traitors" [note on bottom—Oceanside, August 18, 1915]

1915 (November) *American Mercury*, title unknown [no copy—listed in *Readers Guide* 1890-1947 and *Poole's Index*]

1915 (November) *American Magazine*, "Progress" [also published in the *Los Angeles Tribune* (n.d.) along with a review of the poem and a photograph of Marshal South]

1915 ("Christmas") *Oceanside Blade*, "The Messsage"

1915 (December 25) *Army & Navy Call*, "Prepare" [*Army & Navy Call* is the official organ for the American Defense League]

1916 (March 7) *Los Angeles Daily Times*, "Revised National Anthem (Respectfully Submitted for the Consideration of the Anti-Preparedness Party)" [note on bottom—Oceanside, March 4, 1916]

1916 (March 15) *Los Angeles Daily Times*, "America" [note on bottom—Oceanside, March 12, 1916]

1916 (Undated, but probably May 1916) no source, "The Nation's Call: To Theodore Roosevelt"

1916 (May 1) *Los Angeles Daily Times*, "If" [note at bottom—Oceanside, April 17, 1916]

1916 (May 14) *Los Angeles Sunday Times*, "The Battle Fleet"

1916 (June 4) *Los Angeles Sunday Times*, "Rumors" [note on bottom—Oceanside, May 20, 1916]

1916 (June 14) *Los Angeles Daily Times* (Editorial Section), "The Spirit of Preparedness"

1916 (September 8) *Los Angeles Daily Times*, "The Last March" [note at bottom—Douglas, AZ]

1916 (September 22) *Los Angeles Daily Times*, "Song of a Rebel" [note at bottom—Douglas, AZ]

1916 (October 8) *San Diego Union*, "The California Sequoias"

1916 (October 26) *Douglas Daily Dispatch*, "Not Now"

1917 (March) *The Forum*, "The Submarine"

1917 (April) *The Forum*, "Peace"

1917 (May) *The Forum*, "Ruin"

1917 (August) *The Forum*, "Nemesis"

n.d. (published before 1918) *Los Angeles Times*, "The Rule of Power" [reference to this poem in *Desert Magazine's* "Letters to the Editor," March 1940, p. 2]

1918 (January 9) Unpublished poem to Margaret, "The Dearest Girl in All the World"

1922 (December 2) *The Evening Tribune*, "Futility"

1931 (June) Unpublished (?), "Old Indian Trails"

1935 (September 6) *Ranch Romances* (LXIII, No. 2), "When Rita Rides the Range"

1937 (October 22) *Presidio News* (The Big Bend Sentinel issue by Ralph England), "Memories (To my old pal, E.W. King, 'Don Edmundo')"

1937 (November) *Ranch Romances* (76.4), "On the Mexican Line" [unknown if a poem or a story]

1938 (February) *Westways*, "Moonrise on the Desert"

1943 (undated) self-published with the Yaquitepec Press, "The Dixie Pioneers" [written while in St. George, Utah]

1944 (spring or summer) self-published with the Yaquitepec Press, *The House of the Sun* (poem found within the booklet—see Booklets and Greeting Cards, below)

1944 or later, self-published with the Yaquitepec Press, "Giant Cacti" [poem found within this Greeting Card—see below]

1947 (September) unpublished, "The Law" [in response to Tanya's "The Law" published in *Desert Magazine,* September 1947]

NEWSPAPER ARTICLES/ESSAYS/STORIES

1904 (December 23) *Port Augusta Dispatch*, "A Terrible Christmas" [short story]

1905 (February 3) *Port Augusta Dispatch*, "A Dangerous Tale" [short story with a Texas setting]

1905 (March 31) *Port Augusta Dispatch*, "The Second Gun: The Story of a Great Revenge" [short story]

1905 (May 5) *Port Augusta Dispatch*, "The Phantom Steamer!—A Mystery of the Doldrums" [short story with editor's note giving background to Roy B. Richards]

1905 (September 15) *Port Augusta Dispatch*, "The Peril of the Future" [political commentary on the threat posed by Japan and China]

1905 (December 22) *Port Augusta Dispatch*, "The Valley of Death" [original story]

1906 (March 2) *Port Augusta Dispatch*, "The Almighty Dollar" [commentary about America]

1906 (April 27) *Port Augusta Dispatch*, "Is Life Worth Living" [essay. In the May 26 edition of the newspaper there is a line drawing sketch of "Roy—Our Boy Author"]

1906 (June 15) *Port Augusta Dispatch*, "Peace and Australian Defence" [political essay]

1906 (November 2) *Port Augusta Dispatch*, "The Honesty (?) of American Combines: Should Abnormal Incomes Be Taxed?" [essay]

1906 (December 21) *Port Augusta Dispatch*, "A Christmas Reverie: Port Augusta and Its Destiny!" [essay]

1907 (January 3) *Port Augusta Dispatch*, a series of letters to the editor decrying the pace at funerals begins on January 3, signed by "A.B.C." Others follow: August 3 by J. Woodforde; March 15 by A.B.C.; March 22, one by J. Woodforde and the other by Cryptic; March 29 by "Non Itchia Mala Sed Cacoethes"; April 5, one from J. Woodforde and the other by Cryptic; April 13 by Non Itchia; and April 19, one by J. Woodforde and the other by Cryptic—in which it is disclosed that Cryptic is R.B. Richards. In all likelihood all 11 of these writers are R. B. Richards, as the style is similar.

1907 (February 6) *The Gadfly* (Adelaide), "Vengeance" [short humorous story—also printed in the *Port Augusta Dispatch* on February 15, 1907]

1907 (February 27) *The Gadfly* (Adelaide), "A Modern Fairy Tale" [short story—part of a series?]

1907 (March 6) *The Gadfly* (Adelaide), "A Modern Fairy Tale" [short story—part of a series?]

1907 (June 14) *Port Augusta Dispatch*, Letter to the Editor from Pedestrian [in a published poem of July 12, 1907, Marshal strongly suggests that he is Pedestrian]

1914 (August or September n.d.) *Los Angeles Times*, "The Shark" [no copy—reference to it in the September 5, 1914, *Oceanside Blade*]

1916 (April 12) *Los Angeles Daily Times*, "The Rule of Power"

1947 (February) *The Desert Spotlight*, "'The Lost Ship' of the Vanished Sea"

MAGAZINE ARTICLES/STORIES

1914 (May 23) *All Story Cavalier Magazine* (41.5), "The Last Shot" [short story, no copy—reference in *Oceanside Blade* on May 23, 1914]

1915 (January) *Black Cat Magazine*, "Sword of the Flame" [no copy—this short story referenced in the *Oceanside Blade*, January 2, 1915]

1926 (May 15) *Argosy All-Story Weekly* (CLXXVII No. 4), "The Thing That Hunts in the Night"

1927 (August-December) *The Danger Trail: An Illustrated Adventure Magazine*, "The Curse of the Sightless Fish"

August	Part 1: 7.1	pp. 77-107	
September	Part 2: 7.2	pp. 259-272	
October	Part 3: 7.3	pp. 427-440	
November	Part 4: 8.1	pp. 123-131	
December	Part 5: 8.2	pp. 285-291	

1930s (n.y. December 2) *Ranch Romances*, "Written in Flame" [South article listed on front cover of the magazine. Photograph of the magazine cover appears in Jeannette DeWyze's article on South in the San Diego *Reader*, October 7, 1991]

1935 (before this date) unknown, "Child of Fire" [a personal handwritten note by Marshal in the cover of *Child of Fire* states that it was previously published as a magazine serial]

1937 (November) see listing under POEMS for *Ranch Romances*, "On the Mexican Line" [may be a poem—no copy]

1939 (March 11) *Saturday Evening Post*, "Desert Refuge"

1940 (November) *Holland's: The Magazine of the South*, "Desert Housewife" [articles published under the name Tanya South but written by Marshal South]

1943 (May) *Arizona Highways*, "Trail of the Singing Wind" [article followed by a selection of Tanya's poems; a short excerpt of the story was reprinted in *Arizona Highways* May 2000]

1944 (January) *Tomorrow*, "It Can Still Be Done: Present-day Pioneering in the California Desert" [articles published under the name Tanya South but written by Marshal South]

BOOKS (In Cumulative Book Index—nothing in CBI pre-1928, and 1928-1932)

1935 *Child of Fire*, published by John Long, Ltd., London, printed in Great Britain, at the Anchor Press, Tiptree, Essex [Published simultaneously with *Flame of Terrible Valley*]

1935 *Flame of Terrible Valley*, published by John Long, Ltd., London, printed in Great Britain, at the Anchor Press, Tiptree, Essex [Published simultaneously with *Child of Fire*]

1936 *Juanita of the Border Country*, published by John Long, Ltd., London, printed in Great Britain

1936 *Gunsight*, published by John Long, Ltd., London, printed in Great Britain [a "Cheaper Edition" published in 1938]

1939 *The Book of Ona: Desert Child* [unpublished childrens' book—rejected by Farrar & Rinehart, Inc., Publishers]

1943 *Robbery Range*, published by World's Works Ltd., Great Britain [a Master Thriller Adventure Story series]

1944 *Tiburon: The Isle of the Shark*, published by World's Work Ltd, Kingswood, Surrey, Great Britain, at the Windmill Press [a Master Thriller series]

1944 *Gold of the Gods*, published in England, John Long, Ltd., printed in Great Britain

1948 *The Curse of The Sightless Fish*, published by World's Work Ltd, Kingswood, Surrey, Great Britain, at the Windmill Press [a Master Thriller Adventure Story]

BOOKLETS / GREETING CARDS

1945 (spring or summer) *The House of the Sun*, Yaquitepec Press

1940s (undated greeting card) Yaquitepec Press, "Barrel Cacti & Yucca" [essay plus watercolor and linoleum block print]

1940s (undated greeting card) Yaquitepec Press, "Giant Cacti" [poem plus watercolor and linoleum block print. See POEMS above]

SUMMARY OF PUBLISHED AND UNPUBLISHED WORKS (not including *Desert Magazine)*:

Poems: 53 or 54   Newspaper articles/essays/stories: 29
Magazine articles/stories: 10 or 11   Books: 9
Booklets & greeting cards: 3

TOTAL—105

APPENDIX 2

COMMENTS ABOUT THE SOUTHS
AND A LIST OF WRITINGS BY TANYA SOUTH FOUND IN *DESERT MAGAZINE*

DATE		TITLE	AUTHOR	TANYA'S POEMS / ARTICLE	VOL. #
Dec	1939	Writers of the Desert	Randall Henderson		Vol. 3
Feb	1940	Announcing Desert Diary	Randall Henderson		
March	1940	Letters to the Editor	W.H. Marquis		
April	1940	Letters to the Editor	Vance O'Hara		
May	1940	Letters to the Editor	Harriette Stanford		
June	1940	Letters to the Editor	Lee Strobel		
Dec	1940	Letters to the Editor	Rex Vandeventer		
Feb	1941	Letters to the Editor	Earl R. Irey		Vol. 4
Mar	1941	Letters to the Editor	Wallace M. Byam		
May	1941	Faith	Tanya South	*	
		Letters to the Editor	Suzanne C. Dean		
June	1941	Life	Tanya South	*	
July	1941	(untitled)	Tanya South	*	
Aug	1941	(untitled)	Tanya South	*	
		Letters to the Editor	Elsa E. Livingston		
Sept	1941	(untitled)	Tanya South	*	
Oct	1941	Upward	Tanya South	*	
		Letters to the Editor	Wm. C. Chandler		
Dec	1941	Time	Tanya South	*	
Jan	1942	The Prospector	Tanya South	*	Vol. 5
		Letters to the Editor	Robt. Higday		
April	1942	Twilight	Tanya South	*	
		Letters to the Editor	Wm. H. Swartzendruber		
May	1942	Spring	Tanya South	*	
		Letters to the Editor	Charles H. Walker		
June	1942	The Simple Way	Tanya South	*	
		Letters to the Editor	Bill Hibbets		
July	1942	Sincerity	Tanya South	*	
		Letters to the Editor	Myrtle Dougherty		
Aug	1942	About the Souths	Randall Henderson		
		Perfection	Tanya South	*	
Sept	1942	Essentials	Tanya South	*	

——————————(moved from Yaquitepec because of lack of water, articles in Oct 1942-Nov 1943)

DATE		TITLE	AUTHOR	TANYA'S POEMS / ARTICLE	VOL. #
Oct	1942	New Dawns	Tanya South	*	

DATE		TITLE	AUTHOR	TANYA'S POEMS / ARTICLE	VOL. #
Nov	1942	Star Trail	Tanya South	*	
		Letters to the Editor	Kathryne Lawyer		
Dec	1942	Fate	Tanya South	*	
Jan	1943	Ageless	Tanya South	*	Vol. 6
Feb	1943	Path of Empires	Tanya South	*	
		Letters to the Editor	Francis Dickinson		
March	1943	Aspiration	Tanya South	*	
April	1943	Depth	Tanya South	*	
May	1943	Growth	Tanya South	*	
		Letters to the Editor	Capt. H. Lascombe		
June	1943	We Sleep	Tanya South	*	
		Letters to the Editor	Richmond W. Strong		
July	1943	Hope	Tanya South	*	
Aug	1943	Onward	Tanya South	*	
		Pilgrimage to Yaquitepec	Thomas Crocker		
Sept	1943	Purpose	Tanya South	*	
Oct	1943	Persistence	Tanya South	*	
		Letters to the Editor	Anna C. Bostwick		
		"	Alma A. Chessman		
Nov	1943	Contentment	Tanya South	*	
		Letters to the Editor	Merritt W. Boyer		
Dec	1943	Progression	Tanya South	*	
		Letters to the Editor	Kurt Reineman		
		Just Between You & Me	Randall Henderson		
Jan	1944	Substance	Tanya South	*	Vol. 7
		Letters to the Editor	Kathryne Lawyer		
Feb	1944	Handicraft	Tanya South	*	
March	1944	The Clock	Tanya South	*	
April	1944	Freedom	Tanya South	*	
May	1944	Joy of Living	Tanya South	*	
June	1944	Attraction	Tanya South	*	
July	1944	Dawn	Tanya South	*	
Aug	1944	Freedom	Tanya South	*	
		Letters to the Editor	Ralph F. Kreiser		
		"	Mrs. John C. Baur Jr.		
Sept	1944	Yourself	Tanya South	*	
		Letters to the Editor	Ethel York		
Oct	1944	Thus Live	Tanya South	*	
		Letters to the Editor	E.A. Brybacher		
		"	Mrs. C.L. Dobbins		
		"	Susan Groene		
		"	Elmo Proctor		
		"	B. Jay Purdy		
		"	Dora Sessions Lee		
Nov	1944	Purpose	Tanya South	*	
		Letters to the Editor	Ernest F. Edwards		
		"	Alyce Upton		

DATE		TITLE	AUTHOR	TANYA'S POEMS / ARTICLE	VOL. #
		"	Jim Pierce		
		"	Dr. Frank L. Robertson		
Dec	1944	Teachers All	Tanya South	*	
Jan	1945	Little Things	Tanya South	*	Vol. 8
Feb	1945	Oh, Lift Your Hearts	Tanya South	*	
		Just Between You & Me	Randall Henderson		
		Letters to the Editor	James E. Mayberry		
March	1945	Depths	Tanya South	*	
		Letters to the Editor	Rider, Rudyard, & Victoria South		
April	1945	Kindness	Tanya South	*	
May	1945	Effort	Tanya South	*	
		Letters to the Editor	Nellie Keck		
June	1945	I Will	Tanya South	*	
July	1945	Time	Tanya South	*	
Aug	1945	True Greatness	Tanya South	*	
Sept	1945	Security	Tanya South	*	

———————(during the war years, the Navy moved them from Yaquitepec—lived on the Campbell's property—articles from Oct 1945-Aug 1946)

DATE		TITLE	AUTHOR	TANYA'S POEMS / ARTICLE	VOL. #
Oct	1945	Inner Power	Tanya South	*	
Nov	1945	Atonement	Tanya South	*	
Dec	1945	Price	Tanya South	*	
Jan	1946	To Rise	Tanya South	*	Vol. 9
Feb	1946	Man	Tanya South	*	
March	1946	Opportunity	Tanya South	*	
April	1946	Through Integrity	Tanya South	*	
		Letters to the Editor	G.W. Weber		
		"	Mrs. E.J. McCormick		
May	1946	The Little Thing	Tanya South	*	
June	1946	Awakening	Tanya South	*	
July	1946	No Choice	Tanya South	*	
Aug	1946	Courage	Tanya South	*	
		Just Between You & Me	Randall Henderson		
Sept	1946	On Fate	Tanya South	*	
Oct	1946	The Golden Way	Tanya South	*	
Jan	1947	Just Between You & Me	Randall Henderson		Vol. 10
		On the Trek	Tanya South	*	
March	1947	New Morn	Tanya South	*	
April	1947	Just Between You & Me	Randall Henderson		
		Be Content	Tanya South	*	
May	1947	Dawn	Tanya South	*	
June	1947	Seek You	Tanya South	*	
July	1947	The Mind	Tanya South	*	
		Just Between You & Me	Randall Henderson		
Aug	1947	You Still Are You	Tanya South	*	
Sept	1947	The Law	Tanya South	*	

DATE		TITLE	AUTHOR	TANYA'S POEMS / ARTICLE	VOL. #
Oct	1947	Ah, Wisdom	Tanya South	*	
Nov	1947	Ahead	Tanya South	*	
Dec	1947	Hope	Tanya South	*	
		Letters to the Editor	Esther A. Brubacher		
Jan	1948	On the Path	Tanya South	*	Vol. 11
Feb	1948	Flight	Tanya South	*	
		Letters to the Editor	Louis L. Huillier		
		Between You & Me	Randall Henderson		
March	1948	The Dawn	Tanya South	*	
		Letters to the Editor	John H. Richie		
April	1948	Age	Tanya South	*	
May	1948	Lofty Thought	Tanya South	*	
June	1948	To Good Living	Tanya South	*	
July	1948	Take Hope	Tanya South	*	
Aug	1948	Most Important	Tanya South	*	
		Letters to the Editor	Richard Jordan		
Sept	1948	Would We Had!	Tanya South	*	
Oct	1948	To The Young	Tanya South	*	
Nov	1948	Inspiration	Tanya South	*	
Dec	1948	Desert Close-Ups	Randall Henderson		
		Just Between You & Me	Randall Henderson		
		A Great Soul	Tanya South	*	
Jan	1949	Face Life	Tanya South	*	Vol. 12
		Letters to the Editor	R.N. Shuart		
Feb	1949	Forever	Tanya South	*	
March	1949	Oneness	Tanya South	*	
April	1949	Sequel Ghost Mountain	Tanya South	*	
		Glad Choice	Tanya South	*	
May	1949	Hope	Tanya South	*	
June	1949	Oh, Dawn	Tanya South	*	
July	1949	March On	Tanya South	*	
Aug	1949	Take It!	Tanya South	*	
Sept	1949	Your Fate	Tanya South	*	
Oct	1949	Upgrade	Tanya South	*	
Nov	1949	Justice	Tanya South	*	
Dec	1949	Warp & Woof	Tanya South	*	
Jan	1950	Truth	Tanya South	*	Vol. 13
Feb	1950	The Step Ahead	Tanya South	*	
March	1950	Love	Tanya South	*	
April	1950	The Night is Past!	Tanya South	*	
May	1950	Oh Light	Tanya South	*	
June	1950	Hope	Tanya South	*	
July	1950	Advancement	Tanya South	*	
Aug	1950	Glories to Come	Tanya South	*	
Sept	1950	True Worth	Tanya South	*	
Oct	1950	Right Living	Tanya South	*	
Nov	1950	Life	Tanya South	*	

DATE		TITLE	AUTHOR	TANYA'S POEMS / ARTICLE	VOL. #
Dec	1950	Forward	Tanya South	*	
Jan	1951	Eternal	Tanya South	*	Vol. 14
Feb	1951	Fight On!	Tanya South	*	
March	1951	Constancy	Tanya South	*	
April	1951	Pathway	Tanya South	*	
May	1951	In Faith	Tanya South	*	
June	1951	To Grow	Tanya South	*	
July	1951	Earthly	Tanya South	*	
Aug	1951	To Attainment	Tanya South	*	
Sept	1951	Faith	Tanya South	*	
Oct	1951	This Brotherhood	Tanya South	*	
Nov	1951	By the Golden Rule	Tanya South	*	
Dec	1951	Purpose	Tanya South	*	

Tanya's Poetry—Month Published:

1952	Jan, Feb, April, May, June, July, Aug, Sept, Oct, Nov, Dec
1953	Jan, Feb, March, April, May, June, July, Aug, Sept, Oct, Nov, Dec
1954	Jan, Feb, March, April, Sept, Oct, Nov, Dec
1955	Jan, Feb, March, April, May, June, July, Aug, Sept, Oct, Nov, Dec
1956	Jan, Feb, April, May, June, July, Aug, Sept, Oct, Nov, Dec
1957	Jan, Feb, March, April, May, June, July, Aug, Sept, Oct, Nov, Dec
1958	Jan, Feb, March, April, May, June, July Aug, Sept, Oct, Nov, Dec (Henderson defends Tanya's poetry in his "Just Between You and Me" column of June 1958)
1959	Jan, Feb—last one. Henderson steps down as editor and is "advisory" editor beginning with April edition. Tanya would have submitted her last poem to *Desert* in December 1958.

Tanya's Poems—202 (63 published with Marshal South articles)
　　　　Articles—1 (April 1949)

Marshal's Articles and Poems—102 Total (see Table of Contents)
　　　　Desert Diary—12
　　　　Desert Home—3
　　　　Desert Refuge—65
　　　　Desert Trails—11
　　　　Misc. Articles—4
　　　　Poems—7 (one published separately; all the others included with articles)

NOTES

FOREWORD:

ROY BENNETT RICHARDS—THE EARLY YEARS:

Dates were confirmed through South Australian records: birth certificates for Roy Bennett Richards, Norman Afford Richards, and Annie Emma Afford; marriage certificate for Annie Emma Afford and William Charles Bennett Richards; and census surveys. Information about C.B. Richards came from: *Pioneers of the North-West of Australia, 1856-1914* by Norman Alexander Richardson; the *Adelaide Observer* (December 1, 1894; April 23, 1898; and September 26, 1902); the *Adelaide Dispatch* (October 2, 1914); and the *Port Augusta Dispatch* (November 19, 1909, and December 3, 1909). Publications of and information about Roy Richards cited in this section were found in the *Port Augusta Dispatch* (December 23, 1904; May 5, 1905; May 25, 1906; June 28, 1907; and July 12, 1907). Additional information came from Tanya's short biography and interviews with Rider South.

ENTER MARSHAL SOUTH—OCEANSIDE'S POET LAUREATE:

Documents showing England as the place of birth include: birth certificates (Rider South, Rudyard South, and Victoria South); 1920 and 1930 census surveys; death certificates (Annie Emma Richards, Marshal South, and Norman Richards); and Norman's wedding certificate. Tanya's short biography has Australia as Marshal South's birth place.

Articles about B. Richards/Marshal South or his publications that are cited in this section include: the *Los Angeles Tribune* (May 7, 1912, and November 1915—n.d., clipping); the *Oceanside Blade* (December 27, 1913; May 2, 1914; October 3, 1914; October 17, 1914; November 7, 1914; November 14, 1914; September 9, 1914; December 5, 1914; December 26, 1914; January 2, 1915; January 16, 1915; January 25, 1915; January 30, 1915; February 6, 1915; March 27, 1915; April 10, 1915; May 29, 1915; July 10, 1915; July 31, 1915; August 28, 1915; November 6, 1915; March 25, 1916; and May 24, 1916); the *Port Augusta Dispatch* (June 15, 1906, and February 1, 1907); the *Army & Navy Call* (December 25, 1915); and *American Magazine* (November 1915).

It is interesting to note that South's poem "The Emden" was praised by the German Ambassador in 1914. The *Emden* was a German cruiser destroyed by an Australian ship, the *Sydney*, on November 9, 1914. It was Australia's first significant triumph in the war.

A NEW LIFE IN ARIZONA—THE ARMY AND MARGARET:

References to Marshal South or his publications cited in this section include: the *Los Angeles Times* (September 8, 1916); the *Oceanside Blade* (September 16, 1916); the *Presidio News* (October 22, 1937); the *Port Augusta Dispatch* (November 2, 1906); and the *San Diego Tribune* (December 2, 1922). Details about the relationship between Marshal South and Margaret Schweichler are based on personal letters (Marshal to Margaret—January, 1918, and December 18, 1922) provided by Marsha Rasmussen, Marshal Jr.'s daughter. Marsha also shared information she had from conversations with her father. Documents citing dates include:

the wedding license and certificate for Marshal South and Margaret Schweichler; a copy of a notarized statement by Tony Schweichler, dated March 1, 1939, verifying Margaret's place and date of birth; and the 1920 *Douglas City Directory*.

TANYA—A KINDRED SPIRIT?

Tanya's family background is described in her short biography. Her early writings are found in the Rosicrucian Fellowship Magazine *Rays from the Rose Cross*, located at the headquarters of the Rosicrucian Fellowship in Oceanside, California. Marshal's comments about Tanya are found in his letters to Margaret (December 18, 1922 and March—n.d.—1923). Annie Richards' death date is from her death certificate. Dates on early camping trips and comments about "ghosts" at Vallecito are taken from notes written on photographs found in Rider South's family album. Additional information is based on interviews, telephone conversations, and e-mail correspondence with Victoria Morgan and Rider South.

A PRIMITIVE LIFE STYLE—A SOURCE OF INCOME:

Background reasons for moving to the desert were published in: "Desert Refuge" in the *Saturday Evening Post* (March 11, 1939), "Desert Diary" in *Desert Magazine* (March 1940), and "It Can Still Be Done" in *Tomorrow* (January 1944). A contemporary back-to-nature movement in the Palm Springs area by early naturists is outlined in Gordon Kennedy's *Children of the Sun*. Marshal defined the meaning of "Yaquite-pec" in "Desert Refuge," published in *Desert Magazine* in August 1944 (number 38). Copies of correspondence between Marshal South and officials from California State Parks are found in the author's files: South to James A. Snook (September 13, 1936) and Newton B. Drury to South (September 21, 1936).

South's action-packed novels reflect his King's English early training. Perhaps not noticed by his London audience, Americans may find his occasional use of *thou* for "you," *thy* for "your" a little distracting. His use of English spellings and infrequent phrases like "haste thou now and bring my horse" would have been caught and corrected had he an American publisher before going to press.

Details about the activities of Edward R. Burts, who was the inspiration for the Chinese tong in *Flame of Terrible Valley*, can be found in the author's writings (*Anza-Borrego A to Z: People, Places, and Things* published by Sunbelt Publications in 2001, or in "Homesteaders Move into Earthquake Valley in the Early 1900s," published August 22, 2004, in the *Borrego Sun*).

In addition to claims on the jacket copy of his books, Marshal South also told his own children that he had "a drop of Indian blood." He also stated so in "Desert Housewife," published in *Holland's: The Magazine of the South* (November 1940). He wrote that his "great-great-great grandmother" was an Indian.

Dates for the births of the South children, the South's second marriage, and Margaret's divorce from Augusto Carlested are taken from official birth, marriage, and divorce documents. Comments from Letters to the Editor in *Desert Magazine* (see Appendix 2) are taken from the following issues: March 1941, October 1941, May 1942, June 1942, November 1943, August 1944, October 1944, and November 1944. Comments from Editor Randall Henderson are taken from: March 1941, May 1941, and February 1946.

TRAPPED BY AN IMAGE:

Comments published in *Desert Magazine* from Editor Randall Henderson for this section are taken from August 1942 and December 1943 issues. Information about the relationship between Tanya and Marshal is based on interviews and telephone conversations with Victoria Morgan and Rider South. Copies of *The House of the Sun* and the Yaquitepec guest log are found in the author's files.

A copy of Marshal's correspondence to Marshal Jr. (June 27, 1946) is in the author's files (Marsha Rasmussen has the original). Information on Marshal Jr. is based on interviews, telephone conversations, and e-mail correspondence with Marsha Rasmussen. Marsha's mother, Mae Berthelsen South Almond, provided some details about the visit to Ghost Mountain in 1946.

The instructions for driving to Ghost Mountain sent to Marshal Jr. by his father (the same printed instructions sent to all guests) indicate the ways in which Marshal protected the family's privacy on the mountain. The turnoff to Ghost Mountain from what is today the road to Morteros and Pictographs was marked by a "Game Refuge" sign and blocked by "piled yucca trunks." The instructions for guests said to remove them and drive through and then replace them. The next obstruction was a metal sign and two strands of barb wire further down the road. The instructions were to pick up the sign and to unhook the barb wire, drive through, and then replace the barb wire and sign. The driver would then arrive at the parking area where he would find beehives, trailers, and "indications of occupancy." The foot trail to Yaquitepec started from the parking area. A warning sign was found on the trail near the house telling guests that no clothes were worn at Yaquitepec. The instructions also told guests to bring their own bedding and camp equipment as there were no accommodations for guests.

THE MOLD BREAKS—END OF THE EXPERIMENT:

Details about the events that led to the divorce and what occurred immediately after the divorce proceedings began are based on interviews, telephone conversations, and e-mail correspondence with Victoria Morgan, Rider South, and Jeri Botts Wright. A copy of the letter from Marshal South to Judge Arthur L. Mundo (January 21, 1947) is on file at the office of the Superior Court in San Diego County. Comments about the divorce from *Desert Magazine* Editor Randall Henderson are found in the January 1947 issue of the magazine.

Marshal felt the mountain was a safe place to raise children; Tanya thought it wasn't. She always carried a snake bite kit and a forked stick when she roamed for firewood, according to Victoria. If there were coyotes around, she carried a larger stick. Marshal may have thought her fears groundless as he felt a tremendous kinship with all things. Rider also does not recall any real danger from rattlesnakes or coyotes.

Tanya waited a long time before she made the decision to file for divorce. "Suffering" was something she did as a means of evolving spiritually. She wrote in an essay, entitled "Why Is It Necessary for Man to Evolve Through Matter" (Rosicrucian Fellowship Magazine *Rays from the Rose Cross*, August 1920), that "…we are here, not for happiness but for experience which gives us soul-growth. *Suffering* [her emphasis] is one of the most efficient means for gaining experience."

AFTER GHOST MOUNTAIN:

Information about Tanya's and Marshal's life after the interlocutory and final judgments were granted and about Marshal's death are based on interviews, telephone conversations, and e-mail correspondence with Rider South, Victoria Morgan, and Jeri Botts Wright. Additional information comes from comments made by *Desert Magazine* Editor Randall Henderson found in the April 1947, July 1947, and December 1948 issues of the magazine.

Marshal died of heart disease. He knew he had a weak heart when he first came to the desert (*Desert Magazine*, December 1947). He had credited his lifestyle and love for the desert for years of excellent health while he lived on Ghost Mountain. A weak heart and the change in his lifestyle following the separation and divorce led to rapid deterioration and death.

Correspondence about Marshal's death and gravesite include: the letter from Myrtle Botts to Marshal Jr. on January 12, 1965, and the letter from Norman Richards to Margaret Carlstedt Rector and Marshal Jr. on

December 19, 1948. A copy of Tanya's response to the state park system about their inquiry to create a cultural preserve for Yaquitepec (May 1, 1983) is located in the Anza-Borrego Desert State Park research library. Tanya's comments about Margaret are found in her short biography. Documents used to determine dates include the death certificates for Marshal South, Norman Richards, and Tanya South.

Marshal's focus on life may be said to go beyond just seeing "the good things." His philosophy, as written in *Desert Magazine* and in his booklet *The House of the Sun*, reflected some of the key elements found in all great religions: a connection and kinship with all animate creatures; an inner sense of peace, which for him was felt most strongly in the desert; and an intellectual integrity that caused him to act according to his own conscience. The problem was that he had the mentality of a monk with the responsibilities of a family.

INTRODUCTION:

RECOLLECTIONS OF LIFE ON GHOST MOUNTAIN:

A Gift for Victoria:

There is another possibility for the selection of Victoria's name besides the reference to Queen Victoria. In "It Can Still Be Done: Present-day Pioneering in the California Desert," published in *Tomorrow* (January 1944), Marshal stated that Victoria had actually been named "for the Spirit of Victory in a era when the dark furies of storm ride the world,...."

SELECTED BIBLIOGRAPHY

[Editor's note: see Appendix 1 for references to works by Marshal South and Appendix 2 for references to those who made comments about Marshal South in *Desert Magazine*.]

Newspapers:

Adelaide Dispatch (South Australia)
Adelaide Observer (South Australia)
Gadfly (Adelaide, South Australia)
Los Angeles Times
Los Angeles Tribune
Oceanside Blade
Port Augusta Dispatch (South Australia)
San Diego Daily Journal
San Diego Evening Tribune
San Diego Sun
San Diego Union
San Diego Union-Tribune

Websites:

Katz, Bob. "Marshal & Tanya South." http://www.desertusa.com/mag99/mar/papr/mtsouth.html
McCrerey, Tim. "Night on Ghost Mountain." http://www.desertusa.com/mag99/oct/stories/ghostmt.html
Orman, Joe. "Sunrise at Yaquitepec." http://pages.prodigy.net/pam.orman/joeghosts/Ghosts_01.html
Wade, Charles. "Anza-Borrego DSP Ghost Mountain—Blair Valley."
    www.panamintcharlie.com/anza-ghostmountain9-04.html

Interviews/e-mail correspondence/telephone conversations
    (January 1903-November 1904)—copies in author's files:

Almond, Mae Berthelsen South
Morgan, Victoria
Mushet, Gary "Buzz"
Napierskie, Jack
Rasmussen, Mark
Rasmussen, Marsha
South, Lucile
South, Rider
Wright, Jeri Botts

Letters and Unpublished Documents:

Botts, Myrtle. Letter to Marshal South Jr., January 12, 1965. Copy in author's files.

Drury, Newton B. Letter to Marshal South, September 21, 1936. Copy in author's files.

Richards, Norman. Letter to Margaret Carlstedt Rector and Marshal South Jr., December 19, 1948. Copy in author's files.

Schweichler, Tony. "Affidavit as to the Birth Place of Margaret F. South." March 1, 1939. Copy in author's files.

Scouts, Capt. Phil. Letter to Base Quartermaster, September 27, 1917. Copy in author's files.

South, Marshal. Letter to Margaret Schweichler, January 9, 1918. Copy in author's files.

——. Letter to James A. Snook, Chief of Division of Parks, California State Parks, September 13, 1936. Copy in author's files.

——. Letters to Margaret South, December 18, 1922, and March or April 1923 (n.d.—year only). Copy in author's files.

——. Letter to Marshal South Jr., June 27, 1946. Copy in author's files.

——. Letter to C.H. Vinson, American Defense League, December 20, 1915. Archives, San Diego Historical Society.

South, Tanya. Letter to Carol Roland, State Historian, Department of Parks and Recreation, May 1, 1983. In Research Library, Anza-Borrego Desert State Park.

——. Short Biography. Copy in author's files.

Wagner, Katherine. Letter to Marshal South Jr., June 16, 1960. Copy in author's files.

Public Documents:

Birth Certificates: (South Australia) Annie Emma Afford, Roy Bennett Richards, and Norman Afford Richards; (San Diego County, California) Rider Del Sol South, Rudyard Del Sol South, and Victoria Del Sol South; and (Cochise County, Arizona) Marshal South Jr.

Census Records: (San Diego County, California) 1920 and 1930; and (Orange County, California) 1930.

Cochise County (Arizona) Marriages 1911-1920.

Death Certificates: (San Diego County, California) Annie Emma Richards, Norman A. Richards, and Marshal South.

Divorce Judgments: (Los Angeles County, California) Margaret Carlstedt vs. August Carlestedt; and (San Diego County, California) Tanya South vs. Marshal South.

Douglas (Arizona) City Directory 1920.

Marriage Certificates: (South Australia) Annie Emma Afford and William Charles Bennett Richards; (Cochise County, Arizona) Marshal South and Margaret Frieda Schweichler; (Orange County, California) Marshal South and Tanya Lehrer; (San Diego County) Marshal South and Tanya Lehrer, and Norman A. Richards and Gladys L. Smith.

South Australian Births Index, 1842-1906.

South Australian Death Index, 1842-1915.

South Australian Marriage Index, 1842-1916.

Books and Articles:

Baumann, David. "The Ruin on Ghost Mountain." *The Mystery & Adventure Series Review*, 33, 2000.

Bryson, Jamie. "Author Built House on Mountain in Desert, Lived There 16 Years." *San Diego Union*, March 30, 1969.

Crumpler, Hugh. "Yaquitepec Graces Ghost Mountain." *San Diego Union*, December 22, 1988.

De Wyze, Jeannette. "The Hermits of Ghost Mountain." San Diego *Reader*, October 17, 1991.

Gregston, Gene. Monthly column. *San Diego Business Forum*, April 16, 1976.

Hogue, Lawrence. *All the Wild and Lonely Places: Journeys in a Desert Landscape*. Washington, D.C.: Island Press, 2000.

Japenga, Ann. "A Feral Family Album." *Los Angeles Times Magazine*, January 6, 2003.

Kennedy, Gordon. *Children of the Sun: A Pictorial Anthology from Germany to California 1883-1949*. Ojai, CA: Nivaria Press, 1998.

Lehrer, Tanya. "A Vision." Rosicrucian Fellowship Magazine *Rays from the Red Cross*, XIV, November 1922.

——. "Give Me Freedom! Give Me Freedom!" Rosicrucian Fellowship Magazine *Rays from the Red Cross*, XIV, May 1922.

——. "God Loves Us." Rosicrucian Fellowship Magazine *Rays from the Red Cross*, XIV, April 1923.

——. "Illumination." Rosicrucian Fellowship Magazine *Rays from the Red Cross*, XIV, March 1923.

Lehrer, Tessie. "A Parting." Rosicrucian Fellowship Magazine *Rays from the Red Cross*, XIII, June 1921.

——. "I Am Thought." Rosicrucian Fellowship Magazine *Rays from the Red Cross*, XII, December 1920.

——. "Only God." Rosicrucian Fellowship Magazine *Rays from the Red Cross*, XII, August 1920.

——. "Smile." Rosicrucian Fellowship Magazine *Rays from the Red Cross*, XII, May 1920.

——. "Thoughts on Music." Rosicrucian Fellowship Magazine *Rays from the Red Cross*, XIII, June 1921.

——. "Why Invite Spirit Controls?" Rosicrucian Fellowship Magazine *Rays from the Red Cross*, XIII, November 1921.

——. "Why Is It Necessary for Man to Evolve Through Matter?" Rosicrucian Fellowship Magazine *Rays from the Red Cross*, XII, July 1920.

Lindsay, Diana. *Anza-Borrego A to Z: People, Places, and Things*. San Diego: Sunbelt Publications, 2001.

——. "Anza-Borrego Desert: The Story of the Nation's Largest State Park." Master's thesis. San Diego State University, 1973.

——. "Ghost Mountain Image Masks Depth of Marshal South." *Borrego Sun*, November 18, 2004.

——. "Homesteaders Move into Earthquake Valley in the Early 1900s." *Borrego Sun*, August 22, 2004.

——. *Our Historic Desert: The Story of the Anza-Borrego Desert*. San Diego, Copley Books, 1973.

Lindsay, Lowell and Diana Lindsay. *The Anza-Borrego Desert Region*. Berkeley: Wilderness Press, 1998.

Lyons, Priscilla. "Marshal South and Yaquitepec." Colorado Desert District *Tracks*, April 1997.

Perkins, Eloise. "Rocky Ghost Hides Ruins." *Daily Times-Advocate*, October 21, 1973.

Richardson, Norman Alexander. *Pioneers of the North-West of Australia, 1856-1914*. Adelaide: W.K. Thomas & Co., 1925.

Roland, Carol. "Yaquitepec: Marshal South's Chronicle of Life on Ghost Mountain." *California History*, March 1988.

Rowe, Peter. "Write or Wrong: The Legend of Ghost Mountain." *San Diego Union-Tribune*, March 14, 2004.

San Diego Evening Tribune. "Ghost of Days Past Haunts Mountain." September 17, 1973.

Smith, Pete. "A Desert Refuge—1930's California." *Fedco Reporter*, July 1988.

South, Marshal. "Desert Refuge." *Saturday Evening Post*, March 11, 1939.

———. *The House of the Sun*. Yaquitepec Press, 1946.

———. "Trail of the Singing Wind." *Arizona Highways*, May 1943.

South, Tanya. See also Tanya Lehrer and Tessie Lehrer.

———. "Desert Housewife." *Holland's: The Magazine of the South*, November 1940.

———. "It Can Still Be Done: Present-day Pioneering in the California Desert." *Tomorrow*, January 1944.

Surles, Minnie. "Ghost Mountain was Family's Secret Refuge." *Borrego Sun*, January 7, 1988.

———. "The Secret Refuge of Marshal South." *The Mountain Guide*, November 1991.

———. "War Maneuvers on Mountain Beginning of End for Souths." *Borrego Sun*, January 21, 1988.

Winslow, Kent (aka Fred Woodworth). "Hunting for Hidden Books." *The Mystery & Adventure Series Review*, 36, 2003.

Woodworth, Fred, ed. "Desert Reflections: From the Journal of Marshal South." *The Mystery & Adventure Series Review*, 33, 2000.

INDEX

[Editor's note: pages referring to Marshal, Tanya, Rider, Rudyard, Victoria, Yaquitepec, and Ghost Mountain are limited to key entries and to locations of photographs.]

ACKNOWLEDGMENTS

This was a challenging research project. Marshal South and his own family (his mother and brother) changed names, dates, and locations on documents to hide who they were—establishing a pattern of obfuscation. Tanya South would often record these misleading statements on documents. Sometimes Marshal embellished facts to help sell articles. Also many records were destroyed—some deliberately and others through fire—and some key contacts have died.

Tanya destroyed her manuscript about the years on Ghost Mountain after being told that it reflected too much bitterness. A fire in St. Louis in 1973 destroyed 85 percent of all military records for veterans of WWI, WWII, and Korea, including Marshal's military records. San Diego's Cedar fire of October, 2003, destroyed a box of personal articles that once belonged to Marshal (a log book, sketches, documents, personal letters, and published articles in addition to souvenirs from Yaquitepec) that were purchased in a yard sale in Julian from the home of Myrtle Botts after she had died. The box was kept in a private home that burned. Years earlier, a letter that is a source of mystery also was burned. It was a letter that Tanya had given to Marshal Jr. for his mother Margaret. And sadly, Marshal South Jr. died in December 2002 as a result of an accident in which he received third degree burns.

Despite these losses, enough materials have been unearthed thanks to the dedicated efforts of many people. Many members of the South family have enthusiastically supported the project and have willingly shared all documents in their possession. Rider and Lucile South have not only provided the introduction for this book, they have made available all of their photographs and Marshal's poems and articles. They have suffered through my innumerable questions and have provided answers, and in the process they have become dear friends. They are dedicating their author royalties to the Anza-Borrego Foundation to help fund interpretive displays at the visitor center.

Victoria Morgan, Rider's sister, shared her early memories of Ghost Mountain and provided the only known copy of a book cover for *Gunsight*, one of Marshal's novels. She also offered insight about her mother, read through several drafts of the foreword and introduction, and helped to make this book a more balanced and fair presentation of her parents.

Marsha Rasmussen, Marshal South's granddaughter, shared letters that her father (Marshal South Jr.) had saved—written by Marshal South, Myrtle Botts, and others. She also provided documents, photographs and information about Marshal's life with her grandmother, Margaret South Carlstedt Rector. Her son, Mark Rasmussen, initially opened the door to information about Marshal Jr.'s side of the family.

Details of Marshal's early years in South Australia have been researched by Patricia Sumerling, a professional historian in Maylands, South Australia. She was able to find the earliest references to Roy Bennett Richards and provided me copies of his earliest poems, essays, and stories. She was assisted by Robert Martin who was able to get permission from the State Library of South Australia to copy and print Roy's caricature in this book.

Marshal's years in Oceanside, California, have been researched by Kristi Hawthorne, president of the Oceanside Historical Society. She poured through years of the *Oceanside Blade* to glean South's activities and helped me establish that South was born in Australia.

Jeri Botts Wright, daughter of Myrtle and Louis Botts, shared her memories of Marshal South and provided insight into the relationship between Marshal and the Botts family. She also provided an album of photographs for this book.

Alexandra Porter of the Rosicrucian Fellowship of Oceanside searched through documents and photographs for information about Tanya and Marshal South and was able to locate the early poems and writings of "Tessie" Lehrer. David Lewis of Julian, who has been working to reconstruct the names for grave plots in the Julian Cemetery (the original registry was destroyed in a fire), was able to identify the location of Marshal South's grave using the detailed information found in Myrtle Botts' letter to Marshal Jr. As a result of this positive identification, a permanent marker was placed on the grave on January 22, 2005.

Both Bill Worden and Pea Hicks have been an incredible help through this project. Bill provided original scans for all of the *Desert Magazine* articles including photographs and sketches. He also verified the distances to various objects found on Ghost Mountain. Pea has scanned almost all of the original photographs and book covers provided by Rider South. He put together the original 15-minute film about the Souths using the silent 8-minute 1946 Pettinger film of Ghost Mountain, narration by Rider South, and still photographs provided by Rider. This film has been shown at the park visitor center during lectures. Both Bill and Pea have provided me with research materials and have worked to restore old photographs that have been reproduced in this book. Pea also has read the foreword and introduction for errors and has made suggestions for improvement.

Most of the animal and plant illustrations used in this book were drawn by Jon Lindsay. Others were originally commissioned by the Union-Tribune Publishing Company and appeared in Copley Books' 1973 publication of *Our Historic Desert*.

Research documents and newspapers were provided by the staff of Anza-Borrego Desert State Park, the archivists at the San Diego Historical Society, and the librarians of the downtown San Diego Public Library. Individuals who provided additional information or help include: Fred Woodworth for back issues of *The Mystery & Adventure Series Review*; David Baumann for reviewing the foreword and for photographs of the gravesite and the ruins of Ghost Mountain; Dorothy and Buzz Mushet for photographs of the Banner Queen and the Mushet family; Jack Napierskie for remembrances of Marshal South; Lee Fetzer for his careful reading of the introduction and suggestions for improvement; and Jon Rebman of the San Diego Natural History Museum for identification of "ramarillo."

Iris Engstrand, professor of history at the University of San Diego, Mark Jorgensen, superintendent of Anza-Borrego Desert State Park, and Peter Rowe, columnist for the *San Diego Union-Tribune*, read an earlier draft of the manuscript and provided comments for the back cover of the book.

Doc Morgan partnered with me to raise funds to purchase the Pettinger film from eBay. Documentary film maker and Anza-Borrego Foundation Trustee Nicholas Clapp worked with me to fund the restoration of this film. Jim Manner made available another film taken in 1946 by his family that also has scenes from Ghost Mountain and Julian that will be incorporated into a new film that will be created for the Anza-Borrego Desert Visitor Center under the direction of film maker John McDonald. Jim also provided a still photograph from his family's visit to Ghost Mountain.

I would also like to thank the trustees of the Anza-Borrego Foundation and the staff of the Anza-Borrego Desert State Park for supporting this project. Sales of this book support the cost of educational and interpretive displays found at the park visitor center. This book would not be possible without the generous support provided by the following donors to the Anza-Borrego Foundation: Frank

Colver, The Engel Fund of the San Diego Foundation, the Linnie Cooper Foundation, and Jack Napierskie. Their support is greatly appreciated.

W.G. (Bill) Hample and Associates of Bakersfield, California, met the incredibly short deadline I had set before them to prepare the manuscript for publication. I greatly appreciate their diligence and excellent production skills. Joanna Bonomi of Handmade Graphics & Computer Concepts turned a black and white photograph of Marshal South into a stunning front cover. Likewise, the stylized silhouette of Rider and Marshal South, adapted from a photograph, captured some of the magic of this book.

The staff of Sunbelt Publications sheltered me from day-to-day business, which allowed me the time to complete this project. Particular thanks go to Kathy Gouin, vice-president, and Jennifer Redmond, marketing and publications coordinator, who assisted in production tasks. A special thanks is reserved for my life-long friend and spouse, Lowell Lindsay, who saw little of me this past year. Thanks for your long-suffering patience!

I am sure that there are more publications by Marshal South that will be unearthed in the future. If a reader should note one that is not listed in Appendix 1, or if any additional information or corrections need to be made to the text for future editions of this work, please send those to Diana Lindsay, Sunbelt Publications, P.O. Box 191126, San Diego, CA 92020 or e-mail me at dlindsay@sunbeltpub.com.

— Diana Lindsay, December 2004

SUNBELT PUBLICATIONS, incorporated in 1988 with roots in the book business since 1973, produces and distributes publications about "Adventures in Natural History and Cultural Heritage." These include multi-language pictorials, natural science and outdoor guidebooks, regional references, and stories that celebrate the land and its people.

Our publishing program focuses on the Californias, today three states in two nations sharing one Pacific shore. Somewhere in the borderland between reality and imagination, a Spanish novelist called adventurers to this region five centuries ago when he wrote, "Know ye that California lies on the right hand of the Indies, very near to the terrestrial paradise."

Sunbelt books help to discover and conserve the natural and historical heritage of such unique regions on the frontiers of adventure and learning. Our books, with an underlying theme of "journey," guide readers through time and space and into distinctive communities and special places, both natural and man-made. These are the journals of "La Frontera."

Exploring the Southern California Deserts
with
SUNBELT BOOKS
Series Editor—Lowell Lindsay

*Sunbelt books celebrate the land and its people through publications in
natural science, outdoor adventure, and regional interest.*

www.sunbeltbooks.com